The Cambridge Compani.. ..

Hugo Grotius

The Cambridge Companion to Hugo Grotius offers a comprehensive overview of Hugo Grotius (1583–1645) for students, teachers and general readers, while its chapters also draw upon and contribute to recent specialised discussions of Grotius' oeuvre and its later reception. Contributors to this volume cover the width and breadth of Grotius' work and thought, ranging from his literary work, including his historical, theological and political writing, to his seminal legal interventions. While giving these various fields a separate treatment, the book also delves into the underlying conceptions and outlooks that formed Grotius' intellectual map of the world as he understood it, and as he wanted it to become, giving a new political and religious context to his forays into international and domestic law.

Randall Lesaffer is Professor of Legal History at KU Leuven in Belgium and at Tilburg University in the Netherlands. His research focuses on the history of the early-modern law of nations in Europe, as well as the history of modern international law. He is the general editor of *The Cambridge History of International Law*, *Oxford Historical Treaties* and an editor of the *Journal of the History of International Law*. He is president of the Grotiana Foundation (https://grotiana.eu/).

Janne E. Nijman is Professor of History and Theory of International Law at the University of Amsterdam in the Netherlands, and academic director of the T.M.C. Asser Institute in The Hague. She is also Professor of Public International Law at the Graduate Institute of International and Development Studies in Geneva. She has published on Hugo Grotius, and she is an editor on the board of *Grotiana* and a board member of the Grotiana Foundation (https://grotiana.eu/).

Cambridge Companions to Law

Cambridge Companions to Law offers thought-provoking introductions to different legal disciplines, invaluable to both the student and the scholar. Edited by world-leading academics, each offers a collection of essays which both map out the subject and allow the reader to delve deeper. Critical and enlightening, the Companions library represents legal scholarship at its best.

The Cambridge Companion to

Hugo Grotius

Edited by

Randall Lesaffer
KU Leuven and Tilburg University

Janne E. Nijman
University of Amsterdam and The Graduate Institute, Geneva

CAMBRIDGE
UNIVERSITY PRESS

CAMBRIDGE
UNIVERSITY PRESS

University Printing House, Cambridge CB2 8BS, United Kingdom

One Liberty Plaza, 20th Floor, New York, NY 10006, USA

477 Williamstown Road, Port Melbourne, VIC 3207, Australia

314–321, 3rd Floor, Plot 3, Splendor Forum, Jasola District Centre, New Delhi – 110025, India

103 Penang Road, #05–06/07, Visioncrest Commercial, Singapore 238467

Cambridge University Press is part of the University of Cambridge.

It furthers the University's mission by disseminating knowledge in the pursuit of education, learning, and research at the highest international levels of excellence.

www.cambridge.org
Information on this title: www.cambridge.org/9781107198838
DOI: 10.1017/9781108182751

First published 2021

A catalogue record for this publication is available from the British Library.

Library of Congress Cataloging-in-Publication Data
Names: Lesaffer, Randall, editor. | Nijman, Janne Elisabeth, 1972– editor.
Title: The Cambridge companion to Hugo Grotius / edited by Randall Lesaffer,
    Universiteit van Tilburg, The Netherlands; Janne Nijman.
Description: New York, NY : Cambridge University Press, 2019. | Series: Cambridge
    companions to law | Includes bibliographical references and index.
Identifiers: LCCN 2020040542 (print) | LCCN 2020040543 (ebook) |
    ISBN 9781107198838 (hardback) | ISBN 9781316648315 (paperback) |
    ISBN 9781108182751 (epub)
Subjects: LCSH: Grotius, Hugo, 1583-1645. | International law. | International relations.
Classification: LCC KZ2093 .C36 2019 (print) | LCC KZ2093 (ebook) | DDC 340.092–dc23
LC record available at https://lccn.loc.gov/2020040542
LC ebook record available at https://lccn.loc.gov/2020040543

ISBN 978-1-107-19883-8 Hardback
ISBN 978-1-316-64831-5 Paperback

Contents

Contributors

Paolo Astorri is Postdoctoral Researcher at the University of Copenhagen, Centre for Privacy Studies. He studied law at the University of Macerata and canon law at the Pontifical Lateran University. He obtained his PhD from KU Leuven. His research focuses on the interaction between theologians and jurists in the early modern period. He is the author of *Lutheran Theology and Contract Law in Early Modern Germany (ca. 1520–1720)* (Schöningh, 2019).

William Bain is Associate Professor of International Relations at the National University of Singapore. He is the author of *Political Theology of International Order* (Oxford University Press, 2020) and *Between Anarchy and Society: Trusteeship and the Obligations of Power* (Oxford University Press, 2003). He is also editor of, and contributor to, *Medieval Foundations of International Relations* (Routledge, 2016) and *Empire of Security and the Safety of the People* (Routledge, 2006).

Marco Barducci is currently an Honorary Fellow at Durham University's Institute of Medieval and Early Modern Studies, where he was previously appointed as an Assistant Professor (research) and Solway Fellow. Prior to this, after some years spent teaching and researching at the University of Florence, he held fellowships at the Institute for Advanced Studies (Princeton), the Institute of Advanced Studies (Durham), the Interdisciplinary Centre for European Enlightenment Studies (Halle-Wittenberg), the Folger Institute (Washington, DC) and the Fondazione Luigi Firpo (Turin). In 2019, he was elected a FRHistS.

Hans Blom was, upon retiring from Erasmus University Rotterdam, DAAD Professor at the University of Potsdam (2011–13). He has taught at Cambridge University, the University of Buenos Aires and the University of Wisconsin–Madison. His edited works include *Property, Piracy and Punishment: Hugo Grotius on War and Booty in De iure praedae* (Brill, 2009), *Monarchisms in the Age of Enlightenment* (University of Toronto

Press, 2007), *Grotius and the Stoa* (Van Gorcum, 2004), *Hobbes: The Amsterdam Debate* (Olms, 2001) and *Sidney: Court Maxims* (Cambridge University Press, 1996). He is co-editor-in-chief of the journal *Grotiana*.

Camilla Boisen is Lecturer in the Writing Program at New York University, Abu Dhabi. Her main area of research is the political theory of empire including the development of ideas of rights and trusteeship and their influence on contemporary problems such as postcolonial restitution. She is the author of numerous articles in journals such as *The History of European Ideas*, *Settler Colonial Studies*, *Grotiana* and *Journal of International Political Theory*. She also co-edited *Distributive Justice Debates in Political and Social Thought: Perspectives on Finding a Fair Share* (Routledge, 2017).

Peter Borschberg teaches history in the Department of History at the National University of Singapore. He has published widely on Grotius, the just war, the Singapore and Malacca Straits region, as well as Europe–Southeast Asia interaction generally in the early modern period.

William E. Butler is the John Edward Fowler Distinguished Professor of Law, Dickinson Law, Pennsylvania State University; Professor Emeritus of Comparative Law, University College London; Foreign Member of the National Academy of Sciences of Ukraine and of the National Academy of Legal Sciences of Ukraine.

Ignacio de la Rasilla holds the Han Depei Chair in Public International Law and is a Thousand Talents Plan Professor at the Wuhan University Institute of International Law (National Top Think Tank) in China. He was educated in Spain (LLB, 5 years – University Complutense of Madrid); Switzerland (MA and PhD, The Graduate Institute, Geneva); the United States (Fellow in Global Governance, Law and Social Thought, Brown University; LLM, Harvard Law School); and Northern Italy (Post-doctoral Max Weber Fellow in Law, European University Institute, Florence).

Wouter Druwé is Assistant Professor of Roman Law and Legal History at KU Leuven. He studied civil law (LLM 2013, PhD 2018), canon law (JCL 2018) and theology (BA 2013). His publications include two monographs: *Loans and Credit in Consilia and Decisiones in the Low Countries (c. 1500–1680)* (Brill, 2020) and *Scandalum in the Early Bolognese Decretistic and in Papal Decretals (c. 1140–1234)* (Peeters, 2018).

Arthur Eyffinger is classicist and law historian. He was editor of the series *The Poetry of Hugo Grotius*, co-founder and long-standing secretary of the Grotiana Foundation and executive editor of its journal *Grotiana* (1978–2000). He was Head Librarian of the International Court of Justice (1987–2003) and in 2004 founded *Judicap*, centre for publications and presentations on international law and peace studies.

Andrew Fitzmaurice is Professor of the History of Political Thought at Queen Mary University of London. His work focuses on the political ideology of empire. His publications include *Humanism and America: An Intellectual History of English Colonisation, 1500-1625* (Cambridge University Press, 2003) and *Sovereignty, Property and Empire 1500-2000* (Cambridge University Press, 2014).

Francesca Iurlaro is an intellectual historian working on international legal thought, with a distinct focus on the history and reception of natural law theories. She holds a PhD in law from the European University Institute in Florence (2018). She graduated in the history of philosophy (University of Macerata, 2014) and has an LLM in Comparative, European and International Laws (European University Institute, 2015). She is currently an Alexander von Humboldt Postdoctoral Fellow at the Max Planck Institute for Comparative Public Law and International Law (Heidelberg). Her book *The Invention of Custom: Natural Law and the Law of Nations, 1550-1750* is coming out with Oxford University Press.

Meirav Jones is Assistant Professor of Religious Studies at McMaster University. She previously held research and postdoctoral positions at the University of Pennsylvania, Yale University, the Hebrew University of Jerusalem and Tel Aviv University. Her work, generally on the intersection between religious sources and ideas and the foundations of modern politics, has appeared in such venues as *Journal of the History of Ideas, Political Studies, and the Review of International Studies.*

Dennis Klimchuk is Associate Professor of Philosophy at the University of Western Ontario. His main research interests and publications are in the philosophy of law and the history of political philosophy, especially in the early modern period.

Randall Lesaffer is Professor of Legal History at KU Leuven and part-time Professor of Legal History at Tilburg University, where he served as dean of

Tilburg Law School (2008–2012). He is also Visiting Professor of International Law at Catolica Global School of Law, Lisbon. He is general editor of The Cambridge History of International Law, Oxford Historical Treaties and Studies in the History of International Law (Brill/Nijhoff), as well as president of the Grotiana Foundation. He is editor of the *Journal of the History of International Law*, the Global Law series (Cambridge University Press) and a board member of the journal *Grotiana*.

Stephen C. Neff is Professor of War and Peace at the University of Edinburgh School of Law. He is the author of *War and the Law of Nations: A General History* (Cambridge University Press, 2005) and *Justice Among Nations: A History of International Law* (Harvard University Press, 2014). He is also the editor of *On the Law of War and Peace* (Cambridge University Press, 2012).

Henk Nellen is guest researcher of the Huygens Institute for the History of the Netherlands (Amsterdam). He co-edited the five last volumes of the correspondence of Hugo Grotius (17 vols., The Hague, 1928–2001). In addition, he conducted research into other topics in the history of the seventeenth-century scholarly world. He is the author of the biography *Hugo de Groot. Een leven in strijd om de vrede* (Uitgeverij Balans, 2007), of which an English translation by Brill was published. Before his retirement in 2014, he held a chair for the History of Ideas in the Early Modern Period at the Erasmus University Rotterdam.

Janne E. Nijman is Professor of History and Theory of International Law at the University of Amsterdam and academic director of the T.M.C. Asser Institute in The Hague. She is also Professor of Public International Law at the Graduate Institute of International and Development Studies in Geneva. She is the author of a number of papers on Hugo Grotius, an editor on the board of the journal *Grotiana* and board member of the Grotiana Foundation.

Oliver O'Donovan was educated at Oxford and Princeton Universities and is an Anglican priest. From 1982 to 2006, he was Regius Professor of Moral and Pastoral Theology at Oxford, before which he taught in Oxford and Toronto. He was Professor of Christian Ethics at Edinburgh (2006–12), and has been Honorary Professor of Divinity at Saint Andrews University since 2013. A Fellow of the British Academy and of the Royal Society of Edinburgh, he has written on Augustine, on the theological basis of moral concepts, on contemporary bioethical dilemmas, on political theology and on the ethics of war. His books include *The Desire of the Nations, The Ways of Judgment* and *Ethics As Theology*.

Edwin Rabbie studied classics at the University of Amsterdam and law at Leiden University. He is a judge at the Rotterdam District Court and holds an endowed professorship 'Erasmus Studies' at Erasmus University Rotterdam. He has authored many publications on, among others, Grotius and Erasmus.

Peter Schröder is Professor of the History of Political Thought at University College London. He was a visiting professor at universities in Seoul, Rome and Paris and held numerous senior research fellowships. Recent publications include a monograph on *Trust in Early Modern International Political Thought, 1598–1713* (Cambridge University Press, 2017), as well as two edited volumes: a German translation and edition of Hobbes, *Behemoth or the long Parliament* (Meiner, 2015) and a German translation and edition of Filmer's *Patriarcha* (Meiner, 2019).

Mark Somos holds the Deutsche Forschungsgemeinschaft's Heisenberg position at the Max Planck Institute for Comparative Public Law and International Law (Heidelberg). He studied history, political science and law at Cambridge, Harvard, Sussex and Leiden, and taught law and political science at Harvard, Tufts, Sussex and Yale Universities. He wrote *Secularisation and the Leiden Circle* (Brill, 2011) and *American States of Nature: The Origins of Independence, 1761–1775* (Oxford, 2019); co-wrote *The Fabrica of Andreas Vesalius* (Brill, 2018) with Dániel Margócsy and Stephen Joffe; and co-edited *Trust and Happiness in the History of European Political Thought* (Brill, 2017) with László Kontler. Somos is co-editor-in-chief of *Grotiana* and edits the book series, History of European Political and Constitutional Thought (Brill/Nijhoff).

Benjamin Straumann is ERC Professor of History at the University of Zurich and Research Professor of Classics at New York University. He is the author of *Roman Law in the State of Nature: The Classical Foundations of Hugo Grotius' Natural Law* (Cambridge University Press, 2015) and *Crisis and Constitutionalism: Roman Political Thought from the Fall of the Republic to the Age of Revolution* (Oxford University Press, 2016).

Harm-Jan van Dam (PhD in classics, 1984) was Associate Professor of Latin at VU University Amsterdam until his retirement in 2011. Earlier, he worked at the Huygens Institute for the History of the Netherlands (Dutch Royal Academy), preparing an edition of Hugo Grotius' *De imperio summarum potestatum circa sacra* (2001). He is active as a translator of Latin poetry and Erasmus. His present research focuses on neo-Latin poetry. He was member of the board of the Grotiana Foundation and of its journal *Grotiana*.

Gustaaf van Nifterik is Senior Lecturer in Legal History at the law school of the University of Amsterdam. His prime research topic is history of constitutional law, with a focus on topics related to the rule of law. He is member of the board of the Grotiana Foundation and of its journal *Grotiana*.

Jan Waszink studied classics at Leiden University and obtained a MPhil in European Literature from the University of Cambridge and a PhD from the University of Amsterdam. He is the editor and translator of a number of neo-Latin works, including Lipsius' *Politica* and Grotius' *De antiquitate republicae Batavicae*. He has published numerous articles on political thought, in particular Tacitism, in the early modern period. He is member of the board of the Grotiana Foundation and of its journal *Grotiana*.

Bart Wauters is Assistant Professor at IE Law School / IE University (Madrid, Spain), where he teaches European Legal History, Legal Thought and Legal Theory. His latest book is *The History of Law in Europe: an Introduction* (co-author Marco de Benito), published in 2017 by Edward Elgar Publishing.

Alain Wijffels is Senior Research Fellow of the French CNRS at the Centre for Judicial History in Lille. He teaches comparative law and legal history at the universities of Louvain-la-Neuve, Leuven and Leiden. His research focuses on legal scholarship and public governance in the practice of the courts and of political authorities, from the late middle ages until modern times.

Laurens Winkel is Emeritus Professor of Legal History, School of Law, Erasmus University Rotterdam. He was president of the Grotiana Foundation from 2005 to 2015 and has long served as a member of the editorial committee of *The Legal History Review*. He has published numerous studies, in particular in the field of Roman law. He holds an honorary degree of LLD from the University of Edinburgh.

Preface

It remains a mystery why there has not been a *Cambridge Companion to Hugo Grotius* to this point. As a format, the Cambridge Companions have a strong tradition in intellectual history, covering numerous political and theological thinkers from – in particular – Europe's past. It was Stephen Neff (Edinburgh University) who first drew attention to the anomaly that Hugo Grotius, one of the most prolific, versatile and influential voices from Europe's intellectual history, was still awaiting his Cambridge Companion. He suggested that we, as members of the Grotiana Foundation, would take up the task of coordinating this.

It was during a nice afternoon at the National Archives at The Hague that we made the first design for the book. Our proposal, worked out in numerous subsequent conversations, was enthusiastically met by Finola O'Sullivan, law editor at Cambridge University Press, who agreed that Grotius' lasting fame in international law earned him a place in the law list. Nevertheless, the plan to cover the life, thoughts and work of Grotius in all its breadth, transcending the borderlines of modern disciplines, also met with strong approval at the Press. Our special thanks go to Finola and her dedicated team, among others Marianne Nield, Jane Bowbrick, Paul Martin and Sindhuja Sethuraman.

Thanks are due first and foremost to the team of leading international scholars who contributed to this Companion. It has been a fascinating intellectual journey for us editors to learn to know Grotius through the eyes and thoughts of so many specialists from different fields. From the start, we have benefited from the support, expertise, advice and network of the members of the Dutch Grotiana Foundation, the organisation behind the academic journal *Grotiana* (New Series), which has now run successfully since the early 1980s when it restarted. Several of its members also contributed to the volume. We are acutely aware of the gender imbalance of this Companion and regret that not more female scholars have accepted our invitation to contribute a chapter.

Many have tried to characterise Hugo de Groot only to end up with words that convey his elusiveness. For his whole life and *Nachleben*, Grotius has been the subject of controversy, reaping both laudation and revilement. Grotius himself wrote once, 'I do not believe that I am someone who can be [. . .] easily and carelessly denigrated'. Leaving his vanity aside, we can only agree. Reading and studying Grotius' thoughts is an endless story with twists and turns and constant deferral of meaning and judgment. The impalpability of Grotian thought can best be embraced, even if never overcome.

Grotius accompanied his texts with dedications to European kings and princes and to high officials in the Dutch Republic. He used these dedications to express allegiances, seek patronage and make political appeals. We would like to dedicate, dear reader, this Companion to you and hope it will assist you in the study of this extraordinary mind.

Chronology

1618–48	Thirty Years War
1618	Fall of Oldenbarnevelt and Grotius
1618–19	Synod of Dordrecht
1619	Imprisonment of Grotius at Loevestein
1621	Grotius escapes from Loevestein to France
1621	Resumption of war with Spain
1622	*Verantwoordingh/Apologeticus*
1622	*Disquisitio an Pelagiana sint*
1625	First edition of *De jure belli ac pacis*
1627	*De veritate religionis Christianae*
1629	*Grollae obsidio*
1630	Swedish invasion in Germany
1631–2	*Incognito* return to the Republic
1631	Publication of *Inleidinge tot de Hollandsche rechts-geleerdheid*
1632–4	Grotius in Hamburg
1634	Appointment of Grotius as Swedish ambassador to France
1634–59	Franco-Spanish War
1640	*Commentatio de Antichristo*
1641	*Annotationes in libros Evangeliorum & Annotata ad Consultationem Cassandri*
1642	*Animadversiones in Animadversiones Andreae Riveti*
1642	*Votum pro pace ecclesiastica*
1642–3	*De origine gentium Americanarum dissertatio, & altera*
1644	*Annotata ad Vetus Testamentum*
1644	Grotius is called to Sweden
1645	Journey to and from Sweden and death of Grotius at Rostock
1646–50	Publication of *Annotationum in Novum Testamentum tomus* 2 & 3
1647	Publication of *De imperio summarum potestatum circa sacra*
1648	Peace of Münster
1655	Publication of *Historia Gotthorum*
1657	Publication of *Annales & Historiae*
1679	Publication of *Opera omnia theologica*
1687	Publication of *Hugonis Grotii Epistolae quotquot*
1724	Barbeyrac translation of *De jure belli ac pacis*
1864	Discovery *De jure praedae*
1886	Unveiling of statue of Grotius on the Delft marketplace
1899	Grotius' commemoration at Delft during First Hague Peace Conference

Abbreviations and Short Titles of Works by Grotius

AHRB	*Annales et Historiae de rebus Belgicis*
ARpB	*De antiquitate reipublicae Batavicae*
BW	*Briefwisseling van Hugo Grotius* [Correspondence of Hugo Grotius]
CTS	Clive Parry (ed.), *The Consolidated Treaty Series* (Dobbs Ferry, 1969–1981)
CTXI	*Commentarius in Theses XI*
DFP	*De fide et perfidia*
DI	*De imperio summarum potestatum circa sacra*
DJBP	*De jure belli ac pacis*
DJPC	*De jure praedae commentarius*
ICJ Rep.	*International Court of Justice Reports*
IHR	*Inleidinge tot de Hollandsche Rechts-geleerdheid*
ML	*Mare liberum*
OHWP	*Ordinum Hollandiae et Westfrisiae pietas*
OTh	*Opera omnia theologica*
RpE	*De republica emendanda*
UNTS	United Nations Treaty Series, https://treaties.un.org/Pages/Content.aspx?path=DB/UNTS/pageIntro_en.xml

Editions and Translations of Grotius' Work

References throughout the chapters are to these editions and translations, except when indicated otherwise at the end of the chapter.

Sacra in quibus Adamus exul tragoedia (The Hague, 1601).

'Adam's exile', in: W. KirkConnell, *The Celestial Cycle: The Theme of Paradise Lost in World Literature with Translations of the Major Analogues* (Toronto, 1952).

Annotationes in libros evangeliorum. Cum tribus tractatibus et Appendice eo spectantibus (Amsterdam, 1641).

The Antiquity of the Batavian Republic with the Notes by Petrus Scriverius, ed. and transl. J. Waszink (Bibliotheca Latinitatis Novae; Assen, 2000).

P.C. Molhuysen, B.L. Meulenbroek, P.P. Witkam, H.J.M. Nellen and C.M. Ridderikhoff (eds.), *Briefwisseling van Hugo Grotius 1597-1645* (17 vols., The Hague, 1928–2001).

De imperio summarum potestatum circa sacra: Critical Edition with Introduction, English Translation, and Commentary, ed. and transl. H.J. Van Dam (2 vols., Leiden, 2001).

Inleidinge tot de Hollandsche rechts-geleerdheid, eds. F. Dovring, H.F.W.D. Fischer and E.M.Meijers (Leiden, 1952).

The Jurisprudence of Holland, transl. R.W. Lee (Oxford, 1936).

De jure praedae commentarius, ed. H.G. Hamaker (The Hague, 1868).

Commentary on the Law of Prize and Booty, ed. M.J. Van Ittersum (Natural Law and Enlightenment Classics; Indianapolis, 2006).

De iure belli ac pacis libri tres in quibus ius naturae et gentium item iuris publici praecipua explicantur, eds. B.J.A. De Kanter-Van Hettinga Tromp, *annotationes novas addiderunt*, eds. R. Feenstra and C.E. Persenaire (Aalen, 1993).

De jure belli ac pacis libri tres, transl. Francis W. Kelsey (Classics of International Law; Oxford/London, 1925).

The Free Sea, ed. D. Armitage (Natural Law and Enlightenment Classics; Indianapolis, 2004); With the translation of 'Defense of Chapter V of the Mare Liberum'.

Meletius sive de iis quae inter Christianos conveniunt epistola, ed. and transl. G.H.M. Posthumus Meyjes (Leiden, 1988).

Ordinum Hollandiae ac Westfrisiae pietas (1613), Critical Edition with English Translation and Commentary, ed. E. Rabbie (Leiden, 1995).

Poemata collecta et magnam partem nunc primum edita a fratre Gulielmo Grotio (Leiden, 1617).

De republica emendanda; On the Emendation of the Dutch Polity, ed. and transl. A. Eyffinger *et al., Grotiana* NS 5 (1984) 66–121.

Commentarius in Theses XI/Commentary to Eleven Theses, ed. and transl. P. Borschberg, *Hugo Grotius 'Commentarius in Theses XI': An Early Treatise on Sovereignty, the Just War, and the Legitimacy of the Dutch Revolt* (Berne [etc.], 1994), 200-283.

The Truth of Christian Religion: With Jean Le Clerc's Notes and Additions, ed. M.R. Antognazza (Natural Law and Enlightenment Classics; Indianapolis, 2012).

Introduction

Randall Lesaffer and Janne E. Nijman

After 400 years, Hugo Grotius (1583–1645) and his writings still animate debates over a wide range of disciplines. For political and moral philosophers, theologians, intellectual historians and historians of political thought, and international relations and international law scholars, Grotius remains a foremost figure in the history of their disciplines.

In the age of Grotius, these fields had not yet developed into distinct, let alone separate, academic disciplines and were not yet clearly demarcated from the mother and father of all disciplines in early modern Europe, theology and law. The intimate relationship of Grotius' best-seller theological work *De veritate religionis Christianae* (1627) to his major juridical endeavour *De jure belli ac pacis* (1625) testifies to how, for Grotius, theology and jurisprudence were both intertwined and in a process of separation. The period Grotius lived in was one of fundamental changes in the political and legal organisation of Christian Europe and – related to this – in the way Christian Europe thought about the universe and the place of humanity and the individual human being within it. It is no exaggeration to consider Grotius as one of the intellectual trailblazers of modernity, understood as a secular and liberal order premised on conceptions of equality, liberty, tolerance and representative government, and on a much debated relation between self-preservation and universal justice.[1] The theological origins of modern (lega–political) thought,[2] and Grotius' own deep and prolonged involvement with theology and biblical philology, are, however, traditionally overlooked in many of the secular academic disciplines.[3] Recognising these origins is crucial for understanding Grotius and his role in early modern thought. Rendering Grotius his rightful place in intellectual history cannot be done by cutting his writings loose from the fundamental changes that marked his age, or his personal life and career. That said, such a historically contingent approach does not preclude discussions about his manifold contributions to contemporary debates on politics and law, religion and theology, and on humans and their capacity for knowledge and truth.

I.1 Politics and Law

The revolt in the Netherlands against the Spanish monarchy and the formation of the Republic of the United Provinces in the north as an independent state from the 1580s onwards determined the context of much of Grotius' early career and writings. It confronted him with the turmoil that the final collapse of the old order of the *respublica Christiana* and the emergence of the sovereign state brought to much of Europe between the middle of the sixteenth and the middle of the seventeenth centuries, and did so in the most radical of manners.[4]

Grotius contributed to the development of the new Republic as both a legal and political practitioner and a scholar. He plied himself to the cause for the Republic by providing the young polity with its own history and, rooted in that narrative, its own identity. While imprisoned at Loevestein, Grotius wrote the *Inleidinge tot de Hollandsche rechts-geleerdheid* – published a decade later in 1631 – which, more than any other work of legal scholarship, laid the foundations for the Roman-Dutch law that was to dominate the jurisprudence of the Republic until the end of the eighteenth century. The relationship between law and politics in both the domestic and international sphere was subject to debate, as it continues to be to this day. Grotius' legal and political theories made a crucial contribution to later debates on the rule of law, within as well as among states.[5] Amid an international society of emerging sovereign states, Grotius built on the inheritance of patristic writers and late-medieval moral theologians, canonists as well as civilians, and on more recent writers – Spanish neoscholastics and humanist jurisprudents – in redefining the Roman law notion of *jus gentium* into a modern law of nations, or public international law, which applied to sovereign rulers and states. His account of natural law and natural rights has since been at the centre of debates in the history of international thought. Grotius' career and work as an official, as well as his writings until his conviction, imprisonment and exile from the Republic, were very much determined by the Republic's political agenda in the war against Spain and its extra-European maritime and commercial expansion.[6] After his escape from Loevestein, Grotius' political agenda split across his sustained ties through his family with the Republic and its colonial companies, his need to find patrons in France and Sweden, and his desire to foster international and religious peace between the European powers and confessions.

I.2 The Place of Religion

With the Reformations and Counter-Reformation, Christian unity came to an end during the sixteenth century. The confessional struggles dominated many of the societal and political debates in the Dutch Republic and much of Europe. In the Dutch Republic, the confessional rivalry between moderate Arminians and Gomarian Calvinists had deep political consequences. City regents, such as Grotius himself, generally preferred the Erasmian Reformation over Calvinism and sympathised with Jacobus Arminius (1560–1609) and Johannes Wtenbogaert (1567–1644) and their followers. The clash between the two groups provoked discussions about the relationship between Church and state, between religious and political authority. In an attempt to break free from the indurating hermeneutical or exegetical conflicts, Grotius turned to classical philology and 'right reason' as ultimate authority. Grotius' Bible criticism was surely ground-breaking. The historical contextualisation of biblical texts – as if interpreting 'pagan' Roman or Greek texts – that Grotius propagated led him to approach the texts as reflections of ancient Israelite and early Christian thought. This approach paved the way for Baruch Spinoza (1632–77) to redefine Bible exegesis altogether.[7] As a humanist, Grotius took up the position that biblical texts could not be interpreted in contradiction with right reason. Moreover, he contributed to the heated confessional disputes with a mild, non-dogmatic and irenic agenda and a plea for toleration.[8] Socinian and Pelagian slander was, however, the result. Grotius' humanism was manifested in his views on individual liberty in matters of religion and conscience, which was to be protected by secular authority rather than by Church officials, yet within a strong public Church. But, as the identity of this public Church was the object of strife between Arminians and Gomarians, this humanist position did not allow him to bridge the gap.

However much conventional history holds up the myth of religious tolerance within the Dutch Republic, as a statesman Grotius was confronted with the consequences of the criminalisation of heterodoxy at the age of thirty-five. His attempts to carve out a space for a unifying natural religion and a latitudinarian, non-dogmatic Christendom was borne by the importance of toleration also for public peace in the Republic. Time and again, he promoted consistently, both as a public official and a scholar, a limited toleration for the Dutch Republic. Grotius argued for a degree of economic and social autonomy for Amsterdam

Jews, though the 1615 draft Remonstrance did not mean to confer equal formal legal status.[9] He did not speak out against the transatlantic slave trade or slavery.[10] However, he may have contributed to the move of religious belief from the centre of the public to the private realm and, in that sense, to the long-term process of secularisation.

Nevertheless, championing Grotius as the 'great seculariser' is an unhelpful exaggeration when discussing his thought. With *De veritate* and *De jure belli ac pacis*, the humanist Grotius moved beyond neo-scholasticism. He aimed to find common ground amid the confessional struggles in order to point a way towards peace in the Republic and Europe at large. The ongoing scholarly discussion about the relative influence of humanism and scholasticism in Grotius' work is related to this. When Grotius is characterised as a 'modern' jurist who carries the deep imprint of humanist innovation and political thought, it goes to the style and method of his argumentation and to the subjects he addressed in his work: the sovereigns and emerging states as political and legal actors, his conception of natural law in which human nature replaces God as the explicit – though surely not as the ultimate – source of authority, and therewith to his development of the idea of individual rights. Other scholars, however, building on Peter Haggenmacher, emphasise how Grotius drew from late-medieval scholastic thought and was indebted to Spanish neo-scholastic theologians such as Francisco de Vitoria (c. 1483–1546) and Francisco Suárez (1548–1617).[11] To this day, the debate is overtly construed on a narrow distinction between scholastic/theological and humanist/legal–political spheres, which overlooks the obvious fact that neo-scholastics, as well as humanist jurists and political thinkers, were heavily dependent on the legal inheritance of late-medieval civil and canon lawyers. No less than 40 per cent of Grotius' legal sources in *De jure belli ac pacis* date from the eleventh to fifteenth centuries.[12] It also threatens to cloud the eclectic nature of Grotius' use of sources, which flowed from his acceptance, as a humanist, of the historical contingency and the relative authority of the classical text canon of the learned disciplines.[13]

I.3 Human Nature, Epistemology and Methodology

Grotius' influence on the early stages of the European Enlightenment is undisputed.[14] His *De jure belli ac pacis* became the foundational text for a new, 'modern' tradition of natural law in the seventeenth and eighteenth centuries.[15] The idea of human nature, with its defining features of sociability and reason, became the basis for the development of a novel political, moral and legal philosophy. This methodological innovation enabled Grotius to humanise natural law, leading it away from divine command, and to give ethics, morality and law an epistemological foundation in the social and rational human self. The discovery and conquest of the 'New World' by the Europeans contributed moreover to the development of the 'modern' mindset, consciousness and worldview. In *De origine gentium Americanarum dissertatio* (1642), Grotius examined the origins of the native Americans. He seemed fascinated by 'the more highly-refined minds of the Peruvians' for example and suggested that 'their capacity for just and extended government, testif[ied] to a[n] origin, which [. . .] can be no other than from the Chinese, a race of equal elegance and equal ability'.[16] The little tract actually also reads as an examination of how the peoples of the world relate to each other as one human family.[17] While Grotius' approach is interesting to get a sense of his mindset in the turn to the modern, it sold short in terms of the emerging standards of the 'new science'.[18]

New scientific insights coming with, for example, Galileo Galilei's (1564–1642) heliocentrism caused tensions with traditional theological thought and contributed to a profound transformation of prevailing worldviews. With the changing perceptions about the place of the earth, and thus of humankind, in the universe came a shift in the place of religious belief and God in human thought. With the new science came new doubts about how to generate knowledge and how to find truth. Grotius' argument that scripture has to be read in accordance with reason and not as the revelation of the truth was a far-reaching epistemological point too. The early modern European revolution in both the sciences and humanities would invigorate modernity and its rationality. It fuelled the modern worldview with the concept of the rational agent or subject, which became crucial in morality, law and politics.

Grotius lived, worked and thought amid these three major and interrelated fundamental changes – the secession of the northern Netherlands, the religious strife within Christianity and the new scientific outlook – carrying the move from the medieval to the modern world. As a very active member of the Republic of Letters, Grotius was visibly influenced by and in turn influenced these changes and the debates they provoked. The word most often used through the ages to characterise the multifaceted nature of

Grotius' work is 'eclectic'. The 'ambivalence' of his thinking – also often marked – gives room to debate.

In international law, reading and interpreting Grotius has become 'political'. For over a century, since the emergence of modern public international law as an autonomous and established academic discipline in the late nineteenth century, its historiography has been framed as a self-congratulatory narration of (liberal) progress. Recent scholarship, following the seminal work by Richard Tuck, has illuminated the complexity of understanding Hugo Grotius in the context of international law's history. One of today's major discussions on Grotius' ideas on politics and law beyond the state concentrates on his contributions to international law as empire.[19] Among international lawyers, Grotius remains one of the canonical thinkers, yet the images of the Dutch humanist as 'Prophet of Peace' or 'great seculariser' have now – largely – been left behind.[20] The interests behind the 'origins myth' of Grotius as 'father of international law' – or that of his major competitor for the title, Vitoria – have been disclosed.[21] This has liberated Grotius from the concern of international lawyers and international legal historians of overweighing his value for modern international law. Aided by the enduring scholarly interest in the life, thought and work of Grotius by scholars from a variety of disciplines and – by its extension – beyond international law and Grotius' most seminal juridical treatise, international lawyers and other scholars are now able to consider Grotius in his own time and in the 'long pasts' of the various intellectual traditions to which the Dutch humanist contributed. Thereby, we hope the place of Grotius in the tradition of European thought about international order and justice becomes better grounded. At the same time, Grotian studies taking inspiration from Grotius' own use of innovative method and epistemology are not limited to historians. Scholars with a wide variety of methodological leanings may bring the relevance of his thought to contemporary debates nurtured by non-contextualised or more anachronistic readings.[22]

I.4 Scope and Design of the Companion

The Cambridge Companion to Hugo Grotius does not come with the aspiration to bring an end to what has been termed 'the enigma Grotius'.[23] The riddle that Grotius still is to most of us is not due to the absence of a collective synthesis; the surge of research and writing on Grotius in the past few decades has, after all, not solved it either. Everyone has her own Grotius(es), so to speak. And, yet, in spite of this surge, we do think it is time for a *Companion*.

Of the various disciplines and epistemologies to which Hugo Grotius contributed, international law and political thought stand out as those in which his legacy is most acknowledged and debated to this day. Nevertheless, in recent years, his historical, theological and, somewhat less, literary writings and thought have become the subject of revived interest. In the tradition of *Cambridge Companions*, this volume is designed to survey the 'whole Grotius'. This not only means that his theological, historical and literary works are given their rightful place. It also invites questioning of Grotius' views from the totality of his oeuvre, trying to find the entanglements between the different epistemologies and discussing the relations between his life and works, between his *vita activa et contemplativa*.

In order to achieve this, the structure of this volume has been designed in five parts. The first part, 'Grotius in context', covers the biography of Hugo Grotius, in no less than three chapters. Henk Nellen, Grotius' most recent and important biographer, offers a brief survey of Grotius' life whereby he places his major works in the context of his intellectual influencers and his dramatic political, legal and diplomatic careers. Edwin Rabbie traces the rise and fall of Grotius as a Dutch official in the first half of his adult life, unpacking the intertwinement of constitutional and religious tensions that speeded him towards his downfall. Peter Borschberg likewise focuses on the period before Grotius' downfall, but on his engagement to the Dutch commercial and imperial expansion to the Indies. He raises the question what were Grotius' sources of information about the Indies, a crucial key to understanding his political and intellectual involvement with the Dutch undertaking.

The second part, 'Concepts', offers an attempt to tease out the general lines of Grotius' views, throughout his oeuvre, with regards to some key concepts. Making a selection always invites scholarly discussion, and rightly so. Arguably, the concepts selected for this part of the *Companion* play a significant role in Grotius' vast body of work and often ground and shape his arguments in various polemics and scholarly discussions. These chapters are all very rich and introduction here can only be reductive and unjust. But, is it, for example, at all possible to understand Grotius' theological, political and legal ideas without taking his profound reflections on 'virtue' and 'trust' into account? Mark Somos distils Grotius' theory of virtues from various places in his oeuvre as there is no single one work in which Grotius unfolded this theory. The chapter shows the fundamental role of virtues within all of his thinking. Peter Schröder discusses the equally central – though varied – role trust (*fides*) played in Grotius' work in general and in his work on international relations in particular. Also, Meirav Jones' examination of 'natural law as true law' demonstrates how closely entangled law and theology are in Grotius' work. Jones maps the debate about Grotius' contribution to natural law theory, but also points to how God's 'ordered plan of nature' precedes the 'state of nature' in his thinking. She argues that, through Philo, Grotius was able to reconcile voluntarism and rationalism within his conception of natural law. Sociability, of course, then plays a decisive role in Grotius' theory of natural law. Benjamin Straumann puts forward a Ciceronian account of Grotius' conception of 'sociability', which enabled Grotius to argue a legalised, rule-based doctrine of natural law when answering Carneades' denial. For the entry on 'sovereignty', Gustaaf van Nifterik takes a turn to Grotius' ideas on 'internal' sovereignty in *De jure belli ac pacis* to lay bare his constitutional theory and a conception of the people as *persona ficta* with their own rights under natural law. Grotius' Erastian conception of relations between 'Church and state' as expressed in *Ordinum pietas* and *De imperio* is then examined by Harm-Jan van Dam. He shows how, throughout his legal, political, historical and theological work, Grotius argued for a concept of absolute and indivisible sovereignty of state over Church. For Grotius, Van Dam explains, Erasmus had led the Dutch Reformation and he came to draw heavily on Erasmus' irenicism and thinking about toleration and free will. Camilla Boisen examines the relationship between divine will and human freedom in Grotius' work through the lens of 'predestination'. For Grotius, the predestination controversy was a matter of high social and political importance. Boisen shows how a pragmatic Grotius, vested in the Arminian perspective, gave priority to social peace and unity when engaging with theological hot potatoes such as predestination. Not the latter doctrine but natural sociability figured as the foundation for his theory of natural law and natural rights. The concept of 'rights' together with the corollary notion of duties inhabits the heart of Grotius' political and legal philosophical project of peace. The present companion offers two perspectives on this concept of 'rights' so central to current debates on Grotius. Francesca

Iurlaro sheds light on Grotius' use of perfect and imperfect rights from a philosophical perspective. She situates Grotius' theory of subjective rights in particular in relation to the long tradition of Aristotelian commentators and to Michael of Ephesus in particular. She emphasises the fundamental role of *aptitudo* (or moral fitness) and of attributive justice in Grotius' thinking. Another chapter offers a legal-historical perspective; Laurens Winkel provides a Roman law reading of Grotius' theory of rights, and connects the latter to the important debates in intellectual history on the origins of subjective rights. Finally, Andrew Fitzmaurice examines how Grotius reinterpreted 'property, trade and empire' through the changing understanding of human sociability. Drawing on human nature, Grotius claims regulation of trade and property comes naturally and empire of commerce is desirable from the perspective of the sovereign and the principle of self-preservation. This chapter also underscores again how Grotius' conceptual thinking – and the development or reinterpretation of the notions he used in his arguments – was contextual and political. In the course of the editing process, regrettably some chapters fell out of this collection. Yet, concepts so important to Grotius' thinking as charity, liberty, peace and toleration do feature throughout several chapters and the index will assist the reader in savouring these concepts.

The third part, 'Grotius as a man of letters, theologian and political writer' does the opposite of the prior part by carving up Grotius' oeuvre along the lines of modern genres and disciplines, except for the legal works that are saved for the fourth part. The four chapters survey the literary (Arthur Eyffinger), historical (Jan Waszink), theological (Oliver O'Donovan) and political (Hans Blom) works and contributions of Grotius. They introduce numerous, published and unpublished, works by Grotius in chronological order. They situate them against the backdrop of his life and intellectual trajectory, and render a brief account of their major content and contribution to the field.

The fourth part, 'Grotius as a legal scholar', purposely unbalances the holistic approach by singling out Grotius' forays into domestic and international law. This is, however, warranted by the fact that both his *Inleidinge tot de Hollandsche rechts-geleerdheid* and his *De jure belli ac pacis* reached canonical status before the century was out and had an enduring impact on later developments. These two works, together with *De jure praedae commentarius* and its spin-off *Mare liberum*, form the object for the analysis of Grotius' legal thought and methodologies. In the opening chapter, Alain Wijffels reframes the humanist/scholastic-debate by focusing on the legal sources, methodologies and style of discourse of Grotius. Wouter Druwé offers an overview of the major doctrinal views of Grotius with relations to Hollandic-Roman private law in the *Inleidinge*. The next three chapters focus on the international law dimensions of *De jure praedae* and *De jure belli ac pacis*. The first and third leg of the tripod *jus ad bellum/jus in bello/jus post bellum* are discussed by Randall Lesaffer, the second by Stephen Neff. The freedom of the sea, and the legacy of Grotius, is the subject of a chapter by William Butler. In *De jure belli ac pacis*, Grotius fleshed out the notion of just war as an instrument for the enforcement of rights to render a comprehensive overview of natural rights. This led him to discuss major parts of private law, with an expansion into criminal law. Bart Wauters and Paolo Astorri deal with two major themes from private law: property (Wauters) and contract (Astorri). The latter chapter also includes a brief discussion of Grotius' application of contract law – or not – to interstate treaties. Dennis Klimchuck discusses 'crime and punishment' in Grotius.

The fifth part, 'The reception of Grotius', concerns later scholarly receptions, revivals and appropriations of Grotius in different eras and by different disciplines. Marco Barducci revisits the debate on the impact of Grotian thought on the Enlightenment of the later seventeenth and eighteenth centuries, in particular with regards to religion. Ignacio de la Rasilla surveys the different appropriations of Grotius by international lawyers and international legal historians since the late nineteenth century, while William Bain explores Grotius' place in International Relations theory.

I.5 Editions, Translations and References to Grotius' Works

Grotius' published works, both during his life and posthumous, are numerous and many went through several historic and modern editions. A great number of his works still lack critical editions, while a massive amount of manuscripts remain undisclosed in print form in the archives.[24] For the purpose of this volume, a standard edition and/or translation has been selected. References to works of Grotius are in general to these editions and translations, unless it is indicated otherwise at the bottom of the chapter. References are, generally, to books, chapters, sections, paragraphs (so DJBP 1.1.2.1 for *De jure belli ac pacis* Book 1, Chapter 1, Section 2, Paragraph 1) rather than page numbers. This is valid both for references to the original text as to the English translation. Where such a number is followed by a comma, the number after the comma refers to the page number in the edition or translation (e.g. for *Mare liberum*), or the folio of the original manuscript in case of *De jure praedae*. For works without any subdivisions, the sole number refers to the page in the edition or translation, as appropriate; for poetic texts to the line.

For the standard edition of *De jure belli ac pacis*, the version by Robert Feenstra and C.E. Persenaire from 1993 is chosen. This is a reprint of the 1939 edition by B.J.A. De Kanter-Van Hettinga Tromp, with additional annotations[25] and a list of sources.[26] The 1939 edition reproduced the text of the five editions, which Grotius prepared – 1625, 1631 and the octavo editions by Blaeu from 1632, 1642 and 1646 – himself, taking the 1631 editions as its basis. While Feenstra levelled quite some criticism to the choice of the 1631 edition as a basis – instead of the 1646 one as a previous modern edition of 1919 had done –[27] he indicated the inclusion of the critical elements from this 1919 edition in the 1939 as a decisive factor in the latter's favour.[28]

The translation used in most chapters in this volume is the one by Francis W. Kelsey and others, prepared for its inclusion in *The Classics of International Law*, the series of canonical texts of international law designed by James Brown Scott (1866–1943). This translation is based on the 1646 edition, of which the Latin text is also included in *The Classics of International Law*. Absent a translation of the 1939/1993 edition, this unsatisfactory state of affairs is as close one can come in terms of concordance.

Major Works on Grotius

Blom, H. (ed.), *Property, Piracy and Punishment. Hugo Grotius on War and Booty in De iure praedae – Concepts and Contexts* (Leiden and Boston, 2009) [= Grotiana N.S. 26–8 (2005–7)].

Bull, H., B. Kinsbury and A. Roberts (eds.), *Hugo Grotius and International Relations* (Oxford 1990).

Geddert, J.S., *Hugo Grotius and the Modern Theology of Freedom* (London and New York, 2017).

Haggenmacher, P., *Grotius et la doctrine de la guerre juste* (Paris, 1983).

Jefferey, R., *Hugo Grotius in International Thought* (New York, 2006).

Kadelbach, S., *Recht, Krieg und Frieden bei Hugo Grotius* (Stuttgart, 2017).

Knight, W.S.M., *The Life and Works of Hugo Grotius* (London, 1925).

Lévesque de Burigny, J., *Vie de Grotius, avec l'histoire de ses ouvrages* (Amsterdam, 1754).

Nellen, H., *Hugo Grotius. A Lifelong Struggle for Peace in Church and State, 1583–1645* (Leiden and Boston, 2015).

Onuma, Y. (ed.), *A Normative Approach to War. Peace, War, and Justice in Hugo Grotius* (Oxford, 1993).

Straumann, B., *Roman Law in the State of Nature. The Classical Foundations of Hugo Grotius' Natural Law* (Cambridge, 2015).

Stumpf, C.A., *The Grotian Theology of International Law. Hugo Grotius and the Moral Foundations of International Relations* (Berlin, 2006).

Ter Meulen, J. and P.J.J. Diermanse, *Bibliographie des écrits imprimés de Hugo Grotius* (The Hague, 1950).

Ter Meulen, J. and P.J.J. Diermanse, *Bibliographie des écrits sur Hugo Grotius imprimées au XVIIe siècle* (The Hague, 1961).

Tuck, R., *The Rights of War and Peace. Political Thought and International Order from Grotius to Kant* (Oxford, 1999).

Van Beresteyn, E.A., *Iconographie van Hugo Grotius. Met 65 portretten gedeeltelijk in lichtdruk* (The Hague, 1929).

Van Ittersum, M.J., *Profit and Principle. Hugo Grotius, Natural Rights and the Rise of Dutch Power in the East Indies (1595–1615)* (Leiden and Boston, 2006).

Notes

1 See R. Tuck, *The Rights of War and Peace: Political Thought and the International Order from Grotius to Kant* (Oxford, 1999).

2 M.A. Gillespie, *The Theological Origins of Modernity* (Chicago, 2008).

3 Recent exceptions include P. Haggenmacher, 'Sources in the Scholastic Legacy. *Ius naturea* and *ius gentium* revisited by Theologians', in S. Besson and J. d'Aspremont (eds.), *The Oxford Handbook on The Sources of International Law* (Oxford, 2017), 45–63; S. Mortimer, 'Law, justice, and charity in a divided Christendom: 1500–1625' in M. Koskenniemi, M. García-Salmones Rovira and P. Amorosa (eds.), *International Law and Religion. Historical and Comparative Perspectives* (Oxford, 2017), 25–42; J.E. Nijman, 'Grotius's *Imago Dei* anthropology. Grounding *ius naturae et gentium*', in *ibid.*, 87–110; O. O'Donovan, 'The justice of assignment and subjective rights in Grotius', in O. O'Donovan and J. Lockwood O'Donovan (eds.), *Bonds of Imperfection: Christian Politics, Past and Present* (Grand Rapids, MI, 2004), 167–203; C.A. Stumpf, *The Grotian Theology of International Law: Hugo Grotius and the Moral Foundations of International Relations* (Berlin, 2006).

4 J.I. Israel, *The Dutch Republic. Its Rise, Greatness, and Fall 1477–1806* (Oxford, 1995); R. Lesaffer, 'The classical law of nations', in A. Orakhelashvili (ed.), *Research Handbook on the Theory and History of International Law*

(Cheltenham and Northampton, MA, 2011), 408-40; G. Parker, *The Dutch Revolt* (London, 1977).

5 M. Koskenniemi, 'Imagining the rule of law: rereading the Grotian tradition', *European Journal of International Law* 30 (2019) 17-52; H. Lauterpacht, 'The Grotian tradition in international law', *British Yearbook of International Law* 23 (1946) 1-53; J.E. Nijman, 'Images of Grotius, or the international rule of law beyond historiographical oscillation', *Journal of the History of International Law* 17 (2015) 83-137.

6 H. Nellen, *Hugo Grotius. A Lifelong Struggle for Peace in Church and State, 1583-1645* (Leiden and Boston, 2015); M.J. Van Ittersum, *Profit and Principle. Hugo Grotius, Natural Rights Theories and the Rise of the Dutch Power in the East Indies* (Leiden and Boston, 2006).

7 J.I. Israel, *Radical Enlightenment. Philosophy and the Making of Modernity 1650-1670* (Oxford, 2001).

8 In his 'Memorie van mijn Intentiën', Grotius rejected the tendency to dispute unnecessarily ('buyten noodt off nut') and favours toleration towards diverse understandings of dogma, in R.J. Fruin (ed.), *Verhooren en andere bescheiden betreffende het rechtsgeding van Hugo de Groot* (Utrecht, 1871), 3.

9 See e.g. Marc de Wilde on Grotius' *Jodenreglement*: M. de Wilde, 'Offering hospitality to strangers: Hugo Grotius's draft regulations for the Jews', *Legal History Review* 85 (2017) 391-433.

10 G.P. van Nifterik, 'Grotius on slavery', *Grotiana* N.S. 22-3 (2001-2002) 233-44.

11 P. Haggenmacher, *Grotius et la doctrine de la guerre juste* (Paris, 1983); D. Panizza, 'Political theory and jurisprudence in Gentili's *De iure belli*: the great debate between "theological" and "humanist" perspectives from Vitoria to Grotius', in P-M. Dupuy and V. Chetail (eds.), *The Roots of International Law/ Les fondements du droit international. Liber Amicorum Peter Haggenmacher* (Leiden and Boston, 2014), 211-47; B. Straumann, *Roman Law in the State of Nature. The Classical Foundations of Hugo Grotius' Natural Law* (Cambridge, 2015); Tuck, *Rights of War and Peace*.

12 See the edition by R. Feenstra and C. E. Persenaire (Aalen, 1993).

13 R. Lesaffer, *European Legal History. A Cultural and Political Perspective* (Cambridge, 2009), 338-67; idem, 'Roman law and the intellectual history of international law', in A. Orford and F. Hoffmann (eds.), *The Oxford Handbook of the Theory of International Law* (Oxford, 2016), 38-58.

14 J.I. Israel, 'Grotius and the rise of Christian "Radical Enlightenment"', *Grotiana* N.S. 35 (2014) 19-31.

15 T.J. Hochstrasser, *Natural Law Theories in the Early Enlightenment* (Cambridge, 2000).

16 H. Grotius, *On the Origin of the Native Races of America: A Dissertation*, ed. and transl. E. Goldsmid (Bibliotheca Curiosa; Edinburgh, 1884), 18.

17 See also for a monogenic reading L. Janssen, 'In search of the origins of the Native Americans. The story behind Grotius' De origine gentium Americanarum', 44 *Lias* (2017), 89-115.

18 Nellen, *Grotius*, 690.

19 P. Borschberg, *Hugo Grotius, the Portuguese and Free Trade in the East Indies* (Singapore, 2011); O. Hathaway and S. Shapiro, *The Internationalists and their Plan to Outlaw War* (New York/London, 2017); Koskenniemi, 'Rule of law'; Tuck, *Rights of War and Peace*; Van Ittersum, *Profit and Principle*; E. Wilson, *Savage Republic. De Indis of Hugo Grotius, Republicanism and Dutch Hegemony within the Early Modern World-System (c. 1600–1619)* (Leiden and Boston, 2008).

20 M.J. Van Ittersum, 'Hugo Grotius: the making of a founding father of international law', in Orford and Hoffmann, *Oxford Handbook of the Theory of International Law*, 82–100.

21 P. Amorosa, *Rewriting the History of the Law of Nations. How James Brown Scott Made Francisco de Vitoria the Founder of International Law* (Oxford, 2019); W.G. Grewe, 'Grotius – Vater des Völkerrecbts?', *Der Staat* 23 (1984) 161–78; K.-H. Ziegler, 'Grotius als Vater des Völkerrechts', in *Gedächtnißschrift für Wolfgang Martens* (Berlin and New York, 1987), 851–8.

22 See the discussions on method in international legal history, e.g. A. Kemmerer, '"We do not need to always look to Westphalia …" A Conversation with Martti Koskenniemi and Anne Orford', *Journal of the History of International Law* 17 (2015) 1–14; also A. Orford, 'On International legal method', *London Review of International Law* 1 (2013) 166–97.

23 ibid.

24 www.peacepalacelibrary.nl/collection/special-collections/grotius-collection. For a good overview of major works and standard editions, see Nellen, Grotius, 769–71 and 814–16.

25 DJBP, eds. Feenstra and Persenaire, 947–1025.

26 *Ibid.*, 1027–70.

27 H. Grotius, *De iure belli ac pacis libri tres*, ed. P.C. Molhuysen (London, 1919).

28 R. Feenstra, 'Introduction' in DJBP (eds.) Feenstra and Persenaire, 923–45, at 923–6.

Part I

Grotius in Context

Life and Intellectual Development 1

An Introductory Biographical Sketch

Henk Nellen

1.1 Introduction

This outline of Grotius' personal, intellectual and political career is not a pruned version of the author's 2014 biography of Hugo Grotius. It incorporates new material, mainly taken from Grotius' correspondence, and finishes with a succinct description of the *Nachleben* of his works. The story of Grotius' life is interspersed with references to the friendships he cultivated: after his father, Jan de Groot (1554–1640), had guided the child prodigy into the adult world, Josephus Justus Scaliger (1540–1609), Franciscus Junius (1545–1602) and Johannes Wtenbogaert (1557–1644) took over as patrons who helped the young scholar to situate himself in the networks of literature, law and religion. Later on, other friends assisted Grotius in his literary achievements (Daniel Heinsius, 1580–1655), politico-religious debates (Gerardus Joannes Vossius, 1577–1649) and the struggle to reunite the Christian churches (Denis Pétau, 1583–1652). By the same token, the reverse side of Grotius' scholarly life shows the bitter feuds and rivalries that he became embroiled in. Among these, the polemics with the formidable antagonists Sibrandus Lubbertus (1555–1625), Claude Saumaise (1588–1653) and André Rivet (1572–1651) left the most incisive scars.

1.2 A Scholarly Life: Cultural Lineages

The range of cultural lineages that converged in Grotius' personality was so wide that it seems only slightly exaggerated to dub him a 'uomo universale'. First, humanism with its adoration of the classical authors, especially Cicero, dominated his scholarly pursuits. Grotius occupied himself with textual editions of Martianus Capella, Aratus, Lucanus, Tacitus, Seneca, as well as source criticism; disciplines that he also pursued with his antiquarian research in *De antiquitate reipublicae Batavicae* (1610) and *Historia Gotthorum* (1655). Under the aegis of

Scaliger and Bonaventura Vulcanius (1538–1614), he acquired mastery of Latin and Greek. He showcased both skills by publishing an impressive amount of Greek texts that he translated into Latin prose and verse, including Stobaeus' compilation of Greek poets, a collection of excerpts taken from Greek drama, Euripides' *Phoenissae*, fragments from Greek philosophers on Fate and the Greek Anthology.

For his juridical research he owed much to the tradition of the *mos gallicus*, exemplified by legal scholars, philologists and historians such as Andrea Alciato (1492–1540), Jacques Cujas (1520–90), François Baudouin (1520–73) and Hugues Doneau (1527–91). These humanist jurists showed a strong tendency to contextualise, expurgate and systematise the jurisprudence preserved in collections like the *Corpus Justinianeum*. Nevertheless, Grotius also benefited from practical research by the late-medieval commentators of the *mos italicus*. Partaking in this tradition, he endorsed a broad syncretic approach similar to the German *usus modernus pandectarum*, whose representative Matthias Wesembeke (1531–86) he valued highly. This meant that he acquired a sense of the historical development of law as well as of the context in which the laws had been formulated. Also, in accordance with the method of his *alma mater*, Leiden University, he always paid close attention to both the practical application of law as well as its relevance at the time. Another critical facet of Grotius' intellectual signature was his indebtedness to the Thomist-inspired Spanish neo-scholastics, in particular Francisco de Vitoria (c. 1480–1546), Fernando Vázquez de Menchaca (1512–69), Diego de Covarruvias y Leyva (1512–17) and Domingo de Soto (1494–1560), together with their main representative in the Netherlands, Leonardus Lessius (1554–1623), who helped Grotius to develop his understanding of natural law and the law of nations. Since his adolescence, Grotius also studied the Bible and the Church Fathers, and he did so with greater intensity as theological strife began to infect public life. For the informed and intricate interweaving of profane and sacred sources, Grotius' writings should be deemed part of the Christian humanist tradition.

In his advice on how to conduct one's studies, addressed to French diplomat Benjamin Aubéry du Maurier (1566–1636; 1 BW 402), the role of Aristotle, placed alongside Cicero, is remarkable. Grotius underlined the importance of good morals, to be extracted from the *Nicomachean Ethics*, the *Wisdom of Sirach* and other examples of gnomic literature, Theophrastus' *Characters*, Euripides' tragedies, Terence's comedies and Horace's Satires. This reading list represents a broad selection of writings that culminated in the *vade mecum* of every seventeenth-century intellectual, Cicero's *De Officiis*. Furthermore, he recommended to follow personal predilection as a simple recipe for navigating one's way through the overwhelming mass of books on history: 'what we read for pleasure is fixed more firmly in the mind' ('... melius haerent quae libenter legimus'). All in all, Grotius might be characterised as an avid reader who used to pluck from everywhere. His self-declared eclecticism should be taken as a convincing warning against pinning him down to a specific school or confession (6 BW 2421).

Material gain, personal glory and patriotism drove Grotius to deploy his talents for advancing the political, diplomatic and cultural prestige of his fatherland, Holland, which, together with six other Dutch provinces, spearheaded the revolt against Spain. To this end, he was stimulated and coached by his father, Jan de Groot, who assisted his son in several activities, for example in the writing of *Parallelon rerum publicarum liber tertius*, a socio-cultural comparison of Athens, Rome and the Dutch Republic. Without doubt, Grotius' erudition, encyclopaedic memory, formidable command of languages and fluent style, together with his sense of order and accuracy, greatly helped him to advance his career. Tremendous versatility and energy underpin the projects he took on as a politician. As an epistolary intermediary, he greatly enhanced the international reputation of the regime led by the Advocate of the States of Holland, Johan van Oldenbarnevelt (1547–1619). The letters he exchanged with the French historian, Jacques-Auguste de Thou (1553–1617), and his compatriot, the polymath Isaac Casaubon (1559–1614), who had settled in England, are exemplary. The support received from these luminaries clearly shows that Grotius found a niche within a network of powerful relationships that in turn helped him to achieve international fame. From an early age, Grotius found himself at the centre of a finely meshed fabric of family members, learned friends, scribes, amanuenses, printers, patrons, befriended diplomats and functionaries of state.

How did his high societal status impact his behaviour? It is problematic to attempt the construction of a coherent psychological image based on period testimonies, in particular Grotius' official correspondence, which testifies to his constant desire for self-fashioning among the elite. Nonetheless, the sources teem with signs of his abounding enthusiasm, affability, peaceful disposition and eagerness to oblige friends or fellow-scholars; but sometimes Grotius also succumbed to pride and stubbornness. Many of his letters, even letters of consolation, are marked by a strong tendency to place himself in the middle. In later years, as the curse of a life in permanent exile began to take its toll, Grotius increasingly indulged in feelings of self-pity and anger. His sole desire was to retreat from the maddening crowd, so that he could focus on his studies. He put himself on show as a misunderstood genius who heroically adhered to a noble ideal that deserved to be valued above all worldly concerns: the reunification of the Christian churches.

1.3 Youth

Born on Easter Sunday, 10 April 1583, in Delft, Hugo de Groot, or Grotius as he preferred to be called in the international world of scholarship and politics, hailed from a regent family that was celebrated for its history and affiliated kinships ('natus est ... honesta antiquitus ac praeclaris affinita-tibus non semel innexa domo'), as he proudly stated in an autobiography that he wrote for a gallery of Leiden scholars, broadly equivalent of a personal web page today, the *Illustris Academia Lugd-Batava* (1613).[1] Pointing at the humanist learning of his uncle, Cornelis de Groot (1546–1610), and father Jan, Grotius sketched his own life until 1613 as a steeply ascending path that had been cleared from obstacles by a host of powerful patrons, such as Justus Lipsius (1547–1606), Joseph Scaliger, Johan van Oldenbarnevelt, Maurice of Nassau (1567–1625) and French ambassador Paul Choart de Buzanval (d. 1607). From his early years, Grotius portrayed himself as a talented and energetic worker. His exceptional status is attested by many, often legendary stories, for example on his ability to remember the names of all the soldiers of the 'cohortes' that he was asked to muster in the name of the States of Holland.[2] Louis Aubéry du Maurier (1609–87) even considered him the most universal scholar of all time after Aristotle.[3] Grotius' poetry attests to his proverbial precocity. An ode that he had written in the manner of Horace and dedicated to one of his most powerful patrons, Nicolaes de Bie, on the occasion of the latter's wedding, offers a case in point: at the age of eleven, Grotius boldly referred to the consummation of marriage by stating that the bride – like all women – longed for love but eschewed mentioning it.[4] A contemporary testimony, albeit only recorded many years later, stems from King Henry IV of France (1553–1610), who in an audience received the young man and referred to him as 'the miracle of Holland'. Needless to say, Grotius' friends and his father, Jan, but most significantly Oldenbarnevelt, put his talents to good use, and did so with the aim of enhancing the self-consciousness of the Dutch governing elite.

After visiting the Latin school in Delft, Grotius, aged eleven, matriculated at Leiden University on 3 August 1594 in the *artes* faculty. In a Neo-Latin welcome poem, the university's curator, Janus Dousa (1545–1604), ventured to compare the young student with Erasmus and predicted a golden future for him, in which he was destined to rival the ancients and easily surpass the scholars of his time. Together with Scaliger, theology professor Franciscus Junius was his most important mental coach. Grotius resided in his house for some time and may have also benefited from his instruction in biblical Hebrew. Later in life, he declared that he felt much indebted to his former landlord, in whose broad-minded convictions he had taken great delight: Junius was a Calvinist, albeit only in name. With reference to the doctrine of predestination, he assumed a moderate stance.[5] Grotius' studies at university are shrouded in uncertainty. Clues can be found in the letters he wrote to Christiaen Huygens (1629–95), Benjamin Aubéry du Maurier and his brother, Willem de Groot (1597–1662; 17 BW 384A and 1 BW 373 and 402); certain inferences can be made, for example that Grotius' involvement in legal studies organically flowed from the courses he took as an *artes* student. Grotius concluded his studies with a short *peregrinatio academica*, as a member of the entourage in Oldenbarnevelt's embassy that had been despatched to dissuade King Henry IV of France from concluding peace with Spain. The journey lasted from 17 March until the end of May 1598 and brought Grotius and the entire entourage through the northern and western parts of France, Angers, Orléans and also Paris. On 5 May, he was conferred a doctoral degree in law by the University of Orléans. Not long thereafter he probably made friends with Daniel Heinsius, Scaliger's most prized pupil, who embarked on an illustrious career at Leiden University. It is no exaggeration to claim that Grotius and Heinsius were now doomed to become rivals across a range of scholarly fields such as Neo-Latin poetry, letter writing, textual criticism, history and exegesis.

After returning to Delft, Grotius continued his literary and legal studies, until parental pressure made him agree to take the oath of office as a lawyer. He took this before the two institutions that were charged with supreme jurisdiction in Holland and Zeeland, namely the Court of Holland and Zeeland (13 December 1599) and the High Council of

Holland and Zeeland (15 December 1599). Both were based in The Hague. As Junius had done at Leiden in earlier years, the famous preacher Johannes Wtenbogaert, the future leader of the Arminian or Remonstrant party, now kept an eye on Grotius and for some years served as his landlord. In accordance with the privileged position he had enjoyed as a student, Grotius continued to set himself apart from colleagues, in particular in two respects. First, he managed to secure a number of legal cases that enabled him to earn a decent living. This stable income proved important because, at this time or shortly afterwards, Jan de Groot, Hugo's father, encountered serious financial difficulties. The endowments that remunerated Grotius for dedications of recently published works – for example *Pontifex Romanus* (1598) to the States General, and *Syntagma Arateorum* (1600) to the States of Holland – meaningfully added to his earnings. Second, Grotius combined his work as a lawyer with a range of activities that furthered the interests of Holland. He embarked on the ambitious enterprise of penning a history of the Dutch Revolt, under the auspices of the States of Holland, who accorded him an initial stipend on 8 November 1601. In the following years, the aggregate sum accumulated to 1,800 guilders. Around the end of 1604 or at the beginning of 1605, Grotius assumed the office of historiographer of Holland. During the years 1604–5, he wrote a treatise on the right of trade, plunder and lawful defence in the Indies, later called *De jure praedae commentarius*. This, however, remained unpublished until the second half of the nineteenth century, save for a single chapter that appeared anonymously as *Mare liberum* (1609). This is arguably Grotius' most famous publication. The booklet sought to defend the interests of the Dutch East India Company (VOC), whose aggressive policies and actions against Spain and Portugal called for a thorough justification, and to ensure, moreover, that the Republic's allies, France and England, continued their financial and military support.

1.4 Entrance into Dutch Politics

On 7 and 14 December 1607, Grotius was installed as advocate-fiscal, or public prosecutor. In this capacity, he brought civil and criminal cases before the Court of Holland and the High Council.[6] The regular salary attached to this key public office enabled Grotius to secure his marriage to Maria van Reigersberch (1589–1653) on 20 July 1608. Maria's father, a scion of a well-to-do family from Zeeland, had served as burgomaster of Veere. From the children born into this marriage, three sons and two daughters reached adulthood. The office of advocate-fiscal, moreover, gradually tugged Grotius into the maelstrom of Dutch high politics. His scholarly work evidences beyond doubt that he had no qualms about this. The three works *Mare liberum, De antiquitate* (1610) and *Ordinum Hollandiae et Westfrisiae pietas* (1613) are the main fruits of his labours to clean up and advance the tarnished international reputation of the nascent Dutch Republic and also of the federation's largest and most important member, Holland. The treatise *Meletius* was written during the summer of 1611 as a cautious attempt to quell the burgeoning confessional strife in the Republic. Though it remained unpublished, it may be taken as yet another sign of his growing engagement in politics. Already before the publication of *Ordinum pietas*, Grotius had taken the next step in assuming leadership in Dutch politics: on 5 June 1613, he moved from the judiciary to the executive branch ('ita a foro ad rempublicam transiit') with his appointment to the office of pensionary (legal advisor) of the thriving commercial hub of Rotterdam. One of the pensionary's tasks was to accompany the Rotterdam delegates to the meetings of the States of Holland. In this capacity, therefore, he was required to commute between the fatherland of Janus Secundus (The Hague) and the city of Erasmus (Rotterdam) (1 BW 272). This was ever the more important because, until February 1614, he combined his new job with winding up his duties as advocate-fiscal. During this period, he made his next career move by entering the international political arena. As a formally designated ambassador and acknowledged expert in the affairs of the Indies, he assumed leading roles in two Anglo-Dutch colonial conferences. The first was held in London (March–May 1613) and the second in The Hague (February–May 1615).

With visible ease, Grotius steered his ship across the turbulent waters of national and international politics. Analysis of his, gradually swelling, correspondence shows that it was not so much the scholarly or juridical work that consumed most of his time and energy, but his involvement in the politico-religious disputes that incrementally put public life during the Twelve Years Truce (1609–21) into turmoil. This period was shaped by the painful aftermath of the *Ordinum pietas*, written to rebut the Franeker theologian Sibrandus Lubbertus, who had accused the States of Holland of condoning Socinianism with the nomination of theologian Conradus Vorstius (1569–1622) as successor of Jacobus Arminius (1559–1609) at Leiden University. In his book, Grotius made a case for tolerating Arminianism as well as for the submission of the Reformed Church to the secular authorities. It is penned in a Latin style so masterful, compelling and virulent that he brought the already strained tensions to a head. Taken aback by the outspokenly negative response, Grotius resorted to a new polemical strategy. From now on, he took a more cautious approach in publications like *De satisfactione* (1617), *De imperio* (1614–17, published in 1647), *Disquisitio an Pelagiana sint* (1622), *De jure belli ac pacis* (1625), *De veritate* (1627), *Grollae obsidio* (1629) and even in his *Annotationes* to the Bible (1641–50). He remained shackled to his ideas and their free dissemination, but now refrained as much as possible from adding fuel to the political or religious controversies of his day. Instead, he focused on the subject matter itself. For researchers today, this deliberate caution certainly acts as an obstacle to interpreting Grotius' writings. In case of *De satisfactione*, for example, it is not easy to ascertain what triggered him to write this treatise.

As a consequence of Grotius' involvement in the Republic's politico-religious disturbances, a shift in his scholarly endeavours took place in the period up until his imprisonment at Loevestein: his early interest in classical and Neo-Latin literature had begun to wane a bit, though every now and then he indulged in this discipline. An annotated edition of Lucanus' *Pharsalia* (1614) and a large collection of Neo-Latin poetry, the *Poemata collecta* (1617 [=1616]), appeared in print during a period in which Grotius was consumed – nay overwhelmed – by daily worries about the religiously motivated convulsions that were gradually poisoning the public atmosphere. While refraining from polemics and stressing his impartiality, he addressed the imminent collapse of the Republic. The only way to avoid this, he argued, was to uphold and defend the sovereignty of each of the Republic's constituent provinces. To this advice he further added heartfelt pleas for inner-confessional accommodation and toleration. In the eyes of many adversaries, however, Grotius' recommended cure was worse than the disease itself. His complicity with Oldenbarnvelt's cantankerous political style was clear for all to see. As early as September 1614, an English observer dubbed Grotius 'the finger next the thum'. If the Advocate of Holland fell from power, he would take Grotius down with him.

1.5 Internal Strife

By publishing *Mare liberum* (a spin-off of *De jure praedae*) and *De anti-quitate*, Grotius advanced the interests of the Republic, a confederation of seven independent provinces that were waging an exhausting war against the Spanish Habsburgs. But internal dissension was also rearing its head: theological debates had not only infected the Church, but were generating political discord as well. This was true for some parts of the Republic, such as in the provinces of Utrecht and Gelderland, but was most notably occurring in Grotius' home turf, Holland. He presented himself as an honest broker who was interested in reconciling the two quarrelling parties by silencing the extremists on both sides. In the end, however, it was the peacemaker who was given the severest flogging. When theological strife spilled over from the Church into politics, Grotius – who continued to act as a productive writer for Oldenbarnevelt – became embroiled in the raging debates through the power of his pen, and this despite his efforts to rein in the full force of his style and articulation. He became arguably more involved than other champions of Oldenbarnevelt, the polemicists like Petrus Bertius (1565–1629), Jacobus Taurinus (1576–1618) and Caspar Barlaeus (1584–1648), as well as his former landlord, Wtenbogaert. He served as the mouthpiece of the ruling faction, under the aegis and with the ardent support of the magistrates from the Remonstrant bastion, Rotterdam. Apart from many speeches, memoranda and letters, Grotius wrote a series of lengthy learned treatises that lend a clearer picture of his fervent activity: *Ordinum pietas*, *Decretum ordinum Hollandiae* (1614), *Bona fides* (1614), *De imperio* and *De satisfactione*. As a member of the Rotterdam delegation to the States of Holland – on 31 May 1617, he joined the States' executive committee, the *Gecommitteerde Raden* – Grotius was repeatedly ordered to visit cities that were rocked by dissent and in which large segments of the population refused to comply with the States' official policy. But these missions only stirred up indignation and strengthened the resistance of the militant Counter-Remonstrant preachers and the regents who supported them.

Church and state were intricately intertwined at the time. Because the religious strife seriously damaged domestic peace and tranquillity, those in charge of maintaining public order felt compelled to intervene. More often than not, members of the States' delegations, city magistrates and government officials were faithful churchgoers themselves. Just like the common people, they chose a side in the debates, under the spell of preachers who were keen on securing a following that supported their views unreservedly. Theological strife soon became a political impasse. The Counter-Remonstrants or Gomarists deemed it a capital sin to share company in one and the same church with those who adhered to a less rigid interpretation of the doctrine of predestination. The hardliners demanded a Church that strictly conformed to Calvin's teachings. At the other end of the spectrum, the Remonstrant or Arminian preachers sought formal acknowledgement of their less stringent theological stance within the Reformed Church. They appealed to the provincial authorities who, through their spokesman Grotius, for example, imposed religious toleration by the force of law until the States' assembly could arrange for and convene a national synod. This synod would debate the outstanding points of contention and settle the religious differences once and for all. The date for this proposed synod, however, was postponed time and again, because both parties disagreed on the modalities of such a meeting. While the Counter-Remonstrants, representing the majority in the Reformed Church, would not hesitate to ban Remonstrantism, the States of Holland in turn refused to convene a synod for as long as the Oldenbarnevelt-led faction relied on a simple majority in the assembly. Before long, decision-making became so paralysed that even the most pressing business of the day, such as questions relating to the expiry of the Truce, remained unaddressed and unresolved. Seen from this standpoint, Stadholder Maurice of Nassau's decision to break the impasse became unavoidable. He concluded that Oldenbarnevelt's stubborn refusal to abandon his policies of appeasement had brought the Republic to the brink of destruction.

Under the guidance of the land's advocate, Grotius developed different defence-strategies. He pretended to assume a position above the two quarrelling parties and stressed the political necessity of maintaining a united Reformed Church that offered shelter to a broad spectrum of beliefs. The Counter-Remonstrant party rejected his pleas for tolerance and condemned them as disingenuous or even impertinent support for the Remonstrants. In his correspondence, Grotius admitted to subscribing to Remonstrant theology (1 BW 246, 312 and 534). Also, to allay his growing concerns about the outcome of the religious conflict, he appealed to the oath he had sworn. This bound him to his sole superiors, the city magistrates of Rotterdam, who had ordered him to carry on. Finally, he built up a circle of confidential accomplices, who helped him to achieve his goals. From 1613 onwards, the friendship with Daniel Heinsius rapidly cooled down and eventually fell apart after this friend openly sided with the Counter-Remonstrant faction. Heinsius' place was then taken by Gerardus Joannes Vossius, who was a scholar of a very different character, mental outlook and religious affiliation. He was communicative, pliable and versatile, but – most importantly – he possessed an encyclopaedic knowledge of Church history. At Grotius' behest, Vossius was relieved of his dull life as a Dordrecht schoolteacher and nominated regent of the Leiden States College, the academic institute that housed and coached students of theology. Without doubt, Grotius fully trusted that Vossius' administration would soon result in the preparation of Church ministers whose trademark was to blunt and smooth the sharp edges of theological controversy.

1.6 Process, Verdict and Detention

The arrest of Oldenbarnevelt, together with his most prominent helpers, took place in the morning of 29 August 1618. Grotius was incarcerated in the castle at the Binnenhof in The Hague, and his cell was located above the offices of his former employer, the Court of Holland. The investigating judges commenced their interrogations of Grotius on 1 October. This preliminary phase in the trial lasted until 6 March 1619. Next, charges were formulated that supported the verdict, which was pronounced on 18 May. Meanwhile, Oldenbarnevelt was beheaded on 13 May, after hearing the verdict against him the day before. Grotius' own sentencing came as a relief to him because of its relative leniency: life imprisonment and confiscation of property. In the night of 5–6 June 1619, he was taken to Loevestein Castle. Adapting quickly to the less demanding conditions of his imprisonment here, he started working on a wide range of scholarly enterprises, foremost among which are his biblical annotations. These were initially meant to serve as a commentary to a polyglot edition of the Bible being planned by the Leiden Orientalist, Thomas Erpenius (1584–1624). He also wrote a now lost treatise, *De justa defensione, usu gladii et bello,* which, judging by the title may have represented a first sketch of *De jure belli ac pacis* (1625). As if this were not enough, he also finished the manuscript of his compendium of Holland's private law, the *Inleidinge* (published 1631). He further dabbled in various literary activities such as writing Dutch poetry, among which one may include his *Bewijs van den waren godsdienst* (1622), a didactic poem that was later brought into Latin prose and published as *De veritate* (1627).

1.7 A Frustrated Statesman's Life in Exile

Shortly before the expiry of the Truce, on 22 March 1621, Grotius successfully pulled off an escape from Loevestein castle – concealed in a book chest – that left his captors embarrassed and red-faced. He fled via Antwerp to Paris, where he arrived on 13 April 1621. Once firmly settled there, he fell into his old habits and again distinguished himself as the leading apologist of the Oldenbarnevelt faction, soon to be called the Dutch States Party. He was firmly convinced that Maurice's intervention on behalf of the Union of Utrecht – a federation of independent provinces that had been founded in 1579 to repel Spanish violence – represented an unacceptable violation of Holland's sovereignty. This is the thrust of his argument expounded in the *Verantwoordingh* (1622), a book that offers further proof of Grotius' skills as a polemicist. Separately, a Latin and a partial French translation appeared, so as to inform the European reading public that the destruction of the Oldenbarnevelt regime had been illegal. Early in the year 1622, Grotius also opened with a salvo on the theological front with the publication of his *Disquisitio an Pelagiana sint*. In this treatise, he rejected the decisions of the Synod of Dordrecht by arguing that the Counter-Remonstrants had blatantly violated the spirit of the primitive Church, which had always given space to doctrinal positions such as those held by the Arminians or Remonstrants. The *Verantwoordingh* triggered the States General to promulgate a placard that harshly condemned the book as an infamous, seditious and scandalising libel (24 November 1622). The placard confirmed the deep rift that now separated Grotius from his fatherland. Over the next few years, he was repeatedly reminded that the *Verantwoordingh* stood as an obstacle to his return. It was pointless to believe that one day redress could be found and his sentence overturned. Instead of losing heart, Grotius hopefully clutched onto signs that the regime in Holland was about to change. Meanwhile, he focused on his scholarly endeavours. Apart from his ambitious project to collect and edit Greek poetical *sententiae* with ingenuous metrical Latin translations in the famous trilogy

Dicta poetarum (1623), *Excerpta ex tragoediis* (1626) and *Anthologia Graeca* (1795–1822), he also completed within an amazingly short time his *De jure belli ac pacis* (1625).

Both the contents and reception of this monumental work are discussed at length in other chapters of this volume. Suffice it here to mention that discussion of the laws of war and peace was chiefly motivated by Grotius' desire to address the denunciation of natural law by the sceptics: as 'real' law it offered a sufficient basis for a more humane approach to armed conflicts and war. On the other hand, it is important not to overestimate the role of natural, subjective rights in his concept of law. For sure, subjective rights such as self-preservation and respect for property offered a limited range of causes for waging a just war, but Grotius placed these rights within a broader system of justice, that was meant to mitigate the impact of warfare through charity, moderation and personal conscience (*caritas, temperamenta, justitia interna*).[7] A second observation that might be in order here is that *De jure belli ac pacis* completely differed from *De jure praedae* as far as context, perspective, structure, contents and target are concerned. The legal systems of both books concur in many respects and there is some reason to assume that Grotius had the manuscript of *De jure praedae* at his desk when he wrote *De jure belli ac pacis*.[8] But tables had turned during the years of Grotius' detention and exile. Whereas *De jure praedae* was a youthful work that aggressively championed the Republic's struggle for independence against Habsburg Spain, he now adopted an ideal that transcended national interests. Confronted with the grim consequences of continual political and religious strife, he envisaged war as a societal evil that should be drastically checked. He proposed to reduce the catalogue of justified reasons for waging war and developed a complex moral system for humanising war, to be implemented if all attempts to secure peace had failed. Furthermore, according to Grotius, war should be undertaken with the sole aim of achieving an enduring peace. By cultivating the virtues that were rooted in man's natural appetite for a steady community life, violence could be avoided or limited to a minimum.

Using his *Silva ad Thuanum* (1621), a Neo-Latin poem for the young François-Auguste de Thou, as a calling card, Grotius found an open door to the learned circles of Paris. Over the years, he established close relationships with a host of scholars, mostly jurists, philologists and philosophers like Jérôme Bignon (1589–1656), Nicolas-Claude Fabry de Peiresc

(1580–1637), Pierre Gassendi (1592–1655), Nicolas Rigault (1577–1654), Denis Pétau, Claude Saumaise, Guy Patin (1601–72) and Marin Mersenne (1588–1648), who frequented the illustrious *Academia Puteana*, led by the brothers Pierre (1582–1651) and Jacques Dupuy (1591–1656). The circle around the Dupuy brothers was marked by a strong sense of Gallicanism that opted for an independent position of the French state and Church towards Rome. This was also in line with a programme that, during the sixteenth-century wars of religion, had been defended by the *politiques*. The correspondence, however, intimates that a troubled relationship with the fatherland remained the prime topic in Grotius' personal life. During his stay in France, he saw his illusions crushed many times. His bitterness was intensified by the distrust he felt against the authorities in the Dutch Republic. Against all odds, he kept his spirits high in the belief that prospects for an honourable return would emerge soon after Maurice had passed away. He took a letter written by future stadholder Frederick Henry (1584–1647; 2 BW 776) as a trustworthy promise from a mighty patron. Nonetheless, nothing changed after Maurice's death in 1625. With growing impatience, Grotius waited for a lull in the political and religious dissensions. He enjoyed a stipend from the French king – paid irregularly, however – but he undermined his own fragile immigrant status by stubbornly refusing to render any service in an official capacity to the French. For example, when he was invited to make a contribution toward French commercial affairs outside Europe, patriotic scruples stopped him from lending any assistance in founding a new India Company – a domain in which he had acquired considerable expertise.[9] The most important reason why negotiations for his return to the Dutch Republic continued to be delayed was Grotius' outright refusal to compromise, or even just hint at admission, that he may have broken the law during his tenure as pensionary of Rotterdam. The letters from this period reveal a strong sense of ego and self-esteem, which made it difficult for his friends in Holland to assist in his attempts to create a breakthrough.

Eventually, after years of fruitless waiting, Grotius decided to get on his feet and take matters into his own hands. He took his leave from King Louis XIII of France (1601–43), as if he were embarking on a diplomatic mission, and made his way to Rotterdam, where he arrived on 29 October 1631. His first outing was a public pilgrimage to the statue of Erasmus that stood in the marketplace. Dutch friends such as his brother-in-law, Nicolaes van Reigersberch (1584–1654), thought that Grotius' self-assured behaviour was out of place, but his wife Maria supported him resolutely by stating 'that he would be crazy to go there as if into a silent prison'. His appearance in the open was seen as a provocation, and the news spread like wildfire that Holland's most famous exile had dared to make a semi-official homecoming. Grotius was sufficiently content to revel in the relative freedom in Rotterdam and Amsterdam, where a more lenient attitude towards representatives of the former Oldenbarnevelt faction prevailed and where the tense atmosphere that existed during the Truce had now dissipated. But, in the 'Counter-Remonstrant' cities and consequently also in the States of Holland, debates soon flared up on how best to address this explosive homecoming. Although political animosities had subsided to the extent that magistrates from the cities of Rotterdam, Delft and Amsterdam were pleading for granting Grotius permission to settle in Holland, a majority in the assembly, composed of Oldenbarnevelt's old adversaries together with the regents who had assumed power in 1618–19, fiercely resisted any decision that would weaken their standing. Grotius' return reminded them of Homer's story of the Trojan horse; Christ's parable of the prodigal son did not apply to somebody who had penned the *Verantwoordingh* and *Disquisitio*, infamous libels that threatened to destroy the constitutional and religious foundations of the Dutch Republic. This convict, sentenced to life imprisonment, deserved no rehabilitation, especially since he refused to acknowledge any guilt whatsoever and demanded a rescinding of his verdict and condemnation. In the months that followed, the troubles of the Truce appeared to be returning. Grotius thought it best to break off his 'public' stay in Rotterdam and transfer to Amsterdam, where he kept a low profile (arriving on 9 December 1631). Considering that the former exile had found strong support in the main 'Remonstrant' cities, Stadholder Frederick Henry looked for a way out of the gridlock, but his intervention bore no fruit. On 7 April 1632, Grotius was given a clear choice: leave the country or request permission to stay. Asking for permission would have amounted to an admission of guilt, and this was simply out of the question for him. Thrice condemned – in 1619, 1622 and now in 1632 – Grotius decided to leave his fatherland on 17 April 1632 and headed to the city of Hamburg, home to many a Dutch exile. Here he would find a good opportunity to negotiate for future employment in the service of one of the northern European (Protestant) powers.

1.8 Hamburg

After his arrival in Hamburg at the beginning of May 1632, Grotius first stayed in nearby Dockenhuden, at the farm of a befriended Dutch merchant. Later, he moved into the city itself, where he found accommodation in the house of an emigrated Remonstrant preacher. The Hamburg episode has been characterised as a fruitless period in the career of an otherwise very productive scholar. There certainly is a dip in the publications graph, as far as first editions of his works are concerned. Of course, looking for employment that would also enable him to continue his studies took up a good part of Grotius' time, as did getting used to the new environment. The absence of rich libraries and of his personal manuscripts prevented him from continuing with the revision of his annotations to the New Testament (5 BW 1832), but he found time for preparing a Latin drama, the *Sophompaneas*, on the government of Patriarch Joseph in Egypt. The play should be read as a mirror of princes ('vorstenspiegel'), but probably Grotius took interest in the theme because he indulged in musing on the parallels between Joseph's vicissitudes and his own eventful life. Furthermore, the Hamburg period offered Grotius a chance to deepen his acquaintance with adherents of Socinianism, primarily Martinus Ruarus (1587–1657), Johannes Crellius (1590–1633) and Samson Johnson, and also with many German scholars such as Johannes Fredericus Gronovius (1611–71), Fredericus Lindenbrog and Henricus Vagetius, who in turn helped him strengthen ties with Georg Calixt (1586–1656) and Jacobus Lampadius (1593–1649). From the very beginning, the Remonstrants had been accused of sympathising with Socinianism. His earlier publication of *De satisfactione*, written against Faustus Socinus (1539–1604), had not freed Grotius from the task of denying any affiliation between the Remonstrants and Socinians, the more so because he was criticised for failing to answer Crellius' attack on *De satisfactione*. Accusations of Socinianism also popped up every now and again in relation to his *Bewijs van den waren godsdienst* and its Latin version *De veritate*. Perhaps Grotius wrote his most outspoken personal defence, not for the outside world, but rather to allay concerns within the circle of his closest friends and fellow scholars in the form of a couple of informative letters. In these, he confirmed, in accordance to the creed of the primitive Church, the central importance of Christ's role as a mediator in a believer's struggle for salvation (4 BW 1502 and 1503; 8 BW 3390; see also 17 BW 1820A).

Here, Grotius showed himself to be an orthodox Christian who endorsed the core tenets of faith. At the same time, he apodictically rejected the ingrained urge among theologians to codify abstruse dogmas like the Trinity, in the vain hope of suppressing dissent in matters of dogma.

Even before leaving for Hamburg, Grotius had received offers to enter into the Swedish diplomatic service. His response was lukewarm at first, but, during the summer of 1634, more concrete overtures resulted in personal discussions with the Swedish chancellor, Axel Oxenstierna (1583–1654), in whose entourage Grotius travelled in order to attend a conference of the League of Heilbronn of the German Protestants in Frankfurt. During his stay here, he probably also met up with John Dury (1596–1680), the indefatigable promotor of Protestant reunification. Eventually Grotius reached an arrangement with his Swedish superiors, and in particular with Oxenstierna, who entrusted him with the task of representing the young Swedish queen, Christina (1626–89) at the French court. Based on his credentials and instructions dated 6 January 1635 (17 BW 1964A), it is safe to assume that the newly appointed ambassador headed for Paris shortly afterwards. His official entrance into Swedish service probably preceded this date, for remuneration by regular stipend had been granted for the period from May 1634.

1.9 In Swedish Service

After years of waiting and despair, Grotius' career was transformed and experienced a spectacular upsurge. Proudly, but without alluding to the destiny of Patriarch Joseph, he informed his friends and acquaintances on his change of allegiance to his adopted fatherland, Sweden. Still, his earlier life as an exile continued to haunt him. Every now and then he gloomily gibed at his enemies in the former fatherland, who kept him at bay and even sought to thwart his diplomatic career. The frustrations he felt about Holland's obstinacy can be illustrated by highlighting his complex relationship with the English polymath, John Selden (1584–1654). Selden admired Grotius for his *De jure belli ac pacis*. He perused it to write his own *De jure naturali* (1640), a project that he had designed when he prepared his *Mare clausum* (1635) for publication in response to Grotius' *Mare liberum*. After reading *Mare clausum*, Grotius noted not only Selden's benevolence towards him, but also his erudition ('Seldenum legi in me plane humanum et sane eruditum') (6 BW 2431, 2441 and 2583). He did not yield an inch, however, and stubbornly refused to answer the book. As he dismissively put it, he would subject himself to ridicule if he entered the fray for the benefit of a country that had evicted him (7 BW 2613 and 2879). Moreover, he was not prepared to compromise Sweden's interests in the Baltic by championing the cause of the free sea (6 BW 2459; 8 BW 3085). He swallowed his pride, even though Selden at the end of *Mare clausum* maliciously capitalised on an old Neo-Latin poem in which Grotius had glorified King James I/VI's maritime power. His esteem for Selden remained intact (see also 11 BW 4897; 14 BW 6244). In a theatrical display of emotion, Grotius recalled how his patriotism, voiced in treatises like *De antiquitate*, *Mare liberum* and the *Inleidinge*, had resulted in his trial, detention and banishment. *Mare clausum* by contrast restored its author, who had been imprisoned for defending the cause of parliament, into the king's favour.[10] Grotius prudently avoided mentioning his *Ordinum pietas* expressly, obviously because the animosities earlier elicited by the book still lingered, and these in turn made abundantly clear that many of his former compatriots were loath to honour him for it (10 BW 4119, but see DI p. 982, n. 6). Now, after many years in exile, he distanced himself from some of the works he had published during the Twelve Years Truce. He hesitated to re-edit his *Poemata collecta*, embarrassed as he was by the praise that he once had bestowed on dignitaries who later became his adversaries (7 BW 2879; 10 BW 4280); he discarded *Mare liberum* as the unripe fruit of a juvenile spirit: 'Fuit enim meum opus de Mari libero optimo scriptum in patriam animo, sed aetate juvenili' (6 BW 3085), and some years later he dismissed *De antiquitate* as a treatise that spawned from an overzealous love for the old fatherland (14 BW 6051). A host of scholars, including John Selden, Petrus Cunaeus (1586–1638), Dirck Graswinckel (1600–66) and Johannes Isacius Pontanus (1571–1639, mulled over the legal intricacies of the free sea. Grotius, however, preferred to remain in the background and drily hinted at his rivals' propensity to tailor arguments to fit the interests of the state each was serving (8 BW 3085 and 3340).

Grotius' diplomatic career was shaped by four key issues: he had to deal with strong opposition from the French, who took offence at the ambassador's independent and sometimes overtly anti-French disposition; his room for manoeuvre was narrowed down due to the rapidly decreasing Swedish political influence in Europe; the negotiations on an international peace treaty fell outside his work area and he received only lukewarm support from his superiors in Sweden. His embassy started under the inauspicious sign of a personal affront. After his arrival at the outskirts of Paris, the Richelieu government delayed his official entrance, thus revealing to Grotius and the world that the former exile was persona non grata. In his biography of Grotius, Louis Aubéry du Maurier stated that Richelieu instructed all French diplomats who negotiated with representatives of the Swedish crown to request Grotius' recall. Despite these efforts, the ambassador was forbidden to retreat because Chancellor Oxenstierna stubbornly refused to yield to French pressure.[11] Although surely exaggerated, du Maurier's story contains a kernel of truth. Grotius' weekly reports show how squabbles over protocol and precedence ran like a thread through the whole story of his embassy. It took a long time before French manoeuvres to have him removed from his post succeeded. While risking a break with his hosts by resolutely defending Swedish interests, Grotius was also witnessing a steady erosion of Sweden's stature in the European theatre of war. This had begun to set in after the sudden death of King Gustavus Adolphus on the battlefield in 1632. As leader of the Protestant powers in Germany, Chancellor Oxenstierna saw his efforts hampered by a coalition riddled with internal dissensions. To make matters worse, Grotius could not stop the French government from treating Sweden as a satellite power whose aspirations to dominate European politics no longer aligned with the prevailing balance of power. An unexpected journey to Paris, undertaken by Oxenstierna in April and May 1635, aimed at lending his ambassador a helping hand, but otherwise achieved little to improve Grotius' compromised standing.

During the ten years of Grotius' embassy, and certainly after 1641 when preparations for the Westphalian Peace Conference began, the hub of diplomatic negotiations gradually shifted from Paris to central Germany. Of course, Grotius spent considerable time discharging his duties, for example by safeguarding the regular payment of the French war subsidies. He also protected the interests of his Swedish compatriots in Paris and elsewhere in France, and was regularly received for an audience by Louis XIII. The most time-consuming task, however, was his intense, multilingual correspondence with Swedish diplomats posted across Europe and also with relatives in Holland. Every now and then, Grotius' letters intimate that he was unhappy with his position as Swedish ambassador. The source of much of his annoyance was the tepid support he was receiving from his superiors. Oxenstierna, for example, rarely replied to Grotius' letters; instructions from Sweden were ambiguous or overdue and, more importantly, Grotius did not receive his pay regularly, even though maintaining his position as a royal Swedish ambassador came with huge expenses. As if that were not enough, Sweden sent extraordinary emissaries to the French court who, much to Grotius' chagrin, got in the way of performing his official duties. As the ordinary ambassador to the French court, Grotius shot off many angry letters to his superiors in which he grumbled, for example, about the misconduct of the envoys, Peter Abel Schmalz (1610–50) and Marc Duncan de Cerisantes (1612–48). Proud as he was, Grotius could not resist explaining that he had to compete with such unruly, boisterous 'dogs', a situation he described as a blatant dishonour. How long would he have to endure such an abomination? The surprise Swedish attack on Denmark in 1643 certainly triggered a sudden surge in his activities. The war was concluded with the Peace of Brömsebro on 13 August 1645, just a couple of weeks before Grotius' death. The acclaimed author of *De jure belli ac pacis* shrewdly justified the unannounced attack on Denmark to the court of Louis XIII, but the French sharply condemned this military action. They argued that, instead of promoting the common interest, the Swedes were now using French war subsidies to establish hegemony in the Baltic Sea region.

In an official despatch of 30 December 1644/9 January 1645, the Swedish government ordered Ambassador Grotius on behalf of Queen Christina to vacate his post and move to a location that was closer to her ('ad loca nobis propinquiora') (16 BW 7242 and 7366). The Swedes, it would appear, had given in to French pressure for three reasons. First, the benefits of being represented by an ordinary ambassador did not outweigh the high costs of maintaining a permanent presence. To solve his long-standing salary problems, Grotius had been permitted to take his remuneration from the French war subsidies. Second, the relationship with France was in disarray, which meant that Grotius' influence as a representative of the Swedish crown had no impact. Grotius refused to meet Cardinal Richelieu (1585–1642) and, after the cardinal's death, also his successor, Cardinal Jules Mazarin (1602–61), because these dignitaries denied him honour and respect due to him in accordance with diplomatic protocol. Last, but not least, Grotius' publications on the reunification of the Christian churches had seriously damaged his reputation among the conservative Lutheran Swedes. Offended by a refusal to hold services in the

Paris embassy, a debauched Lutheran pastor and fortune seeker named Johann Seiffart attacked Grotius' scheme for unification by spreading false rumours and accusations. These not only greatly discredited the ambassador personally, but also the Swedish government and Queen Christina.

1.10 Farewell to the Fatherland

Around 1637 a biographical turn took place as Grotius readjusted his priorities. He gave up the hope of an honourable return to the old fatherland, while his loyalty to the Swedish authorities began to show some cracks. With growing self-confidence and yet with hesitation, he stepped forward to champion the reunification of the Christian churches. It was an ideal that he had cultivated since he was young and that he now adapted in one important aspect. Until now, the hardline Calvinists, who were mostly rebellious people as he observed in one of his letters (12 BW 5061), had stood in the way of intra-Protestant reunion. Since they would continue to remain an obstacle for the foreseeable future, he proposed a rapprochement of all progressive Reformed believers with French Roman Catholics. This would take place on the basis of a Gallican programme of reform that paved the way for the establishment of a new universal Christian Church.

Grotius displayed a remarkable sense of pragmatism: while dogmatic details would remain open for further discussion, he proposed a union based on a few principal tenets of doctrine and dogma that focused on and confirmed the primacy of Christ's Redemption. In proposing this, Grotius harked back to the primitive Church. In his opinion, the Church of England greatly resembled this ideal. To achieve this goal, he embarked on a series of small but mindful steps. For example, he offered a helping hand to John Dury, a tireless promotor of intra-Protestant unity, and recommended him to Oxenstierna, knowing well that the chancellor was not disinclined toward such a unification scheme. A platform to advance his scheme offered itself when Grotius decided to employ Brendan Daetri, a student of moderate Lutheran theologian Georg Calixt from Helmstedt, to the position of house preacher. Daetri was ordered to hold weekly services for the Swedes and Germans in the French capital. Reformed believers who took offence at their creed's strict tenets of predestination were invited as well. In this way, Grotius' diplomatic post in a Roman-Catholic country enabled two other confessions to interact in a single space. Before long, however, Grotius had to dismiss Daetri on the grounds that he abused his services to rant against Roman Catholicism. When Deatri's religious services were suspended, Grotius felt that he had to account for this decision. He did this anonymously, in *De coenae administratione* (1638), in which he defended Christians who abstained from communion on the grounds of dogma. Apart from the appointment of a non-Calvinist house preacher and publishing a treatise on the Holy Communion, another step in the direction of unification was taken by challenging the claim that the pope was the antichrist. To this end, Grotius anonymously published the treatise *De anti-christo* (1640), which he used to fathom the public mood both in France and Holland. Remarkable is the great circumspection with which Grotius embarked on his 'crusade'. He was obviously aware of the possible conse-quences for his personal life, as well as for his family and reputation. Casual remarks in semi-public letters, formal exhortations in published works, as well as outspoken statements in irenic treatises such as the *Appendix de Antichristo* (July 1641) or *Annotata ad Consultationem Cassandri* (October 1641), reflect a long-term programme that began cautiously and quietly and moved on to openly endorse Christian unity. A couple of pages in the *Votum pro pace ecclesiastica* (1642) provide an account – and even a justification – of Grotius' path or intellectual *Werdegang*.

The exegetical foundations of this reunion were laid out in the *Annotationes* on the Bible, a project that, during his detention in Loevestein, he solemnly swore to publish one day (15 BW 6972). After his escape, Grotius worked on this project intermittently. He considered it his magnum opus, a work that he constantly revised and expanded. He drew on the expertise and assistance of befriended scholars, who were given access to the work while it was still 'in statu nascendi'. His hermeneutic method might be characterised in three keywords, 'phil-ology', 'historicisation' and 'morality'. He compared variants in old translations based on manuscripts that no longer existed. In order to reach a better understanding of the corrupted text, he benefited from the *Codex Alexandrinus*, which had only been recently retrieved at the time. He compared vocabulary and idioms of the original Hebrew and Greek with other ancient sources of the Greco-Roman world. He shed light on Jewish customs, institutions, laws and ceremonies by referring to rabbin-ical literature that, at the time, was becoming more readily accessible in bilingual editions. Apart from their textual corruption, the books of the Bible – a patchwork of texts – contained many flaws, inaccuracies and other, often chronological, inconsistencies, just as the individual books taken on their own. For this reason, Grotius limited the divinely inspired parts to the sayings of the prophets and Christ. In this way, he approached Scripture just as if he were working with a secular text. For example, he annotated the Song of Songs, a poetic colloquy of King Solomon and his Egyptian bride, and in so doing made references to classical writers like Theocritus, Horace, Catullus and Propertius. He did not balk at clarifying the sexual innuendo of the text.

As a classical scholar, Grotius also offered an historical explanation, which is to say that he sought to expound the literal meaning of the text, or uncover authorial intentions. Whereas, according to Reformed tradition, all passages on the antichrist encapsulated the excesses of papal tyranny, Grotius explained them as allusions to moral decay in the Roman Empire. By insisting on what he considered to be the literal meaning, he loosened the historical ties between the Old and New Testaments and, in so doing, undermined the idea of Christ's coming as the fulfilment of the prophesies found in the Old Testament on the coming of the Messiah. Although he acknowledged this fulfilment, he grounded it in a vague, allegorical or theological interpretation, or specifically as a 'sensus mysticus', 'altius', 'abstrusius' or 'sublimior'. This was to be distinguished from the literal sense, the 'sensus primus', 'historicus' or 'apertus', which referred to the meaning as it was understood by the audience at the time. The reader should bear in mind that the prophets generally aimed at satisfying the immediate needs of the audience they were addressing, and did not envision that their words would find fulfilment only many centuries later. All in all, Grotius' philological–historical approach aimed at bringing out the gist of the biblical message, as it was understood in the time of the primitive Church. During the first three centuries CE, ethical values like clemency, selflessness and charity stood at the centre of Christian belief. Church life was not yet shackled to rigid dogmas. In the seventeenth century, the simple morality that Christ and his disciples had offered to their followers was – according to Grotius – still of paramount importance.

During the last phase of his life, Grotius received great services from the Jesuit Denis Pétau. His friendship – or should we say, his alliance – with Pétau remains mostly beneath the surface, but there is no doubt that, as a mental coach, he had replaced Vossius. Pétau revised, for example, drafts of the pamphlets against Rivet and most of the Bible annotations. In an obituary on Pétau, Henri de Valois recalled the Jesuit's ardent attempts to convert Grotius to the Roman-Catholic religion.[12] Together with Peiresc and Gabriel Naudé (1600–53), Pétau features in a long row of militant Roman Catholics who tried to convince Grotius of the advantages that such a conversion would bring, not only for the salvation of his soul, but also in terms of material gain in this world. When Rivet engaged Grotius in an intensive polemical contest, he sharply criticised his adversary for the latter's dependency on Pétau's advice. Mockingly, he assumed that the Swedish authorities would not appreciate this collaboration.[13] Similarly, Claude Saumaise reproached Grotius for his friendship with Pétau; by designating Pétau as 'delicium illud eximium Grotii', 'that special treasure of Grotius', he even insinuated that the two scholars were entertaining a homosexual relationship.[14] Immediately after publication, Grotius studied the volumes of Pétau's pioneering *Theologica dogmata* cover to cover. Although Pétau described the infamous libertine Conradus Vorstius as a Calvinist – a misunderstanding that made him chuckle – Grotius admired the book, and the reason for this is plain to see: through painstaking research into an overwhelming mass of patristic sources, Pétau showed how, in the primitive Church, important tenets of faith such as the Trinity went through formative developments before being articulated and endorsed by Church councils. Once more, Grotius must have concluded that hair-splitting on abstruse doctrines prevented a harmonious coexistence between believers who should abide by the two central commands of their guide, Christ: to honour God and love one's neighbour.

1.11 End of an Eventful Life

Delays in payment, collisions with Swedish rivals and open obstruction on the part of the French authorities: the problems that His Excellency Hugo Grotius had to face as a diplomat made him feel increasingly wary and weary. As he stated in a private letter, the slightest occasion would suffice to make him look for and find a quiet place where he could end his days in good thoughts (12 BW 5452). Once the negotiations for peace had started at Münster and Osnabrück, it was clear to all the world that, contrary to certain rumours, Grotius had not been invited to partake in the talks. The only task left to him was to visit Sweden and discuss the next steps in his career. He left Paris on 26 or 27 April 1645, after having passed the previous weeks by making his testament and meeting his Paris friends and acquaintances, among others Denis Pétau. Then, leaving his wife Maria in France, he travelled via Dieppe by sea to Holland, where he stayed from 3 until 8 May. From Harlingen, he went by ship to Hamburg. Next, he travelled overland to Wismar, a port on the Baltic Sea. Here, he boarded a ship that brought him to Sweden. After deliberations with Queen Christina and members of her Council had failed, they dismissed their obedient servant with a golden chain and a stipend. On 11 August, Grotius left Stockholm for the seaport Dalarö. In a hurry, he travelled back overseas. Did he consider entering the French diplomatic service? We have only tenuous, second-hand information that suggests such an astounding volte-face. On the Baltic Sea, Grotius' ship was taken by a heavy storm. With great toil and labour, he managed to reach the coast. He travelled overland to Rostock, where he died a few days later, on 28 August 1645. According to a report that was divulged in print shortly afterwards, he answered the Lutheran pastor who asked him whether he obeyed the tenets of the Christian faith: 'Nihil intelligo'. Adversaries like André Rivet took these last words to stand as a symbol of Grotius' attitude towards the creed in which he was raised but that he had forsaken later in life, to the great detriment of his former coreligionists.

1.12 Nachleben

At the end of 1645, the year in which Grotius died, the shelves of his study were stacked with important manuscripts that awaited publication. According to Grotius' last wishes, his devoted widow, Maria van Reigersberch, took care of all those works that were ready for press. A collection of ancient testimonies on the compatibility of human free will and divine providence, *De fato* (1648), saw the light with a dedication by Maria to Cardinal Mazarin, as if she wanted to proclaim that these fragments perfectly illustrated Grotius' way of life and career. In the following years, the stream of first editions, collected letters and reprints of earlier publications only swelled, not unlike the mostly vehement refutations and commentaries by his foes and opponents. In two pamphlets, published under the pseudonym Simplicius Verinus, Claude Saumaise angrily dismissed his former friend's struggle for reconciliation with the papacy as a treacherous stab in the back to Reformed believers, mainly on the grounds that Rome would never budge an inch from its traditional stance. Nowadays, Grotius is mostly remembered for his contribution to natural law, the law of nations and the law of the seas. We should not forget, however, that, before the advent of secularisation, Grotius' reputation was also strongly rooted in his theological works.

The story of his *Nachleben* in Germany, France and England is a long one. For his juridical influence, one might point to the significance of his doctrine of subjective rights that underpinned his views on the laws of war. Although the role of these rights in Grotius' system is sometimes exaggerated, it is clear that, by stressing these natural rights, our great scholar cleared the ground for later theorists like Thomas Hobbes (1588–1679), Samuel von Pufendorf (1632–94) and John Locke (1632–1704). For the dissemination and popularisation of his juridical thought, Swiss scholar Jean Barbeyrac (1674–1744) stands out. He re-edited *De jure belli ac pacis* and also published it in a frequently reprinted, extensively annotated, French translation that aligned Grotius' views to the natural law theories of the Enlightenment. But the reception of Grotius' thought also has a dark side. He advocated a powerful government that maintained peace and order by the force of law, whether such law was supernaturally revealed, naturally given, transmitted by custom or recently agreed upon through negotiation and consensus. Grotius was inclined to accept the existing, organically grown state of law as the norm, even if this had resulted in tyranny and the enslavement of peoples. For this, he was later attacked by thinkers of the Enlightenment, including Jean-Jacques Rousseau (1712–78).[15]

If we focus on his religious writings, it is his *Annotationes* to the Bible that stand out as his great intellectual legacy. Countless guardians of Grotius' theological research, for example Henry Hammond (1605–60), Clement Barksdale (1609–87), Jean Leclerc (1657–1736) and Pierre Bayle (1647–1706), attest to his work as a shining example of the strong, resounding impact of the humanist tradition. Instead of seeing Grotius' writings in terms of a pointless accumulation of historical facts and quotations – as later modernist opponents of 'pedantic' humanism would often argue – his broadly secularised literary-historical approach rooted in late humanism proved crucial for uncovering new perspectives on the Bible and developing biblical exegesis in general. He studied the text as a historical and literary source compilation, as if it had been produced by pagan Greek or Roman culture. In this way, Grotius and likeminded scholars were better equipped to peel back the authorial intentions contained in the different books of the Bible. This method soon proved pioneering, because it was adopted, refined and expanded by exegetes like

Etienne de Courcelles (1586–1659), Philipp van Limborch (1633–1712) and Richard Simon (1638–1712). Grotius' exegesis set a new trend in two respects: his restriction of divine inspiration and his literal interpretation of prophecies. The views of Jean Leclerc shall serve here as a concluding assessment. This Swiss theologian was certainly instrumental in promoting Grotius' latitudinarian religious convictions and, in his eyes, Erasmus together with Grotius were the most eminent exegetes of earlier centuries.[16] Grotius, moreover, in an exemplary way had extracted from God's Word an undogmatic Christian belief that was eminently qualified to inspire a morally impeccable life and create a better world.[17]

Notes

1 MS Leiden, UL, Ger. Papenbroeckii Codex no. 11 A.

2 A. Borremansius, *Variarum Lectionum Liber* (Amsterdam, 1676), 11.

3 L. Aubéry du Maurier, *Mémoires pour servir à l'histoire de Hollande* (Paris, 1687), 328–9.

4 *De dichtwerken van Hugo Grotius*, vol. I, 2, pars 1 A-B, ed. B.L. Meulenbroek (Assen, 1972), 14–23 and 7–15.

5 'Iunius, cui multum debeo', OTh 3, 649 A 55; see also *ibid.*, 675 A 38–43 and 730 A 23–25.

6 See in this volume Chapter 2 by Edwin Rabbie.

7 On this broader juridical framework of so-called 'attributive justice', see Jeremy Seth Geddert, *Hugo Grotius and the Modern Theology of Freedom: Transcending Natural Rights* (New York, 2017).

8 Peter Haggenmacher, *Grotius et la doctrine de la guerre juste* (Paris, 1983), 386, n. 1871.

9 Martine van Ittersum, 'The long goodbye: Hugo Grotius' justification of Dutch expansion overseas, 1615-1645', *History of European Ideas* 36 (2010), 386–411, here 387, 393–8.

10 G.J. Toomer, *John Selden: A Life in Scholarship* (Oxford, 2009), vol. 1, 436–7.

11 Aubéry du Maurier, *Mémoires*, 343–4.

12 'Henrici Valesii Oratio in obitum Dionysii Petavii, habita anno 1653', in *Henrici Valesii Emendationum libri quinque*, ed. P. Burmannus (Amsterdam, 1740), second pagination, 43–4.

13 *Andreae Riveti Apologeticus* (Leiden, 1643), 84.

14 F.F. Blok, *Isaac Vossius en zijn kring: Zijn leven tot zijn afscheid van koningin Christina van Zweden, 1618-1655* (Groningen, 1999), 234.

15 See for Grotius' influence in France and England Jacques Le Brun, 'La réception de la théologie de Grotius chez les catholiques de la seconde moitié du XVIIe

siècle', in idem, *La jouissance et le trouble. Recherches sur la littérature chrétienne de l'âge classique* (Geneva, 2004), 217–46, and Marco Barducci, *Hugo Grotius and the Century of Revolution, 1613–1718: Transnational Reception in English Political Thought* (Oxford, 2017), esp. 51, 99–101, 115, 121–3 and 126–32.

16 Henk Nellen and Jan Bloemendal, 'Erasmus's biblical project: Some thoughts and observations on its scope, its impact in the sixteenth century and reception in the seventeenth and eighteenth centuries', *Church History and Religious Culture* 96 (2016), 595–635, here 620–1 and 625–6.

17 Leclerc published a standard-edition of Grotius' *De veritate* (Amsterdam, 1709 and subsequent editions), a *vade mecum* for the moderate Christian believer.

Grotius as Legal, Political and Diplomatic Official in the Dutch Republic 2

Edwin Rabbie

2.1 Introduction

It was Joseph Scaliger (1540–1609) who, already at an early stage, with the sharp look that is perhaps typical of the philologist, foresaw the turn Grotius' career was going to take. In the collection of gossip, table talk and philological observations that, long after his death in 1609, were to be published as *Scaligerana*, the Leiden professor of classics remarked that Grotius, a 'prudent politician, eminent Graecist and jurisprudent', was to pursue a career that would make him pensionary of a city in Holland.[1] Scaliger had already foreseen that neither a career in classical philology nor legal practice would ultimately suffice for Grotius.

From 1607 onwards, until his arrest in 1618, Grotius served the Dutch Republic, more specifically the States of Holland and the city of Rotterdam, as an official in various functions. These activities were preceded by a period in which he did not work in a public position but practiced as an attorney-at-law at The Hague. As a result of the professionalisation of the state administration during the sixteenth century, taking a doctoral degree in law and subsequent practice as an attorney had become a common preparation and an all but obligatory training school for almost every public official in the Republic.[2] For this reason alone, it is useful, by way of introduction, to dwell briefly on Grotius' career as an attorney.

2.2 Advocate at The Hague (1599–1607)

Even if Grotius, in keeping with his early scholarly publications, had aspired to pursue an academic career as a classicist, his father, Jan de Groot (1554–1640), effectively counteracted this at an early stage. At his instigation, the young legal scholar, who had only recently taken his doctorate at Orléans, settled in The Hague at the home of Johannes Wtenbogaert (1557–1644), the court chaplain. There, on 13 December

1599, he took the oath as an advocate before the presiding judge of the Court of Holland. For a little under eight years, Grotius practiced as a lawyer at both tribunals in The Hague, the Court of Holland and Zeeland and the High Council (*Hoge Raad*) of Holland and Zeeland. The Court of Holland was, and had been for a long time, among others, the appellate jurisdiction for both civil and criminal cases in Holland and Zeeland. The High Council, founded in 1582, was originally intended as a replacement of the Great Council of Malines, the highest court of the Netherlands, for all of the Seven Provinces. However, only Holland and Zeeland recognised its authority, thus factually making it into largely a duplication of the other court. Regrettably, there are hardly any sources that allow us to form a picture of how Grotius practiced law. Since these are Grotius' earliest activities in the legal field, we would like to know more about how he acted as a practical lawyer and what, if any, were the connections between his legal practice and his later juridical publications. The reason for this lack of sources is that, according to the rules of civil procedure for both courts, all documents were submitted by the 'procureur' – a term perhaps best trans-lated as court solicitor – and not by the advocate. As a result, the archives do not provide evidence in which trials Grotius played a role. For this reason, we have to put up with the rare statements Grotius made about his legal practice in his correspondence and elsewhere – in one or two con-temporary poems. The gist of these is that, after some initial problems of adaptation, he quickly managed to build up a flourishing practice, in which he was also entrusted with important cases. We know little about his preparation for legal practice either: to begin with, there is no evidence he ever read law while at Leiden university. Here, too, there are only a few indications in his correspondence (2 BW 593; also 17 BW 384A).

Apart from acting at trials, another frequent and, it seems, lucrative activity for lawyers was the writing of legal opinions. Grotius, too, occu-pied himself with this, but of the considerable number – over 100 – of opinions of his that have come down to us,[3] there are hardly any that date demonstrably from the period that he was an advocate; most of them, as far as they are dated, are from the Rotterdam period or were written during his short stay in Amsterdam in 1631. The only exception is the long opinion, written in Latin and probably dating from 1605, about the claim to the domain of Cloppenburg that Stadholder Maurice of Nassau (1567–1625) asserted against the bishop of Münster, an opinion which for the greater part consists of an elaborate treatise on prescription in the case of non-bona fide acquisition of property.[4] On account of both its length and its subject-matter, this opinion cannot be compared to Grotius' other opinions in later years.

In the course of 1606, it became clear that the advocate-fiscal of the Court of Holland, Simon van Veen (c. 1555–1610), who had been in office since 1595 but had indicated already, in June 1604, that he wished to resign,[5] would leave soon. Van Veen was sworn into office as justice in the High Council on 20 March 1607. Thus, a vacancy occurred for an office that was doubtlessly held in high esteem. Only academically educated jurists or advocates with years of experience were qualified for it. As the advocate-fiscal was in charge of pleading before both courts, the office must have ensured public visibility in case of important trials. Initially, the States of Holland postponed the appointment procedure for unstated reasons, but, on 7 November 1607, Stadholder Maurice appointed Grotius as Van Veen's successor from a list of three candidates. The salary amounted to 1,000 guilders per year.[6] Grotius' two rivals – Nicolaas Bakker and Quirijn van Strijen – were likewise advocates at the Court of Holland, both considerably more experienced than Grotius. What motivated those who entrusted this office to Grotius rather than to a reputedly excellent and certainly more experienced lawyer such as van Strijen (1575–1656), who was the son-in-law of resignee Simon van Veen, cannot be established with certainty. It is likely that the protection Grotius enjoyed from the Land's Advocate Johan van Oldenbarnevelt (1547–1619) ever since their voyage together to France in 1598 played a role. The background of this protection may be found in the circumstance that Oldenbarnevelt was an acquaintance of Grotius' father. It seems probable that Oldenbarnevelt became impressed by the capabilities of the Delft prodigy at an early stage. Grotius' and Oldenbarnevelt's careers grew more and more together, the latter's ruin occasioning Grotius' downfall.

2.3 Advocate-Fiscal (1607–1613)

On 7 December 1607, at the age of 24, Grotius was sworn in as advocate-fiscal by the chief justice of the High Council, Reinoud van Brederode (1567–1633); three days later, by the chief justice of the Court of Holland, Pieter de Hinojossa (d. 1616). His public career took off. At the Court of Holland, the advocate-fiscal's tasks were expounded in the instruction dating back to 1531 (articles 25 and 26[7]): he was to plead all cases concerning the prince and draw up all papers and memorandums. Besides this old text, there was the recently (November 1607) revised special instruction for both the advocate-fiscal and the procurator-general at the court.[8] This instruction was bound to cause controversy: previously, the procurator-general had been superior to the advocate-fiscal, but this relation was now reversed. At the time of Grotius' appointment, the procurator-general, Gillis van Florij (c. 1549–c. 1623), was probably about 58 years old and already 21 years in office. It would testify to huge pliability on his side if he had ungrudgingly followed up the young newcomer's instructions. Indeed, it seems he didn't and there seem to have been frictions between procurator-general and advocate-fiscal from the start.

Thanks to the research done in the archives of the Hof van Holland during the 1990s by Rob Huijbrecht,[9] we now have a somewhat more detailed image of Grotius' work as advocate-fiscal. His research has qualified the established – perhaps all too rosy – picture of the 'eminent way' in which Grotius fulfilled his office, presented mainly by older biographical literature. However, as far as the content level of the cases is concerned, the image Huijbrecht sketches is definitely not encouraging: the majority of the lawsuits handled by Grotius were, in his view, 'routine cases' of a simple nature. This holds true for both civil and criminal cases. There is no doubt that Grotius fulfilled his official duties diligently (see also *Verantwoordingh* 19.67, 214), but also there was little opportunity to stand out. On the other hand, the view that only the prospect of a subsequent step in his career made the office bearable is perhaps too gloomy.[10] Apart from the strictly juridical work, the advocate-fiscal, being in charge of land reclamation, also once in a while had to leave The Hague to survey a dike.[11] Judging by the number of cases handled by the advocate-fiscal, his daily duties cannot have been very demanding; according to Huijbrecht's estimation, there were both *in civilibus* and *in criminalibus* about 250 cases each during the period of somewhat over six years that Grotius was in office. If the average workload was that of a routine case, his official activities may not have been so taxing. This also follows from the significant number of publications Grotius managed to prepare after 1607. Thus, in 1612, he put the finishing touch to his voluminous history of the Dutch Revolt, *Annales et Historiae de rebus Belgicis*, which was only published posthumously. All this does not alter the fact that, in a speech to the States of Holland on the occasion of his resignation as advocate-fiscal, Grotius pointed out that especially the number of criminal cases had increased much in recent years, both in number and in weight.[12]

This may, however, in part also be explained by the fact that Grotius' accession to office as advocate-fiscal almost coincides with a serious escalation of the religious conflict within the Dutch Reformed Church, especially in Holland. The conflict started as a dispute on predestination between the Leiden professors of theology, James Arminius (1560–1609) and Franciscus Gomarus (1563–1641), which after the former's death escalated and resulted in schisms within church congregations. Arminius' followers, named Remonstrants after the petition ('remonstrance') they filed with the States of Holland in January 1610, were in the minority and therefore called upon the secular authorities for support against the majority that were designated as Counter-Remonstrants. For a considerable time already, there had been frictions between the secular authorities and the representatives of the Church on matters such as the convocation of a national synod and the degree of influence of the state on the doctrinal authority and the appointment of ecclesiastical officials. Initially, the States of Holland only made cautious interventions in order to keep the conflict under control, but through the years they increasingly interfered with what the Counter-Remonstrants considered the proper domain of the Church.

As a reaction to the Remonstrance, the States on 11 March 1610 issued a missive[13] in which the ministers of both parties, Remonstrants and Counter-Remonstrants, were enjoined to refrain from statements on the office of secular authorities in ecclesiastical matters and on predestination and related subjects until the convocation of a provincial synod. This would prove useless from the very beginning if writers from both sides were to ignore the ban. The unremitting stream of pamphlets shows that this ban remained indeed ineffective. One of the causes of this failure was that both parties constantly felt discriminated against and pleaded this as an excuse to break the rule. The Counter-Remonstrants in particular had qualms about the ban on publications from the outset. Shortly before its promulgation, in February 1610, the States had authorised a publication by Johannes Wtenbogaert, the leader of the Remonstrants, entitled *A Tract on the Duty and Authority of a Supreme Christian Government in Ecclesiastical Affairs* and dedicated to the States.[14] In this book, the author advocated an absolute authority of the government over the Church; anything that tended towards self-rule was convincingly rejected. Wtenbogaert's adversaries considered this development an attempt to silence them.

How was Grotius involved in the dispute during his years as advocate-fiscal? Starting at the end of 1610, there are repeated records in the resolutions of the States of Holland and the *Gecommitteerde Raden* (the States' executive) that indicate that Grotius as advocate-fiscal investigated into or took measures against the publication of pamphlets on ecclesiastical politics or doctrinal disputes. On 20 December 1610, he obtained permission to investigate such publications and to report on them to the States.[15] Three days later, he appeared at the States' meeting and singled out two pamphlets, both directed against Wtenbogaert and his *Tract*.[16] Grotius was ordered to broaden his investigations, to search for contraventions by the other party, too, and 'to do his duty'.[17] The resolutions of the subsequent period time and again mention investigation into, seizure and burning of undesired publications.[18]

Censoring pamphlets was not the only way the States tried to bring the conflict under control. Another measure was the promulgation of resolutions, in which the government exhorted the parties to mutual tolerance and moderation. A first sample from June 1610 calls upon the classes 'not to burden' persons to be ordained during their examination and ministers who already officiate 'with the high mysterious points that today (God forbid) are discussed too much in the churches'.[19] Although there is no direct evidence of Grotius' involvement in the production of this letter, both its tone and its purport are so much on a par with the later resolutions he is known to have been involved with that there can be no real doubt: here we have the origin of what was to become the resolution of tolerance of 1614.

Once appointed, Grotius began to delve into the historical background of the ecclesiastical conflicts. Whether he did so by virtue of his office or out of personal interest is unclear. His publications, especially *Ordinum pietas* of 1613, show a thorough knowledge of the contents of many of the pamphlets exchanged – it appears that the advocate-fiscal not only confiscated them, but also read them. He was likewise warmly interested in the theological questions of the day. In fact, Grotius' statement in a letter to Gomarus of 24 December 1609 (1 BW 181) that he really knows nothing about the conflict between the former and the late Arminius already seems feigned. Four years later, in *Ordinum pietas*, Grotius turns out to be an expert on predestination. His later statement (*Verantwoordingh* 19.10, 176) that, before his accession to the office of pensionary of Rotterdam, he had never involved himself in religious conflicts is perhaps true if taken literally, but does not do full justice to his off-the-record activities. As to the historical background of the ecclesiastical questions in a narrower sense, Grotius as the advocate-fiscal had access *ex officio* to the old archives of the county of Holland. From his posthumous papers, it is evident that, starting at least in early 1613, he collected from those archives documents that bore upon the relationship between Church and state;[20] he had the clerks at the registry make copies of relevant records and he himself took notes from archival documents that seemed important with an eye to publications he was planning. He was soon able to use the fruits of this preliminary work.

2.4 Diplomatic Intermezzo (1611–1613)

Twice Grotius went on a diplomatic mission on behalf of the States General once to East Frisia, in August and September 1611, and once to London in April and May 1613.

The East Frisian mission was the result of a long-term conflict between Count Enno III of East Frisia (1563–1625) and the city of Emden. In May 1611, this controversy had been settled by the intervention of seven deputies on behalf of the States General but, because not all questions had been solved, another arbitration was deemed necessary. In August 1611, Grotius was one of the arbitrators; they passed judgment on 28 September 1611 in Emden.[21] However, in hindsight, the visit he paid on 29 August 1611 from Leeuwarden to the Frisian town of Franeker was of much greater importance than the arbitration itself. While in Franeker 'to look at the university', as he wrote in a letter to his wife Maria van Reigersberch (1 BW 212), Grotius had a conversation with the professor of divinity, Sibrandus Lubbertus (c. 1555–1625). To the great annoyance of Oldenbarnevelt, Lubbertus had intervened in the ecclesiastical conflicts that took place in the Republic. First, he involved himself in the conflict on the convocation of a national synod, before intervening shortly afterwards in the question of the succession of his late Leiden colleague, Arminius. The States of Holland had filled that vacancy by appointing German theologian Conradus Vorstius (1569–1622), a pupil of Theodore Beza (1519–1605) in Geneva and formerly professor at the Gymnasium Academicum in Steinfurt. Lubbertus revealed himself as the most militant of Vorstius' adversaries, accusing him – rightly or wrongly – of various, mainly Socinian, errors and heresies. He did not hesitate to deploy his excellent relations with various theologians abroad to provoke a sentiment against the ecclesiastical policy of the States of Holland. Through George Abbot (1562–1633), the archbishop of Canterbury, he even tried to bring King James I/VI (1566–1625) into action against Vorstius' appointment.[22] We don't know for certain whether the Vorstius affair was a subject of the conversation between Grotius and Lubbertus in August 1611, but it may well have been. The appointment became a matter of prestige for Oldenbarnevelt. Although Grotius tried not to involve himself by avoiding speaking out publicly in favour of Vorstius – 'no-one will defend Vorstius except Vorstius', as he expressed it pithily in a letter to Isaac Casaubon of 1613 (1 BW 294) – his unconditional support for Oldenbarnevelt in other fields – mainly Church policy – made him a champion of Vorstius in the eyes of the other party.[23]

At any rate, Grotius' démarche – doubtless undertaken at Oldenbarnevelt's initiative – came across as an attempt to win Lubbertus over to the Remonstrants' cause. Grotius considered the conversation rather as an attempt to advance tolerance; thus, he adopted the moderate and neutral position we see reflected in the sources (1 BW 299).[24] Soon after his visit to Franeker, however, he must have realised tolerance and Sibrandus Lubbertus didn't match. Consequently, Grotius' attempt to calm Lubbertus came to nothing; on the contrary, during the next few years, the fanatical agitator was to lead the resistance against the ecclesiastical policy of the States of Holland with double effort.

Of much greater impact, and even decisive and ultimately fatal influence, was another diplomatic mission Grotius undertook a couple of years later: his visit to London in the spring of 1613. Grotius passed the major part of April and May 1613 in England as a member of the delegation sent to negotiate about the conflict on East-Indian trade between the Republic and England. Grotius, who had been added to the delegation at a very late stage, had received a secret assignment from Oldenbarnevelt: to hold conversations with King James and his ecclesiastical advisors on the Church policy of the States of Holland and, if possible, to win them over to Oldenbarnevelt's side. Apparently, the importance of Grotius' attendance was so great that the immediate filling of the vacancy of pensionary of Rotterdam, something the city and he had already reached agreement about, had to wait until after this mission.

In the first place, Grotius made optimal use of his good relations with the famous French philologist, Isaac Casaubon (1559–1614). This eminent scholar, a great expert in the field of the history of Christianity, had settled in London after the murder of Henry IV (1553–1610), as one of the major advisors of King James on religious and ecclesiastical affairs.[25] He and Grotius had corresponded for a considerable time, but now they were to meet in person for the first time.

The relationship between the Republic, especially Holland, and England in 1613 was precarious. King James found the appointment of Vorstius at Leiden University unacceptable: here was someone put in charge of educating reformed ministers who, in his publications, trampled on the most fundamental parts of Christian faith. According to James, Vorstius was an unabashed supporter of that most abhorred of all modern heretics, Faustus Socinus (1539–1604). The king considered himself the principal defender of the faith and, for that reason, he decided he had to act against Vorstius. There was a real danger that the king would transfer his aversion from Vorstius to the Remonstrants in general and to those who protected Vorstius; Oldenbarnevelt thought that risk was so great that he devised a scheme to bring James firmly to his side.

The first part of this plan was to submit to James a French translation of the five articles of the Remonstrance, the petition to the States in which the supporters of the late Arminius had expressed their vision on predestination and grace, together with a draft letter for the king's signature to enable him to express himself swiftly on these articles in a favourable way. The plan, prepared and executed by Oldenbarnevelt, Wtenbogaert and the States' ambassador in London, Noel de Caron (d. 1624), succeeded: the translation and the letter were submitted to the king in mid-March 1613. James signed, of his own accord adding the phrase that 'these opinions do not differ so much that they are inconsistent with the truth of Christian faith and the salvation of the souls' (*Ordinum pietas* § 25). Moreover, the king advised the States not to have these questions decided by the ministers or a synod, but to keep the judgment to themselves. Meanwhile, there ought to be a ban imposed on preaching about predestination and grace. Towards the end of March, the letters in which this judgment was included arrived in The Hague. This masterstroke caused much disbelief in Counter-Remonstrant circles, where the king was considered a reliable ally; many suspected Grotius to be the author of this text or at least to have been involved in the plot.[26]

Doubtless, the mystery around his actions in England shortly after, in combination with his later publications, contributed to this suspicion. He himself always adamantly denied any involvement in the scheme.

On 2 April 1613, the States' delegation arrived in London; four days later, it was received in audience by James. Grotius paid several visits to Casaubon, who subsequently arranged meetings with prominent English theologians as well as organising a private audience with the king. Thus, on 28 April, at lunch, Grotius met John Overall (1559–1619), Dean of St Paul's. The day afterwards, he dined at the residence of Lancelot Andrewes (1555–1626), bishop of Ely, in the presence of, among others, John Richardson (1564–1625), Regius Professor of Divinity in Cambridge; on both occasions, there were many and long discussions on topical theological questions. George Abbot, the archbishop of Canterbury, has left us a scathing report of Grotius' attitude at the meeting with Andrewes in a letter to Sir Ralph Winwood (1563–1617), the English ambassador in The Hague. Abbot, who himself was not present at the meeting and who was – like Winwood – no friend of Grotius, painted a sharp image of Grotius as a shallow pedant who had no scruples about dominating the conversation in a company unknown to him and conversing endlessly about the few subjects he was familiar with. According to Abbott, the host, Andrewes, got quite annoyed at Grotius' behaviour,[27] although Andrewes spoke very well about him to Casaubon.[28]

Again, according to Abbot, Grotius had also made an unfavourable impression during his first conversation with the king: 'some pedant, full of words, and of no great judgment', was the royal verdict.[29] Abbot subtly pointed out to Grotius that he ought to adapt his attitude; Grotius followed his advice and thus the private audience of 15 May, lasting two hours, proceeded much better. Grotius and the king first spoke about predestination in general and the five articles of the Remonstrance in particular. Grotius used all of his persuasive powers; as a result, the king actually thought that those articles were in full conformity with orthodox doctrine. They subsequently discussed the question of Church and state. Grotius, who was aware of the king's critical attitude towards the Puritans in his native Scotland and in England, was able to convince the king that the usurpation of the Counter-Remonstrants in the Netherlands was tantamount to the Puritans' actions in Britain. This vouches for Grotius' persuasiveness, for the king had been informed by ambassador Winwood that the identification of Counter-Remonstrants and Puritans was incorrect.

The king even promised that he would instruct Abbot and Winwood to dissociate themselves from the Counter-Remonstrants. When, at the end of the conversation, Grotius expressed his concern that James might recant his letter to the States, the king reassured him, quoting Pilatus: 'What I have written, I have written.' It was surely a favourable sign that His Majesty requested Grotius to convey his greetings to Wtenbogaert.

Thus, Grotius thought he could, as far as the king was concerned, look back on an entirely successful mission. This contrasted, however, with his conversation with Archbishop Abbot two days later. The discussion with this churchman of markedly Puritan sympathies started off awkwardly. Abbot's message to Grotius was clear: the king did not sympathise with Arminius, whom he had earlier called an enemy of God, and his followers; each attempt to represent it otherwise was founded on misrepresentation. In short, with Abbot Grotius got nowhere.

On 21 May 1613, Grotius took leave of the king in another private audience. The course of this talk is exemplary for Grotius' lack of diplomatic feeling. Probably still under the influence of his disappointing experience with Abbot, he gave in to the temptation to make statements to the effect that Abbot did not grasp matters well. An attempt to play off Andrewes and Abbot against one another testifies to his lack of a sense of reality.

Thus, it seemed as if Grotius' English mission, notwithstanding Archbishop Abbot's opposition, had ultimately ended positively, but that was a mere illusion. It is not to Grotius' credit that he seriously thought, even if only for one instance, to be able to drive a wedge between the king and his archbishop. It cost Grotius himself, and also his political sympathisers, dearly. Grotius had only just left England when King James retracted everything that suggested support for the Remonstrants. When, subsequently, in 1617, Stadholder Maurice chose the Counter-Remonstrants' side, the unambiguous support he received from James was the harbinger of the inevitable fall of Oldenbarnevelt and Grotius.

A direct consequence of Grotius' English journey was the publication of the short but hotly debated work *Ordinum pietas* or, with its full title, *Ordinum Hollandiae ac Westfrisiae pietas* ('The Religiousness of the States of Holland and Westfriesland') in October 1613. After all, this book was intended to show once again to (English) readers that the ecclesiastical policy of the States of Holland complied with the demands of (reformed) orthodoxy. The book was explicitly directed against Lubbertus, who had exerted his influence in England, especially with Archbishop Abbot, to create hostility against the States' policy. In his sharp reaction, Grotius discussed three elements of that policy that were under dispute: first of all, the thorny question of Vorstius' appointment as a professor in Leiden, second the question of predestination, where Grotius showed that the Remonstrant point of view was orthodox, and finally – and at the greatest length – the authority of secular authorities in ecclesiastical affairs. There the author defended an Erastian point of view. The first point certainly was the trickiest: King James had expressed himself more than once very negatively about Vorstius.

The title page mentioning the function of advocate-fiscal – as had also been the case with *De antiquitate reipublicae Batavicae*, a historical work Grotius published in 1610 – perhaps indicates that the book enjoyed a somewhat official status. There is, to be sure, no evidence that Grotius wrote the book by virtue of a formal assignment from the States; he did appeal to the fact that defending the honour of the state was the advocate-fiscal's duty (OHWP 1; OTh 3, 132). But, it seems very likely that Oldenbarnevelt assented to Grotius writing the booklet. Perhaps it was even written at his initiative, something Grotius also suggests (1 BW 294). Elsewhere publication is said to have been 'with knowledge and approval' of the *Gecomitteerde Raden*, whose minutes of the year 1613 are, however, lost.[30]

2.5 Pensionary of Rotterdam (1613–1618)

Having served the Court and the Supreme Court for five years, the time was ripe for Grotius to improve his social position. Meanwhile his bosses knew his worth and, when in November 1612 the High Council nominated him as justice, the States preferred to retain him in office as advocate-fiscal. Declining this promotion went with an increase in salary; henceforward the States awarded him the same salary as his predecessor in office, Van Veen, had enjoyed (*Verantwoordingh* 19.3, 174). It was evident, though, that his tenure as advocate-fiscal was coming to an end.

On 20 July 1612, Elias van Oldenbarnevelt (1557–1612) suddenly died in The Hague in the house of his elder brother, Johan, the Land's Advocate. Elias had been pensionary of the city of Rotterdam for more than twenty-five years, an office in which he had succeeded his elder brother. Assiduous consultation about a successor during the first weeks of 1613, in which the strong involvement of Johan van Oldenbarnevelt catches the eye, resulted in a heavyweight candidate: Rombout Hogerbeets (1561–1625), doctor of laws, ex-advocate, with relevant experience – he had been pensionary of the city of Leiden from 1590 to 1596 and, since then, justice in the High Council. Hogerbeets weighed the offer for a little while before turning it down. Again, Oldenbarnevelt came up with a candidate, this time Grotius (March 1613).

Grotius, who later was to state that he had not actively contended for the office (*Verantwoordingh* 19.3, 174), showed himself to be a tough negotiator. Apart from an appointment for life – he himself was allowed to resign, but would not do that rashly – and a salary of 2,000 guilders a year, he managed to stipulate that he would enjoy all the privileges that his predecessor had been entitled to. Among these were free housing in an official residence, freedom from various municipal direct and indirect taxes and duties, and reimbursement of travel expenses. Moreover, he was allowed to settle the current cases as advocate-fiscal until the post had been filled; to this purpose he was permitted to stay a couple of days per week in The Hague for the time being. The possibility of exercising the profitable activity of writing legal advices was subject to negotiation; there were extensive discussions on which categories of litigants he was and was not allowed to assist.[31] Even one day before taking the oath, on 5 June 1613 – the text of the oath had previously been established – the discussions on his legal practice had not been settled.

Grotius' attempts to have his cake and eat it when negotiating his terms of employment are understandable. Unlike the office of advocate-fiscal, that of a pensionary was in most cases the final stage of an official career. The available data show that, for the great majority of advocates-fiscal in the sixteenth and early seventeenth centuries, their appointment was only an intermediate stage that led to the better paid, more honourable and doubtless much more untroubled office of justice in one of the law courts in The Hague. On average, an advocate-fiscal remained in office for less than ten years. On the other hand, the office of justice was usually the final stage of a career. From the small turnover among the pensionaries of the great cities of Holland, it can be deduced that, once a functionary had been appointed to that office, they mostly, like the justices, remained in office until their death.[32] As Grotius had been obliged to turn down an appointment as justice in the High Council, the sudden and unexpected vacancy in Rotterdam was not merely a stroke of luck, it was also completely uncertain when there would be another occasion to be appointed pensionary of a major city.

Johan van Oldenbarnevelt had also started his career as advocate in The Hague and had afterwards been pensionary of Rotterdam, until his appointment as Land's Advocate in 1586. He was already in his late sixties. Did he consider Grotius a ready candidate for his succession and was this the reason he furthered – as an intermediate stage – his appointment in Rotterdam?

The pensionary was the town's highest official and, as the burgomasters under the Republic were no civil servants and held a temporary position, he was, although formally subordinate to them, de facto the best-informed person in the city government. Furthermore, the pensionary, together with the burgomasters, represented the town at the assemblies of the States of Holland in The Hague. The continuity of his position among an ever-changing array of short-term administrators allowed its tenant to build up a degree of expertise and influence. The importance of this office, both in the city and in the Republic, can therefore hardly be overestimated.[33] After his 1618 downfall, Grotius tried to minimise his influence by pointing out that everything he had done as a pensionary had been in the service of and in accordance with the decisions of his Rotterdam superiors. That defence, although technically correct, seems unconvincing in view of the actual situation and Grotius' influential position as Oldenbarnevelt's heir.

On 17 July 1613, Grotius appeared for the first time as pensionary of Rotterdam in the meeting of the States of Holland and took the oath. Henceforth, he was present at almost every States' meeting, albeit always accompanied by one or several burgomasters. Four years later, on 31 May 1617, Grotius was sworn as a member of *Gecomitteerde Raden*, the executive of the States of Holland; he remained a member until his arrest.

Both at the municipal and the provincial level, ecclesiastical politics were the dominant issue on the political agenda. There were, moreover, a number of lingering conflicts between some of the cities of Holland – apart from Rotterdam, Gouda, Haarlem and Dordrecht – about inland navigation and the so-called staple right of Dordrecht. Grotius wrote a memorandum on the question of toll collection, which has not survived.[34]

Rotterdam was in majority a Remonstrant-minded town. This doesn't mean there were no religious conflicts before and during Grotius' time in office. In 1610–11, a schism had arisen within the Rotterdam reformed community; henceforward the dissenters attended church in Schiedam. The city fathers made frantic efforts to prevent the schism, among others by fining those who attended religious gatherings other than the official ones. This proved to be in vain. A Rotterdam conference in November 1615, where an attempt was made to reconciliate the factions and restore the unity of the Church, failed (1 BW 429 and 431). Grotius played an important role at this conference. He drew up the compromise proposal. In the eyes of the Counter-Remonstrants, this text confirmed his support of the Remonstrants.

On ecclesiastical affairs at the provincial level, Grotius became of indispensable support to Oldenbarnevelt, as he seems to have provided the latter's policies with a theological and juridical foundation. By virtue of his unremitting study of mainly contemporary, but also early-Christian, authors on questions of predestination, grace and Church government, he was the obvious person to provide this assistance. Oldenbarnevelt's policy had two main aims: to prevent the convention of a national synod and to promote tolerance between Remonstrants and Counter-Remonstrants in order to prevent a schism within the Church. Both were lost causes: gradually, it became clear that there would be a national synod, which would ultimately lead to a condemnation of the Remonstrants. The promotion of tolerance ended in failure as well: the Remonstrants, the underdog in the majority of cities, needed recognition; the Counter-Remonstrants, who were firmly in control of most congregations, had small reason to grant it. And where this was not the case, they seceded and boycotted the moderate ministers' services.

The States' pursuit of tolerance culminated in the *Resolution for the Peace of the Churches*, which – after endless debates – was passed on 23 January 1614 by the States of Holland. Grotius drafted the text and provided it with a large number of authorities derived from Church Fathers and later theologians. The thrust of the text was to prove that the five articles of the Remonstrance were in conformity with orthodox doctrine. As a starting point, he had taken the third article of the Remonstrance – that man cannot save himself, apart from the grace of God – the only one the Counter-Remonstrants were able to agree with, albeit under restrictions.

The resolution had no result whatsoever – not a single Counter-Remonstrant of standing ever endorsed it – its reception showed that a compromise was impossible for good. A reconfirmation by the States in

March 1616 came to nothing either. Not all cities agreed to the gist of the resolution; the mighty and always rebellious city of Amsterdam, in particular, was obstructive. Grotius was chosen to do the dirty work; he was sent to Amsterdam as the leader of a five-man delegation to justify the policy of the majority of the States. On 23 April 1616, Grotius delivered a long and learned speech that lasted two-and-a-half hours in the Amsterdam town council.[35] In this plea, he again appealed to the – dubious – fact that the king of England vouched for the orthodoxy of the Remonstrance and supported the resistance against a synod; once more he expounded that mutual tolerance was the only way out of the problems. Although it was a tight race, the decision of the Amsterdam city fathers was unfavourable to Grotius: the resolution was not accepted and the city supported the convocation of a synod.

'At this crucial moment Oldenbarnevelt and his faction ought to have accepted that the Counter-Remonstrants were in no mood to be constrained,' Nellen writes, and he is right.[36] Grotius and Oldenbarnevelt's fates were sealed when, after a long period of indecisiveness, Stadholder Maurice finally sprang into action. The first step was his refusal to deploy troops against the riots that resulted from Counter-Remonstrant protests. In July 1617, he made his choice manifest by attending church in the Kloosterkerk in The Hague, a building squatted in by the Counter-Remonstrants – to make the disgrace complete, located next to Oldenbarnevelt's mansion – thus publicly dropping his Remonstrant court chaplain, Wtenbogaert.

In the States of Holland, Oldenbarnevelt still had a majority. On 4 August 1617, the cities adopted the so-called *Sharp Resolution*, which made it possible for cities to act against public disturbances by hiring mercenaries ('waardgelders'). Grotius also defended this resolution in a pamphlet.[37] As Maurice, the commander-in-chief, refused to act against riots, order had to be restored by local forces.

The situation escalated rapidly. When it seemed that the States General were to call a national synod against the will of Holland, Grotius protested violently against this plan in the meeting of November 1617. To his mind, religious affairs belonged to the competence of the provincial States (*Verantwoordingh* 5.1, 48–9). After a disastrous mission to Utrecht led by Grotius in July 1618, the two remaining provinces that had still supported Oldenbarnevelt, Overijssel and Utrecht, switched sides.

After a last attempt by Oldenbarnevelt and Grotius to force the issue of the synod, Grotius finally changed his mind and agreed to its convocation. By then, the concession came too late, even for him to save his own skin. Grotius and Oldenbarnevelt were arrested on 29 August 1618.

In hindsight, Grotius' official and political career seems a variation on the Peter Principle: 'In a hierarchy every employee tends to rise to his level of incompetence.'[38] An eminent jurist, Grotius was the very man for the office of advocate-fiscal, which indeed he filled in an excellent way. As a diplomat, he lacked the necessary feelers and the ability to act tactically while effacing himself. The course of his political career was an outright disaster: by pursuing far too long and with utter misjudgment of the actual situation an ideal that was – with hindsight – foredoomed to failure (unity within a Church that was deeply divided and strong state authority over that of the Church) and thus trying to combine what did not go together – a stance that was only neutral in appearance, with actual support of one faction – he seriously damaged his own credibility and made his political career into a complete failure. His many theoretical demonstrations of the justice of his position do not alter that conclusion.

Further Reading

den Tex, J., *Oldenbarnevelt* (Haarlem, 1966–70), vols. 3–4; Abridged English translation: *Oldenbarnevelt* (Cambridge, 1973), vol. 2.

Israel, J. *The Dutch Republic: Its Rise, Greatness, and Fall 1477–1806* (Oxford, 1995).

Le Bailly, M.-Ch., *Procesgids Hof van Holland, Zeeland en West-Friesland: De hoofdlijnen van procederen in civiele zaken voor het Hof van Holland, Zeeland en West-Friesland zowel in eerste instantie als in hoger beroep* (Hilversum, 2008).

Nellen, H.J.M., *Hugo Grotius: A Lifelong Struggle for Peace in Church and State, 1583–1645* (Leiden, 2015).

Nellen, H.J.M., and J. Trapman (eds.), *De Hollandse jaren van Hugo de Groot (1583–1621): Lezingen van het colloquium ter gelegenheid van de 350-ste sterfdag van Hugo de Groot ('s-Gravenhage, 31 augustus–1 september 1995)* (Hilversum, 1996), especially the contributions by Huijbrecht and Smit.

Platt, E., *Britain and the Bestandstwisten: The Causes, Course and Consequences of British Involvement in the Dutch Religious and Political Disputes of the Early Seventeenth Century* (Göttingen [etc.], 2015).

Notes

1 *Scaligerana, Thuana, Perroniana, Pithoeana et Colomesiana, ou remarques historiques, critiques, morales et litteraires de Jos. Scaliger, J. Aug. de Thou, le Cardinal du Perron, Fr. Pithou et P. Colomiés avec les notes de plusieurs savans* (Amsterdam, 1740), vol. 2, 359.

2 R. Huijbrecht, 'De advocaten en de advocatuur bij het Hof van Holland', in R. Huijbrecht (ed.), *Handelingen van het eerste Hof van Holland symposium gehouden op 24 mei 1996 in het Algemeen Rijksarchief te Den Haag* (Den Haag, 1997), 43–61, at 50.

3 H.F.W.D. Fischer, 'Kort begrip van de gedrukte adviezen van Hugo de Groot', in Hugo de Groot, *Inleidinge tot de Hollandsche rechts-geleerdheid,* eds. F. Dovring, H.F.W.D. Fischer and E.M. Meijers (Leiden, 1965), 350–94; D.P. de Bruyn, *The Opinions of Grotius as Contained in the Hollandsche Consultatien en Advijsen* (London, 1894).

4 *Consultatien, advysen en advertissementen, gegeven en geschreven bij verscheiden treffelijke rechtsgeleerden in Holland en elders* V (Rotterdam, 1664), no. 157 (first count), 459–81.

5 *Register van Holland en Westvriesland van den jare 1604, 1605 en 1606* (n.p., n.y.), 177, 15 June 1604.

6 *Register van Holland 1607–1609*, 168; 340; 970; C. Brandt and A. van Cattenburgh, *Historie van het leven des heeren Huig de Groot I* (Dordrecht/ Amsterdam, 1727), 23–4.

7 *Holland bestuurd: teksten over het bestuur van het Graafschap Holland in het tijdvak 1299–1567,* eds. J.A.M.Y. Bos-Rops, J.G. Smit and E.T. van der Vlist (Den Haag, 2007), 436.

8 'Instructie, nae de welcke soo den Advocaet Fiscael als Procureur Generael heur in't bedienen van heure respective staten sullen moeten reguleren, in't dirigeren van des Graeffelijckheyts saecken', in C. Cau (ed.), *Groot Placaet-Boeck* II ('sGraven-Hage, 1664), 1453–6 (7 November 1606); *Register van Holland 1607–1609*, 341–3 (7 November 1607).

9 R. Huijbrecht, 'Hugo de Groot als advocaat-fiscaal van het Hof van Holland, Zeeland en West-Friesland 1607–1614', in H.J.M. Nellen and J. Trapman (eds.), *De Hollandse jaren van Hugo de Groot (1583–1621): Lezingen van het colloquium ter gelegenheid van de 350-ste sterfdag van Hugo de Groot ('s-Gravenhage, 31 augustus–1 september 1995)* (Hilversum, 1996), 45–56.

10 J. den Tex, *Oldenbarnevelt* (Haarlem, 1966), vol. 3, 286.

11 *Register van Holland 1607–1609*, 940 (5 June 1609).

12 Printed in Brandt and Van Cattenburgh, *Historie van het leven,* vol. 1, 55–7, here 56.

13 *Register van Holland 1610–1612*, 132–3; J. Wtenbogaert, *De Kerckelicke historie, vervatende verscheyden ghedenckwaerdige saken in de Christenheyt voorgevallen* (n.p., 1646), 499.

14 W.P.C. Knuttel, *Catalogus van de pamfletten-verzameling berustende in de Koninklijke Bibliotheek* I-1 ('s-Gravenhage, 1889), no. 1767.

15 *Register van Holland 1610–1612*, 229.

16 Knuttel, nos. 1772 and 1773.

17 *Register van Holland 1610–1612*, 237.

18 *Register van Holland 1610–1612*, 383–4 (20 May 1611); 467 (22 September 1611; Knuttel no. 1844); 481 (21 October 1611; Knuttel nos. 1861–2); 502 (15 November 1611; Knuttel nos. 1864–6; 1868–71); 555 (15 December 1611; Knuttel no. 1863); 684 (13 April 1612; Knuttel no. 1948); 727 (27 June 1612; Knuttel no. 1965).

19 *Register van Holland 1610–1612*, 186 (25 June 1610).

20 Edwin Rabbie (ed.), *Hugo Grotius: Ordinum Hollandiae ac Westfrisiae pietas (1613), Critical Edition with English Translation and Commentary* (Leiden, 1995), 74–82.

21 1 BW 182; H.J.M. Nellen, *Hugo Grotius: A Lifelong Struggle for Peace in Church and State, 1583–1645* (Leiden, 2015), 114–15.

22 E. Platt, 'A re-examination of English participation in the Vorstius Affair', *Holland, Historisch Tijdschrift* 40 (2008) 301–26, at 309–10.

23 R. Fruin (ed.), *Verhooren en andere bescheiden betreffende het rechtsgeding van Hugo de Groot* (Utrecht, 1871), 312.

24 Fruin, *Verhooren*, 184.

25 Paul Botley and Máté Vince (eds.), *The Correspondence of Isaac Casaubon in England* (Genève, 2018), vol. 1, 8–17.

26 The anonymous author of the 'Prefatio ad reformatas Christi ecclesias', in *Acta synodi nationalis in nomine Domini nostri Iesu Christi authoritate illustr. et praepotentum DD. Ordinum Generalium Foederati Belgii provinciarum Dordrechti habitae anno MDCXVIII et MDCXIX* (Dordrecht, 1620), fo. ††† 5r; referred to in *Verantwoordingh* 6.1, 56.

27 Letter of Archbishop Abbot to Sir Ralph Winwood of 1/11 June 1613, *Memorials of Affairs of State in the Reigns of Q. Elizabeth and K. James I, Collected chiefly from the Original Papers of . . . Sir Ralph Winwood* III (London, 1725), 459–60.

28 Cf. Casaubon's letter to Daniel Heinsius of 23 April 1613, Botley and Vince, *Correspondence*, vol. 3, 485.

29 As note 28.

30 Brandt and Van Cattenburgh, *Historie van het leven*, vol. 1, 51.

31 Brandt and Van Cattenburgh, *Historie van het leven*, vol. 1, 44–5; 51–3; 53–5 ('acte van commissie tot het pensionarisschap'); J.G. Smit, 'De Rotterdamse jaren van Hugo de Groot', in Nellen and Trapman, *Hollandse jaren*, 125–43, at 126–7.

32 Cf. Smit, 'Rotterdamse jaren', 130.

33 J. Melles, *Ministers aan de Maas: Geschiedenis van de Rotterdamse pensionarissen met een inleiding over het stedelijk pensionariaat 1508–1795* (Rotterdam [etc.], [1962]), 1–21; J.A.F. de Jongste, 'Hollandse stadspensionarissen tijdens

de Republiek. Notities bij een onderzoek', in S. Groenveld, M.E.H.N. Mout and I. Schöffer (eds.), *Bestuurders en Geleerden: Opstellen over onderwerpen uit de Nederlandse geschiedenis van de zestiende, zeventiende en achttiende eeuw, aangeboden aan Prof. Dr. J.J. Woltjer bij zijn afscheid als hoogleraar van de Rijksuniversiteit te Leiden* (Amsterdam, 1985), 85–96.

34 Smit, 'Rotterdamse jaren', 132–5; Nellen, *Grotius*, 170.

35 *Verhael van de heeren...* (1616), *BG* 844.

36 Nellen, *Grotius*, 214.

37 *Iustificatie vande resolutie der H.M. Heeren de Staten...* (1618), *BG* 861.

38 Laurence J. Peter and Raymond Hull, *The Peter Principle* (New York, 1970), 7.

Grotius and the East Indies 3

Peter Borschberg

3.1 Introduction

The present chapter explores what Grotius came to know about trade, diplomacy and politics in the East Indies. The period under review covers the beginning of his engagement on East Indian affairs around the year 1604 until his arrest and incarceration in August 1618. It focuses on geographically present-day Southeast Asia, especially on the island world of Indonesia, but also areas of the Malay Peninsula and Thailand (Siam). The discussion is aimed at answering the following overarching questions: how and in what capacity did Grotius engage with East Indian affairs? When, from whom and under what circumstances did he acquire his working knowledge about the East Indies?

Historically and thematically, Grotius' knowledge is linked to his early activities as an apologist, lobbyist and negotiator for the Dutch East India Company, the VOC, his work on committees or as a government representative. Over time, Grotius' different activities shaped his views on trade and policy-related issues. In the late nineteenth and early twentieth centuries, researchers were preoccupied with the theoretical, philosophical and legal underpinnings of his ideas and showed little concern, if any at all, for the historic context(s) in which they had been formed.[1]

Research today has not only broadened the scope of questions asked, but also expanded the range of source materials consulted, both of which have helped in reconstructing the evolution of Grotius' ideas. Researchers have trawled Grotius' correspondence, as well as his unpublished reading notes, drafts and fragments found mainly in Dutch depository institutions.[2] The careful evaluation of these materials has yielded invaluable insights on when, why and how Grotius refined his ideas on trade, politics and diplomacy in the East Indies. Researchers have also sharpened their questions of chronology and authorial intentions, as well as Grotius' access to information.[3]

The timeframe under review makes it possible to distinguish four main phases in Grotius' growing familiarity with the trade, politics and diplomacy of the East Indies: the first covers his work on the so-called *Santa Catarina* incident. This spans 1604–6, during which he preoccupied himself with problems of trade, privateering, natural rights and the just war.[4] The second phase, from 1606 to 1609, covers his activities for and on behalf of the VOC in paving the way for the Twelve Years Truce. The synergy developed with one of the VOC directors and fleet commanders, Admiral Cornelis Matelieff (1569–1632), marks the beginning of the third phase, a period from early 1609 until around the middle of 1612, and arguably beyond, during which Grotius acted as an intermediary for the admiral. The fourth and final phase examined in this chapter covers his involvement in the Anglo-Dutch colonial and fisheries conferences (1612–18).

Let us now examine these four individual phases in greater detail. Each section will be structured in a similar way, asking not only when, why and in what context Grotius acquired his knowledge about (southeast) Asia, but also what special insights readers can take away from each period.

3.2 Phase 1: The *Santa Catarina* Incident and Asian Maritime Practices

Grotius' first engagement with the affairs of the East Indies came with his commission to write a defence of the so-called *Santa Catarina* incident. This concerned the seizure of a richly laden Portuguese carrack off the eastern coast of Singapore by Admiral Jacob van Heemskerk (1567–1607) on 25 February 1603. Its cargo was subsequently brought to the Netherlands and sold at a public auction, where it yielded proceeds of over 3.2 million guilders, about half the paid-in capital of the Dutch East India Company (VOC) founded in 1602.[5] The incident and the potential fortunes that could be reaped in conducting trade with China and Japan not only attracted the attention of the merchants of Europe, it also fueled some legal debates about the nature of war at sea: Heemskerk had arguably committed an act of privateering, without proper authorisation or letter of marque.[6]

The carrack was declared a good prize by the Amsterdam admiralty board in a verdict passed on 9 September 1604.[7] Jan den Tex, the biographer of the land's advocate, Johan van Oldenbarnevelt (1547–1619), claimed that Grotius had been working on the *Santa Catarina* case as it was winding its way through the courts.[8] There is no concrete evidence, however, to support this claim. It is clear that Grotius' involvement with the case came only after the verdict had been passed. This insight raises the question as to why the directors resorted to this move to engage his services well after the verdict had been cast in their favour. Some earlier scholars, like Dutch historian Robert Fruin, argued that, by commissioning the work, the directors hoped to appease Mennonite and other Anabaptist shareholders who were concerned by Dutch recourse to violence and the despoliation of the Portuguese under the laws of war.[9]

The 'violent turn' of the VOC, endorsed by its charter of 1602 as well as a resolution of the Dutch States General dating from November 1603, must have caused concern beyond a circle of disgruntled shareholders.[10] After all, the Dutch were now developing the VOC into a private arm in the war waged by the Dutch Republic against its Iberian enemies in the East Indies. It is not evident, moreover, what form this commission assumed. Grotius enjoyed a reputation as an excellent and effective writer – he had been serving as historiographer of Holland since 1604 – so the VOC directors' move to appoint him made perfect sense if they were looking for a piece that defended Heemskerk's actions as a facet of the company's 'violent turn'. It also needed to be concise and published quickly. If such had been the intention of their commission, Grotius did not rise to the occasion. Instead of delivering a short, sharp pamphlet or booklet, he composed a lengthy treatise in Latin on natural rights and the laws of war. This work was drafted and polished over a period of two years, and arguably continually refined over his lifetime. Only one chapter was published in Grotius' own lifetime, as *Mare liberum* (*The Free Sea*).[11] Grotius decided not to proceed with the publication of the full manuscript, which he referred to as *De Indiis* (*On the Indies*) or *De rebus Indicanis* (*On the Affairs of the Indies*) but is now commonly referred to as *De jure praedae commentarius* or *Commentary on the Law of Prize and Booty.*

The aim of this chapter is not to provide detailed arguments developed in this work, but rather to explore when, how, and from where Grotius acquired the knowledge base to write this treatise. Earlier studies made two important assumptions: the first, attributed to Robert Fruin, was that Grotius had been granted access to the archives or document collections of the VOC as well as of its predecessor entities.[12] The second, advanced by Charles H. Alexandrowicz, builds on the following considerations:[13] Asian states or polities had long developed a maritime policy that advocated *mare liberum,* that is the freedom of navigation across maritime spaces.[14]

This Asian practice of free maritime trade, it further transpires from Alexandrowicz's study, sharply contrasts with the situation in Europe before about 1600. With an eye cast on the evolution of Western maritime policies from the seventeenth century onward, Asia was most certainly not inferior to European practices, but arguably more advanced.[15] To secure this Asian legacy for history, Alexandrowicz drew an important conclusion: Grotius, Europe's champion of the freedom of navigation on the high seas, was not only familiar with these Asian practices through his study of materials in the VOC company papers (archives), but significantly took on this principle and presented it for adoption by Western powers.[16] As proof of Grotius' alleged familiarity, Alexandrowicz cited the passage from the treatise *Mare liberum*: 'The Arabians and the Chinese are at the present day still carrying on with the peoples of the East Indies in trading which has been uninterrupted for several centuries.'

It is clear that Grotius was not working with the VOC's document holdings, but instead relied on specific sets of materials forwarded to him by the VOC directors.[17] Judging by the citations in the historic part of *De jure praedae* (chapters 11–15), it is clear that Grotius was working chiefly with the writings of the Greek and Roman geographers as well as some charts, reports and affidavits related to the recent Dutch voyages to the East Indies.[18] According to a note to himself, he was to 'obtain from [Pieter] Plancius the titles of such books on Portuguese trade in the East Indies as may be purchased here [in the United Provinces]' (DJPC app. 2.6). His request went unfulfilled for two likely reasons. First, Portuguese sources were difficult to get hold of in the Dutch Republic – or indeed anywhere outside of Portugal – at the time. Second, Grotius did not cite a single Portuguese source in the whole of *De jure praedae*, even though the *Comentarios de Afonso d'Albuquerque* (*Commentaries of Alfonso de Albuquerque*) or the *Décadas de Asia* (*Decades of Asia*) of João de Barros had been published well before that time.[19] He also failed to cite from travel literature or geographies prepared by scholars of the mid- to late sixteenth century, such as notably the collection of travel accounts published in Venice by Giovanni Battista Ramusio (1554), the geographical discourses of André Thevet (1574) or even from the landmark *Itinerario* and *Reysgeschrift* by Jan Huyghen van Linschoten (1595–6), though in later years he evidently had a copy of that latter work in his library.[20] It was the lack of documentation on the Portuguese in Asia that prompted Grotius to project what he had read about the Spanish in the Americas onto the situation in Asia. For this reason, Francisco de Vitoria's (c. 1480–1546) enquiries into the justness of the Spaniards' wars in the Americas was applied to the Portuguese in the East Indies. This was the reason why other Spanish authors addressing the situation in the Americas are adduced as well, but, on the contrary, not a single Portuguese author is cited in *De jure praedae*. The situation in Asia was most certainly not the same as in the Americas, and Grotius, it seems, recognised this too at some stage when he jotted down a note in the manuscript: 'Alia enim Indiae, alia Americanae ratio est.' (The case of the East Indies and the Americas are different.)[21] One should not get too enthusiastic about Grotius' citations from the Spanish Late Scholastics either. His copy of Vitoria, we learn from later correspondences, had been borrowed from his former study mate at Leiden, Jan ten Grootenhuys (1573–1646), whose elder brother Arendt was a VOC director and a key contact in those early years.[22] As late as 1617, Grotius openly conceded: 'Dominicorum vix legi quemquam' (I have hardly read any of the Dominicans, 1 BW 567). What is he intimating here? Is this a Baroque poise of modesty? Or is he, in fact, conceding that he was not very well versed in the writings of the Spanish Dominicans, or Late Scholastics, at that point in time? The situation would, of course, change when he wrote his *De jure belli ac pacis* (1625) and also some years later when he began to add copious footnotes to his text. The epistolary passage certainly raises some interesting questions about the evolution of his familiarity with the Spanish neo-scholastics.

Readers can take away two main insights relating to this first phase in Grotius' knowledge of and engagement with the East Indies trade. First, Grotius in these early years was working with a far narrower set of sources than had been assumed by scholars in earlier decades. Second, we must be mindful that there is not a shred of evidence to prove that Grotius had familiarised himself with Asian maritime customs. Also, it is highly unlikely that he developed his ideas of *mare liberum* in accordance with Southeast Asian maritime practice. His early knowledge base was overwhelmingly derived from the materials fed to him by the VOC directors and touched mainly on the atrocities inflicted on the Dutch by the Portuguese rather than the mechanisms of trade or maritime customs in Asia. The bottom line is that researchers should be mindful not to over-interpret his source references or even overestimate the expanse of his knowledge of – and familiarity with – the East Indies for the period 1604–1606/7.

3.3 Phase 2: The VOC and the Truce

The second phase in Grotius' involvement with trade and diplomacy in the East Indies came with his efforts to help the VOC position itself in the new global order that would emerge after the conclusion of the Dutch-Iberian truce (1609). This covers the period between 1606/7 and 1609 and saw Grotius help preserve Asian trade for the Dutch Republic. Grotius specifically assisted the consolidation of the VOC's interests in three respects. First, he developed a synergy with the directors and, in late 1607 and early 1608, worked out a blueprint for the Dutch negotiators aimed at safeguarding the VOC's strategic and commercial interests in Asia. Second, after striking a tentative agreement with the Iberian powers over access to marketplaces in Asia, the VOC launched a diplomatic initiative by which it hoped to secure as much of the Asian trading pie as possible. Grotius had a hand in this and drafted letters to some key rulers in Southeast Asia. Third, when the company's Asian interests looked imperilled during the second half of 1608, Grotius, at the encouragement of the VOC directors, pulled out one chapter of his unpublished *De jure praedae*, revised it and published it anonymously as *Mare liberum*. Appended to the treatise are a selection of documents taken from a packet of letters collectively titled 'letters by the king of Spain' that had been forwarded to Grotius by Adriaen ten Haeff (1560–1608) around 17 November 1607.[23] However, due to objections by Oldenbarnevelt voiced in February 1609, the first edition of *Mare liberum* was not immediately released on the market, but only after the signing of the Twelve Years Truce two months later.[24]

The second phase of Grotius' engagement with the East Indies took place in the wake of the VOC's 'violent turn'. The company's explicit mandate to carry out the Dutch war effort in its chartered territory saw a step up in Dutch violence directed against hard and soft targets of their Iberian enemies across Asia. Within a short period, the VOC – subsidised by the home government – was waging a campaign that sought to deny the Iberian powers as much trading revenue as possible. This campaign helped bring Spain to its knees in 1606, when it suspended debt repayments and was forced to negotiate with the Dutch.

But the 'violent turn' had at least one negative impact on the VOC's operations in Asia: it caused security and protection costs to rise dramatically, and these ate into the company's profits. The VOC was constantly begging for subsidies. One of the reasons why Grotius may not have openly supported the truce was because he had become familiar with how Zeeland benefited from privateering activities, and especially how public revenue generated by these had helped Zeeland's finances. Was stepping up privateering a way of improving the VOC's ailing bottom line? What about Holland's public finances? The prospect of a truce also impacted on the outlook of the company. How would the VOC fare in the future? Would the VOC be dissolved as a consequence of the truce? What about the Asian treaty partners? Grotius would address these questions, though admittedly not as a front man, but from behind the scenes. Nellen surmises that he did not want to be seen to openly promote the cause of peace for fear that it might harm his reputation.[25]

First, Grotius helped the directors of the VOC work out their negotiating position. This position is captured in two drafts of a memorandum, complete with notes and a postscript, which survive among Grotius' former working papers at the National Archives in The Hague.[26] His role in working out this document is not clear. Was this memorandum, or was it not, the fruit of synergy? Did Grotius rationalise and systematise ideas that he had collated in conversations and with the different directors?[27] Be this as it may, he left his imprint on the memorandum by working out three scenarios for the impending truce. The first foresaw that the company would be granted freedom of trade and navigation in its chartered territory. The second stipulated a complete withdrawal of the Dutch from Asia – and, consequently, a dissolution of the VOC. The third argued for the status quo in the Indian Ocean and the Pacific: peace in the European theatre, but continued warfare in the south Atlantic and Asia. The first scenario was the preferred option by the directors. The third was seen to be the most likely to materialise, as the first was not acceptable to Philip III of Spain (1578–1621), and the second would damage the overseas trading interests of Holland and Zeeland.

The memorandum was approved by the directors in early February 1608 and accepted by the Dutch negotiators. Although Grotius was unsure whether the negotiations would succeed, there was never any serious doubt that the negotiators would strike a bargain favourable to the company's interests, irrespective of whether the war would continue outside Europe. Once a tentative agreement had been struck after discussions on the East Indies trade, the directors felt sufficiently confident on 11 April 1608 to alert the VOC's network of outposts in Asia of the impending truce.[28] Their message was clear: conclude as many treaties with Asian rulers as possible and grab as much of the trading pie as possible before the truce took effect.[29] The course of events, however, was somewhat different, and there was considerable resistance right until the end in formalising a right of the Dutch to trade in the East Indies.[30]

Among Grotius' papers are a series of draft letters addressed to certain rulers of insular and mainland Southeast Asia. These include the sultans of Ternate, Tidore and Siau, the 'Emperor' of Borneo ('Brunei'), the kings of Johor and Siam, as well as the 'seigneuries' of Ambon and Banda.[31] The letters are undated, but they may have been drafted in conjunction with the diplomatic initiative of April 1608, or perhaps just before that. In terms of content, they share a certain scheme, with cross references made from one to the other, indicating that they must have been written around the same time. The letters to the kings of Johor and Siam, written in the hand of Grotius on different sides of a single sheet of paper, shall serve as a case in point: they attest to the friendship of the Dutch and emphasise mutual interests of commerce and diplomacy.[32] They call on the Asian rulers to join with the Dutch in damaging the interests of the Portuguese, their mutual enemies. Despite the similarities, the letters contain information specific to the VOC's relations with each ruler. The letter to Johor, for example, speaks of joint military action against Malacca (Melaka), and expresses hope that the city will have already been plucked from the Portuguese. This is a reference to the campaign of Admiral Cornelis Matelieff in 1606, the outcome of which was not yet known in the Dutch Republic at the time when Grotius penned this piece. In his letter addressed to the Siamese ruler on the reverse side, Grotius mentions an earlier offer by Siam to join one of their future tributary missions to China. This offer had been extended to Admiral Wijbrand van Warwijk (1566–1615) in 1604 after he had failed to gain access to China with the help of certain overseas Chinese intermediaries. Although Warwijk would have been pleased to take up the offer through the men he had dispatched to Siam's capital, Ayutthaya, the opportunity never arose because no tributary mission was sent to the Ming court for several years. This was due to wars in the north, the unexpected death of Naresuan (1555–1605), the king of Siam, in 1605, as well as events surrounding his successor and brother, Ekathotsarot (1556–1620). Through this letter, Grotius offered to pick up where the Dutch had left off in 1605. He could have hardly known that, just as he was writing these lines, Matelieff carried aboard his ships a delegation of Siamese emissaries destined for the Republic.

What can readers take away from this second phase of Grotius' engagement with the East Indies? He had strengthened his working relationship with the VOC directors and helped them sharpen their negotiating position for the truce talks. The memorandum reflects a synergy and strategic position worked out by Grotius in unison with the directors to safeguard VOC interests in the East Indies. In fact, he would later claim that he had done his utmost to prevent the Iberians from entrenching themselves all over the East Indies.[33] This claim, however, is problematic. Before the ratification of the truce in April 1609, the Dutch States General were planning to include their Asian allies in what may be seen as a collective security arrangement. The matter was discussed before the States General on 18 March 1609, when Siam, Calicut, Bantam [Banten], Johor, Aceh, Pahang, Kedah, Makassar, Banda, Ternate and unspecified 'others' were singled out for inclusion.[34] The arrangement was confirmed by the Anglo-French guarantee, ratified in June 1609. This stipulated that 'France and England also oblige themselves to render assistance during the validity of the Truce, in the event that the Spaniards should harass the Dutch in the East Indies or their allies in that region'.[35]

In addition to helping safeguard the interests of the VOC, Grotius played a role in coordinating the diplomatic initiative by drafting a series of letters to key rulers in the East Indies. This aimed at altering the strategic, diplomatic and commercial realities for the Iberian powers before the truce came into effect in Asia in April 1610. Grotius thus assumed a role in expanding the company's web of alliances, and later delivery contracts, paving the ground for the VOC spice monopoly.

3.4 Phase 3: Matelieff's Intermediary

Cornelis Corneliszoon Matelief(f), or Cornelis Matelief de Jonge, was a director of the Rotterdam chamber of the VOC. He is best remembered for his unsuccessful campaign to seize Malacca from the Portuguese (1606), the first delivery contract with the young Sultan Modafar of Ternate (1607) and recommending reforms of the VOC. Matelieff's reform initiatives were read among government leaders of the Dutch Republic and directors of the VOC. Noteworthy recipients included Oldenbarnevelt and possibly also the stadholder of Holland and Zeeland, Maurice of Nassau

(1567–1625), the Prince of Orange. Signed originals by Matelieff are found among Oldenbarnevelt's working papers preserved in The Hague.[36]

To gain the ear of the land's advocate, Matelieff relied on the services of Grotius. Matelieff had chosen his intermediary carefully. He thought himself to be outspoken and long-winded, and given how busy Oldenbarnevelt always was, these were not traits that would endear him with the land's advocate.[37] This was where Grotius came in: he would pass the written proposals to Oldenbarnevelt with a summary or commentary on their content. Grotius asked for secretarial copies for his own file, and these survive in The Hague and Rotterdam collections. On one of these he wrote as a note to himself: 'Den 23 Maij 1609 aen sijn Ex.tie, ende den Ad.t' (passed on 23 May to his Excellency [Prince Maurice] and the [land's] advocate [Oldenbarnevelt]).[38]

By acting as an intermediary for Matelieff from 1609 through 1610, Grotius developed synergy with the admiral. The memorials yield important information on marketplaces, political conditions, the English and Iberian competition, as well as the need to invest in commercial and military infrastructure, such as forts and factories. In these documents, Matelieff laid down specific recommendations to improve the way the VOC did business in Asia, optimise timings of fleet departures from Europe, assemble an intra-Asian fleet and establish a central base in Asia. Like other fleet commanders of the early VOC, he recognised the advantages that the Iberians gained from their establishments in Goa and Manila. Matelieff's proposal to found a so-called rendezvous, or permanent base, at a central location in Asia should therefore be seen in terms of ensuring that the VOC enjoyed the same financial, commercial and administrative benefits as the Iberians had with their presence in Goa and Manila. Significant also is Matelieff's plan to establish a commercial monopoly at the source of cloves, nutmeg and mace, and inversely to flood the European market with pepper in order to drive the VOC's competitors out of business. Gaastra underscores that Matelieff was 'the first person in the directorate of the Company to think in terms of "empire building"' and also that his ideas were taken seriously.[39] Seen this way, the admiral ranks as one of the early architects of the first Dutch Empire in the East Indies, and he achieved this not least with some help from Grotius.

What can readers conclude from this phase? Matelieff emerged as an important source of information for Grotius on political, economic and strategic issues in the East Indies. In fact, Grotius continued to draw on the admiral's expertise later during the Anglo-Dutch maritime and colonial conferences discussed below. When the English delegates arrived by ship in 1615 for discussions at The Hague, Grotius and Matelieff were together to welcome them.[40]

Matelieff's personal experience in Asia between 1605 and 1608, as well as his vision for transforming the VOC's operations, helped shape the way that Grotius himself would understand the East Indies over the next decade. He also gained access to Matelieff's then still unpublished travelogue, which yields important information on the regions that the admiral had visited directly, including especially the Malay Peninsula, Java, Ternate, coastal China and Champa. Matelieff had grasped the challenge posed by the Iberian powers in Asia, as well as by the emerging competition from the English. Matelieff does not stipulate how his proposed rendezvous was to be founded. The Portuguese did not have a colony like Melaka or Ambon on Java that could be taken as booty of war and, therefore, the base needed to be secured by a treaty as in Johor in 1606.[41] Judging by the notes jotted down in his personal copies of Matelieff's memorials, Grotius must have also been informed of the admiral's proposal to establish a spice monopoly in nutmeg, mace and cloves.[42] He would soon emerge as one of the principal defenders of this budding monopoly at the Anglo-Dutch conferences of 1613 and 1615.

To what extent did Grotius' own vision for the Dutch in the East Indies align with the ideas of Matelieff? His vision for the VOC in Asia was not too far removed from Matelieff's in that he saw Dutch presence and dominance in the East Indies based on commercial and contractual arrangements. The key was to uphold the VOC's twin monopolies: one with the homeland granted by the VOC charter of 1602 and guaranteed by the States General the other a monopoly in the trade of certain spices that was based on a web of delivery contracts and backed by Dutch pledges to protect their Asian treaty partners. To this end, Matelieff's treaty with Ternate served as a model. Grotius, moreover, aimed to tie the VOC's allies closer to the company in a standing arrangement that would keep the VOC's European competitors in check. In a nutshell, the vision of a web of relations supported by commerce was taking shape when Grotius entered the fourth phase under review.

3.5 Phase 4: Anglo-Dutch Conferences

The final phase in Grotius' engagement with East Indies trade and politics is marked by the Anglo-Dutch conferences held in London (1613) and The Hague (1615).[43] The period under review spans from the preparations for the London conference in 1612 up until Grotius' arrest and incarceration in August 1618. A petition by the VOC, prepared by Grotius and submitted to the Dutch States General, argued that the company had incurred heavy expenses on account of its security and infrastructure spending on forts, ports and factories, while the English were seeking to reap the harvest where they had sown nothing. To this, the VOC reacted by excluding the English from certain marketplaces in Southeast Asia, such as in the Moluccas (Maluku). Discussions were held to sort out these problems during the first round of meetings held in London in 1613. The objective from the English vantage point was not to demand reparations for damages suffered from Dutch exclusion, but to obtain guarantees that they could trade without obstruction.[44]

It should be immediately adjoined here that the discussions held between the Dutch and English delegations covered a wide range of both official and unofficial topics. The East Indies represented only one set of issues on the agenda. Other official matters discussed included fishing in the coastal waters of England and Scotland as well as whaling in the North Sea and Spitsbergen. On the unofficial agenda were the mounting problems in the Dutch Republic over religion, specifically the differences between the Arminians or Gomarists, and on what rights the state had in managing their resolution by the force of law.[45] Grotius arrived in London as a key member of the Dutch negotiating team, at the behest of the States of Holland.[46] His performance here during the negotiations – and also in private discussions with leading Anglican divines – left an unfavourable impression of himself on the English.[47] He came across as a pompous, hard-nosed, irritating pedant – not exactly the image we have of him in more recent times. Certainly, any claim that this episode marked 'the high tide of Grotius' political career' and showcased 'the best example of his diplomatic talents' is problematic when seen from the vantage point of the English.[48]

This fourth phase saw a convergence of the preceding three: there was the issue of the just war – specifically against the Iberian powers in Asia – the VOC's diplomatic thrust in Asia, as well as the justification of protection costs through exclusive delivery contracts. Grotius drew on his familiarity with all these issues to justify the VOC's tightening grip on the supply of nutmeg, mace and cloves. Nellen has argued that Grotius sought to defend the Hollanders and Zeelanders in the East Indies, specifically in insular Southeast Asia, and he had a proven track record as a skilled orator and debater.[49] Based on the surviving papers, a number of issues were brought to the table for discussion.[50]

Grotius' opening speech held in the presence of James I/VI on 6 April 1613 set the tone for the London meeting. It was about costs and getting the English to share in the heavy financial burden of security. 'The entire time since we first sailed to the Indies,' Grotius contended in that speech, 'has been spent protecting rather than enjoying our commerce, and the expenses that we have made for the war, apart from trade, amount to many millions of florins.'[51] The Dutch were accusing the English of unduly benefitting from the costly commercial and security infrastructure that the VOC had built up in Asia. To this end, Grotius had solicited the help of his friend Matelieff, who had supplied him with some facts and figures.[52] One way out of the conundrum was to merge the two East India companies, the Dutch and the English, but this did not excite the English delegates. A merger would safeguard English access to spices in the Indies, but, to achieve this merger, the English would need proportionately to contribute toward the cost of existing infrastructure built up by the VOC. Another benefit of the merger was this: an enlarged, united company would stand a better chance of winning a war against the Spanish and Portuguese in Asia. Evidently, however, the English were unimpressed. They resisted contributing toward what they deemed inflated costs of defending the natives, and were loath to be drawn into a new war against Spain.[53] The Dutch, by contrast, had a clearer picture of what would become of this merger. In a letter dated 20 August 1618, Admiral Steven van der Hagen (1563–1621) highlighted: '. . . [W]ith our combined powers we can impede the Portuguese from trading in Surat and along the Coromandel Coast, make us master of the Singapore Straits, and ensure that no junks call at Malacca to trade.'[54]

The merger never materialised in a form that the Dutch had been envisioning and discussions resumed at the next meeting in The Hague.[55] In order to safeguard English commercial and political interests, a cooperation agreement without merger was drawn up. This arrangement, thought to have been a pet project of King James,[56] aimed at creating a 'communion of commerce in the East Indies', but it was only formalised at the meeting in 1619, in other words, after the arrest of Oldenbarnevelt and Grotius in August of the preceding year.[57] The cooperation agreement never worked as intended, as Bassett has testified: '[T]he English directors had reluctantly agreed to an alliance with the "Hollanders" in 1619, by which they were allowed to establish factories alongside the Dutch ones in the Moluccas, the Bandas and Amboyna, in return for bearing one third of the maintenance costs of the Dutch garrisons.'[58] While Grayson claims that the VOC directors were ready 'to give the treaty a fair trial', Governor-General Jan Pieterszoon Coen (1587–1629) was simply not willing to let the agreement work.[59] Tensions rose especially in Asia and, by the so-called Massacre of Amboyna (Ambon) in 1623, the agreement had become unworkable. The fallout caused by the 'massacre' has been discussed by David Bassett and more recently by Adam Clulow. The year 1623 also marked the end of the fourth and last Anglo-Dutch conference that sought to settle outstanding bilateral trade issues in the East Indies as well as in Europe.

Not only did Grotius not see the merger or union of the two companies, he came under serious fire for what the English regarded as Dutch hypocrisy. The English delegates insisted on their right to trade freely in the East Indies, and claimed that Dutch treaties of exclusion worked, in the end, no differently from those of the Iberian powers.[60] They attacked the VOC delivery contracts on two grounds. First, on the grounds that Sir Francis Drake (c. 1540–96) had signed a treaty with the sultan of Ternate well before the Dutch ever arrived in Moluccan waters. English claims to commercial privileges thus predated those of the Dutch. Second, they questioned the validity of Dutch contracts by challenging the conditions by which these had been secured. Concessions by the Moluccan rulers exacted under duress rendered the agreements invalid. In arguing all of this, the English delegates were hurling citations at Grotius that supported free trade and, ironically, which they had plucked from his *Mare liberum*.[61]

Grotius rose to the challenge of defending Dutch interests in the face of these accusations. He described VOC policy in the East Indies as 'coophandel met force', trade supported by armed intervention.[62] The company was facing high security costs in the Indies not least because all of the treaties with the Southeast Asian rulers were wrapped in the language of protection and mutual security.[63] Such security was not only necessary to fend off the common enemy, the Iberian powers, but these security costs had to be paid for, and these expenses were covered by agreeing to an exclusive agreement to supply certain spices to the Dutch. As Grotius explained in his opening address in London: 'Therefore, by way of alliance tribute, they [the East Indian rulers] just promised something that was no trouble to them at all, namely that if we were prepared to buy their spices for a reasonable price, they would not sell them to others ...'[64] The treaties were valid and had to be honoured, irrespective of how these had been secured. 'Pacta sunt servanda', Grotius insisted by invoking a tenet of Roman and canon law, 'contracts must be honoured', and 'nihil tam naturale est quam pacta servare' (nothing is as natural as honouring contracts or treaties).[65] If they were not being honoured, it was not because the contracts were invalid, but because the Asians were 'perfidious'.[66] Under such circumstances, and given the absence of a higher authority to appeal to, it was therefore permissible to act as judge and executioner in one's own case and compel the Asian rulers to honour their treaties.[67]

Referring to the accusation that the Dutch behaved no differently to the Iberians, Grotius begged to differ. VOC exclusion policy was based on a series of alliance and delivery contracts that had been signed with the Southeast Asian rulers, and not on sweeping claims of ownership based on discovery or papal donation. The VOC's contracts with Asian rulers, moreover, were not seen to violate their sovereignty, but, on the contrary, were concluded based on the sovereignty of these rulers. At stake was not sovereignty, but liberty, and this prevails for as long as it is not curtailed by contract or agreement.[68] Every agreement limits natural freedom and freedom of choice – that is true of individuals, rulers and states – and Grotius warned that 'it behooveth all those that will be free to avoid all conditions whereon laws are imposed as those which are next to servitude' (ML 13, 57).

The contractual basis of the Dutch spice monopoly in Asia, moreover, bore two features that clearly set it apart from the policies of the Iberian powers. First, since the contracts were with rulers, they were spatially limited to a few places that were under the suzerainty of their contract partners.[69] This stood in sharp contrast to the claims made by the Iberians. The second was that the monopoly was limited to certain commodities – spices – and not, as in the Iberian case, to all commodities and all forms of trade.[70] From this vantage point, the Dutch could not be accused, strictly speaking, of violating the principle of free trade.[71] Moreover, monopolies were acceptable insofar as they did not lead to price gouging or profiteering, and Grotius underscored that the Dutch were selling their spices to the English at a fair price.[72]

The English negotiators rightly thought Grotius and his team were missing the point as their arguments shared few touchpoints with actual conditions in Asia. In his writings, Grotius did not pause to consider how Asian rulers viewed these treaties. The most powerful among them never signed treaties, and most certainly not with the Dutch, whom they simply regarded as a group of merchants. If the European understanding was one where the parties were expected to honour the conditions despite changing circumstances, Muslim rulers and their jurists held rather different views: altered circumstances reshape the nature of the contract. As Noel James Coulson explained: 'Future circumstances are neither predictable nor controllable, but lie entirely in the hands of the Almighty. In the face of the predetermined mark of events human activity assumes a relative insignificance and the contractual promise becomes a relatively ephemeral thing. If the tide of affairs turns, then the promise naturally floats out with it'.[73] Other rulers saw agreements as a pledge or promise that was made in a personal capacity and were not binding to their successors; they were certainly never understood in Asia to be the international, inter-state contracts Grotius claimed them to be. To their credit, VOC officers in Asia understood this and forged agreements with rulers in their personal capacity.[74] When a given ruler passed on, the company secured a renewal with his successor. A case in point is the treaty signed by Olivier de Vivere with Aceh in January 1607.[75] Upon Ali Ri'ayat Shah's death a few months later, the VOC sought to renew the treaty with his successor, Iskandar Muda (1593–1636), but the latter refused. Renewal was also vital since Southeast Asian rulers acted as the largest, sometimes only, merchant in their own polity and generally retained a monopoly of key exports.[76] In Siam, for example, foreigners could only procure key exports from the king's warehouses, and similar restrictions applied in other parts of Southeast Asia.[77]

What can readers take away from this fourth phase? The VOC directors were pleased with Grotius' performance at the Anglo-Dutch conferences, where he emerged as the champion of an imperial system that was justified by a web of contracts. The security system that emerged, moreover, (nominally) upheld the sovereignty of these contract partners, but not their freedom to choose with whom they trade. To Grotius it was not about curtailing, mitigating or dividing sovereignty, strictly speaking – that seems to have developed at a later stage in the seventeenth century. For Grotius it was primarily about liberty. Rulers are just like individuals in this regard: they are in fact free to sell themselves into slavery. Grotius warned rulers of the consequences of not bothering too much about looking after one's liberty.[78]

3.6 Afterword

Earlier researchers were primarily concerned with dissecting Grotius' ideas found in his published works, especially in his *De jure belli ac pacis*, without consulting his unpublished notes, fragments or correspondence. That has changed, and researchers today pay closer attention to the context and purpose of Grotius' different works, and also how these works build on one another. The growth of Grotius' knowledge about the East Indies must be understood against the backdrop of the different roles he played and the various goals he pursued in dealing with the early Dutch trade with Asia. To this end, his engagement with the East Indies between c. 1604 and 1618 has been divided into four periods: first, the defence of the *Santa Catarina* incident; second, the truce negotiations with Spain together with the VOC's forward diplomatic thrust in Asia; third, Grotius' role as an intermediary or go-between for Matelieff and Oldenbarnevelt; and, fourth, the Anglo-Dutch maritime and colonial conferences after 1613. Right up until his arrest and incarceration in August 1618, Grotius was assuming advisory roles in the talks for the future cooperation between the VOC and the English East India Company, Isaac Le Maire's (1558–1624) dispute with the States General over his – by then defunct – *Austraelsche Compagnie* (Australian Company), as well as for a scheme pursued by Willem Usselincx (1567–1647) to establish a *West-Indische Compagnie* (West Indies Company), or WIC. The year 1618 represents a pivot in Grotius' biography, as it marked the painful end of his political career in the Dutch Republic. This was followed by his escape from prison and the beginning of an itinerant life as a refugee and later a Swedish diplomat. It must be added that, in 1618, Grotius did not abruptly lose interest in the East Indies or Dutch colonialism. He was an acknowledged expert in maritime affairs, which made him an indispensable authority even to his enemies in the Netherlands, and a potential liability should he ever decide – under duress – to sell his knowledge to one of the VOC's competitors. That possibility arose notably when Cardinal Richelieu (1585–1642) was moving to set up a French East India Company.[79]

The VOC's presence in Asia was built on commerce that was sustained by a chartered monopoly from the Dutch States General exclusive delivery contracts with Asian rulers, promises of protection and the exportation of the Dutch struggle for independence from Spain outside the European theatre. In the words of Grotius, the Dutch system in the East Indies was built on 'coophandel met force'.[80] Violence had become an indispensable pillar in this emerging structure right from the start. He supported the evolving Dutch commercial system based on a web of delivery contracts and justified the resulting trade monopoly not with reference to sovereignty, but to liberty and the freedom of choice. In June 1640, Grotius wrote to his brother-in-law, Nicolaas van Reigersberch (1584–1654), explaining why there could never be a union of the English and Dutch East India Companies: the two nations took very different approaches. As merchants, the English were mainly concerned with profits; by contrast, the Dutch resorted to warfare to achieve their long-term objectives.[81] This then is the story of Grotius' life. In later years, he distanced himself from the writings of his youth – including *Mare liberum* – but can it be assumed that he had some regrets about his earlier activities in the service of the fatherland? In chronicling Grotius' involvement in the East Indies, the irony emerges: in an early life involved with stoking the flames of war, he is mostly remembered today as a paragon of peace.

Further Reading

Akvelt, L. (ed.), *Machtsstrijd om Malakka. De reis van VOC-admiraal Cornelis Cornelisz Matelief naar Oost-Azië, 1605–1608* (Zutphen, 2013).

Boxer, C.R., *The Dutch Seaborne Empire, 1600–1800* (London, 1965).

Boxer, C.R., *Jan Compagnie in War and Peace, 1602–1799* (Hong Kong, 1979).

Israel, J., *The Dutch Republic and the Hispanic World, 1606–1661* (Oxford, 1982).

Khalilieh, H., *Islamic Law of the Sea. Freedom of Navigation and Passage Rights in Islamic Thought* (Cambridge, 2019).

Meilink Roelofsz, M.A.P., *Asian Trade and European Influence in the Indonesian Archipelago between 1500 and about 1630* (The Hague, 1962).

Reid, A.J.S., *Southeast Asia in the Age of Commerce, 1450–1680* (2 vols., New Haven and New York, 1988–90).

Wolters, O.W., *History, Culture and Region in Southeast Asian Perspectives* (Singapore, 1982).

Notes

1 Notable exception is Robert Fruin. See Fruin's *Verspreide geschriften met aantekeningen, toevoegsels en verbetering uit des schrijvers nalatenschap*, eds. P.J. Blok and P.L. Muller, 10 vols. (The Hague, 1900–5), vol. 3, 367–412; also 'An Unpublished Work of Hugo Grotius', *Bibliotheca Visseriana* 5 (1925) 3–71.

2 See P.A. Tiele, *Catalogue de manuscrits autographes de Hugo Grotius dont le vente a eu lieu à la Haye le 15. novembre 1864 sous la direction et au domicile de Martinus Nijhoff*, 2nd ed. with annotations by W.J.M. van Eysinga and L.J. Noordhoff (The Hague, 1952); L.J. Noordhoff, *Beschrijving van het zich in Nederland bevindende en nog onbeschreven gedeelte der papieren afkomstig van Huig de Groot welke in 1864 te 's-Gravenhage zijn geveilt* (Groningen-Djakarta, 1953).

3 See for example H.J.M. Nellen, *Hugo Grotius: A Lifelong Struggle for Peace in Church and State* (Leiden, 2014); M.J. van Ittersum, *Profit and Principle: Hugo Grotius, Natural Rights Theories and the Rise of Dutch Power in the East Indies, 1595–1615* (Leiden, 2006).

4 M.J. van Ittersum, 'Dating the Manuscript of *De Jure Praedae*', *History of European Ideas*, 35 (2009) 125–93.

5 P. Borschberg, 'The Seizure of the *Santa Catarina* Revisited', *Journal of Southeast Asian Studies* 33, 1 (2002) 31–62, at 56.

6 *Ibid.*, 48–50; also Van Ittersum, *Profit*.

7 *Ibid.*, 113–15.

8 J. den Tex, *Oldenvarnevelt* (5 vols., Haarlem-Groningen, 1960–72), and its abridged English translation as *Oldenbarnevelt* (2 vols., Cambridge, 1973).

9 For Fruin's works, see n1.

10 On this development see P. Borschberg, 'From Self-Defense to an Instrument of War: Dutch Privateering around the Malay Peninsula in the Early Seventeenth Century', *Journal of Early Modern History* 17 (2013) 35–52.

11 For the history of the publication, see Nellen, *Grotius,* 106–9; M.J. van Ittersum, 'Preparing *Mare Liberum* for the Press: Hugo Grotius' Rewriting of chapter 12 of *De iure praedae* in November–December 1608, *Grotiana* N.S. 27–8 (2005–7) 246–80.

12 Fruin, 'Een onuitgegeven werk', in *Verspreide Geschriften*, vol. 3, 403.

13 C.H. Alexandrowicz, *An Introduction to the History of the Law of Nations in the East Indies* (Oxford, 1967), 65. See also E. Wilson, 'The Alexandrowicz Thesis revisited. Hugo Grotius, divisible sovereignty, and private avengers within the Indian Ocean World System,' K.G. Ooi and A.T. Hoàng (eds.), in *Early Modern Southeast Asia, 1350–1800* (New York and London, 2016), 28–54.

14 Alexandrowicz, *An Introduction,* 44.

15 On this point see also Ram Prakash Anand, 'Maritime Practice in Southeast Asia until 1600 A.D. and the Modern Law of the Sea', *The International and Comparative Law Quarterly* 30, 2 (1981) 440–54, at 443.

16 See Alexandrowicz, *An Introduction*, 61–5; Ram Prakash Anand, *Origin and Development of the Law of the Sea. History of International Law Revisited* (The Hague, 1983), 5.

17 Among the most significant are a collection of affidavits prepared around the time of Grotius' commission. See W.Ph. Coolhaas, 'Een bron van het historische gedeelte van Hugo de Groot's De Jure Praedae', *Bijdragen en Mededelingen van het Historisch Genootschap* 79 (1965) 415–537.

18 P. Borschberg, *Hugo Grotius, the Portuguese and Free Trade in the East Indies* (Singapore and Leiden, 2011).

19 B. de Albuquerque, *Comentarios de Afonso d'Albuqerque*, ed. J. Veríssimo Serrão (text of the 2nd edn. of 1576, 2 vols., Lisbon, 1973); *The Commentaries of the Great A. Dalboquerque, Second Viceroy of India*, transl. W. de Gray Birch (4 vols., London, 1875–95); J. de Barros and D. do Couto, *Da Ásia, Dos feitos que os Portuguezes fizeram no conquista, e descubrimento das terras e mares do oriente* (24 vols., Lisbon, 1778).

20 G.B. Ramusio, *Delle navigationi et viaggi in molti luoghi corretta* ... (Venice, 1554); A. Thevet, *Cosmographie Universelle* (Paris, 1575), vol. 1; J.H. van Linschoten, Itinerario. Voyage ofte Schipvaert van Jan Huygen van Linschoten naer Oost ofte Portugaels Indien, 1579–1592, *and* Reys-geschrift vande navigatiën der Portugaloysers, eds. H. Kern and J.C.M. Warnsinck (2nd edn., The Hague, 1939). For the presence of Linschoten in Grotius' personal library, see van Ittersum, *Profit*, 293–5.

21 Alexandrowicz, *Introduction*, 47 n1.

22 BW 6205, letter to P. Spiring Silvercrona dat. 9 May 1643. On the identity of Grootenhuys, see van Ittersum, *Profit*, 24–5.

23 BW Supp. 107A. The letters are also mentioned in the appendices of *Mare Liberum, sive de iure quod Batavis competit in rebus Indicanis* (Leiden, 1609), where some of them have been published in a partial Latin translation.

24 Nellen, *Grotius*, 108–9.

25 Nellen, *Grotius*, 105; van Ittersum, 'Preparing'.

26 The Hague, National Archives, *Collectie Hugo de Groot Supplement* [1.35.10.02], no. 40, fols. 295–9; 405–13. Source hereafter CHGS.

27 Van Ittersum, *Profit*, 227, 406; also P. Borschberg (ed.), *Journal Memorials and Letters of Cornelis Matelieff de Jonge. Security, Diplomacy and Commerce in 17th-century Southeast Asia* (Singapore, 2015), 37–8; 35–6.

28 The Hague, National Archives, *Collectie Salomon Sweerts, Jeremias van Vliet, en Jacques Specx* [1.10.78], inv. 5, 'Notitiën, missiven en instructiën van Oost-Indische zaken sedert 1602 tot 1644', fols. 60–8; Borschberg, *Journal*, 435–40.

29 The relevant contracts signed in this period have been collected in J.E. Heeres (ed.), 'Corpus Diplomaticum Neërlando-Indicum. Verzameling van politieke contracten en verdere verdragen door de Nederlanders in het Oosten gesloten, van privilegiebrieven, aan hen verleend, enz.', eerste deel (1596–1650), *Bijdragen en Mededelingen van het Koninklijk Instituut voor Taal-, Land- en Volkenkunde* 57 (1907) 1–586. Source hereafter *CD* and the journal *BKI*.

30 J.C. Grayson, *From Protectorate to Partnership, Anglo-Dutch Relations, 1598-1625* (unpublished doctoral dissertation University of London; London, 1978), 116-17. Source hereafter GPP.

31 CHGS, 359-60, 361-2, 364, 430. For the letter to Tidore see DJPC app. II.9, 353-5. For the letters to Siam and Johor with a discussion of their context, see P. Borschberg, 'Cornelis Matelieff, Hugo Grotius and the King of Siam (1605-1616): Agency, Initiative and Diplomacy', *Modern Asian Studies* 54 (2020) 123-56.

32 CHGS, 364.

33 H. Grotius, 'Memorië van mijne intentiën', ed. R. Fruin, *Werken Uitgegeven door het Historisch Genootschap* 14 (1871) 1-80; G.N. Clark and W.J.M. van Eysinga, 'The Colonial Conferences between England and the Netherlands in 1613 and 1615', part 1, *Bibliotheca Visseriana*, 15 (1940) 1-270 at 63, 72. Source hereafter CC.

34 H.P. Rijperman (ed.), *Resolutiën der Staten-Generaal van 1576 tot 1609* (The Hague, 1970), vol. 14, 658.

35 Concerning the Anglo-French guarantee, see Municipal Archives *(Gemeentearchief)* Rotterdam, Buitenlandse Handel, no. 803, fol. 86. See also Grayson, *Protectorate,* 117-19; Nellen, *Grotius,* 104-5.

36 See The Hague, National Archives, *Collectie Johan van Oldenbarnevelt* [3.01.14], no. 3107.

37 Nellen, *Grotius;* 205.

38 Rotterdam, Municipal Archives *(Gemeentearchief)*, Ms. 33.01 no. 3367; Noordhoff, *Beschrijving,* 23, under fols. 510(2)-523.

39 F.S. Gaastra, *The Dutch East India Company. Expansion and Decline* (Zutphen, 2004), 39-40.

40 Clark and van Eysinga 'Colonial Conferences 1', 175.

41 P. Borschberg, 'Left Holding the Bag. The Johor-VOC Alliance and the Twelve Years' Truce (1606-1613)', in R. Lesaffer (ed.), *The Twelve Years Truce (1609). Peace, Truce War and Law in the Low Countries at the Turn of the 17th Century* (Leiden, 2014), 89-120, at 101-4.

42 BVAM, 423-7.

43 See K.N. Chaudhuri, *The English East India Company: The Study of an Early Joint-Stock Company 1600-1640* (New York, 1965), 49-50; also Grayson, *Protectorate,* esp. 241 et seq., esp. 252 et seq.

44 Clark and van Esyinga, 'Colonial Conferences1', 51-2, 58.

45 For Grotius' role in the religious disputes Nellen, *Grotius,* 212-16, and Grayson, *Protectorate,* 137-9. For their impact on Anglo-Dutch relations, see *Ibid.,* 123-41.

46 Clark and van Eysinga, 'Colonial Conferences 1', 84-5; Nellen, *Grotius,* 149.

47 *Ibid.,* 157.

48 J.A. Somers and C.G. Roelofsen, '*Mare Liberum* and the Dutch East India Company', *Grotiana,* N.S. 24-5 (2004-5) 67-76, at 74; and C.G. Roelofsen, 'Hugo de Groot en de VOC', in H.J.M. Nellen and J. Trapman (eds.), *De Hollandse jaren van Hugo de Groot (1582-1621)* (Hilversum, 1996), 63-4.

49 Nellen, *Grotius*, 200.

50 G.N. Clark and W.J.M. van Eysinga, 'The Colonial Conferences between England and the Netherlands', part 2, *Bibliotheca Visseriana* 17 (1951), 1–155.

51 Borschberg, *Free Trade*, 266.

52 Borschberg, *Journal*, 361–6.

53 On this objection, see Grayson, *Protectorate*, 256.

54 P.A. Tiele and J.E. Heeres (ed.), *Bouwstoffen voor de Geschiedenis der Nederlanders in den Maleischen Archipel* (3 vols.,The Hague, 1886–95), vol. 1, 233.

55 *CHGS*, fols. 137–41, 142, 143–4, 145–52. These four documents date from the negotiations at The Hague and list the merits and disadvantages of the merger. The objections of the English are found on fol. 142. Concerning the merger, see also Grayson, *Protectorate* 252 et seq.

56 *Ibid.*, 271. For the thirty articles of this 'accord' see L. van Aitzema, *Saken van Staet En Oorlogh, in, ende omtrent der Vereenighde Nederlanden . . .* (6 vols., The Hague, 1669–72), vol. 1, 206–8.

57 For the Anglo-Dutch conference of 1619, see Grayson, *Protectorate*, 259–71.

58 D.K. Bassett, 'The 'Amboyna Massacre' of 1623', *Journal of South East Asian History* 1, 2 (1960) 1–19, at 4; also A. Clulow, *Amboina, 1623. Fear and Conspiracy at the Edge of Empire* (New York, 2019).

59 Grayson, *Protectorate*, 269; J. van Goor, *Jan Pietersz. Coen, 1587–1629. Koopman-koning in Azië* (Amsterdam, 2015), at 385–466.

60 Clark and van Eysinga, 'Colonial Conferences 1', 49.

61 Borschberg, *Free Trade*, 31.

62 Clark and van Eysinga, 'Colonial Conferences 1', 101.

63 Concerning the background to Grotius' justification of treaties with non-Christians, see the discussion by R. Tuck, 'Alliances with Infidels in the European Imperial Expansion', in S. Muthu (ed.), *Empire and Modern Political Thought* (Cambridge, 2012), 61–83, at 74–5.

64 Clark and van Eysinga, 'Colonial Conferences 1', 89–93; Grayson, *Proctorate*, app. 17, 259–68, citation at 265; also 1 BW 627, 632, 634.

65 D. 2.14.1.pr.; Innocent III, *Liber Extra*, 1.35.1; Clark and van Eysinga, 'Colonial Conferences 2', 104–5; Clark and van Eysinga, 'Colonial Conferences 1', 101, 119; Nellen, *Grotius*, 201.

66 Clark and van Eysinga, 'Colonial Conferences 2', 108.

67 A. Westeijn, '"Love alone is not enough." Treaties in Seventeenth Century Dutch Expansion', in S. Belmoussus (ed.), *Empire by Treaty: Negotiating European Expansion* (Oxford, 2015), 19–44, at 20.

68 Concerning the idea of liberty for Grotius, see also R. Tuck, *Natural Rights Theories. Their Origin and Development* (Cambridge, 1979), 71; Clark and van Eysinga, 'Colonial Conferences 1', 109.

69 Clark and van Eysinga, 'Colonial Conferences 1', 120, 254.

70 Clark and van Eysinga, 'Colonial Conferences 1', 254.

71 Clark and van Eysinga, 'Colonial Conferences 1', 113.

72 Clark and van Eysinga, 'Colonial Conferences 2', 105.

73 N.J. Coulson, *A History of Islamic Law* (Edinburgh, 1964), 81–2. Also T. Miura, 'Islamic Contracts and Courts' in D. Ma and J. Luiten van Zanden (eds.), *Law and Long-Term Economic Change. The Eurasian Perspective* (Stanford, 2011), 193 n. 48.

74 P. Borschberg, 'Lost in Translation? The Languages of Euro-Southeast Asian Diplomacy in the Sixteenth and Early Seventeenth Centuries' in S. Richter, M. Roth and S. Meurer (eds.), *Die Konstruktionen Europas in der frühen Neuzeit* (Heidelberg, 2017), 283–309, at 298.

75 Borschberg, *Journal*, 397–400.

76 This was common in Malaya until the advent of imperialism. See John Crawfurd, *History of the Indian Archipelago* (facsimile edn. of Edinburgh, 1820, 3 vols., London, 1967), vol. 3, 152; A.P. Rubin, 'The Use of Piracy in Malayan Waters', in C.H. Alexandrowicz (ed.), *Grotian Society Papers 1968. Studies in the History of the Law of Nations* (The Hague, 1970), 123; A. Milner, *The Malays* (Oxford, 2008), 72.

77 Concerning Siam, see Charnvit Kasetsiri, 'Origins of a Capital and Seaport: The Early Settlement of Ayutthaya and its East Asian Trade' in K. Breazeale (ed.), *From Japan to Arabia: Ayutthaya's Maritime Relations with Asia* (Bangkok, 1999), 71; C. Baker, Dhiravat na Pombejra, A. van der Kraan and D.K. Wyatt (eds.), *Van Vliet's Siam* (Chiang Mai, 2008), 121.

78 Borschberg, *Free Trade,* 167–8.

79 M.J. van Ittersum, 'The long goodbye: Hugo Grotius' justification of Dutch expansion overseas, 1615-1645', *History of European Ideas* 36 (2010) 386–411, also Nellen, *Grotius,* 203, 278.

80 Borschberg, *Free Trade,* 69.

81 11 BW 4687.

Part II

Concepts

Mark Somos

[I]f a Man owes another any Thing, not in Strictness of Justice but by some other Virtue, suppose Liberality, Gratitude, Compassion, or Charity, he cannot be sued for it in any Court of Judicature, neither can War be made upon on that Account; for to either of these it is not sufficient, that that which is demanded ought for some moral Reason to be performed, but besides it is requisite we should have some Right to it, such a Right as both divine and human Laws do sometimes give us to those Things which are due by other Virtues ...

Hugo Grotius, DJBP 2.22.16

4.1 Introduction

Virtues are indispensable in reconstructions and interpretations of Grotius' thought; yet, without a systematic overview of his relevant texts, it is difficult to grasp his theory of virtues. Grotius' treatments are clear, but scattered over multiple works; many of them are rarely considered in conjunction. Another difficulty is that Grotius shifts between descriptive and prescriptive or normative registers. The shifts are always clear from context, but lost when read in isolation. Consider the following passage:

[M]any Things are said to be of Right and lawful, because they escape Punishment, and partly because Courts of Justice have given them their Authority, tho' they are contrary to the Rules, either of Justice properly so called, or of other Vertues, or at least those, who abstain from such Things, act in a manner more honest and more commendable in the Opinion of good Men.

(DJBP 3.10.1)

Grotius next asserts that the virtue of honesty is the key to the virtues of honour, fairness, justice and to reputation, and that justice and honour are linked via honesty. Citing Seneca at length, he describes the rule of moral duty as being larger than right; and how affection, humanity, liberality, justice, faith, fairness and honesty demand more from us than law does. He concludes that, for actions to be both internally and externally lawful, we need to be virtuous. Thus, Grotius in the same passage describes law (as it is) contrary to virtues; as distinct from virtues (which demand more); and finally as inseparably reliant on virtues (as laws should be).[1] Yet, when we reach the end of the section, his argument is clear: virtues are essential in both assessing the justice of human laws and for guiding human action beyond the domain of such laws. Comprehensive and close reading, noting the context of Grotius' wider argument and shifts between descriptive and prescriptive modes, is essential for understanding the role and function of virtues in his thought.

This chapter aims to provide a systematic overview of Grotius' theory of virtues. Its secondary purpose is to show that his theory of virtues was fundamental to all aspects of his work, from law through drama to biblical criticism, and remained revealingly consistent from his earliest to his final publications. No treatment of any Grotian text or theme can ignore it.[2]

The chapter's next section uncovers the place of Grotius' philosophy of virtue in his ethical foundation for law in peace, and during and after war. It examines the dynamic between virtue and law in Grotius' thought, with virtue as a benchmark for correcting and developing law, and the conditions in which law rightfully ignores the calls of virtue. Grotius' function for virtue in law is then compared to conventional roles assigned to religion in correcting and stimulating law. Section 4.3 shows how Grotius' theory of virtue and law stayed remarkably coherent as he applied it to diverse real-life problems and themes, from Iberian-Dutch encounters through his justification of free trade to the doctrinal minimalism that Grotius regarded as the best chance of saving the United Provinces from religious strife. The distinctive rights and duties of sovereigns, magistrates, soldiers, slaves, citizens and Christians are finally explained in light of Grotius' virtue-law dynamic.

4.2 Virtue as the Ethical Foundation of Law

4.2.1 In Peace

According to Grotius, divinely created nature demonstrates that self-love is beneficial, and also reveals the first principle of natural order (DJPC Prol.). Virtues and self-interest never clash. When you lend somebody something, it is understood that you can retrieve it before the consensual deadline if you need to, because nobody presumes that kindness and friendship extend to harming self-interest (DJBP 2.16.27). It is likewise understandable if someone prefers their own life and property over others' (DJBP 2.25.7).

Animals and humans have self-love and sociability in common. What distinguishes humans is the conscious decision to accept obligations to care for others (DJPC Prol.).[3] Natural justice and property follow from this acceptance. So does social virtue (*virtus socialis*), the foundational nature of which makes us essentially equal. Revenge, and distinctions that raise us above others for reasons unrelated to virtues, can only produce illusory benefits (DJBP 2.22.10).

Freedom of action, and the premise that one's will cannot alter to the extent that it would justify deception, mean that the external statement of one's will is the standard of justice for the promissor's actions. This is the rule of faithfulness or trustworthiness (DJPC Prol.). The political version of this natural liberty and duty enjoins that citizens not only refrain from taking each other's possessions, but that they support their compatriots, as well as the state as a whole. Even in the natural community of mankind, the duty of care is cardinal enough to make neglect and refusal to assist a punishable offense (DJPC 6).[4]

Grotius' formulation of virtues and their operation produces a system in which virtuous conduct generates self-reinforcing rules for beneficial interaction. Faithfulness is obligatory unless the other party breaks faith, which releases the injured party (DJPC 8). Bad faith, shown even once, ruins states and individuals, because it undermines presumptions of good faith (DJPC 12). Veracity is a subset of the cardinal virtue of faithfulness. Language and signs were established to communicate; hence, speech is assumed to be truthful, thus binding (DJBP 2.4.3 and 3.1.11).

Grotian virtues shape laws in non-communicative spheres as well, without promises or external signals. Conscience is coextensive with natural law (DJPC 12). Virtue-driven natural law prescribes sparing an aggressor whose life is valuable to a community, even if the individual right of self-defence allowed punishment. Charity can similarly abrogate self-defence (DJBP 2.1.9).[5] Natural law respects not only strict, expletive justice, but also the virtues of temperance, prudence and fortitude.[6] Justice, honesty and associated virtues apply in civil law as well, and directly fill gaps when applicable law is wanting (*non liquet*) (DJBP 2.12.12). For instance, preventing harm to others is an enforceable duty; failing it is punishable (DJBP 2.21.1).

4.2.2 In War

Grotius' communicative ontology of norms dictates that promises must be kept because words must have significance. Grotius protects faithfulness from logical absurdity and meaninglessness by positing that promises bestow rights (DJBP 2.13.20). Oaths must be kept, even in war, even with pirates, heretics and tyrants, by both sovereigns and private individuals (DJBP 2.13.15 contradicting Cicero, *De officiis* 3.32; DJBP 3.23.1; *De Imperio* 3.7). The society of all humankind is founded on reason and speech; thus, speaking truth is both a logical necessity and an obligation under natural law. The strong presumption of the ever-present virtue of truthfulness provides the faith required to sue for truce or peace. No war can end without it (DJBP 3.19.1–2 and 3.21.1).[7] The need for truthful promises is the reason why fear cannot invalidate promises in war, when it is sensible to seek resolution and be afraid at the same time (DJBP 3.19.11).

Moreover, *honestum* is always *utile*. Even promises made in war are profitable to keep, because a reputation for strict faithfulness encourages strangers to enter trading and military alliances, allies to stay loyal and enemies to surrender. The sovereign's eminent right over the goods and person of his subjects is limited to acts calculated to serve the general interest. Breaking promises to enemies cannot serve public interests (DJBP 3.19.7). Another case when usefulness validates virtues, despite short-term appearances to the contrary, is the Dutch colonial struggle with the Iberians. According to Grotius, when the Dutch know they fight for liberty and justice, defending themselves, their allies and the whole fellowship of humankind against calumny, cruelty and perfidy, then their awareness of virtue and clear conscience will cause their victory (DJPC 15).[8]

Virtues provide standards for laws in war. Imagine agreeing to appoint an arbitrator to settle the war, but disputing the arbitrator's decision. The shared, human understanding of virtues suggests that the arbitrator 'has Force only so far as is conformable to what an honest and equitable Person ought to pronounce'. Arbitrators should also rely on virtues, and mobilise the warring parties' sense of fairness to settle doubtful cases. This is a particularly useful solution among Christians (DJBP 3.20.46–7).

4.2.3 After War

Through reiterations of combat between nomads, and between nomads and civilised nations like the Romans, fairness has historically given rise to proto-international law in the form of fluid, uncodified, yet gradually emerging consensual rules for treating and exchanging prisoners of war, and for *postliminium*. One cannot establish this with pirates, who lack the virtue of fairness (DJBP 3.9.18).

'All Agreements between Enemies depend upon Faith, either expressed or implied' (DJBP 3.20.1). In ending wars, Grotius makes implied faith a remarkably load-bearing device. Other virtues, especially charity, similarly dictate keeping not only explicit but also tacit promises, such as conducting peace negotiations without deceit (DJBP 3.1.18).[9] Given the virtue of humanity, the process of post-war settlement – including apparent breaches of peace and disputes concerning pre-war claims – must be guided by the presumption that the contracting parties sincerely intend to end the war (DJBP 3.20.19). During settlement, 'Goodness, especially Christian Goodness, will more easily forgive small Faults, particularly if they are repented of' (DJBP 3.20.35).[10] Parties are obliged by virtues to reduce their demands to a fair portion (DJBP 3.10.5). In case of complete and unconditional surrender, implied faith sets higher standards of conduct for the conqueror, akin to the master's obligations to slaves, and the sovereign's towards his subjects. Grotius defines this standard in terms of honour, mercy, liberality and other virtues (DJBP 3.20.49–50). Similarly, the implied virtue of friendship is the standard for judging whether acts such as building forts or raising troops violate peace agreements (DJBP 3.20.40).

4.2.4 Semi-Permeability

The best way to understand how Grotian virtues systematically shape divine, natural, civil and international laws is to think of the barrier between ethics and laws as semi-permeable. As we saw, virtues shape laws in several ways. Since laws cannot cover all circumstances with reliable fairness and specificity, virtues must guide particular departures from law. They can do so partly because, by divine design, all humanity shares moral instincts, including those concerning virtues such as faithfulness, benevolence and temperance; partly because Christ's inimitably perfect virtues inform human virtues as aspirational guides to individual and collective action and development;[11] and partly because Grotius defines virtues as relational, never deviating from the common good. Sovereigns' and magistrates' distinctive virtues are defined in relation to subjects, soldiers' virtues in relation to enemies, and so on;[12] and everyone's virtues are defined and assessed in relation to the common society of humankind. The following Grotian arguments illustrate how virtues and laws interact with regard to punishment, war, promises, law, marriage and property.

Modern lawyers and theologians agree on the right to kill thieves, but Grotius recommends charity, which prohibits killing thieves unless they try to kill us. That is how early Christians, persecuted and outlawed, behaved toward thieves (DJBP 2.1.11–13). Charity prefers leniency over rigorously enforcing rights (DJBP 3.1.4). When charity cannot halt retaliation for small injuries, express gospel prohibition should. That said, pagan philosophers and Christians agree on the important virtue of patience in bearing an affront (DJBP 2.1.10).[13] Similarly to charity, the virtue of humanity demands that we spare in war the goods of those who neither caused nor participated in war, but are offered as hostages (DJBP 3.13.4).[14] The rich who enforce laws to deprive debtors of everything are inhuman. Injustice is often associated with another vice, for instance ingratitude. Ingratitude frequently shown attests to a bad character (DJBP Prol.). One's character should be taken into account in criminal determination, prompting the judge to be lenient to offenders with good character. In such cases, virtues shape law conditionally, through the sovereign's discretion (DJBP 2.20.30).[15] However, penal laws cannot be relaxed when doing so would cause wickedness. Grotius provides examples of inexcusable lying, perjury, false witness, breaking promises and breaking faith (De satisfactione 3).

Charity also applies to fatal injuries. Internal justice and the virtues of humanity and fairness proscribe killing or enslaving prisoners of war, even when laws permit it (DJBP 3.14.1–2). And when the virtue of justice allows killing, other virtues, such as goodness, moderation and magnanimity, may not. Those who obey both laws and the rules of virtue will spare their enemies' lives, unless self-defence or another compelling reason, such as an enemy's lawful conviction for a capital crime, dictate otherwise (DJBP 3.11.7 and 3.20.53). It is best to kill in a just war only when all laws and virtues permit it (DJBP 3.11.2). Even though natural law and theologians concur that we can kill an innocent who obstructs our self-preservation, the law of charity says otherwise (DJBP 2.1.4). The virtue of fairness commands sparing those who surrender (DJBP 3.11.15).

To prevent greater injury, can you surrender an innocent as hostage to the enemy? Not by law; but citizens who refuse this role break a rule of charity so important that the breach becomes a crime. The strong link between virtues and law means that sovereigns can oblige citizens even if there is no law, just as sovereigns can oblige citizens to share corn in extreme necessity (DJBP 2.25.3).[16]

When there was or is no law against polygamy or divorce, as in the case of Old Testament Patriarchs and recently discovered non-Europeans, one should recall God's command of strict friendship between husband and wife. This virtue, rightly understood, prescribes monogamy (DJBP 2.5.9, *De veritate* 2.13, *Sophompaneas* 6).

In transferring property, both giver and receiver must externally signal their will to transfer, regardless of pertaining civil laws. External signs are sufficient to bind, given the necessary assumptions of veracity and good faith (DJBP 2.6.2). By the same token, if you hold a thing or person that belongs to me, you have to try to return it. You are not obliged to do the impossible; but signalling that you have someone else's property is the *sine qua non* of good faith (DJBP 2.10.1). Regarding property left behind – distinct from usucaption and prescription – virtues provide the legal standard. When one needs a possibly abandoned perishable good, one should take it, because, irrespective of legal standards used to determine possession, one must charitably suppose that everyone is virtuous and would not allow anyone to suffer for lack of that perishable good (DJBP 2.4.8). As in the case of settling wars, the presumption of universal virtue supplies a self-reinforcing, mutually beneficial and legally binding rule.

This is not to say that virtues always change laws. Virtues permeate the legal sphere, but remain distinct. One way to think about their relationship is to contrast *licet*, what one may lawfully do, with *oportet*, what one should do (DJBP 3.4.2). For instance, Grotius disagrees with Diogenes that one is not obliged to disclose everything relevant to an agreement. According to Grotius, a seller should declare flaws in an object or slave being sold. However, in the classic example of selling grain in port, Grotius does not think it unjust not to reveal that more ships are coming in, which would drive the price down; though it is a breach of charity (DJBP 2.12.9). Cornering the market or otherwise raising the price through unfair competition also violates charity (DJBP 2.12.16). Similarly, reparations for killing someone lawfully are not obligatory, even if the killer acted against charity. One such scenario is when an enemy attacks you and you kill in self-defence instead of fleeing, which you could also have done (DJBP 2.17.13).

Wartime conduct offers numerous illustrations of Grotius' relationship between virtues and laws. The public declaration of solemn wars satisfies extra-legal virtues of generosity and valour – but strict law also requires such declarations (DJBP 3.3.11).[17] Conversely, although international law allows torture in some cases, one should exercise the virtues of magnanimity and self-confidence to refrain from legitimate torture whenever possible (DJBP 3.4.18). The overall aim of *De jure belli ac pacis*, Grotius explains, is to constrain wars within the limits of natural law. Even though his era does not respect virtues, Grotius continues, the virtues – especially moderation and clemency – will forgive him for trying to show that they are useful in law (DJBP 3.12.8).[18]

It is human nature to sin, Grotius admits. Some individuals or groups sin due to innate features – sometimes inherited – or bad customs. Offenses against virtues such as mercy, liberality and gratitude cannot be punished, nor enforced, otherwise they would lose their meaning as virtues. Though virtue is a squarely moral, not a religious or legal, category, it guides decisions concerning punishment, especially severe punishment, the performance of which contradicts charity even when it accords with justice. One punishes when charity suggests that punishment is preferable to forgiveness, for instance to deter or correct offenders (DJBP 2.20.19–22).[19]

Oaths do not bind if the action promised is illegal – but also if it 'hinders any greater moral Good'. We owe it to God to improve ourselves by practising virtues, therefore we cannot renounce the liberty to do all the good we can (DJBP 2.13.6–7). The same function of virtues explains why Cicero is wrong, according to Grotius, and oaths to tyrants and pirates are binding even though, as noted above, pirates lack the virtue of fairness. Virtue's effect on law is not measured merely against this-worldly utility and reciprocity. We owe performance of oaths to God, not to public enemies (DJBP 2.13.15).

4.2.5 Standing in for Religion

Grotius' theory of virtues highlights the intricate relationship between religion and law. Whenever he finds it necessary, Grotius displaces religion with law in order to minimise domestic, European and global tensions. His expansion of *adiaphora*, use of epistemic humility, invocation of early Christians and focus on commonalities among nations and creeds across the ages are systematically directed against sects and doctrines that locked participants in irresolvable conflicts. However, Grotius remains religious. He aims to end religious strife at home and across Christendom. He hopes that Dutch commercial and colonial expansion will spread tolerant, minimal Christianity, a Christianity in which a universal code of practical ethics crowds out the miracles, revelation and rituals that even various Christian denominations, let alone other religions, disagreed about.[20]

As part of this substitution, Grotius explicitly collapses the legal and theological accounts of faithfulness into one (DJPC 7). On the one hand, one sign of a good religion is that it emphasises rewards for faithfulness and punishments for breaking faith, which in turn sustains virtuous cycles of promises exchanged and kept both at home and abroad. On the other hand, even the best laws cannot eliminate religion. The Grotian legal system's aforementioned communicative ontology of norms dictates that promises are kept – otherwise they are not promises. As detailed above, Grotius also shows that it is in the interest of individuals and sovereigns to be faithful, therefore self-interested acts and positive law support faithfulness. Communicative ontology, self-interest and positive laws confirm, but do not replace, the religious precept of faithfulness. However, Grotius praises not only Christianity, but every religion that praises faithfulness, and he does think that any religion enchances the utility of faithfulness (for instance, by adding a universally redeeming quality), only that that religions help to improve compliance and confirm the linguistic and legal proofs of the utility of faithfulness. He also argues that virtues set higher standards than existing religions. As we saw, he rejects Roman, Hebrew and Christian theological views that promises to pirates and tyrants need not be kept. Grotius counters that everyone is entitled to trust as a human being, irrespective of conduct or religion (DFP; DJBP 3.19.2–3).

After uniting legal and theological faith, and preferring his theory of virtue to historical and contemporary religions, Grotius describes Dutch virtues and a very minimal religion as the most useful combination for security and profit. 'The Indian peoples must be shown what it means to be a Christian, in order that they may not believe all Christians to be as the Spaniards are. Let those peoples look upon religion stripped of false symbols, commerce devoid of fraud, arms unattended by injuries' (DJPC

13). Though here he specifies reasons for minimising doctrine, elsewhere Grotius recommends the same policy based on good faith, fortitude, clemency and other virtues, without reference to religion.[21] The corresponding argument in *De jure belli ac pacis* ascribes the same role to virtues and shifts the emphasis further toward religion's practical utility. Religion, Grotius explains, is useful for morals in individual states, but even more so in the great society of humankind. According to Grotius, Cicero is right that fidelity and justice depend on piety. As any religion fulfils these functions, it is best not to insist on Christianity. The closer one gets to four minimalist principles – monotheism, God invisible, engaged with human affairs, created all except himself – the better the virtues (*Meletius*; DJBP 2.20.44–6).[22] The virtue of nations shows how well they preserve the original knowledge of God, and approximate Christian truth even without revelation (*De veritate* 1.3 and 4.12).

Virtues can, but reason cannot, replace religion in Grotius' system. Reason and Scripture agree that one cannot kill someone for things one can dispense with (DJBP 3.20.43). That all acts in unjust wars are unjust is clear from natural reason, and recognised by pagans, Jews, Muslims and Christians (DJBP 3.10.3). When Sallust praised the religion of his ancestors for instilling virtuous conduct in war, he and his ancestors became worthy of Christianity. So are the adages of Aristotle and Cicero on peace as the purpose of war (DJBP 3.15.2). Though Christ proved rituals harmful, Jews could have kept their rituals and still earned salvation through the virtuous core of Christianity alone (*De veritate* 5.12). It is commendable not to enforce the right to punish those who injure us, whether we regard charity as it applies everywhere, or only the virtues expected of Christians. Though Christians in particular should forgive, Grotius derives virtues that stop wars, such as clemency, charity, good-nature and honour, from biblical and pagan sources equally (DJBP 2.24.2–3).

Virtues such as justice supplement, abrogate and rewrite laws, not only civil and international laws made by imperfect humans, but also divine laws, given to imperfect humans (DI 8.15). Grotius warns against mistaking religiosity for virtue. Expiations for sins ruin the state that accepts them instead of ensuring culprits' moral reform (DI 1.13). Religion provides no immunity against vice – it is often corrupted to serve vice (DI 11.12). Regarding the biblical account of virtues, one should note that Hebrew kings occasionally abrogated God's directly pronounced laws because they focused on fairness, and realised that God's own intention is to nullify divine laws in some cases. God can make something just merely through will, which is sufficient cause. However, God also wills things that are intrinsically just, independently from God's will (also DJBP 2.20.4). Instead of ascribing redemptive powers to theology or natural reason, Grotius writes that, when we cannot understand but only instinctively sense God, describable virtues offer the best guidance (*De satisfactione* 5).

De Wilde and Eyffinger argue that good faith becomes Grotius' secular foundation of natural law.[23] This is borne out by evidence, with the modification that good faith in this sense is fundamentally individualistic. It is part of individual virtue, and an inalienable right and duty, to examine religious, political and military commands for oneself.[24] However, there is no necessary conflict between Grotius' Christian faith and his enduring legacy of minimising religion in ethics and law in order to reduce tension between warring religious sects and to build new relations with non-Christians. In *De veritate religionis Christianae*, Grotius denies that virtues are their own reward. They are profitable and we are lost in this world without them, but their primary purpose is to guide us to Heaven (*De veritate* 2.9).[25]

4.3 Coherence, Continuity and Development

The fundamental importance of Grotius' theory of virtues appears from its ubiquity and remarkable continuity. This section is designed to chart themes based on Grotian virtues in a way that brings out their chronological continuity and intellectual coherence. A major theme that already appears in the *Parallelon* and runs through Grotius' five decades of writing is the earthly benefits of moral virtues. Honourable conduct always generates profit (DFP 113).[26] Nor is it a vague maxim that *honestum* is *utile*. In Grotius' definition, *honestum* includes the strategic use of a related virtue, benevolence, in subduing those who resist armed violence (DFP 7, 22).

Grotius expands this connection in *De jure praedae commentarius* (1604-6), with chapter 12 considerably revised and published as *Mare liberum* (1609). He argues that fortitude, companion virtue to justice, means enduring evil (DJPC 7).[27] However, activating the virtue of courage to defend the weak is a part of justice. One has a 'duty to the whole of mankind' to intervene against pirates and tyrants who oppress only their own people (DJPC 7, 9). If the Dutch refused to help the injured, they would offend against the universal bond of human fellowship and against God, and acquire a reputation not for virtuous fortitude or mercy, but for the vice of cruelty (DJPC 14).[28] Virtuous intervention also serves one's self-interest, and prevents oppressors from becoming strong enough for external attack.[29] This is the virtue-based justification why the Dutch can and must help the king of Johore (DJPC 13).[30] The same virtue-driven calculus suggests that the Dutch present themselves as virtuous and religious, but minimise doctrinal elements of Christianity and refrain from proselytising. The combination of fidelity, benevolence and peacefulness will make the natives 'marvel at the faith which forbids that even infidels should be neglected' (DJPC 13).

Similarly to the *Parallelon*, Grotius explicitly describes elements of his theory of virtue in *De jure belli ac pacis*. It is an oversimplification that he rejects Aristotle's theory, which he praises repeatedly.[31] According to Grotius, some Platonists and Christians are right that, in *Nicomachean Ethics* 2.6, Aristotle, though brilliant, erroneously described justice as the midpoint in passion and action. As a result, Aristotle collapses liberality and frugality in order to contrast avarice with both; cannot establish the midpoint for veracity; and misrepresents contempt for pleasure and honour, and insensibility to injuries as vices. The mediocrity principle fails. Aristotle is correct that virtue moderates some passions, but not because that is virtue's function, but merely epiphenomenally as a function of right reason. Virtue always follows right reason, which sets limits to some passions but instructs us to maximise others, such as the love of God, fear of damnation or hatred of sin.[32]

Alongside Dutch special virtues and minimising Christian doctrine, another omnipresent theme is the role of virtues in circumscribing and renegotiating the sphere of law. It is virtuous to use attributive, moral justice to correct expletive or strict legal justice. For instance, if yielding in a conflict does not harm us, it is better to yield than insist on our strict right. This avoids conflict and builds a profitable reputation for patience and good nature (DJBP 3.10.1 and 1.2.8). The virtues of love and kindness toward enemies are not suppressed even by war or well-deserved capital punishment (DJBP 1.2.8).

Coherence and continuity are evident not only in Grotius' general theory of virtue, but also in the special virtues and responsibilities he ascribed in his works to different actors – such as soldiers, rulers and God – who thereby acquired distinctive ethical and legal characteristics.

4.3.1 Dutch Virtues and Iberian Vices

In the *Parallelon*, written around 1600–2, Grotius compares the young Republic of the United Provinces with the ancient Greek and Roman republics. Though unpublished for two centuries, the discussion of virtues in the *Parallelon* reveals remarkable continuities in Grotius' theory of virtues. Particularly relevant are chapter 3 on liberty and slavery, chapter 4 on fortitude and magnanimity, chapter 5 on humanity and ferocity, chapter 6 on faith and perfidy, chapter 7 on justice and injustice, chapter 8 on ambition and its opposite, chapter 9 on avarice and profit, and chapter 10 on beneficence and liberality.

In *De fide et perfidia*, Grotius moves from a comparison of Greek and Roman public faith to a series of diametric juxtapositions of Dutch good faith with Iberian perfidy. During the war for independence, which Grotius classifies as a civil war, the Dutch exhibited faithfulness, fairness or equity, and ancient simplicity, virtues that Cicero connects to fortitude (DFP 7–8). The enemy's conduct was the exact opposite. However, Dutch fairness earned honour, which generated profit, as it always does. Virtuous conduct was particularly important because rebellion is always suspicious; but Dutch virtue brought credibility. The Dutch are loyal to their allies, including France and Britain, and always seek peace. The cruel, treacherous and duplicitous Spanish, inheritors of the notorious *fides Punica*, are perfidious in war, in peace negotiations and toward envoys (DFP 38–72). The Dutch uniquely combine three virtues: unity, intrepid commercial spirit and a sense of justice. Other nations one day may rival their commercial shrewdness – but never their justice (DFP 77, and Eyffinger's 'Introduction', 103). Part of their rare virtuousness derives from the ancient Germans, who were faithful, brave, expelled tyrants and defended religion.[33] All their achievements flowed from the combination of two cardinal virtues: faithfulness and fortitude, a combination inherited by the Dutch and the Swiss (DFP 28–38). The ancient Dutch in particular were saintly; imitating them brings great virtue (DFP; DJPC 14). Presenting Portuguese vileness and false Christianity in opposition to Dutch honour and freedom from greed, Grotius argues that virtue and vice become nationally or racially ingrained over time (DJPC 12).[34]

In both *De jure praedae* and *Mare liberum*, Grotius drew evidence for Iberian perfidy and cruelty and Dutch good faith and benevolence from documents the VOC provided (DJPC, Appendices). A comparison with the

Parallelon shows that the VOC materials simply added further instances to the content and structure of the Dutch-Iberian contrasts, revolving around virtues, that Grotius established to justify the Dutch Revolt.[35] The function of Dutch virtues, invoked in *De fide* to generate Europe-wide credibility and support, is extended in *De jure praedae* and *Mare liberum* to the arena of colonial conflict with Spain and Portugal. In terms of Grotius' detailed analysis of the function of virtues and vices, the Europeans invited in *De fide* to witness Dutch faithfulness, firmness and pristine simplicity, leading to fortitude, are comparable to the Asian powers portrayed in *De jure praedae* and *Mare liberum* as witnesses to Dutch good faith, industry and fortitude. In order to convince Europeans and Asians to support the Dutch, in each text Grotius proposes policies based on these virtues, ranging from scrupulously honouring agreements to extending protection whenever possible. In each text, he marshals evidence of corresponding Iberian vices.

DJPC begins with Grotius' assertion that the Dutch, careful to stay faithful, always proceed more cautiously than others. The Dutch find virtue in the midpoint between extreme vices, such as stolidity and greed. Horace is right, expediency (*utilitatem*) is the mother of justice and fairness. Malevolence is terrible, but ignoring 'true and divinely inspired self-love' is vicious, even if one protects others from injustice (DJPC Prol.). This applies not only to public but also to private acts, as failure to protect private self-interest also harms the public. The vice of self-neglect, which the Dutch would be guilty of if they did not keep the *Santa Catarina*, tries in vain to disguise itself as virtue. Justice is the (Aristotelian) midpoint (DJPC Prol.).

The colonial war with Spain and Portugal highlighted Dutch 'singularly humane qualities', including fortitude, patience and scrupulousness observing commercial rights (DJPC 11).[36] The Dutch are long-suffering, candid and trusting, gentle, endure injuries, patient, and properly blend modesty and goodwill (DJPC 11).[37] Unlike the luxurious Iberians, they are simple and modest, having learned the best use of riches from their frugal ancestors (DJPC 11 and 15). However, Iberians mistake Dutch virtues for weakness and folly. Indeed, Dutch clemency is 'almost excessive' (DJPC 11). In contrast with Portuguese fury and bloodthirst, the Dutch try to instil fear in their enemies only by taking property. The excessive virtue of kindliness has become the vice of timidity. Grotius refuses to even list Dutch acts of self-restraint, as it would damage their reputation (DJPC 12).[38] Iberians mock the Dutch for a flaw that would be mischaracterised as leniency, and potential and actual Asian allies are suspicious. It is a false virtue. Kindness cannot compel Iberians, only fear of retaliation will. Armed engagement is in Asian and Dutch interest, but also in the Iberians', for this is the only effective method for improving their character (DJPC 15). In addition to benevolent Dutch virtues, they are also tough, withstand hunger, cold and hard work. They fight hard, and they are 'true sons of the sea' (DJPC 15). The tangible benefits of Dutch virtues are already evident. Virtues and good faith thwart Iberian schemes. Natives seek alliance and protection because of Dutch credibility (DJPC 11).[39]

By contrast, the Spanish have no moderation (DFP 7). They use cunning, deceit, fraud, treachery, poisoning and assassination, notably of William the Silent in 1584 and in recent attempts against his sons, the king of France and the queen of England.[40] The infernal conduct of Francisco Lopez de Mendoza y Mendoza (1547–1623) encapsulates Iberian vices (DFP 11–12). Their perfidy, greed and cruelty are the perfect inverse of Dutch virtues (DJPC 11). A slightly different catalogue, namely savagery, lust for dominion and destruction of human liberty, is contrasted again with a corresponding list of Dutch virtues (DJPC 11). In a third iteration, Grotius contrasts the Spanish lust for dominion, violence and trickery with Dutch fidelity, benevolence and clemency, which will convert Asians to Christianity in a way that Iberian vices and ferocity never can. Their unique combination of greed, fraud and perfidy stands in sharp contrast with the Dutch combination of justice and fortitude (DJPC 12; on the Dutch combination: DFP 28–38, DJPC 7). Grotius often contrasts specific Dutch virtues with Iberian vices, including luxury (DJPC 11, 15),[41] but his leitmotif is the contrast between Dutch faith and Iberian perfidy (DJPC 11). Iberian bad faith offends God, because it severs the only bond that provides security among those who meet for the first time (DJPC 12).

Iberian perfidy is a declaration of war, which makes their property liable to confiscation (DJPC 8). Their lies, deception and engineering of suspicion injure Dutch reputation so grievously that they warrant an armed response, especially because Dutch reputation is key to breaking into the East India trade (DJPC 11–12).

4.3.2 God and Christ

In *De satisfactione* (1617), Grotius describes God as faithful, and God's virtue in remitting sins as not liberality but mercy, as defined by Seneca and Cicero, and understood as love. Moderating punishment is the source of broad justice, which includes piety, fidelity and friendship (*De satisfactione* 3 and 6). Grotius seems to continue this exact point when he writes in *De jure belli ac pacis* that God's mercy cannot be imitated, as humans are so different from God; but divine mercy can set an example (DJBP 3.1.4).

Similarly, we cannot closely imitate Christ, partly because he was virtuous not only in death but throughout his life. This is one reason why Socinus is wrong to offer Christ as an imitable model of patience and obedience. Christ had no sin, and humans always do (*De satisfactione* 1). Though we cannot fully model ourselves on Christ, his human life serves as an example, and his commands instruct us in virtue (*De satisfactione* 2; *Christus patiens*). Christ commands us to have mercy. This entails not judging those who injured us, but leaving judgment to our sovereign. Even so, we can practice benevolence by not desiring our enemies' just punishment. The same formula is further developed in *De jure belli ac pacis*. We should approximate Christ's superhuman virtues knowing that we cannot reach them and, therefore, cannot be commanded by sovereigns or priests to imitate them (DJBP 1.3.3).[42] The right way to interpret Christ's sacrifice is through the ancient pagan view of forgiveness as neither according to nor against the law, but above it (*De satisfactione* 5).[43] In *De veritate*, Grotius revisits these arguments, adding that God tolerates evil to teach us virtues, either through punishing 'those who were slipt out of the way of Virtue' or creating an 'eminent Example of Patience and Constancy in those who had made a great Progress in Virtue' (*De veritate* 1.19 and 1.21). Idolatry exceeds the scope of God's mercy, and humanity's interest dictates severe punishment (*De veritate* 4.3).

Grotius hints that reason can serve as a necessarily imperfect heuristic device to approximate God. He cites François Connan's (1508–51) opinion that promises without contracts are not binding, but it is laudable to keep them if the acts promised would have been virtuous even without promise. Grotius insists that Connan is misguided. Fidelity means keeping agreed-upon promises. Cicero is right that faithfulness is the foundation of justice. Horace calls faithfulness the sister of justice, Platonists equate justice and truth, Apuleius translates justice as fidelity and Simonides writes that justice means not only returning goods, but also telling the truth. Grotius offers his own addition: 'to perform Promises is a Duty arising from the Nature of immutable Justice, which as it is in GOD, so it is in some Measure common to all such as have the Use of Reason' (DJBP 2.11.1–4).

4.3.3 Sovereign Rulers

In *De imperio summarum potestatum circa sacra*, Grotius agrees with Aristotle that states should optimise citizens' lives and happiness. The sovereign's objective, therefore, is not only peace, but guiding citizens to virtue. Since this requires controlling public religion, the sovereign has the requisite powers (DI 1.5). Not only politics, but everything involving moral good or evil fall under his purview (DI 9.23).

Grotius' technical scheme of virtues is key to regulating individual-sovereign relations. Sovereigns decide on war using virtues specific to them. Citizens judge the justice of war for themselves, then obey or disobey. Declarations of war must be public not only in justice to enemies, but 'so all Mankind, as it were, might judge the Justice of it. Prudence, (according to *Aristotle*) is indeed a Virtue peculiar to the Prince, but Justice belongs to every Man as he is a Man' (DJBP 2.26.4). Unlike citizens, sovereigns need extraordinary virtues. They are responsible not only to other citizens, but to all humankind, and to God. The less one demands one's own property, for instance while recalling debts, the more liberal one is. But when the sovereign exacts punishment, he exercises the virtue of retributive justice (*De satisfactione* 6). Sovereigns must prevent or stop injurious acts. If they fail to, it is as if they approved them (DJBP 2.21.2). Reparations for injuries, including those suffered in an otherwise just war, are the responsibility of the person who commanded the act, which in wars is the sovereign (DJBP 2.17.11).

Prudent self-limitation is a virtue specific to sovereigns (DI 9.21). A virtuous ruler consults with numerous wise men (DI 6.2). His honour sometimes dictates subjecting himself in civil affairs to parliaments or senates, and to pastors in religion. These situations leave his supreme authority intact, as he decides on beginning and ending the arrangement.

Moderation in obtaining empire is another virtue specific to sovereigns. Among other checks on overexpansion, sovereigns should balance the virtues of goodness and indulgence against the vice and public danger they invite by trusting conquered enemies too much, instead of simply recognising their empire's limits (DJBP 3.15.1). However, if the vanquished are trustworthy, sovereigns may exercise moderation by leaving the government of conquered states intact. Doing so fits the virtue of humanity, but it is also profitable, as it minimises transition costs (DJBP 3.15.4, 3.15.7). Whether one replaces or preserves conquered governments, the same rationale dictates treating the vanquished with gentleness, mercy and liberality. The conquering sovereign's use of these virtues will fuse the interests of the conquered with the conqueror's, thereby consolidating order (DJBP 3.15.12). On a smaller scale, following fairness and divine law, we must spare everyone in a city that surrendered. In cities taken by force, it is virtuous and profitable to spare everyone who does not actively violate our rights (DJPC 8).

Sovereigns' faithfulness is comparable to other individuals', with some variation. Although sovereigns need not formally declare war on tyrants, pirates and robbers, or against enemies who already launched an unjust, unproclaimed war, they still need to keep faith with such parties even if they are treacherous. The sovereign is released only regarding particular contracts that enemies have broken. Faithfulness is so fundamental and pervasive that a good faith clause should be understood as implied in all treaties concerning war. While breaking faith is unacceptable, war stratagems that a reasonable enemy should expect are permitted (DFP 12; DJPC 8).

Grotius endows the sovereign with exceptional means to meet extraordinary obligations. Before civil society and courts of justice arose, determining punishments with a view to benefiting all mankind was everyone's duty and privilege; now it is the sovereign's (DJBP 2.20.11). Sovereigns can forego punishment and abrogate penal law generally, or pardon specific individuals. Sovereigns are godlike in this respect, yet always need reasonable justification. A Christian sovereign should imitate God in mercy (DJBP 2.20.24–7).[44] Sovereigns also have greater latitude than non-sovereigns with regard to the virtue of veracity. Anyone can lie to children and madmen for their own good (DJBP 3.1.12). Wise people sometimes lie for the greater good (DJBP 3.1.9). Sovereigns can conceal the truth, and even lie to their subjects (DJBP 3.1.7 and 3.1.15). Yet, there are limits to permissible dissimulation. Not only may sovereigns lie only for the common good, they must never lie to public enemies (DJBP 3.1.17). An extraordinary feature of Grotius' theory that virtue can illuminate is his readiness to divide sovereignty. When the sovereign makes a promise, he cannot break it; with respect to the subject of promise, sovereignty becomes divided (DJBP 1.3.17).

4.3.4 Magistrates

The powers of magistrates was a hotly debated topic. Calvinist anti-absolutist resistance theories attributed to magistrates, rather than the people, the power to test the justice of a sovereign's acts and declare resistible tyranny. Grotius held that magistrates can declare public wars, though not solemn ones that require a formal proclamation. Magistrates can also conduct war, including against private entities, when the war is too small to threaten state stability, or necessity demands a quick response (DJPC 3; DJBP 1.3.1-6). However, collective action entails collective responsibility. Magistrates' mistakes can make a whole people not only suffer wartime ravages, but also become complicit in magisterial transgression. The adage that homicide is virtuous when declared by public authority is a cynical untruth (DJPC 7).

In *De jure praedae* and the dedication of *De antiquitate reipublicae Batavicae* (1610), Grotius praises Dutch magistrates, especially in the States General, as exceedingly virtuous. They ensure that promises are kept, the people are protected according to both natural and civil laws, and that the constitution, including promises in force since time immemorial, remains intact (DJPC 13). This praise disappears from works Grotius composed in prison and exile.

Governors and generals exercise special virtues when it comes to the spoils of war. Pompey, Cicero, Fabricius, Cato or Scipio wished to appear 'exceedingly virtuous', and left their share to the people (DJPC 10). Abraham, like these Roman generals, refused his share 'to vie in virtue with the most virtuous' (DJPC 4). Cato the Elder would 'rather rival the best of Men in Virtue, than the richest in Wealth' (DJBP 3.6.17). Interestingly, in preparing the argument for keeping the *Santa Catarina*, Grotius endows Jacob van Heemskerck (1567-1607), the captain who captured it, with virtues of self-restraint and generosity that resemble those generals' on whom public authority has already bestowed a war prize (DJPC 12).

4.3.5 Slaves and Citizens

Virtues are part of every account of Grotian individualism. Already in *De jure praedae*, Grotius limits the transfer of the natural right of judgment from individual to sovereign. That sovereign authority remains extensive is shown by the fact that Grotius analogises from slavery to civil obedience. His argument runs as follows. Aristotle is right that slaves can exercise virtue in a limited sense, within the scope of obedience. The boundaries of civic virtue are similar. Everyone's safety depends on faithfulness. The special virtue of citizens is obedience, which they owe their sovereign. Citizens cannot disobey when in agreement or doubt, only when their reason categorically exposes a sovereign command as unjust. Their assumption of faithfulness on the sovereign's part, their own good faith in civic obedience, and their faithfulness toward the rest of mankind in resisting when necessary, determine the scope for civic virtue and responsibility. The will that guides action must follow reason, which is why obeying commands is no excuse for individual unjust action (DJPC 7 and 9). Grotius extends this point in *De imperio* (1614–17), best known for asserting secular over ecclesiastical authority. Here Grotius' charge that each individual must use their reason, without systematically challenging political authority, encompasses religion. Citizens who invest the necessary time and attention can disagree with both civic or religious commands (DI 5.13, 6.5; DJBP Prol. 9). In *De jure belli ac pacis*, he adds that another reason why citizens must obey by default is that God has approved sovereignty (DJBP 1.4.4).

The analogy with slaves is revealing. Grotius instructs masters to treat slaves with fairness, conscience, clemency, humanity and beneficence, and free them whenever possible (DJBP 3.14.3–4 and 3.14.6). Masters' virtues must fill the gap left by slaves' diminished agency. While citizens have a greater scope than slaves for virtuous use of reason and conscience, the authority citizens surrender in the polity is matched by the additional virtues expected of sovereigns (DI 3.1).

4.3.6 Soldiers

Soldiers are paradigmatic for Grotius' theory of virtues. They become collectively responsible for unjust acts when they follow commands in an unjust war; and individually for individual unjust acts (DJBP 3.10.4, 3.24.7N). If reason reveals a war as unjust, soldiers must refuse to serve, regardless of consequences. Not only divine, natural, civil and international law apply to acts in war, but also the higher standards of virtue. The fellowship of humanity dictates that virtues limit revenge both within and outside the polity (DJPC 10). The virtuous pursuit of fairness involves sparing those who surrender. Exceptions include those who break faith, or desert their own colours. Grotius cites numerous sources stating that soldiers who remain faithful to their country deserve mercy, creating a virtuous cycle between warring states. Interestingly, Grotius modifies this model by adding that 'country' in such texts refers to the society of all humankind, reducing the equation to the form that all faithful soldiers deserve mercy (DJBP 3.9.16).[45]

Good faith also justifies capturing property. Even if soldiers learn after the war that their cause was unjust, or captured goods should be returned to former enemies for other *postliminium* reasons, the soldiers can keep the goods as long as they fought in good faith (DJPC 8). Unless it becomes apparent after the war that their cause was egregiously unjust, legally (if not ethically) they are entitled to captured property even if they acted in bad faith. In the first scenario, their good faith justifies. In the second, bad faith is insufficient to turn the ethical principle into law applicable to soldiers – but it is sufficient to raise the question of the legal culpability of the sovereign or magistrate who proclaimed the war (DJPC 9).

4.3.7 Christians

In Peace

Christians are exhorted to more noble virtues than non-Christians (DJBP 2.12.20). Regarding how far Christians should refrain from justly punishing those who injure them, Christianity offers rewards greater than nature or politics, and therefore demands virtues higher than bare nature does (DJBP 2.20.10; *De veritate* 2.13). Similarly, to sacrifice ourselves for others is not a natural law, but a Christian duty (DJBP 1.2.6). We find an adroit use of virtues to establish continuity and discontinuity, difference and similarity, when Grotius explains that the same virtues required of Christians were also demanded of Old Testament Jews, but not as strictly (DJBP 1.2.6). Christ abolished only those Mosaic laws that were historically specific. Christ's command to become increasingly virtuous signals that he extended to all nations those Mosaic laws that natural and international law confirm as virtuous. Among these are punishing crimes and repelling injuries by force, which are always laudable, and manifest justice and beneficence (DJBP 1.2.7; *De veritate* 5.7). It is the expansion of the virtuous core of Mosaic laws that led early Christians, whom Grotius considers – alongside the ancient Dutch – to embody the highest standards of virtue, to combine natural laws with Old Testament precepts in order to approximate ideal conduct. Early Christian congregations thereby became pure seminaries of virtue (DJBP 2.5.14, 2.20.49).[46] Their virtues, in turn, attest the truth of Christianity (*De veritate* 2.6, 2.14 and 2.18).[47]

Modern Christians are not only allowed, but encouraged, to form alliances with non-Christians. Such alliances are binding because of our shared humanity, to which religion is irrelevant. They are encouraged because Christ extended the law of charity to all humankind, and alliances give Christians an opportunity to proselytise by demonstrating that Christians are just, kind and otherwise virtuous (DJBP 2.15.9–10). For the same reason, Christians should exercise the virtue of patience, rather than upset pagan or weak minds (DJBP 3.7.6).

At War

In avoiding and conducting war, Christians have a particular duty to exercise the virtues of charity, patience and forgiveness. Everyone should refrain from enforcing rights to punish others for injury, but especially those who follow the example of Christ, especially if enforcing rights might cause war and especially if there is a risk that innocents would die as collateral damage (DJBP 2.24.1–2 and 3.2.6). Extraordinary virtuousness in turn gives Christians the right of conscientious objection. Even when the justice of a war is unquestioned, Christians cannot be forced to participate against their consent, because refraining from war is part of saintliness (DJBP 2.26.5).

When Christians are in a position to take prizes, 'it is not enough that we do nothing against the Rules of rigorous Justice, properly so called; we must also take Care that we offend not against Charity, especially Christian Charity' (DJBP 3.18.4). Similarly, Christians must protect fruit trees, crops and farmers (DJBP 3.12.4). Pagan philosophers correctly insist that virtuous soldiers spare farmers. Canon law dictates that Christians should do so even more, aiming for higher humanity. Christian virtues raise not only moral, but also legal, thresholds against just wartime acts. Prisoners of war cannot be sold into slavery not because of pertaining laws, but because God demands charity (DJBP 3.7.9). Warring Christians must exercise mercy and liberality to allow the exchange or ransom of prisoners of war (DJBP 3.21.23). Plundering almost always violates justice and Christian charity. Christians have a greater bond than ancient Greeks had when they forbade plundering other Greeks (DJBP 3.12.8).

None of this means that wars among Christians are always unjust. When Christians are injured, even theologians agree that punishment for the sake of justice is a virtue. However, those who start such wars fail in their extralegal, Christian duty of love and concord, which surpasses 'the common bond that unites all mankind' (DJPC 3).

4.4 Conclusion

This chapter aimed to show that virtues are fundamental in all aspects of Grotius' work, from law through theology to drama. The fact that he defines them as relational invites a reassessment of his individualism. No history of the rise of individual rights can be told without Grotius, but his natural and civic rights are conferred by promises and guaranteed by the virtue of the parties involved, and by their ability to instantiate self-reinforcing processes that generate language, pre-political communities, states and, he hoped, eventually an international community less bellicose and lawless than in his own time. Grotius did not formulate virtues by analysing the state of nature, or asocial, eremetic versions of *vita contemplativa* aimed at imitating Christ. Moreover, the virtues that are so remarkably fundamental and coherent in Grotius' thought do not derive from sociability or debility, the two conventional motivations given in genealogies of political society.[48] Virtues precede both, and exert a direct influence during and after the creation of the polity, when sociability translates to citizenship and international relations, and debility is remedied by property and laws. The relational or other-regarding character of virtues does not mean that they are not stable. Virtues are fixed insofar as they are established by God, and meant to improve our shared human nature. Through their fixed but relational nature, virtues bind and hold us together. By contrast, laws and Scripture are heuristics that simplify rules, but do not work in every situation. Neither does reason, given man's epistemic limits. Virtues, if correctly followed, unerringly lead to the right solution.

Translation of Grotius' Works Used

The Rights of War and Peace, ed. R. Tuck (Indianapolis, 2005)

Further Reading

Blom, H., 'Hugo Grotius on trust, its causes and effects', in L. Kontler and M. Somos (eds.), *Trust and Happiness in the History of European Political Thought* (Leiden and Boston, 2018), 76–98.

Boisen, C., 'Hugo Grotius, declaration of war, and the international moral order', *Grotiana* N.S. 41 (2020), 282–303.

De Wilde, M., '*Fides publica* in ancient Rome and its reception by Grotius and Locke', *Legal History Review* 79 (2011) 455–87.

Eyffinger, Arthur, 'On trust and treachery', *Grotiana* N.S. 36 (2015) 79–171.

Geddert, J.S., *Hugo Grotius and the Modern Theology of Freedom: Transcending Natural Rights* (London and New York, 2017).

Ramelet, L., 'Political consent, promissory fidelity and rights transfers in Grotius', *Grotiana* N.S. 40 (2019) 123–45.

Straumann, B., *Roman Law in the State of Nature: The Classical Foundations of Hugo Grotius' Natural Law* (Cambridge, 2015).

Stumpf, C., 'Consent and the ethics of international law: revisiting Grotius's system of states in a secular setting', *Grotiana* N.S. 41 (2020), 163–76.

Notes

1 Also see DFP 102 complaining that those in power determine what is vice and virtue. In DJBP Prol. 58 Grotius describes the purpose of DJBP. It is not to show what is profitable but what is just, which is profitable, even though it may not seem to be in this age, when laws are unsatisfactory. As throughout DJBP, here we find clear but unmarked shifts between descriptive and normative registers.

2 Grotius drew on numerous sources for his theory of virtues. For reasons of space, these are only discussed here if they are relevant and not already noted in the editions listed in the bibliography.

3 'Maxime autem in eo consentitur, aliena nobis commoda curanda esse, quia id fere homini proprium est' (DJPC 12). Tuck describes this passage as evidence that Grotius believed that social life distinguishes humans from animals, DJBP Prol. 23. Instead, it is accepting the duty of care that is distinctive. Animals are sociable, many of them care for each other, but they do not consciously accept a binding duty to do so. DJBP Dedication, Prol. on storks; *Sophompaneas* 12; *De veritate* 1.10 and so on. In DJBP Prol., Grotius offers another formulation. Humans differ from animals because they desire to live in a society of other humans that is regulated according to their best understanding. Human relations must be based on justice, which requires both reason and sociability (DJBP Prol. 6, also Prol. 8n2, DJBP 1.1.3, *passim*). While this version differs from DJPC, it agrees with it insofar that it is not limited to sociability alone, *pace* Tuck.

4 Peter describes his vicious denial of Christ, neglect to help him and Judas' perfidy, *Christus patiens*, beginning of Act 2.

5 Also see DJBP 2.1.9n citing Plutarch, 'the principal act of virtue is to preserve him, who preserves every thing else'.

6 Also see DJBP 2.20.2 and 2.20.4.

7 Invoking another virtue, Grotius writes that a generous soul honours wartime treaties even after new injuries (DJBP 3.19.19). DJBP concludes, 'We ought to preserve our Faith for several Reasons, and amongst others, because without that we should have no Hopes of Peace' (DJBP 3.25.1).

8 H. Blom, 'Hugo Grotius on trust, its causes and effects', in L. Kontler and M. Somos (eds.), *Trust and Happiness in the History of European Political Thought* (Leiden and Boston, 2018), 76–98; L. Ramelet, 'Political consent, promissory fidelity and rights transfers in Grotius', *Grotiana* N.S. 40 (2019) 123–45. Also see P. Schröder in this volume.

9 DJBP's last substantive chapter, 3.24, concerns the practical benefits of faithfulness in ending wars.

10 Grotius cites only Seneca, at length, in support.

11 Which laws cannot do, making Grotian virtues function like Hart's secondary rules (DJBP 3.23.5).

12 See section 4.3 below.

13 J.S. Geddert, *Hugo Grotius and the Modern Theology of Freedom: Transcending Natural Rights* (London and New York, 2017), ch. 6.

14 '[T]he Rules of Charity reach farther than those of Right.'

15 Joseph took character into account in his criminal judgments, *Sophompaneas* 23.

16 Grotius paints a terrifying image of the people, defiant of their sovereign, seizing and wasting corn supplies in *Sophompaneas* 19–22. Aristocracy solves this best.

17 C. Boisen, 'Hugo Grotius, declaration of war, and the international moral order', *Grotiana* N.S. 41 (2020), 282–303.

18 DJBP dedication, first sentence: explains that the book is about a virtue called justice. DJBP concludes by calling for faithfulness, clemency and humanity to end wars (DJBP 3.25.1–3).

19 Joseph found this exact balance: *Sophompaneas* 24.

20 *Meletius* and *De veritate* are among Grotius' clearest accounts of how these topics – from Dutch expansion through irenic Christian minimalism to the partial replacement of religion with ethics in law – serve a philosophically unified aim. On law and morality displacing religion see C. Stumpf, 'Consent and the ethics of international law: revisiting Grotius's system of states in a secular setting', *Grotiana* N.S. 41 (2020), 163–76.

21 Also see DJPC 14; Appendix 2, Document 7.549 (VOC instructions). Stoics are right that virtues are connected, DJBP 2.20.29. The rules for exercising one's duties extend through all the virtues and beyond pure right, DI 6.13.

22 Cf. six in *De veritate* 1.2–7: God exists; monotheism; God has all perfection; infinitely so; is eternal, omnipotent, omniscient and completely good; first mover.

23 De Wilde, M., 'Fides publica in ancient Rome and its reception by Grotius and Locke', *Legal History Review* 79 (2011) 455–87; A. Eyffinger, 'On trust and treachery', *Grotiana* N.S. 36 (2015) 79–171, at 99. Also see B. Straumann, *Roman Law in the State of Nature: The Classical Foundations of Hugo Grotius' Natural Law* (Cambridge, 2015), 22, 39, 46, 48, 58, *passim.*

24 DFP 121–3: Attilius' private faith prevails over national interest. Similarly, if the Romans did not think pledges made by individuals were binding, they extradited or ignored them. Individuals authorise the sovereign, who becomes all-powerful (DI 4.13). Individuals must use reason to avoid false action (DI 10.6–7). The unit of analysis in criminal law is the individual, but with collective justice in mind (*De satisfactione* 4).

25 Virtues are not gods: *De veritate* 4.7.

26 Eyffinger, 'On trust', states that this refers to Cicero, and the same sequence appears in DJPC 14. However, in DJPC 14 the Cicero sequence is marshalled to show that everything that is wholly just is also honourable. Unlike in DFP, in DJPC Grotius consistently and explicitly invokes not Cicero, but Aristotle's *Rhetoric* to show that it is also profitable. DJPC 15: everything just is beneficial; everything honourable is beneficial. Conversely, true benefits always adjoin honour and justice.

27 In DJBP Prol. 25, Grotius agrees with the Stoics that fortitude is the virtue that fights for justice, i.e. subservient to it.

28 A detailed discussion is beyond the present scope, but one must note that Grotius is keenly attentive to reputation for virtue and vice, as distinct from virtue and vice. DJPC 15: everyone wants a reputation for virtue.

29 DJPC 14: justice and honour are intrinsically linked or even coterminous. Some say honour and virtue are synonymous; others that honour is inherent in virtue; what is clear is that they cannot be separated. Nothing just can be shameful either because no single virtue can clash with virtue in general, or because the ancients were right (and they were) that the virtue of justice encompasses all virtues. To this Grotius adds his own opinion that keeping the *Santa Catarina* is glorious because it stems from the two most beneficial virtues, justice and fortitude. War is the best test of their combination.

30 DJBP 2.24.4: practising virtues to curtail strict justice in order to stop wars is also often in our self-interest. The same combination of public and private interests characterises private efforts to save a failing state, e.g. through virtuous tyrannicide (DJPC 9).

31 DJPC 14: virtue is as Aristotle's *Rhetoric* describes it; and Aristotle's description is the best.

32 DJBP Prol. 44–6.

33 According to DJPB 3.17.2n, the Goths even had the virtue of moderation.

34 Eyffinger, 'On trust', is right that faith, good or bad, is the best descriptor of national character; DFP 86.

35 Ibid. points out illuminating connections between DFP, written around the end of 1602 with a few lines added in 1604, and DJPC.

36 Also see the end of DJPC 11: humanity makes the Dutch victorious. DJPC 14: the Dutch love peace, violence is their last resort, their heart is always open to peace. Engagements with Prussian and Venetian ships demonstrate Dutch justice, fortitude, fairness, mercy and temperance.

37 Also see DJPC on courage, justice, good faith, gentleness and compassion; DJPC 13 on the Dutch dealing with Portuguese with good faith, exceeding benevolence and liberality.

38 DJPC 15 presumably addressed also to Mennonite VOC shareholders. Compare *De satisfactione* 2: waiving ownership is never unjust. It 'is called, not liberality, but clemency'.

39 DJPC 14: East Indians praise Dutch good faith, industry and valour, declaring the Dutch 'saviours of the Orient'.

40 The same list in DJPC 11: bad faith, assassination, poisoning, treachery.

41 Also see DJPC 11 on treachery and deceit, though elements were already present in Grotius' brief: DJPC Appendix 1, Document 1; Appendix 2, Documents 1 and 4. See DJPC 11 on Iberian cruelty, fraud, torture and oath-breaking; DJPC 15 on avarice.

42 Grotius sets Christ's patience as an example in DJBP 1.4.7 with fewer qualifications.

43 In *Christus patiens*, Peter recounts being rebuked for trying to revenge Christ, and Christ thereby curing his enemies. Those who commit all crimes at once by breaking faith, and their self-flattering minds vainly trust their own virtues, should learn from Peter's mistake. *Christus patiens* 2.15.LL65–8, 16.LL87–92.

44 Also see DI 5.10: no virtue is more worthy of a sovereign than piety. Grotius makes the same point in *Sophompaneas* 5, adding that other virtues flow from piety. DI 6.9: a Christian ruler avoids definitions and uses moderation and prudent silence. Though Grotius writes at length about the virtues of Christians and sovereigns, note that there is little about virtues specific to Christian sovereigns. There is no Grotian equivalent of the structure of Hobbes' *Leviathan*, see Parts 3 and 4.

45 Conversely, faithful soldiers bear their fate with patience and charity, and do not resume hostilities, nor escape if they promised not to (DJBP 3.21.24, 3.23.7–13).

46 Grotius also describes virtues that seem specific to priests in an ideal world; in *De satisfactione* 10, to atone; in DJBP 1.2.10: penitents and early priests were not virtuous, technically. They were chosen from those whose sanctity exceeded normal Christians'.

47 Especially when contrasted with the lack of virtue in the gods and propagators of Greek, Islamic and pagan religions: *De veritate* 2.11, 2.12, 2.13, 2.18 and 4.4. In the dedication of *Sophompaneas*, Grotius praises Vossius for virtues of prudence, diligence and moderation, akin to early Christians'. Grotius notes in the same dedication that Joseph's virtues were beneficial to himself, his household and his state. Joseph's captors loved him for his virtues, *Sophompaneas* 8.

48 See i.a. DJBP Prol.

5 Trust (*Fides*)

Peter Schröder

5.1 Introduction

Trust (*fides*) is already central in some of Grotius' earlier works[1], but it plays a major role in his *De jure belli ac pacis,* where the importance of trust is highlighted right at the beginning in the *Prolegomena.* Perhaps even more importantly, Grotius concludes the treatise with a book-length discussion of trust in chapters 20–25 of the third book. This contribution will discuss the role of trust in Grotius' work. Particular emphasis will be placed on interstate relations and Grotius' attempt to argue for some kind of binding force within the international realm, grounded in a concept of trust. It is here that his concept of punishment plays a crucial, though – as will become clear – problematic, role. Grotius also engages in the ensuing debate about the role of trust within the theories of international commerce. Thus, Grotius has a lot to offer on the various facets of trust and its role within moral, political and even legal thought. His arguments on trust in the religious and domestic political disputes engage to some extent with issues that will not be pursued with the same detail here.[2] The underlying question is how Grotius conceptualises and uses trust in light of the highly conflictual and volatile international sphere. Trust was not a free-standing political doctrine; it was a concept employed in different political writings.[3] Nor was it the dominating concept shaping the political and economic debates in the seventeenth century. The concept of trust was fluid in its use, and the theorising about trust developed not just one coherent argument. In different conceptual contexts, the meaning and importance accorded to trust varied. 'Trust should not be seen as a word with a stable reference', Lagerpetz asserts, 'but as an organising tool for human relations, used in a reasoning context where we wish to justify or challenge behaviour.'[4]

5.2 Aspects of Trust

We need to appreciate the different connotations of trust, since Grotius drew on and developed a whole range of different aspects of trust. We would look in vain for just one single aspect of trust in Grotius' thought. Trust is not a juridical or political term, such as sovereignty or punishment. It is a concept that is much more open-ended, and prone to be charged and occasionally overcharged with different connotations. Grotius was well aware of this. Although he used the Roman concept of *fides* and followed Cicero's argument that 'the keeping of faith is fundamental to justice',[5] he also drew attention to the fact that *fides* in the Roman sense has a twofold meaning. Apart from Cicero's understanding of trust, there is also a very different meaning of *fides* in Roman thought, which always involves an element of coercion and power. The stronger, victorious Romans would receive the vanquished into their *fides* and it would be the Romans who set the conditions. Grotius draws attention to this different use:

> We often meet in *Roman* Histories with these Expressions, *Tradere se in fidem*, To yield themselves to the Faith, *Tradere in fidem & clementiam*, To yield to the Faith and Clemency. (...) But it must be understood, that by these Words is meant an absolute Surrender: And that the Word *Fides* in these Places signifies nothing but the Probity of the Conqueror, to which the Conquered yields himself. (DJBP 3.20.50.3)[6]

However, in Cicero and also for Grotius, these two aspects were related. To yield to the faith of the Romans was not only a euphemism for absolute surrender, but also provided reliable – or trustworthy – Roman protection for those who submitted to Roman rule.

The discussion of trust from the perspective of international political thought faces particular problems, reflecting the volatility of interstate relations when sovereign states confront each other. Grotius took part in an ongoing debate about trust that was entertained within seventeenth-century international political thought, intensified by religious and political conflicts that seemed to confirm the difficulty of actually trusting an adversary. Confessional differences undermined political stability and impeded trust-building. Yet it was recognised that a solution to these conflicts depended ultimately on trust.[7] In various ways, programmes were developed to provide a framework in which mutual trust was both plausible and possible. While searching for a basis for mutual trust, all parties nonetheless sought to protect and preserve their particular confessional identity. In the Netherlands, the inter-confessional dispute between Remonstrants and Counter-Remonstrants shook Dutch political and religious debates to the core. Both parties emphasised existing differences and were thus blocking the search for trust and agreements built on it. Grotius, especially in *De veritate religionis Christianae* and *Meletius*, worked hard to overcome these obstacles.[8]

However, Grotius was also aware of the political currency the reputation of being trustworthy could provide. He did not hesitate to play this political card against the Spanish. In *De fide et perfidia,* he repeatedly contrasts the Dutch faithfulness in their dealings even with their enemies with Spain's perfidy. Grotius emphasises the potential political advantages in observing faithfulness, which would pay off in the long run (DFP 149). He even spins the alleged Dutch trustworthiness into a narrative of patriotic republican virtue: 'our expulsion of tyrants; our advocacy of the true religion; our taking up arms in defence of the Republic (...) the advocacy of Freedom and Faith [*libertatem et fidem*] are in fact tokens of the same mentality' (DFP 137-8.).

Grotius had to address the infamous positions of authors like Carneades or Machiavelli if he wanted to convince his readers of the validity of his own concept of trust. According to Grotius' understanding of trust, Niccolo Machiavelli (1469-1527) had only cynically exploited the appearance and reputation of trustworthiness in his political advice.[9] Without citing him by name, Grotius denounces Machiavelli as undermining good faith: 'They who endeavour to instill into them [the Princes] the Art of Deceiving, practise the same they teach. Their Practices cannot possibly prosper long, which render Men unsociable to Men, and hateful to GOD' (DJBP 3.25.1.3). In order to achieve peace, it was paramount for Grotius to preserve trust between warring parties. That sounds like a contradiction in terms. And Grotius admits that 'any sensible man does well to be forever on his guard against the enemy' (DFP 117). So, how can warring states or princes trust their adversaries? Is such a thing not almost impossible? And, yet, Grotius insists that 'we ought to preserve our Faith for several reasons, and amongst others, because without that we should have no Hopes of Peace' (DJBP 3.25.1.1). Trust is, therefore, central to Grotius' natural law doctrine and crucial for his normative and political arguments about war and peace (DFP 115 and 163).

Nevertheless, trust remains a precarious concept for the organisation of interstate relations. But 'once trust becomes possible, it sustains inter-actions that would otherwise collapse, [and] enhances the quality of cooperation'.[10] At the same time, there existed a tension between trust and interest, as the latter can supersede the keeping of agreements, thereby undermining the fundamental notion of trust. However, the notion of interest can often be oversimplified and misrepresented. For instance, the perception of one's interest can be short-sighted. Grotius argues, therefore, that there was a need to interpret what a state's true interest actually is. And, as we will see, he relates this discussion to the issue of trust. Thus, 'the Faith given' should be observed under all circumstances: 'the Obligation of which [to keep faith] I have proved to be sacred and indispensable. And we ought to be very careful to avoid (. . .) Perfidiousness' (DJBP 3.25.7).[11] Trust was at the heart of Grotius' natural law theory as a moral basis for explaining the beginnings of communal living. We need, therefore, to establish the sometimes even contradictory range of trust to assess what this term might be able to achieve within Grotius' natural law doctrine. It is here that we can discern how Grotius differed from his predecessors and how he developed his argument in contrast to what he had found, for instance, in Jean Bodin (1530–96) or Alberico Gentili (1552–1608).

Grotius wanted to convince his readers that he had the tradition of ancient natural law doctrine on his side. He repeatedly acknowledges the influence of the Stoics and of Cicero. Grotius founds his argument of right and justice on man's 'Desire of Society' (DJBP Prol. 6). He defends his conceptualisation of justice and trust against Carneades and Machiavelli. Grotius would have known about Carneades' famous debate on justice via Lactantius' *Divine institutions*. Carneades had argued opposite positions on successive days, thus effectively challenging the concept of justice for civic and political life.[12] Grotius adopts Cicero's position, and against Carneades he defends the existence of right and justice and declares that 'this sociability (. . .) is the Fountain of Right (. . .) to which belongs (. . .) the Obligation of fulfilling promises, (. . .) and the Merit of Punishment among Men' (DJBP Prol. 8I). Grotius consciously links the obligation of fulfilling promises with the possibility of punishing those who do not keep their obligations. Thus, the enforcement of agreements exists by way of punish-ment, which – according to Grotius – in turn helps to organise interstate relations: trust between states ought to be possible, because punishment will be inflicted on those who break their agreements.

But, for Grotius, trust is more complex and it needs to be advanced towards the adversaries and 'all Agreements between enemies depend upon Faith, either expressed or implied' (DJBP 3.20.1). Grotius reiterates in substance what he had found in Gentili's *De iure belli*. Kingsbury argued rightly that 'the key features of [the] idea of international society' which are central to Grotius' *De jure belli ac pacis* 'are all present in Gentili's work, and Grotius adds little to Gentili's account'.[13] What Grotius does add, however, is a new basis on which to build a theory of universal obligation and trust in the norms, rules and customs of international society, which had plunged into endless warfare throughout Europe.

According to Grotius, Gentili had allegedly failed to observe 'invariable rules of equity and justice' (DJBP Prol. 39) as enshrined in the natural laws. Gentili not only limits 'war to a contest between sovereign powers – whereas Grotius expressly includes private warfare in his definition – he also stresses the idea of legality and regularity which is conspicuously absent from the Dutchman's formula'.[14] The exclusion of those who were not trustworthy was a central part of Gentili's argument – an aspect that he also found in Bodin. Grotius, on the contrary, was prepared to include even pirates in his natural law doctrine. In the chapter 'Concerning Faith between Enemies' of his *De jure belli ac pacis,* Grotius argues that 'such sort of People have not with others that particular Community, which the Law of Nations hath introduced between enemies engaged in solemn and compleat War. But yet, as Man they are to enjoy the common Benefits of the Law of Nature' (DJBP 3.19.2.2). Even with pirates, a relationship of trust is envisaged, since 'it is one of the most inviolable Laws of Nature that we should perform what we promise' (DJBP 3.19.2.2). However, his argument regarding pirates was more balanced and – following Cicero – he conceded a distinction between 'an Enemy in Form (...) and Pirates' (DJBP 2.18.19). Grotius pursues a different and – in many ways – much more ambitious aim than Gentili.[15] His natural law theory claims to be based on justice and to be applicable to all human society. The concept of the sovereign state as developed by Bodin and Gentili was only of limited concern for Grotius' theory. Although the sovereign state is also discussed by Grotius, 'his ultimate frame of reference remains the Ciceronian *humani generis societas* inherited from Stoicism, a society of mankind rather than of states'.[16]

Grotius claims that natural laws are easily intelligible. He stresses that his 'first care was, to refer the Proofs of those Things that belong to the

Law of Nature to some such certain Notions, as none can deny, without doing Violence to his Judgement. For the Principles of that Law, if you rightly consider, are manifest and self-evident' (DJBP Prol. 40). But there remained a fundamental problem: on which basis could a binding force of the natural laws be founded? Grotius needed to answer this essential question. The answer Grotius gives is not much different from Aquinas: 'Natural Right is the Rule and Dictate of Right Reason, shewing the Moral Deformity or Moral Necessity there is in any Act, according to its Suitableness or Unsuitableness to a reasonable Nature, and consequently, that such an Act is either forbid or commanded by GOD, the Author of Nature' (DJBP 1.1.10.1). But, for Grotius, the obligatory force of natural laws does not derive from God's commands, but from right reason. In this respect, he is departing from the scholastic tradition.[17] However, Grotius also shifts the ground of the argument from the political sphere, as found in Bodin and Gentili, towards the realm of morality.

Much has been made of Grotius' proposition that his theory would be valid even if 'we should (...) grant, what without the greatest Wickedness cannot be granted, that there is no God, or that he takes no care of human Affairs' (DJBP Prol. 11). It was not a matter of doubting the existence of God (*De veritate* 31–40). Grotius did not want to advocate a secular natural law theory. Instead, he wanted to argue that natural law would be valid even if there were no God. It is this understanding of the validity of natural law that limits divine voluntarism because even an omnipotent God cannot change the natural laws by his volition.[18] Grotius' view of the normative value of natural law oscillates between the dictates of right reason and God's command:

And this now is another Original of Right, besides that of Nature, being that which proceeds from the free Will of God, to which our Understanding infallibly assures us, we ought to be subject: And even the Law of Nature itself, whether it be that which consists in the Maintenance of Society, or that which in a looser Sense is so called, though it flows from the internal Principles of Man, may notwithstanding be justly ascribed to God, because it was his pleasure that these Principles should be in us'. (DJBP Prol. 12)

Does the obligation of right cease in war? Grotius develops his concept of natural law to demonstrate 'that on the contrary, no War ought to be so much as undertaken but for the obtaining of Right; nor when undertaken, ought it to be carried on beyond the bounds of Justice and Fidelity [*juris ac fidei*]' (DJBP Prol. 26). Trust (*fides*) is thus accorded crucial importance and, following Cicero, perceived as the foundation of justice. Both concepts are seen as means to foster peaceful relations among states. Against the provocative assertions of Carneades and Machiavelli, Grotius needs to rely on justice and trust to compensate for the shortcoming of juridical obligation, and to treat the conduct of war in a way analogous to judicial proceedings: 'to render Wars just, they are to be waged with no less Care and Integrity, than judicial Proceedings' (DJBP Prol. 26). Grotius relies on the natural law and just war theory developed by the Spanish scholastics, but put these to different use, advancing the existing tradition by viewing natural law as universal and above the confessional division of Europe. However, this claim to universality was contested. Depending on the contingent outcome of war, one of the conflicting parties would find itself in the position of being judge over the other.

5.3 Trust and Punishment

Discussion of punishment played a major part in international political thought.[19] Grotius' theory of the 'right of punishment (...) had significant repercussions on the practice of imperialism'.[20] Theologians and jurists alike were readily prepared to consider the exercise of punitive war. In the early seventeenth century, the issue of punishment was taken up by Grotius. He asks whether 'the power to punish [is not] essentially a power which pertains to the state' (DJPC 8, 136), only to deny it emphatically:

Not at all! On the contrary, just as every right of the magistrate comes to him from the state, so has the same right come to the state from private individuals; (...) Therefore, since no one is able to transfer a thing that he never possessed, it is evident that the right of chastisement was held by private persons before it was held by the state. (...) The law of nature, or the law of nations, is the source from which the state receives the power in question. (DJPC 8, 136–7)

Grotius' claim that the right to punish was not a prerogative of the state, but already belonged to private individuals, introduced a different and even more contested notion of punishment into the international sphere. 'From a theoretical standpoint, the greatest challenge was establishing the private right to engage in punishment.'[21] That Grotius was well aware of this challenge is shown by his own caveat, stating that the 'difficult part of our problem lies in the fact that the power to begin a war would not seem to be granted readily to private parties' (DJPC 12, 379). Nevertheless, this understanding of punishment proved very influential throughout Europe in international thought. John Locke (1632–1704) is presumably the most prominent philosopher who took up Grotius' idea of punishment.[22] Grotius' concept of punishment 'legitimated a great deal of European action against native peoples around the world'.[23] As we will see in what follows, Grotius reconsiders his position in his *De jure belli ac pacis*, but he does not substantially change it.[24]

When Grotius turns his attention to the issue of punishment in interstate relations in *De jure belli ac pacis*, he advances a slightly more cautious argument.[25] In the second book, he provides a substantial discussion of punishment engaging with the stoic and scholastic natural law traditions and with the existing views on punishment. He argues that the origin and nature of punishment have been misunderstood and 'given Occasion to many Mistakes' (DJBP 2.20.1.1). Like many of his predecessors, Grotius relates punishment to the concept of justice, since it is a reaction to a wrong that has been done. In agreement with the stoics and scholastics alike, he conceptualises punishment as a means to right a wrong and thereby defend justice. However, the legitimate execution of punishment among states was less straightforward than he presumed. Grotius perceives the right to punish as a natural right that belonged to each human. Punishment is perceived by Grotius as one of the just causes of war: 'Most Men assign *three* just Causes of War, *Defence*, the *Recovery* of what's our own, and *Punishment*' (DJBP 2.1.2.2).

At the same time, he maintained that it was not possible that natural law could determine 'to whom the Right of Punishing belongs. (. . .) For natural reason informs us, that a Malefactor may be punished, but not who ought to punish him' (DJBP 2.20.3.1). Natural law 'suggests indeed so much, that it is the fittest to be done by a Superior. (. . .) The Consequence of which is, that a Man ought not to be punished by one who is equally guilty with himself' (DJBP 2.20.3.1f.). However, Grotius also argues forcefully against the Spanish neo-scholastics. In his view, punishment is allowed everybody against an offender, if an offence against nature was committed. He followed Innocentius IV (1195–1254) and others:

who hold that War is lawful against those who offend against Nature; which is contrary to the Opinion of *Victoria, Vasquez, Azorius, Molina* and others, who seem to require, towards making War just, that he who undertakes it be injured in himself, or in his State, or that he has some Jurisdiction over the Person against whom the War is made. For they assert, the Power of Punishing is properly an Effect of Civil Jurisdiction; whereas our Opinion is, that it proceeds from the Law of Nature'. (DJBP 2.20.40.4)

Such a conceptualisation of just war and punishment has far-reaching consequences. First, the aspect of private punishment is still present in Grotius' *De jure belli ac pacis,* which meant that 'private violence was thus equated to public violence'.[26] But, second and more important, this 'combination of individual punishment, theory of property by occupation, and the right to make treaties with the natives on an equal basis, formed a remarkable set of arguments in support of imperial expansion'.[27] How did Grotius' principle of international punishment influence his concept of trust?

A certain tension in Grotius' theory regarding the concept of punishment can be discerned. The purpose of punishment is to deter future wrong-doing and to right a wrong, not to justify revenge, which would lead to unreasonable and passionate behaviour (DJBP 2.20.5) and enrichment: 'he that has the Justice of the War on his Side, should obtain what he took up Arms for, and also recover his Costs and Damages, but not that he should get any Thing farther by way of Punishment, for that is odious' (DJBP 3.20.11.1). This seems almost to suggest that justice will always be on the victorious side of a war. However, Grotius' argument is more complex here.[28] Although *De jure belli ac pacis* was meant to supply a theory for relations among states, Grotius discusses punishment mainly in relation to the particular state. In this context, only a superior authority that is not party to the conflict ought to punish those who wronged another, the twofold aim being to right the committed wrong and to deter future offences. On this basis, justice would not only depend on the good will of the different actors, but could also be defended. Punishment furnished a framework that would allow trust in other actors, because it provides an incentive to keep obligations. Punishment is instrumental to safeguard the laws and, by doing so, permits trustworthiness among the citizens. Within a state, these concepts avoid the difficulties of interstate relations where a superior authority was lacking. To surmount the problems that come to the fore when considering punishment in interstate relations, Grotius formulates his idea of a *societas humana*. This human society does not replace the sovereign state, but it allows Grotius to apply his natural law theory to the international sphere, shifting away from interstate relations and the structural conflict of sovereign states towards the Ciceronian concept of human society. Regarding punishment and trustworthiness, we need to consider, therefore, what the implications of this concept are.

The subjectivity of the natural right to punish undermined trust and trust-building rather than safeguarding the observance of agreements and promises. The fact that the victorious party of the war assumes the role of judge and executioner of punishment against the former enemy made the notion of a punitive war problematic. As if it were not enough to lose a war, the vanquished enemy was also discriminated against as the culpable and unjust party after the war had been ended. Grotius concedes that 'forasmuch as he that punishes, if he punish justly, must have a Right to punish, which Right arises from the Crime of the Delinquent' (DJBP 2.20.2.3). He who committed a crime was aware of the consequences, 'so that he that commits a Crime, seems voluntarily to submit himself to Punishment' (DJBP 2.20.2.3). But would there be no dispute in interstate relations as to whether the universally valid natural law was breached? Was not the initial problem to decide whether there was a crime committed in the first place? Moreover, if the guilty party is the stronger in any given conflict, it may perhaps even concede the justice of the opponent, thus even admitting its own guilt. But it is hardly conceivable that it will undergo punishment because of any acknowledged guilt. Grotius seems to suggest that these questions are not contested. He goes further and claims 'there being no great Crime that is not punishable; so that he who will directly commit it, is by Consequence willing to incur the Punishment' (DJBP 2.20.2.3). This argument, derived from Thomist natural law doctrine, allows Grotius to maintain that there is no need for interpretation since the delinquent is already anticipating and accepting his punishment. Within a state, those who commit a crime might well be aware of the consequences in the form of a threatened punishment. This notion is, however, problematic when applied to the interstate level. Grotius' argument relies still on the medieval – Thomist – idea of universal justice, which, if undermined by human wrong-doing, is re-established by punishment. Grotius' argument comes full circle:

We must also know, that Kings, and those who are invested with a Power equal to that of Kings, have a Right to exact Punishment, not only for Injuries committed against themselves, or their Subjects, but likewise, for those which do not peculiarly concern them, but which are, in any Person whatsoever, grievous Violations of the Law of Nature or Nations. For the Liberty of consulting the Benefit of human Society, by Punishments, which at first (...) was in every particular Person, does now, since Civil Societies, and Courts of Justice, have been instituted, reside in those who are possessed of the supreme Power, and that properly, not as they have an Authority over others, but as they are in Subjection to none. (DJBP 2.20.40.1)

Grotius realises the problem of being judge in one's own case (*ipse judex*), which he addresses on the level of the state, where he re-introduces the sovereign kings into his argument as the only authorities who could exercise punishment. However, it is still not clear who had the competence to decide in the case of interstate conflicts. The problematic principle of *ipse-judex* remained in force among sovereigns. But, if sovereign states were in subjection to none, then it is difficult to see why one sovereign state would accept punishment from another.

In the end, Grotius was not in a position to provide a convincing foundation for interstate punishment. If punishment ensured the observance of natural and international law, his system either had to remain open to abuse by trespassers, or he would have to accept that those sovereigns who yielded the power to do so would decide when a breach of natural law was committed by a member of the *societas humana*. In the *De jure praedae commentarius,* the notion of the human race also embraced the possibility of private punishment: 'the private avenger has in view the good of the whole human race (...); this goal corresponds exactly to that common good toward which (...) all punishments are directed in nature's plan' (DJPC 8, 139). Grotius argues that the right of punishment enforced natural law in the state of nature. But what was the right interpretation of the laws of nature? Would not both sides to a conflict make the same, hence contradicting, claim? It seems that Carneades' criticism would stand, since this would mean the establishment of right by de facto power. As far as international law is concerned, Grotius uses the concept of punishment to justify a war as just. It is not the just war that puts the victor in the position to punish the enemy, but the right to punish becomes one of the justifications for waging war.

Grotius' natural law doctrine was not able to provide a stable framework for interstate relations. He concedes that the exercise of state sovereignty could not be constrained by natural law. It only provides guidance to the rulers, but there was no superior power over them to enforce natural law, because 'between Kings and Nations (. . .) can be no superior Power' (DJBP 3.20.46.2). Voluntary agreements among sovereign states might regulate interstate relations, but even such an institution as arbitration, which is not part of natural law, finds its limits: 'for it is common agreement that gives the arbiter his authority, and no one is compelled to entrust his rights to this person' (DJPC 8, 145).

Grotius claims that natural law established rules and procedures with universal validity, grounded in an objective justice. But there was no conceptualisation of how a conflict about the very notion of justice could be mediated. The underlying assumption remained that one of the conflicting parties was in the wrong. Grotius' concept of punishment was meant to address this issue, but it was not able to address it satisfactorily. Thus, international politics remained conflictual and volatile, and – as a consequence – trust in interstate relations remained precarious. Despite being only too well aware of this, Grotius maintains throughout his writings that it was nevertheless in the interest and indeed a hallmark of the Dutch to keep their promises and not 'to violate (. . .) the Law of Nations' (DFP 151).

5.4 Trust and International Commerce

Increasing international trade was closely related to these issues. So, we need to assess the question of what extent the discussion of trust within the economic sphere during the seventeenth century influenced the discourse of trust regarding interstate relations. Indeed, Grotius himself asks 'what is there to say with regard to good faith in commercial relations?' (DFP 171). Economic enterprise was taken to be a struggle to gain more access to other markets, while protecting the domestic market to ensure a greater share of the limited economic volume at the cost of competitors. Istvan Hont argued that the legal defence Grotius provided for the 'uninhibited pursuit of trade by the Dutch East India Company became a hallmark of his natural jurisprudence. But his defence of Dutch commerce did not follow from his new legal doctrine of rights'.[29] In view of the increasing conflicts over trade, Hont suggested that 'Grotius' innovation was to raise a bulwark against reason of state from the inside of the idiom itself, without resorting to external doctrinal resources'.[30] Such a reading plays down the importance of Grotius' natural law theory, which was a sophisticated attempt to provide exactly that, i.e. an external doctrinal resource. Grotius forcefully took part in the early modern formulation of commercial and colonial claims of competing European states.

For another contemporary author on commerce, the state should 'not (...) permit a promiscuous, straggling, and dispersed trade'.[31] The role of the state was foremost perceived as safeguarding these conditions of competition. The underlying ideas of mercantilism are best understood 'not as an economic theory, but (...) as part of the theory of the modern State'.[32] Restrictions on foreign traders and merchants were common. Gerard de Malynes (1586–1641) critically observed French restrictions on foreign trade,[33] whereas Jacques Savary (1622–90) complained at 'the ill treatment French merchants suffered in England'.[34] If the political and economic interests of sovereign states were mutually exclusive, can order among states be achieved on such competitive assumptions? Was international trade really advancing peaceful relations between states?

As the Dutch case illustrates, trade was a means of state expansion and hegemony: 'the VOC's mission was founded on the Grotian idea of property, which proved conducive to the expansion of overseas trade into territorial conquest'.[35] However, trade was also seen by Grotius as a means to defend Dutch independence against the Spanish. He is, therefore, happy to advocate the competitive nature of trade, in particular on the open sea: 'Let the Portugals therefore exclaim as much (...) as they list, 'Ye take away our gain!' The Hollanders will answer, 'Nay, we are careful of our own. Are you angry at this, that we take part with the winds and sea? But who hath promised those gains shall remain yours?' (ML 12, 56). His arguments are foremost aimed against European competitors and not the indigenous peoples overseas. Trust between the Spanish and Portuguese and their Dutch competitors was impossible. Can it really be said that trade between foreign states improved trust between them? The VOC was extremely successful in establishing its dominance in the East Asian trade. The contracts and treaties that the VOC signed with the rulers and princes in Indonesia and elsewhere show that the VOC acted on behalf of the Dutch state that thereby acquired extensive trading rights, often close to monopolies, that excluded other foreign merchants. Perhaps it might at least be said that, for a while, trust between the Dutch and Indonesian rulers improved?

Trust and good faith were used in a wide range of registers to serve different interests. In his *Edit du Roy servant de reglement pour le commerce des Negocians*, it was Louis XIV's (1638–1715) intention 'to assure good faith against fraud among merchants'.[36] Regarding commercial agreements, merchants had to negotiate with their foreign counterparts, who were used to different cultural and legal frames of reference. Specific questions were raised by trade relations: were merchants bound only by a signed contract or were they also bound by promises made in good faith? What happened if contracts were broken? These questions were taken up by a range of seventeenth-century authors of whom Malynes is presumably among the most significant. He stressed the importance of custom: 'it plainly appeareth, that the Law Merchant, may well be as ancient as any humane Law, and more ancient than any written Law. The very morall Law it selfe, as written by *Moses*, was long after the customary Law of Merchants'.[37] For Malynes, custom was the regulatory force of the *lex mercatoria*.

Grotius makes a similar argument that trade relations ought to be regulated by custom since rules derived from custom were 'agreeable to the Law of Nature' (DJBP 2.12.25). In Grotius' view, the customary rules would enable the resolution of 'disputes, which could not possibly be decided (...) among those who had no common Judge to appeal to' (DJBP 2.12.26.3). But, as in the dispute over the taking of the Portuguese vessel *Santa Catarina* by the Dutch, Grotius' advocacy on behalf of the VOC on the basis of natural law and custom could not resolve the dispute beyond doubt. The structural difficulties of his natural law theory, which we encountered previously, remained, the private aspect of the natural law being transferred and translated into the public.

The issue of trust regarding tradesmen and merchants was widely discussed in seventeenth-century literature. Richard Baxter (1615–91) noted in his voluminous *Christian Directory*: 'there are no Tradesman or Buyers who will profess that they look not to be trusted, (...) among sober persons in Civil Socciety (...) we must (...) expect some truth and honesty, and not presume them to be all lyars and deceivers (...). Indeed we trust them (...) but with a mixture of distrust.'[38] Anybody writing on commerce knew that a certain risk was always involved when trading with others, especially in the long-distance overseas trade. The vocabulary and structure of the argument of economic thought were often close to natural law doctrine.[39] Cicero returns in Malynes' *Lex Mercatoria*: 'This Law of Merchants (...) in the fundamentals of it, is nothing else but (as Cicero defineth true and just Law) (...): True Law is right Reason, agreeable to Nature in all points, diffused and spread in all Nations, consisting perpetually without abrogation'.[40]

Thus, while not particularly original in his reference to Cicero, Malynes provided one of the more comprehensive economic accounts of his time, demonstrating how recourse to natural law helped build his argument regarding the *lex mercatoria*. The importance Malynes attributed to the role of trust in his argument sheds an interesting light on the structural parallel between Malynes and Grotius' natural law argument. Malynes stressed the need to 'observe the difference between Lawes and Customes according to the description of the said worthy author *Cicero*'.[41] Custom evolves over time and by consent. It gradually gains in strength to oblige. In contrast, law is a command 'by absolute authority of a Prince'.[42] It could be expected, therefore, that law commands a greater force to oblige. But not so for Malynes, who stressed the importance of custom even more than Grotius had done. At the same time, we can detect a striking resonance of the natural law concept of *pacta sunt servanda*, emphasised by Cicero and Grotius alike: 'M. Tully attributes so great a Power to Promises that he calls faithfulness the Foundation of Justice' (DJBP 2.11.1.5). Malynes asserted that 'all agree that *bona fides inter mercatores est servanda*' (good faith needs to be kept among merchants).[43]

Craig Muldrew exaggerates the significance of trust and asserts that the market was not understood by 'contemporaries (...) through the use of a language which stressed self-interest, but rather one which stressed credit relations, trust, obligation and contracts'.[44] Nevertheless, discussion of trust played an important role in seventeenth-century discourses, in which Grotius played a vital part. Contemporary discussion questioned the role trust could play within political and commercial society. William Temple (1628–99), for instance, saw one essential reason for the success of the Dutch in the structures their state provided to safeguard trust: 'Trade cannot live without mutual trust among private Men; so it cannot grow or thrive, to any great degree, without a Confidence both of publick and private Safety, and consequently a Trust in the Government'.[45] Grotius had made a very similar argument before him, claiming that 'other nations may perhaps prove themselves a match to us in commercial shrewdness, but they will never equal us in justice' (DFP 171). We can see that trust was not the dominating concept shaping the political and economic debates in the seventeenth century. Rather it was articulated as a problem and placed within alternative concepts of which interest was certainly one. But, as Grotius as much as Temple were keen to demonstrate, true interest and trust might not have to be mutually exclusive. On the contrary, the interest of trade demanded conditions conducive to trust (DFP 171). Grotius praises the Dutch for their trustworthiness, not without turning this praise at the same time in polemical terms against the Spanish: 'we have earned ourselves a reputation with all nations, and indeed above all other nations. (...) including (...) those peoples, whom the Spanish, in blatant breach of the sacrosanct Law of Nations, have brought under their yoke – partly by surprise attack, partly under the pretence of commerce and with the help of sly fraud' (DFP 171). Trust can become instrumental in achieving political and economic aims.

5.5 Conclusion

When Grotius took up the natural law tradition and explored it further, he was heavily influenced by the Spanish Scholastics. Grotius' programme was bold: he aimed for a universal solution to the confessional and political problems of his time and suggested universally valid norms to achieve this ambitious aim. However, he was not naive and was well aware how complicated and volatile any pacification between warring parties would necessarily be, 'because in treating of a Peace it seldom happens, that either the one or the other of the Enemies owns that he had been in the wrong' (DJBP 3.20.11.2). Notwithstanding such caveats, Grotius believed that natural law provided a normative framework to regulate interstate relations and that it would work as the guiding principle for the conduct of interstate relations. Once – irrespective of Carneades and Machiavelli – such guiding principles were in place, it was – according to Grotius – also possible and reasonable that mutual trust between political adversaries and economic competitors would prevail, even in the international sphere, where there was no higher authority to decide conflicts. Trust was a prerequisite for pacifying warring Europe – the crucial question was how to provide conditions that would allow for trust between the antagonistic actors.

Editions and Translations of Grotius' Works Used

'De fide et perfidia', *Grotiana* 36 N.S. (2015) 106–71

The Rights of War and Peace, ed. R. Tuck (Natural Law and Enlightenment Classics; Indianapolis 2005)

Further Reading

Barducci, M., *Hugo Grotius and the Century of Revolution 1613–1718* (Oxford, 2017).

Blom, H., 'The meaning of trust: *fides* between self-interest and *appetitus societas*', in P.-M. Dupuy and V. Chetail (eds.), *The Roots of International Law/Les fondements du droit international. Liber Amicorum Peter Haggenmacher* (Leiden and Boston, 2014), 39–58.

Blom, H., 'Sociability and Hugo Grotius', *History of European Ideas* 41 (2015) 589–604.

Blom, H., 'Hugo Grotius on trust. Its causes and effects', in L. Kontler and M. Somos (eds.), *Trust and Happiness in the History of Political Thought* (Leiden and Boston, 2018), 76–98.

Boyer, A., *Chose Promise. Études sur la Promesse à partir de Hobbes et de quelques autres* (Paris, 2014).

Eyffinger, A., 'On good faith and bad faith: introductory note' in *Grotiana* N.S. 36 (2015) 79–105.

Fikentscher, W., *De fide et perfidia. Der Treuegedanke in den 'Staatsparallelen' des Hugo Grotius aus heutiger Sicht* (Munich, 1979).

Hartmann, M., *Die Praxis des Vertrauens* (Berlin, 2011).

Hartmann, M., 'On the concept of basic trust' in Behemoth. *A Journal on Civilisation* 8 (2015) 5–23.

Hinshelwood, B., 'Punishment and sovereignty in De Indis *and* De iure belli ac pacis' *in* Grotiana N.S. 38 (2017) 71–103.

Schröder, P., '*Sine fide nulla pax* - Überlegungen zu Vertrauen und Krieg in den politischen Theorien von Machiavelli, Gentili und Grotius', in M. Formisano and H. Böhme (eds.), *War in Words Transformations of War from Antiquity to Clausewitz* (Berlin, 2010), 37–60.

Schröder, P., *Trust in Early Modern International Political Thought, 1598–1713* (Cambridge, 2017).

Schröder, P., 'Fidem observandam esse - trust and fear in Hobbes and Locke', in L. Kontler nad M. Somos (eds.), *Trust and Happiness in the History of Political Thought* (Leiden and Boston, 2018), 99–117.

Straumann, B., *Roman Law in the State of Nature. The Classical Foundations of Hugo Grotius' Natural Law* (Cambridge, 2015).

Notes

1 See, in particular, H. Grotius, 'De fide et perfidia' in *Grotiana* N.S. 36 (2015) 106-71.

2 On this aspect, see M. Somos, 'Virtue' in this volume, as well as H. Blom, 'Sociability and Hugo Grotius' in *History of European Ideas* 41 (2015) 589-604 and H. Blom, 'Hugo Grotius on trust. Its causes and effects', in L. Kontler and M. Soms (eds.), *Trust and Happiness in the History of Political Thought* (Leiden and Boston, 2018), 76-98.

3 See P. Schröder, *Trust in Early Modern International Political Thought, 1598-1713* (Cambridge, 2017). The argument I develop here draws on this previous study of mine.

4 O. Lagerspetz, *Trust, Ethics and Human Reason* (London, 2015), 22-3.

5 Cicero, *On Duties 1.23*, eds. M.T. Griffin and E.M. Atkins (Cambridge 1991), 10.

6 See the discussion in R. Heinze, 'Fides' in R. Heinze, *Vom Geist des Römertums* (Darmstadt, 1960), 59-81; D. Nörr, *Die Fides im römischen Völkerrecht* (Heidelberg, 1991) and M. Hartmann, *Die Praxis des Vertrauens* (Berlin, 2011), 375-405.

7 See R.-P. Fuchs, 'Trust as a concept of religious plurality during the Thirty Years' War', in M. Kontler and M. Somos (eds.), *Trust and Happiness in the History of European Political Thought* (Leiden and Boston, 2018), 302-19.

8 For further discussion of this inter-confessional strife, see C. Boisen's Chapter 10 in this volume.

9 The argument is slightly more complex in Machiavelli and explicitly developed in the infamous chapter 18I of his *The Prince*. N. Machiavelli, *The Prince*, eds. Q. Skinner and R. Price (Cambridge, 2008), 61ff. P. Schröder, '*Sine fide nulla pax* – Überlegungen zu Vertrauen und Krieg in den politischen Theorien von Machiavelli, Gentili und Grotius', in M. Formisano and H. Böhme (eds.), *War in Words Transformations of War from Antiquity to Clausewitz* (Berlin, 2010), 37-60 and E. Benner, 'Natural suspicion and reasonable trust: Machiavelli on trust in politics' in L. Kontler and M. Somos (eds.), *Trust and Happiness in the History of European Political Thought* (Leiden and Boston, 2018), 53-75.

10 M. Kohn, *Trust. Self-Interest and the Common Good* (Oxford, 2008), 38.

11 See also W. Fikentscher, *De fide et perfidia. Der Treuegedanke in den 'Staatsparallelen' des Hugo Grotius aus heutiger Sicht* (Munich, 1979), 79: 'Grotius konnte den Treuegedanken als eine Grundlage des Völkerrechts (...) nehmen'.

12 On Carneades see R. Tuck, 'Grotius, Carneades and Hobbes' in *Grotiana* N.S. 4 (1983) 43-62; B. Straumann, '*Imperium sine fine*: Carneades, the splendid vice of glory and the justice of empire' in M. Koskenniemi, W. Rech and M. Jiménez Fonseca (eds.), *International Law and Empire: Historical Explorations* (Oxford, 2017), 335-58; B. Straumann, *Roman Law in the State of Nature. The Classical*

Foundations of Hugo Grotius' Natural Law (Cambridge, 2015), 55–98 and B. Straumann's Chapter 7 in this volume.

13 B. Kingsbury, 'Confronting Difference: The Puzzling Durability of Gentili's Combination of Pragmatic Pluralism and Normative Judgement', *American Journal of International Law* 92 (1998), 713–32, at 719.

14 P. Haggenmacher, 'Grotius and Gentili: a reassessment of Thomas E. Holland's inaugural lecture' in H. Bull, B. Kingsbury and A. Roberts (eds.), *Hugo Grotius and International Relations* (Oxford, 1990), 133–76, at 169. See with similar argumentation C. Schmitt, *The Nomos of the Earth in International Law of the Jus Publicum Europeum* (New York, 2003), 159–60.

15 See Schröder, *Trust*, 35–44.

16 Haggenmacher, 'Grotius and Gentili',172.

17 See Straumann, *Roman Law*, 39–40. This is controversially debated in the scholarship, see also Boisen's Chapter 10 in this volume.

18 See S. Kadelbach, 'Hugo Grotius: On the conquest of Utopia by systematic Rrasoning' in S. Kadelbach, T. Kleinlein and D. Roth-Isigkeit (eds.), *System, Order, and International Law. The Early History of International Legal Thought from Machiavelli to Hegel* (Oxford, 2017), 134–59, at 140–1. and J.B. Schneewind, *The Invention of Autonomy* (Cambridge, 1998), 66–75.

19 Brad Hinshelwood is situating Grotius' concept of punishment within the humanist and scholastic intellectual context. B. Hinshelwood, 'Punishment and sovereignty in *De Indis* and *De iure belli ac pacis*' in *Grotiana* N.S. 38 (2017) 71–105.

20 M. Barducci, *Hugo Grotius and the Century of Revolution 1613–1718* (Oxford, 2017), 160.

21 Hinshelwood, 'Punishment and sovereignty', 86.

22 See discussion in P. Schröder, 'Fidem observandam esse – trust and fear in Hobbes and Locke', in L. Kontler and M. Somos (eds.), *Trust and Happiness in the History of Political Thought* (Leiden and Boston, 2018), 99–117, at 114–7 and Barducci, *Hugo Grotius*, 167.

23 R. Tuck, *The Rights of War and Peace. Political thought and the international order from Grotius to Kant* (Oxford, 1999), 103.

24 See Kadelbach, 'Hugo Grotius', 138.

25 For the shift of emphasis, see the discussion by Hinshelwood, 'Punishment and sovereignty', 86–103.

26 Barducci, *Hugo Grotius*, 159.

27 Barducci, *Hugo Grotius*, 159.

28 A. Blom, 'Owing punishment: Grotius in right and merit' in *Grotiana* N.S. 36 (2015) 3–27.

29 I. Hont, *Jealousy of Trade. International Competition and the Nation-State in Historical Perspective* (Harvard, 2005), 15.

30 Hont, *Jealousy of Trade*, 15.

31 J. Wheeler, *A Treatise of Commerce* (London, 1601),13. See also J.-F. Melon, *Essai politique sur le commerce* (Paris, 1736), 8–9.

32 M. Koskenniemi, 'International Law and the emergence of mercantile capitalism', in P.-M. Dupuy and V. Chetail (eds.), *The Roots of International Law/Les fondements du droit international. Liber Amicorum Peter Haggenmacher* (Leiden and Boston, 2014), 3–37, at 26.

33 G. de Malynes, *The Maintenance of Free Trade* (London, 1622), 58.

34 J. Savary, *Le Parfait Negociant: ou Instruction générale pour ce qui regarde le commerce des marchandises de France, & des pays étrangers* (Paris, 1679), 114: 'les mauvais traitements que les Marchands François reçoivent en Angleterre'.

35 K. Stapelbroek, 'Trade, chartered companies and mercantile associations', in B. Fassbender and A. Peters (eds.), *The Oxford Handbook of the History of International Law* (Oxford, 2012), 338–58, at 352.

36 P. Bornier (ed.), *Conferences des nouvelles ordonnances de Louis XIV* (Paris, 1694), 376: 'assurer parmi les Negocians la bonne fois contre la fraude'.

37 G. Malynes, *Consuetudo, vel Lex Mercatoria, or the Antient Law-Merchant* (London, 1629), 2.

38 R. Baxter, *Chapters from A Christian Directory or A Summ of Practical Theology and Cases of Conscience*, ed. J. Tawney (London, 1925), 106.

39 C. Larrère, *L'Invention de l'économie au XVIIIe siècle. Du droit naturel à la physiocratie* (Paris, 1992), 95–6.

40 Malynes, *Consuetudo, vel Lex Mercatoria*, 3.

41 Malynes, *Consuetudo, vel Lex Mercatoria*, 4.

42 Malynes, *Consuetudo, vel Lex Mercatoria*, 4.

43 Malynes, *Consuetudo, vel Lex Mercatoria*, 93.

44 C. Muldrew, 'Interpreting the market: The ethics of credit and community relations in early modern England' in *Social History* 18 (1993) 163–83, 163.

45 W. Temple, *Observations upon the United Provinces of the Netherlands* (London, 1673), 214.

6   Natural Law as True Law

Meirav Jones

....

6.1 Introduction

Together with his reputation as 'father of modern international law', Hugo
Grotius is also considered the first modern natural law thinker.[1] That
Grotius took natural law in a new direction was first recognised in his
own time, when John Selden (1584–1654) wrote his major natural law
treatise referencing Grotius' innovation in 'our current age'; Samuel
Pufendorf (1632–94) commented on and took off from Grotius' innovation;
and Jean Barbeyrac (1674–1744) remarked that Grotius 'broke the ice' after
a long winter of Aristotelianism.[2] Grotius' break from scholastic natural law
has commonly been understood through his introduction of a secular
natural law theory at the onset of modernity, with his famous *'etiamsi
daremus'* statement that the principles of natural law would remain the
same even if we should imagine that there is no God or that the affairs of
humans are of no interest to him (DJBP Prol. 11).[3] But there has been so
little agreement on what exactly Grotius' break from scholasticism was,
and the image of Grotius as a secular thinker has been so far-fetched, that
some have concluded that there is no distinctly modern natural law.[4] This is
silently conceded by those who invoke Aquinas' typology in every discussion of natural law. It also reverberates in the writings of those who read
Grotius as transitioning natural law theory towards a doctrine of natural
rights, such that the natural law theory innovated by Grotius at the onset of
modernity is hardly natural law theory at all.[5]

The question of whether there is a modern natural law theory, properly
so named, beginning with Grotius, is an important one. It is equivalent to
the question whether political thinkers who conceived the modern state
and the modern world of states offered a normative standard embedded in
nature or human nature that is equally binding on all, irrespective of belief
or circumstance. Such a standard – an accessible common truth – could
contribute to our understanding of the historical foundations for the idea
of the International Rule of Law that is commonly appealed to today,

somewhat a-historically.[6] Scholars agree that Grotius begins those works in which he seeks a foundation for the laws regulating trade and warfare between nations by articulating a theory of natural law, which he describes as universally binding; as 'command'. The question whether a distinctly modern natural law exists boils down to the question whether Grotius offered anything new by way of a natural law that people and nations hold in common and that could thus regulate norms between states. Thomas Hobbes (1588–1679) famously found states to be in a perpetual state of nature, or war, but did Grotius offer an alternative approach?

With regard to this question, Anglo-American political theory seems often to answer 'no'. Richard Tuck's learned and influential work, which has emphasised the influence of neo-Stoicism on Grotius, has found Grotius' natural law to be normatively thin, amounting to affirming the normative value of the rights of states, such as a right to pre-emptive military strike.[7]

This chapter argues that Grotius does offer a true natural law theory throughout his works, from a different foundation to Hobbes' state of nature, which serves to ground politics in universally-accessible principles of justice that are built into the fabric of the created world. Other than taking sides in an existing debate about modern natural law,[8] the discussion below emphasises two related aspects of Grotius' natural law that have not yet been brought to bear on the discussion.

The first is the extent to which Grotius' understanding of natural law takes off not from a state of nature or from any circumstance imagined or real, but from an 'ordered plan of nature' that is also 'the very design of the creator' (DJPC 2, 5').[9] Readings of Grotius that emphasise the priority of the state of nature rather than the 'plan' or 'design' of nature, see Grotius in light of Hobbes, which is hardly appropriate given that the distance or closeness of Grotius to Hobbes is part of what is at stake. For Grotius, as will be demonstrated below, natural law, or the 'ordered plan of nature' that is also God's design, is prior to any state of nature.[10]

The second aspect of Grotius' work emphasised here is the extent to which his 'ordered plan of nature' introduces a classical approach to natural law into the modern West. This classical approach can be found in the work of Philo Judaeus and, by the time Grotius wrote *De jure belli ac pacis*, he recognised this. He extensively refers to *Philo* in *De jure belli ac pacis*, but, before he encountered *Philo,* he had already developed an approach that was more 'Philonic' than stoic or proto-Hobbesian. It was through this that Grotius positioned himself against Calvinism and broke away from scholasticism. This chapter addresses these aspects of Grotius' natural law in order to make sense of Grotius' statement that natural law is true law, with an independent and prior existence, and is accessible to humanity. While Grotius' natural law holds true for those who do not share his theology, even among sceptics, it does stem from a theology: a Platonic reading of Genesis and a Philonic understanding of the relationship of scripture to law.

Three sections follow. The first section describes Grotius' natural law as introduced in his early work, *De jure praedae commentarius*, where his ideas are considered more voluntarist than rationalist. The emphasis here is on Grotius' discussion of the 'ordered plan of nature', and how divine will, understood as revealed in creation, is considered natural law that is both God's manifest will and right reason. Also explored is how this idea positions Grotius vis-à-vis Calvinism, and the difference between taking this and taking the state of nature as a starting point for natural law. The second section traces the 'ordered plan of nature' in *De jure belli ac pacis*, where *Philo* becomes Grotius' first source for his definition and discussion of natural law. Through *Philo*, the chapter argues that voluntarism persists in the latter work, with will supplemented by and ultimately conforming to reason, such that rationalism and voluntarism coherently come together. The third section looks at how understanding Grotius' natural law as grounded in an ordered plan of nature, which is both divine will and reason manifest, offers a new perspective on Grotius' '*etiamsi daremus*' and on the appeal of his natural law.

6.2 Grotius' 'Ordered Plan of Nature' in *De Jure Praedae*

Grotius' earliest discussion of natural law appears in his first important entry into legal writing, *De jure praedae*. The work, authored in 1604, was not published in its entirety in Grotius' lifetime, though one of its chapters was published in 1609 as *Mare liberum*, presented as the Dutch Republic's case for free trade and navigation on the high seas. For writing *De jure praedae*, Grotius has been called an apologist for the Dutch East India Company (VOC) and, indeed, for war and plunder. There is good reason for this reading: the work was initially written as Grotius' response to a request that he write an apology for questionable plunder – even piracy – by Dutch ships. But Grotius' work went far beyond its commissioned purpose as the young scholar took it upon himself to clarify the universal legal foundations for such discussions. A letter written by Grotius in 1606 that mentions the work is telling:

The little treatise on Indian affairs is complete: but I do not know whether it should be published as it was written or only those parts which pertain to the universal law of war and booty ... I believe that new light can be thrown on the matter with a fixed order of teaching, the right proportion of divine and human law mixed together with the dictates of philosophy. (1 BW 72)[11]

Here, *De jure praedae* is read as an early work of political theory, or a 'fixed order of teaching' written by Grotius, to clarify the legal foundations for people and states to act beyond their borders and to right wrongs by force. The work opens with a meditation on the fact that the Dutch are so virtuous a people that they debate whether it is possible under any circumstances rightfully to despoil an enemy. Grotius sets out to clarify the moral law of nations, positing that this law rebukes not only one extreme form of action, greed or malice, but also an extreme in what might otherwise be considered virtue. War is sometimes commanded, and punishment must be exacted, for the sake of justice and good order. An Aristotelian just mean, a universal moral law, a right possessed by all peoples and the true character of piety according to Augustine are all invoked at the inception of the treatise and come together in a conception of natural law that does not forbid war or its consequences, but sets conditions to it.

Grotius first introduces natural law in a single paragraph in the fourth folio page of his introductory remarks. The paragraph opens with the phrase '[t]he ordered plan of nature to which I referred above'. The reference 'above' was to Lucretius, who a few paragraphs earlier was paraphrased to sustain Grotius' claim that the answer to the question whether or not war is lawful, even considering the 'ills which follow in its train' such as slaughter and plunder, should be derived by no other means but from 'the mien and ordered plan of nature'. To the 'ordered plan of nature' in the introduction, Grotius immediately adds Cicero's explanation. It is 'not written law, but the law sprung from nature'. Grotius then elaborates in the words of Sophocles: 'not those written laws, indeed, but the immutable laws of Heaven'. With the introduction of Baldus, this same law becomes the arbiter between claimants of sovereign power, only this time the judge is 'natural reason' (DJPC 1, 3'–4').

In a single introductory passage amounting to half a paragraph in *De jure praedae*, then, natural law – which is the standard by which the legality of actions should be judged – appears as the ordered plan of nature, 'sprung' from nature, equivalent to the immutable laws of heaven, discoverable by natural reason; and it is unwritten.

There is a hint here already to Grotius' break from scholastic natural law. In the scholastic scheme, the highest law by which other laws should be judged was eternal law. While not all of eternal law was accessible, natural law was the part of eternal law revealed to man through his reason, and divine law was the part of eternal law revealed to man in scripture. Civil law could be informed by both these laws, but was not ultimately limited by either. Grotius' introduction of natural law as 'the immutable laws of Heaven', planned by God and discoverable by reason, collapses the scholastic distinction between eternal law and natural law, as well as between divine will, which was the source of eternal and divine law, and reason, which was the source of natural law. The collapsing of distinctions in Grotius' natural law was to continue throughout Grotius' legal writings, where natural law consistently appears as the highest law and as eternal, true law. That Grotius uses a quote from Lactantius in his introduction to natural law is interesting; it is discussed below.

Grotius' introduction of natural law in *De jure praedae* is, one might argue, as interesting for what it leaves out as for what it includes. First, there is no 'state of nature'. Natural law does not emerge from a state of nature out of which men created sovereign states, but it does appear as prior to any state. It is a 'plan' authored by God according to his will, and willed into creation. As a plan it seems to have an independent existence, and the question of where or how it is to be recovered thus becomes central. Interestingly, where Richard Tuck quotes Grotius on the 'state of nature', the exact quote from Grotius' *De jure belli ac pacis* is 'in nature', which does not necessitate a state of nature, but may refer to the 'ordered plan'. A state of nature does appear in Grotius' text, as implied above, but it is not from this state that natural law is derived. Natural law existed prior; the question in the state of nature is about enforcement, not about the origin of the law. Natural law came from an 'ordered plan'. The Latin term is *ratio naturae*, such that order is reason,

reason behind nature, perhaps. Grotius proceeds, after his description of natural law as an ordered plan, to introduce different ways to recover natural law. He offers Cicero's approach, which is to look to the laws of war and peace, namely to pacts between peoples, kings and foreign tribes. Here Grotius relates agreements between diverse peoples to laws of nature, implying that there is a common denominator between peoples in God's plan that allows them to agree. This is a common theme throughout Grotius' works that generally seek peace and agreement by finding common ground.

Other than in agreement between nations, natural law is contained in 'holy writ', only that caution is necessary to make sure that the civil law of the Hebrews is distinguished from 'divine law' (DJPC 1, 4). Here divine law laid out in scripture is coextensive with natural law, collapsing another scholastic distinction. Grotius rejects the idea that the – Roman – Law of the Twelve Tables (c. 450 BCE) contain natural law, but proposes that it can be found in the 'inmost heart of philosophy', with the Bible as an aid. Grotius' own quest for natural law begins with reasoning from first principles and seeks confirmation of what is discovered by reason in scripture and in the approval of men of wisdom and nations of high repute (DJPC 1, 5). What he seeks when he seeks natural law is what is 'true universally'; a truth with independent and prior existence. There is no separate divine law or eternal law. Divine law is natural law, which is eternal.[12] Reason, scripture and agreement between men all help us arrive at this law, which is one.

We have already seen some of Grotius' argument with scholastic natural law, and if we consider the context in which Grotius wrote, we can discern that Grotius is also arguing with Calvinism and its idea of the Fall through which humans were cut off from access to divine will. Grotius insists that the eternal truth he seeks is both God's manifest will and is accessible to human reason in its own time. After writing that 'man's reason from God's reason takes its being', for which he cites Clement of Alexandria, Grotius writes:

To be sure, this rational faculty has been darkly beclouded by human vice; yet not to such a degree but that rays of the divine light are still clearly visible, manifesting themselves especially in the mutual accord of nations . . . (DJPC 2, 6')

Crucial to Grotius' account of the possibility of human access to God's plan for nature is his reading of the biblical creation narrative in the book of

Genesis. Nature, in Grotius' narrative, does not begin with chaos 'in the beginning' as does the biblical account (Genesis 1.1), nor with a lawless 'state of nature', but it rather begins with God's design and will. The fifth page of Grotius' introduction introduces 'natural properties' willed initially by God and becoming manifest in creation:

Therefore, since God fashioned creation and willed its existence, every individual part thereof has received from Him certain natural properties whereby that existence may be preserved. (DJPC 1, 5)

A few pages later, the second chapter of *De jure praedae*, the *Prolegomena*, opens with the following paragraph, further explaining Grotius' statement about God fashioning creation:

Where should we begin, if not at the very beginning? Accordingly, let us give first place and pre-eminent authority to the following rule: *What God has shown to be His Will, that is law.* This axiom points directly to the cause of law. (DJPC 2, 5-5')

Further, Grotius writes:

The Will of God is revealed, not only through oracles and supernatural portents, but above all in the very design of the Creator; for it is from this last source that the law of nature is derived. (DJPC 2, 5')

In these three proximate passages, natural law is God's design for the world; it is how he chose to fashion creation. The absence of chaos is striking. Prior to God's will there is nothing; the 'very beginning' is God's will. God's will is revealed to humans in nature; the created world and the natural properties of things in it.

In the following chapter, Grotius discusses human beings and their will and reason: as we saw in the first of the three quotes above, each created being has God's intention for it imprinted upon it by God at creation, and in the *Prolegomena* human beings are described as having more. They appear as 'representing the handiwork of God' (DJPC 3, 15-16'). Grotius brings in Epicharmus to explain the harmony of God's design with the collective reason of men, and so to the agreement between nations. 'Man's reason, from God's reason, takes its being.' (DJPC 2, 6'). This opens up, in Grotius' work, the relationship between natural law, human reason and the idea that man was created in the image of God. This is another theme that will connect Grotius' different writings on natural law.[13]

After the introduction and *Prolegomena* in *De jure praedae*, Grotius begins deriving rules and laws of nature from this premise. God designs the creation, which he wills into being, his design is its order or law and all things are designed to survive and to sustain themselves within this order. People thus defend themselves and others, acquire things that are useful to life, protect their gains and the gains of others, set up and maintain states to protect life and gains, and more; all flowing from natural law, which derives from God's will imprinted onto creation. While Grotius lays out nine rules – eight of which pertain to will as constitutive and the ninth to a question of adjudication – and thirteen laws of nature deriving from constitutive will, ultimately the rules and laws seem less important than the method. This method is to expand from the axiom of God's creation at will the principle that will constitutes law, the embeddedness of natural law in the order of the created world to which man has access, and the divine and immutable nature of natural law that returns to its origins (DJPC 2, 6'–14).

From the centrality of will as a constitutive faculty, we can see how *De jure praedae* would be read as a voluntarist approach to natural law. It is crucial, however, to understand that this will is not contrasted with reason, but with purposelessness or chaos, whose absence from Grotius' narrative compared with its presence in Genesis is striking. It is also contrasted with arbitrariness, and with inaccessible eternal law. The relationship between will and reason is not entirely clear, but these themes are continued and clarified in *De jure belli ac pacis*.

The limits of this chapter do not permit us to trace natural law throughout *De jure praedae*, but it is worth looking, as a way of summarising the discussion, at one instance of Grotius' use of natural law in his discussion of private property. Grotius argues that, while there may not have been property, properly speaking, at the earliest stages of human history, yet the establishment of a law on the matter was 'patterned after nature's plan', and that it followed a 'gradual process whose initial steps were taken under the guidance of nature herself' (*De jure praedae* 12, 101–1'). This returns to the centrality of the 'ordered plan of nature' that provides a pattern according to which human behaviour should be fashioned. The ordered plan becomes the foundation from which the rule of law among people and nations is derived.

6.3 *De Jure Belli ac Pacis* and Grotius' Turn to Philo

There are differences between the lists of natural laws Grotius set out in *De jure belli ac pacis* and *De jure praedae*. Yet arguably more interesting than the distinct laws listed is the apparent discrepancy in how natural law is defined in the different texts.

In *De jure belli ac pacis*, Grotius defines natural law thus:

> The law of nature is a dictate of right reason, which points out that an act, according as it is or is not in conformity with rational nature, has in it a quality of moral baseness or moral necessity; and that, in consequence, such an act is either forbidden or enjoined by the author of nature, God. (DJBP 1.1.10.1)

This definition is in reverse order to the definition in *De jure praedae,* which began with God authoring nature according to his will. Some scholarship on Grotius has found that his natural law in the later treatise is not only more rationalist than in the older one, but that natural law is also prior to God, as though God approves natural law because it is morally good rather than that it is morally good because God willed it. That the definition begins with reason seems to support this approach. But now that we have seen that natural law in *De jure praedae* was *ratio naturae*, the ordered plan of nature willed by God and, indeed, the reason in or behind nature, are these definitions in fact distinct? Did Grotius change his approach in *De jure belli ac pacis* to prefer reason over will?

If we read the text of *De jure belli ac pacis* with this question in mind, there is evidence that Grotius did not change his approach. Rather, Grotius' introduction of a non-scholastic, non-biblical and non-Roman source into his natural law theory may be read as harmonising his conception of reason in the second work with his conception of will in the first.

The source is Philo Judaeus, who is cited 114 times in the 1625 edition of *De jure belli ac pacis* and is mentioned as the first source for Grotius' definition of natural law as right reason. Philo lends Grotius' natural law theory in his later work a richness of content and resources, grounding the theory that Grotius had already developed in *De jure praedae* in a textual resource that is both ancient and thus appealing to the humanist, and also perceived as Jewish, such that it brings Grotius' work into a rising Hebraic discourse in seventeenth-century political theory.[14]

Before entering into Philo's natural law and its contribution to Grotius' work, it is worth considering why Philo does not appear in *De jure praedae*.

It seems that Grotius had not read Philo's works, at least not first hand, when he wrote this early work. Philo is absent from all Grotius' works until 1617, even though more than just his natural law theory could have benefited from such reading. His agenda of harmonising different religions through a lowest common denominator in *Meletius*,[15] and his presentation of the Hebrew republic as a model polity in *De republica emendanda*, could have been enriched by Philo's works, as were Jean Bodin's (1530–96) harmonising *Colloquium Heptaplomeres*[16] and Carlo Sigonio's (1524–84) *De republica Hebraeorum*.[17] The first references to Philo in Grotius' writing are in *De imperio summarum potestatum circa sacra*, which was completed in 1617, but which was, like *De jure praedae*, not published during Grotius' lifetime.[18] There is also a letter in Grotius' correspondence, to Gerardus Vossius (1577–1649), dated 28 July 1618, which opens with 'When I got to Rotterdam I looked at Philo' (1 BW 579). We can thus date Grotius' encounter with Philo to between 1613, when Grotius was appointed as pensionary of Rotterdam, and 1617. The fact that Grotius cited Philo far more extensively in *De jure belli ac pacis* than in *De imperio* might be explained by Grotius finding Philo relevant to his natural law theory. With the extensive word-for-word passages from Philo in *De jure belli ac pacis*, it seems that Grotius must have had at least some of Philo's texts with him while writing. However, considering his apologies for quoting long passages only in Latin, perhaps he did not have the text in Greek (DJBP Prol. 6 n. 1).

   To appreciate the fit between Grotius' early natural law thinking and that of Philo, a brief sketch of Philo's natural law theory is in order:[19] According to Philo, before God created the world, he made a blueprint for the world. This blueprint, which God willed into his mind (*logos*) was natural law.[20] This law was then copied in three ways into the world. The first copy was the creation of the world itself, which was created according to the blueprint, with as many kinds and types in the world as in God's mind.[21] The second copy was in the mind of original men, who were given a perfect copy of God's *logos;* this is what it means for man to have been created in God's image, as the entire world was really in the image of God's mind.[22] The third copy was the Torah – the five books of Moses; the first five books of the Hebrew Bible. Notably, not all of the Torah is law, for Philo, but rather the Torah *contains* the law.[23] At the same time, the fact that the Torah begins with creation is more than symbolic. Moses' legislative genius was in the law beginning with creation and creation beginning with the law, with law being eternal and unchanging since creation.[24] Philo goes into detail about the fact that miracles are part of God's plan rather than spontaneous occurrences of divine intervention, and they are hence part of nature properly understood.

Already in this very succinct account we find in Philo's natural law a theory that begins with God and his 'ordered plan of nature' willed into the world, corresponding to Grotius' beginning with God and with creation in *De jure praedae*. Like Grotius' natural law, Philo's natural law was legislated by divine will, inherent to the world, and discoverable by reason and scripture. We find reverence for the Torah, which begins with creation, and we recall Grotius' opening of the *Prolegomena* 'where should we begin, if not at the very beginning?' Opening the law with creation was considered by Philo a stroke of genius on the part of Moses the lawgiver. Grotius might have agreed. Further, just as in Grotius' account in *De jure praedae*, 'man's reason from God's reason takes its being'.[25]

Now that Philo's natural law has been reviewed, it is possible to consider whether and how Grotius draws on him for his later work, which takes reason as the starting point for his theory of natural law. Philo is the first source referred to when Grotius defines natural law as 'right reason', thus giving Grotius' 'ordered plan of nature' willed into the world by God a textual foundation, which was lacking in his earlier work. In fact, Philo's focus on creation as the source of order in the world, as human reason modelled on God's reason, and also the Hebrew Bible containing natural law, were all elements of Grotius' natural law in his voluntarist account in *De jure praedae*. When Philo is cited in *De jure belli ac pacis*, elements of voluntarism are coherently incorporated into Grotius' more rationalist account.

There are two questions that could be raised about Grotius' early theory that Philo helps resolving. The first is the question of why Grotius employs aids other than reason to attain natural law if natural law is accessibly by reason? Grotius seems to have become more comfortable with reason in *De jure belli ac pacis* than he was in *De jure praedae*, but even in the early work he expressed the idea that natural law is accessible to reason while still looking to other sources. According to Philo, the reason conferred on original humans required assistance because of the deterioration of reason over time. This fits both Grotius' reading in *De jure praedae* and his opposition to Calvinism; Grotius finds natural law accessible even after the Fall, but also acknowledges that reason had become somewhat clouded. By consequence, the mutual accord of nations was a better guide to natural law than individual reason in this time. Interestingly, in *De jure belli ac pacis*, where Grotius seems to feel more comfortable with reason, he turns to more, not fewer, sources to confirm his reading of natural law.

The second question is how, if natural law is unwritten law and eternal – God's plan for the world in all places and times, could it be contained within the limited words of a text? For Philo, the question is how natural law could be contained in the limited text of the Torah. The answer Philo gives is that the Torah contains within it the lives of the Patriarchs, including Adam, Noah, Abraham, Isaac, Jacob, Joseph and Moses, all of whom received perfect copies of God's *logos*. Where the Patriarchs are in the text, so are the infinite possibilities contained in their *logos*, which can be better understood by submitting oneself to truly understanding the Patriarchs within the text and their more extensive – even infinitely extensive – minds.[26] The Torah thus has a Trojan horse within, containing in writing that which necessarily cannot be contained in writing, so that when one reads what is written within the text he or she is taken beyond, to infinite possibilities that emerge from studying the lives of the Patriarchs.

The Trojan horse is used by Grotius, even before he encounters Philo, in two ways. First, like Philo, he – in *De jure praedae* – appeals to the biblical 'fathers', and particularly to Abraham whom he discusses fifteen times in the text, studying his behaviour and seeking natural law through interpreting it. Grotius justifies this explicitly:

For, assuming that the actions of just men are properly regarded as just – in other words, assuming that example is of paramount importance in the decision of all questions – I shall cite the following sources: the age when men lived under the guidance of nature, which supplies the example of the warring Abraham; the [Old] Law itself, which gives us Moses and David as examples; New Testament history ... (DJPC 3, 19)

Where Grotius discusses Abraham's behaviour as example, extrapolating natural law from his way of life, he cites not only Greek sources but also Ambrose, who together with Clement of Alexandria – also cited by Grotius throughout his works – is famous for having preserved Philo's writings.[27] Grotius' proximity to Philo may be explained by his first- or second-hand familiarity with patristic sources that brought Philo into Christian thought – in the discussion of *De jure praedae* above we saw Lactantius and Clement of Alexandria appear in Grotius' definitions – by his familiarity with sources that contain ideas similar to those of Philo, such as

Theophilus, or by the fact that he was a student of Joseph Scaliger (1540–1609), who had studied Philo.[28]

Other than turning to the lives of the 'biblical fathers' as Philo did, Grotius had his own method of extending his writing on natural law beyond that which can be encapsulated in a body of written work. After all, Grotius emphasised in *De jure praedae* that natural law is unwritten law, and even as one commits its precepts to writing, natural law remains unwritten. Grotius' method is not to provide a single exhaustive set of laws, but rather a starting point and a methodology that could allow natural laws to be derived as required. For Grotius, like for Philo, natural law cannot be contained in limited words, and he comments on the limitations of language numerous times. We can understand the discrepancy between the list of natural laws provided in Grotius' different texts in this light, as no text should be expected to contain natural law, which is as extensive as God's plan for nature, but natural law can be recovered by starting from sound principles, making deductions with reason and confirming it through additional sources.

To sum up, we have found that, while in *De jure praedae JPC* Grotius' natural law is legislated by an act of God's will at creation, in *De jure belli ac pacis* reason seems to come first. But in citing Philo as his first source for his definition of natural law as right reason, Grotius brings Philo's natural law, which has the same volitional starting point as the definition from *De jure praedae*, back into the later text.[29] In both texts, through Philo, God wills natural law into the fabric of creation. There is nothing prior to the law, which is God's design, and nothing above it. It is eternal and unchanging, there to be recovered as needed.

6.4 Grotius' *Etiamsi Daremus* and True Law

Until now, God has been present in Grotius' conception of natural law, and this dimension was strengthened by the reference to Philo, whose works were preserved by the Church Fathers. Yet, there are two statements in *De jure belli ac pacis* that are often mentioned as evidence of Grotius' secularism and the absence of God from his natural law theory. These seem to run against the account here. The first of these statements, from the *Prolegomena*, has become known as Grotius' '*etiamsi daremus*' or his 'impious hypothesis':[30]

What we have been saying would have a degree of validity even if we should concede that which cannot be conceded without the utmost wickedness, that there is no God, or that the affairs of men are of no concern to him. (DJBP Prol. 11)

The second statement is from the first chapter of the treatise:

The law of nature, again, is unchangeable – even in the sense that it cannot be changed by God. Measureless as is the power of God, nevertheless it can be said that there are certain things over which that power does not extend … Just as even God, then, cannot cause that two times two should not make four, so He cannot cause that which is intrinsically evil be not evil. (DJBP 1.1.10.5)

If the account presented here has been correct that natural law for Grotius is not derived from an imagined state of nature, but from an understanding of an order in nature, designed and willed into the world by God, then it is important to consider these passages together in order to understand what role denying God or limiting God's power played in Grotius' natural law thinking. Is Grotius siding with the sceptics or showing them sympathy, is he being ironic, or is there some other role these statements play? Can these passages even be read in line with the account presented here?

Grotius' first 'impious hypothesis' appears after he spends the first pages of his treatise deriving natural law from reason alone, without mentioning the will of God. After his 'impious hypothesis', Grotius writes that the reason with which we are able to access natural law even in the absence of God derives from God's role in establishing natural law in the world and the fact that he willed these traits in humans that allow them access. There seems to be a contradiction within this statement, but this can be cleared up with the account presented above. If we reverse the order from *De jure belli ac pacis*, God wills the traits into man, which allow him to access natural law. Subsequently, irrespective of whether man believes in God or not, he is able to understand natural law. Grotius' impious hypothesis does not involve the denial that there is order in the world, nor that God created the world with this order in it, but it rather affirms that in this world the order is true irrespective of one's belief. This allows Grotius' natural law to hold true across belief systems, and even among sceptics. This is important particularly in *De jure belli ac pacis*, written to ground a system of law among nations. In the created world, Grotius tells his readers, there is an accessible order; a truth behind nature. Whether or not we agree on the source or origin of the order, we have access to it, just as we have access to the axioms of mathematics.

It is interesting to consider here that Grotius includes the possibility of atheists among those who share in natural law. Hobbes would disagree. For him, natural law is only law, properly so named, when it is considered to have been legislated by God.[31] Grotius seems to be saying that natural law is truth, and access to truth does not require belief in God. Of course, Grotius was a Christian, but he portrays Christian religion not as 'truth' but as 'perfection', (DJBP 1.1.17) whereas he builds political society on truth.

Grotius' second statement that seems to remove God from the equation confirms this reading of '*etiamsi daremus*'. The second statement effectively means that, after creation, God does not alter – and cannot alter – such laws as he initially created in the world. Two times two is four, irrespective of anything God might do. God is, in relation to natural law, irrelevant once the world and its inherent order exists as he willed it to exist.[32] This raises the question of miracles. When Grotius writes that God cannot make intrinsic evil into something good, or make two times two not equal four, he is saying that miracles, as transgressions of the order of nature, do not occur in the created world. Philo's position was that, when we seem to see a miracle, it must be a natural occurrence we have misunderstood. Understood correctly, nothing in the created world transgresses natural law. Even God cannot transgress natural law because it is already manifest in the world. It is so because God willed it, but once created, nature runs according to plan. This is Grotius' position, too.

What role, then, does the hypothetical denial of God's existence or of his power in the world play in Grotius' natural law theory? It strengthens the claim for the truth of natural law, irrespective of beliefs. When Grotius asks his readers to consider that, even if we imagine God not to exist, natural law does not change, he speaks to the absolute nature of God's initial, including both the order willed into the world, and the traits willed into the human mind 'at the beginning'. Creation, in the image of God's plan, becomes truth. Just as two times two equals four, natural law is true law, irrespective of belief.

Returning to the question of this chapter whether Grotius offers a natural law properly so named, a normative standard embedded in nature or human nature that is equally binding on all, irrespective of belief or circumstance law, we are now in a position to answer in the affirmative, with all this implies for the history and foundations – not entirely secular or entirely religious, not entirely volitional or entirely rational – of international law. Natural law, for Grotius, is true law.

Translations of Grotius' Works Used

De Jure Praedae Commentarius: Commentary on the Law of Prize and Booty, transl. Gwladys L. Williams and Walter H. Zeydel (Oxford, 1950)

Further Reading

d'Entreves, A.P., *Natural Law: An Introduction to Legal Philosophy* (London, 1970 [1951]).

Jones, M., 'Philo Judaeus and Hugo Grotius's Modern Natural Law', *Journal of the History of Ideas* 74:3 (2013) 339–60.

Koester, H., 'Nomos Phuseos: the concept of natural law in Greek thought', in J. Neusner (ed.), *Religions in Antiquity: Essays in Memory of Erwin Ramsdell Goodenough* (Leiden, 1968).

Nijman, J.E., 'Images of Grotius, or the international rule of law, beyond historiographical oscillation', *Journal of the History of International Law* 17 (2015) 83–137.

Nijman, J.E., 'Grotius' imago dei anthropology: grounding jus naturae et gentium', in M. Koskenniemi, M. García-Salmones Rovira and P. Amorosa (eds.), *International Law and Religion: Historical and Contemporary Perspectives* (Oxford, 2017) 87–110.

Oakley, F. *Natural Law, Laws of Nature, Natural Rights: Continuity and Discontinuity in the History of Ideas* (New York, 2005).

Runia, D.T., 'Philo of Alexandria and the Beginnings of Christian Thought, Alexandrian and Jew', *Studia Philonica Annual* 7 (1995) 143–60.

Tuck, R. *Natural Rights Theories; Their Origin and Development* (Cambridge, 1979).

Tuck, R., *Philosophy and Government: Philosophy and Government, 1572–1651* (Cambridge, 1993).

Notes

1 K. Haakonsen, 'Hugo Grotius and the history of political thought' *Political Theory* 13 (1985) 239–65, at 239.

2 J. Selden, *De jure naturali et gentium juxta disciplinam Hebraeorum libri septem* (London, 1640) 1.2, 34–5; 1.10, 125; A.P. d'Entreves, *Natural Law: An Introduction to Legal Philosophy* (London, 1970 [1951]), 51–3; S. Pufendorf, *Specimen controversiarum circa jus naturale ipsi nuper motarum* (Uppsala, 1678); R. Tuck, *Philosophy and Government: Philosophy and Government, 1572–1651* (Cambridge, 1993), xv.

3 D'Entreves called Grotius' natural law a 'purely rational construction' in D'Entreves, *Natural Law*, 55. See also C. Courtney, 'Montesquieu and natural

law', in D.W. Carrithers, P.A. Rahe and M.A. Mosher (eds.), *Montequieu's Science of Politics* (Lanham, MD, 2001), 42.

4 F. Oakley, *Natural Law, Laws of Nature, Natural Rights: Continuity and Discontinuity in the History of Ideas* (New York: Continuum, 2005), 64–7. In this respect, Oakley echoes D'Entreves, *Natural Law*, 53–4.

5 This is the position of R. Tuck, *Natural Rights Theories: Their Origin and Development* (Cambridge, 1979), 58–81, at 67–8.

6 J.E. Nijman, 'Images of Grotius, or the international rule of law, beyond historiographical oscillation', *Journal of the History of International Law* 17 (2015) 83–137, at 83–5.

7 Richard Tuck's works are, at the time of this publication, among the most cited – even popular – English-language works on Grotius, indicating the extent to which these works set the tone for how Grotius is commonly understood by scholars and students. Tuck's *Philosophy and Government*, relied on here, was part of the revival of interest in Grotius in recent decades, and has been cited 928 times to date according to a Google scholar search conducted on 13 February 2021. Articles and books presenting alternative approaches such as *Grotius and the Stoa* (Assen, 2004); T. Mautner, 'Grotius and the skeptics', *Journal of the History of Ideas* 66:4 (2005) 577–601 and R. Shaver, 'Grotius on scepticism and self-interest', *Archivfiir Geschichte der Philosophie* 78 (1996) 24–47, are significantly less well-known. Yet, the fact that leading Grotius scholars have contributed to scholarship that questions and offers a nuanced account of Grotius' relationship to stoicism is important.

8 Nijman, 'Images of Grotius'.

9 The English phrase 'ordered plan of nature' appears in the standard English translation of the 1604 manuscript of *De jure praedae* referenced here, to translate *ratio naturae*. The translation does not appear in Tuck's work, but appears in that of Martin van Gelderen. See M. van Gelderen, 'Aristotelians, monarchomachs and republicans: sovereignty and respublica mixta in Dutch and German political thought, 1580–1650', in M. van Gelderen and Q. Skinner (eds.), *Republicanism: A Shared European Heritage, Vol. 1: Republicanism and Constitutionalism in Early Modern Europe* (Cambridge, 2002) 195–217, at 201; M. van Gelderen, 'Contested kingship: conceptions of monarchy and civil power in Spanish and Dutch political thought, 1555–1598' in J. Martínez Millán (ed.), *Felipe II. Europa y la Monarquia Católica* (Madrid, 1998), 365–77, at 373.

10 Benjamin Straumann pointed out the difference between Grotius' and Hobbes' states of nature, where for Grotius it is 'essentially a legal condition, where the norms of natural law are enforced by the holders of subjective natural claim-rights', so that natural law was prior to the state of nature. B. Straumann, 'Ancient caesarian Lawyers in a state of nature: Roman tradition and natural rights in Hugo Grotius's *De Iure Praedae*', *Political Theory* 34 (2006) 328–50, at 329.

11 Hugo Grotius to G. M. Lingelsheim, 1 November 1606. Translation from Hugo Grotius, *Commentary On the Law of Prize and Booty*, ed. M.J. Van Ittersum

(Indianapolis 2006), 'Appendix 2: Archival documents relating to *De Jure Praedae,* transl. M.J. Van Ittersum', xiii.

12 That divine and natural law are coextensive is repeated by Grotius numerous times. See, for example, DJPC 3, 15': 'warfare is compatible with divine law, that is to say, with the law of nature and the law of nations … ' If Grotius continues to use the different categories of divine law and eternal law alongside natural law, this seems to reaffirm that, for Grotius, these categories of divine, natural and eternal law are not distinct and do not exist in separate realms he doesn't touch on, but are different names for the one law he does extensively discuss.

13 On the image of God in Grotius' work, see J.E. Nijman, 'Grotius' imago dei anthropology: grounding jus naturae et gentium', in M. Koskenniemi, M. García-Salmones Rovira and P. Amorosa (eds.), *International Law and Religion: Historical and Contemporary Perspectives* (Oxford, 2017), 87–110.

14 It is beyond the scope of this chapter that Grotius considered Philo a Jewish source. On this, see M. Jones, 'Philo Judaeus and Hugo Grotius's Modern Natural Law', *Journal of the History of Ideas* 74 (2013) 339–60. This article also offers more on the Hebraic context of Grotius' work.

15 Grotius, *Meletius* (1611).

16 J. Bodin, *Colloquium heptaplomeres de rerum sublimium arcanis abditis* (Manuscript, ca. 1588); Jean Bodin, *The Colloquium of the Seven About Secrets of the Sublime,* ed. and transl. M. Leathers Kuntz (Princeton, 1975).

17 C. Sigonio, *The Hebrew Republic* (Jerusalem, 2010). This work, initially published in 1582, contains forty-two references to Philo, according to the Index of the modern edition.

18 In his introduction to the Latin-English edition of *De imperio*, Harm-Jan Van Dam speculates that Grotius read or reread large parts of Philo and Josephus for this work. He notes that, before 1616, references to these authors were rare in Grotius' work. Josephus is cited extensively in *DJP*, while Philo is not cited. See Harm-Jan Van Dam, 'Introduction', in H. Grotius, *De imperio summarum postestatum circa sacra: Critical Edition with Introduction, English Translation, and Commentary* (2 vols., Leiden, 2001) 112 n. 5 and 113.

19 References to Philo are to the *Loeb Classical Library: Philo Judaeus*, transl. F.H. Colson and G.H. Whitaker (11 vols., London, 1929–62). Henceforth, Philo. Numbers refer to section and paragraph numbers in the Greek.

20 *De Opificio Mundi (On The Creation of the World), in Philo,* vol. 1 (henceforth *Opif.*) 6.25.

21 *Opif.* 4.16.

22 *Opif.* 23.69. As man's mind is a copy of God's mind, man's rest from creative work is parallel to God's rest from creative work, making the Sabbath part of the natural order for Philo. This fits with Grotius' understanding in DJBP that Christians are to set aside no more than a seventh of their time for divine worship and a tenth of their income for the support of ministers and similar pious uses, DJBP 1.1.9, 3.14.545.

23 Philo, *De Vita Mosis II* (*On the life of Moses II*), in Philo, Vol. 6 (henceforth *Mos. II*) 8.46–8.

24 Philo, *Opif.*, 1.3.

25 See note 11 above.

26 H. Najman, 'A written copy of the law of nature: an unthinkable paradox?', *Studia Philonica Annual* 15 (2003) 55–73.

27 The patristic context of Grotius' writings is beyond the realm of this chapter. On this see S.P. Bergjan, 'The patristic context in early Grotius', in H. Blom (ed.), *Property, Piracy and Punishment: Hugo Grotius on War and Booty in De iure praedae: Concepts and Contexts* (Leiden, 2009), 127–46, esp. 142ff. where Bergjan discusses Ambrose as a source for Grotius' discussion for Abraham.

28 For Philo in early Christian sources see D.T. Runia, 'Philo of Alexandria and the beginnings of Christian thought, Alexandrian and Jew', *Studia Philonica Annual* 7 (1995) 143–60. For Scaliger's familiarity with Philo, see A. Grafton, 'Joseph Scaliger et l'histoire du Judaïsme Hellénistique', in C. Grell and F. Laplanche (eds.), *La république des lettres et l'histoire de Judaïsme antique, XVIe-XVIIe siècles* (Paris, 1992), 51–63.

29 In light of Philo, differences between the 1625 edition and 1631 editions of DJBP are less dramatic than suggested in R. Tuck, *The Rights of War and Peace: Political Thought and the International Order from Grotius to Kant* (Oxford, 1999), 100–1. A passage that changes from 'proceeding from nature itself or introduced by custom and tacit agreement … ' to 'proceeding from nature itself, or established by divine laws, or introduced by custom and tacit agreement … ' changes only to specify what should have been obvious in the early account, that nature is established by divine laws.

30 D'Entreves, *Natural Law*, 55; Courtney, 'Montesquieu and Natural Law', 42.

31 Thomas Hobbes, *Leviathan, or, The Matter, Forme, and Power of a Common Wealth, Ecclesiasticall and Civil* (London, 1651) 1.15, 38.

32 In a letter to his brother from 1638, defending God's free will despite his statements in DJBP, Grotius wrote: 'God was at full liberty not to create man. The moment he is determined to create man, that is, a nature endowed with reason, and formed for a society of an excellent kind, he necessarily approves of such actions as are suitable to that nature, and as necessarily disapproves of those which was contrary to it.' Letter to William De Groot, 21 May 1638, 9 BW 3586. Translation from Tuck, *Natural Rights Theories*, 76.

Benjamin Straumann

7.1 Introduction

The idea of sociability plays an important role in Hugo Grotius' system of natural law. As we shall see, Grotius adopted an account of moral knowledge and motivation for justice that he found in Cicero, an account that allowed him to connect arguments about self-interest with sociability and ideas concerning natural law. While ultimately Stoic in origin, this Romanised account Grotius used offered some advantages over the Greek Stoic view connected to the doctrine of *oikeiosis*. Unlike the Greek Stoic view, Grotius' Ciceronian account was not teleological or eudaemonist, but made room for a legalised, rule-based doctrine of natural law.

The second section of this chapter shows that, for Grotius, sociability is intended as a counter to Epicurean views of moral motivation, but it does not by itself provide the grounds of validity of natural law, nor does it alone ground the obligatory force of natural law. Rather, it represents an appeal to a basis in human nature for cooperation in the state of nature. This simply allows for the weak claim that human beings could possibly be motivated to cooperate and adhere to the rules of natural law, not that they necessarily are so motivated. But, more importantly, Grotius appreciated that sociability creates its own problems, which he thought could be solved by reason alone.

The third section explains that the basis of sociability in human nature is, for Grotius, not merely instinctual, but also rational; sociability is ultimately based on a respect for the rights to 'first things' such as private property, a respect that itself is motivated by right reason. But, this view of sociability makes Grotius shift from an original concern with our *motivation* for justice to a concern with how we can *know* what is just. By way of conclusion, it is argued that the notion of sociability was to have an important future in the works of later thinkers such as Thomas Hobbes (1588–1679), Samuel Pufendorf (1632–94), Anthony Ashley Cooper, Earl Shaftesbury (1671–1713), Bernard Mandeville (1670–1733), Francis

Hutcheson (1694–1746), David Hume (1711–76), Adam Smith (1723–90) and Immanuel Kant (1724–1804).

7.2 Countering Carneades' Scepticism

Grotius motivated his inquiry into natural law and the law of nations in the *Prolegomena* to his *De jure belli ac pacis* by reference to those who have doubted the very existence of such a law: 'And indeed this Work is the more necessary, since we find some, both in this and in former Ages, so far despising this Sort of Right, as if it were nothing but an empty Name' (DJBP Prol. 3). After giving examples of authors who voiced such doubt, Grotius goes on to say that

> since it would be a vain Undertaking to treat of Right, if there is really no such thing; it will be necessary, in order to shew the Usefulness of our Work, and to establish it on solid Foundations, to confute here in a few Words so dangerous an Error. And that we may not engage with a Multitude at once, let us assign them an Advocate. (DJBP Prol. 5)

The advocate Grotius chooses is the ancient Greek sceptic, Carneades, who, Grotius knows, had argued against the very existence of justice and especially that kind of justice that is Grotius' subject in the *De jure belli ac pacis*. According to Grotius, Carneades' strongest argument was this:

> Laws [*iura*] were instituted by Men for the sake of Interest; and hence it is that they are different, not only in different Countries, according to the Diversity of their Manners, but often in the same Country, according to the Times. As to that which is called Natural Right [*ius naturale*], it is a mere Chimera. Nature prompts all Men, and in general all Animals, to seek their own particular Advantage: So that either there is no Justice at all, or if there is any, it is extreme Folly, because it engages us to procure the Good of others, to our own Prejudice. (DJBP Prol. 5)[1]

Carneades had argued that normative or legal orders (*jura*) merely reflected calculations of interest or utility (*utilitas*), not justice. This is why these calculations of utility result in legal arrangements that are parochial; they are merely local customs and do not reflect any universal propositions of justice. But, Carneades adds as a second claim that it is foolish to be just. At first, there seems to be a tension between the two claims: if the local legal orders reflect calculations of interest, and if this is all there is to justice, how can it at the same time be foolish to be just? As Terence Irwin points out, however, this need not amount to an inconsistency. Carneades should simply be interpreted as saying that legal orders reflect the interest or advantage of the *societies* within which they hold, while it would be foolish from the point of view of any given *individual* to orient himself toward his society's interest, since doing so can be harmful to the individual.[2] Carneades bases his view on a certain anthropology – human beings are no different from other animals in being naturally self-interested. From this descriptive account, Carneades draws a strong normative conclusion: humans have reason to behave in a way consistent with this egoistic anthropology. Breaking the rules that ensure the advantage of a society can be entirely rational for the individual, and adhering to them is irrational, provided that punishment can be escaped. The sophistic views advanced by Glaucon in the second book of Plato's *Republic* loom large.

Grotius responds to Carneades by challenging his anthropological assumptions. Human beings, Grotius holds, unlike other animals, have a strong desire for society. They also have the ability to design peaceful cooperation in society according to reason and so to satisfy their desire for sociability in ways that are suitable to their rational nature. Grotius replies to Carneades thus:

Man is indeed an Animal, but one of a very high Order, and that excels all the other Species of Animals much more than they differ from one another; as the many Actions proper only to Mankind sufficiently demonstrate. Now amongst the Things peculiar to Man, is his Desire of Society [*appetitus societatis*], that is, a certain Inclination to live with those of his own Kind, not in any Manner whatever, but peaceably, and in a Community regulated according to the best of his Understanding; which Disposition the Stoicks termed Oikei/wsin [*oikeiosis*]. Therefore the Saying, that every Creature is led by Nature to seek its own private Advantage [*ad suas utilitates*], expressed thus universally, must not be granted. (DJBP Prol. 6)

Before we proceed, we should discuss a few of the issues this answer to Carneades raises. First of all, both Carneades and Grotius start from what they take to be natural human inclination. Why should this inclination have any normative implications; why, that is, should it be possible to draw from a descriptive account of inclinations any normative conclusions? It is clear from Grotius' allusion to the doctrine of *oikeiosis* that he is arguing here in a Stoic vein, and Carneades is putting forward a sceptical doctrine that is compatible with sophist and maybe Epicurean views. Both start from 'cradle-arguments', where it is assumed that the end of human beings, their highest good, is revealed from uncorrupted inclinations.[3]

There are, of course, hidden normative assumptions at work here, but they are not as problematic as one might think, for, as we will see, both positions proceed to give reason as a natural human feature an exceedingly important role. Indeed, the dispute could be described as one between different views of practical rationality, resulting in differing outlooks regarding the motivation for justice and differing answers to the question whether we have reason to act morally. Is it rational to follow the rules of natural law, can we be motivated to follow it? Given reason's essentially normative nature, the danger of falling into a form of the naturalistic fallacy – drawing normative inferences from purely factual premises – can be avoided. Carneades makes the normative point that we don't just happen to be self-interested, we also have good reasons to seek our own advantage.[4] Grotius replies that not only are we not as egoistically inclined, as an empirical matter, as Carneades maintains, but we also have good reason to find out and acknowledge the rules of natural law given our sociable natures. Neither Carneades' nor Grotius' moral psychology is, therefore, at bottom, sentimentalist.

Grotius claims that this desire for a rule-governed and peaceful society (*appetitus societatis*), an inclination to be sociable and to seek human fellowship, was what the Stoics had called *oikeiosis*.[5] Grotius took his concept of sociability from Cicero's description of the Stoic doctrine of *oikeiosis*, but while Cicero translated *oikeiosis* as *conciliatio*, Grotius chose the term *appetitus societatis*. This term, which Grotius might have taken from the works of Spanish jurist Fernando Vázquez de Menchaca (1512–69),[6] is not frequent in *De jure belli ac pacis*. Grotius introduces it in the passage quoted above. The 'appetite for society' is characterised as a specifically human trait, underlining the fundamental difference between humans and all other living beings. Putting forward this essentially human desire as an anthropological premise serves to refute the Carneadean claim that all animals strive only for their own advantage (DJBP Prol. 6).[7] A distinction between people and animals is, therefore, central to Grotius, as it was for the Stoics.[8]

The original Stoic doctrine of *oikeiosis* is difficult to reconstruct, but to the extent that we can do so, it seems to have assumed the following shape. The process of *oikeiosis*, which is often translated as 'familiarisation' or 'appropriation', designated for the Greek Stoics a natural human develop-ment. Humans, they thought, have immediately after birth certain primary desires, which they seek to satisfy in a bid for self-preservation. As they get older, there is a developmental shift from mere self-preservation to behav-ing virtuously, or other-regarding. This development toward a virtuous disposition goes hand in hand with, and is the result of, the acquisition of a fully rational point of view. The idea is that humans, as soon as they are born, familiarise themselves with themselves qua humans and show a concern with self-preservation; but, under the guidance of reason, they come with time to acquire a view of virtue as the highest, or ultimate, human goal (*summum bonum*). Virtue on this view is sufficient for happiness (*eudaimonia*) and displays an impartial concern for all humans. An important feature of this doctrine lies in its developmental, two-stage character. Newborn humans betray certain behavioural characteristics, which then, as part of natural human development and under the guidance of reason, eventually transform themselves into an exclusive concern with acting for the right reasons and behaving, therefore, virtuously. To what extent this view implies a radical shift from early self-concern to virtue and impartiality, and whether there are, in fact, in the Greek Stoic texts two different kinds of *oikeiosis*, one governing the rational development of self-concern (virtue) and the other that of other-concern (impartiality), those are difficult and much discussed questions that we cannot hope to disentangle here.[9] What is important when it comes to Grotius' use of the doctrine is the fact that he relies almost exclusively on Cicero when putting his own views forward. For the purposes of this chapter, we will therefore have to keep in mind that Grotius, with regard to sociability, although he knew the Greek Stoic texts well himself, is mostly making use of the way Cicero framed Stoic ideas.

Cicero provided a good model for Grotius because he was equally concerned with certain characteristics of human nature on the one hand and natural law and natural justice as the remedy to conflict on the other. Cicero in his philosophical works had provided an answer to Carneades' scepticism that Grotius found convincing; indeed, Grotius could be described as working out the implications of Cicero's reply to Carneades relevant to his own undertaking of detailing a natural, pre-political legal and moral order. For both Cicero and Grotius, a convincing answer to Carneades had to depend on the characteristics of human nature. Was Grotius correct to suggest (DJBP Prol. 8) that human nature showed a specific 'concern for society' (*societatis custodia*)? It is important to remember that Grotius' doctrine of natural law was aimed against an opponent – Carneades – whose own formal doctrine of legal sources also relied on an account of human nature and rationality, an account – of course – at odds with Grotius'.

7.3 Grotius' Argument from Sociability

Now let us look more closely at the various steps of Grotius' argument from sociability. What is sociability supposed to achieve in the framework of Grotius' argument for natural justice? Grotius begins his counterattack on Carneades by seeking to undermine Carneades' claim about animal behaviour in general. Even some of the non-human animals, Grotius says, are not entirely self-interested and betray a concern for others, either their young or other members of the species. But, humans, once they grow up and develop the specifically human faculty of reason, are equipped in a specific way to satisfy their desire for society:

> But it must be owned that a Man grown up, when he has come to learn to act in the same Manner with respect to Things that are alike, has, besides an elevated Desire of Society [*societatis appetitus*], for the Satisfaction of which he alone of all Animals has received from Nature a peculiar Instrument, viz., the Use of Speech; I say, that he has, besides that, a Faculty of knowing and acting, according to some general Principles [*generalia praecepta*]; so that what relates to this Faculty is not common to all Animals, but properly and peculiarly agrees to Mankind [*humanae naturae congruentia*]. (DJBP Prol. 7)[10]

Note that here the Stoic two-stage development required by *oikeiosis* is implied; the focus is here already on the second, fully rational stage of human development. In addition to the desire for society, which is particularly prominent in humans, adult humans have reason. It is when, or even because – the *cum* here is circumstantial or causal, - they have the ability to act in a rule-governed way ('in the same manner with respect to things that are alike') that human beings are able to satisfy properly their desire to live in society. The *appetitus societatis* is an instinct that is, as we have seen, not entirely exclusive to humans, but men as opposed to other animals have instruments to satisfy this desire that are peculiar to them, namely speech and reason.

We may observe that, at this point, the instinctual desire for society is no longer bearing the argumentative weight by itself. Grotius implies that, absent the specifically human features of reason and speech (*ratio et oratio*, or *logos*), the instinctual appetite for society would remain limited to offspring and maybe some other members of the species. In the human case, however, sociability is not simply brought in to solve the problem of how large and stable societies are possible – quite the contrary, Grotius betrays an acute awareness that human sociability is prone to conflict and sometimes war.[11] Indeed, this is what his *De jure belli ac pacis* is, on one level, all about. In short, Grotius seems to suggest that human sociability in and of itself may create as many problems as it, at first sight, might be thought to resolve.

This is a crucial point: sociability, our social nature, is sometimes conceived of as a device Grotius brings in to defeat his sceptical Carneadean opponents and solve the problem of moral motivation.[12] It does, however, not quite play this role; it merely changes the anthropological assumptions and creates the conditions of possibility for natural law. Sociability itself, although originally brought in to counter Carneades' anthropological claims, cannot do all the work associated with a rebuttal of Carneades' scepticism.[13] Reason, and the means of communicating reason, have to be brought in for any normative dimension to open up. The appetite for society only goes as far as it naturally happens to go, and Grotius is not a naturalist in this sense. Grotius' theory is normative, and he is after bigger, normative claims about what we know and have reason to do, given our sociable nature. Sociability presupposes, rather than automatically creates, certain rules of natural law.[14]

This becomes clearer in the subsequent passage from the *Prolegomena*. It is here that Grotius specifies in what way sociability can be said to provide the framework for natural law. Sociability, or the safeguarding of society, is qualified along rationalist lines; not just any desire for society will do, it also has to live up to the requirements of reason. This latter qualification then brings about certain very specific features of the way in which society has to be upheld, if its institutions are to conform to the parameters of reason:

This Sociability, which we have now described in general, or this Care of maintaining Society [*societatis custodia*] in a Manner conformable to the Light of human Understanding, is the Fountain of Right, properly so called; to which belongs the Abstaining from that which is another's [*alieni abstinentia*], and the Restitution [*restitutio*] of what we have of another's, or of the Profit we have made by it, the Obligation [*obligatio*] of fulfilling Promises, the Reparation of a Damage done through our own Default, and the Merit of Punishment among Men. (DJBP Prol. 8)

If we are to maintain society in this specific way, and thus give in to our natural appetite for society 'not in any Manner whatever, but peaceably, and in a community regulated according to the best of our understanding', then we have to heed certain rules of natural law, which Grotius spells out for us with some specificity: abstaining from others' property; giving back what we illegitimately acquired; living up to promises; making whole those we wrongfully damaged; and the punishment of crimes.[15] These rules receive their validity and obligatory nature from the fact that they are required by right reason. The basis of sociability in human nature is, therefore, not merely instinctual, but also rational.

Grotius does not deny that human weakness stands in need of social cooperation, but he does point out, against Carneades, that human sociability requires, in addition to the need for cooperation and conceptually independent of it, a set of rules.[16] This conceptual independence Grotius shows with a counterfactual: even if we did not stand in need of cooperation for mutual advantage and interest, our instinctual sociability, by itself, would require rules by which society can be governed. More importantly, Grotius now turns Carneades' finding of the local and varied nature of legal systems against him: the obligation to abide by these parochial legal systems, their authority, cannot be explained by exclusive reference to interest, since mere self-interest would presumably recommend free-riding and the breaking of promises. The authority of the various civil legal systems must *itself* be explained by reference to an underlying natural law obligation to adhere by promises, otherwise these systems cannot get off the ground. Grotius here exploits Carneades' oscillation between the interest or advantage of a society and the interest of the individual living in the society. But, this allows him to admit Carneades' point that there are many different legal systems, without thereby having to admit the inexistence of natural law; rather, it is only by reference to natural law that the authority of these different legal systems can be explained in the first place. Here is Grotius, a little later in the *Prolegomena*, on the sources of natural and positive law:

Therefore the Saying, not of Carneades only, but of others, Interest [*utilitas*], that Spring of Just and Right [*iusti prope mater et aequi*], if we speak accurately, is not true; for the Mother of Natural Law is human Nature itself, which, though even the Necessity of our Circumstances should not require it, would of itself create in us a mutual Desire of Society [*ad societatem mutuam appetendam ferret*]: And the Mother of Civil Law is that very Obligation which arises from Consent [*ex consensu obligatio*], which deriving its Force from the Law of Nature, Nature may be called as it were, the Great Grandmother of this Law also. (DJBP Prol. 16)

It is human nature that is the 'mother' of natural law, because human nature produces the desire for society, which in turn makes possible and necessary the concept of obligation and (natural) law. The human drive for society is the source of natural law, and not expediency or interest, because the obligation arising from consent cannot be explained in the absence of an underlying account of promise-giving, which itself cannot be contractarian – otherwise an infinite regress looms – but must be, Grotius claims, a natural law account.[17]

Here, however, we should pause and ask ourselves what it is exactly that Grotius puts forward against Carneades. Carneades had started out by claiming that the sheer variety of civil-law arrangements under-mined any unitary account of universal natural law. The civil laws of individual societies simply reflect bargaining arrangements, the advantage of those societies. Grotius replies that this does nothing to under-mine the existence of natural law: those bargaining arrangements need an account of underlying obligation, of promise-giving, and such an account cannot be given simply in terms of an interest-driven con-tractarian outlook.[18] This is where Carneades' second point kicks in: individuals would be stupid if they always adhered by their promises. In the absence of punishment or what Carneades would probably consider the brainwash propounded by Socrates against Glaucon's arguments,[19] it would for Carneades be irrational and foolish not to free-ride on society's cooperative arrangements.[20] It is important to see that Carneades' point about the foolishness of justice is a point about moral psychology, about *motivation*. Remember that Grotius quoted Carneades – from Cicero's *Republic* – as saying that either there is no justice, or it consists in foolishness. That is to say that Carneades admits that we can specify the rules of justice, but there is still a motivational problem of giving people reasons to adhere by these rules.

In what follows, I will seek to show that Grotius, in his reply to Carneades, adopts the Stoic idea, as filtered through Cicero, of a transi-tion from an impulse for self-preservation to the morally right (*honestum*) as something superior to mere self-preservation – but that he does so in a particularly Ciceronian way, ending up with a knowable natural law that amounts to the condition of possibility for sociability. This is unlike the Greek Stoic view, which sees virtue, the disposition to act in morally correct ways, as the ultimate human goal (*telos*) and highest good, understood as happiness. The Greek Stoic view is called eudaemonist, because it justifies and motivates virtue by showing how virtue contributes to the agent's happiness (*eudaimonia*). Such a eudae-monist account of virtue as the highest good and ultimate human end is missing from Grotius; a more rule-oriented, or jural, account of what is morally right takes its place.[21] Grotius took the idea of the transition from self-preservation impulse to the *honestum* from Cicero's exposition of Stoic doctrine in the third book of *On Ends (De finibus)*, which he quoted extensively:

> *Cicero* learnedly proves, both in the third Book of *De finibus*, and in other Places, from the Writings of the *Stoicks*, that there are two Sorts of *natural Principles;* some that go before, and are called by the *Greeks* Τὰ πρῶτα κατὰ φύσιν, *The first Impressions of Nature* [*prima naturae*], and others that come after, but ought to be the Rule of our Actions, preferably to the former. (DJBP 1.2.1.1)[22]

But Grotius also adopted Cicero's account of natural law, as influentially put forward in the *Republic*, the *Laws*, and *On Duties*, and connected it with the Stoic two-stage account of sociability.[23] The doctrine of *oikeiosis* was laid out by Cicero as part of his account of Stoic ethics, while Grotius consulted it and used it to justify his system of natural law. In the second chapter of the first book of *De jure belli ac pacis*, dealing with the lawful-ness of war, Grotius returns to the question of the foundation of natural law. After discussing the first stage of the Stoic account of sociability, that of the primary things according to nature and self-preservation (DJBP 1.2.1.1),[24] Grotius turns to the morally right (*honestum*) as the second stage. He connects the two stages by using the *oikeiosis* model offered by Cicero. Reason plays the leading role, as it does in the original Stoic accounts as well as in Cicero's *On Ends*. But Grotius goes beyond the passage from Cicero by connecting the Stoic two-stage development with natural law:

> After that follows, *(according to the same Author* [i.e. Cicero]*)* the Knowledge of the Conformity of Things with Reason [*convenientia rerum cum ipsa ratio*], which is a Faculty more excellent than the Body; and this Conformity, in

which virtue [*honestum*] consists, ought (*says he* [Cicero]) to be preferred to those Things, which mere natural Desire at first prompts us to; because, tho' the first Impressions of Nature [*prima naturae*] recommend us to Right Reason [*recta ratio*]; yet Right Reason should still be dearer to us than that natural Instinct. Since these Things are undoubtedly true, and easily allowed by Men of solid Judgment, without any farther Demonstration, we must then, in examining the Law of Nature, first consider whether the Point in Question be conformable to the first Impressions of Nature, and afterwards, whether it agrees with the other natural Principle, which, tho' posterior, is more excellent, and ought not only to be embraced when it presents itself, but also by all Means to be sought after. (DJBP 1.2.1.2)

This exposition is also very clearly based on the explanation the Stoic Cato provided in the third book of Cicero's *On Ends*. Cato there explains the shift in the object of *oikeiosis* away from the primary things in accordance with nature and from self-preservation and towards what the Stoics thought was the highest good or goal of life, namely virtue.[25] In Cato's account, the exercise of reason is also seen as the crucial element, leading from early, 'mere natural desire' of *prima naturae* to the appreciation of reason itself. Our rational capacity, then, helps us 'both to recognize [our] common humanity and to see it as the source from which our obligations to our fellow humans flow'.[26]

Grotius bases his account on Cicero when he seeks to justify the steep hierarchy between mere self-preservation, on the one hand, and the superior quality of acting morally, according to natural law, on the other.[27] Acting morally was the product of normative human reason and of the insight derived from it. But Grotius deviates from Cicero's Cato in connecting the two stages of the Stoic doctrine of *oikeiosis* to his discussion of natural law. While, for Cato in *On Ends*, the purpose of reason was to recognise the *summum bonum*, Grotius leaves the Stoic theory of value as reported by Cato entirely out of his account. Instead, he integrates the idea of natural law as found in Cicero's *Laws* and grafts his fine-grained system of natural rights modelled on Praetorian remedies onto it. Grotius, that is, focuses on natural law as that which could be recognised and acknowledged as valid by reason.

Grotius could thus be seen as attempting to build an account of moral motivation on a theory of *oikeiosis*. More important might be the specifically Ciceronian provenance of this account, however. Ironically, by basing sociability on rational respect for the rights to *prima naturae* such as private property, Grotius follows Cicero in giving these 'first things according to nature' the status of a criterion for justice. For the Greek Stoics, they had been merely so-called preferred indifferents, but, for Grotius, they come to occupy the central position that the *summum bonum* had had for the Greek Stoics.[28] As Christopher Brooke has convincingly argued, there is a 'close fit between the general structure of a Ciceronian Stoic natural law theory and the argument that Grotius builds' in *De jure belli ac pacis*, especially in view of 'the organising role that *appetitus societatis/oikeiosis* plays in connecting the arguments about self-interest with the argument about sociability and the argument about property rights'.[29] But Grotius' argument aims at an account of 'natural laws concentrated around the rights of non-interference, especially with regard to property',[30] rather than offering a Greek Stoic view focused on the human *telos* understood as happiness (*eudaimonia*). This should stop us from describing Grotius' view as Stoic in any straightforward way. Grotius makes natural law and the morally right fundamental, and teleological considerations largely drop from view.[31] But the loss of this eudaemonist concern with the happiness of agents as the ultimate end or goal (*summum bonum*) also accounts for a corresponding loss of motivational force and focus. Grotius does maintain, it is true, that both validity and obligatory nature of natural legal rules depend on their being recommended by *recta ratio*, but his adoption of a right to punish in the state of nature suggests that Grotius does worry about a lack of motivation for justice.[32]

This worry may stem from a shift in Grotius' account, where we have gone from an attempt to meet Carneades on the ground of moral *motivation* to an account of how we get to *know* the rules of natural law. Grotius, I think, ultimately gives us an *epistemic* view of the rationality of natural law – natural human rationality allows us knowledge of the rules of natural law – but somewhat neglects what gave rise to the dispute with Carneades in the first place – do we have reason to follow those rules, i.e. a motivational question about the normative pull of natural law. There is *some* motivational purchase in his Stoic claim that humans are naturally social, it is true, hinting as it does at an innate other-regarding inclination. But, this innate other-regarding instinct is merely an empirical fact, if it is one at all, and it reaches only as far as other-regarding instincts happen to be distributed among the population. So far, this does not imply anything in the way of why we should, as a normative matter, give other-regarding reasons their due. Grotius sometimes seems to sketch an additional normative argument along the lines that, given the sociable instinct, there is a specifiable set of rules that applies universally to societies formed by that instinct, and that we should abide by those rules given our instinct. But, here too, the last part, moral motivation, remains underdeveloped and rationalist moral epistemology – our a priori knowledge of these rules via reason – takes over.[33]

Grotius, therefore, starts out by seeking to meet Carneades' challenge on the terrain of moral motivation, but he then largely neglects moral psychology and moves on to epistemic concerns about our ability to successfully say what the rules of natural law are. These epistemic challenges he meets, maybe successfully, but whether or not he has given us reason to observe the dictates of natural law is less clear. The reason this is so, I would suggest, lies in what philosopher Henry Sidgwick has called the 'dualism of practical reason': Grotius acknowledges the force of Carneades' motivational objection, but it is unclear whether his answer goes beyond that suggested already by Cicero. Grotius' sociability does not simply solve the problems Carneades points out. For one thing, as Grotius was clearly aware, the appetite for society creates as many new problems of living peaceably together in society as it seeks to solve other problems of a motivational sort. A desire for society and the desire to free-ride are not only not mutually exclusive, but the latter thrives on the former. The two can also coexist in, say, a gregarious psychopath. Second, while Grotius' account of sociability might, again, be said to offer some motivational support to an anti-Carneadean view of natural law, the aim of Grotius' account is not to provide a view of the good life, but a system of rules – natural law – that human beings may be motivated to observe as rational beings. Grotius' aim, in short, is not eudaemonist.[34] What he puts forward is a 'jural' view of ethics as a rule-governed enterprise without any implications about the highest good or end of human beings.[35] These rules oblige by virtue of being just rather than motivate by an appeal to the agent's happiness. But this throws into sharp relief Sidgwick's observation about the dual nature of practical rationality, where reason may show us how to design rules that make possible our desire for society, on the one hand, but where reason is also ultimately sensitive to the individual agent herself, in a way that can make following those sociable rules, indeed, look foolish.[36]

Grotius' outlook on sociability is, ultimately, at least as Ciceronian as it is Stoic, due to the specific shape that Stoicism received at the hands of

Cicero. As Jacob Klein explains, if 'the eudaimonist framework of earlier Stoicism is neglected, it becomes easier to regard the prescriptions of natural law not simply as principles to which one must adhere in order to live a life that is happy because rational, but as a source of obligation in their own right'. Therefore, 'Cicero's treatment obscures our view of early Stoicism, but it helps to explain how the doctrine preserved in his accounts inspired later, diverse articulations of natural law theory'.[37] This is precisely what we have seen in Grotius' use of Cicero's account of *oikeiosis*. While *oikeiosis* still serves to counter the motivational implications of Epicurean – and later Hobbesian – anthropology, the aim of this doctrine is no longer, as it was for the Greek Stoics, to show what the good life of an agent consists in and to appeal to his *eudaimonia*. For Grotius as for Cicero, the obligatory force of the rules of natural law is based on the idea that these rules are commands of right reason (*recta ratio*).[38] One might say that Grotius is what, today, we call an externalist about moral motivation: Grotius may separate motivation as a contingent psychological or instinctual fact from the content of the natural law. The natural law can be true without anyone being necessarily motivated to act upon it.[39]

But, there is a second, even more important, sense in which Grotius' adaptation of Stoic *oikeiosis* is deeply Ciceronian. Cicero, in his *On Ends*, ultimately professes his own scepticism when it comes to ethical theory and the highest good. He upholds scepticism in the last book of *On Ends* against all the theories that are expounded in that work: Epicureanism, Stoicism and the mix of traditional Academic and Peripatetic theory put forward at the end. But, while Cicero sides, when it comes to theories of the *summum bonum*, with Carneades' scepticism, he defends against Carneades' academic scepticism a political philosophy based on natural law in the *Republic*, the *Laws* and *On Duties*. Cicero, that is, distinguishes between philosophical theories about the ultimate human end, which he regards with scepticism, on the one hand, and theories about what is just in human society, which he believes can be defended against scepticism as true, on the other.[40] In the absence of a convincing account of the *summum bonum* – and Grotius here is at one with Cicero's scepticism as to the highest good – it is the rationality inherent in the natural law rules themselves that must govern society given our sociable appetite.[41] This is why Grotius', and before him Cicero's, answer to Carneades is not eudaemonist, but 'jural'. While we – all of humanity, not just the Stoic sage – can know the rules sociability presupposes, we cannot know the *summum bonum.*[42] This is the deepest sense, then, in which Grotius should be seen as a Ciceronian: a sceptic with regard to our knowledge of the end, Grotius no less than Cicero is convinced that knowledge of the rules that help satisfy peaceful sociability can be successfully insulated from Carneades' scepticism.

7.4 Outlook

Grotius' exploration of the concept of sociability, with its attendant complexities of moral knowledge, motivation, sentiment and reason, proved to be extraordinarily fruitful in the later history of political thought. Both Hobbes and Pufendorf discuss sociability in a way that is very much indebted to Grotius' framework. Hobbes assumes some of Carneades' commitments and insistes on a natural unsociability; Pufendorf agrees with Hobbes on human weakness and neediness in the state of nature, but argues against Hobbes that commerce could create society, including some natural laws and obligations, in the absence of the state. Shaftesbury, Mandeville, the Scottish thinkers of the eighteenth century, as well as Kant, can be read as having drawn out various strands and implications from the argumentative mould presented by Cicero, Grotius, Hobbes and Pufendorf.[43]

Translation of Grotius' Work Used

The Rights of War and Peace, ed. R. Tuck (Indianapolis, 2005).

Further Reading

Blom, H., 'Sociability and Hugo Grotius', *History of European Ideas* 41 (2015) 589–604.

Brooke, C., *Philosophic Pride* (Princeton, 2012).

Darwall, S., 'Grotius at the Creation of Modern Moral Philosophy', *Archiv für Geschichte der Philosophie* 94 (2012) 294–325.

Haggenmacher, P., *Grotius et la doctrine de la guerre juste* (Paris, 1983).

Hont, I., *Jealousy of Trade* (Cambridge, MA, 2005).

Irwin, T., *The Development of Ethics* (Oxford, 2008), vol. 2.

Kingsbury, B. and B. Straumann, 'The state of nature and commercial sociability in early modern international legal thought', *Grotiana* N.S. 31 (2010) 22–43.

Miller, J., 'Stoics, Grotius, and Spinoza on moral deliberation', in J. Miller and B. Inwood (eds.), *Hellenistic and Early Modern Philosophy* (Cambridge, 2003), 116–40.

Piirimäe, E. and A. Schmidt, 'Introduction: between morality and anthropology – sociability in Enlightenment thought', *History of European Ideas* 41 (2015) 571–88.

Sagar, P., *The Opinion of Mankind: Sociability and the Theory of the State from Hobbes to Smith* (Princeton, 2018).

Schaffner, T., '*Societas Humana* bei Hugo Grotius', in T. Altwicker, F. Cheneval and O. Diggelmann (eds.), *Völkerrechtsphilosophie der Frühaufklärung* (Tübingen, 2015), 103–16.

Straumann, B., '*Appetitus societatis* and *oikeiois*: Hugo Grotius' Ciceronian argument for natural law and just war', *Grotiana* N.S. 24/25 (2003/4) 41–66.

Straumann, B., *Roman Law in the State of Nature. The Classical Foundations of Grotius' Natural Law* (Cambridge, 2015).

Tuck, R., 'The 'modern' theory of natural law', in A. Pagden (ed.), *The Languages of Political Theory in Early-Modern Europe* (Cambridge, 1987), 99–119.

Tuck, R., *The Rights of War and Peace. Political Thought and International Order from Grotius to Kant* (Oxford, 1999).

Winkel, L., 'Les origines antiques de l'*appetitus societatis* de Grotius', *Legal History Review* 68 (2000) 393–403.

Notes

1 The passage is known via Lactant. *Div. inst.* 5.16.3 (= Cic. *Rep.* 3.21).

2 T. Irwin, *The Development of Ethics* (Oxford, 2008), vol. 2, 94. Alternatively, Carneades could be taken to claim that there are two kinds of justice. The first kind is one that can be unintentionally realised by a hidden-hand mechanism if all members of society simply look to their own self-interest. But, there is a second kind of justice that amounts to stupidity, the kind that is other-regarding and demands sacrifices, and it is this second kind that Carneades is concerned to attack. But, this would anachronistically ascribe to Carneades a 'private vice, public virtue' outlook, quite apart from the fact that it is not obvious that the first kind of justice can do entirely without elements of the second kind.

3 See for this kind of argument the classic article by J. Brunschwig, 'The cradle argument in Epicureanism and Stoicism', in M. Schofield and G. Striker (eds.), *The Norms of Nature: Studies in Hellenistic Ethics* (Cambridge, 1986), 113–44, at 115–16.

4 He is not arguing, therefore, that we cannot help but act egoistically and that since 'ought implies can' we are shielded from any altruistic duties. Rather, Carneades holds that we can and sometimes do act foolishly by being altruistic.

5 Grotius did not identify his *appetitus societatis* with the technical Stoic term *oikeiosis* until the 1631 edition of his *De jure belli ac pacis*, but there is to my mind no need to give too much weight to the differences between the original 1625 edition and the one from 1631. I cannot engage with *De jure praedae* here for lack of space. See B. Straumann, *Roman Law in the State of Nature. The Classical Foundations of Grotius' Natural Law* (Cambridge, 2015), 34f. See, for a different view, R. Tuck, *The Rights of War and Peace. Political Thought and International Order from Grotius Kant* (Oxford, 1999), 99ff. See also C. Brooke, *Philosophic Pride* (Princeton, 2012), 53-6.

6 Fernando Vázquez de Menchaca used the term *naturalis appetitus societatis* in his *Controversiarum illustrium usuque frequentium libri tres* (1564), with an Aristotelian connotation. The connection with Stoicism is not made until Grotius. This *pace* L. Winkel, 'Les origines antiques de l'appetitus societatis de Grotius', *Legal History Review* 68 (2000) 393-403, at 399ff., who situates the origin of the term in classical antiquity. Cf. also J. Miller, 'Stoics, Grotius, and Spinoza on moral deliberation', in J. Miller and B. Inwood (eds.), *Hellenistic and Early Modern Philosophy* (Cambridge, 2003), 116-40.

7 Cf. M. Pohlenz, *Die Stoa. Geschichte einer geistigen Bewegung* (4th edn., Göttingen, 1970), vol. 2, 229.

8 For the distinction see, e.g., Cic. *Fin.* 3.67, which Grotius knew (DJBP 2.2.2.1).

9 For an excellent recent treatment, offering a survey of the existing literature and an interesting solution to many of these puzzles by giving cognition and self-perception a key role in *oikeiosis*, see J. Klein, 'The Stoic argument from *oikeiôsis*', *Oxford Studies in Ancient Philosophy* 50 (2016), 143-200.

10 The translation has been adapted to reflect the developmental aspect of *cum circa similia similiter agere norit* as well as the fact that the desire for society is not simply 'exquisite', as the original translation has it, but it is actually elevated, or particularly prominent, in humans (*excellens*), according to Grotius.

11 Cf. P. Haggenmacher, *Grotius et la doctrine de la guerre juste* (Paris, 1983), 618, on the centrality of conflict for Grotius; J.B. Schneewind, *The Invention of Autonomy: A History of Modern Moral Philosophy* (Cambridge, 1998), 72f. goes even further.

12 Brooke, *Philosophic Pride*, ch. 2; Straumann, '*Appetitus societatis*'; S. Darwall, 'Grotius at the creation of modern moral philosophy', *Archiv für Geschichte der Philosophie* 94 (2012) 294-325.

13 For a deflationary account of sociability in Grotius, interpreting it as the successor notion of *fides* and a mere 'afterthought' (while not denying its enormous historical impact), see H. Blom, 'Sociability and Hugo Grotius', *History of European Ideas* 41 (2015), 589-604.

14 Cf. Blom, 'Sociability', 602.

15 Grotius gets this specificity by using the procedural remedies that he knew from Roman law, taking them to affirm the basic rights required by natural law, especially property rights. These Roman remedies, then, are taken to be declarative of natural law and to hold – even in the absence of a praetor, far away from the Roman forum – in the state of nature. See Straumann, *Roman Law*, esp. chapters 2 and 7; id., 'A reply to my critics: Adam Smith's unfinished Grotius business, Grotius's novel turn to ancient law, and the genealogical fallacy', *Grotiana* N.SD. 38 (2017) 211–28.

16 Interestingly, Hobbes and Grotius might be closer here than it first appears. Mutual advantage is prominent in Grotius, and Hobbes' point later will be that 'large and lasting' society could not be stably based on advantage-seeking or honour-seeking alone, and in that there's probably agreement with Grotius. See, on the later history of sociability after Grotius, P. Sagar, *The Opinion of Mankind: Sociability and the Theory of the State from Hobbes to Smith* (Princeton, 2018).

17 This Grotius also aims to show by means of a *reductio ad absurdum* – if justice were only aimed at because of its utility, inter-state dealings could not be assessed in terms of justice; but states even externally do need justice understood non-instrumentally as a value in its own right (DJBP Prol. 21).

18 Grotius agrees with Carneades on the role of utility for civil law. Cf. Blom, 'Sociability', 13. But, Grotius theorises already in a sense 'natural' society as opposed to the state, and in this regard anticipates Pufendorf; cf. B. Kingsbury and B. Straumann, 'The state of nature and commercial sociability in early modern international legal thought', *Grotiana* N.S. 31 (2010) 22–43.

19 In book 2 of Plato's *Republic*, Glaucon tells the story of Gyges, a Lydian shepherd who discovers a ring that makes him invisible and proceeds to seduce the queen of Lydia, kill the king and take the throne himself. If one had the ring and the power to commit injustice unpunished, would there be any reason not to do it? Is justice, in other words, an intrinsic good, apart from its consequences, and beneficial to the agent in and of itself? Socrates answers yes, giving a famous account of the disharmony of the psyche of the unjust agent and the health of the just agent (*Rep.* 4.444d).

20 Carneades, in other words, is not convinced by the reasons Socrates offers to Gyges to reject injustice. Justice, for Carneades, is exclusively defined in terms of cooperative strategies. See, for an insightful account of Cicero's reading of Plato and what is at stake in the tale of Gyges' ring, R. Woolf, 'Cicero and Gyges', *Classical Quarterly* 63 (2013) 801–12.

21 For an argument that it is only missing from the natural law treatises, but present in the theological work, see T. Schaffner, 'The eudaemonist ethics of Hugo Grotius (1583–1645). Pre-modern moral philosophy for the twenty-first century?', *Jurisprudence* 7 (2016) 478–522.

22 Cf. Schneewind, *Invention*, 175: Grotius 'sets aside ... questions of the highest good' and 'says nothing about individual perfection'. Schneewind denies therefore that Grotius' natural law deserves to be called Stoic in the sense of

eudaemonist, but leaves open a Ciceronian background. Grotius must have known the formulation *ta prota kata phusin* from Aulus Gellius or from Stobaeus.

23 See Cic. *Rep.* 2.31; 3.34f.; *Leg.* 2.34; *Off.* 1.34ff.

24 This passage is taken straight from Cic. *Fin.* 3.16, 3.17, and 3.20. On Grotius' use of the passage, see Straumann, '*Appetitus societatis*'; Brooke, *Philosophic Pride*, 48–53.

25 Cic. *Fin.* 3.21.

26 R. Woolf, *Cicero: The Philosophy of a Roman Sceptic* (London/New York, 2015), 158.

27 For a view of Grotius that assimilates him to an Epicurean, or Carneadean, outlook centred on self-preservation and a Hobbesian vision of the good, see R. Tuck, 'The 'modern' theory of natural law', in A. Pagden (ed.), *The Languages of Political Theory in Early-Modern Europe* (Cambridge, 1987), 99–119. For counterarguments, see Straumann, '*Appetitus societatis*'; Brooke, *Philosophic Pride*, ch. 2. Hobbes' own view of what right reason requires is indeed indebted to Carneades (cf. *De cive* 2, § 1). This represents a combination of Cicero's natural law (*Leg.* 1.18, 23) with a Carneadean version of *oikeiosis*: see A.R. Dyck, *A Commentary on Cicero, De Legibus* (Ann Arbor, 2004), 35, n.123. For Carneades defending the *primae secundum naturam* as the highest good, see Cic. *Fin.* 5.20.

28 In a sense, then, both Cicero and Grotius design a system of natural justice that is built around a Carneadean account of the good (the *prima naturae*: Cic. *Fin.* 2.35, 42), but, like Carneades', is not conceived as a theory of the good, but subject to scepticism (see below).

29 Brooke, *Philosophic Pride*, 57.

30 Brooke, *Philosophic Pride*, 58.

31 See, for a different view, Schaffner, 'Eudaemonist ethics'.

32 For Grotius' natural right to punish and its influence, see Straumann, *Roman Law*, ch. 9. Fear of punishment and the enforcement of natural law are concessions to the motivational problems Grotius' non-eudaemonist account generates; someone like Gyges or Hobbes' Fool has to be deterred by punishment – by contrast, neither the Stoic nor the Epicurean sage do.

33 This leaves us with the 'puzzle', as Brooke has it, that 'Grotius seems to be fairly cavalier about the origins of justice, at least insofar as it manages to obtain any kind of grip on human psychology'. *Philosophic Pride*, 52.

34 For an argument that it is, see Irwin, *Development*, 93–6 and 98–9. For a view close to the one I offer, see Darwall, 'Grotius'.

35 It is in this sense that it is a recognisably modern, 'jural' outlook, in Henry Sidgwick's terminology: see on this Straumann, *Roman Law*, 84–8.

36 H. Sidgwick, *The Methods of Ethics* (7th edn, London, 1907), 498: 'It would be contrary to Common Sense to deny that the distinction between any one individual and any other is real and fundamental, and that consequently "I" am concerned with the quality of my existence as an individual in a sense,

fundamentally important, in which I am not concerned with the quality of the existence of other individuals: and this being so, I do not see how it can be proved that this distinction is not to be taken as fundamental in determining the ultimate end of rational action for an individual.' This dualism had been absent from Greek ethics, Sidgwick thought: 'In Platonism and Stoicism, and in Greek moral philosophy generally, but one regulative and governing faculty is recognized under the name of Reason – however the regulation of Reason may be understood; in the modern ethical view, when it has worked itself clear, there are found to be two – Universal Reason and Egoistic Reason, or Conscience and Self-love'. Sidgwick, *Outlines of the History of Ethics* (London, 1892), 197. Carneades' dialectical reasoning may be seen as a predecessor of the modern view.

37 J. Klein, 'Stoic eudaimonism and the natural law tradition', in J.A. Jacobs (ed.), *Reason, Religion, and Natural Law: From Plato to Spinoza* (Oxford, 2012), 57–80, at 80. This is why it may be prudent to let the history of the idea of a rule-based natural law, as opposed to natural justice, or virtue-based natural law, begin with Cicero rather than with the Greek Stoics. Cf. G. Striker, 'Origins of the concept of natural law', in idem, *Essays on Hellenistic Epistemology and Ethics* (Cambridge, 1996), 209–20; B. Inwood, 'Commentary on Striker', *Proceedings of the Boston Area Colloquium in Ancient Philosophy* 2 (1987), 95–101.

38 This account of obligation, then, comes to anticipate and resemble Hobbes', where the laws of nature are neither obligatory by virtue of being God's commands, nor simply advice, but based on the authority of reason. But, for Grotius, as opposed to Hobbes, right reason provides motivation beyond merely prudential considerations – this is what the account of *oikeiosis* is designed to achieve. The content of Grotius' commands of right reason differs of course markedly from the content of Hobbes'.

39 See Straumann, 'A reply', 218f., esp. n. 25. Jeffrey Edwards points out to me that this is plausible only insofar as Grotius is in a position to separate motivation from the content of moral judgments; he might also plausibly be said to be an internalist if he thinks that the dictates of right reason (DJBP Prol. 8ff.) are apprehended as *notiones certae*, which are known to us by taking account of the anthropological factors that figure in *oikeiosis*. This may well be true, but I doubt that Grotius is quite as orthodox a Stoic as that (in addition, this still would not solve the problem of Sidgwick's dualism of practical reason). Many thanks to Professor Edwards for the correspondence.

40 For a view that Cicero retains a measure of scepticism even with regard to his political theory, see J.W. Atkins, *Cicero on Politics and the Limits of Reason* (Cambridge, 2013), 176–85.

41 For a vigorous assertion of this scepticism regarding the *summum bonum*, see DJBP 1.3.8.2.

42 For this expansion of the scope of right reason beyond the Stoic sage to all of humanity, see Straumann, *Roman Law*, 107–13. For Grotius' concept of the

society of humankind (*societas humana*), see T. Schaffner, '*Societas Humana bei Hugo Grotius*', in T. Altwicker, F. Cheneval and O. Diggelmann (eds.), *Völkerrechtsphilosophie der Frühaufklärung* (Tübingen, 2015), 103–16.

43 For a survey, see E. Piirimäe and A. Schmidt, 'Introduction: between morality and anthropology – sociability in Enlightenment thought', *History of European Ideas* 41 (2015) 571–88, as well as the other contributions to this issue of *History of European Ideas*. See also, e.g., F. Palladini, 'Pufendorf disciple of Hobbes: The nature of man and the state of nature: The doctrine of *socialitas*', *History of European Ideas* 34 (2008) 26–60; I. Hont, *Jealousy of Trade* (Cambridge, MA, 2005); Blom, 'Sociability'; Kingsbury and Straumann, 'State of nature'; Brooke, *Philosophic Pride*; Sagar, *Opinion*.

8 Sovereignty

Gustaaf van Nifterik

....

8.1 Introduction

Grotius' ideas on sovereignty in *De jure belli ac pacis* are often qualified as 'Janus-faced' and even contradictory, as his theory endorses both absolute monarchy and popular sovereignty, both unaccountability of the sovereign and the right to resist the sovereign in some extreme situations.[1] The conclusion often drawn is that the 'Grotian problem',[2] to admit rebellion while banning private warfare in society, is not solved satisfactorily in his main work, a conclusion that is backed up by pointing out that monarchists, republicans, revolutionaries and others all find useful arguments to support their position in Grotius' theory.[3]

Yet, the 'problem' itself was of acute interest. The Dutch Republic, Grotius' homeland, was the result of a recent and successful revolt of the people against their ruler, Philip II (1528–98), the king of Spain; its internal structure was still under construction. Meanwhile, Europe was on fire, with the Thirty Years War (1618–48) ruining Germany and killing about a third of its population. Rebellion, rights vis-à-vis a legitimate government, and war and peace were matters to be discussed profoundly. How did these topics relate to the idea of sovereignty, both internal and external?

In this chapter, Grotius' ideas on internal sovereignty will be analysed from a legal point of view. It will be shown that, from this perspective, there is no contradiction in the theory in *De jure belli ac pacis*, and that both absolute monarchy and popular sovereignty, both unaccountability of the monarch and the right of resistance, can be deduced from his legal assumptions; the situations in which resistance is allowed are not exceptions to the rule – i.e. 'the law of non-resistance' – but outcomes based on the same principles as the rule itself. Of course, one can question and criticise Grotius' legal assumptions as such, or criticise the outcomes of Grotius' legal reasoning and then point out that, apparently, his assumptions are wrong; we will do so in some concluding remarks. However, inconsistency is a false accusation.

In what follows, the focus will be on Grotius' ideas on internal sovereignty as set forth in his *De jure belli ac pacis*. This focus needs some justification, the more so since Peter Borschberg weaned 'modern researches from their overreliance on Grotius' best-known work'.[4] Yet, also Borschberg considered this work to be 'the result of approximately two decades of intensive research on some of the most fundamental issues in politics, law, and the heritage of all mankind', the result of a long intellectual struggle.[5] Legal reading reveals not just 'snippets of text' removed from their intellectual context and intentionally lacking intellectual coherence, as Borschberg says. It need not be the reader who gives coherence to these snippets.[6] From a legal point of view, the constitutional theory in the treatise seems coherent enough.

However, it is not easy to grasp the coherence since the book was on the law of war and peace, not on constitutional law. Laying bare the underlying constitutional structure, its legal ground-rules and principles, is therefore all the more necessary. Grotius' earlier works can sometimes enlighten us here, if only we are aware that there are some important differences in legal reasoning between his earlier and his later work. Hence a caveat is in place if one tries to use earlier works in order to understand the later one.

8.2 Legal Assumptions and Legal Reasoning: Framing the State

By nature, so runs one of Grotius' basic assumptions, all men are free and no one is subject to (political) power (DJBP 3.7.1: 'Servi natura ... nulli sunt'; 2.22.11: 'Nam libertas cum natura competere hominibus aut populis dicitur, id intelligendum est de iure naturae (...)'; 2.17.2.1: 'Natura homini suum est (...) actiones propriae'). But, people actually did and do live in states and under rulers who have political power over them. The highest ruler with supreme power is he 'whose actions are not subject to the legal control of another, so that they cannot be rendered void by the operation of another human will' (DJBP 1.3.7.1). Grotius used the term supreme power (*summa potestas*), not sovereignty or sovereign power. Borschberg convincingly argued that Grotius wanted to avoid close association with Jean Bodin's (1530–96) ideas on 'souveraineté' (*jus maiestatis* in Latin).[7] As we will see below, Grotius' 'sovereign' is not necessarily freed from the laws, as his supreme power is not necessarily absolute; neither is sovereign power indivisible, according to Grotius, as it was for Bodin.

Obviously, there is a transformation from life in the natural state to life in the political or civil state, and it is also obvious that law ('legal control', *alterius jus*) somehow has to do with this transformation. Grotius' second assumption relevant to our subject says that *potestas*, that is power of man over man, is in fact not unknown in the law of nature. *Potestas* is one of the manifestations of *jus* (the others being *dominium* and *creditum*, DJBP 1.1.5). It can either be power over oneself, called freedom, or power over another. *Potestas in alios* is elaborated in chapter 2.5, where Grotius discussed the rights of parents over their children, the husband over his wife, the (majority in an) association over the individual members, the master over his slave and the state over its subjects. Generation (giving birth), consent and crime are listed as the origins of such powers; consent and punishment are pointed out as the two possible sources of political power (DJBP 2.22.13).

If we focus on consent as the origin of the right to rule, the picture we get is as follows: men are free by nature – they have *potestas in se* – and voluntarily enter into a contract to form an association; the most perfect association is the political, called the state. *Civitas* and *civilis societas* are used synonymously (inter alia DJBP 1.4.2.1 and 2.5.23 ff.); also, *respublica* is used (e.g. DJBP 2.5.24). The political community in its origin is a form of public association by consent (DJBP 2.5.8, 17 and 23).

Before we turn to Grotius' ideas on sovereign power within the state, a few remarks are appropriate on associations in general and on the state being a perfect association specifically. 'All associations have this in common, (...) that in those matters on account of which the association was formed the entire membership, or the majority in the name of the entire membership, may bind the individual members' (DJBP 2.5.17). The quote makes clear that an association is formed on account of something, and that an association may bind its members. The raison d'être for the political association, the reason for men to enter into this most perfect association, is to maintain public tranquillity. The *civilis societas* exists in the interest of public peace and order (DJBP 1.4.2.1: 'ad tuendam tranquillitatem instituta'). The association's power to bind its members is, of course, an important element of political power, to which we will return below.

Grotius used the words *consociatio* and *societas* interchangeably (e.g. DJBP 2.5.17 and 23). *Societas* is a legal institution known from Roman law;[8] something similar was known as 'maetschap' in the law of Holland.[9] But, the *societas* in Roman law was not a legal person and would extinguish with the death of one of the *socii* (partners). Grotius wanted to avoid both implications, and mixed the well-defined legal concept of *societas* with the idea of the community as a *persona repraesentata* or *ficta* that had been familiar since the medieval legists and canonists. Apart from the ideas of the community as a *consociatio* that we also find in the works of Johannes Althusius (1563–1638) – who doesn't figure at all in *De jure belli ac pacis* – there is the idea of the community of a people as a distinct *corpus*, prominent in the works of the Spanish late-scholastics, such as Francisco de Vitoria (*c.* 1480–1546), Domingo de Soto (1494–1560) and Francisco Suárez (1548–1617).[10] According to Grotius, men, sociable and rational – as we read in the *Prolegomena* (DJBP Prol. 6–7), in which Grotius laid out his socio-philosophical foundations – associate and thereby create a moral or artificial body, the people (*populus*). This concept of the people as a moral body can be found in *De jure belli ac pacis* (DJBP 1.3.7.2), with a reference indeed to Vitoria.[11] Elsewhere, the *populus* is called an artificial body (DJBP 2.9.3.1) and, in the notes added to this passage, Grotius referred to Justinian's *Digests*, 5.1.76 (Alfenus), 6.1.23.5 (Paulus) and 41.3.30 (Pomponius), to elucidate the idea of a people belonging 'to the class of bodies that are made up of separate members, but (...) have "a single essential character" (...) or a single spirit (...)'.

Now, the very first 'product' of the associated people is supreme power ('cujus prima pruductio est summum imperium', DJBP 2.9.3.1; something similar can be found in DJBP 1.4.2.1, where it is said that the state 'forthwith' (*statim*) acquires a right over us and our goods), a power that is at the same time the spirit that holds the individuals together, that binds them into one body. We also find the phrase 'jus regendi, qua populus sunt' (DJBP 1.3.12.2); obviously the words 'qua populus sunt' are difficult to interpret, as the translations range from 'in their totality as a people', via 'as they are a people', to 'by which they are a people'.[12] Should the last interpretation be correct – and, in fact, I think it is – the *jus regendi* of DJBP 1.3.12.2 is the same as the *summum imperium* of DJBP 2.9.3.1 and the creation of a political association is a two-sided event, creating both the body (association) and the power to rule and to hold the body together (*summum imperium* or *jus regendi*). The association and supreme power are two sides of the same coin; one cannot have the one without the other.

The idea of the creation of a moral body with sufficient power to hold it together is important, as the association's autonomous right to defend itself and its rights by making war is in fact the execution of the association's natural rights as a distinct legal entity. For, as we read in DJBP 1.5.1 on the question of the efficient cause for private and public wars, 'by nature everyone is the defender of his own rights'. As such, the association has the natural right that also human beings have: the right to defend itself and to foster its wellbeing. What there is to be defended – the precise end or scope of the association and thus of its public power – ultimately depends on the will of the persons associating, as we will see below.

In this line of thought, there is no need for any transfer of (natural) rights from the individual members to the association, state or its ruler(s). The associating individuals do not transfer rights; they create a new body, the association, and natural law provides this newly created body with the rights to defend itself.

This interpretation of Grotius' theory on the origin of sovereign power leads to conclusions that differ from those of various Grotius-scholars on two important points. First, since the individuals do not transfer their rights, there can be no question of how many or how completely the rights are transferred. And, since they don't lose any of their rights, there is no regaining them in situations of extreme necessity. The associates create an overarching association to take care of things, to bind its members by law and, if needed, to punish offenders against the law, including natural law. As soon as people live under state protection, their own individual natural rights to defend their *suum* and to punish, as a result of the mutual contractual promise, lie dormant in their breast, only to be woken up when the body politic is unable or unwilling to act. For, said Grotius, it is certain that much that had been licensed before the establishment of courts has been restricted afterwards (DJBP 1.3.2.1: 'Certe quin restricta multum sit ea quae ante judicia constituta feurat licentia, dubitari non potest'). Within the sphere of the political association, the members mutually agree to make use of the state's lawsuits and judicial settlements to protect and reclaim their rights. Once associated, they are no longer free to protect their own natural rights; this is, indeed, the whole idea of the political association. Only beyond the state do the individual's natural rights wake up and is private war the proper manner to settle disputes (cfr. DJBP 1.3.2.1 and 2.1.2.1: 'ubi judicia deficiunt incipit bellum').

Knud Haakonssen labels the rights that lie dormant 'second-order rights' and focuses exclusively on the 'right to punish'.[13] However, not only the right to punish, but all legitimate titles for war seem relevant here. When the political association is established, men preserve all their natural rights and are bound mutually by contract not to make use of their (second-order) rights to defend their (first-order) rights in the civil state. Grotius meant the natural law *pacta sunt servanda* (DJBP Prol. 8 and 15), where he mentioned that 'the law which forbids a man to seek to recover his own otherwise than through judicial process' – this law being applicable only 'where judicial process has been possible' (DJBP 1.3.2.1). We will see below that, in questions concerning the rights that lie dormant and the situations in which they wake up, Grotius himself did not turn to 'interpretative charity', but to the will of the people who had originally associated. This reading is at odds with Tuck's, who criticises Grotius' theory for the unnecessary renunciation of liberty and the right to self-defence; 'the only thing necessary to create civil society successfully would thus be a transfer of that right [to punish]'.[14] There are, however, no rights transferred at all; a greater body is created, with the natural rights necessary to achieve its end. Its end is the promotion of public order and peace.

The second point of difference that follows from my interpretation is that we can detect a change of mind between the young Grotius writing *De jure praedae commentarius* (around 1604) and the mature man writing *De jure belli ac pacis* (1625). In *De jure praedae*, Grotius indeed talked of rights being transferred ('just as every right of the magistrate comes to him from the state, so has the same right come to the state from private individuals,' DJPC 8, 137) and of the *nemo plus* rule known from Roman law, saying that one cannot transfer to another a greater right than he himself has.[15] By that time, Grotius argued that, since the state has a right to punish transgressors of the law, necessarily the individual members must have (had) this right in the state of nature (DJPC 8, 91 and 137). But, Grotius no longer needed the *nemo plus* rule by the time he was writing his magnum opus, since the rights of the association no longer had to come from its members, as the newly created body or *persona ficta* was provided with its own rights by natural law. The suggestion of Borschberg that reading Grotius' early works might help to better understand *De jure belli ac pacis* is, therefore, questionable, or at least should only be carried out keeping in mind the fundamental difference between the early and the later works.[16]

It is, in fact, specifically on this subject that Grotius' aforementioned long intellectual struggle comes most clearly to the fore. Despite his reliance on the *nemo plus* rule, by the time of writing *De jure praedae*, Grotius was already strongly inspired by the Spanish neo-scholastics, who defended the idea that men cannot survive solitarily and, therefore, given their specific nature, need to associate. Since a body such as an association cannot exist without a head, so ran their argument, also the head of the association and political power as such must be an ordination of God: if, by God's creation, men need to associate and if an association needs a head, the head must be ordained by God also. Therefore, the common-wealth itself and its powers are part of God's creation and have their origin in God and natural law.[17] These Spanish writers consequently didn't need the *nemo plus* argument to derive political power from individual men. In their theories, it is a God-ordained power that is subsequently transferred from the community to the ruler: 'Qui resistit potestati, Dei ordinationi resistit'.[18] Around 1605, Grotius obviously didn't follow the Spaniards all the way to this conclusion.

And he still didn't in 1625. It might have been his familiarity with the ideas of yet another Spanish author, Fernando Vázquez de Menchaca (1512–69), that inspired Grotius not to focus on God and nature only, but to focus more strongly on the will of the associated individuals.[19] Vázquez explicitly attacked neo-scholastic political thought as described above in its fundaments by denying the community the status of an independent, natural entity created by God.[20]

In *De jure belli ac pacis*, Grotius seemed to have come to peace with his intellectual struggle, and combined the ideas of Vitoria, Soto and Suárez with those of their antagonist, Vázquez. Put simply: men come together, establish by contract the kind of association they agreed on and, by doing so, create a body that fits their wishes; nature provides this body with the rights to protect its existence and enable it to foster the end(s) set for it by the (original) associates; or – so Grotius added in DJBP 1.4.8.1 – what they might have arranged at a later moment. Much emphasis is thus laid on the presumed will of the associates. Obviously, Grotius in 1625 didn't go all the way with Vázquez either, who denied the community its status as legal *persona ficta*.

One last point needs to be made before we turn to the substance of the 'sovereign's' right to govern. Since an association is a composed entity, the dangers that possibly threaten its existence can come both from within the association – its members – and from without – all others, especially 'foreign' peoples or rulers. Hence the state's license to use the *jus gladii* against its own citizens, and to make war against other states. It can do so on any of the legitimate causes for war: to defend what is the state's property, to obtain what is its due and to inflict punishment (DJBP 2.1.2), both for its own sake and for the sake of any of its members – or for the sake of natural law itself. For, even if it is not correct to say that the members have transferred their natural rights to the political association, we have already seen that living in a state does limit their liberty (*jus*, as what is not unjust) to make private wars in order to protect or reclaim their subjective rights (see DJBP 1.1.3 ff. for the uses of the word *jus* as right and as law). This is the price they pay for being a member of the *societas*, a citizen.

8.3 The Ruler's *Jus Regendi*

Let us now take a closer look at political power, the faculty of governing the *civitas* (DJBP 1.3.6.1: 'Facultas (...) moralis civitatem gubernandi'). Grotius used the terms *summa potestas*, *jus regendi* (both can be found in DJBP 1.3.8.1), *potestas civilis* (1.3.6.2) and *jus imperandi* (1.3.8.3), and all point to the same power. We have already seen that this power is the 'spirit' of the association, the immaterial element that binds the individuals together and enables them to act as one body, as a people. Grotius also defined the main competences and powers of the highest ruler – legislation; the making of peace, war and treatises, the right to levy taxes, and so on; and the branch called the judicial – and the ways to carry these out (DJBP 1.3.6). We, however, need to move up to a more abstract level, to the level of what political power essentially is.

The essence of the *jus regendi* – I prefer this term as it expresses best what it is about, the right to rule – apparently consists of several interrelated powers, that are for that matter insufficiently distinguished analytically by Grotius himself (see for instance DJBP 1.3.6.2). One faculty, a consequence of the state being an overarching association, is the superior right over the persons comprising the association and their property, a *jus* (in the sense of *facultas*) *eminens*, that is an eminent *potestas* and *dominium*, for the sake of the association's end: to maintain public tranquillity (DJBP 1.1.5 and 6, 1.3.6.2 and 1.4.2.1). A second faculty, as already indicated above, is the natural right to make (public) war on behalf of the association as a distinct body or entity to defend its *suum*, both externally and internally, on any of the natural titles (or causes) of war (see DJBP 2.1.2). Later in the treatise, we read that a king may deprive his subjects of their rights either by way of punishment, or by virtue of his eminent *dominium* (DJBP 2.14.7: 'sciendum est, posse subditis jus etiam quaesitum auferri per regem duplici modo, aut in poenam aut ex vi supereminentis dominii'). And, finally, the state as an association has the right to make and execute laws that bind its members and to take care of the administration of justice (DJBP 2.5.17, quoted above), to the advantage of its members, the citizens.

The next move in Grotius' theory is that the *jus regendi*, the supreme power over the association and its members, can be wielded by the members collectively – that is, by the entire people – or be transferred to a few, or to one man. It is for the people to decide, and the outcome of this choice leads to one of the *tres gubernandi formas* (DJBP 1.3.8.9),[21] systems of government, that we may call democracy, aristocracy and monarchy. The *civitas*, as a moral body or legal entity, will always be the common subject (*subjectum commune*) of the state's power; the many, or some, or one person to whom the right to rule is transferred, its special or proper subject (*subjectum proprium*). To elucidate the sense of common and proper, Grotius used the parable of the body: the body is the common subject of sight, the eye is the proper subject (DJBP 1.3.7.3).

Grotius suggested several legal forms for the transfer of the association's supreme power to the ruler(s) (DJBP 1.3.11). If the right to wield this power is transferred to a few or to one man, they or he can either receive a revocable right (*jus precarium*) in the *summa potestas*, or a usufructuary right or ownership of it. The difference between the last two is the transferability of the power received: according to law, a property right may be sold and transferred, whereas a usufructuary right may not. The difference between these two rights and a *jus precarium* is more substantial, since the people can at all times revoke a precarious right, but not a property or usufructuary right; consequently, he who has a precarious right does not have genuine supreme power, as the persistence of his position depends on the will of those who can revoke the precarious right (DJBP 1.3.11.3).

Except in cases where the right to rule is the execution of punishment imposed on the people over which it is wielded, the legal form of the ruler's right – a precarious, usufructuary or property right in the supreme power – ultimately depends on the pact underlying the transfer of power from the people (association) to the ruler. Although, according to Grotius, some kings do have a property right in sovereign power, either transferred to them or acquired in a lawful war against the people they rule over, most kings hold their right as a usufruct (DJBP 1.3.11.1). It is at this point that Daniel Lee goes wrong in his defence of Grotius' theory against republican critique, attributing the weak and indeed 'non-sovereign' position of a ruler with a precarious right to the typical king with a usufructuary right.[22] Lee's account of Grotius' ideas as a theory of a free and sovereign people under monarchical rule is consequently unsustainable: if the monarch is a king with a usufructuary right in the *jus regendi*, only he, and not the people, has supreme power to rule. Generally speaking, the people under a king are not free; even less could it be considered 'sovereign'.

There are yet a few other 'constitutional' varieties, in addition to the legal variations mentioned above, with regards to the right that is transferred and the quantity of persons to whom it is transferred. For the right to rule can be transferred either completely or partially. The people might well have wished to transfer only one part of the power and to preserve another for themselves to be wielded collectively, for instance the power to approve or reject taxes. Or the transfer might have been conditional and a right of resistance against the ruler included, for instance if he should violate the laws of the land. We find these and a few other 'constitutional' varieties in chapter 4 of the first book of the treatise. They lead to the conclusion (made explicit in DJBP 2.5.31) that the subjection of the people to the king might very well be a complete subjection (*perfecta subjectio*), but that degrees of subjection less complete are also conceivable, either in the manner of holding power or in the plenitude of it ('aut habendi modo, aut quoad imperandi plenitudinem'). Notwithstanding the conclusion in the chapter that, generally speaking, resistance cannot legitimately be made against those who hold supreme power, the so called 'law of non-resistance', constitutional varieties do mitigate this 'law' (DJBP 1.4).

We can deduce that subjection in the Grotian approach to constitutional law does not necessarily entail a lasting contractual relationship between the people and the ruler after the transfer of the *jus regendi*. One should, therefore, not read the principle of *pacta sunt servanda* into the relationship between the people and its ruler unreservedly.[23] Based on a preliminary contract by which the right – precarious, usufructuary or property – is determined and the exact scope of it defined, an absolute right – absolute in the legal sense of being enforceable against everyone – is transferred to the ruler. After the transfer, the contract dissolves as the parties have fulfilled their contractual obligations. Things were different in Grotius' early work, *Theses LVI* (first decade of the seventeenth century), where we find the possibility that the power is mandated to the republic's ruler, alongside the possibility of a transfer of power (*Theses LVI* 40: 'Potest autem respublica aut mandare totum imperium alieni, aut transferre').[24] In case of a mandate, there would indeed be a lasting contractual relationship between the prince and the associated people, but not in case of a transfer. But, ruling by mandate is no longer found in *De jure belli ac pacis*; the precarious right in supreme power has taken its place. In the later treatise, the adage *pacta sunt servanda* only plays a role when promises are made between the ruler and the people concerning the *exercise* of the power transferred; then, indeed, the ruler might be bound to 'certain rules, to which kings would not be bound without a promise' (DJBP 1.3.16.2).

8.4 Law of Non-Resistance and the War of Subjects against Their Superiors

Chapter 1.4 of the *De jure belli ac pacis* deals with the question of whether the subjects may rebel against their superiors (*De bello subditorum in superiors*). The fact that Grotius here thought of war (*De bello* . . .) already indicates that, to him, 'resistance' has its place beyond the civil state, when judicial settlement is no longer possible and war begins, where parties face each other in their natural condition. 'Legitimate resistance' is, accordingly, a *contradictio in terminis*: if it is legitimate, it is no longer resistance to a ruler, but a 'war', private or public, to curb illegal behaviour. Grotius himself was aware of this as he remarked that we are, in fact, dealing with situations in which the rule of non-resistance simply does not apply, for reasons that the ruler has not acted within his right (DJBP 1.4.7.15). This, of course, doesn't solve questions of who is to decide on the legitimacy of the ruler's actions, which is crucial for the legitimacy of the war by the people against him as well. Robert Filmer (1588–1653), in his *Observations upon H. Grotius de Iure belli ac Pacis* (1652), already pointed out that Grotius is not all too clear on this particular question.

This being said, in chapter 1.4, at the end of the long seventh section, Grotius came to the conclusion that resistance cannot rightfully be made to him who holds supreme power, the aforementioned law of non-resistance (*lex de non resistendo*, DJBP 1.4.7.1). Although, by nature, all men have the right to resist in order to ward off injury, the moment that the civil association was instituted, the association or *civitas* acquired a greater right over the associates and their goods – Grotius obviously referred to his idea of the state's *jus eminens*. The state can limit the 'unregulated' (*promiscuus*) right of resistance for the sake of public peace and order, which should not surprise us, since peace and order are the very raisons d'être of the state. And it will limit this right indeed, for otherwise the state would, presumably, not be able to achieve its end (DJBP 1.4.2). As Grotius explained, the order of bearing rule and rendering obedience necessary for securing peace cannot coexist with the individual license to offer resistance (DJBP 1.4.4.5).

This prompts us to delve a little deeper into the question of the precise end of the state. This is an interesting question indeed, and Grotius answered it prudently, triggered by the question on the force of the law of non-resistance in cases of extreme or eminent peril (DJBP 1.4.7.1). The answer to this question is pre-digested in a statement that is crucial for understanding Grotius' theory of sovereignty: 'Now this law which we are discussing – the law of non-resistance – seems to draw its validity from the will of those who associate themselves together in the first place to form a civil society ('pendere videtur a voluntate eorum, qui se primum in societatem civile consociant'); from the same source, furthermore, derives the right which passes into the hands of those who govern.' (DJBP 1.4.7.2) The end of a specific state, and thus – since the power over others is related to the end of the association – of the exact scope of the state's power, and consequently also of the range of the law of non-resistance in situations of extreme or eminent peril, ultimately depend on what the people had wished for at the time the association was instituted, or might have arranged at a later moment. Were we in a position to ask them whether they had unconditionally wanted the obligation to prefer death rather than to take up arms to ward off an injury by their sovereign, Grotius was not quite so sure on the answer we would get: 'nescio' (DJBP 1.4.7.2).

Notwithstanding the conclusion in chapter 1.4 that, generally speaking, resistance cannot legitimately be made to him or them who hold(s) supreme power, the constitutional varieties discussed above can lead to grounds for resistance in several situations, since they might limit the supreme power of the ruler. The key to the puzzle of the idea of 'limited supreme power' lies hidden in DJBP 1.3.16.2: according to Grotius, power can be supreme (*summa*), that is not subject to the legal control of another, even if it is limited. The limitation can concern the exercise of power, or the power itself. The first is the case when a promise was made (not) to make use of power in a certain way; an act contrary to the promise is unjust. But, as we have seen, also the power itself can be limited, in the sense of not being complete. In fact, the typical situation of a king with a usufructuary right in the association's power is an example of limited supreme power, since this king may not alienate his power. Should he do so, it would implicate a change in the manner of holding power, a competence that is usually not comprised in the supreme power transferred to a king; therefore, the people are licensed to resist him should he try to sell and alienate his power (DJBP 1.4.10). In either situation – the limitation concerns the exercise of power, or the power itself – if the subject of limited supreme power acts beyond the limits, Grotius would say that it's not 'the legal control of another' that nullifies the act, but law itself (*ipso jure*): the act will be unjust (*injustus*) or void on account of lack of power ('nullus defectu facultatis', DJBP 1.3.16.2). Therefore, the power that is thus limited might still be called 'supreme', since it was exclusively the absence of 'the operation of another human will' (DJBP 1.3.7.1) that marked supreme power.

Apart from stipulated situations in which resistance might be legitimate, there is still one important general restriction on the power of any ruler and any government. It says that, if the ruler openly shows himself as an enemy of the people, he may be resisted, irrespective of whatever right he may have in the supreme power (DJBP 1.4.11). By showing himself as an enemy of the people, said Grotius, he has already renounced and forfeited his kingdom. The will to rule, that is to foster the association's goal of public peace and order and to defend the association in its being and its rights, logically cannot coexist with the will to destroy the association or its members, the people.

To complete the picture, we must read Grotius' ideas on resistance in connection with his general maxim on the right of war and peace, which reads that 'War begins where judicial settlement fails' (DJBP 2.1.2.1). This goes for international public wars, and it goes for private wars in the state of nature. It also goes for civil wars. If the association is in great danger, or the supreme ruler fails to defend the mere existence of the people, or doesn't provide for proper and appeasing law and justice, or acts beyond his competences, there is in fact no longer a *civil* order, since there is no effective court or institution one could turn to in order to settle the dispute or issue. The association and its members then – temporarily – fall back into the state of nature, the natural order. In this situation, the people can lawfully begin a war against their superior, 'subditorum in superiores'. Not entirely clear is exactly *who* may offer resistance to the superior in a situation as described: any individual member of the association, or only the people collectively? The argument itself seems to entail that the association as such is entitled to fight the tyrant, for the associated individual members are still reciprocally bound by their collective will to act as one body.

8.5 Conclusion: How to Appreciate Grotius' Theory

Individual men associate, whereby a moral entity or body is created with the power to bind its members, with an eminent *dominium* and with the natural rights to defend itself. What there is to defend depends on the kind of association the individuals have willed for themselves, on how thoroughly they want their life and existence to be ruled by the association. The next move is that the association chooses who should wield the association's power and on which legal title they should do so; the choice of the association is decisive for the power of the ruler(s). Grotius' ruler is bestowed with absolute power if the people so wished, bound to the laws if they wished otherwise; bestowed with all the power needed to protect the association, or only a part of it; with unrestricted or conditional power. But, whatever the scope of power and whatever the form of government, the legitimacy of the government's rule depends on the will and ability to strive for the ultimate end of the association, that is: public peace and order.

Is this the ruler 'whose actions are not subject to the legal control of another, so that they cannot be rendered void by the operation of another human will' (DJBP 1.3.7.1)? It seems proper to say that not so much the subject, but only the power itself, could possibly be called 'supreme' – as Grotius himself indeed did (DJBP 1.3.7.1). Power can be supreme (*summa*) even if it is limited (DJBP 1.3.16.2). If the subject of limited supreme power acts beyond the limits, the act will be void on account of lack of power. On the other hand, limited supreme power can be held 'absolutely' ('pleno jure', DJBP 1.3.17.1).

The theory might be legally consistent, but how to appreciate it? After all, it does make room for absolute power and, as is often pointed out, political enslavement of a people. Grotius (in DJBP 1.3.8) attacked the opinion of many that the supreme power always resides in the people. In order to get there, he used the analogy of the people and the individual: as it is permitted for any person to enslave himself, why would it not be permitted for a people to enslave themselves?

Jean-Jacques Rousseau (1712–78) is well known for his fierce critique on Grotius' ideas concerning this issue in his *Du Contrat Social* (1762). An act by which a man gives himself for nothing – that is, enslaves himself – said Rousseau, is null and illegitimate for the simple reason that this man must be out of his mind; and madness, he added, does not confer rights. John Locke (1632–1704), too, without reference to Grotius, denies man the possibility to enslave himself to anyone, to part from his freedom and subject himself to the absolute, arbitrary power of someone else. The 'fundamental, sacred, and unalterable law of self-preservation', said Locke, stands between a man and anyone who invades his means of preservation.[25]

According to Grotius, however, individual voluntary slavery is not a form of submission 'for nothing', as Rousseau said, since he calculated a serious repayment: a lasting certainty of support (DJBP 2.5.27.2). The exchange of lifelong services in return for nourishment and other necessities of life in itself does not seem a sign of insanity. Moreover, just as Locke would do some decades later,[26] Grotius held that a man's life, body and limbs are his own (*suum*) 'not to destroy, but to safeguard' (DJBP 2.17.2.1 and 2.21.11.2). One can think of situations in which voluntary enslavement might be the only way to safeguard one's life. The more so if we take into account that, according to Grotius, a master does not have the right of life and death over his slaves (notwithstanding that the master might often go unpunished according to the laws of some people if he killed his slave for whatever reason, DJBP 2.5.28). The same goes for the ruler and his people, however unrestrained the ruler's power might be (DJBP 2.5.28). Voluntary slavery might, according to Grotius, be a reasonable option in situations of threats to one's preservation, and this is precisely the situation in DJBP 1.3.8.3, where Grotius discussed the option for a people to transfer its *jus imperandi* completely and unrestrictedly to a ruler, thereby creating absolute power and subjection, a form of political slavery.

However, Grotius, in the same paragraph, also discussed the possibility that a people are so constituted that they understand better how to be ruled than to rule, a reminder of Aristotle's account of slaves by nature.[27] Another people might be impressed by examples of men living happily and prosperous under their absolute rulers (DJBP 1.3.8.4–5). Complete voluntary submission might seem attractive to such peoples even without being in a situation of eminent threat – and Grotius, former spokesman of the VOC, would not withhold them. In addition to these voluntary forms of slavery, there is (political) slavery as a result of being conquered in a war that had been legitimate on the side of the conqueror (DJBP 1.3.8.6, against which Rousseau likewise objected in *Du Contrat Social* 1.4).

What Grotius tried to refute in DJBP 1.3.8 was the opinion that the *summa potestas* always resides in the people. The possibility of a complete and absolute submission, that is political slavery, is one of his arguments against it. Indeed, it might not convince us, but it seems too severe to say with Rousseau that all constitutions in which the people are not sovereign are a definite sign of madness.

Another possible attack on Grotius' theory is that not necessarily everything is open for trade. A free man (*homo liber*) was sometimes explicitly said to be *extra commercium*, for instance by the aforementioned Spaniard, Fernando Vázquez,[28] and by Frenchman Francois Hotman (1524–90),[29] with reference to D. 45.1.103. Grotius refers to the latter (DJBP 1.3.12.1–2). But, for both Hotman and Grotius, the point of saying that men are or are not *extra commercium* concerns the question of whether or not the right to govern can be sold and transferred by the ruler without the subjects' approval; it is not on the relation between the ruler and individuals he rules over – in fact, Vázquez's ideas on this topic were more promising. For Grotius, the question of sale and transferability is settled by the right the ruler has in the *jus regendi*: property or an usufructuary right; in the first case, the right may be sold and transferred, in the second case not. Still, Grotius answered to Hotman, even if the ruler holds the *jus regendi* in property and would thus be authorised to sell and transfer this right, it is not the people who are subject to trade, but only the right to govern them. This *homo liber* discourse doesn't lead us anywhere.

One could object to Grotius that not all natural rights of man – or of the people as a legal *persona ficta* in natural law – necessarily are for sale or trade. This, of course, is the idea that some such rights might be inalienable, the theory ascribed to John Locke and found in the American

Declaration of Independence (1776) and the French *Déclaration des droits de l'homme et du citoyen* (1789). With respect to the rights, not of the individual but of the people, the inalienability of power had a strong defender in Johannes Althusius, who insists that the power of the people was *proprium & incommunicabile* and that the king's power was only a *precarium* given by contract to the commissioned king, and undertaken by him ('precarium ex contractu mandate regi datum & susceptum').[30]

Grotius himself, at first sight, came close to the very idea of inalienable rights when he, in *The jurisprudence of Holland* (written around 1619, published 1631), differentiates between alienable and inalienable things (IHR 2.1.41–8, '(on)wandelbare zaken', in Latin in the margin to the text: *(in)alienabiles*). Life, body, freedom and honour are inalienable. But, what Grotius meant by a thing being 'inalienable' is that a thing can belong to one man in a way that it cannot possibly belong to anybody else. When I give up my life, or my freedom, there cannot be somebody else who acquires it. In *De jure belli ac pacis*, we find another example of an inalienable right, the right of a father over his children (*jus patrium*; DJBP 3.7.4); it is striking that, in the only section in the *Two treatises* in which Locke came close to the term 'inalienable',[31] we also read that 'a father cannot alien the power he has over his child'.

Even if we take into account that, according to Grotius, people do not 'alienate' their natural rights when they enter the association, he was definitely not looking for a theory that would exclude slavery, or indeed absolutism or political slavery. Quite the opposite, as Annabel Brett has pointed out, focusing on the political: 'Individual right was conceived in an almost commercial vein as natural man's original capital, to be spent on advantage: and the man who bought citizenship with his rights could not then claim those same rights against the city.'[32]

It was not Grotius' aim to prescribe one form of government or another – his theory was analytical, rather than normative (cfr. DJBP 1.3.8.1). Instead, he provided the legal ground for a whole spectrum of constitutional arrangements, from a free people ruling themselves to complete political slavery under an absolute ruler.

Translation of Grotius' Work Used

Het recht van oorlog en vrede, transl. J.F. Lindemans (Baarn, 1993). *The Rights of War and Peace*, ed. R. Tuck (Indianapolis, 2005)

Further Reading

Barducci, M., *Hugo Grotius and the Century of Revolution 1613-1718. Transnational Reception in English Political Thought* (Oxford, 2017).

Baumgold, D., *Contract Theory in Historical Context. Essays on Grotius, Hobbes and Locke* (Leiden and Boston, 2010).

Brett, A.S., 'The development of the idea of citizens' rights', in Q. Skinner and B. Strath (eds.), *States and Citizens, History, Theory, Prospects* (Cambridge, 2003), 97-112.

Brett, A.S., *Changes of State. Nature and the Limits of the City in Early Modern Natural Law* (Princeton and Oxford, 2011).

Brett, A.S., 'The subject of sovereignty: law, politics and moral reasoning in Hugo Grotius', *Modern Intellectual History* 4 (2019) 1-27.

Feenstra, R., 'Expropriation et *dominium eminens* chez Grotius', in *l'Expropriation/ Exrpropriation* (Recueils de la société Jean Bodin pour l'histoire comparative des institutions/Transactions of the Jean Bodin society for comparative institutional history 66.1; *Brussels*, 1999), 133-53.

Grunert, F., 'Sovereignty and resistance: the development of the right of resistance in German natural law', in I. Hunter and D. Saunders (eds.), *Natural Law and Civil Sovereignty. Moral Right and State Authority in Early Modern Political Thought* (Basingstoke and New York, 2002), 123-38.

Haakonssen, K., 'Hugo Grotius and the history of political thought', *Political Theory* 13 (1985), 239-65.

Hinshelwood, B., 'Punishment and sovereignty in De Indis *and* De iure belli ac pacis', Grotiana N.S. 38 (2017) 71-105.

Konegen N., and P. Nitschke (eds.), *Staat bei Hugo Grotius* (Baden-Baden, 2005)

Lee, D., 'Popular liberty, princely government, and the Roman law in Hugo Grotius' *De Jure Belli ac Pacis*', *Journal of the History of Ideas* 72 (2011) 371-92.

Straumann, B, 'Early modern sovereignty and its limits', *Theoretical Inquiries in Law* 16 (2015) 423-46.

Van Gelderen, M., 'From Domingo de Soto to Hugo Grotius: theories of monarchy and civil power in Spanish and Dutch political thought, 1555-1609', *Pensiero Politico* 32 (1999), 186-205.

Van Nifterik, G., 'Hugo Grotius on slavery', in H.W. Blom and L.C. Winkel (eds.), *Grotius and the Stoa* (Assen, 2004), 233-43.

Van Nifterik, G., 'Grotius and the origin of the ruler's right to punish', in H.W. Blom (ed.), *Property, Piracy and Punishment* (Leiden and Boston, 2009), 396-415.

Notes

1 Most influential has been R. Tuck, *Natural Rights Theories. Their Origin and Development* (Cambridge, 1978), 79: 'The book is Janus-faced, and its two mouths speak the language of both absolutism and liberty.'

2 D. Baumgold, 'Pacifying politics: resistance, violence, and accountability in seventeenth-century contract theory', *Political Theory* 21 (1993) 6–27. The text is also published as chapter 2in D. Baumgold, *Contract Theory in Historical Context. Essays on Grotius, Hobbes and Locke* (Leiden and Boston, 2010).

3 Recently in this sense M. Barducci, *Hugo Grotius and the Century of Revolution 1613–1718. Transnational Reception in English Political Thought* (Oxford, 2017).

4 P. Borschberg, 'Grotius, the social contract and political resistance. A study of the unpublished *Theses LVI*', *IILJ Working Paper 2006/7. History and Theory of International Law Series*, 70.

5 P. Borschberg, *Hugo Grotius 'Commentarius in Theses XI'. An Early Treatise on Sovereignty, the Just War, and the Legitimacy of the Dutch Revolt* (Berne [etc.], 1994), 199 and Borschberg, 'Grotius, the Social Contract and Political Resistance', 59.

6 See Borschberg. 'Grotius, the Social Contract and Political Resistance', 28.

7 Borschberg, *Hugo Grotius*, 116 ff. and Borschberg, 'Grotius, the Social Contract and Political Resistance', 49 ff.

8 D. 17.2.

9 See H. Grotius, *Inleidinge tot de Hollandsche rechtsgeleerdheid* (1631) 3.21 on 'maetschap'.

10 The topic is discussed by A.S. Brett, *Changes of State. Nature and the Limits of the City in Early Modern Natural Law* (Princeton and Oxford, 2011), 122 ff. See for instance F. de Vitoria, *De potestate civili* (1528): 'respublica, societas, corpus humanum, communitas'; D. de Soto, *De justitia et iure* (1556) 4.4.1: 'congregatio, respublica, corpus & membra reipublicae'; F. Suárez, *De legibus ac Deo legislatore* (1612) 3.1: 'communitas (perfecta / politica), corpus', 3.3: 'corpus politicum hominum, communitas humana/hominum, respublica'.

11 F. de Vitoria, *De jure belli* 7.

12 These phrases are taken from Kelsey in his translation of DJBP; the translation in the edition by R. Tuck (Indianapolis, 2005) and by Jan Frans Lindemans in his Dutch translation. In Dutch it reads: 'waardoor zij juist een volk zijn'.

13 K. Haakonssen, 'Hugo Grotius and the history of political thought', *Political Theory* 13 (1985) 239–65, at 246.

14 Tuck, *Natural rights theories*, 79 ff. Interpretative charity at 80.

15 D. 50.17.54.

16 Borschberg, 'Grotius, the social contract and political resistance', 40.

17 Vitoria, *De potestate civili*, esp. par. 7 ff; Soto, *De justitia et iure* 4.4.1; Suárez, *De legibus ac Deo legislatore*, 3.3.

18 Romans 13.2.

19 Yet, other authors that might have influenced Grotius on these issues also come to the fore, as the Jesuit Luis de Molina (1535–1600). According to Hasso Höpfl, *Jesuit Political Thought. The Society of Jesus and the State, c. 1540-1630* (Cambridge, 2006) 229 Molina 'asserted that the extent of any prince's *potestas* depended on the decision of the commonwealth "at the first creation of the kingdom"'.

20 He did so most clearly in *Controversiae illustres* (1564) 1.13.2 and 16, an 1.21, with reference to, and extensively quoting from D. de Soto, *De justitia et jure* 4.4.1.

21 With reference to Seneca, *Moral letters to Luculius*, Letter 14.

22 D. Lee, 'Popular liberty, princely government, and the Roman law in Hugo Grotius' *De Jure Belli ac Pacis'*, *Journal of the History of Ideas* 72 (2011) 371–92; also published as chapter 8 in his *Popular Sovereignty in Early Modern Constitutional Thought* (Oxford, 2016), at 387.

23 As does F. Grunert, 'Der Vertrag als rechtliches Medium sozialer Gestaltung: Zum Kontraktualismus bei Hugo Grotius', in N. Konegen and P. Nitschke (eds.), *Staat bei Hugo Grotius* (Staatsverständnisse 9; Baden-Baden, 2005), 125–37, at 130.

24 The text can be found in P. Borschberg, 'Grotius, the social contract and political resistance', 55.

25 J. Locke, *Two Treatises on Government* (1689) 2.4.23 and 24, 2.13.149.

26 Locke, *Two Treatises* 2.2.6.

27 *Politics 1.5, 1254a17.*

28 F. Vázquez de Menchaca, *Controversiae illustres* (1564) 2.82.13.

29 F. Hotman, *Questionum illustrium liber* (1573), q.1.

30 *Politica* 18.104; transl. F.S. Carney, *The Politics of Johannes Althusius. An Abridged Translation of the Third Edition of Politica Methodice Digesta* (London 1964), 109.

31 Locke, *Two Treatises* 1.100.

32 A.S. Brett, 'The development of the idea of citizens' rights', in Q. Skinner and B. Strath (eds.), *States and Citizens, History, Theory, Prospects* (Cambridge, 2003), 97–112, at 104–5.

9 Church and State

Harm-Jan van Dam

9.1 Introduction

In the Dutch Republic around 1600, a nascent state where the new, reformed religion had recently been adopted, relations between Church and state – a relevant issue in most of Europe at the time – gained extra importance. Hugo Grotius, both a political thinker and a politician, made a serious contribution to the debate. By and large, Grotius' lifelong ideal was, as we shall see, that of a state with a Christian public Church, where toleration of religious differences was practised. In that state, all power – both in secular and religious matters – should rest with the secular authorities, the 'supreme ruler', the sovereign government. This needs some clarification: for Grotius and his contemporaries, the Church was divided into the 'invisible' church of Christ, the universal community of believers, on the one hand; and, on the other hand, the visible church, that is the concrete institutional body on earth that preaches the gospel and administers the sacraments. The 'public church' is the visible church, and by 'public' Grotius referred to an established Christian church or state church, which is officially recognised and subsidised. In the Dutch United Provinces, this was the Dutch Reformed Church, but, in speaking of England or the Late Roman Empire, Grotius likewise referred to the Church of England, or the early Christian state church, as the 'public church'. 'Supreme ruler' is one of the (Latin) terms that Grotius used in speaking of the 'state', of sovereign government. Other terms are 'highest power(s)', 'sovereign', 'authorities' or 'civil magistrates'. According to Grotius, there is always one and only one highest power or sovereign government. This may be a person, such as a king; or a pair, such as the two Roman consuls; or a representative body of men, such as the Dutch States. According to his works that were written when he lived in the Netherlands, the States of each of the Seven Provinces were the sovereign government in all practical instances regarding religion. In Grotius' case, therefore, this was the States of Holland, not the States General. The proposition that each province was sovereign in the field of religion was contained in Article 13 of the Union of Utrecht (1579), the founding text of the new state, but it was much disputed. In discussing Grotius' views on Church and state, some scholars, such as Quentin Skinner, tend to see the two as opposing forces in Grotius' work or in his time, judging that the state became 'modern' as it became secular.[1] Others, such as Charles Prior, claim that religion and government, or politics, continued to belong firmly together, especially in the first century after the Reformation.[2] I tend to agree more with the latter position, because – in my view – Grotius himself could not imagine living in a state without a Christian Church, but I will come back to this issue in discussing divine and natural law later and directly below in discussing secularisation.

For Grotius, there existed no fundamental difference between his historical, political, theological or legal work: in the introduction to his *Annotationes* on the Old Testament, he referred the reader to *De jure belli ac pacis*, and references to that work abound in his late Bible commentaries. On a larger scale, blending theology with law and history is the essence of some of his works, such as *De satisfactione Christi* (*On the satisfaction of Christ*, 1617). In my view, Grotius' major work on Church and state, *De imperio summarum potestatum circa sacra* (*On the Authority of the Supreme Powers in Matters of Religion*; finished in 1617, published in 1647), is a compound of political science, ecclesiology/theology and law, which anticipates *De jure belli ac pacis* in a number of respects. A different view, that of Grotius' 'removal of theology from law', is held by Mark Somos, who argues mainly from Grotius' unpublished *De jure praedae commentarius*.[3] It is often claimed that this work is a forerunner of the 'essentially secular, new system of laws that we find in *De Jure Belli ac Pacis*', but this 'secularity' is open to some modification: in both *De imperio* (DI 1.13) and *De jure belli ac pacis* (DJBP 2.20.44.3), Grotius quotes a number of ancient authorities to prove that 'religion is the base of human society' ('religio humanae societatis fundamentum', ascribed to Cicero). Peter Haggenmacher warns against seeing Grotius as the strictly secular, rational forerunner of the Enlightenment who liberated law from its theological shackles.[4] Richard Tuck holds a different view.[5] Grotius undoubtedly played a part in Europe's secularisation, seen as a process during which the Church lost its exclusive control over society; he did so mainly by his historical, or rather philological, approach to biblical studies. However, we must guard against linking 'philological criticism with philosophical rejection of tradition'.[6] That secularisation was the outcome of a process to which Grotius contributed does not of itself mean that he intended a society without Christianity at its heart to come about, as I argue against Jonathan Israel and Mark Somos.[7] Grotius' philological approach to the Bible was well aligned with his irenic ideals, as Dirk van Miert claims.[8]

In the following, I will first sketch an historical background of Grotius' views on Church and state. Then I will go into their intellectual background, sources and key factors. Other sources will come up in the main discussion. Subsequently, I will discuss Grotius' opinions on the relations between Church and state regarding a number of specific aspects, such as the qualities of the supreme power and its status; lawgiving; the right of resistance by the Church to the supreme power; synods; jurisdiction; the appointment of ministers and ecclesiastical hierarchy; and, finally, divine and natural law.

9.2 Historical Background: The Dutch Revolt and Religious Troubles

From 1588, five years after Grotius was born, the Dutch Revolt against Spain was pursued by the United Provinces of the North, more or less sovereign states. They delegated representatives to the States General a body that took on a number of executive functions. In practice, Holland, by far the most powerful and richest of the provinces, was in charge. From 1586 until his execution in 1619, the highest-ranking civil servant was the so-called Grand Pensionary, Johan van Oldenbarnevelt (1547–1619). In theory, he was only the leader of the States of Holland and Zeeland, but, in practice, he was the most powerful man in the Republic, together with its commander-in-chief, Stadholder Maurice of Orange (1567–1625).

In 1613, Grotius was delegated by the burgomasters of Rotterdam as their representative in the States of Holland, the civil government of the province. There he became Oldenbarnevelt's right-hand man. It was, therefore, as a civil servant in peacetime that Grotius had to deal with the troubles within the United Provinces. For, during the Twelve Years Truce with Spain (1609–21), serious conflicts broke out that divided the young republic. These conflicts, which intensified during the Truce, were both religious and political. The doctrinal divergence was over the nature of predestination: when and how did God choose between the souls to be saved and those eternally damned – not merely an academic question at a time when infant mortality was huge.[9] It originated with the appointment of Jacobus Arminius (1559–1609) as professor of theology at Leiden in 1603 and the ensuing clash with his colleague, Franciscus Gomarus (1563–1641). However, the differences soon took a political turn and infected the whole republic: the appointment of preachers, which was the task of the civil authorities, involved a theological choice. Therefore, the followers of Gomarus demanded that the States of Holland convoke a general synod of the Dutch Reformed Church, in order to decide on the doctrine. The States, on the other hand, tried to avoid a synod at all costs. Then Arminius' spiritual successor, Grotius' friend and mentor Johannes Wtenbogaert (1557–1644), drew up the so-called Remonstrance, five articles of belief that were presented to the States of Holland in 1610.[10] This body made the political decision to base the examination and appointment of future ministers on the religious views of the Remonstrance. Since the presentation of the Remonstrance, Arminians and Gomarists were also known as Remonstrants and Counter-Remonstrants.

The States of Holland charged Grotius with investigating the nature and causes of the troubles. The chief matters at issue were: would it be possible to have a public church in which toleration of religious differences was practised? For the States, the existence of one, and only one, Dutch Reformed (state-)Church was imperative; but many Dutch Christians rejected the enforced toleration of different religious views that this implied. Moreover, should a national synod be convoked and, if so, by whom? Most ministers and many members of the States General were in favour of such a synod, but the States of Holland obstructed this for a long time, arguing that they were sovereign in this matter. The third, and perhaps most important, question concerned the supremacy of magistrate or minister, 'state' or 'Church', or rather the extent of the sovereign's power over the Church. Most regents, members of the States and city councils, argued that in a public church, where ministers were trained and paid out of public means, obedience of the ministers was due to the Christian magistrate. They saw the wish of ecclesiastics for a Church with its own authority as 'collaterality', the existence of two equal powers, Church and state, as something that was associated with Roman Catholicism.

Grotius not only investigated matters on the ground, but also composed many works in which he gave his views on the issues that were at the root of the troubles. There are two sides to Grotius' work on Church and state, especially in the 'Dutch years': first of all, he was a great scholar and a sharp and profound thinker. Scripture and the Church Fathers laid the fundament for his views: the Old Testament, with the Jewish constitution described in it, and the New Testament, as evidence for the institution of the early Church with its apostles, pastors, lay elders and other offices and rules, showed, according to Grotius, that his views were in accordance with the Christian faith, and were true. The practice of the early Church under the Roman Christian emperors from Constantine the Great onwards (r. 306–37), as it was represented by the Fathers, strengthened his case. For the later period, he based himself on anti-papal writings from the medieval struggle for power between the popes and the emperors, especially by Marsilius of Padova (1275/1290–1343). To Grotius, such historical examples and instances offered conclusive arguments if they were firmly founded on philology and after they were sifted by his scholarship and reasoning. On the other hand, his views of the superiority of the civil government largely coincided with those of the States of Holland, his masters. As a result, there is also a streak of propaganda in the work of this period and there are more or less veiled references to contemporary questions.

9.3 Intellectual Background

As his works from 1610 onwards show, Grotius was familiar with canon-ical ancient texts, legal works up to his own time, and medieval and contemporary Church history and theology. Moreover, he kept himself up to date, in Holland and later in France, by reading recent, relevant literature, such as the books and pamphlets published during the Dutch troubles. Therefore, identifying specific influences and sources is some-what arbitrary, but three important elements in Grotius' views on Church and state should be mentioned here. They are Grotius' ideal of toleration and its roots, his views on Jewish history and its relevance to the Dutch Republic, and the theories on Church and State of the Swiss theologian Erastus, which Grotius largely adopted.

First, Grotius' personal ideal throughout his life was that of toleration of different religious convictions, and of unity in the Christian Church; his early unpublished works *De Pace* (*On Peace* 1600–10) and *Meletius* already testify to it. In *Ordinum pietas* (90), Grotius placed Desiderius Erasmus (1466–1536) at the head of a specific Dutch form of the Reformation, not without somewhat special pleading, and quoted from Erasmus that harmony in the Christian state can only exist if theological definitions are avoided as much as possible.[11] This was another of Grotius' lifelong convictions, comparable to the ancient maxim on legal definitions: 'Every definition in the civil law is dangerous' (DI 6.9).[12] According to Grotius and his fellow Remonstrants, there were only a few essential articles of faith, and those could and should be shared among all Christians. Accepting this view was a necessary condition for a unified Christian Church.

Grotius always supported the unity of the Church, when he lived in Holland and in France. In the *Dedication* of *De jure belli ac pacis* to King Louis XIII (1601–43), he commended the unification of the Christian churches, 'in somewhat veiled terms, with some restrictions', as he wrote to his brother-in-law on 4 April 1625 (2 BW 963); and toleration, freedom of thought, is the theme of *De jure belli ac pacis* 2.20.[13] The sovereign's objective is the common good, that is salvation, and he will attain that goal by fostering religion. For Grotius' argument, this sovereign is not necessarily a Christian. Grotius went further than most of his contemporaries in arguing that all persecution based on religious convictions is wrong, Christians persecuting non-Christians as well as the other way around. Since his appointment as Sweden's Ambassador in Paris in 1635, Grotius was particularly concerned with the reunion of the Christian churches. This is clear from his treatise of around 1638, *De dogmatis, ritibus et gubernatione ecclesiae Christi* (*On doctrine, ritual and government of the Christian church*). At the same time, this ideal of reunion implied Grotius was drifting away from orthodox Protestantism.[14] Church and state remain important in his writings on dogma, belief and ecclesiology of that later period insofar as toleration is one of their main themes. However, Grotius always was rather vague about the exact relations between Church and state in a reunited Christian Church.

According to Grotius, the few essential, and necessary, articles of the Christian faith are to be found in the early Christian Church, which the Anglican Church resembled most: it is best always to follow the early Church, even if a change would be an improvement but is unnecessary, as Grotius thought (DI 6). This conservative attitude is also at the base of his views on ecclesiastical hierarchy.

Grotius often mentioned his one-time landlord, François du Jon (Franciscus Junius, 1545–1602), professor of divinity at Leiden from 1592 until his death, as his prime example for toleration. When Grotius was cross-examined during his imprisonment in 1618, he stated: 'For what I needed of theology I have based myself on the late doctor Junius, whose conviction of the need for tolerance is known well enough from his *Eirenicum*.' There is no doubt that Grotius' ideal of toleration was a strong personal conviction, but there is a social and political side to toleration as well. Most historians nowadays consider toleration as the pre-eminent characteristic of the Dutch Republic.[15] Even during the troubles, freedom of conscience and of religious belief was always an unquestioned principle, both for Grotius and for strict Calvinists. As Grotius put it in legal terminology: internal, purely mental processes are not liable to punishment (DI 3.1, see also DJBP 2.4.3, 2.6.1 and 2.20.18). However, freedom of conscience does not mean freedom of religious practice. Where external, public matters are concerned, the civil government steps in, according to Grotius' philosophy; and according to contemporary practice as well: in the first decades of the seventeenth century, the civil authorities thought the unity of the public church all-important. Therefore, the States of Holland decided to enforce toleration: in 1614, they issued the so-called Toleration Decree (*Decretum pro pace ecclesiarum*); it laid down what the ministers were allowed to teach on predestination. This official, political (short) text was written by Grotius, who was also responsible for most of its over 130 pages of justificatory quotations, taken from Scripture, the Church Fathers and the reformers.[16]

Second, in Grotius' time the comparison of the Dutch and their revolt with Habsburg Spain to the people of Israel led out of Egypt was frequently made: 'a unified socio-political ideology expressed in the metaphor of the New Israel'.[17] Moreover, many reformed scholars of the late sixteenth century read the Old Testament not only as the history of the Jewish people, but as containing a political constitution, a body of law given by God to his people, with Moses as his lawgiver. In this view, God's laws embraced both civil and religious law, to be administered by the civil magistrate of the Hebrew state, the most perfect state on earth until the coming of Christ. The study of Hebrew and of Talmudic sources was especially developed in Holland: Grotius' friend, Petrus Cunaeus (1586–1638), published his *Hebrew Republic* in 1617. Grotius himself consulted sources on Jewish history, including Talmudic literature in secondary sources and Jewish specialists in person. Arguments based on the Jewish constitution and examples taken from the Old Testament abound in *De jure belli ac pacis*, in *De imperio* and elsewhere. In fact, as Eric Nelson argues, both parties in the troubles shared the – European – view of the Hebrew State as a model for the modern, that is the Christian, state. And they agreed that the civil ruler had received law from God, including religious law.[18] In one of his earliest writings, *De republica emendanda* (*To improve the Dutch Republic*, c. 1600), Grotius brought up for the first time the subject of Church and state. In this connection, he briefly discussed the Jewish Sanhedrin, the Great Council. He claimed, not for the last time, that it possessed the supreme power and was undivided, until Roman Emperor Theodosius I (r. 379–95) abolished it.[19] In this early work, Grotius compared the Sanhedrin to the Dutch Republic's State Council, and he argued for a shift of power to that Council. However, not long afterwards he changed his mind and suppressed the book, which was published only in the twentieth century. After that, he defended the sovereignty of the States. The point of his repeated, longer discussions of the Jewish constitution and the Sanhedrin in later works always is that it was one body, the sovereign government, invested with temporal and religious power and that it should be an example for the Christian state in this respect.

Third, Grotius' strong conviction that all power rests with the supreme ruler may be called 'Erastian'. It is useful, however, to qualify that term, which is most frequently used in connection with English history in the years 1640–60. Thomas Erastus (1524–83) himself, a Swiss Zwinglian theologian and physician, composed one famous book in 1568 that was published posthumously in 1589 in England, *A treatise on excommunication ...* (*Explicatio gravissimae quaestionis...*).[20] Its leading thought is that excommunication in the sense of exclusion from the sacraments is a Roman-Catholic practice without any foundation in the Bible. Two other propositions were more or less corollary to this: that there should be only one, that is, a civil, jurisdiction within the state. And, second, that this should be similar to the Jewish Sanhedrin. Views like that of Erastus had been put forward by other Swiss theologians, such as Hulrych Zwingli (1484–1531) and Heinrich Bullinger (1504–75), but never in such a compelling way.[21] In English usage, 'Erastianism' has mostly lost its connection with excommunication and may refer more generally to one or more of three propositions: 1) state authority prevails over Church authority, 2) religious authorities do not have any independent disciplinary role within a Christian state, 3) the civil magistrate has the absolute right to determine religious policy regardless of his personal orthodoxy. In the Dutch context, these views, in pure form, are first found in the 1610 Dutch work on Church and state by Grotius' mentor, Johannes Wytenbogaert: *Tractaet van t'Ampt ende Authoriteyt eener Hoogher Christelicker Overheydt in Kerckelicke saecken* (*A treatise on the office and authority of the supreme Christian government in ecclesiastical affairs*).[22] Grotius knew this book well and used it in his own writings, but he also read and quoted Erastus' Latin work, and possessed a copy. He agreed with Erastus on the role of the Sanhedrin, and also on the point of civil jurisdiction; but he took that one step further by allowing the civil authority to decide on doctrinal matters. In the Dutch Republic, this was the States of each Province. This means that Grotius also approved of two consequences of the propositions mentioned above: that all binding religious law is civil law, and that the civil sovereign should only make religious laws that are politically necessary; and, also, that he is obliged to do so. It is in this sense that Grotius' views as expressed especially in *Ordinum pietas* and *De imperio* may be called 'Erastian'.

9.4 Works

Grotius wrote his works dealing more or less exclusively with Church and state in the years 1610–18.[23] The most important are *Ordinum Hollandiae et Westfrisae pietas*, published around 21 October 1613; the *Oration* he held in April 1616 in a vain attempt to persuade the Amsterdam magistrates to adopt the politics of the States of Holland; and *De imperio summarum potestatum circa sacra* in 1617. This leaves aside the notes, letters, statutes, drafts and similar papers Grotius wrote for the States in direct consequence of his office. There, the political purpose is evident; but, in the other works, it is not always simple to distinguish what is dictated by current political demands from detached scholarship or Grotius' personal convictions. Church and state retained Grotius' attention after his escape from prison in 1620, first in his *Apologeticus* (*Justification of the lawful government of Holland* 1622), the political apology that he started writing immediately after his imprisonment. It remains an important issue in *De jure belli ac pacis* (1625) and in his annotations to the Bible of the 1640s, as well as in a number of treatises written during the years 1638–40.

Ordinum pietas had its origin in a particular occasion: the Frisian orthodox Calvinist theologian, Sibrandus Lubbertus (1555–1625), had charged the States of Holland and Westfrisia with impiety, in a massive book dedicated to the Anglican Archbishop George Abbot (1562–1633). With *Ordinum pietas*, Grotius tried to defend his masters against this charge. In its last part, he discussed topical questions on Church and state. Here he argued for the first time that the sovereign or supreme magistrate alone judges on the public religion (§ 118). In fact, Lubbertus had hardly touched upon the relation of Church and state in his book. One reason for Grotius' introduction of the subject was that he expected English churchmen and the king to read his book. By drawing the parallel between the Dutch Counter-Remonstrants and the English Puritans, he hoped to set up King James I/VI (1566–1625) against the Counter-Remonstrants. However, *Ordinum pietas* backfired because of its fierceness and its outspoken Remonstrant views. King James completely rejected the idea that the civil authorities decide on religious doctrine. Grotius immediately tried to repair the damage by composing a more scholarly, detached work: a first, unpublished version was finished in August 1614: *Tractatus de jure magistratuum circa ecclesiastica* (*Treatise on the right of the rulers in ecclesiastical matters*, TJME). The final version of this was *De imperio*. This is an exhaustive monograph on Church and state in which a scholarly, abstract approach based on Aristotelian logic and scholastic distinctions is combined with more concrete questions of Church policy. Grotius himself repeatedly stressed that *De imperio* was a theoretical, methodical book, a full treatment of Church government. A mass of over 2,000 quotations and examples supplied historical proof of the truth of Grotius' views. Many of them had been used earlier and were recycled later. They demonstrate that, for Grotius and many contemporaries, philology was an indispensable tool in deciding questions of Church policy, ecclesiastical hierarchy or doctrine. Correct texts of reliable authors from the past, the more the better, were fundamental. Of contemporary sources, works by English churchmen, also by King James, were the most frequent – but only works in Latin, for Grotius did not know English. The book's first half is general and theoretical. Here, Grotius distinguished, for instance, between different kinds of rule or directing/commanding (*regimen*), dividing it into 'constitutive rule', that is binding law, and 'directive rule', which merely voices an opinion, like the counsel of a physician or a pastor. In much the same way, judgment (*iudicium*) is divided into 'imperative' and 'directive' judgments in administering justice. The practical and topical issues in the rest of the book concern a range of subjects such as synods, the appointment of ministers or ecclesiastical hierarchy. Even this detached, scholarly monograph is, up to a point, a topical and partisan book: in speaking of the 'sovereign' or 'supreme power', Grotius often means 'the States of Holland' and the historical evidence about Church councils is geared to the conclusion that such a synod cannot be convoked without the support of the States.

De imperio was more or less ready for printing when Grotius was arrested in August 1618, and it remained unpublished until three years after Grotius' death, though it circulated in manuscript in scholarly circles in Paris and England. During his exile, Grotius returned from time to time to the theme of Church and state: for example, around 1625, when *De jure belli ac pacis* was published. At that time, there was a demand in France for an edition of *De imperio*, provided that quotations from Protestants were removed. However, Grotius considered this unacceptable.[24] Just as in the case of *De imperio*, Grotius claimed that his objective in *De jure belli ac pacis* was that what he wrote 'would apply always and everywhere' (2 BW 998, 1 August 1625). And, in fact, that book contains even less references to contemporary events than *De imperio*. In *De jure belli ac pacis*, the relationship between Church and state is not discussed at any length, but its background remains the same, and Grotius' views on sovereignty and the absolute power of the civil government, on legislation, jurisdiction and the organisation of the Church are presupposed; this is highlighted by the many common sources and quotations. His great commentaries on the Bible are philological and historical in character. The views found there are similar to those of the pre-1620 period, but less outspoken, for instance in his notes on Matthew regarding exclusion from the sacraments. The focus of the discussion there is not on the relationship between Church and state. Grotius plays down his earlier views on the Church without, however, taking them back.

9.5 The Supreme Power and the Church

In his unpublished early *Commentarius in theses XI*, Grotius still defined 'supreme power' as a right (*jus*); in *Ordinum pietas*, he left it undefined.

Since 1614, however, Grotius defined 'the supreme power', sovereign government, to be one indivisible person or body placed above other men and
subject to God alone. He based this view on Paul,[25] Aristotle and a long line
of medieval and early modern philosophers (TJME, DI 1.1, DJBP 1.3.7.1). The
sovereign has the highest authority over all offices, both those to which he
appoints deputies and the unrelated but inferior offices, such as physicians,
pastors or judges. Governors are both subject and deputy, pastors as such are
subject but not deputy. Pastors and other churchmen, just like physicians,
have their own tasks and responsibilities, but they can never overrule the
sovereign. For rule (authority, *imperium*) and office (*functio*) are different
things, and only the sovereign possesses the 'constitutive rule' (above, DI
2.1–2, 6.1, 4.6 ff., again based on Aristotelian arguments). Since there is only
one sovereign government, religion is its (main) concern. Its first decision
should be determining the official religion (OHWP 68–70, 98). This is the
principle of '*cuius regio eius religio*', 'whose realm, his religion', accepted at
the Peace of Augsburg in 1555. That is to say, the sovereign lays down the
state religion: Lutheran or Calvinist or Roman Catholic, etc. The principle
originates in natural law, and was accepted by Lutherans and Anglicans,
and also by the Dutch Remonstrants, but abhorred by orthodox Counter-
Remonstrants. Determining the official religion includes the removal of false
beliefs and heresy. 'It is the duty of the king *qua* king to protect the true
doctrine with laws and suppress its opposite. For he must also be the judge of
doctrine itself', Grotius wrote (1 BW 438, also expressed in DI 7.14–6, 8.2 ff.
and elsewhere).

   In defence of his view that religion is the most important office of the
sovereign, Grotius quoted, in his *Apologeticus* and elsewhere, Justus
Lipsius (1547–1606) and a number of German political and theological
authors, and also 'English theologians'. Characteristic of Grotius' use of
quotations and their importance to him is how he repeatedly cites a phrase
from the fourth-century Church historian, Socrates Scholasticus: 'from the
time the emperors began to profess the Christian religion, the affairs of the
Church have depended on them'. For Grotius, this amounts to proof that
the Christian Church has always been subordinate to the civil authorities.
The central question during the Dutch troubles was, as Grotius' gentle
opponent Anthonius Walaeus (1573–1639) expressed it, not 'whether
management, care and power in matters of religion belong to the sovereign – we all agree on this – , but whether this care is entrusted to the
sovereign in such a way that he alone is directly subject to God and his

Word and the ministers are not'.[26] It is this last proposition that Grotius emphatically affirms in all his relevant writings before 1618 and somewhat more gently in his later work. Decisions of the visible Church as a whole give rise to an obligation that is valid only as long as it does not conflict with obligations created by commands of the civil government; and individual pastors must obey the sovereign. There is only one exception, and that is valid for all individuals, including the sovereign: nobody may act against God's commands or refrain from doing what God commands (DI 4.1–2). In other words, in sacred as in profane matters, actions are impermissible or obligatory because of natural or divine positive law; only indefinite actions are subject to the authority of the sovereign, who cannot forbid what God has commanded – which includes natural law – or vice versa. In sum, the sovereign is above the earthly, visible Church (DI 1.3, repeated in DJBP 1.3.8.8 ff., see 2.20.8.2 and DI 10.2). Like all men, he is subject to God, but, unlike others, he is subject *only* to God. To Him alone he will render account.

One implication of this view, that the sovereign is above the earthly Church, is that he is also above positive law, that is, exempt from all laws made by others and also by himself. This doctrine originates in the second century CE,[27] and was frequently used by medieval canonists and philosophers in the struggle for control between the emperors and popes.[28] Grotius often adduces this doctrine as proof of the supremacy of the secular ruler (e.g. OHWP 155, DJBP 2.20.24.1–2, see also 2.14.1.2). The Church, on the other hand, has no legislative power: if the civil authorities grant the Church some power to legislate, they may later rescind or correct the laws made by the Church. And, if they declare themselves bound to certain canonical laws, this is a statement of their intent, not an abdication of their right. Grotius frequently compared this statement of intent to clauses added to wills (DI 8.12; in a series of letters on wills of 1615 to his brother, 1 BW 427, 430, 432, 433, and in DJBP 1.3.18.1–2).[29]

If the sovereign is the highest authority in matters of religion, he could also be the highest priest. According to Grotius, natural law does not forbid it and this situation was current in the whole world for 2,500 years, but God changed that when he instituted Mosaic law and assigned the priesthood to Aaron and his descendants. When Christ abolished Mosaic law, it remained not 'right that the supreme authority and the priestly office … should be combined in one person' (DI on Mosaic law, see also DJBP 1.1.15–7). Roman Catholics defended the opposite view: the supremacy of one person, the pope, in both civil and secular matters. Grotius completely rejected this. Throughout his life, he stuck to the view that a host of ancient and medieval authorities, and contemporary English authors, proved its falseness. (cf. DI 2.5–7, 4.5, 4.8, DJBP 1.1.16.6 ff., *De veritate* 5.6–12, *Commentary on Mt.* 5:17 in OTh vol. 2,1.34 and 1.36 a 41, *on Act.* 15 in OTh vol. 1 618 b 51 ff., esp. 621 b 10 ff.). Towards 1640, Grotius published two decidedly anti-papal treatises: *De summo sacerdotio* (*The highest priesthood*, 1638) and an anonymous pamphlet *De Antichristo* (*On the Antichrist*, 1640).[30] This may seem somewhat strange, since Grotius was occupied with the union of the Christian churches at the same time. However, Grotius aimed primarily at the reunion of Protestantism with the Catholic Church of France, with its rather anti-papal and nationalist persuasions.

The sovereign cannot forbid what God has commanded, or vice versa. On the other hand, if he uses force, resistance is forbidden, let alone that lower magistrates are allowed to resist their superiors. Grotius had voiced this principle already in *Theses XI* and *Meletius*, and discussed it at length in *De imperio* (DI 3.5–8, 3.14) and *De jure belli ac pacis* (DJBP 1.4.1–7, especially 6–7 and 3.7.7). It is in accordance with the views of the early Church: although natural law allows to repel force with force (DI 3.6, DJBP 1.2.1 ff., see 3.1.2.1),[31] all resistance against the Christian sovereign is strictly forbidden. This goes for both resistance by private citizens and resistance by lower magistrates. As the ultimate ground for this prohibition, Grotius adduced divine law as it is expressed in *Romans* 13: 'Let every soul be subject unto the higher powers. For there is no power but of God: the powers that be are ordained of God. Whosoever therefore resisteth the power, resisteth the ordinance of God.'[32] On the other hand, John Calvin (1509–64) taught that magistrates may resist a tyrant and this was also argued at length by French jurists of the later sixteenth century. The issue is often discussed, recently by Martin van Gelderen and in this volume by Guus van Nifterik.[33] Although Grotius adduced many scholarly arguments, his views on this subject were largely determined by events of his own time and of the generation before him: the reign of terror in the Calvinist Republic in Flanders in 1577–9, and the influx of rigid and 'unruly' Calvinist ministers in the North after 1585. In his posthumously published polemic with French theologian André Rivet (1572–1651), Grotius still lashed out against tyrannicides ('monarchomachs') and strict Calvinist ministers who refuse to obey the magistrates' authority. In short, sovereign government is invulnerable from below, but exposed to God's final judgment.

9.6 Synods or Church Councils

As the question of convoking a national synod became ever more urgent in the years 1610–18, Grotius expressed his views on the role of the sovereign in councils of the Church in many works of the period (OHWP 100–33, DI 7). On the one hand, Grotius' views, especially in *De imperio*, follow from his systematic discussion of sovereignty on a philosophical and legal basis; they are presented in abstract terms and bolstered by historical examples. On the other hand, on this subject Grotius clearly expresses the politics of the States of Holland. The most important questions were: who has the right to convoke a council (or forego it)? Who presides? Who decides? The answer to all these questions is the supreme power, the sovereign government. For synods fall under human law: it is the ruler's right to choose the delegates. Defining the place, time and agenda of synods has always been done by the Christian Roman emperors. Accepting, rejecting and changing proposals of the synod is the sovereign's prerogative, for it is a matter of imperative judgment. One of Grotius' main authorities for this view is Marsilius of Padova, a political philosopher with revolutionary ideas on Church and state and a dedicated opponent of papal authority. His *Defensor pacis* (1329)[34] was composed during the struggle for power between Pope John XXII (1244–1334) and Emperor Elect Ludwig IV of Bavaria (1282–1347). In it, he argued that the pope was subordinate to the emperor, that Church councils were superior to the pope and that they had to be convoked by the civil authorities.

The States of Holland considered themselves sovereign in matters of religion, and so did Grotius. Therefore, the States of Holland judged that they could resist the convocation of a national synod despatched by the States General where the Counter-Remonstrants were certain to win the day. Grotius himself had always wished for an international synod of Protestant churches, with the union of these churches as the ultimate goal (*Apologeticus* 122). Not long before he was imprisoned in August 1618, he composed for the States letters and documents to the kings of France and England, the German Protestant princes and the deputies of the French Protestant Church. In a last attempt to forestall the inevitable national synod, he argued that the upcoming synod was illegal, as his research proved. Here, Grotius the scholar or thinker and Grotius the politician coalesce.

9.7 Jurisdiction

Since the sovereign is above the Church and the law, he cannot be subject
to the jurisdiction of the Church, that is: the practical authority to administer justice within a defined field of responsibility. The sovereign may
gracefully yield to ecclesiastical discipline, but Grotius deems this unwise
in general, and rejects the subjection of kings to papal authority in the
middle ages. On this subject, as on the appointment of churchmen, Grotius
founded his views on medieval anti-papal sources, again in particular on
Marsilius of Padova. However, in theory, pastors might have jurisdiction
over others. This is emphatically denied by Grotius, in accordance with his
Erastian views: some actions by churchmen do resemble formal acts of
judgment, such as pastors who punish by denying people the sacraments,
or, as it was expressed at the time, by using 'the keys'. This refers to three
passages from the New Testament,[35] where Jesus offers the keys of heaven
to the apostles. Their interpretation was hotly debated in the middle ages
between the partisans of the emperor and the pope, later between Catholics
and Protestants.[36] According to Grotius, it is God or Christ who judges and
punishes errant believers. Priests can only declare, and this is true for
ecclesiastical discipline in general: judgment is involved, but no real
jurisdiction. For this is always exercised by a superior over an inferior
(DI 9.6–7, 1 BW 539 and 543, and still in the Bible Commentaries: OTh
vol. 2, 2 780, b 21–29, II 2 852 b 3–7, II 2 861 b 1 and 8–12). Here, Grotius
drew on the medieval philosopher Petrus Lombardus (1096–1160), on
Erastus and also on one of his favourite sources: Thomas Bilson's
(1547–1616) *De perpetua ecclesiae Christi gubernatione* (1611), a Latin
translation of his earlier *The Perpetuall Government of Christs Church*
(1593). Grotius called the author of this heavy, repetitive book 'the most
reliable authority on the history of the early church'. In other words,
pastors possess no jurisdiction based on natural or divine law, and crimes
committed against religious laws are liable to punishment by the secular
authorities, just as other crimes are. Therefore, ministers in the Republic
could not legally use exclusion from sacraments as a weapon. For this is
what they did during the Dutch religious troubles. However, Grotius' view
was much more than just a comment on contemporary events. This is also
shown by his similar interpretation of the same biblical passages in his
commentaries composed in the 1640s. The Erastian indivisibility of civil

and religious law under one highest power is also supported by Grotius' view on the Jewish constitution with its one sovereign council.

9.8 Ecclesiastical Officials and Ecclesiastical Hierarchy

In the concrete situation of the Dutch troubles, the right to appoint ministers in the public church was a bone of contention between regents (city magistrates and members of the States) and Church ministers. In Grotius' extensive discussion in *De imperio* and elsewhere, his approach is legal and historical: this right cannot belong to the faithful, nor to the pastors themselves, for electing pastors does not belong to natural or divine law, except for the general divine law that God does not want disorder in the Church. Grotius claimed that, just as in all other areas of human law, it belongs to the supreme power, as it has done throughout history: the Church Fathers left countless instances of Roman emperors appointing ecclesiastical officials, which Grotius copied from Bilson's book, and Marsilius of Padova supplied material for denying the claims of medieval popes to this right. Indeed, the sovereign authority may delegate or substitute others in the appointment of pastors, but this does not detract from its right to the final decision. And its right, like all the sovereign's rights, remains in force even if the sovereign is a pagan or bad ruler. The popular contemporary argument that pastors in the public church are paid by public money and therefore must be elected by the supreme power is often expressed by Grotius (in OHWP 118, DI 1.7, 1 BW 304). This may look like a practical political argument to please his masters, the States, but Grotius still kept to it in the late *De dogmatis, ritibus et gubernatione* (OTh vol. 3, 752a).

In contrast to the Lutheran and Anglican Church, the Dutch Reformed Church did not have bishops. In discussing the (dis)advantages of this office in *Ordinum pietas* and *De imperio*, Grotius again tried to reconcile differences in his pursuit of toleration and unity between all Protestant churches, with a practical eye on winning over the Anglicans: by arguing that the Church may either have bishops or go without them. For, on the one hand, episcopacy is not commanded by divine law and there is much to be said in favour of a Church without bishops. The many abuses by bishops were good reasons for suspending episcopacy in the Reformation. On the other hand, the office is ancient, very useful for the Church and approved by God. Although in later years Grotius was seldom explicit on this point, his ever more passionate pursuit of the unity of the churches strengthened his belief in this middle position.

9.9 Divine and Natural Law: Sources and Interpretations

Many sources on Church and state, and arguments quoted in support, are shared between Grotius' works *De jure praedae, Ordinum pietas, De imperio* and *De jure belli ac pacis*. There are over forty common sources and over 100 citations between the last two.[37] Of these shared sources, Thomas Aquinas' *Summa* is important: Grotius possessed and annotated a copy of it and, in 1615, he recommended Thomas for instruction in the moral principles of public and international law (1 BW 386, cf. DJBP 1.1.10.1 n. 6). And, as it is well known from the works of Robert Feenstra and others, Grotius used the commentators and followers of Thomas, most of them generally known as the Spanish scholastics, both in his politico-theological and in his legal work, from the early years of the century: Tommaso Caietano (1469–1534), Diego Covarrubias (1512–77), Domingo de Soto (1494–1560), Fernando Vázquez de Menchaca (1512–69) and Francisco de Vitoria (c. 1480–1546).[38] Richard Tuck has claimed that *De jure belli ac pacis* and other Grotian works have an anti-Aristotelian character, because their eclectic philosophy aims primarily at challenging scepticism, but the Aristotelian, scholastic approach itself seems undeniable, just as does Grotius' admiration of Aristotle.[39] Around 1615, Grotius also knew the works of the great philosopher and theologian, Francisco Suárez (1548–1617), including his masterpiece *De legibus*.

These sources are relevant for the part played by divine and natural law in the discussion about Church and state, in particular in *De jure belli ac pacis* and *De imperio*. In this respect, Grotius' views on natural, divine and human law in the two books are akin – though not about the relationship of natural law to politics and the law of nations. In *De imperio*, Grotius distinguishes – absolute – natural law from positive divine law: natural law consists of general, moral rules valid for all humanity and conforming to right reason, such as worshipping God or loving one's parents (DI 1.9, 2.3, 3.3, 7.2, 9.3). Positive divine law is given by God directly to individuals, to a people – the Jewish people in particular (DI 3.3, DJBP 1.1.15.2) – or to all humanity. By natural law, things are obligatory or impermissible by their own nature, while they are obligatory or impermissible by divine law because God has made them so: 'volitional divine law does not enjoin or forbid those things which in themselves and by their own nature are obligatory or not permissible, but by forbidding things it makes them unlawful, and by commanding things it makes them obligatory' (DJBP 1.1.10.2, see Prol. 12, 1.1.15.1, also *De satisfactione* 5.1). In *De imperio*, there seems to be more room for voluntarism than in *De jure belli ac pacis*, since natural law is presented there as given by God (DI 3.5, 3.12), while in the later treatise natural law perhaps seems somewhat more connected to human right reason (DJBP 1.1.10.2). But, in fact, the two views sometimes coalesce in both books; as Grotius put it himself: 'I have shown in the prolegomena and in Book One of *The Rights of War and Peace* that the laws of nature are rightly ascribed to God' (*Florum sparsio* 12). Therefore, binary oppositions such as that of Roman Catholic, scholastic, intellectualist, natural law versus Reformation, belief, voluntarism, divine law should be avoided, since Grotius is more subtle or more eclectic, for instance in defending the divine right of the sovereign to judge in doctrinal matters.[40] There seems to be more truth in the view that Grotius 'is returning natural law to theology rather than secularising divine law', as Chroust claimed.[41]

9.10 Conclusion

Grotius developed his views on Church and state under growing political pressure in the Dutch Republic, but in his final word on the subject during the religious troubles, *De imperio*, contemporary events stay in the background: in this theoretical work, law, history, theology and politics coalesce in order to prove the absolute supremacy of state over Church, of sovereign over priests. There is only one, indivisible sovereign government, and it is civil government. This does not interfere with personal faith, for everyone is free to believe what they want, but all external acts in the public space are subject to the sovereign government. The possibility of abuse by the sovereign of his absolute power is restricted by the fact that they have to render account to God, and their main duty is to foster religion in society. Toleration of different religious convictions is essential. Grotius' views were based on the Jewish constitution and especially the early Christian Church as described in Scripture and the early Church

Fathers. Medieval anti-papal writings, as predecessors of the Reformation, strengthened his case, but Grotius went beyond the dichotomy emperor-pope and the political philosophies connected to it; for him, there existed only civil sovereign governments side by side. All this was included in a well-balanced system of natural, divine and human law; in combination with Grotius' razor-sharp mind, the whole formed a more or less complete theory of the relations of Church and state, ranging from abstract considerations to the concrete details of ecclesiastical hierarchy. These views remain valid for *De jure belli ac pacis*, a book with a different objective but presupposing the same views on Church and state and sovereignty, and with similar legal concepts. In the years after 1635, as the ambassador of Sweden, Grotius' lifelong convictions that peace and quiet in the state are the highest good, and that toleration of differences is essential, shaped his ultimate goal, the reconciliation of Christian churches. This made him less inclined to insist on the supremacy of the state, but there are no indications that his views had changed. Dedicating more and more energy to the unification of the Christian churches, Grotius came to experience this as his mission in life for which he was prepared to die. Therefore, he was also willing to meet the Roman Catholic Church half way, provided that it was also willing to take some steps, which it was not. Grotius' sudden death in 1645 put an end to his ideals.

Further Reading

Brett, A.S. and J. Tully (eds)., *Rethinking the Foundations of Modern Political Thought* (Cambridge, 2010).

Grotiana N.S. 34 (2013): *Dossier: Ordinum Pietas.*

Gunnoe, C., *Thomas Erastus and the Palatinate* (Leiden, 2011).

Haggenmacher, P., *Grotius et la doctrine de guerre juste* (Paris, 1983).

Heckel, M., *Staat und Kirche nach den Lehren der evangelischen Juristen Deutschlands in der ersten Hälfte des 17. Jahrhunderts* (Munich,1968).

Nellen, H.J. and E. Rabbie (eds.), *Hugo Grotius Theologian. Essays in Honour of G.H.M. Posthumus Meyjes* (Leiden, 1994).

Nelson, E., *The Hebrew Republic. Jewish Sources and the Transformation of European Political Thought* (Cambridge, MA, 2010).

Skinner, Q., *The Foundations of Modern Political Thought* (2 vols., Cambridge, 1978).

Solt, L.F., *Church and State in Early Modern England 1509–1646* (Oxford and New York, 1990).

Notes

1 See Q. Skinner, *The Foundations of Modern Political Thought* (Cambridge, 1978), vol. 2 ch. 14, and the literature in Prior (below, note 2).

2 C. Prior, '"The Highest Powers": Grotius and the Internationalization of Church and State', *Grotiana* N.S. 34 (2013) 91–106, at 92–3 and the literature quoted in notes 5–6.

3 M. Somos, *Secularisation and the Leiden Circle* (Leiden and Boston, 2011), chapter 5, the quotation at 387.

4 P. Haggenmacher *Grotius et la doctrine de guerre juste* (Paris, 1983), 469–70 and 510.

5 R. Tuck, 'The modern theory of natural law', in A. Pagden (ed.), *The Languages of Political Theory in Early Modern Europe* (Cambridge, 1987), 99–119; Tuck, *Philosophy and Government 1572–1651* (Cambridge, 1993), ch. 5.

6 H.J.M. Nellen and P.M.L. Steenbakkers, 'Introduction', in H.J.M. Nellen, D.M. van Miert, P. Steenbakkers and J. Touber (eds.), *Scriptural Authority and Biblical Criticism in the Dutch Golden Age: God's Word Questioned* (Oxford, 2017).

7 J. Israel, 'Grotius and the rise of Christian 'Radical Enlightenment', *Grotiana* N.S. 35 (2014):19–31; Somos *Secularisation*. See also H.J.M. Nellen, *Hugo Grotius. A Lifelong Struggle for Peace in Church and State* (Leiden and Boston, 2015), 373–4.

8 D.M. van Miert, *The Emancipation of Biblical Philology in the Dutch Republic, 1590–1670* (Oxford, 2018), ch. 5.

9 See infra Chapter 15.

10 Its text is in https://www.remonstranten.nl/wiki/remonstranten-vroeger/remonstrantie-1610. For an English translation, see https://arminiusinstituut.remonstranten.nl/wp-content/uploads/sites/32/2017/08/Remonstrantie-Orginal-Act-English.pdf.

11 J. Trapman, 'Grotius and Erasmus', in H.J.M. Nellen and E. Rabbie (eds.), *Essays in Honour of G.H.M. Posthumus Meyjes* (Leiden, 1994), 77–98; H.J.M. Nellen, 'A Rotterdammer teaches the World how to reform : the Image of Erasmus in remonstrant and counter-remonstrant Propaganda', in M.E.H.N. Mout, H. Smolinsky and J. Trapman (eds.), *Erasmianism: Idea and Reality* (Amsterdam, 1997), 177–87.

12 D. 50.17.202 *Omnis definitio in jure civili periculosa est.*

13 See Nellen, *Grotius*, 374–75.

14 See Nellen, *Grotius* 643–56, and below.

15 W. Frijhoff, 'Religious toleration in the United Provinces: from 'case' to 'model', in R. Po-Chia Hsia & H. Van Nierop (eds.), *Calvinism and Religious Toleration in the Dutch Golden Age* (Cambridge, 2002), 27–52; A. Pettegree, 'The politics of toleration in the Free Netherlands 1572–1620', in O.P. Grell and B. Scribner (eds.), *Tolerance and Intolerance in the European Reformation* (Cambridge, 1997), 182–98.

16 The Latin and the Dutch version of the *Decretum* with all its quotations appeared simultaneously, see J. ter Meulen and P.J.J. Diermanse *Bibliographie des écrits publics de Hugo Grotius* (The Hague, 1950), 826–38. The Latin text is in OTh vol. 3 139–73; without its supporting quotations also in Rabbie's edition of *Ordinum Pietas, Appendix* XII (628–9). There is an English translation in W.E. Beckwith, *The Theology of Hugo Grotius, Jurist-Theologian* (Diss. Boston University, 1959) 168–70; older ones also in G. Brandt *History of the Reformation* (translation 1719) 2.138–9 and (less reliable) in H. Vreeland, *Hugo Grotius* (New York, 1917), 244–6.

17 Frijhoff, 'Religious Toleration' 39, see also 50–1; S. Schama, *The Embarrassment of Riches*, Dutch Translation (1988) 68, 93–125.

18 E. Nelson, *The Hebrew Republic. Jewish Sources and the Transformation of European Political Thought* (Cambridge, MA, 2010), *Introduction*, pp. 88 ff., see also below.

19 Its first edition is H. Grotius, *De republica emendanda*, ed. A. Eyffinger, in collab. with P.A.H. de Boer, J.Th. de Smidt and L.E. van Holk', *Grotiana* NS 5 (1984).

20 *Explicatio gravissimae quaestionis utrum excommunicatio, quatenus religionem intelligentes et amplexantes, a sacramentorum usu, propter admissum facinus arcet, mandato nitatur divino, an excogitata sit ab hominibus* (Pesclavii [= London], 1589).

21 C. Gunnoe, *Thomas Erastus and the Palatinate: A Renaissance Physician in the Second Reformation* (Leiden, 2011), esp. ch. 5–6, 135 ff. and (The Netherlands) 394 ff.

22 See D. Nobbs, *Theocracy and Toleration. A Study of the Disputes in Dutch Calvinism from 1600 to 1650* (Cambridge, 2012), ch. 2. It was immediately translated into English by John Douglas, army chaplain to Colonel Sir John Ogle, and offered to King James by Bishop Lancelot Andrewes in 1614; the manuscript is in London, see my Introduction to *De imperio,* n. 53.

23 For an analysis of Grotius' theological and political works during his days in Holland, from *Meletius* to *De imperio*, see also F. Mühlegger, *Hugo Grotius. Ein christlicher Humanist in politischer Verantwortung* (Berlin and New York, 2007).

24 See the letters 2 BW *BW* 998, 1 August 1625; 3 BW 1062, 13 March 1626; 3 BW 1087, 1 July 1 626; 9 BW 3510, 29 March 1638; 9 BW 3524; 9 BW 3530 26 April 1638; and my edition of *De imperio,* 44–5.

25 Rom. 13.

26 A. Walaeus, *Het Ampt der Kerckendienaren* (Middelburg, 1615), 44.

27 D. 1.3.31 and elsewhere.

28 J. Wyduckel, *Princeps legibus solutus. Eine Untersuchung zur frühmodernen Rechts- und Staatslehre* (Berlin, 1979); see Baldus on X. 2.1.12.3, ST I^a II^{ae} q. 96 a 5 ad 3.

29 See also below on jurisdiction.

30 See Nellen, *Grotius,* 608–18.

31 With reference to D. 4.2.12.1, D. 43.16.1.27, D. 9.2.45.4.

32 *King James Bible.*

33 See G. van Nifterik in this volume; M. van Gelderen, '"So meerly humane":
    theories of resistance in early-modern Europe', in A.S. Brett and J. Tully (eds.),
    Rethinking the Foundations of Modern Political Thought (Cambridge, 2010),
    149–70.

34 *Marsilius of Padua. The Defender of the Peace*, transl. and commentary by
    A.S. Brett (Cambridge, 2005).

35 Mt. 16.19, 18.18 and Jn 20.22–3.

36 See e.g. W.D. Davies and D.C. Allison Jr,. *A Critical and Exegetical Commentary
    on the Gospel according to St. Matthew* (Edinburgh, 1991), 634–47, with
    extensive bibliography.

37 For a comprehensive survey of the sources of OHWP, see Rabbie's edition,
    73–82. For those of *De imperio*, see my edition, 108–31. On intermediate
    sources: H. Grotius, *Defensio fidei catholicae de satisfactione Christi adversus
    Faustum Socinum Senensem*, ed. E. Rabbie and transl. H. Mulder (Assen, 1990),
    54, DI 108–9.

38 See Feenstra's edition of DJBP (Aalen: Scientia 1993), 929–34, 1045.

39 R. Tuck, 'Grotius, Carneades and Hobbes' in *Grotiana* N.S. 4 (1983) 35–42;
    Tuck, *The Sleeping Sovereign. The Invention of Modern Democracy* (Cambridge,
    2015), ch. 2, see DJBP Prol. 42.

40 Haggenmacher *Grotius*, 466–510, especially 466 ff., 496–9; and for a different
    view Q. Skinner and A.S. Brett, 'Scholastic political thought and the concept of
    the modern state', in Brett and Tully, *Rethinking*, 130–48.

41 'Hugo Grotius and the scholastic natural law Tradition', *The New Scholasticism*
    17 (1943), 101–33, quotation at 128.

Camilla Boisen

10.1 Introduction

The doctrine of predestination, or election, has divided Christians for centuries. When the British monk, Pelagius (c. 360–418), rejected the
Augustinian conception of grace by asserting that humankind was not
inherently depraved, he exposed a fundamental tension in Christian thought
between divine will and human freedom.[1] By the time of the Protestant
Reformation, the Pelagian controversy took on renewed significance as
Europe was thrown into violent religious and political strife. Here, the
doctrine of predestination struck a chord with early modern anxiety about
an issue that is central to Christianity: salvation. Inherent to the doctrine of
predestination is a message of salvation. It is there in Luther: 'Whoever hates
sin is already outside sin and belongs to the elect.'[2] While Martin Luther
(1483–1546) and his followers took great comfort in justification by faith
alone through God's grace, affirming God's predestination of humanity for
salvation or damnation and stipulating the bondage of free will, it was that
other great Lutheran reformer, Philipp Melanchthon (1497–1560), who
became dissatisfied with an unqualified doctrine of predestination. He
suggested that not only did the unadulterated logic of predestination make
God the author of sin, it also aligned too closely to the erroneous fatalism of
the Stoics and the dualistic Gnosticism of Manichaeism.[3] Grotius' project of
appeasement with the Calvinist orthodoxy lay in avoiding such heretical
epithets as he called for religious concord.

   In the Dutch Republic, the doctrine of predestination was central to the
intra-confessional dispute between the Remonstrants, the followers of
Jacobus Arminius (1560–1609), and the Counter-Remonstrants, in which
Grotius found himself embroiled. Arminius, eminent professor of theology at
the University of Leiden, had contested the orthodox Calvinist teaching of
double predestination; the idea that some had been elected for salvation,
while others, the reprobates, had been elected for damnation. The idea of
double predestination was the ultimate religious determinism, and this,

Arminius contended, made God the author of evil. Furthermore, Arminius sought to affirm the freedom of the human will by making predestination conditional, not absolute. God had chosen to give each individual a self-determining free will through prevenient grace. In this way, each person has a choice of either accepting or rejecting God's offer of salvation and, hence, God, as remunerator, allows humankind a role in the determination of his or her salvation. The Arminian troubles fuelled debates about religious toleration, political and ecclesiastical representation, and the division of Church and state. By the time the Synod of Dort (1618–19) had declared his teachings heretical, Arminius was long dead. Johan van Oldenbarnevelt (1547–1619), the foremost political supporter of the Remonstrants, as the members of the Arminian party became known, was executed and Grotius imprisoned.

Grotius was deeply vested in the Arminian cause. He was initially hesitant to get involved in the theological dispute but, later, he launched attacks against the Counter-Remonstrants, most notably in *Ordinum Hollandiae ac Westfrisiae pietas* (*The Religiousness of the States of Holland and Westerfriesland*) in 1613. Rather than solving any religious dogmatic disputes, it is argued here that Grotius' involvement in the Dutch predestination debates is a unique opportunity to explore some of the philosophical connections between Grotius' religious and political ideas. His two central writings on religious matters, *Meletius* and *De veritate religionis Christianae*, stress an irenicism that aligns with his broader political philosophical project of formulating a set of universal rights and duties that would secure peace by constraining states in their internal and external relations. From investigating Grotius' broader intellectual involvement with the doctrine of predestination, two key aspects of Grotius' political theory – natural sociability and the impious hypothesis – emerge in a new critical light. Arguably, from Grotius' engagement with predestinarian doctrinal controversy in, particularly, *Meletius*, but also *Ordinum pietas*, emerges an account of socialisation independent of the predestination question. Grotius thinks that we have a natural propensity for social cooperation, that is, we are naturally sociable (DJBP Prol. 6), from where he deduces a whole array of rights and duties. As we are inclined to cultivate social life, certain protections have to be afforded: the minimalist foundations required for such cultivation. In *Meletius* and *Ordinum pietas*, we get a sense of a moral pragmatist, who is acutely aware that the maintenance of social order requires commitment to religious toleration, and hence a deliberate marginalisation of the doctrine of predestination; a marginalisation that ultimately served his strong irenicism and made Grotius one of the early modern period's most prominent defenders of religious toleration. If anything, Grotius' Arminian proclivities liberated him from the constraints of orthodox Calvinism as he espoused central natural law precepts about humankind's natural equity, inherent moral capacity, autonomy, political freedom and sociability in order to cement a universal moral order independent of religious convictions.

Grotius' – unprofessed – Arminianism also gives further credence to why he rejected metaethical theological voluntarism – that God, by absolute degree, created justice – most starkly articulated in his 'etiamsi daremus' statement (DJBP Prol. 11). 'The impious hypothesis' was already a standard part of scholastic discussions going back at least to Gregory of Rimini (1300–58), and raised questions of why we are committed to pursue justice, and the ultimate sources of our obligations. In the now infamous 'etiamsi daremus', Grotius does imply that the source of obligation is human nature, endowed by God. Predestination debates about God's authority related in a very concrete way to the obligation argument in natural law, that is in specifying the content of God's authority and how it is directed. An emphasis on God's absolute sovereignty is a fundamental commitment in orthodox Calvinism. That commitment also leads one to both have a strong view of predestination and a voluntarist view of natural law. Thus, this careful contextualisation of predestination in Grotius' religious oeuvre enables us to reassess this most disputed statement of his and further establish it as an obligation device that served his quest for religious and political accord.

Grotius's project, then, of building political consensus by conceiving of a set of moral principles that everyone could accept, despite fierce confessional and political conflict, left no space for state-sanctioned religious orthodoxy. Of course, religious consensus somehow had to be sought. The genius of Grotius was to stipulate that religious consensus arose out of the idea of religion itself without having to speak to divisive religious dogma, such as the doctrine of predestination. Such deliberate repudiation of what Grotius believed to be adiaphoristic, that is theologically non-essential, religious principles challenges even the most astute of Grotius' readers, who set out to examine his intellectual evolution with predestination. The challenge here lies in excavating Grotius' theology of the very doctrine whose religious importance he sought to renounce. The success of such an intellectual undertaking will be not to approach Grotius from a denominational angle, as one leading scholar aptly observes, but instead to regard him as a Christian humanist,[4] who believed that inherent to the practice of Christianity were human freedom, individual conscience and unfettered rational inquiry.

10.2 Grotius and the Arminian Crisis

In the *Prolegomena* to *De jure praedae commentarius*, Grotius writes:

For God created man αὐτεξούσιον, 'free and sui iuris', so that the actions of each individual and the use of his possessions were made subject not to another's will but to his own. Moreover, this view is sanctioned by the common consent of all nations. For what is that well-known concept, 'natural liberty,' other than the power of the individual to act in accordance with his own will? And liberty in regard to action is equivalent to ownership in regard to property. (DJPC, 2, 33–4)

Asserting, as Grotius does here, that human beings are morally free and autonomous agents is, from a theological standpoint, not unproblematic.[5] Even Arminius was adamant that there can be no such occurrence as 'perfect independence or complete freedom of action'. Such agency 'appertains to God alone'.[6] By affirming the absolute majesty, or sovereignty, of God as judge over God's mercy as a loving father, reformed theology – and its later abstruse theological technicalities in conceptualising predestinarian models – had re-exposed the polarity of the Christian message as Augustine (354–430) had done centuries before.[7] The ultimate question of how humans relate to God and whether they have an ability to cooperate with Divine providence demarcates the theological lines between human depravity – that is, the corruption of the human condition – and human free will and personal responsibility. Answering this question proved especially divisive in the Low Countries,[8] where Calvinism became inextricably tied to the Dutch fight for independence. It was in these so-called 'Arminian Troubles' that debates over 'freedom of conscience', 'predestination' and 'human free will' threatened to tear the newly formed Dutch Republic apart. The Twelve Years Truce of 1609 with their former Spanish overlords was unpopular among orthodox Calvinists, as it made impossible all hope of recovering the Southern Provinces from where the 1560s Calvinist dissent had originated.[9]

Here we can roughly draw the battlelines between Oldenbarnenevelt-Grotius Remonstrants, who wanted toleration for the various Reformed denominational factions, and the Counter-Remonstrant Calvinist hardliners who sought to use state power to promote religious uniformity. The Church was fully free and autonomous from the States General, the highest federal institution, which wanted a national synod to settle all theological disputes, thereby denouncing public space for confessional diversity.[10] For the Remonstrants, as the Arminian faction became known, 'freedom of conscience' laid at the heart of the Dutch protest against Spanish oppression. The Spanish king had tyrannised the Dutch people by 'exacting from them slavish compliance', while seeking 'opportunities to infringe their ancient customs and privileges'.[11] The Dutch Revolt was seen by many, including Grotius, as a fight for freedom, and his early writings were fervently patriotic, championing the cause of the Dutch against Spain,[12] pointing toward his later claims of freedom as foundational for human flourishing.

When Arminius took up a position at Leiden University to teach theology in 1603 – with Grotius' backing – as a student of Theodore Beza (1519–1605), the 'doge' of Calvinist orthodoxy, he seemed the most unlikely of candidates to reject the doctrine of predestination. But, his bitter dispute over predestination with Franciscus Gomarus (1563–1641), another Leiden University theology professor, exposed a fragile Reformed Church, and left it vulnerable to a schism. Arminius related salvation with human faith and he opposed Gomarus' dogma that divine grace was not contingent on human agency; that is, it could not be resisted or lost. Although orthodox Calvinists such as Gomarus had a concept of human freedom, the issue at stake was really whether a person was free to choose the good. The answer to this question was a complicated one, and depended not only on how 'freedom' and the 'good' were defined, but ultimately on the extent to which God's saving grace was imposed on the human condition. Arminius' goal was to mediate between divine providence and human freedom in salvation, and he adopted an infinitely less pessimistic view of human capacity for living a virtuous life that guaranteed salvation. God had bestowed upon humanity a gift of faith upon which salvation rested. God had foreknowledge of human action that embraced faith and, as such, election was conditional on faith. Only the unbelievers were rejected in Arminius' predestination system.[13]

Grotius had become entangled in the dispute early on despite a desire to keep a firm distance from both theologians by playing religious peace-maker.[14] He sums up the religious disputes between the two Leiden professors as follows:

> *Arminius* blaming *Gomarus*, that he ascribed to God the Causes of Sinne, and by a strong persuasion made Mens Minds obstinue: And *Gomarus* finding fault with *Arminius*, that he fill'd men with Arrogance, far more than the *Decrees* of the *Romanists*, and would not suffer a good *Conscience*, which is a Man's greatest Concern, to be acceptable to God. (AHRB, 950)

After Arminius' death, Grotius sought political and religious mediation, but his professed impartiality was a smokescreen as he continued to voice his annoyance with what he perceived to be the pugnacious intolerance of the Counter-Remonstrant theologians.[15] There is little doubt as to where his theological and political allegiance lay, although it would be erroneous to think that Grotius' 'religious feelings were completely in accord with Arminianism'.[16] It is Grotius' 1609 funeral poem in honour of Arminius that provides us with the first insight into his theological attitude to the doctrine of predestination and his desire for religious consensus.[17] Grotius never received any formal education in theology and admits he was not 'well informed on the finer theological points of the controversy'.[18] His epicedium shows an averseness to religious dogma – a view that charac-terised all of his religious writings, professing it to be divisive and unnecessary for religious purposes. People are clouded with ignorance on these matters; 'how insignificant is that which we call knowing here', Grotius professed, 'on account which we haughty people lift up our heads to heaven; we trample on others and in turn are trampled on'. The blind fury of doctrine that enrages people makes the 'holy Truth, friend of holy Peace, [flee] far away, and appears to be invisible to those who fight' (*Arminius Poem*, 175).

Grotius laments the hopelessness of the whole endeavour. People, over-taken by dogmatic 'aggressive fury', are 'glad to pursue what is refused to be understood'. Only the enemies of Christianity profit from such divisive-ness. As we tear ourselves asunder, Grotius remarks, 'the Moor laughs and the Jew rejoices'. Religion does not require of us to understand fully its doctrinal fineries, nor should we try and understand in what way God who, Grotius is quick to interject, 'has no share in evil', might direct or reject evil (*Arminius Poem*, 177). God's providence, Grotius would later write in his

'Memorial of my intention' while imprisoned in Loevestein Castle, 'ought to be more worshipped than examined; in the knowledge that God uses His supreme freedom with supreme wisdom, the reasons of which [wisdom] are largely incomprehensible to us' (*Memorie*, 5). Grotius' concern over the corruptibility of natural reason, either through sin, inability or sheer ignorance, to assure the certainty of our moral reasoning featured in his later natural law writings. In *De jure belli ac pacis*, he is acutely aware that our moral reasoning cannot be as certain as mathematical demonstrations because the situation in which we weigh what is right is frequently clouded by circumstantial issues (DJPB 2.23.1). He professes in the epicedium that religious tolerance is necessarily brought forth by the limitations of human knowledge. A true believer refrains from remarking on salvation or damnation; 'he walks with subdued footsteps along dangerous detours, persistently following the threads of [Scripture]'. Even though 'condemned by others', he or she 'whose freedom, moderated by grace, exerts [him or herself] to stay in harmony with those who disagree' by not condemning others and knowing when to stay silent (*Arminius Poem*, 178–9).

10.3 Nascent Irenicism: Meletius

Grotius' call for religious tolerance was systematised in his more mature theological treatise, *Meletius* (1611), the message of which he hoped would appease, if not transcend, the Dutch predestination controversy. Through his mouthpiece, the Eastern Patriarch Meletius, Grotius seeks to define the truth of the Christian religion itself as a common denominator of love and rapprochement. Impressing on his audience the necessity of reflecting on their Christian commonalities, rather than dogmatic differences, is the first purpose of *Meletius*. Its second aim is to remind readers that right conduct is more important than dogmatic doctrine.[19] That being said, Grotius did not think that setting aside dogma would lead to harmony (*Meletius*, 133). In quoting Seneca's lament 'everybody prefers discussing to living', Grotius reveals a scepticism for the metaphysical that would characterise his later political philosophy. As a faithful reader of Aristotle (384–321 BCE), Grotius knows that the absolute certainty and verification of metaphysics is impossible, and he questions how we can obtain that which is true knowledge. The only thing we can be certain of is the existence of God and the truth of the Christian religion. Grotius establishes all other dogmas relating to religion as adiaphoric, especially the doctrine of predestination, and reasons that there are many more dogmas formulated 'than ethics requires'. To rectify this societal ill, only self-evident concerns for religion should be addressed. That means limiting 'the number of necessary articles of faith to those few that are most self-evident' (*Meletius*, 133). Inquiry into the finer doctrinal points of religion should only be done under the auspice of the Holy Scripture and be guided by Christian love (*Meletius*, 133–43).[20] As a way of conclusion, Grotius advises against punishing unbelievers and instead speaks of tolerance and forgiveness against those whose impiousness leads them to sin. They believe in the righteousness of their own conviction and thus err in good faith (*Meletius*, 134).[21]

Grotius' insistence in *Meletius* that religious dogmas rarely concern matters of true religion is the crux of his irenicism. It is a serious fallacy to assume that dogmas constitute the most singular parts of religion when, in fact, they 'subserve [ethical] precepts and lead up to them' (*Meletius*, 133).[22] Grotius' promotion of what he would later refer to in *Ordinum pietas* (1613) as an 'absolute minimum' as the basis of religious consensus, where 'each party adapts itself somewhat to the other' (*Ordinum pietas*, 169), demonstrates a philosophical consistency between his religious and political writings. Van Gelderen rightly remarks, 'in theology, as in civil philosophy, Grotius seeks to solve conflicts by a quest for the universally shared theological and philosophical foundations for peace and concord'. What guarantees their universal acceptance is that they have gone through a process of rational deliberation.[23] Human beings' capacity for rationality is integral to Grotius' understanding and affirmation of human free will, which in turn is a requirement for human socialisation. God has instilled reason in man to make His will intelligible so that humans can live according to His commandments, bestowing on them dignity, worth and the responsibility to participate in their own salvation. The virtuous conduct underlying the demands of one's own salvation is not something that can be dictated by explicit conduct or mandatory religious distributive schemes. Grotius would make clear in his later political writings that, without God, individuals would have no obligation to undertake the conduct of ensuring duties to themselves and others, thus leaving no room for socialisation.[24]

Meletius is not a firm Remonstrant anti-predestinarian endorsement; instead, it is an indirect second best in Grotius' strong defence of free will, in God as well as in humankind. God has made humans rational beings with free will (*Meletius*, 106). He made humans free agents capable of reflection and deliberation to choose a course of action for himself or herself. But, the root cause of evil lies in people's freedom and not in God's volition – 'who of their own volition deviated from the law of their maker' (*Meletius*, 112). Religion is there to guide human conduct in doing what is right and good, and 'concerns actions based on free choice'. It 'necessarily consists of two parts: the one theoretical, the other practical. The former is made up of dogmas, the latter of ethical precepts' (*Meletius*, 109). As an intermediary between God and people, religion serves ethics; that is, it may ground and motivate right action. As we find in *De jure belli ac pacis*, Grotius might not care so much why conduct is good, but that whatever good it serves makes it right. The metaphysical purpose is what makes it good, but only in so far as it leads to right conduct, which is conducive to social behaviour:

> Now whenever there is a fight over precepts, it hardly ever involves ethics – for these have definite and unequivocal rules – but deals with those matters which everybody establishes for himself for the sake of preserving order, and in which a short cut to concord is to leave every man to his own discretion. (*Meletius*, 133)

Later, in *De imperio summarum potestatum circa sacra* (1617), a work that addressed the relationship between religious and secular authorities, Grotius, with his usual prudence, sought to avoid issues of moral and religious relativism by espousing the importance of the doctrinal truths of Christianity.

> [We] must not think that religion has an effect on society only in so far as it gives moral precepts and sanctions them with threats and promises; for doctrines or ceremonies are also of great importance to morality and public happiness. (*De Imperio*, 177)

False beliefs, of which the most troubling is God as the cause of evil, can never be regarded as moral, and might even be harmful to the state (*De imperio*, 179).

Grotius' fervent commitment to, if not religious inclusion, then religious non-exclusion apprise his later reverence evident in *De jure belli ac pacis* for demarcating the boundaries between the ethical and the moral community. Grotius takes seriously the ethical implications of conventionalising a moral community that might be unable to innovate and adapt to religious plurality of his own time. For Grotius, a political community where there is more than one account of the good life requires a more inclusive social space to authenticate those individual comprehensive goods. He is reluctant to speak on the conception of the good life, as he wants to establish foundations for coexistent and different religious groups – both of which aimed to pursue a good life based on the rule of law. Grotius believes that the necessity of maintaining social order is fundamental to law. This non-interventionist account of individual liberty is most evident in how Grotius uses sociability as a common good to individuals. '[P]eculiar to Man', Grotius contends, 'is his Desire of Society' (DJBP Prol. 6). The desire to lead a sociable life is derived from divine design, to satisfy our material needs within society; and we are constrained by our lack of things to be more inclined to cultivate the social life.[25] Grotius' 'rudimentary theory of sociability' has been the object of much scholarly debate, partly over Grotius' ambiguous corollary answer of what commits men to the pursuit of justice.[26] As Hans Blom shows, Grotius' own lack of retractions and changing strategies, which is certainly evident in some of his religious writings discussed here, indicate his deep commitment to understanding and explaining what should or should not motivate individuals to create a better world for themselves.[27]

Grotius never gives a comprehensive account of what counts as a good social life, like a particular form of Christianity, the capabilities required to fulfil it or the specific ways in which it fulfils human flourishing.[28] In fact, Grotius' religious writings outline good reasons to desist from any prescription as to what constitutes the good social life, beyond being a good Christian. What Grotius instead makes clear, most evident in *De jure belli ac pacis*, is the reason why we are sociable and have sociability, which obligates us to actions of human fellowship rooted in a sense of religion and an account of human dignity, something that is a point of consensus but is not left to be defined by that consensus. As long as their conduct does not violate the preservation of society, individuals are obligated (by God) to be virtuous people – kind, charitable and empathetic. Governments serve only to ensure that people can live this kind of life, not to compel them to conduct in keeping with ideal virtues. The point to be made here, and which we will return to in the discussion of Grotius' 'impious hypothesis', is the philosophical cohesiveness of Grotius' conception of natural sociability in his later political writings, and the minimalist concept of Christianity he presents.[29] The rights Grotius' individuals have to lead a virtuous life do not dictate explicit types of conduct, privilege or entitlement, nor is it exact what that virtuous life, social or private, might be. Benjamin Straumann has observed that Grotius is sparse, negative and minimal rather than prescriptive in what people owe to one another in terms of social capacity.[30]

Grotius' general opinion against fanatical partisanship in favour of his irenic programme of religious tolerance does somewhat inundate his own religious convictions. To excavate them, we need briefly to consider the specific historical circumstances in which both *Meletius* and *Ordinum pietas* were written. Arminius' death did not quell the theological disputes about predestination and human free will in the Dutch Republic. If anything, they were intensified by the controversial appointment of his successor as professor of Leiden University, Conradus Vorstius (1569–1622), a Socinian sympathiser. Socianism, or Antitrinitarianism, was particularly despised as it essentially denounced the divinity of Christ. Such heresy was tantamount to atheism. Vorstius' nomination had been backed by the Remonstrant faction, including Grotius' friend and collaborator, Johannes Wtenbogaert (1557–1644), the leader of the Remonstrant cause. To them and the university's administrators, the Vorstius affair became a matter of principle to assert the right of civil authorities to freely make university appointments. *Meletius*, as Henk Nellen points out, was written to pacify these theological controversies and enlist James I/VI (1567–1625) for their pacification.[31] James I was especially attuned to Grotius' championing of the unconditional power of secular authorities over a public church built on the broad confessional understandings of the early Church.[32] Nevertheless, Grotius failed on both accounts, and in the end decided not to publish *Meletius*. The decisive issue not to publish was, perhaps not surprisingly, the question of free will and its relationship to grace. On this Grotius writes:

[I]t follows that logically we acknowledge God as legislator. For if God has a free will, then so has man. But God is superior, man inferior. And the superior influences the inferior since the superior is destined to act and the inferior to be acted upon. Consequently, God acts upon man according to His free choice. This activity, then, of superior free agent toward inferior free choice as such is nothing but the law of authority. That this is true is proved by man's conscience more forcefully than by any other evidence. (*Meletius*, 106)

Grotius' somewhat pragmatic approach to what was considered a serious doctrinal issue was criticised by the Middelburg Calvinist minister, Antonius Walaeus (1573–1639). But, how could Grotius have been more explicit, given the book's conciliatory purpose? Anything beyond emphasising the common factor of religion, 'what people have in common', that is the very *idea* of consensus, would be partisan. Grotius had sent the manuscript to a select few, including Walaeus, which sparked an intense correspondence between the two learned men. Walaeus listed key objections to the *Meletius* manuscript: Grotius' reduction of essential tenets, which opened the door too wide to heresies such as Anti-trinitarianism, his reticence about the Holy Trinity and the doctrine of predestination. Walaeus shrewdly noted that the latter ultimately hinged on the delicate balance of not affirming God's complicity in sin on the one side, and not making humans the cause of their own salvation on the other.[33] Walaeus reckoned that theological discussions that would keep within the boundaries of these two extremes could be tolerated within a broader Church. But, Grotius' defence of the Remonstrants' Article 1 on God's conditional election, that is election based on people's response to God's offer of salvation, *fides praevisa*, or foreknowledge of faith, which principally excluded predestination, was a notion too flawed ever to appease Grotius' orthodox Calvinist readers.[34] The Canons of Dort would later affirm that notions of foreseen faith inevitably impeded divine election and God's sovereign decree, making salvation an individual choice as opposed to divine appointment.[35]

10.4 Committed Remonstrant Crusader? *Ordinum Pietas*

Following the completion of *Meletius*, Grotius' Remonstrant leanings grew more thinly veiled as he prepared to pen *Ordinum pietas*. Against Calvinist disciplinarians, he defended the Remonstrant alternative understandings of predestination – if only indirectly in *Ordinum pietas* then directly in his correspondence, the supreme authority of secular authorities in religious matters and the policy of the States of Holland in the Vorstius affair.[36] Grotius had already defied Gomarus and other orthodox Calvinists. In *Annales et Historiae de rebus Belgicis*, written before *Ordinum pietas* but only published after Grotius's death, Grotius expresses his astonishment at the Dutch orthodox Calvinists' unwillingness to tolerate dissenting voices, given the long history of predestination.[37] To Grotius, Arminius and his followers were hardly doctrinal trendsetters as they were successors to a long line of theologians from Augustine to Luther, Erasmus (1466–1536), Melanchthon and Calvin (1509–64) who freely discussed predestinarian arguments. And, even here, Grotius argues, a belief in absolute predestination must be considered an exceptional occurrence in the history of the Church.[38] Conflicts of theological matters, such as predestination, demands prudent political practicality by tolerating 'diversity of sentiment' that 'were not absolutely vital for salvation'.[39] A commitment to religious tolerance left little room for theological semantics and, parroting his 'compatriot Erasmus', allowed defining only the 'absolute minimum and leave to each individual his own free judgement on many questions, because many things are very obscure' (OHWP 90).[40] Grotius sternly warns against the futility of surrendering our good judgment to our emotions by persisting in 'deciding yes or no' on every controversial point and excluding from the body of the Church or from the ministry those who do not comply (OHWP 90). We have only to turn to our most recent history of religious schisms to understand why such doctrinal wrangling is 'harmful both to the Church and to the state'. Due to 'the fatal hatred of theologians; the Reformed will again split up into other sects and those sects will at last also divide into new parties and thus nothing will be left but shattered limbs, and nowhere the form of a real body' (OHWP 91). We are left in no doubt which theologians Grotius refers to here: the orthodox Calvinist faction of Gomarus and Sibrandus Lubbertus (c. 1555–1625).

Grotius' challenge in *Ordinum pietas* was, then, to carefully heed Walaeus' advice, and avoid the two extremes of first 'that we do not ascribe the causes of sin to God, or damnation to fatal necessity, second, that we do not trace back the origin of salutary good to the powers of our depraved nature' (OHWP 35). As such, we never get a firm independent outline of the doctrine of predestination from Grotius. His defence of Remonstrant tenets rests on his own refusal to accept that the early Church grounded the question of predestination in any particular orthodoxy. Grotius advocates that, as long as the two aforementioned extremes are avoided, the Dutch Reformed Church is broad enough to accommodate different theological opinions. He argues that Article 3 of the Remonstrance 'demolishes Pelagianism' because salvation necessitates the mitigation of divine grace; (OHWP 41) but, on the very question of election, where the Remonstrants appeal to God's foreknowledge of faith, Grotius is on the defence: 'I do not yet ask what [elections of certain persons to the foreknowledge of faith] is true; I ask whether it is Pelagian or Socinian to think thus, whether it is intolerable' (OHWP 44). To orthodox Calvinists, as noted above, it most certainly was, as election would then be determined by the faithful – that is, human's future response to God, as opposed to God's unconditional choice. Furthermore, for the orthodox Calvinists, it compromised divine time-lessness by insinuating that God was somehow constrained by time.[41] Grotius' pursuit of mutual toleration on the predestination controversy by attempting to appease orthodox Calvinists through condemning doc-trinal protrusions of Pelaginism and Socianism had come to a hold; and his Remonstrant tendencies were exposed. But, we need only look at a letter to Isaac Casaubon (1559–1614) from the previous year for evidence of Grotius' rejection of the doctrine of predestination. He writes that not only did the Counter-Remonstrants err by reviving the fatalism of the Stoics, their excessive emphasis on predestination to damnation made God the author of sin.[42] Grotius' plea for toleration of 'the diversity of sentiment' is his antidote to the destructive forces of predestination arguments that 'were not absolutely vital for salvation'.[43] Further indi-cation of Grotius' cloistered rejection of predestination can be found in his device for formulating a natural law that sought to eschew theo-logical controversies. I turn next to the so-called 'impious hypothesis'.

10.5 Predestination, Human Free Will and Grotian Natural Law

Some contemporary studies of Grotius' 'political' writings disregard his religious works, partly to promote him as a pioneer of modernity, who laid the foundations for modern international law.[44] From such siloed treat-ment of his works emerges a somewhat contradictory ahistorical Grotius. Grotius' reconstitution of natural law theory in Protestant political thought clearly required reconciling the idea of a predestinarian system with the universal moral principles of human natural goodness and moral capacity. As we have seen, Grotius' solution was the affirmation of free human will, which made predestination conditional, not absolute. But, such affirm-ation was not without intellectual problems, and here we must turn to one of the most disputed passages in Grotian scholarship, the so-called 'impious hypothesis', to understand why. Predestination debates about God's authority related in a very concrete way to the obligation argument in natural law, that is in specifying the content of God's authority and how it is directed. An emphasis on God's absolute sovereignty is a fundamental commitment in orthodox Calvinism. That commitment also leads one to both have a strong view of predestination and a voluntarist view of natural law. In fact, the above contextualisation of predestination in Grotius' religious oeuvre enables us to shed a further critical light on this most disputed statement of his, which seemed to render the obligatory force of the natural law independent of God's existence. Natural law, for Grotius, might be self-evident, the proof of which is found in human sociability. It was so inextricably tied to human nature that, even if it was the case that God did not have an interest in the welfare of humanity, the law prescribing this welfare would remain valid:

And indeed, all we have now said would take place, though we should even grant, what without the greatest Wickedness cannot be granted, that there is no God, or that he takes no Care of human Affairs. (DJBP Prol. 11)

It is not surprising that much controversy should have arisen from this passage.[45] Modern scholarly controversy over this statement rests on whether or not it marked the secularisation of the natural law tradition, which signalled a need for a natural law theory based upon natural rights.[46] The purpose of the law of nations and civil law, then, as David Boucher argues, was to protect and facilitate the free use of these rights.[47] But, the statement in question was obviously not a disavowal of the existence of God, because in the next sentence Grotius goes on to say: '[...] God, as being our Creator, and to whom we owe our Being, and all that we have, ought to be obeyed by us all in all Things without Exception [...]' (DJBP Prol. 11). Grotius further contends that there are compelling reasons for ascribing the principles of natural law to God. He has made them so evident and clear, Grotius writes, even to those 'less capable of strict Reasoning, and has forbid us to give way to those impetuous Passions which are contrary to our own Interests and that of others', and which deviates us from following the rules of reason (DJBP, Prol. 13). In the 'Defence of Chapter V of the *Mare Liberum*', Grotius is even more forthcoming on this point, and writes that God has directly implanted certain precepts into men's minds, which are 'sufficient to induce obligation even if no reason is apparent' (ML, *Defense,* 105).

To Grotius' early modern audience, the 'impious hypothesis' was controversial as it obfuscated Grotius' understanding of God's power and authority regarding human action. Grotius' translator and commentator, Jean Barbeyrac (1674–1744), was so perturbed by this statement to offer a qualification: 'The Duty and Obligation', Barbeyrac comments, '[. . .] necessarily supposes a superior Power, a supreme Master of Mankind, who can be no other than the Creator, or supreme Divinity' (DJBP, Prol., 11 n. 1). Knud Haakonssen and Michael Seidler convincingly argue that Grotius did not intend the 'impious hypothesis' to be a deep philosophical examination of obligation or God's existence. Instead, he sought to avoid potential religious differences over the basis of the natural law from which disputes about rights were to be settled. Grotius conceded, *pace* the neo-scholastics, that natural law was not entrenched in a system of divine eternal law.[48] Grotius' contemporary, Spanish theologian Francisco Suárez (1548–1617), saw, for example, natural law as tied to eternal law.[49] The question of the source of our obligations, how they are prescribed by natural law and why we are obliged to act upon them had been a longstanding debate in medieval theology long before Grotius. This gave rise to two opposing positions: voluntarism and intellectualism. Voluntarism was the position that derived moral standards from the divine will, whereas intellectualists believed that the divine will was determined or guided by independent standards. For the voluntarist, God is the absolute power and His actions need not be explained or rationalised. It is a divine will that ordains all things. The good is good because God has willed it. By an act of will, God created morality. For the intellectualist, God wills the good because it is intrinsically good and can thus be logically verified.[50]

The answer to that main question that predestination debates turned around, 'to what extent does human freedom pose limitations on God's sovereign control over earthly affairs?', was to be found somewhere on the continuum between these two ideal positions.[51] On the voluntarist side of the spectrum where 'God ordains all things', we find some of the early Protestant reformers such as Luther and Calvin. For Calvin, the power and will of God remains unchangeable: 'of all the things which happen, the first cause is to be understood to be His will, because He so governs the natures created by Him, as to determine all the counsels and the actions of men to the end decreed by Him'.[52] By purporting the absolute and arbitrary willpower of God, Gomarus and the Counter-Remonstrants are also to be found here. Moving further to the middle of the continuum toward an intellectual ideal, we find the view that 'God limits his powers' in line with more classical Arminian urgings. To protect divine love, God's omnipotence must be restricted to ascribe evil and sin to the volitional actions of His human creations.[53] This Arminian mediating position is consistent with how Grotius understands God's design for and relationship to humans. John Finnis has argued that Grotius was not adopting a firm intellectualist position, as the German natural lawyer, Samuel Pufendorf (1632–94), later understood him to do. Rather, Finnis sees Grotius' natural law theory as mediating between voluntarism and intellectualism. For Finnis, the specific content of natural law may be determined independently, but its obligatory force derives from divine will.[54] Thus, the source of natural law is undeniably God, however, its contents are based upon and emanate from human nature and those traits that are implanted in us by God. Grotius' mediation between two doctrines of God here fully serves his notion of religious consensus and, as such, we might even understand Grotius' 'impious hypothesis' as a manifestation of Arminianism.

10.6 Conclusion

By appealing for moderation in the predestination controversy, Grotius purposefully re-framed questions from doctrinal certainty to how proclaimed orthodoxy and heresy should be solved in a shared society. He looked to what he presented as the accommodating heterodoxy of the early Christian Church as a model in the shared spirit of the conflicting doctrinal perspectives.[55] Here, issues of practice over theory weighed higher on Grotius' scale of moderation. As we have seen, religion served a practical purpose of promoting those ethical precepts for human conduct vital for societal welfare and commodious living. Grotius is trying to accomplish these dual tasks and reconcile these irreconcilably disparate parties in his political theory, which meant he had to take a pragmatic and more nuanced approach to the predestinarian debates that threatened to break up the fabric of societal cohesion. In many ways, it was an impossible project, and one doomed to fail. But Grotius' pragmatic attitude to these debates illuminates not only the political delicacy of his position, but also his claims about sociability and natural justice we find in his later and, today, arguably more widely circulated political writings. Against the back drop of religious controversy, Grotius sought to develop a kind of theory of political and social harmony and took the concept of natural sociability and worked it into a pluralistic minimal approach to social justice.

Achieving political and social harmony entailed accepting the metaphysical divide, while appreciating its depth and even acknowledging the potentially mandatory nature of daring to possess a personal opinion on such controversial matters as he shows in his own writing. Yet, as we can see from his consideration on issues of predestination, he desired to reconcile these sides politically by insinuating politics as a space where the structure must reflect what is needed for these moral debates of consciousness to happen. Notwithstanding, for the parties he was dealing with, the right way to live was similar in character, a point often lost on those who seek Grotius as a precursory for a plural liberal political order.[56] For Grotius, rules that enable social unity take primacy over religious doctrines and their dogmatic certainty; but, without question, a very specific God stood as author of either religious doctrine or the principle of sociability, and the obligations they engendered. Ultimately, Grotius showed how an overlap in religious consensus could be socially fulfilled and be broad enough to ensure human flourishing. Sociability was natural, but Grotius was acutely aware that societies were structured in the image of the individuals they served. The predestination controversy exposed the intricate balance that the social realities of his time demanded be struck – which is an idea worth considering even if the specific obligations Grotius suggests we have to balance those social realities with are very much a product of his time.

Translations of Grotius' Works Used

The Rights of War and Peace, ed. R. Tuck (Indianapolis, 2005)

Annales et historiae de rebus Belgicis or, The annals and history of the Low-Country-warrs wherein is manifested, that the United Netherlands are indebted for the glory of their conquests, to the valour of the English, under whose protection the poor distressed states, have exalted themselves to the title of the high and mighty . . ., transl. T. Manley, (London, 1665)

'A chloliambic poem by Hugo Grotius on the death of the venerable, most erudite Jacob Arminius, Professor of Divinity at Leiden Academy', transl. M. van Oosterhout, in J. Bloemendal, A. Dixhoorn and E. Strietman (eds.), *Literary Cultures and Public Opinion in the Low Countries 1450-1650* (Leiden, 2011), 175-9 (*Arminius Poem*)

'Memorie van mijne Intention', R. Fruin (ed.), in *Verhooren en andere bescheiden betreffende het rechtsgeding van Hugo de Groot* (Utrecht, 1871), 1-34 (*Memorie*)

Further Reading

Mulsow, M. and J. Rohls (eds.), *Socinianism and Arminianism, Antitrinitarians, Calvinists and Cultural Exchange in Seventeenth-Century Europe* (Leiden, 2005).

Nellen, H.J.M. and E. Rabbie (eds.), *Hugo Grotius Theologian – Essays in Honour of G.H.M. Posthumus Meyjes* (Leiden, 1994).

Stanglin, K.D., *Arminius on the Assurance of Salvation; The Context, Roots, and Shape of the Leiden Debate, 1603-1609* (Leiden, 2007).

Van Gelderen, M., 'Freedom fighters: The Act of Abjuration, Hugo Grotius and the Dutch debates on liberty', in P. Brood and R. Kubben (eds.) *The Act of Abjuration – Inspired and Inspirational* (Nijmegen, 2011), 155-72.

Van Gelderen, M., 'Arminian trouble: Calvinist debates on freedom', in Q. Skinner and M. van Gelderen (eds.), *Freedom and the Construction of Europe: Religious Freedom and Civil Liberty* (Cambridge, 2013), vol. 1, 21-37.

Wetzel, J., 'Predestination, Pelagianism and foreknowledge' in E. Stump and N. Kretzmann (eds.), *The Cambridge Companion to Augustine* (Cambridge, 2001), 49-58.

Notes

1 See J. Wetzel, 'Predestination, Pelagianism and foreknowledge' in E. Stump and N. Kretzmann (eds.), *The Cambridge Companion to Augustine* (Cambridge, 2001), 49-58.

2 Cited in D. MacCulloch, *Reformation – Europe's House Divided 1490-1700* (London, 2003), 118.

3 Ibid., p. 242. On Luther and Melanchthon see J. Witte Jr., *Law and Protestantism – the Legal Teachings of the Lutheran Reformation* (Cambridge, 2002).

4 G.H.M. Posthumus Meyjes, 'Grotius as a theologian', in *Hugo Grotius. A Great European 1583-1645. Contributions concerning his Activities as a Humanist Scholar* (Delft, 1983), 51-8, at 52.

5 M. van Gelderen, 'Freedom fighters: The Act of Abjuration, Hugo Grotius and the Dutch debates on liberty', in P. Brood and R. Kubben (eds.) *The Act of Abjuration – Inspired and Inspirational* (Nijmegen, 2011), 155-72, at 162.

6 Ibid.

7 MacCulloch, *Reformation*, 109.

8 The divine grace controversy proved equally controversial between the Jesuits and Dominicans as can be seen in the extraordinary De Auxiliis meetings convened by order of Pope Clement VIII.

9 Ibid., 374.

10 After the consolidation of the rebellious provinces, two major conflicts concerning the Church came to light: Confessional/Catechism and Church/State. For more on this see E. Rabbie, 'Introduction', in *Ordinum pietas*, 12–13.

11 The Act of Abjuration 1581 http://www.age-of-the-sage.org/history/dutch_ independence_1581.html (accessed 1 April 2016).

12 See for instance his *Parallelon Rerumpublicarum* (*Comparison of Commonwealths*, 1601–2), which, as Arthur Eyffinger notes, 'reads like an electoral pamphlet'. See A. Eyffinger, 'On good faith and bad faith: introductory notes', *Grotiana* N.S. 36 (2015), 79–105, at 84.

13 H.J.M. Nellen, *Hugo Grotius. A Lifelong Struggle for Peace in Church and State, 1583–1645* (Leiden and Boston, 2015), 124. See also K.D. Stanglin, *Arminius on the Assurance of Salvation; The Context, Roots, and Shape of the Leiden Debate, 1603–1609* (Leiden, 2007) for a more in depth discussion of Arminius and Gomarus's debate.

14 Nellen, *Grotius*, 128.

15 Ibid., 135.

16 Posthumus Meyjes, 'Grotius as a theologian', 51. For a detail account of Grotius's involvement in the Remonstrant/Counter-Remonstrant controversy see Nellen, *Grotius,* ch. 5.

17 M. van Oosterhout, 'Hugo Grotius in Parise of Jacobus Arminius: Arminian readers of an epicedium in the Dutch Republic and England', in J. Bloemendal, A. Dixhoorn and E. Strietman (eds.), *Literary Cultures and Public Opinion in the Low Countries 1450–1650* (Leidenl, 2011), 151–80, at 159.

18 Nellen, *Grotius*, 128.

19 Posthumus Meyjes, 'Introduction', in *Meletrius*, 24.

20 See also F. Mühlegger, 'Pluralization and authority in Grotius's early works,' in M. Mulsow and J. Rohls (eds.) *Socinianism and Arminianism, Antitrinitarians, Calvinists and Cultural Exchange in Seventeenth-Century Europe* (Leiden, 2005), 99–120, at 107.

21 For an excellent and in-depth discussion on Grotius' changing concept of punishment from his religious works and DJBP, see H.W. Blom, 'Grotius and Socinianism', in Muslow and Rohls, *Socianism,* 121–47.

22 See also Mühlegger, 'Pluralization'.

23 M. van Gelderen, 'Arminian trouble: Calvinist debates on freedom', in Q. Skinner and M. van Gelderen (eds.), *Freedom and the Construction of Europe: Religious Freedom and Civil Liberty* (Cambridge, 2013), vol. 1, 21–37, at 32.

24 In Grotian scholarship, there is some debate of the extent to which the obligatory force of the natural law derives from right reason not God. See for instance

B. Straumann, *Roman Law in the State of Nature. The Classical Foundations of Hugo Grotius' Natural Law* (Cambridge, 2015).

25 See especially Grotius early 1625 edition of DJBP 1.1.10.2.

26 H.W. Blom, 'Sociability and Hugo Grotius', *History of European Ideas* 41 (2015) 589–604, at 589.

27 Ibid.

28 See C. Boisen and M.C. Murray, 'Dignity, sociability and capability: exploring Nussbaum's interpretation of Grotius', in C. Boisen and M.C. Murray (eds.) *Distributive Justice Debates in Political and Social Thought: Perspectives on Finding a Fair Share* (New York, 2016), 79–106.

29 Barbara Knieper is only marginally convincing when arguing that Grotius turned to the natural law as a foundational framework to unite Christendom, having been unsuccessful with his religious writings. See F. Mühlegger, *Hugo Grotius: Ein christlicher Humanist in politischer Verantwortung* (Berlin, 2007), 62–5.

30 Straumann, *Roman Law in the State of Nature*, 4. See Straumann ch. 8 in this companion.

31 For a comprehensive in-depth discussion of the 'Vorstius affair' see Nellen, *Grotius*, ch. 5. See also Posthumous Meyjes 'Introduction'; P.G. Lake, 'Calvinism and the English Church 1570-1635', *Past and Present* 114 (1987) 32–76; F. Shriver, 'Orthodoxy and diplomacy: James I and the Vorstius affair', *The English Historical Review* 85 (1970) 449–74.

32 Nellen, *Grotius*, 155.

33 Posthumus Meyjes, 'Introduction', 44–60.

34 Rabbie,'Introduction', in *Ordinum Pietas*, 9 n. 1 and 10. In 1610, the Remonstrants stipulated five theological propositions to rebut the five point of Calvinism.

35 *The Articles of the Synod of Dort*, transl. and annotated T. Scott and intro. S. Miller (Philadelphia, 1841), 272–8.

36 Nellen, *Grotius*, 142–3 and 171.

37 J. Trapman, 'Grotius and Erasmus', in H.J.M. Nellen and E. Rabbie (eds.), *Hugo Grotius Theologian. Essays in Honour of G.H.M. Posthumus Meyjes* (Leiden, 1994), 77–98, at 80–2.

38 Ibid.

39 Grotius cited in van Gelderen, 'Arminian trouble', 32.

40 On the intellectual relationship between Grotius and Erasmus see in particular Trapman, 'Grotius and Erasmus'.

41 F. LeRon Shults, *Reforming the Doctrine of God* (Cambridge, 2005), 211.

42 Nellen, *Grotius*, 183. See also letter from Grotius to Wilhelm Grotius 22 Sept 1617, 1 BW 534.

43 Grotius in *Oratie vanden hooch-geleerden voortreffeycken Meester Hugo de Groot...* [1622] cited in M. van Gelderen, 'Hot Protestants: predestination, the freedom of will and the making of the modern European mind', in G. van den Brink (ed.) *Calvinism and the Making of the European Mind* (Leiden, 2014), 131–54, at 144.

44 For a good exploration of the connection between Grotius' theology and international relations see Will Bain's forthcoming monograph *Political Theology of International Order*.

45 See e.g. D. Boucher, *The Limits of Ethics in International Relations: Natural Law, Natural Rights and Human Rights in Transition* (Oxford, 2009); K. Haakonssen, *Natural Law and Moral Philosophy. From Grotius to the Scottish Enlightenment* (Cambridge, 1996); B. Tierney, *The Idea of Natural Rights. Studies on Natural Rights, Natural Law and Church Law 1150–1625* (Cambridge, 2001); R. Tuck, *The Rights of War and Peace. Political Thought and the International Order from Grotius to Kant* (Oxford, 1999).

46 For a helpful discussion of scholastic antecedents of the 'impious hypothesis' see J. St.Leger, *The 'etiamsi daremus' of Hugo Grotius: a study in the origins of international law* (Rome, 1962). See also J.E. Nijman, 'Images of Grotius, or the international rule of law beyond historiographical oscillation' in *Journal of the history of International Law* 17 (2015), 83–137 and her 'Grotius' Imago Dei Anthropology Grounding Ius Naturae et Gentium' in M. Koskenniemi, M. García-Salmones Rovira, and P. Amorosa (eds.), *International Law and Religion: Historical and Contemporary Perspectives* (Oxford, 2017), 87–110.

47 D. Boucher, *Political Theories of International Relations: From Thucydides to the Present* (Oxford, 1998), 209.

48 K. Haakonssen and M.J. Seidler, 'Natural law: law, rights and duties', in R. Whatmore and B. Young (eds.), *A Companion to Intellectual History* (Oxford, 2016), 377–401, at 385.

49 F. Suárez, *Selections from Three Works*, ed. T. Pink (Indianapolis, 2015), 2 Introduction'; 2.8.3 and 7; 2.10.1.

50 N.E. Simmonds, 'Grotius and Pufendorf', in S. Nadler (ed.) *A Companion to Early Modern Philosophy* (Oxford, 2002), 216–24.

51 LeRon Shults, *Reforming the Doctrine of God*, 211. For an in-depth discussion see also L. Besselink, 'The impious hypothesis revisited', *Grotiana* N.S. 9 (1988) 3–63.

52 Calvin cited in LeRon Schultz, *Reforming the Doctrine of God*, 240.

53 LeRon Shults, *Reforming the Doctrine of God*, 238–41.

54 J. Finnis, *Natural Law and Natural Rights*, (Oxford, 1980), 44.

55 S.-P. Bergjan, 'The patristic context in early Grotius', in H.W. Blom (ed), *Property, Piracy and Punishment: Hugo Grotius on War and Booty in de Iure Praedae – Concept and Contexts* (Leiden, 2014), 128–46, at 133–4.

56 See M.C. Nussbaum, *Frontiers of Justice: Disability, Nationality, Species Membership* (Cambridge, MA, 2006); R. Tuck, *Natural Rights Theories: Their Origins and Development* (Cambridge, 1979).

Rights (I) 11

Francesca Iurlaro

11.1 Introduction

In a recent article on the *National Review*, John Yoo wrote, in support of the US killing of Iranian general Qasem Suleimani, that such killing was justified by the laws of war. 'As Hugo Grotius, the father of modern international law, observed in 1646, it is permissible to kill an enemy.'[1] Historical inaccuracy aside – Grotius died in 1645 – it is interesting that, in times of dire international crisis, the name of Grotius is still evoked as an authoritative voice to argue for punishment as a natural right, calling into question the contemporary relevance of his intellectual legacy for understanding the global order and its foundations.

The issue of the 'Grotian tradition of international law' is, hence, still a crucial one.[2] What is the legacy of his doctrinal efforts, and how did they impact on current structures of international law? Was he providing a natural law foundation for the global order, or rather an instrument of power for sovereigns to assert their political and commercial dominion over the world? To attempt an answer to these questions, scholars from different fields and disciplinary perspectives have engaged with Grotius' doctrine of natural law and rights, one of the most contested and crucial aspects of his intellectual enterprise. More specifically, on the one hand, Grotius' natural law seems to provide a universal framework of justice, a rule of law for the global world based on right reason and sociability (objective law); at the same time, Grotius originally introduces a system of natural, individual (subjective) rights, strongly building on an anthropology of free will and contractual self-determination.

Whereas some scholars have emphasised one aspect over the other, more recent interpretations suggest that objective justice and individual rights are not in conflict in Grotius' legal doctrine. Rather, natural rights are entrenched into a natural law system that provides them with a normative framework of justice.

Along these lines, in this chapter I argue that a more careful reading of Grotius' engagement with the Aristotelian tradition might cast new light on his conception of justice. Famously, Aristotle provides a moral justification for human freedom fully integrated into a moral paradigm of virtue ethics. However, I also argue that, rather than just looking at Grotius' reading of Aristotle himself, engaging with a long tradition of Aristotelian commentators with whom he shows full acquaintance, might help us to fully grasp the nuances of Grotius' legal doctrine. Grotius argues that *jus* is 'a moral quality annexed to the person, enabling him to have, or do, something justly'. Grotius observes that when this 'moral quality' is perfect, it is called *facultas*, and it entitles its owner to demand respect from others; when it is imperfect, it is called *aptitudo*, and it designs a more generic account of merit and moral fitness. Far from being discarded as a 'minor' or 'deficient' source of right, aptitude plays a fundamental role in this context. I will thus analyse this concept through Grotius' reading and translating of the Aristotelian commentator, Michael of Ephesus. Such close reading will allow us to see the connection of Grotius' thin conception of right as aptitude with the idea of fitness as a heuristic requirement for right reason.

11.2 Natural Law and Natural Rights: Challenges in the Interpretation of Grotius

As recently pointed out,[3] two opposite narratives coexist in the interpretation of Grotius' doctrines: the first one insisting on the distinctively 'liberal' features of Grotius' legal thought, and a second one claiming that Grotius' innovation in conceding subjective rights to individuals does not, by any means, imply a denial of a more universal system of justice, which was, in fact, granted by natural law and its inherently coercive, normative power. In Grotius' iconic formulation, natural law is a conceptual device so powerful that it would still be in place even if God would not exist.[4]

Concerning the first, 'liberal' interpretation, its starting point consists in acknowledging Grotius' original contribution to the birth of subjective natural rights in the European legal tradition.[5] By channelling a body of theological and juridical sources from the medieval past into the present,[6] Grotius contributed to shape a conception of rights as entitlements conferred upon individuals, as opposed to – but not in contradiction with, as many have rightly pointed out – an objective, universal conception of justice. According to such an interpretation, Grotius is one of the first natural law theorists to articulate the liberty of the moderns and its individualistic features, as opposed to the more 'collective' dimension of the liberty of the ancients.[7] Scholars have drawn different consequences from this insight. Richard Tuck has interpreted Grotius' anthropology of self-preservation against the background of his critique of moral scepticism. According to Tuck, in an anti-Aristotelian move, Grotius openly criticises scholasticism – according to which, we can simply deduce human nature from God-given *naturalis ratio* – as well as scepticism – whose fundamental claim goes: if we are not able to reduce the whole body of ethics into a system, then we should simply give up striving for any kind of systematic attempt whatsoever.[8] Turning Grotius into a pre-Hobbesian author, Tuck suggests that Grotius' most fundamental theoretical move is to put self-preservation and reason of state at the apex of the international legal order, as the only universal principles capable of regulating human conduct.[9] Scepticism provides, thus, a theoretical justification behind Grotius' alleged reason of state approach, animated by a profound disbelief that justice can be determined objectively, and that, instead, the only rule of the law of nations is self-preservation – what Tuck has referred to as 'moral minimalism'.

As it has been observed, however, Tuck's moral minimalism fails to grasp Grotius' inherently normative project. Rather than being a 'war-hawk'[10] or a relentless defender of the Dutch East India Company's (VOC) commercial practices,[11] Grotius was also providing a universalistic foundation of the law of nations through natural law. This leads us to the second, 'conciliatory' interpretation of Grotius' doctrine of right. In the twentieth century, authors such as Cornelis van Vollenhoven (1874–1933) and Hersch Lauterpacht (1897–1960) have overemphasised the 'pacifist' afflatus of the Grotian tradition, in an attempt to provide a counter-narrative to the dominant political realism of their contemporaries and to vindicate international law's irenic stance in times of war.[12] However, their reading fails to grasp the complexity of Grotius' thought, just as much as the radicalness of the liberal interpretation insists, on the other end of the spectrum, on picturing Grotius as a champion of individual rights and unrestrained sovereign interest. Instead, contemporary interpreters have focused on his contribution to the conceptualisation of the international rule of law, while seeking to reconcile

Grotius' innovative doctrine of natural rights with the universal afflatus of his natural law theory.[13] For example, Janne Nijman has criticised the view that Grotius' political theory is 'individual rights-based and rests on the expansive notion of individual autonomy, [...] that is, a system of rights rather than objective law that guides and constrains state conduct. [...] where states are free and exploitive agents'.[14] Furthermore, Anthony Carty and Janne Nijman have argued that it is possible to retrace a tradition of northern humanism in Grotius, emphasising the importance of Erasmian concepts such as grace and *caritas* in the construction of Grotius' law of nations.[15]

Similarly, recent scholarship on Grotius' reliance on Stoic sources has offered a new insight on how his account of self-preservation should be understood in connection with *oikeiosis*. It is by relying on this Stoic concept that Grotius elaborates his famous doctrine of *appetitus societatis*. *Oikeiosis* constitutes Grotius' starting point – if not the fundamental principle – of his doctrine of natural law, providing a corrective to the potential dangers of unlimited inclination towards self-preservation. According to this famous Stoic doctrine, humans have a feeling of self-appreciation that leads them both to self-preservation and to the 'appreciation of the human species as being akin to the individual human being'.[16] Notably, in Grotius' account, the two meanings of *oikeiosis* merge together: the instinct of preservation already contains the germs of *sociabilitas*, and vice versa (DJBP Prol. 19).[17] Quoting Seneca's *De ira*, Grotius writes that society 'cannot subsist but by a mutual love and defence of its parts' ('salva enim esse societas nisi amore et custodia partium non potest', DJBP 1.1.3). Accordingly, 'rather than to embrace the universal right of self-preservation as the basis of a wide-ranging set of unlimited natural rights, Grotius entrenches natural rights within natural law and justice'.[18] As also claimed by Tierney, 'individual rights could flourish only in a well-ordered society; but a society could flourish only if the individual members cared, not only for their own well-being, but for that of their fellow members and of the whole community'.[19]

In other words, it is impossible to grasp the complexity of Grotius' intellectual enterprise by focusing exclusively on one aspect or the other. Both – universal justice and individual rights – coexist in Grotius' legal thought.[20] Several factors might have contributed, however, to the misunderstanding of this crucial aspect, as I will explain in the next section.

In this sense, the 'conciliatory' interpretation of Grotius' theory of rights might respond to an urge to look at his theory of rights in a less predatory fashion.[21] It is, thus, intuitively easy to detect in this need a sign of the times. Adopting the 'liberal' paradigm seemed crucial critically to understand how Grotius used the language of natural law to justify commercial and colonial expansion, and allows us to contextualise the global turn of modernity. In a similar manner, it is now urgent to make sense of this cumbersome historical legacy, in times in which structures of dominion all over the world are leading us towards self-destruction and to the destruction of the planet. The allegedly natural universality of the Grotian instinct of self-preservation seems to have left room for a Freudian death drive, instead.

11.3 Grotius and Aristotelianism(s): Right, *Facultas* and *Aptitudo*

No wonder, then, that in times of political and existential bleakness like ours, scholars have turned to Aristotle and his account of virtue ethics to try and make sense of the international legal order. From a theoretical perspective, it can also be argued that one of the reasons of this polarisation in the interpretation of Grotius' doctrine of rights might be the lack of acknowledgment of his debt towards the Aristotelian tradition – perhaps another consequence of Tuck's influential account of Grotius as an 'anti-Aristotelian'. It has recently been argued by Annabel Brett that Grotius' doctrine of moral necessitation is fundamental to understanding the interplay between natural law and natural rights.[22] Humans have subjective rights, as granted by natural law, but, when those rights are violated, an anomaly is introduced into the whole system. Punishment plays a fundamental role in Grotius' doctrinal architecture.[23] Punishment works, in Grotius' doctrine of rights, as the natural police of moral necessitation: once there is no way back from wrongful human action, there *must* be a way to restore order and peace. Against the dogmatism of Calvinism, Grotius, a follower of Jacob Arminius (1560–1609), believed that humans enjoy total free will, and there is no fate or divine predestination governing their actions. Humans must have free will; otherwise, they would not be accountable for their deeds. Law and legal obligation thus become the 'legal *proprium*' of humanity – what makes humans different from animals.[24]

All these conceptual innovations are channelled by Grotius through a re-interpretation of Aristotelian philosophy. As recently claimed by Brett, 'appreciating the complex triangulation between scholastic casuistry, Aristotelian philosophy and Aristotle himself is vital to the understanding of morality in Grotius' thought'.[25] In that respect, more research should be done concerning the kind of Aristotelianism that Grotius was voicing, not only as far as his relationship with Aristotelian texts and their scholastic reception is concerned[26]. It is also necessary to engage into a more critical scrutiny of the Aristotelian commentators Grotius was reading and actively re-interpreting.[27] For example, I have elsewhere showed Grotius' intellectual debt towards one of the greatest Aristotelian commentators, Alexander of Aphrodisias (c. 200 CE). Grotius translates Alexander's famous *De fato* – a text whose early modern reception was crucial and often instrumental to challenge the idea of predestination.[28] The main purpose of this text is to provide an Aristotelian reading of the concept of fate (a concept, itself, absent from Aristotle's vocabulary) and to settle the question by providing a rational account of responsibility and an interpretation of fate as, in proper Aristotelian terms, what mostly happens by nature. Alexander's conceptual strategies are particularly useful to understand Grotius' attempt at reconciling natural order and human accountability, natural justice and free will. This reconciliatory approach is also at the basis of his posthumous *Philosophorum sententiae de Fato* (1648), a collection of excerpts from different philosophical schools of the past he uses to 'demonstrate the compatibility of free will and divine providence'.[29] Grotius creates an original connection between the legal dimension of fate and human will, which is made even stronger in his patently juridical translation of the concept of *autoexiouson*, 'free according to his own right'. This concept, already present in Grotius' *De jure praedae commentarius* (DJPC Prol. 2), indicates that man is free and has dominion over himself and his choices. In the passage from Alexander of Aphrodisias where this expression is present, Grotius translates the concept as *sui juris*.[30] Human freedom, however, is constrained by the law of fatal consequences: once bad choices are made, there is no turning back and punishment is the only way to restore order. From this perspective, Grotius' reading of Alexander suggests the existence of an overarching set of universal rules, to which individual actions and claims of rights should conform, to avoid disorder and unnatural deviations.

11.4 The Legal Dimension of Aptitude: Grotius' Reading of Michael of Ephesus

Another example, relevant to the purposes of this contribution, is Grotius' citation of Michael of Ephesus (1070–1129), a Byzantine commentator of Aristotle working under the princess and scholar Anna Comnena (1083–1153) at the beginning of the twelfth century.[31] Reading Michael's rendition of Aristotle's concept of attributive justice in his commentary to book V of *Nicomachean Ethics* is particularly revealing to understand the entanglements between the subjective and the objective dimension of Grotius' account of law.

Famously, Grotius presents a tripartite definition of *jus* in the first chapter of the first book of *De jure belli ac pacis*. Grotius says that *jus* is 1) 'merely that which is just, and that too rather in a negative than a positive sense' (DJBP 1.1.3); 2) 'a moral quality annexed to the person, enabling him to have, or do, something justly' (DJBP 1.1.4); 3) 'a rule of moral actions, obliging us to that which is good and commendable' (DJBP 1.1.9). Let us focus on the second definition, which is the one introducing the tension between subjective and objective rights we have been discussing so far. Grotius observes that, when this 'moral quality' is perfect, it is called *facultas*; when it is imperfect, it is called *aptitudo*. In Aristotelian terms, whereas *facultas* is an act (hence, a complete, perfect right requiring no further actualisation), aptitude belongs to the realm of potentiality (i.e. it is an imperfect right):

Aristotle calls *Aptitude* or *Capacity*, ἀξίαν, *Worth*, or Merit: And Michael of Ephesus terms that which is called Equal or Right, according to that Merit, τὸ προσάρμοζον καὶ τὸ πρέπον, *Fit and Decent*. *(aptitudinem vero ἀξίαν, id est dignitatem vocat Aristoteles. Michael Ephesius id quod secundum eam aequale dicitur interpretatur τὸ προσάρμοζον καὶ τὸ πρέπον, id quod convenit, p. 141)*

Consequently, Grotius continues, 'attributive justice, styled by Aristotle διανεμητικὴ, Distributive, respects Aptitude or imperfect right, the attendant of those virtues that are beneficial to others, as liberality, mercy and prudent administration of government' (DJBP 1.1.8). For these reasons, Grotius writes, civil lawyers only consider *facultas* as right in the proper sense. This polemic specification seems to imply Grotius' distancing from such position, and, rather, his intention not to underestimate the value of aptitude as a valid form of *jus*.

In the interpretation of the passage on ἀξία, it is interesting to note Grotius' translation of Michel of Ephesus. *Aptitudo* is Grotius' translation for the Aristotelian term ἀξία, which is often rendered with the Latin *dignitas* ('aptitudinem vero ἀξίαν, id est dignitatem vocat Aristoteles'). Let us compare his translation with Iohannis Bernardus Felicianus' Latin rendition of Michael of Ephesus' commentary:

> nam in politicis et talem quondam aequalitatem commemorate, et eam etiam quam diximus. Aequale enim unicuique illud est quod pro dignitate traditur. Nam cum apud geometras ea sint aequalia, quae alicui ita accomodantur atque aptantur (τὰ προσαρμόζοντα), ut neque excedant neque deficient.[32]

Although Grotius does not report the exact reference to this passage – he quotes τὸ προσάρμοζον instead of τὰ προσαρμόζοντα – he emphasises the semantic affinity between the verb προσάρμοζω and *aptitudo*, as we can see from Feliciano's Latin translation of this expression ('quae ... *aptantur'*). Grotius chooses the word *aptitudo* to give a better sense of fitness, while disregarding the importance of the distinction between arithmetic and geometric proportion (DJBP 1.1.8). Second, the term *aptitudo* very well conveys the idea that individual behaviour needs to be 'adapted' according to a natural criterion of fitness; but, the very fact that an adjustment is needed means that not all individual actions are necessarily and inherently just – aptitude and equality always need a means of comparison to be evaluated and equated with – as humans have freedom of choice and their lives are not entirely governed by God's predestination. Rather, humans engage into a negotiation between individual behaviour and ideals of virtue. Aptitude is, thus, a matter of judgment and appreciation.[33]

Interestingly, Grotius rejects Aristotle's view that 'attributive justice is exercised about things belonging to the whole community; and expletive about things belonging to private persons' (DJBP 1.1.8); both private and public persons can administer the two kinds of justice indifferently.[34] Similarly, we find another quote from Michel of Ephesus in the chapter on punishments, in which Grotius asks whether punishment belongs to expletive or attributive justice. He writes that 'the true nature of attributive justice consists, neither in such an equality, nor in a procession from the whole to a part, properly speaking'; rather, it consists in 'considering an aptitude or merit, which doth not contain in it a right strictly so called, but gives occasion to it' (DJBP 2.20.2). On the other hand, expletive justice, being based on strict right, implies that 'he that commits a crime, seems voluntarily to submit himself to punishment ... [...] he who will directly commit it, is by consequence willing to incur the punishment', as a result of the nature of contracts (DJBP 2.20.2). In other words, the world of perfect rights seems to be governed by moral necessitation, once they have been violated. Instead, while implying that attributive justice provides the necessary normative framework for perfect rights to emerge, Grotius suggests that more options are available for individuals, peoples and sovereigns to determine what those rights are.

The dichotomy between perfect and imperfect rights, between expletive and attributive justice, with the first being overlapped by the second, has been misunderstood for a variety of reasons. First, from an historical point of view, one contributing factor might have been the further reception of Grotius' doctrine of rights. Later authors seem to attach a value judgment to the dichotomy between perfect and imperfect rights. For example, according to Emer de Vattel (1714–67) – who, in turn, relies on a reading of Gottfried Leibniz (1646–1716) and Christian Wolff's (1679–1754) natural law doctrines – imperfect rights need to be activated and turned into positive agreements to become perfect obligations, for which it is possible to demand respect.[35] There must be, in other words, a corrective to the constitutional 'deficiency' of imperfect rights. Instead, far from being a qualitative distinction of more or less 'deficient' rights, Grotius' notion of perfect rights does not disqualify imperfect ones; rather, respect just cannot be demanded from certain type of rights (mercy, *caritas*, kindness), but this does not make them less important. Moral evaluation of these rights guarantees a certain space of freedom for the community; conversely, any attempt at turning 'merits' and *aptitudo* into perfect obligations would be problematic. This aspect is crucial to later solidarist approaches towards international law, as witnessed by representatives of French solidarism such as Léon Duguit (1859–1928)[36] or, before them, by the nineteenth-century tradition of Catholic social thinkers. For example, the Italian Luigi Taparelli D'Azeglio (1793–1862) was very aware of this problem, which he perceived as the plague of Protestant natural law, and introduced a general duty of love into the international society.[37]

Second, from a more contemporary perspective, the misinterpretation of Grotius' theory of justice might also be a result of the kind of mentality introduced by neo-liberal approaches towards international law, which have fetishised 'enforceable contract' and 'individual will and consent', and prioritised 'private over public international law'.[38] Consequently, critical appraisals of Grotius and, more in general, of the international order have focused on deconstructing these, but without producing a constructive theory of universal justice, which is considered to be as problematic as the lack of it. According to Oliver O'Donovan, Grotius' elaboration of the concept of fitness:

> was to look in the opposite direction from later theorists, such as Locke and Pufendorf, who attempted to derive the whole nature of a society of rational beings from the original right of the individual, the *dominium sui*. It brought forward the notion of a non-entitling fitness, a correspondence of actor to social role, that must be prudently discerned in assigning benefits and burdens, and this belonged every bit as much to the justice required of law as proprietary right itself did. With assignative justice Grotius lifted the law of war out of the marketplace of private claims.[39]

In my view, O'Donovan's interpretation exaggerates the impact of Grotius' doctrine of attributive justice, just as the neo-liberals undermine it. Indeterminacy concerning the core of fundamental values tenets, while being considered better than providing a very clear definition of them, paradoxically leaves the international community with the cynicism and despair of those who do not believe in any value whatsoever.[40] However, based on and consistent with these assumptions, this does not mean that aptitude and attributive justice do not play a fundamental role in Grotius' enterprise: rather, there is a strong connection between fitness and Grotius' third definition of *jus*. Thus, 'natural right is the rule and dictate of right reason, shewing the moral deformity or moral necessity there is in any act, according to its suitableness or unsuitableness to a reasonable nature' (DJBP 1.1.10). Grotius insists on the normative value of natural law: 'right in this sense does not belong to the matter of justice alone (such as I have before explained it), but also to that of other virtues' (DJBP 1.1.9).

11.5 Conclusion

This short overview of the concept of aptitude shows that, according to Grotius, individual behaviour needs to be 'adapted' according to a natural criterion of fitness; but, the very fact that an adjustment is needed means that humans have freedom of choice and their lives are not entirely governed by God's predestination. Rather, they engage into a constant negotiation between individual behaviour and ideals of virtue. Aptitude is, thus, a matter of judgment and appreciation.[41] While unrestrained human freedom should still be considered the core of his theoretical endeavour, Grotius' focus on virtue should not be overlooked. As such, virtue has an incredibly useful heuristic value: it leads Grotius to the discovery of the definition of 'natural right as the rule and dictate of right reason', proof of which must also be provided according to criteria of fitness 'with a reasonable and sociable nature' (DJBP 1.1.12).

To conclude, two final considerations on the value of the Grotian tradition need to be evoked. First, it can be argued that natural law was, for Grotius, more of a progressive force than it is in our contemporary mentality: it often voices and organises changes in society into an understandable and desirable vocabulary of rights, rather than merely justifying conservative policies – as Grotius says in another one of his quotes of Michael of Ephesus (DJBP 2.5.13). There is, in other words, faith that virtue can be achieved in this world, and that the language of rights can help us do so. One could wonder whether the extension of the vocabulary of rights to non-human beings to respond to the challenges of climate change and environmental sustainability, as suggested by many contemporary scholars, seems justified by a similar faith in the 'virtuousness' of such language.

Second, this calls into question the role of freedom. Reflecting on the implications of free will on the patterns of domination it has helped to construct in the contemporary legal order (against the Weberian myth of the Protestant ethics of predestination) might help us disrupt narratives crafted to suggest the inevitability of such a process of construction.[42] Whether this suffices to bring justice in and out of war and the marketplace, however, remains a challenge more for us than it was for Grotius – whose individual anthropology[43] could only exist in the presence of an unshakeable faith for universal order.

Translation of Grotius' works used

The Rights of War and Peace, ed. R. Tuck (Indianapolis, 2005)

Further Reading

Blom, H., *Property, Piracy and Punishment: Hugo Grotius on War and Booty in* De jure praedae: *Concepts and Contexts* (Leiden and Boston, 2009).

Haggenmacher, P., *Grotius et la doctrine de la guerre juste* (Paris, 1983).

Nijman, J.E., 'Images of Grotius, or the international rule of Law beyond historiographical oscillation', *Journal of the History of International Law* 17 (2015) 83–137.

Straumann, B., *Roman Law in the State of Nature: The Classical Foundations of Hugo Grotius's Natural Law* (Cambridge, 2015).

Tierney, B., *The Idea of Natural Rights* (Michigan and Cambridge, 1997).

Tuck, R., *The Rights of War and Peace. Political Thought and International Order from Grotius to Kant* (Oxford, 1999).

Notes

1   John Yoo, 'The Soleimani strike: The president has the constitution and precedent on his side', *National Review*, 6 January 2020, retrieved from: www .nationalreview.com/2020/01/qasem-soleimani-strike-president-trump-has-constitution-precedent-on-his-side/ (page consulted on the 20 January 2020).

2   H. Lauterpacht, 'The Grotian tradition in international law', *British Yearbook of International Law* 23 (1946) 1–53; B. Kingsbury, 'A Grotian tradition of theory and practice?: Grotius, law and moral skepticism in the thought of Hedley Bull', *Quinnipac Law Review* 17 (1997) 3–33; E. Keene, 'The reception of Hugo Grotius in international relations theory', *Grotiana* N.S. 20 (1999) 135–58; R. Lesaffer, 'The Grotian tradition revisited: change and continuity in the history of international law', *British Yearbook of International Law* 73 (2003) 103–39; M. Koskenniemi, 'Imagining the rule of law: rereading the Grotian tradition', *European Journal of International Law* 30 (2019) 17–52. See replies to Koskenniemi's *Foreword* in the last issue of *European Journal of International Law*: J.E. Nijman, 'Grotius, rule of law and the human sense of justice: an afterword to Martti Koskenniemi's foreword', 30 (2019) 1105–14; F. Iurlaro, 'International legal histories as orders: an afterword to Martti Koskenniemi's foreword', 30 (2019) 1115–19; B. Straumann, 'The rule of law: sociology or normative theory? An afterword to Martti Koskenniemi's foreword', *European Journal of International Law* 30 (2019) 1121–7.

3   J.E. Nijman, 'Images of Grotius, or the international rule of law beyond historiographical oscillation', *Journal of the History of International Law* 17 (2015) 83–137; A. Del Vecchio, 'Tendenze e problemi delle ricerche contemporanee su Ugo Grozio', *Filosofia Politica* 3 (2019) 509–20.

4   J.St. Leger, *The etiamsi daremus of Hugo Grotius: a Study in the Origins of International Law* (Rome, 1962).

5 M. Villey, 'Les origines de la notion de droit subjectif', *Revue historique de droit français et étranger* (1946) 201-27; M. Villey, *La formation de la pensée juridique moderne* (Cours d'histoire de la philosophie du droit, 1961-6; Paris, 1975); R. Tuck, *Natural Rights Theories. Their Origin and Development* (Cambridge, 1979), 58-82; P. Haggenmacher, 'Droit subjectifs et système juridique chez Grotius', in L. Foisneau (ed.), *Politique, droit et théologie chez Bodin, Grotius, et Hobbes* (Paris, 1997), 73-130; A. Brett, 'Natural right and civil community: the civil philosophy of Hugo Grotius', *Historical Journal* 45 (2002) 31-51.

6 B. Tierney, *The Idea of Natural Rights* (Michigan and Cambridge, 1997), 342.

7 Benjamin Straumann has tackled this narrative, 'Is modern liberty ancient? Roman remedies and natural rights in Hugo Grotius' early works on natural law', *Law and History Review* 27 (2009) 55-85.

8 On this, see R. Tuck, 'Grotius, Carneades, and Hobbes', *Grotiana* N.S. 4 (1983), 43-62, at 44.

9 Tuck, 'Grotius, Carneades and Hobbes', 58. See also, from the same author, *The Rights of War and Peace: Political Thought and International Order from Grotius to Kant* (Oxford, 1999).

10 Nijman, 'Images of Grotius', 85.

11 P. Borschberg, 'Hugo Grotius, East India trade and the king of Johor', *Journal of Southeast Asian Studies* 30 (1999) 225-48; M. van Ittersum, *Profit and Principle: Hugo Grotius, Natural Rights Theories and the Rise of Dutch Power in the East Indies, 1595-1615* (Leiden and Boston, 2006); M. Koskenniemi, 'International law and the emergence of mercantile capitalism: Grotius to Smith', in P.M. Dupuy and V. Chetail (eds.), *The Roots of international law/ Les Fondements du Droit International: Liber Amicorum Peter Haggenmacher* (Leiden and Boston, 2013), 3-38; O. Hathaway and S. Shapiro, *The Internationalists: How a Radical Plan to Outlaw War Remade the World* (New York, 2017), 3-37.

12 Lauterpacht, 'The Grotian tradition', 1-53; C. van Vollenhoven, 'Grotius and Geneva (1925)', *Bibliotheca Visseriana* 6 (1926) 1-81.

13 Nijman, 'Images of Grotius', 86; A. Carty and J.E. Nijman, 'The moral responsibility of rulers: going back beyond the liberal rule of law for world order', in A. Carty and J.E. Nijman (eds.), *Morals and Responsibility of Rulers: European and Chinese Origins of a Rule of Law as Justice for World Order* (Oxford, 2018) 1-52; C. Stumpf, 'Hugo Grotius and the universal rule of law', in Ibid., 187-200.

14 Nijman, 'Images of Grotius', 96.

15 Carty and Nijman, 'The moral responsibility of rulers', 22.

16 H. Blom and L. Winkel, 'Grotius and the Stoa: Introduction', in H. Blom and L. Winkel (eds.), *Grotius at the Stoa* (Assen, 2004), 3-20, at 9.

17 On self-interest and *lex charitatis*, see R. Shaver, 'Grotius on scepticism and self-interest', *Archiv für Geschichte der Philosophie* 78 (1996), 27-47.

18 Nijman, 'Images of Grotius', at 109. See also B. Straumann, 'Ancient Caesarian lawyers in a state of nature: Roman tradition and natural rights in Hugo Grotius' De jure praedae', *Political Theory* 34 (2006) 328-50, at 344.

19 Tierney, *The Idea of Natural Rights*, 336.

20 Recent studies on Grotius' argumentative methods and rhetorical tradition also bear witness to this: the more universal a principle of natural law is, the more applicable (subjective and objective coincide); the less universal, the more controversial its identification is (because the correspondence between the subjective and the objective must be ascertained). See B. Straumann, *Roman Law in the State of Nature: The Classical Foundations of Hugo Grotius' Natural Law* (Cambridge, 2015), 51–82; F. Iurlaro, 'Grotius, Dio Chrysostom and the 'Invention' of Customary *Jus Gentium*', *Grotiana* N.S. 39 (2018) 15–44.

21 O. O' Donovan, 'The justice of assignment and subjective rights in Grotius', in O. O' Donovan and J. Lockwood O'Donovan (eds.), *Bonds of Imperfection. Christian Politics, Past and Present* (Cambridge, 2004), 167–203, at 168–9.

22 A.S. Brett, 'The subject of sovereignty: law, politics, and moral reasoning in Hugo Grotius', *Modern Intellectual History* (2019) 1–27.

23 See contributions from H. Blom, *Property, Piracy and Punishment: Hugo Grotius on War and Booty in De jure praedae: Concepts and Contexts* (Leiden and Boston, 2009); J.S. Geddert, 'Too subtle to satisfy many: was Grotius' teleology of punishment predestined to fail', *Grotiana* N.S. 38 (2017) 46–69; P. Kalmanovitz, 'Hugo Grotius on war, punishment and the different sovereignty makes', in M. Bergsmo and E.J. Buis (eds.), *Philosophical Foundations of International Criminal Law: Correlating Thinkers* (Brussels, 2018), 193–212.

24 Koskenniemi, 'Imagining the rule of law', 35; I addressed the relationship between predestination, fate and punishment in F. Iurlaro, 'Divine decrees and human choices: Grotius on the law of fate and punishment', *Grotiana* N.S. 40 (2019) 76–101. I refer to this contribution for further bibliographical references.

25 Brett, 'The subject of sovereignty', 6.

26 On this debate, see P. Haggenmacher, *Grotius et la doctrine de la guerre juste* (Paris, 1983); F. Todescan, '*Sequuntur dogmatica De jure praedae*: law and theology in Grotius' use of sources in the De jure praedae', in Blom, *Property, Piracy and Punishment,* 281–309; also see, for more references, W. Decock and C. Birr, *Recht und Moral in der Scholastik der Frühen Neuzeit 1500–1750* (Berlin, 2016), 77–81. For a recent comparison between Francisco Suárez' and Grotius' conception of imperfect rights, and their relationship with an Aristotelian notion of justice, see J. Olsthoorn, 'Francisco Suárez and Hugo Grotius on distributive justice and imperfect rights', *History of Political Thought* 41 (2020) 96–119.

27 On the variety of traditions of Aristotelianisms and the importance of later commentators of Aristotle, see R. Sorabji, *Aristotle Transformed: the Ancient Commentators and Their Influence* (London, 2019); idem, *Aristotle Reinterpreted: New Findings on Seven Hundred Years of the Ancient commentators* (London, 2016).

28 Iurlaro, 'Divine decrees and human choices', 79. See also C. Boisen's contribution to this volume.

29 D. Levitin, *Ancient Wisdom in the Age of New Science* (Cambridge, 2015) 52.
30 Iurlaro, 'Divine decrees and human choices', 97–8.
31 On Michael of Ephesus, see R. Sorabji, 'Michael of Ephesus on Books 5, 9 and 10', in Sorabji, *Aristotle Transformed*, 464–71. On other potential points of contact with Grotius, that should deserve further investigation, see J. García-Huidobro, 'Michael of Ephesus and the Byzantine reception of the Aristotelian doctrine of natural justice', *Archiv für Geschichte der Philosophie* 94 (2012) 274–95; also, on the epistemic status of moral science, see K. Ierodiakonou, 'Byzantine commentators on the epistemic status of ethics', *Bulletin of the Institute of Classical Studies* 83 (2004) 221–38.
32 *Aristotelis Stagiritae, summi philosophi ethicorum sive moralium nicomachorum libri decem, una cum Eustratii, Aspasii, Michaelis Ephesii, Nonnullorumque aliorum graecorum explanationibus nuper a ioanne bernardo Feliciano latinitate donati* (Basileae, 1542), 177; the passage in question is a comment to *Nichomachean Ethics* 5.3.7. The Greek edition Grotius might have referred to is *Eustratii et Aliorum Insignium Peripateticorum Commentaria in Libros Decem Aristotelis de Moribus ad Nicomachum* (Venetiae, 1536), 64. Here's the entire passage: 'λέγει γὰρ ἐν ταῖς Πολιτείαις καὶ τοιαύτην ἰσότητα, λέγει καὶ τὴν εἰρημένην· τὸ γὰρ κατ' ἀξίαν διδόμενόν τινι ἴσον ἐκείνῳ ἐστίν. ἐπεὶ γὰρ ἴσα ἐστὶ κατὰ τοὺς γεωμέτρας τὰ προσαρμόζοντα καὶ μήθ' ὑπερέχοντα μήτ' ἐλλείποντα, εἰ ἔστιν ὁ Ἀχιλλεὺς διπλασίων τοῦ Αἴαντος, δοθῇ δὲ τῷ μὲν Ἀχιλλεῖ νομίσματα η, τῷ δ' Αἴαντι δ, τὰ κατ' ἀξίαν λαβὼν ἕκαστος τὸ ἴσον ἑαυτῷ ἔλαβε· κείσθω γὰρ τὸν Ἀχιλλέα μήτε πλείω τῶν η μήτε ἐλάττω λαβεῖν ἄξιον εἶναι, ὁμοίως καὶ τὸν Αἴαντα', in *Michaelis Ephesii in librum 5 Ethicorum Nicomacheorum commentarium*, ed. M. Hayduck (Berlin, 1901), 20. See also 273–4: 'τὸ πρέπον καὶ ἁρμοζον', at 143 in the Aldine edition.
33 A point also made by Nijman, 'Images of Grotius', 116–17.
34 To elucidate this point, Grotius quotes an interesting *exemplum* from Xenophon's *Cyropaedia*, in which Cyrus talks about his legal education: 'the case was like this: a big boy with a little tunic, finding a little boy with a big tunic on, took it off him and put his own tunic on him, while he himself put on the other's. So, when I tried their case, I decided that it was better for them both that each should keep the tunic that fitted him. And thereupon the master flogged me, saying that when I was a judge of a good fit, I should do as I had done; but when it was my duty to decide whose tunic it was, I had this question, he said to consider – whose title was the rightful one; whether it was right that he who took it away by force should keep it, or that he who had had it made for himself or had bought it should own it', Xenophon, *Cyropaedia* 1.17, trans. Loeb Classical Edition, 41–3.
35 See S. Zurbuchen's reconstruction in 'Vattel's law of nations and the principle of non-intervention', *Grotiana* N.S. 31 (2010) 69–84.
36 See Léon Duguit's famous essay 'Objective law', *Columbia Law Review* 20 (1920) 817–31.

37 On Luigi Taparelli's solidarism, as developed in his influential *Saggio teoretico di diritto naturale appoggiato sul fatto* (Palermo, 1840-3), see the recent T. Behr, *Social Justice and Subsidiarity: Luigi Taparelli and the Origins of Modern Catholic Social Thought* (Washington DC, 2019); also, F. Iurlaro, 'The law of international love: Luigi Taparelli D'Azeglio on Catholic natural law and the law of nations', in E. Fiocchi Malaspina and G. Silvestrini (eds.), *Natural Law and the Law of Nations in the 18th century Italian Peninsula: Teaching and Circulations of Ideas* (Leiden and Boston, *forthcoming*).

38 U. Özsu, 'Neoliberalism and the New International Economic Order: a history of contemporary legal thought', in J. Desaustels-Stein and C. Tomlins (eds.), *Searching for Contemporary Legal Thought* (Cambridge, 2017), 330-47, at 330.

39 O'Donovan, 'The justice of assignment', 202-3.

40 See M. Koskenniemi, 'International law and the far right: reflections on law and cynicism' (The Annual T.M.C. Asser Lecture; The Hague, 2019), 1-53.

41 A point also made by Nijman, 'Images of Grotius', 116-7.

42 A similar argument is made in W. Decock, *Le marché du mérite: penser le droit et l'économie avec Léonard Lessius* (Paris, 2019).

43 See J.E. Nijman, 'Grotius' *Imago* Dei anthropology: *grounding jus naturae et gentium*', in M. Koskenniemi, M. García-Salmones Rovira and P. Amorosa (eds.), *International Law and Religion: Historical and Contemporary Perspectives* (Oxford, 2017), 87-110.

Laurens Winkel

12.1 Introduction

This chapter concentrates on Grotius' views on rights in a large sense, but with a special emphasis on his doctrine of subjective rights. In doing so, it is necessary to pay attention to systematisation in law in the sixteenth and seventeenth centuries as well. This chapter is divided as follows. After some general remarks on the rise of the concept of subjective rights in the history of legal ideas, we will examine their elaboration by Grotius, especially in his most extensive legal treatise, *De jure belli ac pacis*. Then we will turn to the oldest legal treatise of Grotius, *De jure praedae commentarius*, of which for a long time only one chapter (XII) was available, better known as the treatise *Mare liberum*.[1] In this work, the idea of a subjective right is not yet fully developed. Then we will deal with *De jure belli ac pacis* and briefly with the *Inleidinge tot de Hollandsche Rechtsgeleerdheid*. We will conclude with some equally brief remarks on the *Florum sparsio ad jus Justinianeum*.

12.2 General Part: *Jus* as a Polyvalent Notion

There is an influential opinion on the rise of the notion of subjective rights in the middle ages. It is based on research done by the French legal philosopher and legal historian, Michel Villey,[2] and the British scholar on the history of ideas, Richard Tuck,[3] who – as a specialist in intellectual history – is an enthusiastic follower of Villey. In their view, the notion of subjective rights is originated in the medieval theology of the Franciscan order. The legal elaboration of this notion is supposed to have taken place in Spanish neo-scholastic literature in the fifteenth and sixteenth centuries, which in its turn was of great importance to Grotius. Of course, the fact that Grotius is under the spell of the Spanish neo-scholastic school is undeniable, but the history of (legal) ideas is much too complicated to be summarised in such a simple way. In this chapter, we will follow a slightly different approach, which is more compatible with the inner legal structure of Roman law in the different phases of its development in Antiquity and during the long-term process of the so-called reception of Roman law in medieval theology and jurisprudence until the sixteenth century. This so-called reception started with the first teaching of Roman law at the University of Bologna (founded 1088) and spread over Europe with the creation of other universities.

This chapter argues, moreover, for taking into account that the real basis of our understanding of Roman law lies in the evolution of procedural law. All too often we tend to forget that, originally, Roman law is embodied in legal procedures and, to a very small part only, as it is today, in substantial legal norms. This chapter follows the views of Giovanni Pugliese[4] for Antiquity and those of K.W. Nörr[5] and some others on medieval legal doctrine in an attempt to avoid a further series of misunderstandings on this topic caused by the all too enthusiastic use of modern concepts in legal history. An important legal historian and Romanist, H.R. Hoetink, has rightly warned against this phenomenon.[6] Most modern legal scholars are, indeed, not aware of the fact that subjective rights as we know them in modern law could not exist in pre-classical and classical Roman law for rather simple reasons following from the essence of Roman procedural law,[7] where originally fixed structures were present. In the earliest stages, we find them in the very formal *legis actiones*. From the second century BCE onwards, we find them in the form of *formulae*, in the annual edict of the praetor, which stand at the basis of the more advanced procedure *per formulas*. When legal protection is promised in the edict to a claimant, there is no more than a promise, a pre-figuration of a subjective right, that is confined to the rather strict framework of a concrete procedure, whether *per legum actiones* or *per formulas*.

In the past, even in Grotius' time, such misunderstandings could be explained and excused, because a full survey of the historical development of Roman procedural law was not yet available. The discovery of the more or less full text of the *Institutes* of Gaius, which served as a model for the *Institutes* of Justinian, was decisive here. However, the manuscript with this text was not yet available in the seventeenth century; it was published only in 1816 by a pupil of Friedrich Carl von Savigny (1779–1861), Barthold Georg Niebuhr (1776–1831).[8] Before that year, the whole work of Gaius was not known, except for a few fragments.[9] It is only through

Gaius that we have a clear outline of the historical development of Roman procedural law. In the middle ages, the legislation of Justinian was available and, in this respect, the *Institutes* of Justinian (*c.* 530 CE) are relevant. They are a kind of half-hearted update of Gaius' *Institutes* fitted to the structure of Roman law and procedures in the sixth century, but are stripped of the historical information from Gaius' work.[10] Justinian's *Institutes* remained known before the revival of Roman law scholarship in Bologna near the end of the twelfth century.

The Roman procedure, the so-called *cognitio extraordinaria*, which originated from the first century CE under the early empire, gradually became the normal form of legal procedure in late Antiquity. It was the only surviving form of procedure during the Dominate (end of the third century CE) and the epoch of Justinian (sixth century). The judge, who can be equated with the imperial administration, was only loosely bound by the form of the claim of the plaintiff and the appreciation of the case was very much within the discretion of the judge, that is the imperial chancery. There was no such thing as a list of guaranteed legal remedies as formerly laid down in the *Edictum Perpetuum* (138 CE) for the procedure *per formulas*. The shorthand for the older legal procedures was in Latin *ubi remedium ibi ius* (if there is a legal remedy then there is a substantial right). In the *cognitio extraordinaria*, one sees a transition towards the inverse proverb *ubi ius ibi remedium* (if there is a substantial right, then there is a legal remedy).

Only then and there, in this *cognitio*, does something emerge that can be compared with subjective rights in post-classical Roman law. However, during Antiquity, this notion was never elaborated clearly by Roman jurists. There was only one word, *jus*, with a wide variety of meanings and there was simply no need for a precise concept of subjective rights. Moreover, Justinian wanted to restore classical Roman law as much as possible, hence the rather ambivalent structure of procedural law in his *Corpus Juris Civilis*. For these reasons, the notion of subjective rights can only be traced back vaguely to later Antiquity[11] and certainly not to the period of classical Roman law (first century BCE until 250 CE).

Grotius was not so much innovative in comparison to the medieval legal scholars with whom the notion of subjective rights took shape. In medieval and early-modern jurisprudence, there was no longer a need for a procedural approach of legal norms as embodied in the *Corpus Juris Civilis*. The Spanish neo-scholastic school transmitted the notions of late-medieval legal science to Grotius, but – of course – the *Glossa Ordinaria* by Accursius (first half of the thirteenth century) on the legislation of Justinian, the *Corpus Juris Civilis* and the so-called post-glossators, such as Bartolus de Saxoferrato (1313–57) and Baldus de Ubaldis (1327–1400), and several scholars of canon law were equally important for him.[12]

However, Grotius' special importance lays in the transfer of the system and the notions of private law of his time to a construction of international law. For that purpose, he used the system from the *Institutes* of Justinian and the rules of Roman law as conceived by medieval and neo-scholastic jurisprudence. This can be demonstrated in many quotations of *De jure belli ac pacis*. Not only does he use the system of the *Institutes*, but also several of its other key concepts. In the earlier work, *De jure praedae*, this is not yet the case. The form of argumentation after chapter 2 is around the rather traditional question whether a war and warlike acts can be just (*justum bellum*) and the prize of the vessel *Santa Catarina* in 1603 was argued to constitute a just prize.[13] The only modern and innovative element comes from chapter 2, in which a series of abstract rules are developed.

In *De jure belli ac pacis,* the legal system is much more elaborated. It is systematically visible in the division of the work, which is dependent on the main divisions of Justinian's *Institutes, personae – res – actiones*. It also appears in the divisions of this work in chapters and paragraphs. In the first book of the treatise, basic definitions of war and law (*jus*) are given and important distinctions are made, e.g. between private and public war. In the last part of Book 1, a kind of 'law of persons' can be found, where the question is dealt with who can lawfully wage a war (*Qui bellum licite gerant*). In the second Book, we find a further expatiation on the 'law of persons', followed by the ways of acquiring ownership and the role of promises, contracts and treaties. In the third Book, rules are given for warfare and the role of *fides* is fully explained.[14]

This is not the only link between private law and international law. Many notions of private law were elaborated by Grotius to fit in a parallel structure for public international law. One of the most familiar examples is 'contract' in private law and 'treaty' in international law. A further striking example is 'ownership' in private law and 'sovereignty' in international law, tort in private law and international law. The question must be answered what kind of reasoning Grotius used to establish this link. For him, re-definitions are necessary of the three traditional notions *jus naturale* (natural law), *jus gentium* (law between nations) and *jus civile* (internal law), in order to build a conceptual framework for international law in analogy with the conceptual framework of private law.

12.3 Playing Around with the Broad Meaning of Jus Gentium

The connecting link between private law and international law in Latin terminology lays in Grotius' works on the notion of *jus gentium* in classical Roman law, in Roman legal terminology an ambivalent term with purely private law connotations at one hand – i.e. in opposition to the notion *jus civile* – and philosophical connotations in the relation between Roman citizens and privileged foreigners.[15] However, first we need to consider the not necessarily religious aspects of *jus gentium*. We find in *De jure belli ac pacis* the following famous statement:

Et haec quidem quae iam diximus, locum aliquem haberent, *etiamsi daremus*, quod sine summo scelere dari nequit, *non esse Deum*, aut non curari ab eo negotia humana : cuius comtrarium cum nobis *partim ratio, partim traditio perpetua*, inseverint confiment vero et argumenta multa et miracula ab omnibus saeculis testata, sequitur iam ipsi Deo, ut opifici et cui nos nostraque omnia debeamus, sine exceptione parendum nobis esse, praecipue cum is se multis modis et optimum et potestissimum ostenderit, ita ut sibi obedientibus praemia reddere maxima, etiam aeterna quippe aeternus ipse possit, et voluisse credi debeat multoque magis si id desertis verbis promiserit : quod Christiani indubitata testimoniorum fide convicti credimus.

What we have been saying would have a degree of validity *even if we should concede* that which cannot be conceded without the utmost wickedness, *that there is no God*, or that the affairs of men are of no concern to Him. The very opposite of this view has been implanted in us *partly by reason, partly by unbroken tradition*, and confirmed by many proofs as well as by miracles attested by all ages. Hence it follows that we must without exception render obedience to God as our Creator, to Whom we owe all that we are and have; especially since, in manifold ways, He has shown Himself supremely good and supremely powerful, so that to those who obey Him He is able to give supremely great rewards, even awards that are eternal, since He Himself is eternal. We ought, moreover, to believe that He has willed to give rewards, and all the more should we cherish such a belief if He has so promised in plain words; that He has done this, we Christians believe, convinced by the indubitable assurance of testimonies. (DJBP Prol. 11, my emphasis)

This text must be read in relation to the theological and philosophical opinions of Grotius.[16] It is a very first step of secularisation and rationalisation of international law. Grotius was a follower of the theology of Jacobus Arminius (1560–1609) and, therefore, he rejected the Calvinistic doctrine of predestination that could have influenced his theory of legal imputation.[17] At the same time, Grotius was adhering to neo-Stoic philosophy in other domains. Stoic philosophy was put forward by the works of Justus Lipsius (1547–1606), professor in Leuven. Stoicism was of growing importance for Grotius,[18] as his doctrine of *appetitus societatis* would testify.[19] This held implications, not only for the construction of 'civil society', but also for a legal framework of international law and international relations. Stoic philosophy is, in essence, cosmo-political and therefore a cornerstone for building an international legal order. A central notion of Stoic philosophy is *ratio*, which is accessible for all human beings. In other words: with rational capacities, it is possible to have immediate knowledge of fundamental legal principles valid for all human beings.

12.4 Grotius Starts a New Systematisation of Natural Law

The starting points for Grotius are new definitions of *jus naturale* and *jus gentium*, terms that were used in traditional Roman legal sources, albeit in a confusing way because of the different philosophical backgrounds of the Roman jurists.[20] The traditional trichotomy *jus naturale/jus gentium/jus civile* is redefined in the following text:

Et eatenus sententiam sequimur Innocentii, et aliorum qui bello aiunt peti posse eos qui in naturam delinquunt: contra quam sentiunt Victoria, Vasquius, Azolius, Molina, alii, qui ad justitiam belli requirere videntur, ut qui suscipit aut laesus sit in se aut republica sua, aut ut in eum qui bello impetitur jurisdictionem habeat. Ponunt enim illi puniendi potestatem esse effectum proprium jurisdictionis civilis, cum nos eam sentiamus venire etiam ex jure naturali (. . .)

Thus far we follow the opinion of Innocent, and others who say that a war may be waged upon those who sin against nature. The contrary view is held by Victoria, Vásquez, Azor, Molina and others, who in justification of war seem to demand that who undertakes it should have suffered injury either in his person or his state, or that he should have jurisdiction over him who is attacked. For they claim that the power of punishing is the proper effect of civil jurisdiction, while we hold that it is derived from the law of nature (. . .) (DJBP 2.20.40.4)

Grotius is creating a body of universally binding legal norms of a higher order, *jus naturale*, based in human nature, that can be applied in the relations between nations: in other words, international law. This also follows from the following, key text:

Grotius, *De iure belli ac pacis* I, 2,4,1–2:De iure naturali ergo, quod et gentium dici potest, satis constat eo bella non omnia improbari. Iure autem Gentium voluntario itidem non damnari bella satis nos docent historiae, et omnium populorum leges ac mores. Imo iure gentium introducta esse bella dixit Hermogenianus: quod paulo aliter quam vulgo accipi solet interpretandum censeo: nempe ut certa bellorum forma a iure gentium sit introducta, quam formam quae habeant bella ea peculiares ex iure gentium effectus consequantur (. . .)

It is sufficiently well established, therefore, that not all wars are at variance with the law of nature; and this may also be said to be true of the law of nations. That wars, moreover, are not condemned by the volitional law of nations, histories, and the laws and customs of all peoples fully teach us. Rather, Hermogenianus said that wars were introduced by the law of nations; but I think that this statement ought to be understood as having a meaning slightly different from that ordinarily given to it, namely, that a definite formality in the conduct of war was introduced by the law of nations, and that particular effects follow wars waged in accordance with such formality under the law of nations (. . .) (DJBP 1.2.4.1–2)

This quotation proves the new place for *jus gentium*: *jus gentium* is a body of norms that must be volitional, i.e. it can be created by sovereign nations in treaties. The last part of this text is a clear hint to the formalities of declarations of war.[21] Grotius quotes here a text from *Digest* 1.1.5.1:

Hermogenianus, libro primo iuris epitomarum. Ex hoc iure gentium introducta bella, discretae gentes, regna condita, dominia distincta, agris termini positi, aedificia collocata, commercium, emptiones venditiones, locationes conductiones, obligationes institutae; exceptis quibusdam quae iure civili introductae sunt.

Hermogenian, Survey of law, Book I. As a consequence of this *ius gentium*, wars were introduced, nations differentiated, kingdoms founded, properties individuated, estate boundaries settled, buildings put up, and commerce established, including contracts of buying and selling and letting and hiring, except for certain contractual elements established through *jus civile*.[22]

In this text, the ambivalent nature of the notion of *jus gentium*, already in post-classical Roman law, becomes clearly visible. *Jus gentium* is, for Hermogenian,[23] a kind of rainbow-notion encompassing phenomena of public and private law alike. For Grotius, this broadly defined *jus gentium* is a vehicle to define international law in analogy with private law notions.

This transfer is extensively dealt with by Hersch Lauterpacht (1897–1960) in his very interesting dissertation of 1927.[24] His main purpose was to widen the number of sources of international law and to combat the narrow positivistic approach to international law in which only treaty and custom were recognised as a source of law. According to Lauterpacht, there are far more sources of international law. He tried to re-establish the link with the natural law school and with a much greater diversity of sources of international law, as well as with legal doctrine as a source of international law. He rightly stressed the analogies between international law and private law, but he did not try to explain the reason for this analogy, which was to be found in some ambivalent texts in the Roman legal tradition.

As far as we can see, the following text was meant by Grotius to indicate a parallel between judicial settlements and disputes in the international sphere that are settled by waging a war:

Ac plane quot actionum forensium sunt fontes, totidem sunt belli: *nam ubi iudicia deficiunt incipit bellum.* Dantur autem actiones aut ob iniuriam non factam aut ob factam. Ob non factam , ut qua petitur cautio de non offendendo, item damni infecti, et interdicta alia ne vis fiat. Factam, aut ut reparetur, aut ut puniatur. <quos duos obligationum fontes recte distinguit Plato nono de legibus>. It is evident that the sources from which wars arise are as numerous as those from which lawsuits spring; *for where judicial settlement fails, war begins.* Actions, further-more, lie either for wrongs not yet committed, or for wrongs already done. An action lies for a wrong not yet committed in case where a guarantee is sought against a threatened wrong, or security against an anticipated injury, or an interdict of different sort against the use of violence [cfr. *interdictum unde vi* lw]. An action for a wrong committed lies where a reparation for injury, or the punishment of the wrong-doer, is sought. <These two sources of legal obligations were rightly distinguished by Plato in the Ninth book of the Laws> (<> *added in the 1631 and later editions*) (DJBP 2.1.2.1, my emphasis)

Apart from the proverbial status of *ubi iudicia deficiunt incipit bellum*,[25] this text is, in the first place, referring to legal systematisation. In inter-national relations, there is in last instance no judicial remedy, as there is in private law, but the remedy is war. At the end of the text, we can also see a very significant addition showing Grotius' gradual wider knowledge of the philosophical literature of Antiquity. Indeed, Aristotle had been far better known since the twelfth century than Plato, who regained importance in the Renaissance.

Further Grotian systematisation in analogy with private law can be found in a text from the *Prolegomena* of *De jure belli ac pacis*:

Ego cum ob eas quas iam dixi rationes compertissimum haberem, esse aliquod inter populos ius commune *quod et ad bella et in bellis valeret*, cur de eo instituerem scriptionem causas habui multas ac graves. Videbam per Christianum orbem vel barbaris gentibus pudendam bellandi licentiam: levibus aut nullis de causis ad arma procurri, quibus semel sumtis nullam iam divini, nullam humani iuris reverentiam, plane quasi uno edicto ad omnia scelera emisso furore.

Fully convinced, by the considerations which I have advanced, that there is a common law among all nations, *which is valid alike for war and in war*, I have had many and weighty reasons for undertaking to write upon this subject. Throughout the Christian world I observed a lack of restraint in relation to war, such as even barbarous races should be ashamed of; I observed that men rush to arms for slight causes, or no cause at all, and that when arms have once been taken up there is no longer any respect for law, divine or human; it is as if, in accordance with a general decree, frenzy had openly been let loose for committing of all crimes. (DJBP Prol. 28, my emphasis)

This is a key text for a very important development in international law and also for a striking parallel between private law and international law. At the same time, it illustrates the ongoing conceptualisation of international law by Grotius as once described by Hersch Lauterpacht in his 1927 dissertation. Grotius' text above is very significant for a fundamental change in the terminology of international law. Until *De jure bell ac pacis,* the discussion in the literature on international law focused on the question whether a war was just (*bellum justum*). Following Grotius' treatise, the approach becomes different: a clear distinction is made between the (subjective) right to wage a war and the legal rules that apply in wartime between belligerent nations. The first is in shorthand *jus ad bellum*, the second *jus in bello*. We would advocate the view that the Latin terminology *jus ad rem* is rephrased by Grotius in *jus ad bellum* and *jus in re* is rephrased in *jus in bello*. Apart from the grammatical structure of it, this also hints on a substantial parallel. This is a very interesting question, which touches upon the essence of the two branches of law: private law and international law. Lauterpacht paid attention to these phenomena.

Whereas he sketched the parallel between private law and international law, he did not deal with the intrinsic and historical reason why there were so many striking parallels between the two. Lauterpacht did not write as a legal historian. He did not go into the historical development of international law, which was modelled by Grotius on the basis of private law. The main problem here is the ambiguous notion of *jus gentium*, on the one hand private law between Roman citizens and foreigners, on the other hand law that, through the Stoic notion of reason, was alike for every people gifted with rational capacities.

Grotius attempts in his *De jure belli ac pacis*, and also in the *Inleidinge tot de Hollandsche Rechts-geleerdheid* (1619/1631), a systematisation of law; in *De jure belli ac pacis*, of international law, in the *Inleidinge* of the law of the province of Holland. In both cases, he did so with the help of the institutional system, which was developed in medieval legal science on the basis of Justinian's *Institutes*.[26] The model of the *Institutes* regained importance through the work of legal humanists, where a systematic approach of the Roman legal sources is joined to the historical approach. This implies that the *ordo legum* in which the Roman legal sources were studied in medieval legal scholarship is abandoned by leading legal scholars of the Renaissance. This starts with Hugues Doneau (1527–91), who was the teacher of the teacher – Gerard Tuning – of Grotius at Leiden University.[27]

In the *Prolegomena* of *De jure belli ac pacis*, we find at the beginning general principles, followed by Book 1, which discusses the actors in (international) law. This is comparable with the Law of Persons in the *Institutes*. Book 2 covers the *jus ad bellum* and Book 3 the *jus in bello* (DJBP Prol. 28). These general titles are, therefore, by no means original, there is most probably an analogy between, at one hand, private law and, at the other, international law, so that *jus in re* equates *jus in bello*, and *jus ad bellum* equates *jus ad rem*. In the language of sixteenth-century private law, *jus in re* is shorthand for real rights, *jus ad rem* for personal rights. The first category, *jus in bello*, encompasses the legal rules applicable in wartime between belligerent nations; under the second heading, *jus ad bellum*, we find a restatement of the question of just war, but now in the form of a 'subjective right' of a sovereign to wage a war.

How can we explain this new terminology? As far as we can see, it flows from the use of a new vocabulary in the study of Roman private law by legal humanists. A dogmatic distinction is made there between *jus ad rem*, implying a subjective right, and *jus in re*, an absolute right of ownership.

Here we rely on an important publication of the late Robert Feenstra, at first published only in Dutch, but later also in English.[28] According to him, the distinction between *jus in re* and *jus ad rem* was coined, not by Grotius, but a century before by Johannes Apel (1485–1536).[29] Grotius uses this distinction in several instances. Hence, the transition construed by him to a well-developed system of international law based on the system of private law. In this respect, the dissertation by Lauterpacht remains very important, where he describes the sources of international law.[30]

Grotius' *De jure belli ac pacis* must be read with two layers of interpretation – and here we follow a train of thought developed by Feenstra in his inaugural lecture at Leiden.[31] Feenstra drew attention to the fact that historical texts in different stages are interpreted in different ways. Therefore, we can read *De jure belli ac pacis* either from the perspective of private law or from that of international law. In this way, we are able to see how Grotius has worked. He starts from concepts of Roman, i.e. mainly private, Law, and he constructs a dogmatic framework of international law as a kind of mirror to private law.

In Grotius' legal works, we can find the main characteristics of legal humanism as stated in standard works on the subject cited in *De jure belli ac pacis*: the return *ad fontes*, back to the classical sources in Antiquity, and *Graeca leguntur*, Greek sources are mentioned. Next to Aristotle, Plato is quoted. Further we find a critical approach of the sources, and a reconstruction of legal science, through the redefinition of the notion of *jus gentium*. Grotius' works stand at the very core of the Dutch form of legal humanism. The 1625 treatise, in particular, contains lots of references to legal and non-legal sources of Antiquity, but is at the same time very innovative in its systematisation.

12.5 De Jure Praedae Commentarius

Grotius' earlier legal treatise, *De jure praedae* (1604–6), was written at the behest of the East India Company (VOC) after the capture of a Portuguese vessel in the Strait of Singapore in 1603.[32] Only one chapter, chapter 12, named *Mare liberum*, from this work was printed and published in the seventeenth century, in 1609.[33] Nellen has argued that this chapter was published for political reasons.[34] A complete, albeit not too reliable, version of *De jure praedae* was published by H.G. Hamaker in 1868. In an earlier article, we concluded that the treatise is still quite dependent on the old medieval topics. The main question is a traditional one: whether the war of independence against Spain was a just war and the seizing of the *Santa Catarina* therefore a just prize. Nevertheless, it starts at the beginning as the outline in some respects of a general treatise on international law, though this train of thought is not further developed.

12.6 Inleidinge tot de Hollandsche Rechtsgeleerd-heid

First printed in 1631, this book is an introduction to Dutch jurisprudence and was written between 1619 and 1621, when Grotius was imprisoned in Loevestein. It was conceived for his sons as a guide for their legal study at Leiden University. The textual transmission of this work is somewhat problematic, because the normal protection of the author (privilege of the author) was absent as a consequence of Grotius' imprisonment after 1619 and his subsequent escape to France. Therefore, the modern edition of 1952 is more reliable than the older ones of the seventeenth and eighteenth centuries. Also, in this work we find a delicate balance between 'system' and 'history'. In fact, it is a systematic survey of private law in the province of Holland after the reception of Roman law. As such, it was a precious instrument for much later codification of private law in the Netherlands (1838). The very important division between absolute rights, *beheeringe* (Book 2), and personal rights, *inschuld* (Book 3), is the root of its systematisation. The *Inleidinge* is a prefiguration of the divisions in modern civil codes and, at the same time, an echo of the system of the *Institutes* of Justinian, just as we have seen for *De jure belli ac pacis*. Written in Dutch, it was much less influential than the 1625 treatise. Nevertheless, it was of fundamental importance for the School of Roman-Dutch Law that was leading in the later seventeenth and eighteenth centuries in Europe.[35] Arnold Vinnius (1588–1657) made use of it in his works written in Latin and so some of the content of the *Inleidinge* became known to non-Dutch speaking jurists.[36] A Latin translation was made by Johannes van der Linden (c. 1805), which was only published in 1962. There is an English translation by R.W. Lee, *The Jurisprudence of Holland*, from Oxford, 1926, which is still important for countries and legal orders where Roman Dutch Law is relevant, such as South Africa.[37]

12.7 A Note on *Florum Sparsio ad Jus Justinianeum* (1642)

This work lacks an independent systematisation and can be considered as a series of notes on passages of the *Corpus Juris Civilis*. In this way, it can be compared with the *Paratitla* of the French humanist, Jacques Cujas (1520–90) and it certainly is influenced by Denis Godefroy (1549–1622), one generation before Grotius. The work has been largely neglected in modern scholarship. *Florum sparsio* has not yet been edited according to modern standards. As far as we can see, Grotius did not pay special attention to systematisation, not even when texts of the systematic *Institutes* of Justinian are being commented upon. This conclusion sounds negative, but this valuable work with interesting references is an example of humanistic scholarship and still waits to be analysed in a more detailed manner.

12.8 Conclusion

In *De jure belli ac pacis*, Grotius redefines the relations between natural law (*jus naturale*), law between nations (*jus gentium*) and internal law (*jus civile*) in order to put an end to ambivalences around these concepts in the Roman legal tradition. These ambivalences stem from the complicated way in which Justinian and his compilators in the sixth century tried to give an overview in the *Corpus Juris Civilis* of previous Roman legal literature and legislation. Grotius uses an analogy between two newly invented expressions in private law: *jus ad rem* – personal right – and *jus in re* – absolute right – and transplants these conveniently to describe international law, a field that until then focused on the question whether a war was just or not. In this way, Grotius provided international law with a firm dogmatic framework distinguishing between *jus ad bellum*, the sovereign right to wage a war, and *jus in bello*, the law applicable between belligerent nations in wartime. From there onwards, there developed in legal scholarship an articulated debate on questions of war and peace and on the behaviour of belligerent nations in wartime. For this, Grotius may be considered as the father of modern international law.

Editions of Grotius' Works Used

Mare liberum, eds. R. Feenstra and J. Vervliet (Leiden, 2009)

Further Reading

Blom, H.W. and L. Winkel, 'Grotius and the Stoa: Introduction', *Grotiana* N.S. 22–3 (2001–2), 3–19.

Donahue, C. , 'Ius in the subjective sense in Roman law, reflections on Villey and Tierney', in A Ennio Cortese (ed.), *Scritti promossi da Domenico Maffei* (Rome, 2001), vol. 1, 506–35.

Haggenmacher, P., *Grotius et la doctrine de la guerre juste* (Paris, 1983).

Lauterpacht, H., *Private Law Sources and Analogies in International Law* (London, 1927).

Lee, R.W., *The Jurisprudence of Holland by Hugo Grotius*, vol. 1: Text (Oxford, 1926); vol. 2: Commentary (Oxford, 1936).

Nörr, K.W., 'Zur Frage des subjektiven Rechts in der mittelalterlichen Rechtwissenschaft', in *Festschrift für Hermann Lange* (Stuttgart etc., 1992), 193–204.

Olivecrona, K., 'The concept of a right according to Grotius and Pufendorf', in *Festschrift A. Germann* (Bern, 1969), 175–97.

Schrage, E.J.H., *Actio en subjectief recht – over Romeinse en middeleeuwse wortels van een modern begrip* ([Amsterdam], 1977).

Ter Meulen, J. and Diermanse, P.J.J., *Bibliographie des écrits imprimés de Hugo Grotius* (The Hague, 1950).

Vermeulen, B.P. and G.A. van der Wal, 'Grotius, Aquinas and Hobbes, Grotian natural law between *lex aeterna* and natural rights', *Grotiana* N.S. 16–17 (1995–6), 55–84.

Wubbe F.B.J., '*Ius in re*', *Paulys Realencyclpopädie der classischen ALtrtumswissenschaften*, ed. G. Wissowa, Suppl. 10 (Stuttgart, 1965), 333–43, reprinted in F.B.J. Wubbe, *Ius vigilantibus scriptum est – Ausgewählte Schriften/Oeuvres choisies*, ed. P. Pichonnaz (Fribourg, 2003), 65–77.

Notes

1 Henk Nellen, *Hugo Grotius. A Lifelong Struggle for Peace in Church and State 1583–1645* (Leiden and Boston, 2015), 92 ff.

2 M. Villey, 'L'idée du droit subjectif et les systèmes juridiques romains', *Revue historique du droit français et étranger*, IV 24–5 (1946–7) 201–27; Villey, 'Le sens de l'expression jus in re en droit romain classique', *Revue international des droits de l'antiquité* 3 (1949) 417–36.

3 R. Tuck, *Natural Rights Theories. Their Origin and Development* (Cambridge, 1979); idem, *The Rights of War and Peace. Political thought and the international order from Grotius to Kant* (Oxford, 1999), esp. 78–108.

4 G. Pugliese, *Actio e diritto subjettivo*, eds. L. Vacca and M. Brutti (Milan, 1939; repr. Naples, 2006); Pugliese, '*Res corporales, res incorporales* e il problema del

diritto soggettivo', in *Studi in onore di Vincenzo Arangio-Ruiz* (Naples, 1953), vol. 3, 223–60.

5 E.J.H. Schrage, *Actio en subjectief recht – over Romeinse en middeleeuwse wortels van een modern begrip* (Amsterdam, 1977).

6 H.R. Hoetink, 'Les notions anachroniques dans l'historiographie du droit', *Legal History Review* 23 (1955) 1–20 = *Opera selecta* (Zutphen, 1986), 216–37.

7 M. Kaser and K. Hackl, *Das römische Zivilprozessrecht* (2nd edn., Munich, 1996) for *legis actio* see 25 ff; for the procedure *per formulas* see 151 ff; for *cognitio* see 435 ff.

8 W. Kunkel, *Römische Rechtsgeschichte* (5th edn., Köln and Graz, 1967), 116 ff.

9 Except for a few fragments, see W. Kunkel and Th. Mayer-Maly, *Römisches Recht* (Berlin, 1987), 34.

10 Gaius' historical interest follows e.g. from his commentaries on the Law of the Twelve Tables (510 BCE), in his days no more of practical importance.

11 M. Kaser, 'Zum "ius" Begriff der Römer', in *Essays in honour of B. Beinart* (Cape Town and Johannesburg, 1979), vol. 2, 3–81. See again the serious warnings by Hoetink, 'Notions anachroniques'.

12 P. Haggenmacher, *Grotius et la doctrine de la guerre juste* (Paris, 1983), 462 ff.

13 L. Winkel, 'Problems of legal systematisation from *De iure praedae* to *De iure belli ac pacis*: *De iure praedae* chapter II and the *Prolegomena of De iure belli ac pacis* compared', *Grotiana* N.S. 26–8 (2005–7) 61–78.

14 See on *fides* or Trust, chapter by P. Schröder in this volume.

15 For a recent survey see M. Kaser, *Ius gentium* (Köln, Weimar and Wien, 1993).

16 L. Besselink, 'The impious hypothesis revisited', *Grotiana* N.S. 9 (1988) 3–63.

17 See also the chapter by C. Boisen in this volume.

18 See A. Eyffinger, '*Amoena gravitate morum spectabilis*, Justus Lipsius and Hugo Grotius', in M. Laureys *et alii* (eds.), *The world of Justus Lipsius: A contribution towards his intellectual biography* (Brussels and Rome, 1998), 297–327, at 300 ff.

19 L. Winkel, 'Les origines antiques de l'*appetitus societatis* de Grotius', *Legal History Review* 68 (2000) 393–403.

20 See my articles 'Einige Bemerkungen über *ius naturale* und *ius gentium*', in '*Ius est ars boni et aequi*', *Festschrift für Wolfgang Waldstein* (Stuttgart, 1993), 443–9 and 'Le droit romain et la philosophie grecque, quelques problèmes de méthode', *Legal History Review* 65 (1997) 373–84.

21 See on the declaration of war P. Haggenmacher, *Grotius et la doctrine de la guerre juste*, Paris 1983, 226 ff. (DJPC), Haggenmacher, 575 ff (DJBP).

22 Translation A. Watson, *The Digest of Justinian* (Philadelphia, 1985).

23 A post-classical Roman jurist, ± 300 CE, living in any case quite long after he promulgation of the *Constitutio Antoniniana* (212 CE) in which nearly all free inhabitants of the Roman Empire acquired Roman citizenship.

24 H. Lauterpacht, *Private Law Sources and Analogies of International Law* (Cambridge, 1927), on Grotius, see 12 ff.

25 On the wall of the Dutch Supreme Court since 1938, see J. Huizinga, *Briefwisseling* (Utrecht and Antwerpen, 1991), vol. 3, 129–31.

26 This system can still be traced in nearly every modern codification of private law. It consists in the separation of the law of persons, patrimonial law (to be subdivided between absolute and personal rights) and procedural law in Latin: *personae, res, actiones*. See P.G. Stein, 'The fate of the institutional system', in Stein, *The Character and Influence of Roman Civil Law. Historical Essays* (London, 1988), 73–82.

27 See more in detail R. Feenstra, 'Hugues Doneau et les juristes néerlandais du XVIIe siècle: L'influence de son "système" sur l'évolution du droit privé avant le Pandectisme', in: B. Schmidlin and A. Dufour (eds.), *Jacques Godefroy (1587–1652) et l'Humanisme juridique à Genève* (Basel and Frankfurt, 1991), 461–74 = R. Feenstra, *Legal Scholarship and Doctrines of Private Law, 13th–18th Centuries* (Aldershot, 1996), IV and R. Feenstra, 'La systématique du droit dans l'oeuvre de Grotius', in *La sistematica giuridica: Storia, teoria e problemi attuali* (Rome, 1991) = R. Feenstra, *Legal Scholarship and Doctrines of Private Law, 13th–18th Centuries* (Aldershot, 1996), VII.

28 R. Feenstra, *'Ius in re', Het begrip zakelijk recht in historisch perspectief* (Zwolle, 1979); an elaborated version: R. Feenstra, *'Dominium and ius in re aliena*: the origins of a civil law distinction, legal scholarship and doctrines of private law', in P. Birks (ed.), *New Perspectives in the Roman Law of Property, Essays for Barry Nicholas* (Oxford, 1989), 111–22 = R. Feenstra, *Legal Scholarship and Doctrines of Private Law, 13th–18th Centuries* (Aldershot, 1996), III.

29 J. Apel, *Methodica dialectices ratio ad jurisprudentiam adcommodata*. See F. Wieacker, *Privatrechtsgeschichte der Neuzeit* (2nd edn., Göttingen, 1967), 157 and Feenstra, *'Ius in re'*, 17; Feenstra, *'Dominium and ius in re'*, 114.

30 An interesting question that cannot be answered here is whether the *Prolegomena* is kind of a prefiguration of the General Part in codifications of private law of the German kind.

31 R. Feenstra, *Interpretatio multiplex* (Inaugural lecture; Leiden, 1952).

32 http://arkyves.org/view/DeIurePraedae.

33 See J. ter Meulen and P.J.J. Diermanse, *Bibliographie des écrits imprimés de Hugo Grotius* (The Hague, 1950), 210 ff.

34 Nellen, *Grotius*, 106–9.

35 An overview in R. Feenstra & R. Zimmermann (eds.), *Das Römisch-Holländische Recht, Fortschritte des Zivilrechts im 17. und 18. Jahrhundert* (Berlin, 1992).

36 R. Zimmermann, *Das römisch-holländische Recht* (Berlin, 1992), 42 f. with further references.

37 A modern French translation by Dominique Gaurier (Nantes) will soon be available electronically.

Property, Trade and Empire 13

Andrew Fitzmaurice

13.1 Introduction

Relations between European sovereigns were never tranquil, but the Reformation brought violence and instability on an unprecedented scale as cities, empires and states experienced chronic conflicts between each other and internally. These wars were driven, or at least justified, by the various parties defending their understandings of true religion. Prior to the Reformation, Europeans were able to believe that their communities were held together by bonds of love or friendship, and that humans were, therefore, naturally sociable creatures. Following the Reformation, in an epoch characterised by extraordinary violence, it was no longer possible to maintain such an optimistic understanding of humanity. Writing during the English Civil Wars – one of the many theatres in which the Reformation was played out – and in an extreme revision of the theory of natural sociability, Thomas Hobbes (1588–1679) argued that it was not mutual love that drove humanity into the social contracts that formed communities, but their mutual distrust and dislike.[1] The transformation in the understanding of human sociability that prevailed by the time Hobbes wrote had to a very large degree been shaped in the late sixteenth and early seventeenth centuries by writers on the society of nations, and by writers on the law of nations in particular. Hugo Grotius was the most important figure among those writers. Such a dramatic shift in the understanding of humanity had profound implications for the laws and conventions that governed relations between humans and it was Grotius who did more than any other thinker to draw out those conclusions. According to Grotius, property, trade and empire were central to human relations and he reinterpreted each of these concepts in terms of the changing understanding of human sociability.

13.2 Sociability and Self-Preservation

Aristotle (384–322 BCE) described humans as 'political animals' because, he argued, 'the impulse to form a partnership of this kind [the city] is present in all men by nature'.[2] This view dominated ancient Europe. It was echoed, for example, by Cicero (106–43 BCE) who argued that, because bees 'are gregarious by nature' they 'gather together' and that 'in the same way, but to a much greater extent, men, living naturally in groups, exercise their ingenuity'. Moreover, Cicero denied what Grotius would later sustain: namely, that 'it is not true' that 'men embarked upon communal life and fellowship in order to provide for life's necessities'.[3] Medieval and Renaissance Europeans inherited this perspective. It was articulated by Thomas Aquinas (c. 1225–74) who declared 'it is natural for man to live in fellowship with many others' and that 'all are united by the bond of friendship'.[4] Although they made much of their differences with scholastic philosophers, Renaissance humanists concurred on the importance of human sociability. Playing upon the idea, Francesco Petrarch (1304–74), a great admirer of Cicero, thought deeply about friendship and wrote that he had never 'willingly sat down to table without a companion'.[5] For the humanists, a world drawn together by mutual affection could be governed by the virtuous and selfless action of citizens. Before the Reformation broke upon Europe in the sixteenth century, Niccolo Machiavelli (1469–1527) had already poured scorn upon the notion that fellowship was driven by mutual affection and he radically redefined the understanding of virtue. Writing during the Italian Wars, he described human character as self-interested, and bestial.[6] 'Love', argued Machiavelli, 'is sustained by a bond of gratitude which, because men are excessively self-interested, is broken whenever they see a chance to benefit themselves.'[7] Nevertheless, in the early years of the Reformation, the idea of amicable sociability continued to dominate discussions of the nature of human communities and their relations with each other. Theologian Francisco de Vitoria (c. 1483–1546), trained in scholastic philosophy and the *studia humanitatis*, was the most notable author in this vein and he asserted 'amity (*amicitia*) between men is part of natural law', from which he drew the conclusion that 'it is a law of nature to welcome strangers'.[8]

It was not only the extraordinary bloodshed of the Reformation that undermined such notions, it was also the fact that the violence prevailed in communities that had previously not seen civil strife at such levels – for example, in the French Wars of Religion. Moreover, it was difficult to take the rule of virtue or honour seriously when the violence was frequently believed to be treacherous, for example in the Massacre of Saint Bartholomew's Day in 1572 or the 1618 Defenestration of Prague. In order to make sense of such events, and of their duration over many decades, contemporaries began to revise their understanding of the bonds that held together human society. This did not mean, however, that they rapidly drew the deeply pessimistic conclusions Hobbes came to during the English Civil Wars. Michel de Montaigne (1533–92), whose entire adult life was spent within the French Wars of Religion, wrote about the great import-ance of friendship, and virtue, at the same time that he coldly analysed the motivations of self-interest in human affairs and recognised that virtuous behaviour in public could be a form of auto-destruction. By the late sixteenth century, writers such as Montaigne and Justus Lipsius (1547–1606) had come to the view that, in a dangerous and corrupt world, individuals were driven by the desire for self-preservation and they accordingly gave far greater weight to interest and expedience when calibrated against virtue as a guide for action.[9]

Hugo Grotius was similarly ambivalent about sociability in the face of such change. He, too, wrote in response to the religiously-inspired conflicts that defined the moment, both that which pitted the Protestant Netherlands against Spain and also the conflict between Calvinist factions within the Netherlands that almost cost him his life and led to his exile. Like Montaigne, Grotius struggled with the classical account of human fellowship. In his earliest work on the law of nations, he agreed that human communities are drawn together by love. 'The old poets and philosophers', he argued, 'have rightly deduced that love ... is the first principle of the whole natural order.' He radically revised this Aristotelian account of human sociability, however, by echoing Machiavelli with the claim that love's 'primary force and action are directed to self-interest', thereby reconciling the motivation of expedience with natural sociability (DJPC 2, 5'). He justified this position, bringing Cicero to his aid, the most respectable of humanist sources, by declaring that 'all things in nature, as Cicero repeatedly insists, are tenderly regardful of self, and seek their own happiness and security' (DJPC 2, 5'a). Citing the Academic sceptics, he added that 'expediency might perhaps be called the mother of justice and equity' (DJPC 2, 5'a). The reason separate human societies came into existence, therefore, and were separated from the 'universal society' that Grotius argued was constituted by all humankind, was not because the bonds of mutual affection drew people together but because, even where love played a role, expedience governed. And the primary expedience of creating separate human societies, or civil societies, was to ensure the survival of their members.

Grotius took an Augustinian – and Protestant – view regarding the inherent sinfulness of humans and therefore concluded that, in a world without civil society – 'such is the evil growing out of the corrupt nature of some men!' – 'many persons . . . assailed the fortunes and the very lives of others' (DJPC 2, 10'). Such a dangerous condition of life required a remedy that would 'fortify that universal society by a more dependable means of protection' (DJPC 2, 10'). This 'smaller social unit' was 'formed by general agreement'. Its purpose was 'self-protection through mutual aid, and through equal acquisition of the necessities of life' and it was 'called a commonwealth [*Respublica*]'. The purpose of civil society, therefore, was the highest order of expedience – namely, survival – and, from this first principle, Grotius extrapolated the laws that governed relations between societies. Although Grotius was concerned with refuting the sceptic Carneades' claim that the universal rule of expedience proved the inexistence of both justice and the law of nature, he was only able to do so by subordinating the law of nature and justice to expedience. Grotius softened these arguments in his more mature work on the law of nations, *De jure belli ac pacis*, but the innovative nature of his thought remained salient. In this later work, he repeated Carneades' claim that 'Expediency is, as it were, the mother/ Of what is just and fair', and argued this was 'not true, if we wish to speak accurately'. Even without expedience, he now conjectured, 'the mutual relations of society' were to be found in 'the very nature of man'. Nevertheless, he conceded that 'the law of nature has the reinforcement of expediency' and 'that law is not founded on expediency alone', finding a correspondence between natural law and expediency rather than simply reducing natural law to expediency (DJBP Prol. 16 and 22). In all his works on international society, with such a revolutionary starting point, Grotius would completely rewrite the understanding of relations between peoples that theologians, notably Vitoria, had explored. Expedience and survival animate each of the laws that he understood to govern relations between peoples, including those regarding trade and property.

13.3 Expansion and Empire

Grotius understood each sovereignty, whether a principality, empire or state, to be an autonomous entity or, as he put it: 'the state is a self-sufficient aggregation' (DJPC 2, 13). These aggregations he described as 'moral bodies', drawing an analogy with natural bodies.[10] This understanding of states as self-sufficient aggregations drew upon a medieval tradition, stemming from Bartolus (1314–57) and the post-Glossators, which saw the Italian cities as *sibi princeps*, or as emperors unto themselves, but it was even more indebted to Jean Bodin's (1530–96) sixteenth-century account of sovereignty as absolute and indivisible.[11] Bodin wrote that account in response to the Wars of Religion in his native France. For Bodin, indivisible and absolute sovereignty was an antidote to the religious conflict in which each party claimed to possess a cause more important than the law. Grotius defined sovereignty accordingly: 'That power is called sovereign whose actions are not subject to the legal control of another, so that they cannot be rendered void by the operation of another human will' (DJBP 1.3.7).

The society of sovereigns, therefore, was a society of such independent moral bodies. It was a society without government analogous to that which natural persons inhabited prior to the establishment of civil societies. Grotius' society of sovereigns, like the pre-civil state of natural persons, was not, however, a Hobbesian natural state in which a war of all against all prevailed. Although it was not a harmonious condition, certain laws and rights were observed and, foremost among those, as we shall see, were the right of self-preservation and the right over property – initially common property and subsequently particular property – which furthered self-preservation. Grotius argued that the original society of natural persons, prior to their formation into communities, was unable to persist because, in order to do so, humans would have to be able to live on 'terms of mutual affection' that, he noted, 'rarely appears' (DJBP 2.2.1). Moreover, he added, people would have to be satisfied with the 'great simplicity' of that life. But the harmony of that rather prelapsarian condition was destroyed by the vice of 'ambition' (DJBP 2.2.3). The absence of mutual affection and prevalence of ambition were also characteristic of the society of states, but, in contrast to the progression from the original 'simple' 'state of the first men' to a civil state, the persons – states who behave as persons – who made up the society of states would not submit to world government, even if they did acknowledge certain natural laws that constrained their behaviour. For this reason, sovereigns were obliged to take measures to ensure their own survival.

For Grotius, this question of survival in the society of nations was of the utmost immediate practical relevance. He was profoundly conscious of the fact that the continued existence of both the Dutch Republic and reformed religion were in constant peril from the Spanish empire and he wrote his first extensive treatise on the law of nations, *De Indiis*, or *De jure praedae commentarius* as it is more commonly known, in response to precisely that threat. He began that treatise by observing that 'the savage insolence of the Iberian peoples will swell to immeasurable proportions' such that 'the shores of the whole world will soon be blocked off' (DJPC 1, 2). Grotius' solution to this peril was entirely in tune with a number of his contemporaries. If sovereigns were to survive in the dangerous world of post-Reformation politics, they must extend their resources. The most notable proponent of this view was Giovanni Botero (1544–1617), an apologist for the Habsburgs, who domesticated Machiavelli's controversial political prescriptions, took seriously the role of expedience – which Botero referred to by the term 'interest' that he popularised – in political affairs and developed the notion of 'reason of state'.[12] Botero argued that states could only preserve themselves if they pursued greatness. And greatness would be achieved by acquiring empires. Walter Raleigh (1552–1618), who read Botero, had similarly urged the English to extend their empire, warning that it was not the trade in 'Civil Orenges' that had made Phillip II (1528–98) the most powerful sovereign in Europe.[13] Importantly, however, Botero warned against the pursuit of gold and silver as the basis of greatness because he had seen the inflation that it had caused in the Spanish empire. Rather, he argued, arts and commerce should be the foundation of empire and greatness.[14] Grotius, who has frequently been understood to be a critic of the Machiavellian tradition, was remarkably close to Botero in his advice to the Dutch Republic in *De jure praedae*, albeit that he did not acknowledge Botero. 'The wealth of our state is chiefly if not entirely sustained', he declared, by 'commerce with Asia.' An empire of commerce, rather than the conquest of specie, was the source of Dutch power. At the same time, he added, 'If the Dutch choose to avail themselves of their good fortune, God has provided a weapon against the inmost heart of the enemy's power, nor is there any weapon that offers a surer hope of liberty' (DJPC 1, 2).

13.4 Trade and Communication

Empire, for Grotius, was permissible, therefore, even desirable, because it was essential to the self-preservation of the sovereign in the dangerous world of post-Reformation international society. His discussions of property and trade derived from that necessity and they can be seen, in that sense, as arguments based upon the reason of state tradition as much as natural law. In part because Grotius was seeking in *Mare liberum* to refute the imperial claims of Portugal and Spain, he based his argument to a large degree upon the authority of Spanish theologians, notably Vitoria, declaring in his Preface that 'In this controversy we appeal to those jurists among the Spanish themselves who are especially skilled in divine and human law' (ML Dedication, 4). *Mare liberum* reads like a gloss on Vitoria's lectures on the Indies. For Vitoria, communication and trade were fundamental rights of all humans because they were expressions of natural sociability, which was the foundation of understanding *jus gentium*.[15] He argued, therefore, that while the Spanish had no right to conquer the Americans with swords, they did have the right to go among them to preach and trade – trade was seen to be fundamental to sociability, as reflected in the dual meanings of the term 'commerce'. Grotius seized upon this argument to refute the claims of the Portuguese, relying partly on the Treaty of Tordesillas (1494), to exclude all other nations from the right to trade in the East. He asked: 'Can any one nation have the right to prevent other nations which so desire, from selling to one another, from bartering with one another, actually from communicating with one another?' (ML Dedication, 4) The question itself revealed the nexus between trade and communication. He answered that question with 'an unimpeachable axiom of the Law of Nations, called a primary rule or first principle': namely, 'Every nation is free to travel to every other nation, and to trade with it' (ML 1, 7).

Grotius, however, was living in a very different moment from that in which Vitoria had given his lectures, and it was no longer possible to understand the right of communication as arising from a natural human affection alone. Grotius argued that there were 'those' who would 'neglect justice on the pretext of expedience', but they would have to 'unlearn the lesson of injustice at their own expense': that is, they would soon discover that justice was wedded to expediency (ML Dedication, 6). If the bonds of human fellowship were not formed by mutual affection, they must be driven by need. He portrayed humans as creatures who were not 'intire of themselves', as John Donne (1572–1631) would put it, needing each other in order to become complete.[16] Nor was any place on the globe capable of providing 'all the necessaries of life' – again the emphasis was upon necessity (ML 1, 7). 'Human friendships', therefore, were driven by 'mutual needs and resources' (ML 1, 7). 'It ought not to be supposed', therefore, 'that trade was invented for the benefit of a few, but in order that the lack of one would be counterbalanced by the oversupply of another' (ML 1, 7). This need for trade and communication was not only a matter of human perfectibility; it was also a question of obtaining the resources needed for self-preservation.

Vitoria had cited Virgil to illustrate the 'law of hospitality' that obliged all people to welcome all others in need. This obligation, for Vitoria, was a question of amity: 'What men, what monsters, what inhuman race,/ What laws, what barbarous customs of the place,/ Shut up a desert shore to drowning men,/ And drive us to the cruel seas again!'[17] Grotius, too, cited the same passage from Virgil on this question of human fellowship as the basis of trade and he explicitly acknowledge Vitoria on the question: 'Vitoria holds that the Spaniards could have shown just reasons for making war upon Aztecs and the Indians in America' if they were 'prevented from travelling' among those peoples and if they 'were denied the right to share in those things which by the Law of Nature or Custom are common to all' (ML 1, 9). Such resources were necessary to self-preservation and, to underline this point, when citing Virgil on sanctuary, Grotius added some further lines that Vitoria had not included and which related, not to amity, but to survival: 'To beg what you without your want may spare- / The common water and the air' (ML 1, 8). Because the common resources of the earth had been given by God to all for their self-preservation, it was a violation of the law of nature to deny access to anybody in pursuit of those resources.

Grotius later reiterated this point in *De jure belli ac pacis* under the title 'The right to such acts as human life requires'. He declared that all people had rights 'in respect to acts indispensable for the obtaining of the things without which life cannot be comfortably lived'. 'Now all men have absolutely a right to do such or such acts as are necessary to provide whatever is essential to the existence or convenience of life' (DJBP 2.2.18). He accordingly condemned anybody who would 'destroy that commerce which is the very support of life'. Again, the reason that commerce and communication were a matter of right in these circumstances was not because they reflected human sociability, but because they supported self-preservation. In the final chapter of *Mare liberum*, Grotius underlined this point by arguing that any nation could go to war to protect their access to common property as much as to protect their particular property (ML 13). Common goods, he argued, were for the 'common benefit of the human race' and it was a 'most stable law of nature' that any act to the detriment of that benefit could be punished (ML 13, 76).

13.5 Property

Grotius' objective in *Mare liberum* and *De jure praedae*, of which it originally formed a chapter, was to make a positive case for the Dutch being able to trade in the East Indies, but that argument depended to a large degree on a negative case as to why the Portuguese did not hold property over the East and so could not exclude competitors. The Portuguese claim to the East, Grotius argued, must arise from either a right over the seas or a right over the territories of the 'Indies'. His aim, again, was to show that rights over property were derived from the right to preserve oneself. The Portuguese claim, therefore, was a violation of all other peoples' rights to preserve themselves. To make this case, Grotius reconstructed the idea of property from first principles.

In 'ancient times', he began, 'all things were held in common', and he repeats that 'primitive men held everything in common (ML 5, 23).[18] God, he argued, did not give 'all things' to particular individuals but, rather, to all people and this meant that all people were sovereigns over all things and the same things (ML 5, 24). This situation, he argued, changed gradually. In *Mare liberum*, he stated that the cause of the change was that there are some things which, when used, become 'used up', although in *De jure belli ac pacis,* he deepened his analysis of the cause of the change to include ambition and the loss of innocence through the acquisition of knowledge (ML 5, 24; DJBP 2.2.2–3). Certain things, for example food and drink, when used are consumed. The use of property 'began in connection with bodily needs': that is, it was a product of each person's need to preserve her or himself (ML 5, 25). By meeting such needs, property that was consumed, or property (such as land) that was used to make consumables, was transformed from being common to being the property of individuals. The name for this process by which common property was transformed into particular, or individual, property was 'occupation', from the Roman law concept of *occupatio* (DJBP 2.3.1).[19] The occupation of movable goods, such as wild beasts, was a form of seizure, while the occupation immovables, notably land, required the demarcation of fields and the erection of buildings (ML 5, 25–6). Individual ownership could involve things being taken from the common by a body-politic, in which case such things became public property, or it could involve such things being taken by natural persons, in which case the things became private property (ML 5, 26).

These premises led Grotius to the conclusion that 'that which cannot be occupied, or which has never been occupied, cannot be the property of anyone, because all property has arisen from occupation' (ML 5, 27). Even if such common property served the use of one person that fact did not change its service for 'the common use of all other persons'. It was the use of such common property, he argued, citing Cicero, that 'unites together men as men, and all to all' (ML 5, 27). Human fellowship, therefore, was not based upon amity but upon use, or expedience: that is, upon the 'common right to all things' that would serve 'the common use of man' (ML 5, 27). Grotius singled out two kinds of common property, in particular, for analysis: namely, the air and the sea. The air, he pointed out, is 'not susceptible of occupation' and its use was 'destined for all men' (ML 5, 28). Similarly, the sea 'is common to all, because it is so limitless that it cannot become a possession of any one, and because it is adapted for the use of all' for the purposes of both fishing and navigation (ML 5, 28; DJBP, 2.2.1). By the 'common consent of all mankind', which reflected natural reason, the sea was 'forever exempt' from 'private ownership' on account of its 'susceptibility to universal use' (ML 5, 29). Moreover, he added in *De jure belli ac pacis*, 'occupation takes place only in the case of a thing which has definite limits', because occupation requires seizure (DJBP 2.3.1–2). No 'one person' could take any part of the sea 'any more than what is mine can be taken away from me by you' (ML 5, 29). The inviolability of property applied as much to common property as to private property. For this reason, it was not possible even to drive 'piles' into the sea and so enclose a part of it, or to build a breakwater, if to do so was 'prejudicial to the interests of any one', because to do so was to build upon common property (ML 5, 31). These principles governed both individual persons and nations, or 'peoples', because 'from the point of view of the whole human race peoples are treated as individuals', so 'neither a nation nor an individual can establish any right of private ownership over the sea itself' (ML 5, 36–7). Navigation and fishing on the seas were to remain absolutely free, albeit that – when fish were seized – they were effectively occupied and so could pass into private ownership (ML 5, 33).

The reason Grotius so carefully constructed this theory of property was in order to demonstrate that the Portuguese claim to a monopoly on the sea routes to the East was not only unjust but 'barbarous and inhuman': 'it may be seen that the Portuguese have not established private ownership over the sea by which people go to the East Indies' (ML 5, 37). He demanded whether the Portuguese had 'completely covered the ocean' by 'laying out estates' in the same manner that 'we do on land' (ML 5, 39). What are we to say of a person, he asked, who prevents others from using something that incurs 'no loss to himself' (ML 5, 38). As Grotius repeatedly stated in *De jure belli ac pacis*, the purpose of the common ownership of resources that could not become individual property, due to their unlimited nature, was to enable each person to take what 'he' needed 'for his own needs' (DJBP 2.2.1.1). By denying other nations free navigation of the sea, the Portuguese were not merely denying access to common property but, in so doing, denying the right of those peoples to use common resources for their own self-preservation.

If the Portuguese had not established property over the sea, the question remained whether they could exclude other peoples from the East by virtue of their own possession of the territories there. Here Grotius turned even more to Vitoria. In chapter 2 of *Mare liberum*, entitled 'The Portuguese have no right by title of discovery to sovereignty over the East Indies', Grotius proposed that 'The Portuguese are not sovereigns of those parts of the East Indies to which the Dutch sail'. 'No one', he argued, 'is sovereign of a thing which he himself has never possessed' (ML 2, 11). The Portuguese had never possessed territories in the East Indies, because those countries 'have and always have had their own kings, their own government, their own laws, and their own legal systems'. Here he glossed Vitoria's dismissal of the 'Third unjust title' of the Spaniards to the Americas: namely, 'that possession of these countries is by right of discovery'. Vitoria similarly argued that this title was invalid because 'the barbarians possessed true public and private dominion'. Vitoria added that 'the law of nations ... expressly states that goods which belong to no owner pass to the occupier' whereas 'the goods in question here had an owner'.[20]

Grotius developed this reasoning. He began by defining discovery, which, he said, was not merely 'to seize' a thing 'with the eyes but take real possession thereof', so that 'to discover' and 'to occupy' have the same signification. Moreover, discovery and occupation, he pointed out, could only lead to legal rights over things in cases where 'before the alleged discovery they were *res nullius*': that is, in cases where those things belonged to nobody (ML 2, 13).[21] By contrast, 'these Indians of the East, on the arrival of the Portuguese, although some of them were idolaters, and others Mohammedans, and therefore sunk in grievous sin, had none the less perfect public and private ownership of their goods and possessions' (ML 2, 13). Sinfulness, however, was not a bar to ownership. 'The Spanish writer Vitoria', had shown that Christians 'cannot deprive infidels of their civil power and sovereignty merely on the ground that they are infidels' (ML 2, 13). At the time Grotius wrote, both Catholic and Protestant sovereigns were disturbed by the heretical argument that the only just society is a godly society, an argument that licensed religious rebellions and left the question of godliness, and legitimate sovereignty, to the conscience of each person. 'Religious belief', Grotius argued citing Aquinas, 'does not do away with either natural or human law from which sovereignty is derived' (ML 5, 25). It was therefore 'a heresy to believe that infidels are not masters of their own property'. Again glossing Vitoria, he noted that 'Nor are the East Indians stupid and unthinking; on the contrary, they are intelligent and shrewd', so that there could be no problem for them in recognising and exploiting natural laws in order to establish their own systems of property, law and sovereignty (ML 2, 13–4). He concluded 'Vitoria then is right in saying that the Spaniards have no more legal right over the East Indians because of their religion, than East Indians would have had over the Spaniards if they had happened to be the first foreigners to come to Spain' (ML 2, 13).

Again, for Grotius, this understanding of private property was driven by the right of self-preservation. He argued, citing Cicero, that every person could acquire 'for himself . . . whatever contributes to the advantage of life; and in this there is no conflict with nature' (DJBP 2.2.5). Moreover, by arguing that the basis of private property was occupation, and that the justification for occupation was the 'advantage' it gives to the occupier, Grotius submitted justice, at least in the matter of property, to expedience. In doing so, he addressed the ancient debate on the relative merits of honour or '*honestas*', including justice, on the one hand and expedience, '*utilitas*', or advantage, on the other. He resolved the tensions between these two objectives by bringing them into line, so what was expedient was also just. Such an argument was not entirely consistent with reason of state discourse, which also arose in response to the religious wars of the sixteenth and seventeenth centuries, because reason of state dictated that justice could be dispensed with in cases of necessity or expedience. Nevertheless, both reason of state and Grotius' submission of justice to expedience were part of a broader shift in moral philosophy in the late sixteenth and seventeenth century, which saw the rise of interest as the primary consideration in political discourse, whereas virtue had dominated ancient, medieval and Renaissance thinking. The central question in the politics of interest was self-preservation, and, for most early modern writers on law and politics, greatness was understood to be the means of ensuring self-preservation.[22] Both these modes of thinking – in terms of interest and greatness – made a deep impression upon Grotius' account of the law of nations.

13.6 Conclusion

It has been argued that the theologians of the sixteenth-century School of Salamanca, foremost among whom was Vitoria, provided the philosophical foundations for a law of nations that would not only justify, but even inspire, the European empires of the following 500 years.[23] There is much merit in this argument. The School of Salamanca did indeed furnish a theory of a *jus gentium* that universalised European norms, even while theologians – including Vitoria and Domingo de Soto (1494–1560) – were critical of Spanish empire in the Americas. It provided a theory of *dominium*, both property (*dominium rerum*) and sovereignty (*dominium jurisdictionis*), that was extended over the globe through the *jus gentium*, allowing the appropriation of the goods and imperium of other peoples. And, finally, those theologians provided a theory of just war that would sanction this understanding of the universality of *dominium*. Each of these elements would be fundamental to the justification of empire. But this Salamanca School account of the law of nations lacked the most important element to drive those empires: namely, ambition. The ambition for empire came from the traumatic experience of religious war in Europe and the brutal lessons of those wars had not been learnt by the Salamanca generation, even if Vitoria and Soto were themselves concerned with refuting

Protestant heresies in the early years of the Reformation. By the early seventeenth century, however, Europeans were beginning to understand that the most important qualities in political life were survival and interest, rather than virtue. Indeed, the Renaissance valorisation of virtue had partly driven the confessional conflict. The politics of self-preservation and interest inspired Grotius' understanding of the law of nations in a manner that was not evident in the discussions of the Salamanca authors – whose discussions of expedience rested in a classical mould. His argument that the means to self-preservation was the extension of the state's power through overseas trade and empire was entirely consistent with the thinking of many of his contemporaries, even while it ironically rested upon an assertion of the rights of property and sovereignty of non-European peoples. His unique contribution, however, was to present a new understanding of the law of nations, including central concepts within the law of nations such as property and the right of communication and trade, in terms of this new regime of interest and greatness and in a critique of the ancient world attachment to a world bound by love and friendship.

Translations of Grotius' Works Used

H. Grotius, *The Freedom of the Seas, or the Right Which Belongs to the Dutch to take part in the East Indian Trade,* transl. Ralph Van Deman Magoffin (New York, 1916)

Further Reading

Borschberg, P., 'Hugo Grotius, East India trade and the king of Johor', *Journal of Southeast Asian Studies* 30 (1999) 225–48.

Borschberg, P., 'The seizure of the Sta. Catarina revisited: the Portuguese Empire in Asia, VOC politics and the origins of the Dutch-Johor alliance (1602–c.1616)', *Journal of Southeast Asian Studies* 33 (2002) 31–62.

Fitzmaurice, A., *Sovereignty, Property, and Empire 1500–2000* (Cambridge, 2014).

Keene, E. *Beyond the Anarchical Society: Grotius, Colonialism and Order in World Politics* (Oxford, 2002).

Tuck, R., *Philosophy and Government 1572–1651* (Cambridge, 1993).

Tuck, R., *The Rights of War and Peace: Political Thought and the International Order from Grotius to Kant* (Oxford, 2001).

Van Ittersum, M.J., *Profit and Principle: Hugo Grotius, Natural Rights Theories and the Rise of Dutch Power in the East Indies (1595–1615)* (Leiden, 2006).

Notes

1 T. Hobbes, *Leviathan*, ed. Richard Tuck (Cambridge, 1991), 117–9.

2 Aristotle, *Politics*, transl. H. Rackham (Loeb Classical Library; London, 1932), 1.1.12.

3 Cicero, *On duties*, eds. M.T. Griffin and E.M. Atkins (Cambridge, 1991), vol. 1, 157–8.

4 Aquinas, *De regimine principum, in Political writings*, ed. R.W. Dyson (Cambridge, 2002), 7 and 31.

5 Petrarch, *Letter to posterity, in Petrarch: The first modern scholar and man of letters ed.* and transl. J.H. Robinson (New York, 1898), 61.

6 N. Machiavelli, *The Prince* eds. Q. Skinner and R. Price (Cambridge, 1990), 61.

7 Machiavelli, *The Prince*, 59. This view was summarised in his observation in the same chapter that: 'men forget sooner the killing of a father than the loss of their patrimony', 59.

8 F. de Vitoria, *On the American Indians, in Political writings* eds. A. Pagden and J. Lawrance (Cambridge, 1991), 3.1.2.

9 R. Tuck, *Philosophy and Government 1572–1651* (Cambridge, 1993) provides the best account of Montaigne and Lipsius in this context.

10 See, for example, DJBP 2.9.1. Tuck provides a thoughtful analysis of this Grotian analogy between natural persons and states when both are understood to be autonomous rights-bearing individuals: R. Tuck, *The Rights of War and Peace: Political Thought and the International Order from Grotius to Kant* (Oxford, 2001), 84.

11 On Bartolus, see: Q. Skinner, *The Foundations of Modern Political Thought* (Cambridge, 1978), vol.1, 11–12. For Bodin: Skinner, *Foundations*, vol.1, 284–301.

12 On Botero, see: A. Fitzmaurice, 'The commercial ideology of colonisation in Jacobean England: Robert Johnson, Giovanni Botero and the pursuit of greatness', *William and Mary Quarterly* 64 (2007) 791–820.

13 W. Raleigh, *The discoverie of the large, rich and bewtiful Empyre of Guiana*, ed. N.L. Whitehead (Norman, 1997), 127.

14 G. Botero, *A treatise, Concerning the causes of the Magnifencie and Greatnes of Cities*, transl. R. Peterson (London, 1606).

15 Vitoria, *On the American Indians* 3.1.

16 J. Donne, Devotions upon Emergent Occasions, Meditation XVII, *in Donne, John Donne Poetry and Prose*, ed. Frank J. Warnke (New York, 1967), 339. Donne possibly employed Grotius in his 1622 sermon to the Virginia Company, while he certainly employed the Roman law of occupation: John Donne, *A Sermon Preached to the Honourable Company of the Virginian Plantation* (London, 1622), 25–7, arguing that a person does not 'become proprietary of the Sea, because he hath two or three Boats, fishing on it' and 'In the law of Nature and Nations, a land never inhabited, by any, or utterly derelicted and immemorially abandoned by the former Inhabitants, becomes theirs that will possesse it'.

17 Vitoria, *On the American Indians* 3.1.2

18 See also: DJBP, 2.2.1–2.

19 On occupation, see: A. Fitzmaurice, *Sovereignty, Property, and Empire 1500–2000* (Cambridge, 2014).

20 Vitoria, *On the American Indians* 2.3.1.

21 In his Latin text here Grotius uses simply '*nullius*' rather than '*res nullius*'.

22 The most notable exception to this perspective was Thomas Hobbes, who argued against the 'vain-glory' of states and derided 'the insatiable appetite, or *Bulimia*, of enlarging Dominion': Hobbes, *Leviathan*, 230. On Hobbes and the bulimia of empires, see: I. Hont, *Jealousy of Trade: International Competition and the Nation-State in Historical Perspective* (Cambridge, MA, 2005); and Fitzmaurice, *Sovereignty,* 104. For Hobbes's familiarity with the literature on greatness and reason of state and his sympathy with some of its themes, despite his disdain for 'pretenders to Political Prudence', see N. Malcolm, *Reason of State, Propaganda and the Thirty Years' War: An Unknown Translation by Thomas Hobbes* (Oxford, 2007), 109–23.

23 M. Koskenniemi, 'Empire and international law: the real Spanish contribution', *University of Toronto Law Journal*, 61 (2011) 1–36.

Part III

Grotius as a Man of Letters, Theologian and Political Writer

Arthur Eyffinger

14.1 An Ambitious Programme

In a volume that aims to get across the substance, merits and pertinence to our times of Hugo Grotius' intellectual legacy, the chapter that highlights the Dutchman's poetical outpourings might at first glance strike as a mere side issue. What intrigues the intellectual discourse of our times is Grotius' normative approach to human understanding and the global intercourse. From that perspective, the humanist world of letters must appear a closed chapter from a distant past. But, then, appearances can be deceptive. This chapter has a double objective: to advance the social, moral and political pertinence of Grotius' literary oeuvre and to substantiate its quintessential status within his overall philosophy. To drive this message home, this contribution will focus on the most productive and rewarding period of Grotius' intellectual life and address his ambitious programme of comprehensive social reform to overcome the incisive moral and intellectual crisis of his day and age. These high aspirations prompted Grotius' seminal masterpieces and theorems in the legal and theological domains. Less well-known, they also triggered a series of impressive literary outpourings of eminent socio-political pertinence.

For five years, between 1613 and 1618, Grotius had been a major protagonist in the politico-religious strife in the Republic that tragically wrecked both his line of policy and his career. He endured three years of grim but purifying incarceration, made a spectacular escape into exile, got frustration off his chest by writing an embittered *Apologeticus* *(Verantwoordingh*, 1622), then let bygones be bygones, resolutely looked forwards and shifted interest towards the international arena and its many predicaments. The outcome was an intellectual outpouring of imposing width and depth. Its substance encompassed the whole social spectrum in a concerted effort to put human intercourse on a new footing. The roughly five years the project took him (1622–7) were intellectually the most stimulating period of his life.

In a three-pronged endeavour from a single overbearing perspective, Grotius tackles the many challenges posed to a world uprooted by the discovery of new continents, the unsettling new paradigms of science, technology and a sceptical outlook on life, the rise of the modern state system and, last but not least, the moral onslaught of the Reformation. His answers are clear-cut and consistent, in urgent appeal to the *fontes* and the common ground left in the massive onslaught. In his magisterial *De jure belli ac pacis* (1625) and his great apology for Christianity, *De veritate religionis Christianae* (1627), he proclaims his intellectual response to war, the scourge of his times, and to religious dissent, the evil at its root, by insisting on the common legal tradition and the core creed of the early Church respectively. The normative precepts he defines to bolster political consensus and religious peace are the rule of law and the principles of ecumenism and toleration. In this chapter, we will address Grotius' third proposition to put Europe onto a new track: his insistence on the pertinence of the great moral legacy of the classical tradition. Two major treatises are at the heart of his conviction in this sphere during the stipulated span of years (1623, 1626) and we will discuss them presently. They were to prove the opening move to a lifelong line of research.

14.2 Classical Literary Theory

Two distinct, complementary elements underpin the claims made above: the prevailing literary theory of his times and Grotius' personal outlook on literature. The rationale of classical literary theory in Grotius' days differed substantially from the one that took hold in the nineteenth century. To Grotius' contemporaries, poetry was not the sublimation of individuality, but precisely the bearer of universal values and ethical norms. Its province was not so much the private sphere as rather the public domain. We will illustrate this. In 1615, the French envoy to The Hague, Benjamin Aubery du Maurier (1566–1636), an ambitious lawyer and diplomat, consulted Grotius on how best to optimise his professional expertise.

In an 'open letter' (1 BW 384, 13 May 1615),[1] reprinted under the programmatic heading *De studiis instituendis*, Grotius recommends his acquaintance first to secure a solid philosophical basis in ethics and political sciences.[2] Next comes rhetoric and literature, notably the *poemata moralia*, which, 'as in a mirror', presented the human condition. Grotius exemplifies Aristotle's *Rhetorics*, the speeches of Demosthenes and Cicero, along with the latter's *De officiis*, quite possibly the work he himself valued most in all literature. Turning to poetry, he recommends Euripides, Terence, Horace and Seneca. He then suggests reading political historians such as Tacitus and Sallust. Once one has grasped the general principles, he argues, one can easily assign the point at issue in each case to its proper category. Tellingly, this is exactly Grotius' own procedure in his majestic history of the Dutch Revolt (*Annales et Historiae de rebus Belgicis*, published posthumously 1657). Once having accomplished the above, Du Maurier should turn to the law.

And I mean not private law, out of which shysters and pettifoggers (*legulei et rabulae*) make their living,[3] but the law of nations and public law, which Cicero, who calls it a pre-eminent science, says consists of the treaties, truces and covenants of peoples, kings and nations – in short, of the whole law of war and peace (. . .) and the laws based on the *moralis sapientia* as exposed in Plato's and Cicero's *Laws*.

Grotius' views were familiar enough among humanist-lawyers such as Guillaume Budé (1467–1540), Jean Bodin (1530–96) or Alberico Gentili (1552–1608),[4] but we should stress that the same conviction inspired prominent jurists in subsequent centuries. Thus, the celebrated American jurist, Billings Learned Hand (1872–1961), commented:

I venture to believe that it is as important to a judge called upon a question of constitutional law, to have at least a bowing acquaintance with Acton and Maitland, with Thucydides, Gibbon and Carlyle, with Homer, Dante, Shakespeare and Milton, with Machiavelli, Montaigne and Rabelais, with Plato, Bacon, Hume and Kant, as with the books which have been specifically written on the subject.[5]

In Cambridge, Arnold McNair (1885–1975) put his pupil – and, later, successor, both in the Whewell Chair of International Law and in the Presidency of the International Court of Justice – Sir Robert Jennings (1913–2004) on the track with Sir Walter Scott's words that proudly served as motto to Sir Robert's *Festschrift* in 1996:

A lawyer without history or literature is a mechanic, a mere working mason; if he possesses some knowledge of these, he may venture to call himself an architect.[6]

The rationale of this conviction was, as Oliver Wendell Holmes (1841–1935), the law philosopher and US Supreme Court judge, famously argued, that 'the life of the law has not been logic; it has been experience'.[7] Or, as his colleague on the bench, Benjamin Cardozo (1870–1938) once observed, at times a single page of history equals a volume of logic.[8] Percy Shelley (1772–1822) held that poets participated in 'the infinite, the eternal and the one' and were the 'unacknowledged legislators of mankind'.[9]

This element precisely constituted the link between law and literature in the classical perception. Greek cities impeccably boasted a poet-legislator among their founding fathers – men such as Solon, Thales, Lycurgus or Draco – and prided themselves on their νομῳδοί, law-singers. Early legislations were mostly put in verse.[10] Didactic purposes, mnemonic devises and aesthetic considerations all had their say, but, in essence, the Greek νομός – in philosophical terms expressive of 'customary law' as opposed to θέμις, 'the divine ordinance' – embodied the overall idea of *discipline*, as opposed to the Dionysian element.[11] Apollo, Law and Order incarnate, conducted the band of Muses, 'the first educators of man' in Plato's perception,[12] his advice couched in the elusive formulas and 'riddling rhymes' of the Pythian oracle.

14.3 Grotius' Outlook on Poetry

The domain of letters was at the heart of Grotius' studies all his life. Among his peers, he was well-known for his insistence on the issue. To him, the pertinence of the classical tradition was a given, whether one touched upon Cicero's discourse on the *honestum et utile*, Horace's *utile dulci* or the moral authority of classical playwrights (*auctoritas poetarum*). If 'the Dutch Selden' – Leiden's most gifted lawyer of the period, Petrus Cunaeus (1586–1638) – is to be our judge, around 1615 Grotius' stature at home as man of state, law and letters was perfectly unique. The day Grotius became head of state, Cunaeus mused, would be a day of bliss for Holland.[13] Cunaeus was impeccably right on one tag: Grotius was the embodiment of the beneficial fusion of disciplines and interests. In his poetry, this asserted itself in a distinct moral and political outlook.

Grotius may well have been the best Latinist the Netherlands produced. From his student days onwards, he was the master of all genres, be this poetry or prose. His Ciceronian letters, his Tacitean history or his dramas in the Senecan amble, invariably reveal the same authenticity and identification with the model; with Grotius, Latin seemed to flow naturally. It was the accomplishment of an eminently fertile and versatile brain. Neither was Grotius' predilection for the epigram a matter of incident; the genre offered the ultimate challenge to his intellectual genius and linguistic brilliance. And one other faculty stood him in good stead, his photographic memory. The strictly literary merits of Grotius' first Neo-Latin tragedy, on the Fall (*Adamus exul,* 1601), may be open to argument, but the way the youngster appropriated Seneca's idiom and wove his model's every Stoic turn of thought into a religious garb was an intellectual *tour de force.*[14]

The play also exemplifies another seminal character trait, Grotius' deep religiosity. Genuine faith and sincere piety, averse to hair-splitting polemics, inspired Grotius' life, as his poetry amply attests. It accords with his hallmark of seriousness throughout: Grotius never was the light-hearted type of man. Born on Easter Sunday, he composed verses in honour of the Christian heyday on numerous occasions,[15] eminently so in his play on Christ's Passion (*Christus patiens,* 1608). Time and again, he turns his hand to biblical paraphrase, notably the Psalms.[16] Religiosity, if anything, typifies his small corpus of poetry in the vernacular.[17] Reliance on the Lord carried him through the years of harsh imprisonment, when his mind wavered and his physique surrendered.

And this leads us to a last character-trait that assesses itself in Grotius' poetry, his sensitivity. Grotius was a hyper-intelligent, but rather anxious and timid, man. We have his own word for it that the military and the navy were never his thing.[18] The records of his alleged mental collapse under physical torture ring true enough. His poetry shows the brighter flipside of the medal: Grotius' ability to express empathy with suffering positively struck contemporaries. His poetry emphatically confirms the impression his calls for moderation in *De jure belli ac pacis* adumbrate.[19]

14.4 Dutch Years

Ninety per cent of Grotius' original poetry in Latin stems from the years between 1598 and 1608. His prolific production over this decade covers all genres and literary models in reflection on political, academic and private circumstance. The verses address military campaigns as readily as weddings, funerals, publications and appointments. They impeccably answer to eminent technical standards, without invariably complying with modern criteria of poetry.[20] Still, jurists may be charmed by his paraphrases in hexameters of Justinian's *Institutes* in the best tradition of didactic poetry (*De rerum divisione,* 1597–1600; 575 ll., based on *Instit.*

2.1.1–10)[21] or epigrams addressing the integrity of barrister and judge (*De officio advocati*, 1602; *Formidare Deum, Ps. 82*, 1602).

Two elements may be highlighted. No Dutch publicist even came close to the repute young Grotius built himself abroad – through panegyrics and ingenious epigrams on history prints – as advocate of his nation's political ambitions, eulogist of the House of Orange or champion of the feats of arms, military engineering and mathematical research of Maurice of Nassau (1567–1625).[22] It lends drama to the fatal clash between the prince and his then foremost legal adviser a decade later, recalling that of Henry VIII (1491–1547) and Thomas More (1478–1535). Speaking of Britain, perhaps no poem among Grotius' poetry is as teeming with learning – adroitly pinched from William Camden (1551–1623) – as his long panegyric (*c.* 600 lines) on the coronation of James I/VI (1566–1625) in 1603. It includes a friendly piece of political counsel[23] that did not fare better than Grotius' notorious advice to James in 1613 that heralded Grotius' political fall from grace.[24]

Indeed, up to *Mare liberum* (1609), Grotius' European renown as a child prodigy rested precisely on his poetry and the philological treatises he produced under the aegis of his director of studies, Justus Scaliger (1540–1609).[25] Admittedly, his most ambitious projects over the years 1595–1610 addressed the domains of politics (*Parallelon rerumpublicarum, De republica emendanda)*, the law *(Philarchaeus, Sex leges damnatae, De jure praedae commentarius)* and historiography (*Annales et Historiae)*. But, then, for one reason or another, none of these treatises ever appeared in print during Grotius' lifetime; some were lost altogether. The first tracts outside the sphere of letters to make it to publication were *Mare liberum* (1609) and *De antiquitate reipublicae Batavicae* (1610), the latter being an apology of the Dutch Commonwealth and its theorem within the political cauldron of the nascent State system. Various treatises eminently convey Grotius' conceptual programme to link the Dutch confederal system ideologically to the Israelite tribes and present the Republic as the zenith of a historical process of political and cultural evolution.

14.5 The Playwright

Grotius aimed high in all domains of study; his focus on classical drama is a case in point. Discussing the genre will help us carry the above-mentioned moral and political function of poetry one step further. The rediscovery of Aristotle's *Poetica,* around 1500, inspired wide theoretical speculation – and polemics – on the primacy of genres.[26] In a world of letters dominated by the epic tradition, Aristotle claimed pride of place for tragedy. To underpin this claim, he insisted on the genre's eminent moral and political pertinence, in that it reflected on ethical dilemmas on the plane of rulers and princes, as in the Theban cycle and Oedipus plays.[27] Tragedy portrayed man at the crossroads, faced with the choice between two evils or confronted with the traumatic consequences of unintentional failure. The genre mirrored the human condition. To learn of the pangs and scruples of heads of state had a therapeutic effect on the soul.[28] Aristotle came up with a whole range of props and devices to enhance the dramatic effect of tragedy and its purifying impact.[29]

The political context and moral implications of the genre[30] appealed to humanist scholars who often served as counsel to princes and as tutors to dauphins. In their hands, the genre grew into the poetic counterpart of the *Institutio principis* and *Fürstenspiegel.* Dramas were composed as *pièces à clé,* an indirect way of censuring morals and tackling *raison d'état,* the way Senecan drama had served Imperial Rome.[31] One of Grotius' models, the Scottish playwright George Buchanan (1506–82), in his play *Jephthes,* criticised the making of rash vows and implicitly addressed the institute of oblates, celibacy and bona fides as such. In *Baptistes,* he censured the beheading of state counsels – read Thomas More.[32] Grotius' colleague, Daniel Heinsius (1580–1655), produced the play *Auriacus* (1600) on the exemplary, but tragic, life of the ideal ruler, William the Silent, Prince of Orange (1533–84),[33] then to portray its counterpart in *Herodes infanticida* (first, unpublished version 1608). In 1616, in the midst of political strife, playwright and historian Pieter Corneliszoon Hooft (1581–1647) enquired with Grotius whether or not he should conclude his political history play, *Baeto* (1617, on the mythical founder of the Batavian nation), with the chieftain's elevation on the shield – in contemporary terms: to have Maurice of Orange invested with the principate.[34] Grotius' three tragedies (*Adamus exul, Christus patiens, Sophompaneas* on Joseph in Egypt) link biblical themes to socio-political topicality and moral dilemma.

14.6 *Adamus Exul* (1601)

Grotius' first drama, *Adamus exul,* on the Fall, was produced at a juncture when polemics on predestination, free will and the Lord's grace – nothing new in Church history – escalated among orthodox Leiden professors of divinity to increasingly stir up social unrest.[35] Whether or not the drama inspired John Milton (1608–74), it bears witness to Grotius' in-depth knowledge of natural law, physics and metaphysics, astrology and ethics. We will leave this aside, and exclusively focus on the play's social pertinence and Grotius' typology of Adam and Eve in their blessed state of innocence as the sole owners of the world (*Adamus exul* 74–9). Grotius presents the couple placed between virtue and vice (85–9). Satan typifies Adam as unaware of sin, his step guided by his free will – and precisely this faculty he seeks to exploit (176–81) in Adam's fickle and self-indulgent partner, the female (192–6). The choir, the moral yardstick in classical drama, falls in with the above evaluation: man is positioned at the crossroads (305–8). He is blessed in that he joins reason to the worship of God (332–5), unlike the rest of creation that lacks intellect, speech, religion or the soul that directs man's senses (350–5). Precisely on account of his soul and reason, man can be said to be born 'in the image of God': human reason is the impression of the divine mind and testimony to man's participation in the eternal law (68–9).[36] An angel emphatically confirms Adam's perception of God's nature as the alpha and omega of all good (392) and of His infallible loving care for the world;[37] the human will serves God's will of its own accord (406–10). Eve muses on the social appetite of man: happiness rests on partnership and sharing (649–55 and 682–4).

Satan's ruse is intentionally aimed at fraud and *mala fides* (862–3). Adam firmly holds him at bay, scolding Satan's rebellion and perfidy (878–9). He and Satan are like lamb and wolf: worlds apart (898–9). Satan then assails Eve along three lines: first, with an appeal to preordained fate and God's eternal and immutable law: a mere bite cannot possibly change this status (1074–80). Second, with reference to God's obvious insincerity. At variance with His promise, God has not offered man the world unconditionally, making reservations for tree and apple. He might reclaim more any day, until at last His so-called gift will be nullified altogether (1122–4). Were God's generosity consistent, creation should never be modified (1125–6). Better for man not to exist at all than to serve as slave at the whim of a tyrant (1137–8). Third and most clever, Satan appeals to Eve's ignorance of good and evil. As he argues, it was from sheer envy that God withheld man this vital knowledge (1129–31), the very prerequisite to the search for truth, man's ultimate fulfilment (1171–8): Eve would do best to anticipate God's deceit (1210).

Struggling to balance obeisance with her innate curiosity and inner desire – 'Why did I receive longing after all?' – Eve takes the bite (1223–4). Confronted by Adam, she owns up that God's prohibition made the apple appeal to her (1345–6). The incident addresses the core of the human dilemma in Grotius' concept: the conflict of will and intellect turns free will into the source of evil.[38] Eve ironically implores Adam not to condemn her too rashly (1363–5) and invokes the sanctity of their marriage bond (1395). Adam gets confused, can't make up his mind – and actually deplores his free will: if only others could choose for him (1442–7)! But, then, what was the loss of a mere apple to God? Shouldn't the marriage bond prevail (1456–60)?

In the aftermath of sin, Adam is a total wreck; he is barely kept from suicide and making the human species extinct (1771). Eve, on her part, remains on top of affairs and, time and again, implores Adam to let common sense prevail (1612–18, II. 1756–60). Adam gives in (1811–12), then, denounced by God, devolves guilt onto Eve (1865). She brazenly confronts God: wasn't He the one who created the serpent in the first place, against whose ruse a guileless woman stood no chance (1871)? Having read the verdict, merciful God reassures the pair that He will leave in their minds a spark of the former light, a foreboding of salvation to come (1903–11),[39] then dismisses the couple, thus to prevent them from stealing the apple from that other tree that would secure them longevity. To forestall their return, He puts Eden on fire (2005 ff.). If Grotius is to be believed, the first man was a lawyer. More to the point, at eighteen, Grotius had already given ample thought to a number of pertinent issues in the social debate that, within two decades, would tear the nation apart. Indeed, *Adamus exul* reaches well beyond the above dilemmas to also include Grotius' position on such quintessential issues as eternal and natural law, virtue and truth, will and intellect, promise and *fides*.

14.7 *Christus Patiens* (1608)

Grotius' second drama appeared at one of the most critical junctures in Dutch history. By 1608, the Dutch Revolt had reached a military deadlock, with the Dutch East India Company (VOC) balancing on the verge of bankruptcy. Being the Company's foremost legal counsel, Grotius was involved in diplomacy on two fronts, to sound a merger of the English and Dutch East India Companies and to prevent the launch of a competing India Company in France. He had just entered his public office as advocate-fiscal (1607), was putting the last hand to *Mare liberum* and was about to get married. *Christus patiens* appeared in the midst of protracted peace talks between the war-weary parties in Madrid, Brussels and The Hague. Negotiations involved the domains of politics, religion and economy; they hinged on sovereignty, toleration and the trade with the Indies. The deadlock was never solved; negotiations ended in procrastination: the Twelve Years Truce of 9 April 1609. It proved a fatal miscalculation; soon conflict turned inwards into the Remonstrant troubles that wrecked Grotius' career.

Adamus exul had been dedicated to the French Dauphin; *Christus patiens* was dedicated to Pierre Jeannin (1540–1623), the French diplomat who played a prominent role as mediator in the recalcitrant negotiations. It was a political statement in itself; the French mediation was not uncontroversial. In his *Lectori*, Grotius highlighted the religious overtones of the drama that, as he argued, touched upon the quintessence of the Christian creed that allowed for no ambiguity. Christ's Gospel of Love preached conciliation among all denominations. Truth be told, this lofty goal Grotius definitely meant to reach on his own political terms. In his portrayal of Pharisees and Sadducees, he makes short shrift of the stern Calvinist professors of divinity, the intransigent clergy and their helpless toy, the fickle mob. Later on, he blamed the irreconcilable Jesuits and Calvinist clergy for wrecking the peace negotiations. Neither had the proud scion of a Delft regent class family much patience with the fanatic Calvinist bursar students in Leiden, sons of Flemish and Huguenot refugees mostly. The play likewise censures politicians, be this Herodes' cynicism or Pontius Pilate's raison d'état under the veil of *force majeure*.

Grotius' play has several layers. In two dramas,[40] Seneca had portrayed Hercules, the epitome of virtue and son of Zeus (out of wedlock), accomplishing the twelve labours revengeful Juno had ordered. Never satisfied, the goddess made Hercules confront Cerberus in hell, and finally struck him with insanity. In his play, Grotius unfavourably compares the fury of the hero of Stoicism who revolts against fate (*Hercules furens*) with Christ's patient endurance of his Passion (*Christus patiens*). He contrasts Hercules' Labours and Christ's Miracles, their mothers Hecuba and Maria and trusted friends Hyllus and Johannes, finally Hercules' insanity and Christ's triumph, all to underpin the superiority of the Christian dogma. Much criticised by hair-splitters at home, the innovative play was highly praised abroad, soon rendered into German and English, frequently staged and taken for a model by theoreticians. Grotius' identification with the Senecan idiom was astounding. The Latinist was as much *hors concours* as was the lawyer and barrister.

14.8 The Greek Moral Legacy

We will now turn to Grotius' years in exile and enlarge on the literary or cultural component of the comprehensive programme of social reform we alluded to in our opening paragraphs. Grotius' position in Paris was not to be envied. Courted by king and pope alike, he stuck to the Reformed faith out of principle and confident of a speedy recall home. As years went by, his status became a matter of embarrassment, his mental frame despondent. Still, already in prison, he had started a critical edition and translation into Latin verse of Stobaeus' *Dicta poetarum*, a fifth-century anthology of the *sententiae* on physics and ethics in Greek poetry that was published in 1623. The project marks his growing leaning towards the Greek intellectual and moral legacy. Three years later, the treatise was complemented by a personal selection of the gist of moral, political and legal sayings of Greek playwrights. In these *Excerpta ex tragoediis et comoediis Graecis* (1626), consistent reference is made to the edition of Stobaeus[41] to underscore the programmatic unity.[42] Fragments are ordered thematically to anticipate the book's use as *vademecum*.[43]

The two treatises proved the opening move of many years of preoccupation with Greek drama. But then, the quantity of excerpts from Aeschylus, Sophocles and Euripides in *Excerpta* is fairly unbalanced, being in the proportion of 1:2:6.[44] Its rationale bespeaks Grotius' distinct predilection for Euripides' sententious style and 'political' approach to the genre. This preference was not to be taken for granted. Daniel Heinsius, Grotius' literary counterpart, deemed Sophocles' style superior by far. Grotius did not necessarily disagree, but in the last resort matters of style were of minor concern to him. In the *Lectori* to *Excerpta* he observes that each playwright's particular virtues reflected his status and experience in life.

Aeschylus had served at Marathon, Salamis and Plataea[45] – and one hears the harsh clamour of battle reverberating in his ponderous and rugged lines. With him, one would search in vain for wordplay, wisdom or emotion. Sophocles, by comparison, had been a dignified citizen, conversant with Pericles and Thucydides. His social status was reflected in his eminently polished, elegant and melodious verse that had rightly given him the surname *The Bee*. However, the best playwright by far, Grotius opined on Aristotle's authority, was Euripides. Anaxagoras had impressed natural law on him, the sophist Prodicus refined his style, Socrates himself informed him on morals; Euripides spoke with their combined tongues. Plato himself had impeccably relied on his wise verdict: Euripides was a man of deep insight and unparalleled persuasiveness, the master of emotions and penetrating dialogue.

In short, what counted most to Grotius was an author's moral and political output. Three years earlier, in his *Lectori* to *Stobaeus*, he intimated that he had always liked Stobaeus' third book best, as it dealt with ethics. Being himself well-known to be biased towards moral poetry, he appealed to Cicero's appraisal that to him Euripides' moral sayings were veritable oracles of wisdom. Or Quintilian's verdict that he had hardly ever met anything in the philosophers that matched Euripides' wisdom – to which Clemens of Alexandria had heartily agreed. Or, as Emperor Augustus had once owned up, neither in Greek nor in Latin literature had he ever found anything of similar pertinence to his private and public life. He recommended Euripides to his servants, governors and generals alike.

As Grotius avowed in 1623, from the moment he had been called to public office, he had felt the same. As he stated, he had long felt the urge, as Cicero before him, to render the best quotes from playwrights into Latin to have them at his fingertips in the courtroom or for his philosophical writings. Rendering these texts into Latin had been his foremost comfort in the solitude of state prison ('optimum mihi solatium paravi') – until, that is, he had been deprived of writing material. Still, he had persevered and the *Excerpta* were the result.

In 1630, Grotius drew the obvious conclusion from this observation and produced an exemplary edition of what he considered the best play by the best author on the most pertinent theme, Euripides' *Phoenissae*. The appraisal is debatable, as commentators then and now will agree, but Grotius had very pertinent grounds for his verdict: *Phoenissae* is Antiquity's ultimate play on fratricide and exile. Grotius had started work on the text back in Loevestein; tellingly, he had the edition published in 1630 on the eve of his clandestine return to Holland (1631–2).[46] It was perhaps as far as he ever went to reach the hand of forgiveness to his implacable antagonists at home. Almost on a sideline, Grotius' tender Latin verse is simply the best Latin rendering ever of the Greek original. Again, his lengthy *Introductory Note* on principle stands witness to his technical expertise and the primacy he awarded the genre. Translations of three more plays, Euripides' *Supplices* and *Iphigeneia Taurica*, along with Sophocles' *Electra*, have been lost, but are amply attested to in his correspondence.[47] A corollary objective of his in all these endeavours was to preserve the Greek heritage from being lost in the maelstrom of time; the vernacular tongues rapidly overtook classical languages. To that extent, the objective of his work equalled that of Stobaeus'.

14.9 *Joseph in Egypt* (1635)

The political miscalculation of his return to Holland at the perhaps unwise invitation of befriended men of letters, such as Joost van den Vondel (1587–1679), Caspar Barlaeus (1584–1648) and Pieter Corneliszoon Hooft, who saw in him the ideal rector and law professor for the envisaged *Athenaeum Illustre* (f. 1632) in Amsterdam, forms another sad moment in Grotius' dramatic life. His stealthy flight in the dead of night, the dire straits in Hamburg, then his glorious return to Paris in the capacity of Swedish ambassador at King Gustave Adolph's (1594–1632) invitation readily suggested to biblical humanists the parallel with arch-father Joseph. Grotius took up the gauntlet and produced a play on Joseph's record as viceroy in Egypt: fratricide and exile all over again.

Sophompaneas reads like 'Trial and Retribution', teeming with political connotations.[48] The play presents Joseph the ruler as νόμος ἔμψυχος, the living law, in the *tricolon* of shepherd, husband and man of state. In this interpretation, Grotius harks back to Philo Judaeus, that exponent of Alexandrian syncretism and Stoic outlook, who, in his *De Josepho, βίος τοῦ πολιτικοῦ*, gives an essentially political turn to the Patriarch's record.[49] Highlighting the pre-Mosaic phase of Hebraism and Noah's legislation of universal, rather than exclusively Hebrew, purport, Grotius also kept true to the solemn pledge he had made to Justus Lipsius (1547–1606) back in 1601, that all his works would breathe the καθολικὸν καὶ οἰκουμενικόν.[50]

Grotius probes the truth of Joseph's rule from various angles. He has him quench revolt and curb the fickle mobs with a stern but righteous hand, then has him reform Egyptian society the way Grotius himself would have loved to reform Holland. He enlarges on Joseph's granary policies, land distribution and the concept of *lustrum*, vexed items in Grotius' day and age – and not just in Britain. As he argues in *De jure belli ac pacis*, intervention by public authorities is a beneficial instrument to prevent abuse and exploitation by private parties. Central authorities might curb the import of commodities or buy up harvests, to impose economic checks and balances.[51] In a critical move, Grotius makes Joseph, from his position of power, reach the hand of mercy to his brothers and dramatically exploits the element of ἀναγνώρισις. Awaiting their interview with the viceroy, the brothers inspect a gallery celebrating his feats, never realising they review their brother's life, then to learn the truth in a masterfully orchestrated 'interrogation at court'.

The above must suffice to illustrate one side of the medal, the prominent part ethics and politics took in Grotius' poetry. To conclude, we will summarily address the flipside, the way these findings from drama found their way into Grotius' legal tracts and overall philosophy.

14.10 Law and Literature

Lawyers have questioned Grotius' procedure to insert quotations from poets in his legal treatises. In the 1940s, it was suggested to purify *De jure belli ac pacis* from this ill-considered ballast.[52] One might perhaps give Grotius more credit for his alleged 'fallacy' that is first observed in *De jure praedae* and only gets 'worse' with every new edition of *De jure belli ac pacis*. The *Prolegomena* hands us a clue to the pertinence of his respective sources (DJBP, Prol. 46–55, esp. 46–7). In Grotius' appraisal, historical references contributed in two ways: first, by providing *examples*; second, by providing *judgments*. The authority of the *examples* depended on their times and provenance and, with Grotius, Graeco-Roman sources took obvious precedence. *Judgments* were equally relevant, the more so where they concurred. Human agreement suggested concordance with natural law[53] and the pertinence of the judgment as primary source of the law of nations. Pronouncements by poets, by comparison, while lacking the authority of objectivity, reflected human experience and added eloquence.

The *Prolegomena* from 1625 is not our only source on the issue. In his *Lectori* from 1623, Grotius amply addresses the hierarchy of sources and the status of poetry and poets. In the tracks of Epicurus, he observes,

Stobaeus divided the search for wisdom in a natural and a moral part – and justly so, as these were entirely different arenas. To ethics and as a guide to life, reason as expressed in moral treatises was of great impact. Wisdom streamlined in verse had the additional asset of being easier to pick up and memorise. This is why, in early times, precepts of wisdom were invariably put in verse.[54]

More pertinent to us, the intuitive wisdom of the poets, Grotius argues, constituted the first highlight in man's search for truth, indeed the upbeat to the next stage, the stricter tenets of philosophy. Presenting the assembled harvest of human reason, their joint findings were the counterpart to the – superior – truth of divine revelation propounded by prophets and evangelists. Whatever passed the test before the joint tribunal of reason and revelation must needs ring true. Grotius then fills well over twenty closely written pages to illustrate the point, advancing a host of instances of congruity of the wisdom of Hebrew and Christian authors with the findings of Greek playwrights, philosophers and moralists. It tellingly recalls his procedure in 1598, when, in his Socratic dialogue *Philarchaeus* (*Sacra in quibus Adamus exul,* 1604, *Lectori*), he seeks to corroborate Moses' legislation with reference to Egyptian, Phoenician orphic and Pythagorean theology or, more pertinent, the underpinning of his methodology in his great apology of Christianity, *De veritate.*[55]

In 1626, in his *Lectori* to *Excerpta,* Grotius once more raises the issue. Just like painters, he puts it here, poets drew both straight and curved lines. They reproduced their own views and those that served their characters. He hands two instances. He recalls how one day, in Athens, an actor who unduly praised financial gains was assaulted by the theatre audience. To appease the public, Euripides himself had appeared on stage, admonishing them to bide their time and see what the outcome of this character would be. On another occasion, Euripides himself faced a court order in reprimand of a notorious line in *Hippolytus*: 'Iurata lingua est, mente iuratum nihil' ('My tongue did swear this oath, not my heart').[56] As the playwright pointed out in court, the magistrate should not take offence: the line belonged to the theatre, not to the court of law. Playwrights, Grotius argues, were only human and, like philosophers, bound to fail when dealing with matters divine. Their merits shone best in the domain of ethics, not just in their clear-cut statements but no less in *obiter dicta* and so-called *rhemata.*

14.11 Citations from Playwrights

As Grotius insists in 1626, he had been conversant with classical playwrights from the days he first turned to public office. The reference may well be to 1607, when he became advocate-fiscal, as the first quotes from playwrights feature in *De jure praedae* – henceforth to explode. In *De jure praedae*, no quotations from Aeschylus are found, five from Sophocles, six from Euripides. They concern such issues as: the precedence of natural law over positive law;[57] the eternity of divine law;[58] the role of court decrees;[59] the will of states being tantamount to law;[60] the inviolability of ambassadors; burial rights;[61] the reverence due to the God-given king;[62] the slaying of public enemies;[63] the use of armed force;[64] the sparing of prisoners of war;[65] the law of prize.[66] On top of this, fifteen references to Stobaus address the concepts of (self-)justice and morals, acquisition and spoils in warfare.

By 1625, the harvest had grown considerably. *De jure belli ac pacis* contains fourteen fragments from Sophocles, twenty-seven from Sophocles and an impressive seventy-seven citations from Euripides. They cover virtually all morals in the private and public spheres and the laws of war and peace at that, as a tentative listing of major items may illustrate:

The Private Sphere:

Asylum;[67] Burial rights;[68] Exile;[69] Justice;[70] Marriage, Polygamy;[71] Oaths;[72] Parents, Rights over children;[73] Punishment;[74] Voting Rights;[75] Last Wills.[76]

The Public Sphere:

Ambassadors[77]; Law of Nations/Natural law;[78] *Droit de bris* (Wreckage);[79] Sovereignty.[80]

The Laws of War:

Declaration of War;[81] Fraud in War;[82] Hostilities;[83] Justification and Lawfulness of War;[84] Moderation in war;[85] Non-resistance;[86] Peace Treaties;[87] Prize Law;[88] Punitive War;[89] Unjust War;[90] War of Assistance to Allies, Friendly States;[91] War *vs.* Diplomacy.[92]

Many of the above issues are likewise covered in the, by then, forty-six quotes from Stobaeus' *Florilegium*. Grotius' procedure in other works is much similar.[93] Elsewhere I have elaborated on his debt to Greek playwrights in his biblical dramas.[94] Grotius' correspondence features close to twenty citations from Sophocles, well over thirty from Euripides and scores of references to *Stobaeus* and *Excerpta*. Among these adoptions are some all-time favourites of Euripides and Grotius alike, such as their reliance on

God: 'τῶν ἀδοκήτων πόρον εὗρε θέος' ('for God makes things come to pass one least expects to happen … ').[95]

A career as barrister, magistrate and diplomat, along with the lifelong, ardent study of letters, had satisfied Grotius that, in the last resort, wisdom in all provinces of life boiled down to insight into human nature and experience. This wisdom could be gained from pulpit or political arena, from classroom or court hall, but likewise in the theatre, on the authority of the intuitive judges of human morals. Lawyers and political scientists keen on analysing Grotius' social philosophy stand as much to gain from this treasure-trove as do philologists.[96]

Translations of Grotius' Work Used

The poetry of Hugo Grotius; Original Poetry/Dichtwerken van Hugo Grotius; Oorspronkelijke Dichtwerken; successive eds. B.L. Meulenbroek, A. Eyffinger and E. Rabbie (9 vols.; Assen 1971–92)

Further Reading

Bloemendal, J., and H. Norland (eds.), *Neo-Latin Drama in Early Modern Europe* (Drama and Theatre in Early Modern Europe 3; Leiden, 2013).

Bloemendal, J., and N. Smith (eds.), *Politics and Aesthetics in European Baroque and Classicism Theory* (Leiden, 2016).

Ford, P., and A. Taylor (eds.), *The Early Modern Cultures of Neo-Latin Drama* (Leuven, 2013).

Van Oosterhout, M., *Hugo Grotius' Occasional Poetry (1609–1645* (Nijmegen, unpublished dissertation, 2009).

Parente, J.A., *Religious Drama and the Humanist Tradition. Christian Theatre in Germany and the Netherlands 1500–1680* (Leiden, 1987).

Notes

1 *De studiis instituendis* (1626) was reproduced in R.S. Reeves, 'Grotius on the training of an ambassador', in *American Journal of International Law* 23 (1929) 619–25.

2 'Philosophia moralis et civilis'. Grotius suggested the *Nicomachean Ethics*, the schools of Academy, Stoa and Epicureans, Epictetus and Theophrastus.

3 Grotius' being appalled at the pettiness and lack of culture of colleagues at the bar in The Hague is well-documented; 1 BW 44, 21 July 1603. His move from the literary coterie in Leiden came as a rude awakening.

4 Grotius held that Bodin first linked the law to history. Cf. G. Budé, *Annotationes in XXIV. libros Pandectarum* (Lyon, 1551), 545–9; S. Gentilis, *Parerga ad Pandectas* (Francfurt,1588).

5 'Sources of tolerance', in *University of Pennsylvania Law Review* 79 (1930), 1–14.

6 V. Lowe and M. Fitzmaurice (eds.), *Fifty Years of the International Court of Justice: Essays in Honour of Sir Robert Jennings* (Cambridge, 1996), xv. Sir Robert Jennings (1913–2004) was Whewell Professor of International Law (1955–82) and Judge (1982–95) and President (1991–4) of the International Court of Justice. I have enlarged on these issues in *The Early Modern Cultures of Neo-Latin Drama* (2013); see Further Reading.

7 *The Common Law* (1881) 1.

8 R. Cardozo, *The Nature of the Judicial Process* (New Haven, 1921).

9 *A Defense of Poetry* (1821), concluding line.

10 Cf. Aelian, *Varia Historia* 2.39 (Crete); Strabo, *Geographica* 3.1.6 (Spain).

11 Mythical bards by their lyrics reputedly upheld culture: in taming lion or tiger like Orpheus, quenching revolt like Terpander or banning plagues like Thales. The concept of the poet as *vates* is found from Landino and Gentili to Huizinga and Heidegger.

12 Plato, *Nomoi* 654A. For Plato's views on music in education *Protagoras* 326B; *Politika* 376C, 424–5; *Nomoi* 656C.

13 1 BW 341, 29 May 1614; for the context A. Eyffinger, 'Introduction', in P. Wyetzner (ed.), *Petrus Cunaeus, The Hebrew Republic* (Jerusalem and New York, 2006), xxxiii.

14 The play reads like a *cento*, but this is an accomplishment in itself.

15 Grotius consistently celebrated his birthday on Eastern; he produced a *Carmen Paschale* (1601), *In Pascha* (1606), *Pascha* (1613,) *Pascha* (1614).

16 In 1601 paraphrases on *Psalms* 51, 88, 114, 130, 137; *Luke* 1 and 6; *Matthew* 1 and 5; *Mark* 1; John 1; *Acts* 7 and 17. In 1602 on *Psalms* 82, 113, 134. In 1606 on *Jeremiah* 10, *Job* 1 and 2, in 1609 on *Jonah* 1. Concepts on *Psalms* 13, 14, 20, 117 and 150 are documented.

17 Grotius' corpus of vernacular poetry is relatively meagre; it was collected in *Nederduitsche Gedichten* (1844). Noteworthy amid prayers, religious songs and biblical paraphrases, as on the Commandments, is an interrogation on Baptism for his daughter, a dialogue between father and son on the virtue of sparing words and a Complaint about divided Christianity. It also includes *Bewijs van de Ware Godsdienst*, the basis for Grotius' majestic prose apology of Christianity in Latin, *De veritate*. In England the apology was reprinted every three years, in Latin or English, for well over two centuries.

18 Cf. *e.g.* 'Non ego doctrinae, non duro Marte probati / Roboris exemplum, sed pietatis ero', in the Preface to the *Parallelon Rerumpublicarum*, ed. J. Meerman (4 vols., The Hague, 1801–3).

19 Witness his anapests on the demise of his younger brother Francis (1604); his *Oratio Consolatoria* to his father on the occasion; or the *Silva ad Thuanum* (Paris, 1621). Famous in the public sphere was his complaint of the besieged citadel of Ostend, *Ostenda Loquitur* (1603).

20 Grotius was acutely aware of genre doctrine; he emulates with the Golden (Catullus, Tibullus, Ovid)) and Silver Latinity (Lucan, Statius, Claudian) indiscriminately.

21 See B.L. Meulenbroek (ed.), *The Poetry of Hugo Grotius* (Assen, 1971), vol. 1.2a.2, at 17–49.

22 We exemplify, first, *Genealogia Nassovii* (1599), which addresses the history of the House of Orange; in a definite political statement, William the Silent is modelled after Pompey, the hero of Roman aristocracy, in Lucan's *Pharsalia*. Next, poetry on the campaigns of Prince Maurice (1588-98), e.g. the *Maurice Epigrams* (c. 1600) that circulated abroad on history prints in four languages. Finally, *Mathematica* (1604) on the prince's scientific research and poetry on the triumph of engineering, the *Sailing Chariot* (1602).

23 *Inauguratio* 614 ll. (1603): 'Make sure, Your Majesty, that the coast opposite your coast will never be occupied by a nation that is opposed to your nation!' The plea was in vain; in 1604 James concluded the Treaty of London.

24 The reference is to the failure of Grotius' interviews with James I on the Remonstrant Troubles in the wake of his successful diplomacy at the Bilateral Conference on Fisheries in London (1613).

25 Grotius' editions of Martianus Capella's fifth-century *Satyricon* (1599), which covered astronomy and the liberal arts (*De nuptiis Philologiae et Mercurii libri duo* and the *De septem artibus liberalibus libri singulares*) was as exemplary as his *Syntagma Arateorum* (1600), a compilation of seven centuries of classical astronomy. In 1614, Grotius produced a critical edition of Lucanus' *Pharsalia*.

26 Aristotle's text prompted a host of editions, commentaries and translations of Greek playwrights, both in Latin and the vernacular. Robortello, Segni, Maggi and Vettori researched text and genre theory. Authoritative in Grotius' days was Daniel Heinsius' *De Tragica Constitutione* (1611); See *Daniel Heinsius, On Plot in Tragedy*, eds. P.R. Sellin and J.J. McManmon (San Fernando Valley State College, 1971).

27 Notably so in its display of ῥήματα (*sententiae*) and the quasi forensic altercation between protagonists, the στιχομυθία.

28 Called κάθαρσις.

29 Aristotle recommended, first, the strictest thematic unity, which was facilitated by restricting the time of action and the location of the setting. Second, with respect to structure, to gradually thicken the plot (δέσις), then work towards its dénouement (λύσις). Third, he handed means to intensify the play's therapeutic effect, as by inserting a shock-effect, e.g. the recognition (ἀναγνώρισις) of a person's true identity that entailed a complete overhaul of perspective (περιπέτεια).

30 Tragedy was the *imitatio actionum humanarum*, the reflection of true life.

31 Tacitus, Dialogus de Oratoribus 2.10 on the political impact of plays in Imperial Rome.

32 P.J. Ford, *George Buchanan, Prince of Poets* (Aberdeen, 1982).

33 J. Bloemendal (ed.), *Daniel Heinsius: Auriacus, sive Libertas Saucia* (1602) (2 vols., Voorthuizen, 1997).

34 I BW 476, 23 September 1616.

35 In February 1602 the drama was staged in France in honour of its dedicatee, Prince Henri de Bourbon, heir presumptive to the throne.

36 On the wider context of the concept in Grotius' writings see J.E. Nijman, 'Grotius' Imago Dei Anthropology: Grounding Ius Naturae et Gentium', in M. Koskenniemi, M. Garcia-Salmones Rovira and P Amorosa (eds.), *International Law and Religion: Historical and Contemporary Perspectives* (Oxford, 2017), 87–110.

37 An interesting observation in the context of DJBP, Prol. 11.

38 As Grotius puts it in DJBP 1.1 and 1.10, action can be prompted either by the will or the intellect, virtuous action only by the latter.

39 DJBP 2.9 and Regula II; DJBP 1.1.10.1; the same image in Lipsius' *Politica* (1589) and Junius' *Protoktisia* (1603).

40 *Hercules Oetaeus* and *Hercules Furens*.

41 Witness his *Lectori* to *Excerpta*: 'Volo enim hanc nostram collectionem illius Stobaeanae quasi supplementum quoddam esse.'

42 In his correspondence, Grotius often refers to a third stage of his project, the *Anthologia Graeca*, a massive collection of epigrams (first ed. 1494). Grotius' edition was only published posthumously, H. de Bosch (ed.) (4 vols., Utrecht 1795–1822).

43 In striking parallel with Lipsius' *Politica* (1589) or Grotius' own *De Fato* (1648).

44 Fragments from Aeschylus cover pp. 2–57; Sophocles pp. 58–153; Euripides pp. 154–435.

45 Major incidents in the wars between the Greeks and the Persian Empire, in 490, 480 and 479 BCE respectively.

46 See Grotius' *Prolegomena* to *Euripides Tragoedia Phoenissae* (1630), dedicatory letter to the French politician Henri de Mesmes; reprinted in 4 BW 1509, 1 June 1630.

47 A. Eyffinger (ed.), *Inventory of the Poetry of Hugo Grotius* (Assen 1982), 'Introduction'.

48 A. Eyffinger (ed.), *The Poetry of Hugo Grotius: Original Poetry* (Assen 1992), 1. 4 A/B (*Sophompaneas*).

49 A. Eyffinger, 'The Fourth Man, Stoic Tradition in Grotian Drama', in H.W. Blom and L.C. Winkel (eds.), *Grotius and the Stoa* (Assen, 2004), 117–56, at 130–3.

50 1 BW 25, 1 January 1601.

51 In DJBP 2.2.2.4. Grotius discusses granary policies, a very sensitive topic at the time, witness e.g. D. Graswinckel, *Placaet-Boeck op 't Stuck van de Lijftocht: graanpolitiek* (Leiden, 1651).

52 At the instigation of the expert Leiden scholar B.M. Telders (1903–45) and resulting in the 'Extract' edition of DJBP, ed. Barents and Douma, The Hague 1948; for Telders' argument see *Grotiana* 8 (1940) 30–40: 'Pour qu'on lise Grotius'.

53 As Grotius had suggested in DJBP Prol. 40.

54 Cf. Aelian *Varia Historia* 2.39 (Crete); Strabo, *Geographica*. 3.1.6 (Spain).

55 Cf. J.P. Heering, *Hugo Grotius as Apologist for the Christian Religion* (Studies in the History of Christian Thought 111 (Leiden, 2004), ch. 4, notably at 83ff.

56 Euripides *Hippolytus* 612. Grotius records the line in DJBP 2.13.2.1.

57 Sophocles *Antigone* 454–5.

58 Sophocles *Antigone* 456–7.

59 Euripides *Heraclides* 142–3, with respect to Grotius' Law XII.

60 Sophocles *Ajax* 666–8.

61 Euripides *Phoenissae* 296.

62 Sophocles *Ajax* 1356–7; Euripides *Phoenissae* 296 and 393.

63 Euripides *Ion* 1334.

64 Euripides *Supplices* 347.

65 The reference in DJPC 8, 49 to Euripides *Heraclides* 1009 seems spurious.

66 Euripides *Rhesus* 181–3.

67 Sophocles *Oedipus in Colonus* 462, 512, 558, 904–9; Euripides *Heraclides* 330–2.

68 Sophocles *Ajax* 1110–14, 1346–9; *Antigone* passim; Euripides *Alcestis* 365–72; *Hippolytus* 393; *Supplices* 373–80, 523–42, 563.

69 Euripides *Heraclides* 181–202.

70 Euripides *Erechtheus* 44; *Helena* 905–24; *Phoenissae* 68.

71 Euripides *Alcestis* 305; *Andromache* 170–80 and 214–22.

72 Aeschylus *Agamemnon* 1070; *Supplices* 124; *Oedipus in Colonus* 645–51; Euripides *Hippolytus* 612.

73 Aeschylus *Fragments* 34; Euripides *Andromache* 987.

74 Euripides *Iphigenia in Aulis* 375; *Orestes* 491–506.

75 Euripides *Electra* 1267–9; *Iphigenia* 1470.

76 Sophocles *Trachiniae* 1157–78; Euripides *Alcestis* 280–325; *Andromache* 418.

77 Euripides Fragments 317.

78 Euripides *Phoenissae* 497–502.

79 Euripides *Helena* 456.

80 Aeschylus Fragments from *Suppliants, Persae, Prometheus*; Sophocles *Antigone* 734–45; Euripides *Heracles Furens* 26–35; *Ion* 69–74 and 578.

81 Euripides *Supplices* 381–94.

82 Aeschylus *Prometheus* passim; Sophocles *Philoctetes* 84–96 and 108–11; Fragment from *Creusa*; Euripides *Hecuba*. 251–5; *Rhesus* 510–20.

83 Sophocles *Oedipus* 139; Euripides *Ion* 1334; Fragments 429.

84 Sophocles *Trachiniae* 274–80; Euripides *Orestes* 507–19; Fragments 390.

85 Aeschylus Fragment from *Persae*; Euripides *Heraclides* 961–6; *Supplices* 873–80; *Troades* 95–7.

86 Aeschylus *Trachiniae*; Sophocles *Ajax* 677; Euripides *Cyclops* 120; *Phoenissae* 396.

87 Euripides *Heraclides* 804; *Phoenissae* passim.

88 Euripides *Troades* 28–39.

89 Euripides *Supplices* 334–58.

90 Euripides *Iphigenia in Aulis* 1384–1402.

91 Euripides *Heraclides* 135; *Supplices* 253, 623.

92 Euripides *Helena* 734–43; *Iphigenia in Aulis* 1014–23; *Phoenissae* 515–25; *Supplices* 473–93.

93 Thus, Grotius' irenical tract *Meletius* (1611) contains quotations from Aeschylus on the nature of God (Aesch. *Frgm. Nauck* 145 = Stob. 10), from Sophocles on religious ceremony (Soph. *Frgm. Nauck* 753 = Stob. 26) and from Euripides on the sanctity of matrimony (*Andromache* 177), a major theme throughout Grotius' works and recurrent in his three plays.

94 Notably in *Sophompaneas* (1635); *Poetry*, 1.4; 'The Fourth Man' 154–6.

95 The concluding line of the chorus in *Alcestis* 1162; also *Andromache* 1287, *Bacchae* 1391, *Helena* 1691, *Medea* 1418. The line is met thrice in Grotius' correspondence: 8 BW p. 665; 10 BW p. 106; 11 BW p. 204. Other favourite *passus* stem from Euripides' *Supplices* and *Phoenissae* and from Sophocles' *Ajax* and *Antigone*.

96 Passages were invoked by Grotius in successive stages of his career; they reveal variant readings and ever more accomplished Latin renderings.

Jan Waszink

15.1 Introduction

Although Grotius' historiographical activity spanned most of his lifetime, his true historical works occupy a less prominent place in his published oeuvre: only the relatively short treatise *De Antiquitate reipublicae Batavicae* of 1610 has attracted wider attention in the scholarship, as the *Annales et Historiaede rebus Belgicis* has done to a degree. As a result, Grotius the historian is a much less prominent figure in the general perception today than Grotius the lawyer or Grotius the advocate for Christian unity. Other historical works published during Grotius' lifetime are less studied, such as *Grollae obsidio* on the siege of Groenlo of 1629[1] and the treatise *De origine gentium Americanarum* of 1642. Although the *Parallelon rerumpublicarum*[2] of c. 1600 has not even survived in full and may never have been intended for printed publication, the *Annales et Historiae de rebus Belgicis* on the Dutch Revolt and the *Historia Gotthorum*[3] were ready for publication at any time, but were left in manuscript form at their author's death. The *Annales et Historiae de rebus Belgicis* is arguably Grotius' main historical work and, while he was preparing it for publication in the 1630s[4] as part of a collection of his own most important works, he expressed the expectation that it would bring him lasting fame with posterity.[5] In most of Grotius' other main works, historical sections, approaches or methods figure prominently, ranging from the important historical chapters in *De jure praedae commentarius* (1604–6) to the advanced use of classical and biblical history in *De jure belli ac pacis* (1625) and the *Annotationes in libros Evangeliorum,* his annotations to the New Testament (1641).

It is often rightly pointed out that, throughout his oeuvre, Grotius' approach remained that of the humanist, in the sense of the 'Late humanism' of Justus Lipsius (1547–1606) and Joseph Scaliger (1540–1609), that informed the interests and approaches within the Arts faculty in the University of Leiden during Grotius' years of study there. This approach gave particular prominence to the study of history, combining it with the naturalist, or 'realist', tendencies of the time, which were also present in such varied fields as astronomy, physics, medicine – e.g. anatomy and botany – politics and law. The influence of this realism, and its manifestation as 'reason of state' in the study of history and politics, is one of the major influences on Grotius' thought – not only his scholarly thought, but also his stance in the actual politics of the province of Holland in the 1610s. In contrast to the traditional humanist historiography, with its stress on exemplarity, these late humanist writers brought a far more critical and sceptical approach from their reading of history to their consideration of politics. They rejected the idea of an inherent connection between virtue and success, thus proposing a fundamentally different and controversial view of the relationship between ethics and politics.[6] The 'secularising' tendencies – in the sense of the opposite force to confessionalisation – that can be perceived in Grotius' life and works must also be viewed in this connection. Thus, given the pivotal place of the relationships between natural law, sociability, scepticism and reason of state in the current debate on Grotius' thought as a whole, it is evident that a consideration of his historical thought must be included. Another, related, aspect of Grotius' oeuvre that the study of his historical thought brings to light is the flexibility of his political and rhetorical positions, i.e. the caveat that each of his works should be interpreted within its own discursive and historical context, as will appear below.

15.2 Two Approaches to Ethics, Law and Reason of State

A major tension within Grotius' oeuvre is that between the two approaches to reason of state that it embodies.[7] This bipolarity reflects what is perhaps the most crucial issue at stake in the methodological debates on history and politics of his time: the division between legal normativity and moral optimism on the one hand and scepticism, moral pessimism and reason of state on the other. The constitutional line of thought in *De antiquitate* expresses a legitimation, and in effect a glorification, of the Dutch Revolt, which also appears in the historical chapter 11 of the unpublished *De jure praedae* and in *Commentarius in Theses XI*.[8] A chief mark of Grotius' reasoning here is the 'constitutional optimism' that it expresses. The well-being of all is secured if the magistrates and social elites stand up to defend the rules and liberties laid down in the age-old privileges of the provinces, towns and nobility against the rulers eager for domination. Much in the spirit of Renaissance civic humanism, this is also a call to the elites in society to take their responsibilities as a ruling class seriously, submit private to common interests and avoid the dangers of *luxuria*.

This view of politics and history leaves little space for the legal and constitutional flexibility inherent in Machiavellism and reason of state thought. This rejection is combined with a patriotic rhetoric. The mental world of Lipsius' *Politica* and the *politique* reception of Niccolo Machiavelli (1469–1527) and Tacitus – which put political concerns over religious and constitutional ones – is far away from these texts; as is the 'Tacitist' scepticism regarding man's social nature and moral motivation. Also, religious policy and the religious aspect of the Dutch Revolt remain unmentioned. The Revolt is depicted as an exclusively political conflict over liberties, taxation and constitutional rights. From the perspective of Grotius' oeuvre as a whole, it seems only logical to connect these views with the rejection of 'Carneades' in the later *Prolegomena* to *De jure belli ac pacis* (DJBP Prol. 3–6) and the Grotian view of human reason and sociability.

On the other hand, however, and at precisely the same time, Grotius' *Annales et Historiae* (written between 1600 and 1612) present a sceptical and 'realist' account of politics and history, which produces a different, and distinctly unglorifying, image of the early Dutch Revolt. Here the chief sources of inspiration appear to be precisely Lipsius' political thought and his turn to Tacitism. The title, *Annales et Historiae*, is a direct and unmistakable reference to Tacitus, and indeed the work brings in the full package of reason of state thought from Tacitism as represented by Lipsius, with its sceptical and *politique* ideas about religious policy and the characteristic disenchanted picture of man's moral motivation, self-interestedness and political psychology. The literary style of the *Annales et Historiae* is a highly accomplished imitation of Tacitus' *Histories* and *Annals* on Roman society under the emperors of the first century. This style is characterised – among other things – by brevity and compression, unusual diction and grammar, *sententiae* and euphemism.[9] The resulting picture of the Dutch Revolt, at least in the *Annales*, puts the emphasis not on virtue, glory or faith on either side, but on their failure: lack of solidarity and commitment, selfishness, naivety, religious obstinacy[10] and just bad luck on the Dutch side; arrogance, rigidity and cruelty on the Spanish side; and political gambling or aloofness with the French and the English. Any sense of heroism or patriotism is conspicuously absent from these pages. This distinctly unglorifying image of the Revolt sits uneasily with the spirit of the years around 1610 when the Twelve Years Truce with Spain had given *de facto* recognition to the Dutch Republic as a new state on the European political stage – precisely the sentiment expressed by Grotius himself in the simultaneously written *De antiquitate*.

15.3 Religious Policy

Throughout the *Annales et Historiae*, organised religion, whether Catholic or Protestant, is presented in a negative light, as a source of division, intransigence and chaos in society. This depiction starts early in Book 1:

[In the middle ages] the bishops of Rome (...) established a virtual dominion over religion, with overall control for themselves, cardinals as associates, and thence a long series of connected authorities. (...) These Romans made everything religious their province, issued new decrees, ruled anew on established matters, took Scripture from the hands of the common people, declaring it pernicious if untaught curiosity should form judgments about the most important matter of all. Thus it was easy to arrange everything for their own authority and profit; and priestly license descended to such a degree of vice that they themselves admitted the need for remedies. (AHRB *Annales* 1.22)

And, although originally the Reformation might have brought improvement,[11] these promises were never lived up to:

Not much different from [Lutheranism] was another doctrine, distinguished by Zwingly's talent and that of Calvin, which would have united with that of Augsburg a long time ago if in religious matters it weren't an established fact that everything leans more to stubbornness than concord. (AHRB *Annales* 1.55)

This view of organised religion is complemented by a conception of religious policy as a political tool that governments employ for secular purposes, depending entirely on political circumstances. Grotius thus follows again the lines set out by Lipsius in the *Politica* of 1589. That this perception extends beyond the pages of the *Annales* is shown by the policy principles formulated in the Amsterdam oration of 1616 about the religious troubles in the Dutch Republic, where the very same logic is turned into political counsel.[12]

In the *Annales,* Philip II's (1527–98) refusal of any compromise regarding Catholic faith is depicted not as religious zeal, but as a tactical error that hardened the resistance against his rule and legitimised it in the eyes of his subjects. Moreover, Grotius presents Philip in a Machiavellian light by presenting his submission to the pope as disingenuous and determined by political opportunism:

As the real reason [behind his religious policies] it can be conjectured that Philip had decided to let the pope's authority work for him in many matters. (. . .) Now Philip had turned the Pope into his instrument by showing docility, and the most trusted people around him by largesse; and this seemed to provide abundant warranty and pretext. (AHRB *Annales* 1.31)

Nevertheless, Grotius makes an even stronger claim of Machiavellian behaviour by the greatest hero of the Dutch Revolt, William of Orange (1533–84). He writes that, during the Cologne peace negotiations of 1579, Orange feigned a zeal for Protestantism as a cover for his own political purposes:

(. . .) the Emperor, to whom as we said the attempt to arrange peace was entrusted, had sent delegates to Cologne. [. . .] Orange however, who had never doubted that any peace with the King would result in danger to him, since the Low Countries were then divided and he himself was right in the middle between all these parties, and was therefore hated, feared not without reason that he would be surrendered to foreign and domestic enemies alike. On the other hand, to turn away from the negotiations and the German referees was difficult and damaging to his reputation. More in the dark, to achieve the same, he made sure the religious issue would be insisted upon, and other things which no one expected the King to agree with. (AHRB *Annales* 3.25)[13]

Grotius makes a comparable claim regarding Queen Elizabeth (1533–1603) in 1585:

But the wise woman foresaw the accusation of having pilfered someone else's dominion: and avoided the involvement of her own fame and fortune by such a close tie in doubtful circumstances. It seemed wiser to have secret bases of support spread over the Low Countries, [. . .]. However, she promised help, [. . .]. At the same time, she pretended to act for the sake of religion, the security of which she demonstrated, by referring to the events in France and Scotland, to be entrusted to her without any desire for another one's possessions. (AHRB *Annales* 5.7)

Grotius thus shows himself unafraid of introducing flavours of reason of state and outright Machiavellism into his analysis of the Revolt and its politics.

15.4 Divine Providence in Grotius' View of History

Grotius' position on the question whether there is divine supervision over human historical events varies according to the genre he is writing in. Here, poetic and rhetorical levels must be distinguished from philosophical and historical ones. In his poetry, the notion of divine supervision is freely admitted in the text, for example in his *Induciae Batavicae* on the Twelve Years Truce (1609–21).[14] On the wings of literary imagination, and often of an elegiac tone, God or a personification of Faith can be given a direct role in the mechanics of history. This mode of speaking is perfectly comparable with that in contemporary poetic reflections of the Revolt, such as for example the various tragedies on William the Silent[15] or the Virgilian epos on his exploits by Georgius Benedicti Werteloo.[16] It is not evident, however, that such literary tropes represent Grotius' actual historical thinking.

Similarly, the highly rhetorical dedication in *De antiquitate* presents the hardships of the Revolt as a deliberate trial by God of a nation that He has destined for glory.[17] Although this seems to be largely rhetorical in nature and purpose, one might argue that the statement could also, and at the same time, express a deeper-seated faith in God's ultimate intentions for His creation; evidently Grotius was not an irreligious person. On the other hand, *De antiquitate* contains no other references to a divine plan or influence, or any other connection between Providence and the Revolt that takes this connection to a level firmly beyond the rhetorical.

The work in which we should expect to find Grotius' most fundamental thinking on the philosophical aspects of history and historiography is the *Annales et Historiae*.[18] In this work, references to a divine influence can be found only at a few places, such as the following one on God's help towards the lifting of the siege of Leiden:

[This siege] brought everything into peril, as the Spanish had taken hold of the heart of Holland, and there was no force to resist them except God's help and a stubborn hatred of the faithless tyranny (...) (AHRB *Annales* 2.53)[19]

Apart, however, from conventional phrases like these, the idea of a divine supervision of events is hardly ever brought into the narrative. The role of a divine will or providence in history remains very limited, and where it appears in less commonplace phrasings, their purpose seems rather to complicate or deny the idea of a divine 'agenda' behind the events than to assert it.[20] This is exemplified by the following passage on the events right before the capture of the town of Den Briel in 1572 by the unruly 'Sea-Beggars' – a chance event that would re-launch the war and consequently acquired a status as one of the founding moments of the Republic:

At that point in time however the Almighty's Providence decided to employ this lot as her helpers: in the history of the Low Countries war it has pleased her almost invariably to deceive human planning and confidence in such a way that great hopes and a happy outcome were never together in the same place. (AHRB *Annales* 2.25)

A comparable passage that marks the transition between the *Annales* and the *Historiae* at the very beginning of the latter part of the work plays with a cosmic perspective on events:

The fifteen hundred and eighty-eighth year to Christ's name was on its course down, foresaid by the astrological calculators to become the last year of humankind –whether accessing the future be a futile skill, and one that doesn't reach beyond our credulity; or that prediction an error from human miscalculation of Fate's magnitude, and part of Heavens' threats a colossal fleet: which the Spanish, from great hopes as much as from great anger, now that there was peace both with France and the Turks, hastened to completion, equipped with arms against themselves. (AHRB *Historiae* 1.1)

This sentence introduces the spectacular story of the Spanish Armada. The location of the Netherlands struggle in a cosmic perspective is deliberately tragic and religious in tone and its emplacement at the central hinge point of the work suggests quite definitely that the idea of presenting the Revolt's history in this kind of perspective has indeed occurred to Grotius. But only the idea: for the passage actually mocks those who regard human religion and knowledge as a basis for reliable knowledge of the Creator's will and plans. This connects the sentence with the previous quoted passage, and indicates that Grotius is, in fact, resisting such religious interpretations of the Revolt. This squares entirely with the Tacitean, secular interpretation of politics, and the sceptical element in that strand of thought. And, in turn, this *realpolitische* reading of the Revolt squares with his *Staatsgezinde* parti-pris in the political and intellectual controversies of the Truce and beyond.

15.5 Grotius' Ideal of the Statesman-Historian

In the *Annales et Historiae*, the scholarly and political concerns in the tense period of the Truce intertwine in a striking and intense manner. Grotius attempted to employ his knowledge of literature, especially that of Tacitus, the *magister in politicis*,[21] to exert a conciliatory influence on the quarrels in the Republic by demonstrating what he saw as the true character of the Revolt. The problem of consolidating the government's position in a context of increasing opposition occupied Grotius' thought intensely. His attempt to help restore concord and unity was first and foremost a scholarly endeavour and characterises the world of thought that had produced him. In the *Annales et Historiae*, Grotius presents himself as a political insider and historian at the same time, who hopes to build bridges between the warring factions by presenting the truth of a solid historical analysis of the Revolt.[22]

Remarks on the project of the *Annales et Historiae* in Grotius' correspondence inform us about his views of the historian's role in politics, which appears to be something very specific.[23] First, a remark on the selection of facts to be presented refers to an important dichotomy in historiography as seen by the humanists: that between mere narrations of facts, chronicles – the 'lower' form of historiography – and the 'higher' historiography that is based on it, i.e. the historiography that produces narratives with a literary and philosophical flavour, in which moral judgments are passed, praise and blame are meted out, and insight is granted into the deeper truths of history. Thus, the selection and combination of the available material, the development of historical explanations and vision, and the phrasing of the Revolt's story in Tacitus' style, which presupposes a certain judgment and 'insight', belong to the higher historian's task.

When discussing the usefulness (*fructus*) of the *Annales et Historiae*, Grotius makes a direct connection between the Leicester period (1585–7) and the Truce controversies. In a 1614 letter to one of his informers, Jean Hotman de Villiers (1552–1636), who had been Leicester's secretary in the

Low Countries, Grotius emphasises the usefulness of Hotman's material in the present circumstances; it appears that, in his view, he might serve the public peace and the *Staatsgezinde* cause alike by spreading his interpretation of the Revolt (1BW 389).

During the years in which he wrote the *Annales et Historiae*, Grotius communicated his thoughts on historiography in letters to people such as the Heidelberg councillor, Georg Lingelsheim (ca. 1557–1636), and the great French politician and historian, Jacques-Auguste de Thou (1553–1617). These letters indicate that it was Grotius' ambition to become a statesman-and-contemporary historian after the ideal image he cherished of De Thou.[24] However, Grotius takes the traditional humanist uses of history[25] a significant step further. The classical *topos* held that an Achilles needs a Homer in order to secure his fame with posterity. When Grotius, pensionary of Rotterdam and a member of the States of Holland, writes to De Thou that he wants to help overcome the Truce controversies by means of his historical writings, Achilles (the statesman) and Homer (the historian) merge into one and the same person. His inside knowledge of the actual events and their backgrounds, combined with his insight into the true motives and causations, inform and define not only his historical work, but also steer the events themselves. The choice of Tacitus' political and psychological *acumen* as his model works both on the political stage and in the historical work. Thus, in this ideal, the Tacitean statesman-historian occupies a pivotal place in politics and society: through his person and work, the events and contemporary historiography influence each other. For Grotius, historiography is no longer merely a related activity for the educated councillor, with or without political implications, but a direct instrument of government for rulers.[26]

To Grotius, his older contemporary De Thou came close to this ideal. It is clear from their correspondence that, at the time, Grotius aspired to become such a statesman-historian himself. He repeatedly compares himself to De Thou and complains about his own uneducated compatriots.[27] This bold ideal is characteristic of the high ambitions and expectations that Grotius fostered in his 'Holland years'. Tacitean *acumen* belongs to the core of his ambitions on *both* the political and the historiographical level.

From the late seventeenth to the early nineteenth century, the *Annales et Historiae* enjoyed a solid reputation as historiographical work. Eighteenth-century historians valued Grotius' impartiality and his Tacitean judgment regarding the true causes and motives of events.[28] The turning point seems to come with the great Dutch historian, Robert Fruin (1823–99), who wrote extensively on Grotius, but very little on the *Annales et Historiae* or any other of Grotius' historical works. Fruin's judgment on Grotius as a historian shows that he saw him primarily as a humanist, that is, a literary, scholar, who produced a literary rendition of a period of history, rather than a critical historical investigation in the sense that the term had for Fruin, who was an admirer of the 'historical positivism' of Leopold von Ranke (1795–1886).[29] Given Fruin's influence, his judgment has undoubtedly contributed to the relative obscurity of the *Annales et Historiae* since the nineteenth century, in addition to the fact that – near the end of that century – Grotius was 'canonised' as foundational thinker of the then-emerging international law. This development put his juridical oeuvre at the foreground and made the author primarily a jurist in the public perception.

15.6 Historical Approaches in *De Jure Belli ac Pacis* (1625) and the *Annationes in Libros Evangeliorum* (1641)

In these works, Grotius brings in historical issues and perspectives on virtually every page. With respect to his historiographical aims, his concerns are those of the 'cultural historian' in the humanist sense of the word. He employs ancient circumstances and cultural, religious or legal practices to explain classical or biblical texts and languages. Grotius is less occupied with the identification of specific items of geography or chronology in the way Antiquarian scholars of his age were.

Dating from the later period of his life, *De jure belli ac pacis* and the *Annotationes* display many similarities on the level of method and approach, and legal and theological thought appear to overlap in many places. The opening page of the *Annotationes*, for example – addressing the Greek title, Ἡ καινὴ διαθήκη, The New Testament – is an exposition of the basic theory of legal obligations, whereas – conversely – chapters 1.1–2 of *De jure belli ac pacis* are to a large extent a theological enquiry into the legitimacy of war as such.

The historical aspect of Grotius' work on the New Testament is among its most important characteristics. In his 1983 study on Grotius as an interpreter of the New Testament, Henk-Jan de Jonge labels Grotius the most successful of the seventeenth-century commentators on the New

Testament because of precisely this contextual, historicising approach. According to De Jonge, Grotius:

endeavoured to understand the books of the New Testament as a product of the time when they were written; to this end he tested and revised traditional ideas on their genesis by the application of other known historical data." By contrast, other 17th-century exegetes tried only "to use the ancient texts to underpin a modern dogmatic system and to counter the dogmatic systems of those of different persuasions." For De Jonge, this difference makes Grotius' *Annotationes* "indeed the most important 17th-century explanation of the New Testament and the only commentary of those times that is still regularly referred to.[30]

Significantly, Grotius' biblical exegesis does not belong to the tradition of theological exegesis, but to the tradition of philological annotation such as had been conducted since the 15th century by Christian humanists with linguistic and historical interests.[31]

For example, De Jonge points at Grotius' demonstration that 2 Peter cannot have been written by Peter the Apostle, but must stem from the time of Trajan (r. 98–117), and that 2 Thessalonians was written earlier than 1 Thessalonians. Another example is Grotius' discussion, at the opening of his notes on the Gospel of Luke, of some methodological problems with establishing the truth about the historical figure of Christ, especially that of distinguishing between the relative reliability of the various available accounts, since some of the biblical authors themselves had faced the exact same problem and dealt with it with varying degrees of success – a reasoning that also underscores the man-made nature of the Scriptural text. According to Grotius:

at the time Luke was writing there was already a considerable number of books about the deeds of Christ; obviously the weight of events had drawn many to the topic. But while several people were collecting whatever information went around, not surprisingly they mixed truths and non-truths, like the oldest author of the Egyptian Gospel did. (...) Others however, like Matthew and Mark, wrote down what they knew from observation or had heard from reliable authors; and since they were far beyond any accusation of negligence themselves, they have not closed off the possibility to add something to the fruit of their work on such a rich topic to another who might wish to do so. Add to this the fact that it is likely that at this time, Matthew's book existed only in Hebrew; while Mark, writing in Greek, wrote a summary overview of events rather than a proper history. Nevertheless I do not believe, as some do, that Luke wrote at an earlier time than Matthew and Mark (...) (*Annotationes*, 594)

15.7 History in *De Jure Belli ac Pacis*

Grotius uses a wealth of historical illustrations in *De jure belli ac pacis*. Moreover, the programmatic rejection of 'Carneades' at the very opening of the work connects it directly to late-humanist debates on moral scepticism and reason of state that arose from, and centred on, the interpretation and use of the historical record. Given the evidence adduced so far – especially the role of reason of state in the *Annales et Historiae* and in the politics of the period of the Truce – it becomes clear that this rejection is the result of a continuous development of Grotius' judgments and ideas, and that *De jure belli ac pacis* is also indebted to the tradition of reason of state-thought in several ways. We can, thus, expect to find many elements of late-humanist realism, and indeed reason of state itself, in the treatise of 1625.

First, Grotius' use of historical information is a clear case in point. His approach to history is of the 'realist' or naturalist and not the 'exemplary' type. The historical record of mankind constitutes a body of factual knowledge, a kind of raw data set from which lessons for the present can be derived, which – as for Lipsius – may provide effective rulers with an understanding of human behaviour and the nature of evil, precisely in order to combat it better. Along similar lines – and just as in the commentary on the New Testament – *De jure belli ac pacis* uses historical information and classical literature in general to observe and understand practices and ideas in the past, with a view to identifying the unchanging basic principles of the relations between human individuals and communities. The choice of ancient history and literature to fulfil this role is not only explained by Grotius' deep familiarity with this literature, but also by the fact that ancient history provided both a common cultural basis and point of reference for all European nations beyond the partialities of contemporary conflicts.

To give just one example from *De jure belli ac pacis*, Grotius writes on the question whether subjects of one prince may serve under another:

Another query is often made, whether it be all one, if subjects take up arms, not by themselves, but fight under others engaged in war. The Cerites in Livy clear themselves, by saying, their subjects took up arms without any publick Order. The same was the defence of the Rhodians. And indeed the best founded opinion is, that such a thing ought not to be deemed permitted, unless there are apparent reasons for believing that there was an intention to permit it; as we see now that is sometimes practiced, in Imitation of the old Aetolians, who accounted it lawful, "to plunder the plunderer" (Gellius). (DJBP 3.20.31)

Regardless of its origins in the sceptical spheres of late humanism, this use of history as a neutral, non-exemplary dataset on human behaviour remains perfectly compatible with Grotius' notion of sociability in his natural law thought, and the normative and moral outlook of the *Prolegomena*. For the sake of a streamlined discussion, Grotius herds the entire complex of ideas from scepticism, Machiavellism and reason of state under the single common denominator of the sceptical philosopher, Carneades (214–129 BCE),[32] and then states his programmatic rejection of this straw man's view of politics and international relations (DJBP Prol. 3–6).

Nevertheless, elements of reason of state logic are not absent from *De jure belli ac pacis*. The obvious example is the pivotal role of the principle of self-interest in Grotius' natural law thought – though balanced by man's reason and sociability, which is generally understood as stemming from the very same spheres of thought that Grotius refers to by the label 'Carneades'. However, more specific examples are in evidence too, in *De jure belli ac pacis*, such as Grotius' view of the admissibility of a pre-emptive strike:

But I can by no means approve of what some authors have advanced, that by the law of nations it is permitted to take up arms to reduce the growing power of a prince or state, which if too much augmented, may possibly injure us. I grant, that in deliberating whether a war ought to be undertaken or not, that consideration may enter, not as a justifying reason, but as a motive of interest. *So that where we have any other just cause for making war, it may for this reason too be thought prudently undertaken.* And this is all that the authors before cited do in effect say; but to pretend to have a right to injure another, merely from a possibility that he may injure me, is repugnant to all the justice in the world: For such is the condition of the present life, that we can never be in perfect security. It is not in the way of force, but in the protection of Providence, and in innocent precautions, that we are to seek for relief against uncertain fear. (DJBP 2.1.17, my emphasis)

Thus, while emphatically and elaborately denying the moral and legal legitimacy of pre-emptive strike, Grotius allows space for it in practice by suggesting a 'prudently undertaken' workaround.

15.8 Grotius and the Antiquarian Tradition

The analysis of *De antiquitate* showed it to be both relevant and alien to the then-innovative antiquarian tradition of scholarship. This picture is more or less confirmed by the treatises on the American peoples that Grotius wrote towards the end of his life, *De origine gentium Americanarum* from 1641 and *De origine gentium Americanarum dissertatio altera* from 1643.[33]

The two treatises provide a fascinating, and perhaps paradoxical, opportunity to observe Grotius' basic approach and reflexes as a historian.[34] It should be noted first that the treatises are not presented as proper works of history or even scholarship. The original treatise has the format of a pamphlet; it holds a very brief and sketchy argument of just thirteen pages; its conclusions are emphatically presented as provisional (*'probabiliora'* and *'coniecturae'*) rather than definitive and scholarly. There are no notes of any kind and the work is written in a very simple and accessible Latin style, noticeably different from Grotius' usual scholarly style. The format, too, is extremely simple and sober; the pamphlet carries only author, title and year on the title page, no publisher, place, dedicatee or other information.[35] The whole looks like an intervention in a public or political debate rather than a contribution to a scholarly one – although the omission of metadata makes it very difficult for a reader to identify which parti-pris Grotius' intervention would have been supposed to serve.

In 1641, Grotius finished a draft of the treatise and requested through his network to have it 'peer-reviewed', anonymously, by Johannes de Laet (1581–1649), who was recognised as a leading specialist on the Americas. He was one of the directors of the Dutch West India Company (WIC) and author of a 'Yearly Report' on the progress of the WIC in the period from 1621 to 1636.[36] From 1619 to 1621, the passionate Counter-Remonstrant De Laet sat on the Synod of Dordt, the Church council that had sealed the victory of Calvinism over the politics and theology of Grotius' States party. This might explain Grotius' move to ask for his treatise to be reviewed anonymously. De Laet made suggestions for improvements that Grotius ignored. After the publication of *De origine*, De Laet then wrote a treatise to oppose it,[37] which was answered by Grotius with the *Dissertatio altera*, to which De Laet wrote another reply. This controversy has attracted a fair deal of attention in modern scholarship.[38]

In the original *Dissertatio*, Grotius claims to be the first to raise the question of the origins of the original inhabitants of the Americas.

Characteristically, he begins by turning to classical history. Throughout the two treatises, there is a concern to harmonise and connect recent discoveries and observations from the New World with classical, biblical and medieval history and language from the Old World. This, however, does not exclude a critical approach to Scripture and the classics, but, characteristically for the humanist, there is little interest in information outside the sphere of language and literature, and indeed even Grotius' use of those sources looks haphazard and selective.

A heavy emphasis is put on the supposed Norwegian origins of the original inhabitants of North America, which is curious as Grotius was the Swedish ambassador in Paris at the time. For Central America, Grotius proposes that the inhabitants arrived from Ethiopia; and that those of South America originally came from southeast Asia via the largely hypothetical 'Southland' beyond Strait Magelhães.[39]

Following some of De Laet's own remarks, several modern authors view the controversy in terms of the 'querelle des anciens et des modernes', i.e. between – old-fashioned – humanist scholarship and – progressive – sceptical and empirical research.[40] After pointing out that the question of the origins of the inhabitants of the Americas has indeed been discussed before by the Jesuit explorer, José de Acosta (1540–1600), and observing that these peoples display enormously varied and different languages and cultures, De Laet writes 'with the result that in this case there is no place for the customary research approach using resemblances in language, character and practices'.[41] In this manner, he opens a distinction between humanist scholarship and a different type of research.

Grotius' conclusions about the origins of the inhabitants of South America illustrate the controversy in a nutshell. The fact that Grotius claims to have turned to contemporary descriptions, eye-witness accounts and maps suggests that he was aware of the dangers involved in his usual humanist approach.[42] At his time of writing, the 'Southland', or at least some outlines of it, still appeared on world maps as 'Terra Australis Incognita' or 'Magellanica'. Thus, at least, Grotius' geography was potentially plausible and founded on recent empirical documentation, as it was available when he wrote.[43] It is fascinating to note that this Southland began to disappear from the maps precisely after 1640. De Laet points out that the idea is becoming outdated since recent explorations have revealed that, beyond the islands southeast of Strait Magelhaes and the Strait of Lemaire, there seems to be just a wide sea leading into the ocean; which makes the very idea of a land connection with southeast Asia question-able.[44] In fact, this is the recurring tenor of De Laet's objections to Grotius' views: that the latter is insufficiently informed about the actual situation and the newest reports from the New World. So, although Grotius did indeed turn to contemporary and first-hand information, he was insufficiently aware of the pace at which the new knowledge was changing and expanding. One might suspect that it was this new phenomenon of *changing* facts and *developing* knowledge that he was insufficiently awake to, rather than a lack of openness to 'unclassical' sources of information.

Current scholarship has failed so far to come up with an explanation why Grotius wrote these treatises.[45] Nellen and others suppose that Grotius' aim was to show that all inhabitants of the Americas came from known territories in the Old World, in order to save the biblical worldview that all humans descended from Adam. Against Grotius' view, that of De Laet, who followed Acosta in this, would allow for the possibility of a kind of 'polygenetism'. It seems highly unlikely, however, that this was the issue at stake. First, Acosta and De Laet took the hypothesis that a migration from the Old World to the New had happened via an, as yet undiscovered, passage at the east end of the Eurasian continent as their starting point: thus, their theory in no way excluded the possibility of a common descent from Adam. Conversely, Grotius' 'Southland' hypothesis for the origins of the South Americans complicated, or even excluded, a 'monogenetic' explanation rather than supporting it. Moreover, this supposed intention with Grotius to save the literal truth of the biblical account is neither expressed in the text nor supported by his free and secularising approach to Scripture elsewhere in his oeuvre. Finally, it remains unexplained why Grotius would find a sketchy pamphlet the best format to contribute to this type of scholarly debate.

Unfortunately, Scandinavia's contemporary political map fails to provide clear answers as well. Grotius was Sweden's ambassador to France at the time, and Sweden's most important activity in the Americas was the foundation, in 1638, of a colony on the Delaware.[46] However, it is not easy to see how claiming Norwegian descent for the inhabitants of Northern America would have served Swedish interests at a time when Sweden and Denmark-Norway were regularly in and out of war. The Second Treaty of Brömsebro in 1645 awarded three Norwegian provinces to Sweden but, in so far as any territorial claims were involved at all, this occurred too late to help explain Grotius' pamphlet of 1641.

15.9 Conclusion: Grotius and the Discipline of History; an Innovator?

With respect to the historical aspect of Grotius' oeuvre, five main themes have emerged: (1) the polarity, in his historical works proper, between constitutionalism and patriotism on the one hand, and reason of state and scepticism on the other; (2) Grotius' 'secularising' reading of history; (3) the close correlation between scholarship and politics; (4) Grotius' use of sources and his relation to contemporary developments in antiquarianism; and (5) the important role of historical perspectives in his other works, such as *De jure belli ac pacis* and the *Annotationes* on the New Testament.

Although, for Grotius, history was always subservient to political ends and this led him to creative overinterpretation of sources in some cases, this does not mean he has not contributed to the discipline as such or to its methods. For him, the progress of the historical discipline lay in the movement towards secularism and realism/naturalism, not so much in the antiquarian direction. In his correspondence of the 1630s, Grotius includes the *Annales et Historiae* among his chief achievements and expresses his expectation that the work would earn him a lasting fame with posterity. The chief methodological thrust of the work is an attempt at analysis of the true logic behind human history; i.e. of the real causes, motives and effects, regardless of the demands of moral exemplarity and religious teleology. Obviously, this separation runs parallel to the rise of reason of state in politics itself and the gradual 'emancipation' of politics from the demands of ethics and religion; as Grotius' ideas on the statesman-historian show, politics and the writing of history were intimately connected activities. The belated publication of the *Annales et Historiae* in 1657, however, robbed Grotius of a good part of his actual influence on the field, for, by that time, the secular and realist view of history and politics was no longer as controversial as it had been in the period around 1610. Nevertheless, the work's quality of realist analysis ensured that it enjoyed a reputation as 'the' work on the Dutch Revolt from its publication up to some point in the eighteenth century. These conclusions apply to the *interpretation* of the historical record.

On the other hand, it is also obvious that, with respect to the *creation* of the historical record, Fruin's judgment of Grotius makes sense. Grotius' approach to his task is not that of a critical historical researcher in the 'modern' sense of the word, but that of the (late-)humanist. Although he uses a wide array of sources, these are limited to written materials: composed historical narratives – ancient, medieval and modern ones – documentary sources such as letters, diaries, treaties, decrees, laws or pamphlets, as well as etymological and linguistic evidence.[47] Grotius displays only limited interest in information outside these realms, and never really adopts the innovations of the antiquarian branch of scholarship. The antiquarian notes to *De antiquitate* were written and added, not by himself, but by Petrus Scriverius (1576–1660). The recent characterisation of the *Historia Gotthorum* as a work in the antiquarian tradition has been criticised as questionable if one takes the concern with physical objects and data as a defining mark of antiquarianism, for indeed the work indicates scant use of such information to confront the written record with. The same might be said of *De origine gentium Americanarum*, although in that work Grotius' use of new empirical evidence is less limited than some of the scholarship suggests.

15.10 Addendum: Consistency within Grotius' Oeuvre

A recurrent problem also highlighted by this historical cross-section is the internal consistency within Grotius' oeuvre.[48] A good part of the older scholarship on Grotius is built on a conception of his life and works as one continuous effort to promote justice and peace. The ongoing study of his

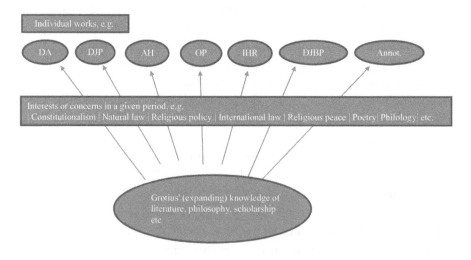

individual works, however, especially those from before 1618, has been making it progressively difficult to uphold this idea of principled consistency. In this chapter, we have seen the very different approaches to political ethics between two perfectly contemporary works, *De antiquitate* and the *Annales*.

For the interpretation of Grotius' works, this question is urgent since it concerns the question if or to what extent we can use the content of one of his works to understand that of another. On the practical level, there seems to exist a difference of approach between scholars who examine Grotius' work from a strictly 'historical' perspective, aspiring to reconstruct and understand the author's actual thought processes when he composed a given work at a given time, and those who approach the works or the oeuvre from a more 'philosophical' perspective, looking for its value for thought and debate in the present. In this approach, elements or arguments from a different work may legitimately be invoked, or perhaps even elements from another author with whom Grotius may reasonably be understood as being 'in conversation' on the given topic. But however this may be, in each case we do need some vision of the nature of the relationships between Grotius' works. Since they are all products of the same mind, they cannot be entirely disconnected from each other.

To understand these relationships, I propose the model above which consists of three levels. The basic level is Grotius' enormous knowledge, expanding over the course of his life, and built up from his reading of literature, scholarship, philosophy plus everything else such as the news facts of his time. The impetus towards the composition of the individual works is the middle level, that of the concerns or pursuits that entertained him at any given time, some of which have a permanent presence throughout his life, and some of which are more limited to particular periods. For example, the concern with constitutionalism and the legitimacy of the Dutch Revolt properly pertains to his earlier life, whereas the struggle for inter-confessional peace or even integration is a concern of his later years. The third level is that of individual works. Their content is rooted in the first level, that of Grotius' wide reading and knowledge, and informed and prompted into being by the concerns of the middle level. Many of Grotius' individual works are strongly tied to their particular, political and discursive, contexts, audiences and purposes – for example, *De antiquitate*, *De jure praedae*, *Mare liberum*, *Annales et Historiae*, *Ordinum pietas*, *Historia Gothorum*. As a result, there is no 'direct' consistency between the individual works at the third level: any coherence or overlap they may have only derives from their common basis in the first level and, in some cases, from their connections at the middle level. It follows that great circumspection is required when we use elements from one work to explain another.

One may ask whether this means that a greater degree of consistency should be expected between the works with a less direct relation with a particular interest at the time of writing – *De jure belli ac pacis*, the *Annotationes* to the New Testament, perhaps the plays and other theological works.[49] Obviously, in principle, this model could be valid for any author. A remaining question is whether or to what extent Grotius is exceptional with respect to (in) consistency within his oeuvre. In Grotius' case, this question can only be approached through collaborative and interdisciplinary efforts.

Translations of Grotius' Works Used

Annals of the War in the Low Countries, ed. J. Waszink (Bibliotheca Latinitatis Novae; Assen, forthcoming)
The Rights of War and Peace, ed. R. Tuck (Natural Law and Enlightenment Classics; Indianapolis, 2005)

Further Reading

Damon, D., D. den Hengst , M. van der Poel, J. Waszink,: 'Dossier: Tacitus and Grotius', *Grotiana* N.S. 29 (2008) and 30 (2009).
Waszink, J., 'Tacitism in Holland: Hugo Grotius' *Annales et Historiae de rebus Belgicis*', in Rhoda Schnur (ed.), *Acta Conventus Neo-Latini Bonnensis: Proceedings of the 12th International Congress of Neo-Latin Studies* (Bonn, 2003; Medieval & Renaissance Texts & Studies 315, 2006).
Waszink, J., 'Lipsius and Grotius: Tacitism', *History of European Ideas* 39 (2013) 151–68.

Notes

1 Celebrating the conquest of Groenlo by the Dutch Stadholder Frederick Henry (1584–1645) in 1627, it was written with the purpose of currying the Stadholder's favour with a view to Grotius' aspired return to Holland; see

H.J.M. Nellen, 'The significance of *Grollae Obsidio* in the development of Grotius' relations with the fatherland', *Lias* 11 (1984) 1–17; and J. Pluijm, 'Grollae Obsidio', *Grols verleden, Tijdschrift voor de historie van Groenlo en directe omgeving* (2008).

2 The *Parallelon* probably circulated in manuscript among Grotius' acquaintances, and was only published in 1801–3. It appears that, by 1605, Grotius had lost interest in having it printed, A. Eyffinger, 'Het Parallelon Rerumpublicarum van Hugo de Groot', in Z. von Martels, P. Steenbakkers and A. Vanderjagt (eds.), *Limae Labor et Mora. Opstellen voor Fokke Akkerman ter gelegenheid van zijn zeventigste verjaardag* (Leende, 2000), 127–44, at 132. The work makes a strong connection between the virtuousness of a society and its historical success; its rhetorical brilliance, however, seems to carry more weight than any attempt at serious historical investigation. Eyffinger argues that it should be read as a serious critical analysis of and warning against rising moral defects in Dutch society around 1600 resulting from the success of the Revolt, i.e. especially *luxuria* and lack of unity.

3 See L. Janssen, *Hugo Grotius, Antiquarianism and the Gothic Myth. A Critical Study of the Ideological Dimension and Methodological Foundation of the Historia Gotthorum* (1655) (Leuven, unpublished dissertation, 2016) and the forthcoming edition of Grotius' foreword to the HG in Bibliotheca Latinitatis Novae.

4 First finished in 1612, published 1657; see 'Nawoord' to Grotius, *Kroniek van de Nederlandse Oorlog. De Opstand 1559–1588*, transl. J. Waszink (Nijmegen, 2014); and the forthcoming edition of the *Annals* (see 'Translations of Grotius' Works Used').

5 See the references in note 49.

6 As expressed in the strongly sceptical opening chapter of *Politica* book 4; see J. Waszink, 'Introduction' to J. Lipsius, *Politica. Six books of Politics or Political Instruction.* ed. and transl. J. Waszink (Assen, 2004), 81, 207; Waszink, 'Lipsius and Grotius: Tacitism', *History of European Ideas* 39 (2013) 151–68; Waszink, 'Henry Savile's Tacitus and the English role on the Continent: Leicester, Hotman, Lipsius', *History of European Ideas* 42 (2016) 303–19, at 11–12.

7 See the related debate between readers of Grotius, such as Richard Tuck, who emphasise the role of self-interest in Grotius' 'system', and those who focus on Grotius' assertion of a principle of sociability; a summary of this discussion in C. Brooke, 'Grotius, Stoicism and 'Oikeiosis', *Grotiana* N.S. 29 (2008), 25–50, at 25–31.

8 See P. Borschberg, ' "Commentarius in Theses XI". Ein unveröffentlichtes Kurzwerk von Hugo Grotius', *Zeitschrift der Savigny-Stiftung für Rechtsgeschichte, Romanistische Abteilung* 109 (1992) 450–74; Borschberg, "Grotius, the social contract and political resistance. A study of the Unpublished Theses LVI' in: *IILJ Working Paper* 2006/7.

9 For further discussion see J. Waszink, 'Tacitism in Holland: Hugo Grotius' Annales et Historiae de rebus Belgicis', in Rhoda Schnur (ed.), *Acta Conventus*

Neo-Latini Bonnensis: Proceedings of the 12th International Congress of Neo-Latin Studies (Bonn, 2003) (Medieval & Renaissance Texts & Studies 315; 2006); Waszink, 'Your Tacitism or mine? Modern and early-modern conceptions of Tacitus and Tacitism', *History of European Ideas* 36 (2010), 375–85.

10 A view of Dutch society also expressed in Lipsius' (in)famous 1595 advice-letter to the Archdukes, see *Iusti Lipsi Epistolae* (ILE) vol. 8, ed. J. Delandtsheer (Brussel, 2004), no. 950102S and Waszink, intro to Lipsius, *Politica* 27–8, 127.

11 E.g. AHRB *Annales* 1.23.

12 Waszink, J., 'Lipsius and Grotius: Tacitism', *History of European Ideas* 39 (2013) 151–68, 13–4.

13 For a fuller discussion of this and the next passage, see Waszink, 'Tacitism in Holland' and Waszink, 'Lipsius & Grotius'. On the absence of sources for this claim by Grotius, see Grotius, *Kroniek*, 246–7.

14 H. Grotius, *Occasional poetry (1609–1645)* ed. M. van Oosterhout (Nijmegen, unpublished dissertation, 2009), e.g. chapter 4 on the Truce, 305 sqq, e.g. 310 r. 280 '*Adstabat Pietas*' etc.

15 See ref. in Waszink, 'Your Tacitism or Mine', 383, n. 48.

16 G.B. Werteloo, *De Krijgsdaden van Willem van Oranje*, ed. coll. class c.n. E.D.E.P.O.L. (Leiden, 1990), e.g. the allegorical *Religio* in book 1, vs. 158–238.

17 Grotius, *De Antiquitate*, Ded. § 2.

18 Whether Grotius perceives a direct divine influence on historical events partly overlaps with the question whether there is 'dramatic structuring' in the AHRB; see Waszink, 'Your Tacitism or mine', 382–4.

19 Similarly *Annals* 2.21.

20 Compare Lipsius' characterisation of Tacitus' works as serious, useful, political discussion rather than interesting stories 'which serve more to delight the reader than to instruct him' in the dedication to Maximilian in *Taciti Historiarum et Annalium libri qui exstant* (Antwerp,) 1574), also printed as *Iusti Lipsi Epistolae* 1, 74 07 00M.

21 Characterisation by Lipsius.

22 For a fuller discussion and lit. reff., see J. Waszink, 'The ideal of the Statesman-Historian. The case of Hugo Grotius' in: J. Hartman, J. Nieuwstraten en M. Reinders (eds.), *Public Offices, Personal Demands: Capability in Governance in the Seventeenth-Century Dutch Republic* (Newcastle, 2009), 101–23.

23 For Grotius's correspondence regarding the AHRB, see J. Waszink, 'Hugo Grotius' *Annales et Historiae de rebus Belgicis* from the Evidence in his Correspondence, 1604–1644', *Lias* 31–2 (2004) 249–68.

24 Waszink, 'Correspondence'; Waszink, 'Tacitism in Holland'.

25 E.g. intellectual *fructus*; the creation of *gloria* and of *exempla* to the living; guidance in political deliberations.

26 Grotius, BW 1, ep. 315 of 5 February 1614 and ep. 409 of 5 June 1615 (both to J.A. de Thou).

27 BW 1, ep. 128 (1608), 169 (1609), 409 (1615); the complaint in ep. 22 (1601).

28 E.g. Jean Leclerc and Jan Wagenaar, as well as Grotius' biographers Brandt and Cattenburgh, C. Brandt en A. van Cattenburgh, *Historie van het leven des heren Huig de Groot* [..] (Dordrecht en Amsterdam, 1732); the latter praise the AHRB extensively as a successful emulation of Tacitus and Thucydides (p. 34–5). On the reception of the AHRB see further A. Janssen, 'Grotius als Geschichtsschreiber' in: *The World of Hugo Grotius (1583–1645)* (Amsterdam, 1984), 161–78, esp. 164–7; H. Muller, *De Groots Annales et Historiae* (Utrecht, unpublished dissertation, 1919), chapter 5; Grotius, *Kroniek*, 248–52 and notes.

29 'History, as understood by Grotius, belonged to the sphere of philology; its main aspect was form, and this had to modelled on the examples from Antiquity. In-depth and extensive research, [and] critical evaluation of transmitted information was less important. This is why Grotius considered himself fit to write history, and was seen as such by others,' R. Fruin, *Verspreide Geschriften*, eds. P. Blok, P. Muller and S. Muller Fz. (The Hague, 1901), vol. 3, 405–6; see also Muller, *De Groots Annales et Historiae*, 159–61.

30 H.J. de Jonge, 'Grotius as an interpreter of the Bible, particularly the New Testament', in: R. Feenstra et al. (eds.), *Hugo Grotius: A Great European 1583–1645* (Delft, 1983), 59–65, esp. at 64 and 59; de Jonge, 'The study of the New Testament', in: *Leiden University in the seventeenth century. An exchange of learning* (Leiden, 1975), 113–29. I thank prof. De Jonge for his comments on this paragraph.

31 Ibid., 60–1. De Jonge's view has been contested recently by N. Hardy, *Criticism and Confession, the Bible in the Seventeenth Century Republic of Letters* (Oxford, 2017), esp. ch. 5. For Hardy, Grotius was as entangled in confessional controversy as other theologians of his day, only less systematic and more eclectic than orthodox Calvinist or Catholic theologians, 230–40; a point that may be true without detracting from the above-mentioned methodological merits of Grotius' work on Scripture. Hardy is right, however, in pointing out that Grotius' view of the power relation between states and churches 'was informed in large part by historical scholarship', 239–40.

32 For this reading, see e.g. A. Eyffinger and B. Vermeulen, *Hugo de Groot. Denken over Oorlog en Vrede* (Baarn, 1991), 25–7; A. Droetto, 'Il Tacitismo nella storiografia Groziana', in *Studi Groziani di Antonio Droetto*, (Torino, 1968), 101–51, at 149; and see C. Brooke, 'Grotius, Stoicism and 'Oikeiosis', *Grotiana* N.S. 29 (2008) 25–50.

33 See H.J.M. Nellen, *Hugo Grotius. A Lifelong Struggle for Peace in Church and State, 1583–1645* (Leiden, 2015), 684–90 and lit. notes there.

34 See C. Laes and T. Van Houdt, 'Over Goten Germanen en Indianen: de controverse Grotius-De Laet', *De Zeventiende Eeuw* 25 (2009) 120–36, at 125, for a similar point; they analyse the controversy from the perspective of its rhetoric, 131–36.

35 There are at least two impressions, as appears from differences in the typesetting between the digital copy at The Internet Archive (https://archive.org/details/hugonisgrotiideo00grot), and that in Leiden UL.

36 Published as *Iaerlyck Verhael van de verrichtinghen der geoctroyeerde West-Indische Compagnie* in Leiden in 1644.

37 Ioannis de Laet Antuerpiani, *Notae ad dissertationem Hugonis Grotii De Origine Gentium Americanarum: et Observationes aliquot ad meliorem indaginem difficillimae illius Quaestionis* (Amsterdam, 1643).

38 See B. Schmidt, 'Space, time, travel: Hugo de Groot, Johannes de Laet, and the advancement of geographic learning', *Lias* 25 (1998), 177–99; Van Houdt and Laes, 'Goten, Germanen, Indianen', notes for lit. reff.

39 Nellen, *Grotius*, 687–8, incorrectly simplifies Grotius' view to one that 'the peoples of the Americas (. . .) had arrived from Norway (via Greenland), parts of Africa and the Far East'.

40 Esp. Schmidt, 'Time, space, travel', 195–8; followed by Nellen, *Grotius,* 688.

41 'Quo fiebat, ut usitatae indagandi viae per linguarum aut morum institutionumque similitudinem, hic nullum haberent locum', p. A2–3.

42 See Grotius' defence of his method in the reply to the critics in the *Dissertatio altera*, 6–7.

43 See R. Shirley, *The Mapping of the World. Early Printed World Maps 1472–1700* (Holland Press Cartographica 9; London, 1983), vol. 9, 350–400.

44 De Laet, *Notae,* 59. Although on 16 he still calls the idea of a land connection with New Guinea a '*communis et versimilis opinio*'.

45 Van Houdt and Laes, 'Goten, Germanen, Indianen', 123–5; Nellen, *Grotius,* 684.

46 In cooperation with Dutch and German stakeholders, Sweden founded New Sweden on the Delaware and brought settlers to expand it in the subsequent period. After 1648 there was competition with Dutch attempts to settle in the area, which led to a Dutch takeover in 1654. The Swedish settlements however remained in place as an 'independent' Swedish nation until they came under English rule in 1681; see P.S. Craig, 'Chronology of colonial Swedes on the Delaware 1638–1713', *Swedish Colonial News* 2.5 (2001).

47 On Grotius' use of sources in the AHRB, see Grotius, *Kroniek,* 244–8.

48 This paragraph comes out of discussions at the conference *The intellectual lives of Hugo Grotius* at Princeton, 4–6 May 2018. I thank the organisers, Leo Russel and Morgens Laerke, and especially Timothy Harrison, Jane Raisch, Freya Sierhuis, Eric Nelson and Mary Nyquist for their comments on this topic.

49 In this respect, it is relevant to see Grotius' plans for publication of his main legacy. The idea comes up in May 1639, 10BW 4119 and 4132. In November 1639, 10 BW 4367, he formulates a list: the *Annotationes in Libros Evangeliorum, Anthologia Graeca, Annales et Historiae, Historia Gothorum* (none of these had been published at the time). The development of this project, to be executed by Blaeu in Amsterdam, keeps figuring in the correspondence until his death. From 1640 onwards, the discussion includes a new edition of DJBP; see Waszink, 'Correspondence', 263.

Theological Writings 16

Oliver O'Donovan

16.1 Introduction

The great controversy that sucked Hugo Grotius into its slipstream early in his career and shaped his life was a theological one. His theological stance is woven through his whole literary output, not just in the works that were designated 'theological' with the publication of his *Opera omnia Theologica* in 1679. It was a controversy about 'Calvinism', which for these purposes meant the form of Christian teaching that became normative among French-speaking Protestants in the generations after John Calvin's (1509–64) death, marked by strong doctrines of double predestination, selective atonement and the indefectibility of the elect. The term needs careful definition, since it can be used both more narrowly, of teachings directly attributable to Calvin himself, and more broadly of the wider Reformed strand in German and English-speaking Protestantism.

This intellectual wave was gaining strength in the early decades of the Dutch Revolt against Spanish rule, so that many of the French-trained pastors who assumed the running of the Dutch Church were shaped by it. The immediate problem it presented concerned the limits of doctrinal conformity: whether assent to Calvinist doctrines could be required of a Christian population or could be made a necessary condition of service in the Church's ministry. In high Christendom, which tied civil and ecclesiastical status closely together, non-conformity had serious implications for civil rights. So, Grotius upheld the view that it befell civil and not ecclesiastical government to set the limits of Christian conformity, though always subject to the law of the Church, in which civil lawyers were expected to be competent.[1] In defence of this power of civil jurisdiction, he resisted the Calvinist demands for synodical autonomy. Grotius' positions were by no means original to the circle around Jacobus Arminius (1559–1609), with which Grotius developed some sympathy. They had been commonplace in the wider German and English Reformation and had roots in the medieval theory of imperial power in Christendom. The problem that vexed the newly Protestant state, then, was the same one that had vexed the Christian late Roman Empire: if it was to exercise a quasi-theological jurisdiction partly independent of ecclesiastical authorities, by what theological norms could it be held to account? Grotius' unswerving answer was, again, the traditional one: the norms were to be found in the canons and teachings of the undivided Church of the first four centuries.

The age in which Grotius wrote theology, between the early stages of the Dutch Revolt and the Peace of Westphalia (1567–1648), was no longer, in our conventional classifications, the age of 'Reformation', but was not yet the age of 'Enlightenment'. It was an age in which much theology was written in Europe, but principally by the clergy of the various ecclesiastical factions. Grotius was unusual in writing theology as a layman. He was unusual, too, in the seamless continuity with which he blended his theology with classical studies and his work on jurisprudence and historiography. This was also an age of high learning, in which classical philology and the study of history attained new heights, when great libraries and colleges were founded, and when the observational sciences, especially astronomy and medicine, struggled out of their chrysalis. In Church and state, it was an age when the need for reform had given place to an urgent need for consolidation; the recovery of the 'catholic' – as distinct from the 'papal' – was becoming a watchword of European Protestant theology. The great fault-lines had changed, dividing rival conceptions of a re-consolidated European religion and culture. The age also saw an important growth in political theory, partly generated by the experience of colonisation. Yet, political theory was still theo-political, for the age of modern European philosophy had not yet dawned. Not long before his death, Grotius read – with distaste – Hobbes' *De cive*. In the same period of his life, he could have read, or heard discussed, Descartes' *Discourse on Method*. These were two early birds of the philosophical spring, the era of scepticism and re-foundation, which vested its justifications of the *status quo ante* on careful argument from unquestionable axioms.[2] In Grotius' generation, however, the principles of research were wholly different. Learning, not reasoning, was their foundation, gathering witnesses and testimony from every period and civilisation that could be known about. The eclectic mass of citations that accompany all of Grotius' writings was, in his contemporaries' view, the supreme achievement of a learned civilisation. Yet, he also possessed a rarer and less purely quantitative intellectual virtue, a crystalline clarity of mind that could articulate a potent idea with sharp precision. The logical status of the law of nations, the conditions for authentic Christian unity, the power of a judicial analogy to illuminate the central mystery of Christian faith, the need for a religion of revelation to rest upon testimonies of history – these conceptions of his were the great legacy of his mind, all of them more or less dependent on theology.

16.2 Political Theology

Grotius entered the lists of theological controversy, then, on the question of political theology – not, that is, on what the true Christian doctrines *mean*, but on what doctrines *should be normative* for the task of securing Christian society. His earliest published interventions, the annotated *Decretum pro pace ecclesiarum, Ordinum Hollandiae ac Westfrisiae pietas, Bona fides Sibrandi Lubberti* and the Amsterdam oration, were occasional pamphlets intended to justify the conduct of religious affairs by the States of Holland, both in its permissive aspect, allowing wider doctrinal liberty than Calvinism could tolerate, and in its restrictive aspect, refusing consent to a national synod designed to expel non-Calvinist ministers.

Three comments serve to elaborate the logic of Grotius' position. (*a*) It held to a version of the primitive simplicity of the Church, rejecting the idea of a normative development in which new requirements of belief could evolve. This had been an element in the mainstream Reformation critique of papal government. The patristic era embracing the first four councils of the fourth and fifth centuries had been treated as normative by earlier Protestants, but respect for the post-apostolic age was now falling out of fashion among Calvinists. Grotius was among those who asserted the authority of the patristic era as a whole, allowing a special status to the pre-Constantinian centuries.[3] (*b*) Responsibility for resisting doctrinal development lay with civil magistrates, always presumed to be Christians. Here, again, was a position established in the first generation of Reformation from which the now regnant Calvinism had departed. (*c*) In the local context, the sovereign to whom Grotius ascribed the right of defending Christian freedom in his native land was none other than the small body of men to which he himself belonged, the States of Holland. This element in his position proved to be its political Achilles' heel, since many contemporaries, Stadholder Maurice of Nassau (1567–1625) among them, thought a more centralised and monarchical disposition of sovereignty necessary for the young republic's security.

It would be a mistake to treat Grotius' politico-theological doctrine as no more than a cover for more fundamental theological disagreements with Calvinism. The political points were of central importance to him. The Protestant idea of the sovereign magistrate in Christendom as directly answerable to the law of God, without mediation of ecclesiastical authority, was the ground on which he founded his most important idea, the real existence of a law of nations lying behind statutes, convention and custom. It was also the theme of the longest and most carefully researched work of his Dutch period, *De imperio summarum potestatum circa sacra,* completed in 1617, but overtaken by the disaster that befell him and so never published in his lifetime.[4] This work deserves to be read alongside *De jure belli ac pacis,* of which it forms, as it were, a companion-piece on Church-state relations, making *De jure belli ac pacis* look more like a defence of Christendom than it has often been taken to be. But *De imperio* also deserves to be read on its own terms, as the fullest and most lucid presentation of a Reformed ecclesiology arising from outside the Calvinist stream.

It would equally be a mistake to suppose that Grotius stood only for politico-theological principles and had no primary theological convictions. When the *Meletius* of 1611 came to light in 1988, its discoverer and editor, Guillaume Posthumus-Meyjes, saw at once its significance as proof that Grotius' earliest involvement in the theological controversy had more than political aspects in view. That essay, composed in the literary form of a speech placed in the mouth of a recent Patriarch of Alexandria, presents an ecumenical account of Christian belief, urging the universal duty of Christians to pursue unity on that basis. It appeals to the traditional Greek distinction between *dogma* and *theologoumenon* (theological opinion), the former defined by the Church, the latter open to respectful disagreement and discussion. We learn from his preparatory notes that Grotius intended to identify some permissible, but non-binding, *theologoumena,* placing the doctrine of predestination in the same category as the question that had divided East and West on the status of the *filioque* clause in the Nicene Creed.[5] That element of the plan was never executed, perhaps to avoid alienating moderate Calvinist support.

Posthumus-Meyjes interpreted the essay as illustrating an anti-dogmatic conception of Christian belief. We ought, however, to be hesitant about the use of this term. One feature of the piece that has passed unnoticed is the difference of focus between the preface and conclusion, on the one hand, and the four numbered sections that form the main body of the text on the other. References to Patriarch Meletius and to the programme of 'restricting necessary items of belief to a few obvious ones' are confined to the preface and conclusion. But these comprise only eight of the ninety-one numbered paragraphs, and the rest of the work, supposedly the content of Meletius' speech, makes no mention of Christian disagreements. It presents Christianity as the supreme religious truth, preserving what is best in ancient philosophy and religion while correcting their mistakes in the light of revelation. Christian doctrines and moral principles are pitted against classical pagan alternatives, not against other Christian teachings. The third section (*Meletius* 19–58), itemising essential doctrines of Christianity, lists, on a conservative count, no fewer than twenty-six such *decreta*, including such disputable propositions as 'all things are created for the sake of man' and 'one man, not several, was originally created'. Here, Grotius identifies *decreta* with the Greek *dogmata*.[6] The conclusion seems irresistible that the use of the essay was an opportunistic adaptation of a text originally conceived as an *apologia* for Christianity, addressed to contemporaries with a classical education, anticipating the later *De veritate religionis Christianae*, though with the important difference that Grotius had not clarified his later distinction between apologetics and doctrine. The effect of the adapted composition was less to insist that doctrines be 'few' than that they be 'essential'. *Meletius* was a protest not against doctrine, but against doctrinal innovation.

16.3 The Death of Christ

A passage of *Meletius* (47–8) on the redemption effected by Christ's death looks forward to the major achievement of the Dutch period, *Defensio fidei catholicae de satisfactione* (1617). Why, at the height of the crisis that was to end his political career and come close to ending his life, Grotius took the time required to compose this attack on the views of the sixteenth-century anti-Trinitarian Faustus Socinus (1539–1604) on the atoning death of Christ is a question to which recent historians offer only the lamest of answers.[7] It is said to be his defence against the charge of

Socinianism, an explanation that explains rather little. Although Socinus had undoubtedly handled the death of Christ in an unorthodox manner, it was not that which primarily drew the wrath of orthodox Protestants, but his subversion of the doctrine of the Trinity. If Grotius' project had been politically driven, why would it not have targeted Socinus' most vulnerable point? And one has only to weigh the *De satifactione* in hand to wonder whether there was not a simpler way for Grotius to distance himself from that heresy. For this is a toughly argued and seriously detailed work of scholarship and criticism, of considerable originality besides. Socinus is useful to Grotius mainly as a foil for reflections on a theme that bulked large within his own theological culture. He wrote the book for the reason great thinkers usually write things: the development of his mind required it. And he wrote it in this way for a reason typical of his personal temperament: his ideas found stimulus in polemical engagement.

Grotius' preoccupation with the theme of Christ's death goes back at least to 1608, the year that saw the composition of his Latin tragedy, *Christus patiens,* where the penal and substitutionary character of the passion is expressed in the long opening speech of Christ: 'The threatening thunder of my father's wrath bursts all around and over me, but my flock is spared. That the world may perish not, I perish; to the penalties of every land I submit' (*Poemata* (1639) 403). A letter written in the same year to his intended brother-in-law, Nicholas Reigersberch (1584–1654), shows how Grotius was publicly known to hold distinctive views on the subject. It describes a meeting of the States of Holland at which the preachers Franciscus Gomarus (1563–1641) and Arminius were summoned to give an account of their controversy over predestination (1 BW 137, 6 August 1608). Gomarus had seized the opportunity of a holiday period, Grotius reports, to launch a new tirade against heterodoxy, diverting his fire away from points at issue with Arminius to attack the view that Christ's death was the 'meritorious cause' of justification and human faith its 'material cause'. Grotius understood himself to be the target of this attack, and, indeed, those are precisely the terms in which he later expressed the doctrine in *De satisfactione.* In his appearance before the States, Grotius reports, Gomarus 'went on and on about me in explaining the term "imputation"'. By 1608, then, the outlines of Grotius' soteriology were in place, known and criticised. They did not change with the years. 'Imputation' would still be a sore point between him and André Rivet (1572–1651) in 1643.

Yet, *De satisfactione* by no means aroused suspicion in all who identified themselves as Calvinists; Antonius Walaeus (1573–1639), from whom Grotius often sought reasoned criticism on the Calvinist side, warmly appreciated the draft he saw (1 BW 412, 15 June 1615).

De satisfactione is hard going for a modern reader, much of it consisting of relentless exegetical pursuit of Socinus' *De Jesu Christo Salvatore* through the New Testament, text by text and word by word. From the opening pages, with their painstaking review of the Greek prepositions *dia*, *huper* and *anti*, it is clear that the heart of the enterprise is not jurisprudence, as the preface suggests, but philological exegesis. It was the solidity of that exegetical labour that made this work a force to be reckoned with among Protestants subsequently, not least in many circles where the author's name was not a recommendation. It made its appeal to a public whose theological seriousness was expressed in the detailed reading of the New Testament, and whose professional clergy proved their competence by discoursing on the Greek text. Grotius' purchase on the vocabulary and syntax of redemption and sacrifice, so superior in subtlety to anything else available, made it the gold standard for discussions of the atonement up to and including the nineteenth century.

On the back of this exegesis, Grotius commended his theory, of the type commonly known as 'penal substitution'. Its thesis is this: in the complex biblical imagery surrounding redemption, sacrifice and the forgiveness of sins, the language of punishment affords the clearest central paradigm that allows other images to be grouped intelligibly. That is because punishment is a juridical act in pursuit of justice, the only motivation by which we could conceive of a loving God as being in any sense restrained in his generous and forgiving response to human sin. God is understood, then, as a ruler who mitigates the implementation of his justice by accepting a representative punishment in place of the destruction of the whole human world. As a theorist of punishment, Grotius was undoubtedly important. The account of that topic in *De jure belli ac pacis* (DJBP 2.20), for which *De satisfactione* is a preparation, is probably the most powerful and comprehensive to be offered before Friedrich Wilhelm Hegel (1770–1831), whom in some ways it anticipates.[8] If we have doubts about the application of this theory to the central mystery of Christian faith, they may probably turn not on the notions of substitution or satisfaction, but on its most innovatory idea: divine mercy expressed as mitigation, rather than as full forgiveness.

16.4 The Apologetic Enterprise

From as early as 1611, as we have seen, Grotius was engaged with an apologetic-cum-catechetical project. The catechetical aspect occupied his attention during his imprisonment, and the apologetic side of the ambition came to fruition in the first Paris period, in the *Bewijs* of 1622 and then, supremely, in *De veritate religionis Christianae* of 1626. The latter work's full title illustrates the question as to how the work is to be understood: is it *True Christianity*, or *Christianity the True Religion*? It has often been presented as a contribution to his programme of restoring Christian belief to primitive simplicity. On that account, its argument is taken to be that the truest account of Christian doctrine is one that is most self-evident and open to natural reason. Such a reading goes back to the eighteenth-century Remonstrants, and is detectable in Le Clerc's edition of 1709, which was influential on the reception of the work in England.[9] But it is explicitly denied by the author, who declared his purpose 'not to present a sum of Christian doctrines, but to demonstrate that Christianity as a religion is the truest and the most certain' (*De veritate* 2.1 OTh 4.33a). Critics, or advocates, who worried, or delighted, in its silence about the Trinity should also have noticed its silence about the life and death of Christ and the moral transformation wrought through faith, topics on which – in other contexts – Grotius could hardly insist strongly enough. But, *De veritate* is a self-conscious exercise in natural theology, pushing it to its limits and pointing to where those limits demand attention to revelation. An age that has listened to Kierkegaard finds such a project disconcerting in its assumption that Christian faith can be recommended on the basis of purely external indications. It is commonly referred to as 'rationalist', a term that may be serviceable enough if broadly construed, though Grotius' argument from antecedent probabilities is nothing like what 'rationalism' was to become in the hands of René Descartes (1596–1650). Distrustful of apologists who had found too great an anticipation of Christian revelation in ancient pagan philosophy – especially the Huguenot leader, Philippe du Plessis-Mornay (1549–1623), a perpetual *bête noire* – Grotius strictly demarcated the propaedeutics of faith from its content and restricted himself to bare apologetics without catechesis.[10]

The work therefore concentrates on the inter-cultural consensus on the transcendence of God and the immortality of the soul, on defending the historical facticity of the person and works of Jesus, on defending the historical credibility of Scriptural testimony and, most strikingly, on presenting Christianity as the best and supreme example of the genus 'religion'. The appearance of 'religion' as a sociological and cultural category – *religio,* not *pietas,* which is 'religion' as a personal virtue – tells us that an important shift of perspective had occurred since the sixteenth century. The seventeenth century felt the need for an apologetic for Christianity, as it had not been felt, perhaps, since the days of Thomas Aquinas' (*c.* 1225–74) *Contra Gentes.* Christendom had become conscious of its historical and geographical boundaries; it knew that it occupied a world containing other and rival religious traditions. Christians travelling abroad encountered the cultural *massifs* of deeply-rooted non-Christian beliefs. Whether they encountered them successfully depended, Grotius urged, on an attitude of serious prayer and Bible study, missionary enter-prise and the care for Christian unity (*De veritate* 6.11 OTh 4.94). With *De veritate,* Grotius had in view a more popular readership than he usually addressed, which makes its style simpler than much of his writing. In his sights was the educated, but essentially practical, merchant-class to which his own family belonged, who in travel and trade encountered a wider world and greater challenges to understanding than their stay-at-home pastors were equipped to meet, merchant sailors who, on their long voy-ages to the Far East, might be taught to become lay-missionaries among their trading partners (*De veritate* 1.1 OTh 4.3). The awareness of a world-context shaped the book, even though the only non-Western religion Grotius discussed in detail was Islam, his knowledge of which was limited.

The other religions marked out for special discussion were Judaism – a religious presence at the heart of Europe – and, surprisingly, the ancient paganism with which Augustine (354–430) had argued more than a mil-lennium earlier, equally European but hardly contemporary. That decision was not merely nostalgic, for it was not only merchants that Grotius wrote for, but, as always, people like himself, an educated elite, who might count sociologically as Catholics or Calvinists, but whose minds were formed chiefly by the encounter with classical antiquity. The sudden inrush of a world of new learning made pagan Antiquity seem more real to the imagination than the unedifying confusions of Christendom. Sensitive pastors such as Richard Baxter (1615–91), regretting the fierce intra-Protestant controversies of the mid-century, diagnosed a concealed unbelief as the real temptation of the age, and insisted on 'a methodical procedure in maintaining the doctrine of Christianity, and of beginning at natural verities, as presupposed fundamentally to supernatural'.[11] To these readers, Grotius wished to emphasise the great historical fact that the classical world had been the scene of God's personal intervention in human history. When, in 1679, Grotius' son placed *De veritate* at the head of the fourth volume of the *Opera omnia Theologica*, it was an indication that it had found its readership and come to be seen as his most influential religious work. And that was due less to its appeal to merchants than to the accuracy with which it had targeted the religious deficit among this educated class.

16.5 The Second Paris Period

The works of Grotius' last period fall into two connected, but distinct, groups. On the one hand, occupying three volumes of the four-volume *Opera omnia Theologica*, is the work on which Grotius lavished more care than on any other, his exegetical notes on the whole Bible, begun long before, during his imprisonment, and published in stages, the New Testament Epistles appearing only after his death. On the other hand, there is a disparate collection of occasional works united by the general aim of renewing the late sixteenth century quest for Christian unity. The latter group itself subdivides into four distinct sub-groups. First came short exegetical pamphlets on New Testament texts central to the dispute between Rome and Reform (*De fide et operibus*, on the verbal disagreement between Paul and James on faith and works; *Commentatio de Antichristo*, on why the antichrist in the Apocalypse should not be read as a prediction of the papacy). Second, two pamphlets, *De coenae administratione* and *An semper communicandum per symbola*, reflected on the dilemma of those who, like himself, were denied access to the communion of a recognised church, arguing for principled abstention from sacramental life. Third, there was the core enterprise of the period, the *Via ad pacem ecclesiasticam*, a proposal for the reconciliation of Christendom, which involved the re-publication, with commentary, of sixteenth-century documents, especially the so-called Consultation of Cassander, in which the Roman-Catholic theologian George Cassander (1513–66) had measured the Augsburg Confession against the Catholic tradition and found the gap to be bridgeable. This gave rise, fourth, to a heated exchange of polemics with the Leiden theologian, André Rivet, in which, whoever may be judged to

have had the last word intellectually, Rivet had the last word chronologic-
ally, composing and publishing his final rebuttal after Grotius' death.

16.6 The Biblical Commentary

Grotius began writing his exegetical notes on the Synoptic Gospels in
1619 while committed to prison, apparently for life. But what might have
been conceived as a work of purely private study and devotion was fashioned
in the fires of his indignation to assume a public shape, and from early in its
composition there is no question that he intended his *Annotationes* to be
widely read. They would be a demonstration of how the Scriptural text could
be interpreted in a church founded objectively on the doctrines of the undivided Church of the first four centuries. Yet, the exegesis we find throughout
this remarkable and largely unprecedented work studiously avoids polemics.[12]
Grotius wished to make the Scriptural text accessible to all Christians of good
will, enabling them to read without dogmatic prejudice and with the fullest
insight gained from historical and philological research. He was, of course, a
pre-eminent exponent of any ancient Greek text, and especially of the Greek
New Testament, which he had known intimately from childhood. His sense of
how the Greek language worked was intuitive, and he had good enough
Hebrew to appreciate the colour that their Jewish background lent to the
apostles' language. It was not difficult for him to bring philological clarification to bear upon passages that had been tormented by dogmatic controversy,
with powerful solvent effect. His comment on Romans 8.29, for example,
'Those whom he foreknew he also predestined ... ', that bone of contention
that had caused such bad blood between Gomarus and Arminius, is a model of
demystifying lucidity: 'foreknew' is a Hebraism for 'approved'; 'predestined' is
simply 'designed'; the phrase beginning 'those ... ' is generic, not particular.
God's design was to bring believers into his kingdom by conforming them to
the cross of Christ (OTh 3.723b). It is not the least important testimony to the
strength of his exegetical work that, when theologians of the twentieth century
undertook to reconstruct the ideas of election and predestination, the lines on
which they did so followed this exposition closely.

   Together with philological insight, Grotius brought a strong sense of the
historical background to the text. The principle that no apostle or prophet
wrote anything not intended to mean something to his contemporaries,
whatever further meanings it may justly be thought to contain, seems

self-evident to us today, but was at the time a liberation from the toils of many bad exegetical traditions. A first- or second-century application of the antichrist imagery in the Apocalypse must be favoured over a seventeenth-century one. The Christological significance of such passages as Isaiah's prophecy of the virgin's child, though it was intended by the Holy Spirit, was not the primary reference of the text in its setting of the mid-eighth century BCE. Here, too, we can see a natural link between Grotius and the early reformers' concern to vindicate the 'literal', i.e. historical, sense of Scripture. In the service of this principle, Grotius makes full use of the Judaica of the first century, of Philo of Alexandria (25 BCE–50 CE), the rabbis and the apocryphal writings as witnesses to the language and conceptuality of the New Testament. It is easy to form the impression that we are, for the first time, among familiar landmarks of modern biblical commentary, especially in matters of New Testament authorship: the author of the Epistle to the Hebrews is unknown, for its style and vocabulary exclude Paul; 2 and 3 John cannot come from the same pen as 1 John. Yet, caution is needed: Grotius' speculations follow the lines of patristic reception very closely, and include a defence of the apostolic authorship of the Apocalypse. As for the multiple problems of authorship in the Old Testament prophetic books, Grotius is largely unconscious of them.

For all the scholarly distance enabled by his philological and historical sense, Grotius never attempted to detach himself from the theological contents of the text. As he observed, he could not disentangle *verba* from *res*. The aim of the project was the Protestant one of establishing in full seriousness the authority of the Biblical text over dogmatic constructions. Not that he thought that the exposition should confine itself to repeating biblical vocabulary and concepts. In the exposition of Matthew 5.17, for example, 'Do not think that I have come to set the law aside … ', Grotius introduced a lengthy review of the differences between 'civil' and 'natural' law that played such a large part in his legal theory (OTh 2.34a–36a). Developed conceptual frameworks were not to be done away with, but brought before the bar of the text to answer for their fidelity and usefulness.

16.7 The Ecumenical Project

It is characteristic of Grotius that, at the end of his life, he took up a cause that had had eminent advocates before, but now appeared hopelessly outdated, the reunion of Christendom. In the generation in which he grew up, the hope of an orderly approach to healing the gulf left by the Reformation had been a lively one. Two of his heroes in London, Isaac Casaubon (1559–1614) and King James I/VI (1566–1625), had been powerful supporters of this project, and the Synod of Dordrecht (1618) itself had been envisaged by King James as a step to its implementation.[13] In retrospect, the divisive outcome of that Synod, together with the political coup that exploited it, was the mortal wound from which the project of reunion never recovered. This was all the more reason for Grotius to return to an earlier stage of the project. His professed aim was to outflank the spoiling behaviour of the Dortian Calvinists, who had set themselves against the peace of the Church, but he was perfectly aware that he also had to outflank the regnant orthodoxy in Rome. Despite, or perhaps because of, his friendship with the Jesuit, Denis Pétau (1583–1652), Grotius shared a general public suspicion of the ultra-montane effect of excessive Jesuit influence. The coming together he looked for, then, involved recovery of an earlier, more generous Catholic consciousness together with an earlier, more generous Reformed consciousness. Medieval corruptions of doctrine and practice were to be purged. Excesses of the Reformation – essentially, the equality of ministers and the abolition of episcopacy – were to be renounced. The consensus of the undivided Church of the first five centuries was to be the arbiter of differences. The tactic, well-considered, of republishing from the 1580s the imperially-commissioned findings of George Cassander that the Augsburg Confession was not far from the Catholic tradition brought into play an old-fashioned Catholic humanism independent of the dogmatic decrees of the Council of Trent (1545–61). These formed the basis of Grotius' own *Annotata ad consultationem Cassandri*, in which Cassander's accommodating reading of Augsburg was matched with an equally accommodating reading of Trent. For this, he draws upon the – to him – anonymous *History of the Council of Trent*, written by Venice's Paulo Sarpi (1552–1623), condemned at Rome and published by King James in London. Did Grotius regard his strategy as a practical proposition? It is difficult to say. He would often declare that the reconciliation of the churches could be accomplished 'easily', but that was bravado. He had hopes for initiatives from Archbishop William Laud (1573–1645) in England, even from Cardinal Richelieu (1585–1642) in France, which in either case remained unrealised.[14] An insuppressibly active man, condemned, as he saw himself, to inactivity, Grotius longed for some large practical accomplishment. At the same time, he pursued this project for the same reason he pursued his other intellectual projects: the development of his mind required it. And we can only be struck by how the conservative of one age may be the prophet of a later one: the ground so painfully defended in the seventeenth century, to the incredulity and derision of Grotius' friends and foes, was to lie at the centre of the great ecumenical re-opening of the twentieth century.

The speculation promoted at every opportunity by the embittered Claude Saumaise (1588–1653) that Grotius' polemics with Rivet had set him on course to become a Roman Catholic simply extended the logic of Calvinist objections that there was no ground to stand on between the Gospel and the antichrist.[15] It deserves little credit, though rhetorically these last writings were aimed at delivering an intense shock to Protestant sensibilities, to 'punch through the elephant's hide, bone and vitals'. There is, however, less substantial difference between Grotius' earlier and later theological positions than can appear. The son of a Roman-Catholic mother, he had always taken the view that the Catholic Church was a legitimate, though unreformed, expression of Western Christianity. He had never believed that the pope fulfilled prophecies of the antichrist. He had never regarded the piety of ordinary Catholic Christians as heretical fanaticism (*Votum* OTh 4.653a). On four points, however, Grotius' thought developed in ways that diverged from his Dutch period, offering more hospitality to Catholic views. (i) His view of the ordained ministry, starting from the Reformed principle of the equality of ministers as qualified by a principle of presidency, leaned increasingly towards the hierarchical structure of bishops, metropolitans and patriarchs (*Annotata Cassandri* ad 14, OTh 4.621b). (ii) He came to defend the ideal position of the See of Rome as the senior patriarchate in a united Church (*Annotata Cassandri* ad 7, OTh 4.617b). (iii) He became committed to the language of 'real presence' in relation to the Eucharist (*Votum* OTh 4.656b). These three points hardly took him beyond other Protestant theorists of Church unity, but he was more adventurous in (iv) supposing an oral apostolic tradition, parallel with Scripture, giving authority to patristic models of worship and government (*Annotata Cassandri* ad 7, OTh 4.617b; *Discussio* OTh 4.685b).

Together with these Catholic themes, there was much in Grotius' thought that resisted Romanising, not least his unflagging zeal for the historic rights of Christian secular rulers, opposed, as he recognised, no less in Rome than in Geneva. There are, he repeatedly states, two kinds of 'catholic': those who uphold such rights and those who undermine them with ultra-montane pretensions (*Discussio* OTh 4.679a, on Baudouin). The kind of Catholicism towards which he felt warmly was that which opposed the bolder pretensions of papacy, that of imperialist and conciliarist theorists who had provided the ground for Gallican liberties. He never ceased asserting that the doctrinal woes of the Church originated in the Aristotelian corruption of scholastic doctrine. Occasional grudging expressions of respect for Aquinas, whose treatise on justice had shaped the revisions of *De jure praedae commentarius* in his youth, would reward closer and more detailed study.[16]

If Cassander's work taught Grotius that there was a Catholic viewpoint not far removed from his own, it also taught him to appreciate the ecumenical possibilities of the Protestant Augsburg Confession. The two reformers for whom he had the greatest respect, Philip Melanchthon (1497–1560) and Martin Bucer (1491–1551), were associated with the reception of this document. If the Church was to be coaxed towards reunification on the basis of patristic norms, a first step might be for Protestants to abandon their multiplicity of doctrinal statements and agree to re-group around this founding document, which appeared accepting of, and acceptable to, the mainstream Catholic tradition. This gives force to almost the last words he published in his lifetime, where he clearly identified himself with 'the adherents of the Augsburg Confession'.[17] On the role of Scripture, moreover, the scholarly exegesis of which was his key to Christian unity, Grotius was in essential continuity with the Reformation, only insisting that its authority must be understood as a function of its prophetic and apostolic authorship, and that this did not rule out, but actually implied, a diversity of literary practice in Scriptural books of different *genres*. Though Scripture was never to be read 'alone', but always in the light of (apostolic) tradition, it contained the apostolic and prophetic witness authorised by God and Christ, a witness upheld by continuities of practice in the Church derived from apostolic practice.[18]

But the chief reason to doubt any thought on Grotius' part of becoming a Roman Catholic is that it would have abandoned his flagship theopolitical principle, the normativity of the patristic age for all Christian practice. To substitute the authority of Rome for the authority of the 'ancients' would have been to cut his life's unifying thread. In youth he had, like many Protestant thinkers, championed the patristic norm with only a modest acquaintance with the texts, depending on *florilegia* compiled for him by his friend, Gerardus Vossius (1577–1649). By his later years, Grotius knew the literature extensively at first hand, and had a much less simplified and idealised idea of the purity of the undivided Church. That broadened the range of views to which he could allow a place within the Church, and it was broadened even further by occasional inadvertent use of medieval pseudepigrapha transmitted under the names of major fathers. But while he ended up defending much that Reformed Christians usually attacked, even clerical celibacy, everything conformed to the ruling principle: what was allowed in the patristic Church must be allowed today; what was uniformly insisted on in the patristic Church must be insisted on today. Protestants sympathetic to his goal of unity feared that the programme of patristic norms would mean the sacrifice of much that they saw the Reformation had gained for Church liberty.[19]

16.8 The Critique of an Amoral Calvinism

Grotius, like Augustine, ended his days locked in bitter polemical exchanges with an adroit adversary whose ill-will spared him nothing. In a moment of self-pity, he wondered aloud whether André Rivet wanted him burned at the stake (*Discussio* OTh 4.683a). What Rivet did seem to have wanted, and to all intents achieved, was to make Grotius' ambassadorial position at the French court untenable in the heat of the religious controversy. Four times, Rivet wrote paragraph-by-paragraph, sentence-by-sentence attacks on Grotius' writings; three times, Grotius rose to the bait and wrote paragraph-by-paragraph, sentence-by-sentence counter-attacks (*Animadversiones in animadversiones Andreae Riveti, Votum pro pace eccclestica, Rivetiani apologetici discussio,* in *Opera omnia Theoligica*). Having announced in the second response that he would take the controversy no further, he returned to it again, writing of himself in the third person as though he were someone else. His friends were dismayed, and it is hard to read these works without sharing their sense that Grotius had been swept off course by his combativeness, and that this hostile barrage could only hurt the cause he believed in. As before, we must seek his real motivations in an inner intellectual life that demanded expression. Rivet offered him the opportunity to pursue a question he had lived with all his life, that of the authenticity of Calvinism itself as an expression of Christianity. Early in the first Paris period, he had written *Disquisitio an*

Pelagiana sint ea dogmata, essentially a supportive review of Vossius' *History of the Pelagians,* which emphasised the historical arbitrariness with which the Synod of Dordrecht employed the term 'Pelagian' against the Remonstrants.[20] At the beginning of the second Paris period, he had published an exposition of the New Testament texts on faith and works, intended to correct the conventional Calvinist account. Now was the time to present an account of Calvinism as such, and to reposition himself away from his youthful account of its views as legitimate, but non-binding, *theologoumena.* Calvinism was an amoral fatalism, a heterodox Stoicising retrogression from Christian discipleship.

Grotius' later writings formulate much of what was to become a standard hostile paradigm of Calvinism, except in one respect: he does not accuse Calvinism of being moralistic, but of subverting morality, both by promoting the false assurance of a certainty of election and by failing to integrate religious and moral duties, so that what are taken to be religious duties impose themselves with a peremptory immediacy that makes the law of charity unintelligible. Before all else a master of jurisprudence and a theorist of law, Grotius was offended at demands that left no room for thoughtful legal application. The command in the Decalogue prohibiting graven images, used as a justification for iconoclastic riots, was, he thought, given arbitrary precedence over the other nine commands, subject to no interpretation, qualification or discretion, not read in context as part of the prohibition of worship of false gods, not read historically as part of the positive law of Israel that was suited in the needs of its time and place, but treated as though it were a universal datum of natural law.[21] The actual history of Calvinist rebellions in France, the Rhineland and the Netherlands, a history repeated at the end of Grotius' life in the English Civil Wars, bore the stamp of an obsessive reactiveness that failed to consider the good of human life in community. 'Nothing disturbs civil peace so much as the doctrine professed by the so-called Reformed that the cause of religion licenses armed rebellion against governments' (*Discussio* OTh 4.701b). In formulating a right of rebellion on religious grounds, the Calvinists of his day adventured onto moral ground never before occupied by Christians.

Grotius' view of Calvin himself, whose commentaries on Scripture he respected for their philological and exegetical competence, also hardened. Though never believing him to have taught the full Dortian Calvinism of his own day, he did think of him as having been the model for an embittered and violent spirit among his followers (*Votum* OTh 4.655b).

As his view of Calvin became darker, so his view of Augustine became lighter. Where once he had seen Augustine's later anti-Pelagian writings as an ominous first defection from the patristic consensus on free will, deeper reading made him confident that Augustine had built into his account of divine predestination a firewall to protect human freedom. He found Augustine 'no stranger to changes of mind, not always for the better', but protected by his very inconsistencies from the fatalism into which Calvinism fell (*Discussio* OTh 4.704a, 728a). The extent of these changes of mind was exaggerated by pseudepigrapha, sometimes reeking of high medievalism, which Grotius treated with more confidence than his scholarly judgment might have allowed, were it not driven by a need to marshal every last bit of evidence against his opponent. The great work of clarifying Augustine's authentic corpus, to be accomplished by the Maurist editors not a mile from his home in the Faubourg Saint Germain, was thirty years in the future when Grotius died.

At the heart of his complaint lay the doctrine, upheld by Rivet as by many Calvinist teachers, that Christ's righteousness was 'imputed' to the believer – the theme of Gomarus' attack on him back in 1608.

'Imputed righteousness', so called, is not found in Holy Scripture, and the doctrine expressed in those terms flatters the flesh and poisons the soul … Why is it so popular? The reason is obvious: we want nothing so much as to learn that we shall attain eternal joys by external propulsion with no effort of our own, and that those sayings about the narrow path and the need for righteous works in all, and for deeds of repentance in the fallen, need not trouble us. (*Discussio* OTh 4.701a)

The concept of substitution belongs to Christ's death as penalty for sin; it cannot be transferred to the believer's relation to Christ's life, which must be one of active participation.[22] Through the drama of redemption, mankind's relation to the Redeemer changes from passive to active. So, Grotius' most typically Protestant theme, of Christ's substitutionary death, connects directly with his most 'Arminian' theme, the insistence that faith in the Gospel feeds practical reason. The necessary conditions of human action are preserved intact in believers, among them the ignorance in which agents necessarily stand of the future, including their own moral destiny. Christian confidence in relation to the future is one of hope founded in God's promises, not of knowledge. Each day presents them with the question of their ultimate salvation afresh. Faith is understood by Grotius, again in faithfulness to the early reformers, as the root of action, the source of a righteous life and the particular object of God's approval. The gift of the Holy Spirit, he thought, was subsequent to faith (*Annotata Cassandri* ad 5, OTh 4.617a). And he defended the possibility of a real, though always dependent, holiness and perfection of the saints in this life.

Grotius was no metaphysician – that is the valid point misleadingly made in calling him 'undogmatic'. The controversy that mattered more to him than any other concerned the shape of Christian doctrine; but his interest in doctrines about the eternal and unchanging was very much less than his interest in doctrines about time and history. He thought deeply on redemption and the Church, but accepted the orthodox doctrine of God largely as it stood in the tradition (cf. *Animadversiones* ad 1, OTh 4.639b). His dislike of Calvinism and Thomism were parallel reactions to two schemes of Christian belief that did not hesitate to probe the eternal and the absolute. It is a fixed ground for Grotius that God relates to his human creatures on a political model, as ruler to subjects – he does not even think of these predicates as an analogy. It is not unreasonable to complain that his understanding of God's grace lacked that sense of divine decisiveness that captivated the imagination of Martin Luther (1483–1546). But equally recoverable from Luther was a vital sense of the organic relation of Gospel to ethics, in which Grotius was not mistaken in thinking that early seventeenth-century Calvinists were weak. If this resulted, for him, in an elevation of natural law – which is one truth, but not the sole truth, about the foundations of Grotius' ethics as he also assigned a major role to divine positive law – it was not, as is often suggested, because natural law relegated God to the sidelines, but because it integrated divine action so closely into the created order of the human moral world. It was not given to Grotius, nor to anyone of his age, to discern how divine agency and human agency might be combined effectively other than through a concept of cooperation.[23] Ethics in the seventeenth century was grounded in acts of will and in law; not until eighteenth-century moralists extended it to the dispositions and affections could room be found for more subtle understandings of divine-human interaction.

16.9 The Theological Location of Grotius

Grotius' status as a lay theologian, rarer in his day than in ours, did much to determine the way he wrote. Grotius commonly appealed to his non-professional status to recommend his arguments beyond the limits of the settled Church establishments.[24] This opened him to a multiplicity of appropriations, and yet it was a liability, too. His thought lacked the stirring and inspiring qualities that other theologians of his era acquired from the exercise of pastoral care and preaching. Religious passion, never lacking, found poetic expression in his verse, but in his prose it took the form of combativeness and didacticism.

From the viewpoint of the early nineteenth century, Grotius' legacy in the later seventeenth and throughout the eighteenth century ran out into established latitudinarian Christianity. As good a judge as Samuel Taylor Coleridge (1772–1834) wrote that, with the restoration of episcopacy in England with Charles II (1630–85), the doctrines of 'Luther, Zwinglius and the first Reformers collectively' were 'exchanged for what is commonly entitled Arminianism, but which ... would be both historically and theologically more accurate to call *Grotianism*'.[25] In retrospect, that summary looks one-sided, coloured by the reaction of the romantic era against what it saw as rationalism and Erastianism, the understandable reaction of a generation brought up in deductive logic by the Enlightenment, now thirsty for the emotional depths of religion.[26]

But before Grotius can be claimed as a forerunner of later streams of Protestant Christianity, he must be located in terms of his own age, an age which was pregnant, perhaps, with the great conflicting movements that would bring the storms of *odium theologicum* to unprecedented heights, but which in its conscious purposes was solely intent on mastering the troubled legacy it had inherited. In his day, Grotius appeared as an odd-man-out, stateless and allied with none of the most powerful Christian communities, relating to *patria* and *ecclesia* nostalgically across the frontiers of dislocation. That appearance may conceal from us how central he was to the concerns of his time, and how much he draws on longer political-theological traditions of European legitimation running back at least to the twelfth century. For him, as for the tradition, the framing question in theology and statecraft concerned the norms of law that conferred authority on institutions and practices. His appeal is to an unbroken channel of authority through essentially unbroken institutions of law. In rejecting scholastic theology for its observably schismatic effects, he can reach over its head to a greater authority than Aristotle in the medieval world, that of the twelfth-century canon lawyer, Gratian. The new plurality of Western Christian confessions was a fact that he hoped to render insignificant in the longer view. His opponents, offering a more apocalyptic and irreversible reading of European history as a disclosure of antichrist, gave a more radical answer to the framing question, locating the source of institutional authority within the gathered community of the godly. But neither he nor they, nor any of their contemporaries, could foresee the imminent replacement of that framing-question by a different one, which would ask about the sources of meaning from which the individual might construct a world and a life.

The Remonstrants, who alone could claim institutional connection with him, hoped to find in him support for their eighteenth-century retreat from the creedal norms of Western Christianity that he had stubbornly upheld. In England, his authority was claimed by advocates of the restored episcopacy. Yet, an equally discernible line connects Grotius with pietism, which, by merging with a growing Reformed interest in moral psychology, fuelled the popular explosion of revival and holiness enthusiasms. The evangelicalism of John (1703–91) and Charles (1707–88) Wesley, dubbed 'Arminian' by their contemporaries, was known for controversial claims about moral 'perfection' already clearly articulated by Grotius (*Discussio* OTh 4.682a, 689–90). Pietist and Reformed circles embraced his understanding of atonement, while, in a later age, the protests of the nineteenth century – Coleridge, Søren Kierkegaard etc. – against the demoralising effects of bad understandings of grace may be heard to repeat his concerns about Calvinism. Grotius' understanding of the divinely-governed course of world history, seeing Christian revelation as a decisive critical reflection on, but not a wholesale repudiation of, pagan culture, would be taken up in a variety of guises in the nineteenth century, that last great heyday of Christendom. The normative role of patristic doctrine, meanwhile, on which he was neither the first nor the last to insist, but which he programmatised more fully than anyone else, has constantly been appealed to by Western Christian communities not wholly at ease with their sixteenth-century heritage. Yet, it is not too much to suggest that the bold renewal of the ecumenical venture in the twentieth century could hardly have been conceived without the witness of that earlier irenical tradition, of which Grotius was the last spokesman.

Grotius' religious writings make a claim on our admiration in that they addressed questions of great urgency to his Christian contemporaries, and offered answers of thoroughgoing consistency. If we would overcome Grotius, we must tackle him at the points he himself thought of most importance, not merely try to catch him out, as his opponents did and modern critics still sometimes do, in incautiously phrased remarks. We will begin, perhaps, by recognising that his polymathic ambitions as an outstanding jurist and a historical philologist created difficulties. There were serious problems in his attempt to use patristic literature as a source for determining ecclesiastical law: the materials were too diverse in period, context, authorial intention and, let it be said, theological competence to be put to the jurisdictional uses he had in mind for them – as though every Christian author from the first five centuries of the era could be treated as a judge whose rulings constituted legal precedents. Pressing the unending catena of patristic texts into the service of his cause, Grotius gives the impression of reading them superficially, without inhabiting their rhetorical world and social context – quite the opposite, in fact, of the profound historical and cultural awareness that he brought to bear on the authors of the New Testament – and the Old, to the extent that he was capable – and on the writers of classical Antiquity to whom he gave his focused critical attention. To use patristic writings effectively to argue for a mainstream Christian tradition in Antiquity, we must be content to confine our use of them to a narrow range of questions, to handle them with less legalism and more discrimination in deciding what each text is capable of telling us. In the second place, we are bound to question the theological-political matrix within which Grotius sought to accommodate the deepest thoughts about the relation of man to God. It is not simply that the hypothesis of Christendom, that the civil magistrate was responsible for determining orthodox terms of religious participation and humane terms of toleration of non-conformity, was to undergo progressive erosion in the generations that followed. More profoundly, later centuries felt increasingly uncomfortable with the political analogy for talking about God as ruler and lawmaker, which, if pressed beyond its proper sphere of application, could yield unintelligible results. With the recovery of political theology in the later twentieth century, a greater awareness has been required of the limits of that analogy.

'Him from whom perhaps every man of learning has learned something' was Samuel Johnson's (1709–84) verdict on Grotius.[27] To which it follows as a corollary, perhaps, that very few who have been glad to acknowledge that they have learned from Grotius have been able to accept more than a portion of what he would have liked to teach them.

Further Reading

De Jonge, H.J. 'Grotius as an interpreter of the Bible', in *Hugo Grotius, a Great European 1583-1645* (Delft, 1983), 59-65.

Geddert, J.S., *Hugo Grotius and the Modern Theology of Freedom: Transcending Natural Rights* (New York, 2017).

Nellen, H.J.M., and E. Rabbie (eds.), *Hugo Grotius - Theologian: Essays in Honour of G.H.M. Posthumus Meyjes* (Leiden, 1994).

O'Donovan, O., 'Attributive Justice in Grotius', in J. Lockwood O'Donovan and O. O'Donovan, *Bonds of Imperfection. Christian Politics, Past and Present* (Grand Rapids, 2006), 167-203.

Patterson, W.P., *King James VI and I and the Reunion of Christendom* (Cambridge, 1997).

Notes

1 Cf. 1 BW 345, 16 June 1614, J. Utenbogaert: 'Each individual must make his mind up conscientiously about the truth of a doctrine, and reach a judgment before he believes in it; similarly, the Church as a community must make its mind up about its common faith and doctrine. But which faith and doctrine is to be publicly defended and promoted must be strictly a matter for the magistrate's judgment.'

2 On Hobbes, see H.J.M. Nellen, *Hugo Grotius, a Lifelong Struggle for Peace in Church and State 1583-1645* (Leiden and Boston, 2015), 601, 659.

3 *Discussio* OTh 4.681b, writing of Vincent of Lérins: 'How can one be a Semipelagian if one acknowledges the initiative of divine grace in all salvific good, and never departs from the orthodox writers of the three first centuries, among them many martyrs and other defenders of God's grace in their doctrine and of its strength in their lives, as their lives and deaths showed?'

4 The story of how a copy survived in the hands of John Overall (1559-1619), Bishop of Lichfield, who entrusted it to John Cosin (1594-1672), the later Bishop of Durham, and how it was returned to the author, who decided not to publish it, is admirably reconstructed and recounted in the edition of H.J. van Dam (Leiden, 2001) 31-45. See also van Dam's chapter, 'Church and state' in this volume.

5 It is again to G.H.M. Posthumus-Meyjes that we owe the documentary evidence. See 'Some remarks on Grotius' *Excerpta Theologica*, especially concerning his *Meletius*', in H.J.M. Nellen and E. Rabbie (eds.), *Hugo Grotius Theologian* (Leiden, 1994), 1-17. But the assertion of this scholar, in whose debt we all stand, that the sphere of *adiaphora* extends to the 'dogma of Trinity', goes well beyond the evidence.

6 Users of Postumus-Meyjes' invaluable edition (Leiden, 1988) need to be warned of its idiosyncratic translation of *decreta* as 'principles'. The editor holds that 'the term is used in a general philosophical sense, not in a specifically Christian one' (35), a judgment for which it is hard to see the foundation.

7 See the introduction to Edwin Rabbie's major edition (Assen/Mastricht, 1990), 10–19; also Nellen, *Grotius*, 232–9. I may perhaps be allowed the suggestion that the contribution of Socinus to Grotius' thought – the question arises again in connection with *De veritate* – has occupied the minds of modern scholars, as of contemporary opponents, more than it deserves. It would be mean-spirited, however, to let the work of this recent generation of historians and editors, who have effected something of a renaissance in Grotius studies, pass with this critical observation. If readers from other disciplines can venture a dissenting judgment from time to time, it is because they have been presented with outstanding historical and textual work to build on.

8 See the chapter in this volume 'Punishment and Crime', by Dennis Klimchuk.

9 Le Clerc was rash enough to add to Grotius' six books two of his own, purporting to supply similarly 'undogmatic' reasons why the Anglican Church was preferable to all others.

10 On Du Plessis-Mornay's apologetics cf. *Discussio* OTh 4.678b: 'Hermes and the Sibylline Oracles ... appear as authorities on almost every page of his.'

11 *Reliquiae Baxterianae, Or, Mr. Richard Baxters Narrative of the Most Memorable Passages of His Life and Times* (London, 1696), 128.

12 For a judicious assessment of what Grotius added to the Renaissance tradition of biblical annotation, see H.J. de Jonge, 'Grotius as an interpreter of the Bible', in *Hugo Grotius, a Great European 1583–1645* (Delft, 1983), 59–65.

13 See W.P. Patterson, *King James VI and I and the Reunion of Christendom* (Cambridge, 1997).

14 On these see Nellen, *Grotius,* 556–9 and 612–14.

15 Especially in Jakob Laurensz' *Grotius Papizans* (Amsterdam, 1642). On these speculations see Nellen, *Grotius*, 659–60, 709 and 740–5.

16 Cf. 1 BW 402, 13May 1615 to B.A. du Maurier: 'Among the scholastics it is no bad thing to read Thomas Aquinas – if not the whole of him, II-2 of the *Summa Theologiae* is worth a look, especially the treatment of justice and the laws.' For the impact of this text on the revisions of DJBP see my 'Attributive justice in Grotius', in Joan Lockwood O'Donovan and Oliver O'Donovan, *Bonds of Imperfection. Christian Politics, Past and Present* (Grand Rapids, 2006), 167–203, 174–7.

17 *Discussio* OTh 4.745b: 'Grotius spends what time he can spare from public duties in making Catholics understand that adherents of the Augsburg Confession are not so far removed as never to be reunited in a single body.'

18 It will be seen that I regard Nellen's inferences from *Discussio* OTh 4.723, *Grotius*, 706, as needing caution. Grotius there makes a distinction between speech given by the *afflatus Dei*, typical of prophets, and the work of historical enquiry undertaken by the Evangelists. Scriptural authors are all inspired by the

Holy Spirit and authoritative for the Church, but go about their task in different ways. It is not the written form of Scripture, but its connection with the acts and words of God, that is decisive. 'What the apostles wrote, Christ must be understood to have commanded – not that he commanded them to *write* it, but that they wrote down *what* he had commanded, reckoning that to be of use to the churches, which it was, and is.' Cf. also his comment on 1 Tim. 3:15 (OTh 3.968–9).

19 Cf. Richard Baxter, *Reliquiae Baxterianae*, 132: 'I have thought and thought again of the way of the moderating Papists, Cassander, Grotius, Baldwin etc., and of those that would have all reduced to the state of the times of Gregory the First, before the division of the Greek and Latin churches, that the Pope might have his primacy and govern all the Church by the canons of the councils with a salvo to the rights of kings and patriarchs and prelates, and that the doctrines and worship which then were received might prevail. And for my own part, if I lived in such a state of the Church, I would live peaceably, as glad of unity, though lamenting the corruption and tyranny.'

20 On the circumstances of the publication of this work, see Nellen, *Grotius,* 335–40.

21 *Discussio* OTh 4.707b–708b. On the false assurance offered by Calvinist spiritual directors cf. 728b (on Johannes Bogerman).

22 Cf., from much earlier, 1 BW 412, 29 June 1615, A. Walaeus: 'It seems to me that while Christ's κατορθώματα (righteous deeds) establish merit, only his passion, by virtue of being punishment, makes satisfaction.'

23 To this generalisation an exception may be the exploratory attempt of John Cameron (1580–1625) to conceive of the operation of practical reason without a distinct act of will to implement its conclusion. Grotius, not always a supporter of Cameron, responded sympathetically to this idea in 1613, 1 BW 252 to S. Episcopius.

24 See Vossius' prefatory letter to *De satisfactione,* presenting the author as a 'Christian lawyer ... writing not as a theologian but a Christian man', with Edmund Rabbie's report (11, 12) on the suggestions of Grotius behind this presentation. For his sense of distance from the professional theologians see also *Discussio* OTh 4.702b–703a.

25 *Aids to Reflection* [1825] (London, 1913), 106f.

26 A curious glimpse of the reception of Grotius at the dawn of the nineteenth century is given us in Thomas de Quincey's autobiographical *Confessions of an English Opium-Eater* [1821]. On the day he entered Manchester Grammar School in 1800, de Quincey recounts, he found his fellow-scholars discussing *De veritate*. All were disdainful, finding its depiction of Islam dated and its reasoning inconclusive – except for one student who had a striking insight into Grotius' argumentative strategy. The use of *De veritate* as a textbook, we are told, was discontinued very soon after.

27 James Boswell, *Life of Samuel Johnson* (1791), vol. 2, 19 July 1777.

17 Political Writings

Hans Blom

17.1 Introduction

As a political actor and a humanist trained to articulate the conceptual world behind his actions, Hugo Grotius had an important voice on the Dutch and the European stage and beyond. His purview ranged from the theory of political action and political virtue to the principles of social organisation and society and state, covering principles of toleration, political freedom and political obedience. Grotius also discussed the role of the economy in politics and that of politics in the economy. Republican by humanist predilection, he nonetheless was open to the idea that political societies can take many forms and an important part of his writings is devoted to describing and explaining these constitutional variations and showing their political consequences.

A long-standing tradition has attempted to locate Grotius within different schools of political thought, making him at variance into an Aristotelian, a scholastic, a Stoic, an Epicurean, a 'modern', such as a contract thinker, even a liberal or an absolutist. Grotius himself qualified his eclectic position in a letter to Benjamin Aubéry du Maurier (1566–1636): 'In the Ethics, however, you should observe particularly the differences between the sects, noting carefully the teachings of Pythagoras, of the stern Portico, of the Old and the New Academy, and of the Garden of Epicurus' (1 BW 402, 13 May 1615).[1] These classifications are important in their own right, but can also illuminate our understanding of Grotius' thought, 'for if we are ignorant of these distinctions a thick mist rises before us when we try to read the books of ancient writers, and their value is lost'. Qualified use of authorities by reference, explicitly or implicitly, to their philosophical sect enhances their value. A typical case is Grotius' defence of self-preservation as formulated in the first two laws in *De jure praedae commentarius*:

[N]o member of any sect of philosophers, when embarking upon a discussion of the ends [of good and evil], has ever failed to lay down these two laws first of all as indisputable axioms. For on this point the Stoics, the Epicureans, and the Peripatetics are in complete agreement, and apparently even the Academics have entertained no doubt. (DJPC 2, 6)

Less careful readers reproach Grotius for being 'glaringly selective and self-serving in his choice of references.'[2]

Grotius seems to be aware that sensitivity to context is a sure way to become eclectic. As an eclectic, Grotius was never shy to borrow from original thinkers, with no particular qualms to put their arguments to his own, often clearly different, use. Grotius claims to look for the truth under the sectarian biases, and thus to recover perennial wisdom. To trace the presence of major political thinkers in Grotius might be valuable, as long as one sees them as part of the larger mosaic of Grotius' eclecticism. I will argue that this eclecticism allows Grotius to combine a realist view on politics as the effective and efficient management of society with a normative view on justice as the guiding principle for a peaceful society. Consequently, Grotius' politics is not about ideal states or utopias, but about the variety of actually existing or historical societies, their origins, development and challenges. The nature of political corruption, its causes and remedies, is a central topic in Grotius' politics. In modern terms, Grotius is intrigued by the issue of political sustainability. Since war is the greatest threat to political stability, and just war is the likely answer to persistent injustice, a political order that is just in a strict sense is more likely to be sustainable. Given the minimal requirements this condition poses, many different political arrangements may possibly lead to the desired goal. In sum, Grotius' eclecticism allows him to stay away from end-state political normativity.

The 'political writings' of Grotius are taken in a broad sense here and include all those published and unpublished writings that provide essential information on Grotius' political thought. Obviously, relevant parts of *De jure belli ac pacis* and *De jure praedae* are central to the analysis, but also central claims in *Adamus exul* and *De imperio summarum potestatum circa sacra* are given consideration. Next to that, the historical works *Annales et Historiae* and *De antiquitate reipublicae Batavicae*, as well as the programmatic *De republica emendanda* and the *Parallelon rerumpublicarum* are important sources.

The argument of the chapter, however, will be programmatic, concentrating on Grotius' analysis of the highest powers – *summa potestas* – in a self-sufficient polity – *civitas perfecta* – its causes and effects.

Both the terms 'political thought' and 'political writings' require some explication in relation to Hugo Grotius. First of all, Grotius did not think of himself as a political thinker, but as a humanist who – apart from having a vivid interest in theology and Bible studies as well as law – was also actively involved in politics in one way or another, by devising day-to-day policies in the city government of Rotterdam, the States of Holland or as Swedish ambassador to the king of France. In addition, he would more often than not translate his political involvement into more detached, theoretical informed writings on the Dutch political system, on Dutch commercial interests, on war and peace and on Swedish history. Differently from other humanists, he never wrote a commentary on Aristotle, or a treatise *De republica*. He did not aim at developing an integrated view of the political world, nor a philosophical system to approach that world. Yet, Grotius was interested in and an avid reader of ancient philosophy and history – Plato, Aristotle, Cicero, Thucydides, Tacitus, among many others, the Church Fathers – Lactantius, Augustine, Aquinas and their commentators, the neo-scholastic writers as much as the Protestant political thinkers – Vitoria, Suárez and Althusius; Arnisaeus, Bodin. Of course, the political significance of the study of law did not escape him in addressing Roman law, its reception and modern developments. He himself wrote about many important political issues, and numerous were his contributions to sorting out the pressing problems of his time: the religious troubles that plagued the young Dutch Republic, the wars of religion and the broader issue of war and peace, also in a colonial context, the presence of political and religious order in the Old Testament and its possible meaning for his own age. On all of these topics, Grotius was speaking out, most of the time dressing himself in the cloak of scholarly erudition, and always aiming to take a broader view and a nuanced perspective. But, erudition does not preclude political engagement, nor political activism. Increasingly engaged in the attempts of the States party around Johan Oldenbarnevelt (1547–1619), Grotius not only wrote two books on Church-state relations, he also took a stance in this polemic before the city government of Amsterdam through his *Oratio* of 23 April 1616. Together with his justification of the political programme and the actions it gave rise to in the *Apologia* (1622), the *Oratio* forms his most personal and outspoken political intervention.

What would be easier, one might think, to deduct therefrom a coherent view of politics and of the political order from his political writings? Many have tried, but few have succeeded in formulating a dominant interpretation. This chapter draws a few lines that might be helpful in looking in a coherent way at Grotius' political writings. First, an attempt is made to distinguish Grotius the political thinker from Grotius the jurist; then, his relevant writings are introduced and discussed in their chronological order.

17.2 Political Thought

How do the juridical differ from the political, law from power, justice from utility in Grotius' writings? One might be tempted to identify the texts that Grotius wrote in order to address a practical political problem and declare these the prototype of his political writings. Yet, since Grotius' style of writing is forensic and very much that of a legal counsel, we still would need a reconstruction of the underlying theory. For Grotius the *jurist*, such reconstruction has been a constant endeavour of scholars ever since Jean Barbeyrac (1674–1744) wrote his short history of natural law.[3] For Grotius the *political thinker,* there are studies that place him in the history of contract theories of the state,[4] of unsocial sociability,[5] of early-modern Aristotelianism[6] or consider him in the light of the development of Roman law-based theories of the public and international sphere.[7]

Grotius himself makes the distinction between law and political thought at the end of the *Prolegomena* of *De jure belli ac pacis,* where he writes:

In my work as a whole [–] I have refrained from discussing topics which belong to another subject, such as those that teach what may be advantageous in practice [quod ex usu sit facere]. For such topics have their own special field, that of politics, [quia ista suam habent artem specialem politicam] which Aristotle rightly treats by itself, without introducing extraneous matter into it. Bodin, on the contrary mixed up politics with the body of law with which we are concerned [haec ars cum iuris nostri arte confunditur]. (DJBP Prol. 56–7)

A similar passage can be found in *De imperio*:

In this whole treatment I just want to work out one thing, what is lawful [quid liceat], not what is expedient at any single moment [quid unoquoque tempore expediat]. (DI 10.31)

However, this claim comes with two provisos. First of all, Grotius does not exclude that, here and there, he actually did discuss what is expedient to do ('quod utile est feci'), but only in passing and in order to distinguish it more clearly from what is lawful ('iusti quaestione'). Second, Grotius vehemently rejects that he is writing as a polemicist and aims to take a stance in actual or foreseeable controversies. He claims to have aimed at such a style that both the sorts of controversies and the theoretical principles for deciding these are laid out in one go to his target audience, a readership of those who play an active part in public affairs ('qui negotia publica tractant') (DJBP Prol. 58–9).[8]

The two *artes* of politics and justice are distinguished as *utile* and *quaestio iusti*. In distinguishing between actual controversies and types of controversies, Grotius clearly intends to separate the *ars politica* from practical politics. In *De antiquitate*, Grotius lists 'religion, justice and agreement ('religionem, iustitiam, atque concordiam') as the surest safeguards of the state' (ARpB, Introduction), thus joining the theological to the legal and the political. *Concordia* is the subject matter of the *ars politica*, and is achieved through the exercise of sovereignty.

Negotia publica is an interesting term, with its moral overtones of a worthy life dedicated to serving the commonwealth. Different from *res publica*, a term that indicates an object or range of objects, *negotia publica* refers to an activity or range of activities. Underlying it is the Grotian distinction between private and public. This distinction is a helpful entry into the *ars politica*, since it allows outlining of the proper subject matter of politics independently from the legal treatment of social relations. Of course, politics is not separate from questions of legal rights. Yet, political activities proper are neither about litigation nor jurisdiction. By consequence, it would be better to distinguish – just like between justice in a strict sense and a wider sense – between politics in a strict sense and in a wider sense. In a wider sense, political activity (*potestas civilis*) is also about safeguarding jurisdiction in the actual world and about articulating a political community's legal claims and position:

Aristotle distinguishes three parts in the government of a state [*in administranda republica*]: deliberation in regard to matters of common interest; the choice of officials; and the administration of justice. (DJBP 1.3.6.1)

However, it seems proper to say that politics in a strict sense is about making authoritative decisions for a political community: it is the *exercise* of sovereignty. It is important to underline that Grotius effectively separates the provision of justice from the provision of authoritative decisions, even if the former can fall under the purview of the latter. By claiming that, in the absence of specific arrangements for the provision of justice, everyone has a right and a duty to provide for justice (DJPC 7, 30; DJBP 1.4.16), Grotius is on a track that differs from both that of Jean Bodin (1530–96) before him and Thomas Hobbes (1588–1679) after him, who both reckon the provision as well as the establishment of justice as a prerogative of the sovereign. We will come back to this issue when discussing the different elaborations of sovereignty from *Parallelon* up to *De jure belli ac pacis*. For now, we will trace this perspective of two takes on social life in Grotius' writings. On the one hand, a political perspective, on the other a juridical one; the first arguing that taking care of public affairs is to rule, and the other that to take care of public affairs is to provide justice. Of course, a wise and prudent ruler provides for justice, but in order to distinguish the political thought of Grotius from amid his other interests, it is useful to think of the exercise of sovereignty, *regimen imperativum* or rule, τὸ κράτος , as a topic in its own right. Grotius also argues the reverse, i.e. that 'by the very law of nature leadership is conferred on him who acts justly' (DJBP 2.20.9.2). This underlines the close connection between the legal and the political perspectives. Yet, Grotius introduces τὸ κράτος as equivalent to sovereignty: 'The sovereignty [*summum imperium*] [in the Low Countries] was with the States if not in practice, certainly in principle as we have demonstrated before [in *De antiquitate*]. [–] In the German lands τὸ κράτος is equally with the States [Ordines]' (1 BW 528, to Lingelsheim, 3 September 1617). It exhibits the *kratos-ethos* distinction that Meinecke made the leading idea of his history of reason of state, and is present in Grotius' use of the notion of necessity, in the extreme case of 'necessity breaking the law', and in the various ways in which the necessity of circumstance generates a justified claim to individual or state.[9]

The wielding of power and the logic of necessity are not limited to the state. There is another natural source of power: the *pater familias*, the head of the household, whom Grotius introduces in *De jure praedae*, expands on in *De imperio* and makes part of the history of state formation in *De jure belli ac pacis*. Grotius hesitates between two positions. He emphasises the natural legitimacy of paternal rule, and the 'might makes right' aspect of paternal rule – *potestas patria* – in opposition to the legality that might, but not necessarily does, reign in the state, according to *De jure praedae*. *In De imperio*, we read a more outspoken defence of the legitimacy of parental rule: 'There is only one ordinary, permanent and primitive form of power which is placed below the supreme power without being derived from it, that of the head of a household' (DI 4.6). To bring the argument home, Grotius adds: 'the power of the tutor and of the guardian have their origin in that', i.e. the power of the *pater familias* is not explained from his being a tutor or guardian, but from the father's natural command over that which is naturally his. Here we encounter a beginning of a conjectural history of social organisation. At various places, Grotius takes this up to explain the origins of property or the role of the state in Church matters. Grotius seems to be more Aristotelian here than either Johannes Althusius (1563–1638), who sees the family as a consociation initiated by a special pact for the purpose of holding in common a particular interest,[10] or Bodin, who defines the family as a lawful government of many subjects under a *pater familias*.[11] For Grotius, the family is a natural necessity for the procreation of the human species, and the command of the *pater familias* – the *potestas patria* – is that of the creator of this entity. In terms of Roman law, it is only by *mancipatio* that the children, and/or the servants and slaves, obtain a life of their own. In *De jure belli ac pacis*, Grotius systematises the various notions of power in a threefold classification of *potestas* (*patria*, *domenica* and *in se*), as well as a division in private and public.

A second general consideration concerns Grotius' understanding of social organisation. For all his realism, Grotius at times expresses his hope or belief that justice wins in the end. This does not signify that he denies that human societies originate and develop in all sorts of ways, in the interplay of violence and warfare, fundamental legislation, migration, suppression and submission. In *De jure belli ac pacis* (DJBP 1.4 and 2.9), he provides a plethora of examples of this. It is often said that *De jure praedae* presents a utility-driven systematisation of state formation, in which individuals unite in order to promote their private interest, while, conversely, that the later juridical treatise builds on man's fellow feeling as the basis for sociability. The differences maybe are less stark, considering the importance of fellow feeling in the prior work (DJPC 15, 154v): 'Throughout the whole universe, there is nothing – save for immortal God – more beneficial to man than man himself, so that the most beneficial of all achievements is the winning of human goodwill', and of utility and necessity throughout all his writings. The difference seems to hinge rather on the changing understanding of public virtue in relation to justice. Anyhow, the Grotian idea is that of natural sociability. Although the state is a human creation, it has its roots in human nature and nature in general. The unequal distribution of resources over the earth forces mankind to cooperation:

No one, in fact, has the right to hinder any nation from carrying on commerce with any other nation at a distance. That such permission be accorded is in the interest of human society and does not involve loss to any one. (DJBP 2.2.13.5)

Such cooperation can take the form of commerce, or that of a *civitas*, the aggregation of a multitude for the purpose of living under common laws and for common defence. If successful, it may lead to the establishment of a self-reliant commonwealth, fit for self-defence and therefore endowed with sovereignty. It needs to be noticed that the state is not created by a sovereign, nor is state formation identical to the establishment of a sovereign, but sovereignty is acquired in the process of the *civitas* becoming perfected – the term in *De jure praedae* – or self-sufficient – in *De jure belli ac pacis*. Sovereignty is an attribute of the state – which is its *subjectum commune* – and executed by the person(s) designated by the fundamental laws who are the *subjectum proprium* of sovereignty (DJBP 1.3.7.1–3). The fountain of justice is sociability (DJBP Prol. 8). What is the fountain of sovereignty? According to *De imperio*, the *patria potestas* is an original power and antecedent to the genesis of political rule (DI 4.6).

Aristotle himself, the author chiefly relied upon by those who hold the contrary view [i.e. that the state is natural], writes as follows:

   For man is by nature a conjugal creature to a greater extent than he is a political creature, in that the family is in truth an earlier and more necessary institution than the state, and the procreation of children a more general characteristic of the animal kingdom [than the gregarious instinct]. (DJPC 8, 40)

The family or household is run by the *pater familias* who only learns to deal with equals through contacts with other patriarchs. Thus, hierarchy reappears in the prefect society, after the establishment of a commonwealth by patriarchs who unite for a common purpose:

An association [*consociatio*] in which many fathers of families unite into a single people [*populus*] and state [*civitas*] gives the greatest right to the corporate body [*corpus*] over its members [*partes*]. This in fact is the most perfect society [*societas*]. There is no lawful act of men which does not have relation to this association either of itself or by reason of the circumstances. (DJBP 2.5.23)

17.3 Political Writings

A substantial part of Grotius' political writings was – for various reasons – only published posthumously. His political works deal with the nature and actual organisation of political power in societies, from the theory of sovereignty, all the way to issues such as toleration and the governance of churches. They include historical analyses of actual states, as well as perspectives on their future development. Of course, a large part of these writings discusses the extent to and ways in which justice is helpful to achieve sustainable political regimes. Notwithstanding his general endorsement of the Ciceronian union of the *honestum* and *utile*, a moral stance is a necessary, but not a sufficient, condition for effective politics. In *Parallelon rerumpublicarum liber tertius. De moribus ingenioque populorum Atheniensium, Romanorum, Batavorum*, Grotius criticises Cicero for calling honourable what is useful for the state. What is not honourable can never be useful, retorts Grotius (*Parallelon* 7, 150). Yet, throughout his writings, Grotius explains the workings of power and discusses the relative advantages of different political regimes. Moreover, he accepts throughout that states are the product of history, the outcome of human action, though not of human design. There is no political regime without its shortcomings, most of all because, for sovereign rule to be effective, it should not meet with resistance from the citizens.

In his first publication, *Adamus exul*, Grotius gives a supra-lapsarian account of the origins of sin. Adam is made to understand by Jehovah that he was foregoing his duty by not correcting Eve when she took an apple from the tree of knowledge. Adam admits to Eve: 'I believed thee once too often' (*Adamus exul* 1736). And the *vox Dei* speaks:

He whom thou hast betray'd. Beneath his yoke thou'lt learn

His orders to obey; and he shall be thy lord. [*Iussibus parere disces, ille te imperio reget.*] (1938–43)

Here *potestas patria* appears as punishment for original sin. Most likely, *Adam exul* was written after another text that was almost lost to posterity: *De republica emendanda*, in which the young Grotius compared the early United Provinces to the Hebrew state.[12] Relying on Flavius Josephus' history of the Jewish war,[13] Grotius describes the nature and critical aspects of political rule in the Jewish theocracy, as he calls it. Comparing it to the Republic, he finds many similarities: the organisation in terms of cities, provinces/tribes and commonwealth, the mixed constitution that is ruled by an aristocracy with the *sanhedrin*/state council ruling, God's providence that saves the commonwealth and punishes its enemies. Explaining the ambivalence of the word *princeps*, Grotius distinguishes responsive from exploitive government, an approach that Grotius' friend and colleague, Petrus Cunaeus (1586–1638), would elaborate upon in his *De republica Hebraeorum* (1617). Grotius thus belongs to the current in political theory known as political Hebraism, to which his teacher, Franciscus Junius (1545–1602), is also reckoned. In *De republica emendanda*, Grotius laments the federative organisation of the United Provinces, their lack of decisiveness and the prevalence of particularism. He pleads for a stronger, more authoritative and more effective Council of State as the central ruling body of the Republic. Thus, this early work contrasts with the more positive take on federalism of *De antiquitate reipublicae Batavicae* and, in particular, the later defence of provincial sovereignty of the States of Holland in the *Apology* of 1622. It is a distinct possibility that, in the later treatises, Grotius wrote in defence of provincial sovereignty out of a realistic despair about the limits for changes within the Dutch political system, since he more than once complained about the centrifugal forces of provincial particularism. In *Annales et Historiae de rebus Belgicis,* completed in 1612, indeed, concerns about provincial particularism reappear. At the end of the fifth and last book of the *Annales*, Grotius laments about provincial particularism, luxuriousness flowing from the economic successes of the Republic and the ensuing moral decay. This is all not very original, but is informative about Grotius' registers as a political writer.

As a true humanist, Grotius had a penchant for comparative history, as is demonstrated in *Parallelon rerumrepublicarum liber tertium. De moribus ingenioque populorum Atheniensium, Romanorum, Batavorum* (written in 1602). In this wide-ranging comparative study of Greek and Roman political history with ancient and modern Batavia – the Low Countries, Grotius brings together a coherent view of *civitas* and *respublica*, against the background of a moral psychology of political ambition. As before, Grotius subscribes to the unity of the *honestum* and *utile*, yet gives full reign to the idea that corrupt political systems do exist and can thrive, up to a point, only to be countered by the armed resistance of commonwealths that suffer from their transgressions. In particular, in the chapter *De fide et perfidia*, it looks as if nature corrects itself: political corruption leads to injustice towards other states, which in turn wage just wars against their oppressors. History shows, according to Grotius, that – in this way – corrupt systems decay and disappear. Corrupt regimes are not sustainable: therefore, it is in the interest of a state to fight corruption. 'Give God that we will have always, as an expression of our character, this desire for virtue, and that nobody will ridicule vices or considers it wordly-wise to corrupt each other' (*Parallelon* 7, 148).

There is no paradise on earth as *Adamus exul* had shown,[14] but there can be a workable order of *concordia* in which citizens, among themselves and in cooperation with the government, manage to agree on the important matters, and thus on what the important matters are. *Concordia*, in Grotius' view, is something empirical, achieved by gradual adjustment, and is as such the defining criterion of a *societas*, be it of *socii* in a joint economic enterprise or of citizens in a political entity – a city, a state, the community of mankind. Chapter 24 of the work also makes generous use of the expression *humanum genus* as a term to denote what convictions and interests we humans have in common. Other core concepts in *Parallelon* are *fides*, justice, trade and crafts (the economy), prudence, military and mental strength and, finally, tolerance.

Not surprisingly, the controversialist thrust of *Parallelon* was to provide an ideological perspective on the Dutch Revolt after it entered into a new phase with its decisive victory over the forces of the Habsburg archdukes at the Battle of Nieuwpoort (1600). The merits of the Dutch Republic as a commercial nation are praised and explained from the political liberty that the citizens enjoy and their trustworthiness, in the marketplace and in politics alike. The generosity of the province of Holland is highlighted: 'They [the other provinces] share with us [Holland] the liberty, and also have an equal share in the government, even while they contribute less' (Parallelon 6, 126). A separate chapter is devoted to maritime matters. This chapter brings together fishery, trade and commerce, and shipbuilding, praising the strong network economy that these interlocking trades brought about. An important part of the section on trade is reserved for the Asian trade, describing the various parts of East India that were frequented by Dutch merchant ships.

Only two years later, Grotius wrote another – also unpublished – text, *De jure praedae*, that brought his considerations from *Parallelon* to a new point, defending warfare against the Portuguese merchant fleet in the East Indies as a case of just war. As a political argument, *De jure praedae* is an intriguing exercise at the interface of *civitas* and rule. Here also, Grotius maintains that, although 'human society does indeed have its origin in nature', 'civil society as such is derived from deliberate design' (DJPC 8, 40). It is the kind of design that is behind *concordia*, some form of agreement that produces a peaceful and rational society, yet open to various further considerations. One of these pertains to the relative autonomy of the citizens, who are as much a driving force behind the commonwealth as they are guided by the sovereign. As a *societas*, the *civitas* is guided as if through a single spirit: 'Since there is in a nation as a whole a certain agreement of spirit and genius, which is not in any individual member of that nation, but can be found in the unity of the common body' (*Parallelon* 1, 20). In the Preface to *De antiquitate*, Grotius holds that 'there is not immediately another republic, as long as the supreme force of rule and the supreme power, and that mind, so to speak, that moves and keeps the whole body politic, remains one and the same'. A similar idea is found in *De jure praedae*: 'Thus a household consists, as it were, in a multitude of bodies directed by one mind' (DJPC 6, 27v).

This sociological view of the commonwealth will culminate two decades later in *De jure belli ac pacis*:

Isocrates and, after him the Emperor Julian, said that states are immortal; that is, they can continue to exist because a people belongs to the class of bodies that are made up of separate members, but are comprehended under a single name, for the reason that they have 'a single essential character' [ἕξιν μίαν], as Plutarch says, or a single spirit [spiritum unum], as Paul the jurist says. Now that spirit or 'essential character' [*spiritus sive* ἕξις] in a people is the full and perfect union [*consociatio plena atque perfecta*] of civic life, the first *product* [my italics] of which is sovereign power [*summum imperium*]; that is the bond which binds the state together, that is the breath of life which so many thousands breathe, as Seneca says. These artificial bodies, moreover, are clearly similar to a natural body; and a natural body, though its particles little by little are changed, does not cease to be the same if the form remains unchanged, as Alfenus argues after the philosophers. [. . .]

Again, it is not an empty name merely that remains, but 'the essential character' [ἕξις], which [the ancient Greek general] Conon defines as an 'inherent bodily character' [ἕξιν σώματος συνεκτικὴν], Philo as a 'spiritual bond' [πνευματικὸν συνέχον], and the Latins as a spirit [*spiritum*]'. (DJBP 2.9.3.1)

In this sequence of fragments from *De jure belli ac pacis,* Grotius brings together his previous attempts to identify the results of living together, most importantly connecting the *consociatio perfecta* with the *civitas* and with sovereign power. The 'single essential character' that causes this to happen might best be understood – in hindsight – as a constitution. *Summum imperium* thus is the production of *consociatio perfecta.*

That is only seen in hindsight, since Grotius made effective self-defence a defining element of the *civitas perfecta.* This existentialist element – in order to be a good citizen, or state, is first to exist, second to exist in a sustainable fashion – is strongly present in the whole of the *Parallelon,* particularly in its chapter 21 on military matters: the core term is *necessitas.* As Grotius states in *De jure praedae*: 'But if a given state lacked power to wage war, it would not be self-sufficient for purposes of defense' (DJPC 6, 27v). Here, Grotius elaborates on early-modern notions of liberty: defending one's city by way of a citizens' city militia, dramatically demonstrated in 1618 when Prince Maurice of Nassau (1567–1625) disbanded the city militia of Utrecht to bring the town to heel as part of his coup against Oldenbarnevelt.

Just as the local is never far away in the global, so the general strategy of *De jure praedae* of justifying private war to correct injustice in the colonies fits very much into a republican political theory of 'all for one (commonwealth) and one for all'. In order to make his approach work, Grotius devotes a lot of effort to articulating the connections between individual, society and state. He distinguishes the multitude from the organised *civitas* (DJPC 2, 10v): 'Truly, there is no greater power [*majus nullum imperium*] set over the state, since the state is a self-sufficient aggregation [*per se sufficiens multitudo*]' (DJPC 2, 13). Thus arises a concept of state sovereignty, in that the self-sufficient multitude is, as such, the incumbent of sovereign powers, 'that is to say, possessed of its own laws, courts, revenue, and magistrates; something endowed with its own council and its own authority' (DJPC 6, 27v). Interestingly, Grotius adds that this does not exclude that the 'self-sufficient multitude' could be part of a larger political entity and could have a prince in common with other *civitates*. This move to federalism, where autonomous entities unite in a larger whole, goes beyond the classical Batavian myth of Dutch autonomy, in that it emphasises the basic autonomy of the commonwealth and considers the acceptance of a foreign ruler as a matter of international affairs. This seems to refer to the actual situation of the Northern Netherlands after the abjuration of Philip II (1528–98) in 1581, followed by a fleeting experiment with François, Duke of Anjou (1555–84) and an experiment with Robert Dudley, Earl of Leicester (1532–88), who represented Queen Elisabeth of England (1533–1603).

The philosophical presuppositions of the overall argument *of De jure praedae* are meant to deliver a justification of war, i.e. a concept of just war that covers the 1603 merchants' piracy in the Strait of Singapore. In achieving that, however, a political theory steps in, expanding on the private-public distinction and the correlated anthropology. Having created man the way He did:

God wills that we should protect ourselves, retain our hold on the necessities of life, obtain that which is our due, punish transgressors, and at the same time defend the state, executing its orders as well as the commands of its magistrates. (DJPC 3, 14v)

The human being who recognises and accepts the divine commands is free, autonomous, active and useful to others. However, human choices are conditioned by circumstances and, 'in cases of necessity and for the purpose of preventing the loss of our rights, many things are permitted which otherwise would not be permitted; and when one recourse fails, we turn to another' (DJPC 9, 42), writes Grotius with reference to Baldus' pupil, Paulus Castrensis (d. 1441). Historical circumstance and human need produce a plethora of political regimes, of which two stand out: the monarchical regime and the commonwealth, *regimen regale* and *regimen politicum* (DJPC 12, 99).

Together, the constructions of an original rule of the *pater familias* and of collective responsibility produce the argument for rightful punishment by individuals of individual members of a rogue state. Being in the world, for Grotius, presupposes being powerful, as a family, as a commonwealth. Strong, sustainable communities are in harmony, i.e. there is agreement among the citizens about their aspirations. In the early writings of Grotius, this political model operates on the fault-line between a good and a bad state. It is the Netherlands versus Spain, *fides* versus *perfidia*, commerce to the benefit of all versus extortion. In 1609, with the publication of *Mare liberum*, Grotius settles the European debate on early modern commercial colonialism with a natural law argument about unhampered access to trading places and trade goods. The connection between individual property and politics, punishment and politics, trade and politics has been established once and for all. The harmonious society goes global.

At the time, Grotius was forced to act locally. The Twelve Years Truce with Spain of 1609 forced the Dutch leadership to focus on internal disagreements, for which the predestination debate was the ideological *pars pro toto*. More was brewing, however. Grotius himself described the desolate situation of the Republic in these words in a letter to Pierre Jeannin (1540–1623):

[T]he mutual understanding between the various provinces leaves much to be desired. There is incessant quarrelling with the Zealanders. ... the authority of the States General is held in contempt and the common bond jeopardized. (1 BW 107, 18 September 1609)[15]

Some Zealanders wanted to leave the Union and Grotius did not expect anything good to flow from this. It is with Zealand friends that Grotius engages when he composes a text on toleration. In this, at the time unpublished, text, he pleas for mutual understanding and toleration. For this, he sets up the Greek-Orthodox patriarch, Meletius Pegas (1549–1601), who had been frequented by several friends of Grotius during their stay in Constantinople, as an example.

The political message of *Meletius* is one of concord and tolerance. The argumentation is theological: it condemns dissension and quarrel as unchristian and claims that the rules of life are eternal and straightforward. Debate about religious doctrine should be limited to the issues that are unequivocally necessary for salvation. *Meletius* gives an overview of the essentials of Christian belief and lists the duties that come along with it. Reflecting the irenicism of Grotius' Leiden teacher, Franciscus Junius, *Meletius* is a predecessor of *De veritate religionis Christianae*, and constructs one of the two planks of Grotius' position in the Church-state debates. The other plank is that of sovereignty as developed in *De imperio*.

In *De jure praedae*, Grotius presented a notion of state sovereignty, the *summa potestas* as an attribute of the *civitas*, connected to its institutions and conditioned upon its effectiveness in assuring self-defence. In *De imperio*, he identified sovereignty as an attribute of the ruler(s) of the state. 'I understand the 'supreme power' ('Summam potestatem intellego') to mean a person or a body having authority over the people, and subject only to the authority of God Himself' (DI 1.1). In the Dutch context wherein the regents of Holland were addressed as 'Hoogmogende Heren' (Supreme Lords), this rhetorical trick might work. The discrepancy with *De jure praedae* is understandable as the former book was about sovereignty between states, while the latter book concerned the supreme power of the state over its citizens. *In De jure belli ac pacis*, Grotius might be said to harmonise these two conceptions of sovereignty, not by making the distinction between internal and external sovereignty, but by constructing a theory of *potestas*, first, and second by a distinction between sovereignty's common subject (i.e. the self-sufficient *civitas*) and its special subject (i.e. the person(s) of the sovereign). Thus, sovereignty remains an attribute of the self-sufficient state; it is about the autonomy of the body politic. Yet, the state acts authoritatively only through its supreme rulers.

Grotius deviates here from the positions of Bodin, and those later of Hobbes and Jean-Jacques Rousseau (1712–78), who distinguished between the sovereign who appoints the government and the administration of sovereignty by the latter. Richard Tuck speaks of a sleeping sovereign, who only 'wakes up' when a new administration has to be appointed.[16] The obvious candidate for the sleeping sovereign is the multitude of citizens, acting as *constitutive power*. This is not how Grotius understands things: he compares the common/special distinction to that between the body as the common acting subject of sight and the eye as its special subject: 'The subject of a power is either common or special. Just as the body is a common, the eye a special subject of the power of sight, so the state, which we have defined above as a perfect association, is the common subject of sovereignty' (DJBP 1.3.7.1). There is no foundational relationship between body and eye, other than that the spirit of the body politic – the constitution – stipulates who is to be the person of the sovereign. With one exception: in case the constitutional sovereign intends to alienate part of the commonwealth, he can do so only with the permission of the body of citizens, but that is because the citizens' freedom and property is involved, not because they can limit the authority of the sovereign. This position is not without problems and will continue to be discussed under the heading of '*lex regia*', among others by Ulrich Huber (1636–94).[17] Grotius thus holds an extraordinary position within the tradition of constitutional contract theory. One may even ask whether his theory of sovereignty is a contract theory at all.

Ever since the predestination debate and the attempts of Oldenbarnevelt, Grotius and others to defuse that debate by making the case for moderation, as Grotius so eloquently formulated in his address to the Amsterdam city council of 23 April 1616, it became evident that Grotius' natural law theory had not considered the actual ways in which God's rule of the world and secular rule by man cohere. How is the authoritative interpretation of God's will achieved in a polity? How much of it can we understand through the study of human nature and its implied teleology? The general idea of harmony between reason and revelation is challenged by the disagreements among different interpreters of God's word and their position in society. From *Ordinum pietas* to *De imperio*, Grotius develops his position, trying first his hand at an Erastian position. In *De imperio*, however, few limitations pertain to the authority of the sovereign power in matters of religious organisation. Political obedience is due to commands of the sovereign, not because citizens agree with their decision, but because it is issued by the sovereign. Things that cannot be commanded – matters of belief or matters of logic – must be left to man's conscience and man's reason. All other matters are indisputably within the discretion of the sovereign, even if he is advised by ministers of the Church. It is up to the sovereign to determine if it is God who is speaking through his ministers. Only what is truly God's word can prevail. This is the situation as far as the dominant Church – the Dutch Reformed Church – is concerned. Toleration of heterodox religious organisations takes place outside the bond of religious conviction, and is only driven by, on the one hand, the principle that conscience cannot be forced, and on the other hand by care for public peace. On the latter grounds, Grotius was sceptical of the Mennonites, whose abstinence of politics he considered hypocritical. In the *Remonstrantie*, which he drafted in 1615 to suggest rules for the admission of Jews to the cities in the province of Holland, he defined his task as to determine whether the Jews should be tolerated, and also whether they should be free to exercise their religion. Last and most important, Grotius set out to give regulations to prevent negative effects on the Christian religion and the public peace. With arguments out of *Mare liberum*, Grotius defends the right of Jews to be admitted to the country; to allow them the practice of their religion in unobtrusive buildings is a matter of benevolence and political prudence. The negative effects can be managed by forbidding proselytisation and inter-confessional marriages on the one hand, and by strict regulation of places of worship on the other. Holland did not give heed to Grotius' proposals that otherwise did not deviate much from the practice in cities such as Rotterdam and Haarlem.

In *De jure belli ac pacis*, the empirical approach to political regimes takes a relativist turn: 'no matter what form of government you may devise, you will never be free from difficulties and dangers' (DJBP 1.3.8.1). In particular, Grotius advises to prefer life over civil freedom, if the latter can only be obtained by warfare.

Life, to be sure, which affords the basis for all temporal and the occasion for eternal blessings, is of greater value than liberty. This holds true whether you consider each aspect in the case of an individual or of a whole people. (DJBP 2.24.6.2)

Not that Grotius would not defend the natural rights of man, the value of equality and equity, but the variety of human organisation and the necessity occasioned by the circumstances often point towards survival where more heroic persons would have dreamt of resistance. *Ars politica* is the art of the possible, and Grotius' analysis of sovereignty delineates its contours. Grotius the humanist would have been the first to add that the *ars politica* is only part of the story and that the theological perspective of eternal happiness and the legal perspective of justice should be added to provide the full picture. But, that is not to diminish the singular importance of a naturalist, 'sociological' understanding of political order and its underlying processes. Without a separate study of private and public utility, the study of justice would remain sterile.

Editions and Translations of Grotius' Works Used

Parallelon rerumpublicarum liber tertius. De moribus ingenioque populorum Atheniensium, Romanorum, Batavorum (ca. 1602; Haarlem, 1801–3)

Annales et historiae de rebus Belgicis (ca. 1612; Amsterdam, 1657)

Ordinum Hollandiae ac Westfrisiae pietas (Leiden, 1613)

Decretum pro pace ecclesiarum (Leiden, 1614)

Remonstrance concerning the order that should be imposed upon the Jews in the territory of Holland and Westfriesland, ed. and transl. D. Kromhout and A. Offenberg (Leiden, 2019)

De imperio summarum potestatum circa sacra (ca. 1615; Paris, 1647)

Oratio in Senatu Amstelredamensi [Address to the Council of Amsterdam] (Frankfort/M, 1616)

Apologeticvs eorvm qvi Hollandiœ VVestfrisiœqve et vicinis quibusdam nationibus ex legibus prœfuerunt ante mutationem quœ evenit anno 1618 (Paris, 1622)

De jure belli ac pacis libri tres (Paris, 1625)

De origine gentium Americanarum dissertatio (Paris, 1642)

Further Reading

Brett, A.S., 'Natural right and civil community. The civil philosophy of Hugo Grotius', *The Historical Journal* 45 (2002) 31–51.

Eyffinger, A., 'Introduction' to 'De Republica Emendanda; a juvenile tract by Hugo Grotius on the emendation of the Dutch polity', *Grotiana NS* 5 (1984) 5–56.

Fukuoka, A., *The Sovereign and the Prophets. Spinoza on Grotian and Hobbesian Biblical Argumentation* (Leiden, 2018).

Grotiana NS 21–22 (2001-2) *Grotius and the Stoa*; 26–28 (2005-7) on *De jure praedae*.

Hont, I., *Jealousy of Trade: International Competition and the Nation-State in Historical Perspective* (Cambridge, MA, 2006).

Lee, D., *Popular Sovereignty in Early Modern Constitutional Thought* (Oxford, 2016).

Nelson, E., *The Hebrew Republic. Jewish Sources and the Transformation of European Political Thought* (Cambridge MA, 2011).

Somos, M., *Secularisation and the Leiden Circle* (Leiden, 2011).

Tuck, R., *Natural Rights Theories: Their Origin and Development* (Cambridge 1979).

Tuck, R., *The Sleeping Sovereign. The Invention of Modern Democracy* (Cambridge, 2016).

Van Dam, H.-J., 'Introduction' in Van Dam (ed.), *Hugo Grotius, De imperio summarum potestatum circa sacra* (Leiden, 2001), 1–151.

Notes

1 Published as *Hugonis Grotii epistola de studio politico vel iuris publici recte instituendo* (Upsala, 1626); reprinted in *H. Grotii et aliorum Dissertationes De studiis instituendis* (Amsterdam, 1645). I follow the translation in *American Journal of International Law* 23 (1929) 621–5.

2 Edward Gordon (review), in *American Journal of International Law* 89 (1995) 461–3, at 463.

3 In the introduction 'Preface du traducteur', to his French edition of Samuel Pufendorf, *Le Droit de la Nature et des Gens* (Amsterdam, 1706), i-xliii.

4 E.g. R. Tuck, *Natural Rights Theories: Their Origin and Development* (Cambridge, 1979).

5 E.g. I. Hont, *Jealousy of Trade: International Competition and the Nation-State in Historical Perspective* (Cambridge, MA, 2006).

6 E.g. A.S. Brett, 'Natural right and civil community. The civil philosophy of Hugo Grotius', *The Historical Journal* 45 (2002) 31-51.

7 E.g. B. Straumann, *Roman Law in the State of Nature. The Classical Foundations of Hugo Grotius' Natural Law* (Cambridge, 2015); M. Koskenniemi, 'Miserable comforters. International relations as a new natural law', *European Journal of International Relations* 15 (2009) 395-422; Koskenniemi, 'Vocabularies of sovereignty – powers of a paradox', in Q. Skinner and H. Kalmo (eds.), *Sovereignty in Fragments* (Cambridge, 2011), 222-42.

8 See Cicero, *De Officiis* 3.1 for the term *negotia publica* as the opposite of *otium*.

9 F. Meinecke, *Die Idee der Staatsräson in der neueren Geschichte* (Munich, 1924); See also R. Tuck, *The Rights of War and Peace. Political Thought and the International Order from Grotius to Kant* (Oxford, 1999), esp. ch. 3.

10 J. Althusius, *Politica Methodice Digesta* (Herborn, 1600), 2.2.

11 J. Bodin, *Les six livres de la République* (Paris, 1576), 1.2.

12 See for the circumstances of its discovery and the grounds for attributing it to Grotius the editor's introduction: A. Eyffinger, 'Introduction' to 'De Republica Emendanda; a juvenile tract by Hugo Grotius on the emendation of the Dutch polity', *Grotiana* NS 5 (1984) 5-56.

13 Flavius Josephus, *De Bello Judaico,in: Flavii Josephi Operum tomus secundus: quo continentur authoris Vita, De bello Judaico libri vii, De antiquitate Judaeorum libri ii, Peri autokratoros logismou seu De imperio rationis lib. i* (Geneva, 1595).

14 See for the opposite interpretation of *Adamus exul* – i.e. that of perfectibility – J.E. Nijman, 'Grotius' Imago Dei anthropology: grounding Ius naturae et gentium', in M. Koskenniemi , M.García-Salmones Rovira and P. Amorosa (eds.), *International Law and Religion : Historical and Contemporary Perspectives* (Oxford, 2017), 87-110.

15 Quoted from *Meletius,* ed. and transl. H. Posthumus Meyjes (Leiden, 1988), 14.

16 R. Tuck, *The Sleeping Sovereign. The Invention of Modern Democracy* (Cambridge, 2016), 4, where the importance is signalled of the distinction between sovereignty and administration by Rousseau and the praise thereof by Hume and Dupont de Nemours.

17 See T. Veen, 'Interpretations of Inst. 1,2,6, D. 1,4,1 and D. 1,3,31: Huber's historical, juridical and political-theoretical reflections on the lex Regia', *Tijdschrift voor Rechtsgeschiedenis*, 53 (1985) 357-77 and recently: G. van Nifterik, 'Ulrik Huber on fundamental laws: a European Perspective', *Comparative Legal History*, 4 (2016) 2-18.

Part IV

Grotius as a Legal Scholar

Legal Scholastic and Humanist Influences 18
on Grotius
Alain Wijffels

18.1 Introduction

Between the mid-sixteenth and the mid-seventeenth century, legal methods and legal literature in the Western civil law tradition underwent momentous transformations. Hugo Grotius' legal works reflect those changes. As a prominent legal writer, whose works were highly influential and became leading books of reference and authority, Grotius was also instrumental in contributing to the emergence of a new legal literature.[1] However, there is no general consensus on the typology and properties of various currents of early modern legal science. In the absence of a conventional legal historiography, it is therefore necessary to set out in what sense some common classifications are to be understood in the context of the present chapter. The reader should be warned that, although the terminology of the classification may follow standard historiographical labels, their significance is controversial among legal historians. As hermeneutical props, these labels remain indispensable nonetheless when assessing Grotius' legal scholarship against the backdrop of the evolving legal science of his time.

18.2 Scholastic and Humanistic Jurisprudence

Three broad paradigms of legal methods may help to recognise some structure in the development of legal science during the era of political and cultural transition spanning the fifteenth to seventeenth centuries.[2] The first has often been referred to in legal historiography as the Italian method (*mos italicus*). One may also refer to it as the (medieval) scholastic legal method, mainly represented in civil law literature through the Accursian Gloss, late-medieval commentaries on various parts of the *Corpus Juris Civilis*, collections of *consilia* and comparatively minor genres such as *summae, repetitiones* and treatises. The scholastic method remained influential in sixteenth-century legal scholarship and its most important late-medieval authorities continued to be reprinted until the first quarter of the seventeenth century. That enduring fortune may at least partly be explained by the fact that, throughout Western Europe, practitioners in civil law courts continued to rely heavily on the *mos italicus* authorities for buttressing their forensic arguments.

The second paradigm is usually referred to as legal humanism; or, sometimes, because a few prominent centres of humanist learning and scholars were established in France, as the French method, *mos gallicus*. Legal humanists championed a more authentic understanding of ancient Roman law, which entailed a critical philological and historical overhaul of Roman law sources. Those achievements, in turn, moved some legal humanists to criticise in more or less strong polemical terms the readings and doctrines of the traditional scholastic method. The rivalry between the Italian method and legal humanism has long been a favourite theme of legal historians. Since the later twentieth century, legal historians often prefer to emphasise that, beyond the polemics, most sixteenth-century jurists tried to steer a middle course, combining elements from the two brands of authorities and approaches. Even so, there is little evidence that, in the courts' practice, even by the end of the sixteenth century, legal humanistic method had made much headway against the enduring ascendancy of the Italian method and authorities.

One generation before Grotius, Alberico Gentili's work illustrates the staying power of the Italian method. Gentili (1552–1608) had been educated at the law faculty of Perugia, where some of the most illustrious late-medieval jurists had taught and worked. He spent most of his career as a Protestant exile in England, where he was appointed to the Regius Chair of Civil Law at Oxford and wrote treatises on topics of Roman law and international law. At the beginning of his academic career, in the early 1580s, Gentili still championed the Italian method and argued against the use of legal humanism by lawyers; by the mid-1580s, and in his subsequent works, he adopted both the style and the expertise of legal humanism, without ever jettisoning the traditional late-medieval learning. In the aftermath of the Anglo-Spanish peace treaty of 1604 – around the same time as the young Grotius made his mark writing *De jure praedae commentarius* – Gentili was involved as a consultant in litigation about privateering and maritime warfare, and his scholarly treatment of the issues show how, at that stage of his intellectual trajectory, he was attempting to reconcile scholastic and humanistic methods by seeking a new arrangement of the issues he dealt with by subject matter.

18.3 *Ac Tertium Datur*

Gentili's attempts are a fair illustration of the state of the art in civil law, and its extension to international law issues, at the time when Grotius was entering the field of jurisprudence as a professional lawyer. Throughout the sixteenth century, legal science had been exploring various ways of systematising legal thinking. The key to systematisation, largely inspired by the pre-existing sources and newly-developed legal literature on private law issues, was eventually worked out along a classification by subject matter. Significantly, the historiography of early modern European legal scholarship does not offer a common label or even a consistent character-isation of what developed, beyond political and religious fault-lines, as a – to some degree – common approach among civil lawyers. Teleological national perspectives often tend to overlook the enduring reality of a European civil-law based *jus commune* during the seventeenth and eight-eenth centuries. This is perhaps the result of the paradox of early modern civil law scholarship. On the one hand, its systematic approach to legal topics conceived and arranged by subject matter aimed at merging, within a jurisdiction, civil law and that jurisdiction's particular laws, thus produ-cing and highlighting a differentiation between legal systems from one jurisdiction to the other. On the other hand, the same early modern scholarship also contributed decisively, by its proto-positivistic approach, to shift the meaning of *jus commune* to that of rules of substantive law inspired by Roman law, potentially or effectively applicable in most European legal systems.

   Grotius' education and career coincided with the emergence of that early modern legal scholarship that would eventually supersede as a mainstream legal method both the Italian tradition and legal humanism. The symptoms of the transformation, which was still hesitant during the second half of the sixteenth century, but which gained momentum during the first half of the following century, are manifold. One way to gauge the gradual changes is by having a look at the developments on the legal book market. Not only did the reprints of the major works of reference of the Italian method peter out during the first decades of the seventeenth century, the appearance of a new literature and the strengthening of subject-related books during the sixteenth century, and their growing importance in legal literature as a whole, show that legal humanistic scholarship was not the only jurisprudential strain competing with the Italian method. The development of legal treatises provides a rough indication of the greater interest for the systematic treatment of a particular subject matter. The genre was not unknown in the middle ages, and many medieval treatises were incorporated – along with more recent ones – in the multi-volume collections published at Lyons in the 1530s and 1540s, or in the extensive Venice edition of 1584, but, as a main format of legal literature, it only acquired a greater importance during the latter years of the sixteenth century. At the same time, the treatise-format was used by some authors in order to explore themes that had not – or very rarely – been handled systematically before. For example, in the area of what would later become international law, the second half of the sixteenth century witnessed the publication of a string of treaties on the law of embassies and on the law of war. Other, more traditional genres of legal literature also reflected the shift to a subject-related approach. Commentaries, for example, were increasingly more determinedly arranged by topic than according to the *ordo legalis* of the individual collections of the *Digest* or the *Code*. Concomitantly, early modern commentaries on the *Institutes* – the order of which inspired a comprehensive systematisation of the law, known as the 'Institutional system' – became more popular and relevant than in medieval legal science.

Another way to follow the general development of legal thinking – even at the level of grass-root practitioners in day-to-day litigation – is by analysing the types of legal arguments and reasoning submitted by advocates in their written memoranda and in learned opinions. Whereas the absence of a comprehensive systematisation in the Italian method allowed a relatively free use of legal principles regardless of the specific legal context in which a rule had been expressed, the new insistence on subject matter implied a more rigid discipline in which the use of rules – and, by extension, authorities – was strictly bound by their subject matter. In the civil law tradition, much depended on the extent to which the sources of the *Corpus Juris* covered a particular topic. International law issues, for example, are mostly relatively poorly covered by explicit texts in the *Digest* and *Code*. Hence, the first generations of early modern legal writers on international law – not least Grotius himself – continued to borrow a great deal from private law institutions,[3] which they transposed to an international law setting. Once such a transposition had been carried out and the book on an international law topic had become a standard authority, as was the case with Grotius' *De jure belli ac pacis*, the former private law rules gradually became, in international law arguments, rules of public international law in their own right.[4]

18.4 The Open Triangle of Scholastic Tradition, Legal-Humanistic Innovation and Modern Systematisation-in-Progress

Grotius' achievements as a legal scholar may, therefore, be appraised in the light of these three broad paradigms: the traditional heritage of the scholastic Italian method, the alternative call of legal humanism and the progress of a new mainstream early modern method, which integrated much learning of the two previous methods while, at the same time, transcending them as a new, distinctive model. Beyond this brief outline of the early development of legal scholarship from the perspective of intellectual history, any assessment of Grotius' positioning in the changing scholarly approaches of his time cannot be attempted without referring also to the 'Great Game' that occupied the scholars of his era. The political and religious changes that reshaped Europe, both in domestic politics and in international relations, between the fifteenth and seventeenth centuries also affected the relations between the sciences. The 'Great Game' is a metaphor for the struggle for prominence and distinctiveness that different areas of scholarship vied for in their endeavours to play a decisive part in public governance. In the late-medieval city-states, where the Western civil law tradition originated, legists and canonists had succeeded in moulding jurisprudence as an art of governance. Their success was not least due to their prestige as experts of justice, which was deemed to be an essential feature of good governance. They always faced the competition of theologians and, arguably, the theologians' efforts after the Reformation, both among Roman-Catholic and Protestant theologians, were to a large extent directed at recovering lost ground in the governance of an increasingly secularised, or, more accurately, less clergy-influenced polity. A new competition arose from the development of a distinct scholarship on political theory, no longer anchored in theology. Many early modern writers on political theory had a legal background, but their political writings were not integrated in the legal-literary canon, nor in the established academic legal curriculum. On the whole, the association between civil law expertise and public governance became more ambivalent in early modern times. In some areas, such as private law, the connection with public governance was slackened, while in others, such as international law, it was maintained or strengthened. Any assessment of an early modern jurist's scholarly work implies an assessment of that jurist in the 'Great Game', and his commitment to adjust his work to the needs of public governance in a changed political context. The demise of the Italian method was arguably partly due to its dependency on a political rule-of-law culture that no longer prevailed in early modern political theory and practice.

Late sixteenth-century and early seventeenth-century legal authors were aware of developments and differentiation in legal thinking and could express or reflect their own intellectual and ideological preferences in elaborating a legal argument or a scholarly monograph on a series of topics. That was definitely the case with Grotius, who not only was able to master various currents of legal thinking, both new and old, and other areas of scholarship, but who appears to have been acutely aware of how these currents could be channelled into a method that offered the potential of establishing a new and lasting canon of legal scholarship. That achievement was obviously most successfully reached by Grotius in his work on international law, as *De jure belli ac pacis* became for several generations of jurists, statesmen, diplomats and other public figures a fundamental work of reference. His *Inleidinge tot de Hollandsche Rechtsgeleerdheid*, purportedly a primer for young lawyers who needed a general introduction to the domestic laws of Holland, was also a seminal work in the development of Roman-Dutch law.

Dietrich Heinrich Ludwig Von Ompteda's (1746–1803) late eighteenth-century bibliography on the law of nations mirrors the enlightened beliefs and biases of the age. In his historical survey of international law, he takes a striking leap from Antiquity to Grotius – briefly pausing to mention a few sixteenth-century authors of monographs on topics of international law and dismissing the whole intermediate period as the dark ages of legal scholarship. Modern scholarship of international law, in that view, started with Grotius. Von Ompteda's opinions may have been prompted by a combination of prejudices against a civilisation that had not yet been impressed by the Reformation, humanism and mathematical-scientific rationalism. At the same time, Ompteda's perception of the development of legal scholarship on international law betrays a paradox, for the author's *damnatio memoriae* towards medieval scholastic legal literature required him to turn a blind eye to a very substantial part of legal scholarship that Grotius had used and quoted in his legal works.[5] Admittedly, in Ompteda's time, that scholastic legal literature had been obsolete for a long time. The new literature that had replaced it from the seventeenth century onwards had often extensively used the scholastic authorities, but, at the same time, recycled it in a modern framework. Once that framework was in place, new generations of lawyers no longer felt the need to hark back systematically to those pre-modern sources. Thus, the scholastic tradition became a hidden layer of legal science buried under early modern scholarship. The covering was all the more effective because the old literature had produced very few immediately recognisable books on topics of international law; its doctrines and principles on such topics were widely scattered over the commentaries and *consilia*, for which even the more detailed indexes in early modern imprints – usually based on the summaries inserted by editors at the beginning of a commentary on an individual *lex* or chapter, or preceding an individual *consilium* – were not entirely reliable signposts. More fundamentally, many of the old doctrines, taken at face value, no longer seemed to fit in the systematic methods and classifications of early modern scholarly thinking. Another, more ideological, reason why late-medieval literature became unfashionable and ineffectual from the seventeenth century onwards is probably linked with the new model of sovereignty in political theory. The early modern ruler was, ideally, an exclusive sovereign in his territory, a concept at odds with the late-medieval representation and acceptance of a multi-layered public governance. From the seventeenth century onwards, the recognition of a heterogeneous international community of legitimate actors intervening at different levels of international relations was gradually cancelled out in favour of a conception of international law where only sovereign states were acknowledged as proper subjects.

Grotius' work on international law operated as a hinge in the transition between legal thinking of the late-medieval political order and legal science of the early modern polity. In that sense, Ompteda's use of Grotius for a periodisation of international law scholarship was justified. The obvious disadvantage and shortcoming of his historiographical construct was that it failed to convey the extent and quality of scholastic learning incorporated in Grotius' work, and consequently the 'transference' of the medieval legal heritage into early modern legal science. That shortcoming has been more systematically amended by recent legal historiography. Where modern legal historiography still falls short of unfolding the distinctiveness of Grotius' legal work is its inadequacy to offer an understanding of that distinctiveness in the broader context of the emergence of a new paradigm of legal scholarship. The new paradigm drew from the scholastic legal heritage and from sixteenth-century legal humanism, but at the same time used those materials in a new mainstream mould of legal thinking, which comprised both conservative and progressive characteristics. It is true that, after Grotius, pre-Grotian legal authorities on international law issues, especially those authorities that were associated with 'bartolism', became swiftly out-dated, but the same observation can be made for seventeenth-century civil law scholarship in general.

Grotius famously outlined his own overview of relevant sources, at least for international law scholarship, in the *Prolegomena* of *De jure belli ac pacis* (DJBP Prol. 47 ss). The legal authorities are discussed in Paragraphs 53 to 55, but the somewhat arbitrary subdivision in paragraphs and punctuation – in later editions – have inspired divergent interpretations from Grotian scholars. Various translations have added to the confusion. The now most commonly accepted understanding of that part of Grotius' outline is that in Paragraphs 54 and 55, not all the authors he refers to fit in one of the three classes of jurists he mentions.[6] The first class are the ancient Roman lawyers whose names, works and opinions are mentioned in the compilations of the *Corpus Juris Civilis*. The second class comprises the medieval civil lawyers who were trained or who taught in the universities, and who sometimes took into consideration canon law. The third class appears to refer to authors who are usually categorised in modern historiography as legal humanists, but, as the text makes clear, in a more restrictive sense than conventional histori-ography does. Grotius praises the jurists of the first class, and he acknow-ledges the merits of the better jurists of the second class, who, in spite of their often misguided understanding of the Roman law texts, were able to seek equity ('bonum et aequum'). The jurists of the third class, Grotius states, have focused on Roman law without extending their attention to the common law of nations, and are therefore hardly useful for his purpose. Grotius' text in Paragraph 55 then makes a somewhat abrupt transition to other groups of writers, not included in the previous classification. He commends Diego Covarruvias (1512–77) and Fernando Vázquez de Menchaca (1512–69) as scholars who have combined 'scholastic subtilty' with 'knowledge of the Roman laws and of the canons';[7] in addition, there are two French authors whom he commends for having included historical expertise ('historiae') in their legal works: Jean Bodin (1530–96) and François Hotman (1524–90). These last four authors should, therefore, not be seen, in Grotius' categorisation, as representatives of the third class – *viz.* legal humanists – which he defines restrictively. On the other hand, he does not categorise them as a separate and distinctive fourth class. The categorisation expressed by Grotius in this passage is not an absolute one: it appears to be specifically taking into account the relevance of various forms of legal scholarship, ancient and modern, for Grotius' purpose of writing comprehensively and systematically on the law of nations. By pinpointing the last four comparatively recent authors, Grotius emphasises two features he found especially useful for dealing with international law: the combination of legal scholarship with the doctrines of the scholastics – by which he may be understood to refer to scholastic theologians – and the incorporation of historical studies in legal reasoning. On those two counts, that passage of the *Prolegomena* therefore appears to be programmatic with respect to Grotius' own method and characteristic use of sources in *De jure belli ac pacis*.[8]

18.5 Revisiting the *Inleidinge*

An indication of Grotius' mindset outside the area of international law and at a later stage of his life may be inferred from his annotations to the *Inleidinge tot de Hollandsche Rechtsgeleerdheid* written in 1639 and probably intended for a new edition of the work. Grotius' handwritten annotations, kept in Lund, were published in 1952.[9] The *Inleidinge* belongs to the genre of general surveys of a jurisdiction's particular (private) law following the arrangement of the Roman law *Institutes*. It represents early modern legal scholarship combining civil law jurisprudence with the systematisation of particular law rules. In so far as Grotius' introduction is mostly rule-based, it also displays the characteristic proto-positivistic approach of many such early modern works. In that sense, the translation of the phrase *rechts-geleerdheid* of the title as 'jurisprudence' in English is misleading, since Grotius' book does not purport to present a legal theory beyond the system and rules of positive law. Apart from various corrections and mostly brief additions, Grotius also included a limited number of references to legal authorities in his annotations. His choice of authorities no doubt expresses the practical and educational purpose of the *Inleidinge,* and maybe the selection also reflects the availability of legal books while he was planning to revise the *Inleidinge*. Even so, Grotius would not have included such references simply because a legal book happened to be available to him at the time. The references had to fit in his outline of the law of Holland. Most of these references are to primary sources of law: Dutch statute law and regulations; old German law – above all frequent and sustained references to the Mirror of the Saxons – and occasionally also French customs – Paris, Normandy, Sens; Scottish law and laws from Southern Italy. In addition, Grotius also referred to texts of both the *Corpus Juris Civilis* and *Canonici*. The references to legal literature suggest that, for this practical work, Grotius, who here also referred extensively to his own works, avoided almost entirely any of the late-medieval scholastic legal authors – apart from Durantis' *Speculum judiciale*. Among the approximately fifteen other authors mentioned in the Lund notes, only Jacques Cujas (1522–90) stands out as a representative of legal humanism, but only because of his commentary on feudal law. Three English authors – Thomas de Littleton (*c.* 1407–81), Thomas Smith (1513–77) and H. Spelman (*c.* 1562–1641) – make an unusual appearance in a civil law work of that epoch, but, as for the references to commentaries on French customs – by Charles Dumoulin (1500–66) and Jacques Joly (seventeenth century), they illustrate the comparative interest of the author even when dealing specifically with the particular law of Holland. The other authors all belong more conventionally to early modern *jus commune* literature. These are sixteenth-century practice-orientated works: collections of *consilia* such as those by Nicolaas Everaerts 'praeses' (1462–1532), Pietro Paolo Parisio (1473–1545) or Lodovico Giunti (sixteenth century); and case reports such as those by A. Gail (1526–87), Th. Grammatico (*c.* 1474–1556), Georges Louet (*c.* 1540–1608) or Jean Papon (1507–90). Grotius also referred to treaties such as Pieter Peck (1529–89) on testaments and Benvenuto Stracca (1509–78) on commercial law. Papon's reports and, at a distance, Everardus' *consilia* and Gail's reports are the works that the annotations refer to more than occasionally. As practical works, all these books still conveyed much scholastic learning, but their outlook and sometimes their structure fitted in the early modern insistence on literature that provided positive rules and rulings related to specific issues and topics of substantive law. The novelty of the *Inleidinge* and its immediate impact on domestic Dutch literature probably owed more to its all-round systematic and rule-based outline of Hollandic law and to the discipline such a systematic approach entailed than to any innovative doctrinal theories.

18.6 Practice in the Dutch Courts: Legal Opinions

Legal opinions attributed to Grotius in the collection of *Consultatien* – most of which are written in Dutch – only occasionally contain references to civil law and literature.[10] In a few important, and sometimes politically sensitive, cases, the language and style of the opinion's argumentation become far more elaborate and the opinion is buttressed by a wider range of doctrinal authorities. In some cases, it even discusses doctrinal controversies. In so far as one can rely on the dates of the opinions and on the attribution of authorship provided by the seventeenth-century editors of those collections, most opinions appear to have been written during the years preceding the 1618 cataclysm, while another batch was apparently written during and around Grotius' brief return to Holland in 1631–2.

As may be expected, and reflecting legal practice in the Low Countries since the sixteenth century, most opinions that do include references to legal literature refer to traditional late-medieval authorities – mainly commentaries, many *in utroque jure*, and *consilia* – or to more recent authorities reflecting legal practice – *consilia* and reports of courts' decisions – or to works that had set out to systematise legal learning. Frequently recurrent early modern works include Giulio Claro's (1525–75) *Receptae sententiae*, various works by Didaco Covarruvias (1512–77), Andrea Fachinei's (*c.* 1555–1608) *Controversies*, Andrea Gail's reports and Tommaso Grammatico's reports and consultations. However, depending on the issues at stake in a particular litigation, Grotius could draw on a far wider range of authorities, which he only refers to in specific cases. In one opinion dated from early 1631 in Paris, where the issue of the investor of capital in a company is discussed, Grotius adduces several legal and theological authors, some fairly common authorities, others who are only very rarely to be encountered in forensic practice or even in Grotius' own scholarly work.[11] Occasionally, as in a case of more exceptional importance that involved foreign interests, such as a controversy between the prince of Orange and the bishop of Münster over certain lordships, the opinion is written in Latin and covers a much wider range of argumentative registers. In addition to traditional learning, Grotius refers at length to a case of Cujas' historical editing of a Roman constitution.[12] In general, no contrast is sought between humanistic and scholastic arguments: thus, in the same opinion, a quote of Cicero on the value of an oath in warfare is followed by a reference to Baldus' (1327–1400) commentary, who is said to agree fully with Cicero's opinion. And when, on a different question, the opinion expressed by Bartolus (1313/14–57), who appeared to rely on Innocent IV's (Sinibaldo Fieschi, 1195–1254) opinions in the latter's commentary, is rejected, Grotius discusses the controversy by relying on the works of more recent authors, Antonio Gabrieli (*ob.* 1555) and Andrea Fachinei, the latter of whom is exulted as 'doctissimus utriusque juris'. The endeavours of these final two authors had been to bring some degree of control over doctrinal controversies, rather than to break away from the heritage of traditional learning. A similar picture may be drawn from the short memorandum Grotius wrote in 1607 on the prospects of negotiations towards a Dutch-Spanish truce.[13] Framed by moral-political quotations of Livy and Cicero, Grotius' main political argumentation in this case refers mostly to recent authors' opinions on public and international law – Baltasar de Ayala (1548–84), Jean Bodin, Alberico Gentili, François Hotman and Fernando Vázquez de Menchaca. His line of argument also brings him to refer to texts of the *Libri Feudorum*, and hence to medieval learned commentaries on feudal law, namely Baldus, and indirectly Iacopo di Belviso (1270–1335) and Andrea d'Isernia(*ob. ca.* 1316).

18.7 *Commentarius in Theses XI*

Grotius' legal justification of the position of the Estates of Holland in the insurrection and war against the Spanish crown may primarily have served political and diplomatic purposes. In spite of his emphasis on the ancient Dutch political liberties, it was arguably the living constitution in his day that was at stake, but Grotius' use of legal authorities in those polemical writings did not differ from his usual method of arguing a point of law. The *Commentarius in Theses XI*, which was an apology of the States of Holland for waging a 'just public war' against Philip II (1527–98), and a counterblast against the Spanish crown's claims to exercise exclusive and unchecked sovereignty in the Low Countries, is thought to have been written at some time between 1603 and 1609.[14] Within the limits of this short treatise, one recognises the argumentative technique Grotius displayed on a greater scale in his major works of international law. The authorities he used included some of the best-known medieval authors of civil and canon law, such as the gloss, Bartolus de Saxoferrato, Baldus de Ubaldis, Henricus Segosius (c. 1200–71) or Innocent IV; a favourite repertory of canonistic and moral-theological scholastic learning (the *Summa Sylvestrina*); Covarruvias as a modern and Spanish legal work of reference; a sustained strategic use of Francisco de Vitoria (1483–1546); and, to a lesser extent, of Cajetanus (Tommaso de Vio, 1469–1534). For some of the political-theoretical discussions in the *Commentarius*, Grotius also used, without sharing those authors' theories on royal sovereignty, the *Six Books on the Republic* by Bodin and James I/VI's (1566–1625) *De lege absolutae monarchiae.*

18.8 *De Jure Praedae* and *Mare Liberum*

Whereas the Lund annotations on the *Inleidinge* express the author's concern to train the reader's attention on particular law and its practice, Grotius' major works on international law, *De jure praedae commentarius* (1604) and *De jure belli ac pacis libri tres* (1625, with later amendments and additions) addressed issues of international public governance and, primarily, the audience of rulers and office-holders professionally involved in public governance. The works were written in Latin and their register aimed at impressing the reader through a combination of state-of-the-art legal science and expertise or informed understanding in a wide range of relevant subjects. Both works have a central theme that commands their structure: the legitimation of the Dutch East India Company's claims to trade and protect their trade in the East Indies in the case of *De jure praedae*; the regulation of international relations through a state-transcending normativity in the case of *De jure belli ac pacis,* centred around the just war as the ultimate legitimate sanction in international law.

A recent annotated reprint of the *Mare liberum* provides a few provisional indications of Grotius' use of legal authorities at that early stage of his career. The general argumentative purpose of *De jure praedae* notwithstanding,[15] *Mare liberum* – as well as the whole work in which it originally figured – has the modern treaty-like composition of a systematic dissertation on a specific topic. Its style and use of non-legal sources also differentiate it radically from former scholastic works. Nevertheless, a survey of the legal literature it mentions reveals at least a score of late-medieval authors, mostly the prominent authorities of the Italian method in civil law, canon law and learned feudal law. Commentaries prevail, other genres such as *consilia* are somewhat less represented. In contrast, more recent, sixteenth-century authors represent only half that number of references in Grotius' marginal notes. Typical representatives of legal humanists, such as Andrea Alciato (1492–1540) or Cujas, have no prominent position in that small group, which consists mainly of legal writers who had assimilated legal-humanistic methods, but were already heading towards a more innovative substantive synthesis of the topics they discussed along more systematic lines. These authors included Ayala, François Connan (1508–51), Covarruvias, Hugues Doneau (1527–91),[16] François Le Douaren (1509–59), Fachinei, Gentili and Vázquez de Menchaca. Significantly, among these, Covarruvias, a typical and influential figure of the early modernist movement whose work was conducive in conveying the late-medieval doctrinal legal heritage, is the most frequently quoted authority. That small sample of legal references in *Mare liberum* barely provides a very rough indication, but it is nonetheless adequate to show that Grotius was not so much eclectic in his choice of references, but rather followed a strategy of scholarly discourse with a practical, and political, purpose that required him to muster in a consistent argument both the authorities of a tradition that, in his day, had not quite vanished yet, and the works perceived to herald a new age in legal science, more adjusted to general ways of modern thinking on various subjects. Moreover, the impact of legal humanism is identifiable through other means than references to specific works. Reliable indicators of how Grotius had assimilated the (legal-) humanistic agenda in his writing and reasoning are the Neo-Latin register of his style, the frequent quotations and references to non-legal ancient sources and their use in the course of the argument, and, in a more distinct legal register, the way opinions of ancient Roman jurists are discussed, sometimes in contrast to later (scholastic) interpretations, or in order to assert Grotius' understanding of Roman aw rules in their ancient historical context. Factual information and common perceptions relating to the ancient world are typically also recurrently drawn from the ancient poets.

A survey of legal literature mentioned in the whole of *De jure praedae* confirms, on the whole, these findings restricted to *Mare liberum*. Inevitably, the range of authors is larger, and the ratio between medieval legal authors and sixteenth-century legal writers is more balanced: some

28 names among the latter against 35 among the former. To a limited extent, Grotius was able to draw from the more recent literature in his time that had been published specifically on the law of war and the law of the sea – Ayala, Pierino Belli (1502–75) and Francisco Suárez (1548–1617) – but, overall, much of the argumentation was still borrowed and transposed from private Roman law texts and related doctrines.

18.9 *Florum Sparsio ad Jus Justinianeum*

These annotations (1642) on the *Institutes*, the *Digest*, the *Code*, the *Novellae* and the *Libri Feudorum* match more closely the approach conventionally associated with legal humanism.[17] In particular for the first three of these collections, Grotius adduces mostly ancient Roman and Greek sources, to a large extent non-legal sources, which may contribute, however summarily, to a more contextualised understanding of the annotated Roman law texts. References to legal literature and scholarship tend to be scarce. Grotius altogether avoids late-medieval scholastic authorities, but even legal-humanistic scholarship is relatively rarely quoted. When this occurs, in true humanistic philological–historical fashion, it is mainly in order to make a point about a specific textual edition or amendment. One rather exceptional example is a passage on a text of the *Lex Rhodia*, where a textual amendment is mentioned with reference to John Selden (1584–1654), Denys Godefroy (1549–1622), Samuel Petit (1594–1653) and Claude Saumaise (1588–1653). In other passages, Grotius mentions Andrea Alciato, Barnabé Brisson (1531–91), Cujas, Pierre du Faur de Saint-Jory (c. 1532–1600), Antoine Favre (1557–1624), Hotman, Antoine Leconte (1517–86), Johannes Löwenklau (1541–94), Giulio Cesare Scaligero (1484–1558) and Jacques Sirmond (1559–1651) – referring to the latter's additions to the edition of Theodosius' *Code*, published in Paris in 1631 – but most of these authors only occur on a single occasion and none serves as a regular source or authority. Grotius refers more often to ancient Germanic law, to some medieval imperial constitutions and to Neapolitan law. The annotations on feudal law rely consistently on medieval sources, both legal and non-legal. Apart from the many references to Greek sources, Grotius also includes several references to Hebrew law, for which he mostly quotes 'Baba Kama', possibly through the edition by Constantin Lempereur (1591–1648) that he used in his own additions to

De jure belli ac pacis, and occasionally he also refers to John Selden. The *Florum sparsio* often also refers the reader to specific passages in Grotius' own *De jure belli ac pacis*, enhancing – as such – the latter treatise's legal-humanistic features.

18.10 *De Jure Belli ac Pacis*

In a modern reprint of *De jure belli ac pacis* (1993), Robert Feenstra *c.s.* have given special attention to Grotius' legal references, with separate indications on references added in the 1631 and 1642 editions, so that we now have a more accurate overview of the explicitly mentioned legal sources in Grotius' most famous book.[18]

Overall, and allowing for approximations, since not every author can be classified as a lawyer or as a scholar from a different discipline, about 40 per cent of the legal writers cited by Grotius were medieval jurists. They are almost all Italian, and a clear majority of them can be numbered among the conventional, most commonly encountered jurists of the Italian method. Almost a quarter of these medieval authors were canonists, while feudists appear only exceptionally. As one may expect, the range of early modern legal authors and works is significantly broader. Apart from Italians, French and Spanish jurists appear prominently, as well as, to a lesser extent, jurists from the German territories and from the Low Countries. Other jurisdictions remain entirely or largely absent – there are, for example, only a small handful of authors from the British Isles. A broader, and largely new, range of legal literature is being introduced. These include genres that had been initiated by medieval scholarship, but became far more popular and wider spread in the sixteenth century with the advent of the printing press – *consilia*, reports, treatise . . . – and which were often vectors of medieval learning. Some of these declined in importance by the early-seventeenth century. Conversely, a new type of specialised, and therefore more systematic, literature on specific topics, including a small array of books on questions of international law, is drawn to Grotius' reservoir of legal authorities. Specifically humanistic works touching on historical and philological questions remain relatively rare. The medieval commentaries and legal literature, which were no longer systematically reprinted from the 1620s onwards, make up only a small proportion of the references in the 1642 additions. The proportion of canonistic literature is, in these 1642 additions, much reduced. On the other hand, Grotius' increased interests in old Germanic law sources, documented directly through early modern editions or through chronicles and other 'histories',[19] are here also very much in evidence.

18.11 Conclusion

Grotius' main legal works reflect both scholastic and humanistic influences, but in different ways. The legal authorities appearing in those works – most of which may be assumed to have been consulted first-hand by the author –[20] belong in large part to the late-medieval tradition, and to practice-based legal literature, such as reports or *consilia*, which, until Grotius' time, was still heavily dependent on the late-medieval method. Another substantial, and over the years increasing, part of the legal authorities cited by Grotius are works that did not focus primarily on the historical, philological or antiquarian agenda of sixteenth- and seventeenth-century legal humanism, but rather on the less radical synthesis of civil law scholarship that asserted itself as the mainstream method of legal thinking in Grotius' lifetime. Explicit references to authors and works involved in the philological and historical revision of, mostly, Roman law sources remain, on the whole, comparatively rare.

While explicit references to legal-humanistic literature tend to be far less numerous, Grotius' legal work is nonetheless much more steeped in the humanistic method than in scholastic learning. The most obvious evidence of this humanist learning, which marks the contrast with scholastic legal learning, is Grotius' style and language registers. Beyond a humanist Neo-Latin style in his works on Roman law and international law, Grotius also incorporates many ancient – mostly, but not exclusively, classical – non-legal sources that contribute to put the legal principles and concepts, in particular derived from Roman law, in a wider cultural, social and political context. That contextualisation is, in the humanist spirit, both historical and timeless, as it refers to values and attitudes drawn from ancient history that are presented as universal, or at least as universal standards of good and bad behaviour.

In Grotius' time, precisely because legal-humanistic scholarship could not provide a comprehensive alternative system that would have replaced scholastic learning, but also because the normativity of international relations, in spite of fundamental changes in the structure and nature of the international community and its members, was still principally governed by the scholastic tradition, that tradition had still to be conveyed and recycled into a new systematisation. In that sense, *De jure belli ac pacis* functioned in some way as a draft doctrinal codification of international law in its time, casting and adjusting, as most codifications do, much of the available legal heritage in a new mould. The mould – in this case, largely shaped by legal humanism – provided a new format for pre-existing rules, as those rules acquired a new normative value in the codified system. Severed from their original scholastic context, and exposed to a different environment of political relations, the rules were not simply transposed, but to some degree transformed.

Finally, any assessment of the respective influence of medieval legal scholarship and legal-humanist methods should not be viewed solely from the vantage point of the intellectual history of jurisprudence. Behind such works as *De jure belli ac pacis*, one can recognise the early modern scramble among scholars to secure for their expertise a central position in public governance, in the case of Grotius' book specifically in the area of international public governance or, from the sovereigns' viewpoint, of foreign affairs. Grotius' work highlights the standards of legal scholarship required for a lawyer to play a part in that governance. At the same time, both his legal works and his non-legal works emphasise the need for the ideal courtier, councillor or ambassador to develop a command in other areas of expertise, in particular in the disciplines of theology, history, rhetoric and, increasingly, secular political theory. In all these other disciplines, the critical methods developed by humanist learning proved essential tools in forging a new scholarly paradigm. Moreover, humanist learning tended to impose an integrated pluridisciplinary approach to issues of governance, as a necessary path for transcending the political and religious divides of the era in domestic and international politics.

Primary Sources Other than by Grotius

Consultatien, advysen en advertissementen, Gegeven en geschreven bij verscheiden Treffelijke rechtsgeleerden in Holland en Elders. Het derde Deel (Rotterdam, 1688)

Consultatien, advysen en advertissementen, Gegeven en geschreven bij verscheiden Treffelijke rechtsgeleerden in Holland en Elders. Het vijfde Deel (Rotterdam, 1664)

Consultatien, advysen en advertissementen, Gegeven en geschreven bij verscheiden Treffelijke rechtsgeleerden in Holland en Elders. Sesde Deel (Rotterdam, 1685)

Further Reading

Borschberg, P., *Hugo Grotius 'Commentarius in Theses XI'. An Early Treatise on Sovereignty, the Just War, and the Legitimacy of the Dutch Revolt* (Bern et al., 1994).

Feenstra, R., 'L'influence de la scolastique espagnole sur Grotius en droit privé: quelques expériences dans des questions de fond et de forme, concernant notamment les doctrines de l'erreur et de l'enrichissement sans cause', in R. Feenstra, *Fata Iuris Romani. Etudes d'histoire du droit* (Leiden, 1974), 338-63 [originally published in 1973].

Feenstra, R., 'Quelques remarques sur les sources utilisées par Grotius dans ses travaux de droit naturel', in *The World of Grotius (1583-1645). Proceedings of the International Colloquium organized by the Grotius Committee of the Royal Netherlands Academy of Arts and Sciences, Rotterdam 6-9 April 1983* (Amsterdam and Maarssen, 1984), 65-81.

Feenstra, R., 'The Most Usable Editions of Grotius' Main Legal Works', *Grotiana* N.S. 11 (1990) 66-71.

Feenstra, R., 'La systématique du droit dans l'oeuvre de Grotius', in R. Feenstra, *Legal Scholarship and Doctrines of Private Law, 13th-18th Centuries* (Aldershot, 1996), 333-43, No. VII [reprinted from *La sistematica giuridica: Storia, teoria e problemi attuali* (Biblioteca internazionale di cultura 22; Rome, 1991).

Haggenmacher, P., *Grotius et la doctrine de la guerre juste* (Paris, 1983).

Sampson, J., *The Historical Foundations of Grotius' Analysis of Delict* (Leiden and Boston, 2018).

Notes

1 The present chapter deals almost exclusively with legal authorities. In particular with regard to international legal scholarship, Grotius recognised the need to widen the range of authorities, especially to theological and historical scholarship. He also refers in his works on international law to other non-legal sources, for example various, mainly classical literary, sources. All these non-legal

sources are beyond the brief of the present chapter, though I would gainsay that such sources were only included as ornamental devices. The theological authorities played a special role in Grotius' time, as will be briefly mentioned in the text hereafter. Although in recent Grotian studies, the importance of Grotius' theological sources is generally acknowledged, its precise role remains somewhat controversial. This is particularly the case for medieval Thomist scholarship and for the early modern neo-scholastics. To some extent, especially in the field of international law, Grotius' extensive use of Spanish and Roman-Catholic theologians may have been a strategic device in the Dutch-Spanish, or more in general, Protestant–Roman-Catholic polemics and exchanges; however, it may also be viewed as part of an attempt to transcend those divides in order to find universal or common fundamental principles for organising international relations. That idea would then have been worked out in a potentially more secular form as a theory of natural law.

2 A. Wijffels, 'Early-modern scholarship on international law', in A. Orakhelashvili (ed.), *Research Handbook on the Theory and History of International Law* (2nd edn., Cheltenham and Northhampton, MA, 2020), 19–57.

3 That was a characteristic feature of late-medieval legal scholarship, which ignored a systematisation of the law and relied heavily on general principles or analogies that could be drawn from rules appearing in an entirely different context. The method could be applied for arguments in other areas of scholarship. This is to some extent the case in Grotius' refutation of a theological argument by Faustus Socinus (1539–1604): E. Schrage, 'Having Made Peace through the Blood of the Cross. On legal arguments in Grotius' *De satisfactione Christi, Grotiana* N.S. 38 (2017) 28–45.

4 Nevertheless, it is common in legal historiography and in Grotian studies to seek in *De jure belli ac pacis* also a general legal theory – perhaps inspired by concepts of natural law – that would be applicable both in international law and in various areas of domestic law, such as private law. I am not sure whether such an undifferentiated use of general principles is fully warranted in assessing Grotius' work. Transposing principles borrowed from private law to the law of nations was not quite the same in Grotius' time as it had been in the medieval *mos italicus*. For a critical historical assessment of the 'reception' of Roman law in the formation of international public law, see R. Lesaffer, 'Roman Law and the Intellectual History of International Law', in A. Orford and F. Hoffmann (eds.), *The Oxford Handbook of the Theory of International Law* (Oxford, 2016), 38–58.

5 Grotius' reliance on late-medieval scholarship in his works on international law was highlighted by P. Haggenmacher, *Grotius et la doctrine de la guerre juste* (Paris, 1983).

6 R. Feenstra, 'Hugo de Groots oordeel over 16e eeuwse beoefenaars van het Romeinse recht: een herinterpretatie van § 55 der Prolegomena van De iure belli ac pacis', in *Na oorlog en vrede. Twaalf opstellen bij het dertiende lustrum van Societas Iuridica Grotius en de vierhonderdste geboortedag van Grotius* (Arnhem, 1984), 23–9.

7 On those two authors as references in Grotius' international law scholarship: R. Feenstra, 'Ius commune et droit comparé chez Grotius. Nouvelles remarques sur les sources citées dans ses ouvrages juridiques à propos d'une réimpression du *De iure belli ac pacis'*, in R. Feenstra, *Legal Scholarship and Doctrines of Private Law, 13th-18th Centuries* (Aldershot and Brookfield, VT, 1996), No. 6, 20.

8 My own understanding is that the passage expresses Grotius' views specifically about the law of nations, and that there is only a degree of overlapping with other areas of the law. The overlapping, moreover, may differ depending on the notions and principles at stake. Even so, it is still fashionable in Grotian studies to seek a strong degree of commonality in discussing Grotius' doctrines specifically on private law, e.g. in the *Inleidinge,* and on international law, as in *De jure praedae* or *De jure belli ac pacis*. As a result, Grotius' use of non-legal scholarship – in particular, theological scholarship – is sought for discussing his views on concepts and principles to be found both in private law and in international law. A recent example is J. Sampson, *The Historical Foundations of Grotius' Analysis of Delict* (Leiden and Boston, 2018), who emphasises Grotius' reliance on Thomist writers – possibly more so than directly on Roman law, except in order to tie up loose ends on specific points of Thomist doctrine – in delictual liability in private law. See also R. Feenstra, 'Théorie sur la responsabilité civile en cas d'homicide et en cas de lésion corporelle avant Grotius', in R. Feenstra, *Fata Iuris Romani. Études d'histoire du droit* (Leiden, 1974), 323-37 [originally published in 1959]. Other examples are Grotius' doctrine on property: R. Feenstra, 'Der Eigentumsbegriff bei Hugo Grotius im Licht einiger mittelalterlicher und spätscholastischer Quellen', in O. Behrends, M. Dießelhorst, H. Lange, D. Liebs, J.G. Wolf and C. Wollschläger (eds.), *Festschrift für Franz Wieacker zum 70. Geburtstag* (Göttingen, 1974), 209-34, and B. Wauters, 'Grotius, necessity and the sixteenth-century scholastic tradition', *Grotiana* N.S. 38 (2017) 129-47; on restitution: R. Feenstra, 'L'influence de la scolastique espagnole sur Grotius en droit privé: quelques expériences dans des questions de fond et de forme, concernant notamment les doctrines de l'erreur et de l'enrichissement sans cause', in R. Feenstra, *Fata iuris romani. Études d'histoire du droit* (Leiden, 1974), 338-63 [originally published in 1973]; on frustration: R. Feenstra, 'Impossibilitas and Clausula rebus sic stantibus. Some aspects of frustration of contract in continental legal history up to Grotius', in Feenstra, 'Impossibilitas and Clausula rebus sic stantibus', 364-91.

9 The standard edition is Hugo de Groot, *Inleidinge tot de Hollandsche rechts-geleerdheid. Met de te Lund teruggevonden verbeteringen, aanvullingen en opmerkingen van den schrijver en met verwijzing naar zijn andere geschriften uitgegeven en van aantekeningen en bijlagen voorzien*, ed. F. Dovring, H.F.W.D. Fischer and E.M. Meijers (2nd edn., Leiden, 1965).

10 As the opinions here referred to are merely examples, I have not checked Grotius' opinions in later supplements to the *Consultatien*. *Cf*. D.P. De Bruyn,

The opinions of Grotius as contained in the Hollandsche Consultatien en Advysen (London, 1894).

11 *Consultatien, advysen en advertissementen, Gegeven en geschreven bij verscheiden Treffelijke rechtsgeleerden in Holland en Elders. Het derde Deel* (Rotterdam, 1688), No. 303.

12 *Consultatien, advysen en advertissementen, Gegeven en geschreven bij verscheiden Treffelijke rechtsgeleerden in Holland en Elders. Het vijfde Deel* (Rotterdam, 1664), No. 157.

13 W.J.M. van Eysinga, 'Ene onuitgegeven nota van De Groot', in F.M. baron van Asbeck, E.N. van Kleffens, K.P. van der Mandele and J.R. Stellinga J.R. (eds.), *Sparsa collecta. Een aantal verspreide geschriften van Jonkheer Mr. W.J.M. van Eysinga* (Leiden, 1958), 488–504, [first published in *Mededeelingen der Nederlandsche Akademie van Wetenschappen,* Afd. Letterkunde N.S. 18 (1955) 235–52].

14 P. Borschberg, *Hugo Grotius 'Commentarius in Theses XI'. An Early Treatise on Sovereignty, the Just War, and the Legitimacy of the Dutch Revolt* (Bern et al., 1994), with the Latin text of the Commentarius and an English translation, 203–84.

15 P. Borschberg, 'Hugo Grotius' theory of trans-oceanic trade regulation. Revisiting Mare liberum (1609)', *Itinerario* 29/3 (2005) 31–49.

16 Hugues Doneau has been identified by Grotian scholars as a major, though often 'hidden' source of Grotius, also in his later work, see e.g., R. Feenstra, 'La systématique du droit dans l'oeuvre de Grotius', in: *Feenstra, Legal Scholarship and Doctrines of Private Law,* 333–43, No. VII.

17 Hugo Grotius, *Florum sparsio ad ius Justinianeum* (*ed.pr.* Paris, 1642).

18 Hugo Grotius, *De iure belli ac pacis libri tres in quibus ius naturae et gentium item iuris publici praecipua explicantur,* ed. B.J.A. de Kanter-van Hettinga Tromp. *Editionis anni 1939 quae Lugduni Batavorum in aedibus E.J. Brill emissa est exemplar photomechanice iteratum, annotationes novas addiderunt R. Feenstra et C.E. Persenaire, adiuvante E. Arps-de Wilde* (Aalen, 1993).

19 Grotius' interest for old Germanic laws at that time has been linked to his position as ambassador of the Swedish Crown: W.J.M. van Eysinga, 'Quelques observations sur Grotius et le droit romain', in F.M. baron van Asbeck, E.N. Kleffens, K.P. van der Mandele and J.R. Stellinga (eds.), *Sparsa collecta. Een aantal verspreide geschriften van Jonkheer Mr. W.J.M. van Eysinga* (Leiden, 1958) 373–81, at 374–5 [first published in *Symbolae Van Oven,* Leiden, 1946]; W.J.M. van Eysinga, 'Ene onuitgegeven nota van De Groot'. The interest was ultimately triggered by Grotius' political-historiographical ambition to write an antiquarian 'national' history of Sweden, L. Janssen, 'Hugo Grotius in dialogue with his colleagues. Intertextuality and polemics in *Historia Gotthorum* (1655)', *Grotiana* N.S. 38 (2017), 148–75.

20 E. Rabbie, 'The history and reconstruction of Hugo Grotius' library, a survey of the results of former studies with an indication of new lines of approach', in E. Canone (ed.), *Bibliothecae selectae da Cusano a Leopardi* (Florence, 1993), 119–37, with references to earlier studies on books owned by Grotius at various stages of his career.

Wouter Druwé

19.1 Introduction

On 5 June 1619, Hugo Grotius was sentenced to life imprisonment and brought to the castle of Loevestein near Zaltbommel in the south of the Republic of the United Provinces. As a consequence of this unexpected imprisonment, which would last until his remarkable escape on 22 March 1621, Grotius was finally granted some time to dedicate himself again to scholarship, albeit in difficult circumstances. His nearly two years behind bars were very productive in terms of scholarly output. He wrote religious poetry,[1] but also found the time to author the first-ever comprehensive introductory textbook on Hollandic (private) law and jurisprudence in the Dutch language. The *Inleidinge tot de Hollandsche rechts-geleerdheid* became one of the key and even founding texts in the tradition of Roman-Dutch law. That was the law that was taught at Dutch universities until the late-eighteenth century, and that long remained influential in some former Dutch colonies, too, including the South African territories. This contribution will focus on the writing and publication of the *Inleidinge* in 1631, on the aim, style and structure of the work, on its content, and on its fate and influence after Grotius' death.

19.2 The Writing and Publication Process

As from the foundation of the first European universities, law students had almost exclusively been introduced to Roman and canon law. Royal or princely ordinances, local customs and statutes, as well as feudal law, were, in principle, not taught in academia. This focus on the so-called 'written law or learned law was upheld by the early modern universities, also in the Low Countries. When, however, in the late sixteenth and early seventeenth centuries, princely, regional and local regulations became ever more dominant in legal practice, criticism grew against the teaching system that arguably did not prepare the students well for their future roles as legal practitioners. Some professors tried to overcome these criticisms by introducing elements of particular law into their courses. For that intellectual task of integration of particular law into the learned legal system, they could draw inspiration from their consultation practice: in *consilia*, generations of law professors – in the Low Countries definitely as of the mid-fifteenth century – had learned to apply Roman legal rules to specific cases, also taking into account particular laws.[2] The first printed volume of *consilia* in the Low Countries appeared in 1554, and contained advice by Nicolaas Everaerts (1462–1532). Among the first learned legal treatises in the Low Countries that substantially took into account particular law were those by Petrus Gudelinus (1550–1619) and Paulus Busius (1570–1610).[3] Both of them still wrote in Latin. In the early seventeenth century, only very few published legal writings were available in Dutch, although most courts proceeded almost exclusively in the vernacular. Important exceptions were some procedural works, for instance by Filips Wielant (1441–1520), Joos de Damhouder (1507–81) and Paulus Merula (1558–1607).[4]

Hugo Grotius was well aware of the lack of an introductory textbook to the law that was applied in the Hollandic courts. When his younger brother, Willem (1597–1662), was studying law at the University of Leiden, Hugo wanted to assist him. In a letter of 18 May 1615 to his brother, he suggested possible criteria for a systematisation of Hollandic law (1 BW 405). In those years, however, Grotius was very active as pensionary of Rotterdam and involved in politics: he did not find the time to write a textbook. It was only during his imprisonment in 1619 that he finally started working on his overview of Hollandic jurisprudence. For the main categorisation criteria, he built upon his earlier reflections, for instance in the aforementioned letter of 1615. A notice of 17 July 1619 proves that Grotius was working on a textbook on Hollandic law.[5]

After Hugo had fled Loevestein and went into exile, his brother Willem repeatedly suggested that the *Inleidinge* be printed. On 10 April 1627, Hugo indicated that he first wanted to consult some learned lawyers, well versed in legal practice, as he had lacked that legal practice for several years and had not enjoyed access to sufficient sources during his time in prison (3 BW 1143). Although it is uncertain whether he actually managed to consult those experts, he finally consented to the publication in a letter of 11 February 1628, most of all because he had been informed that parts of the manuscript had been copied for private use by several legal practitioners (3 BW 1222).

Grotius sent his brother the final manuscript on 9 January 1629. This manuscript included six synoptic tables and an alphabetical index of the titles. Grotius remained, however, in doubt about the preface (4 BW 1364). We know of a letter of dedication to his children that was originally meant as the preface, but in the end was not included and only published much later in 1720,[6] as well as of three manuscripts entitled *Prolegomena juri hollandico praemittenda* and therefore possibly meant as a preface to the *Inleidinge* too, even if that is controversial.[7] The preface that would eventually be included in the printed edition was inspired by the letter of dedication, but put in the third person singular instead.

In February 1629, Willem had tried to obtain a privilege from the States General but his request was rejected and the manuscript only returned in November. The printer, Jacob Elsevier, who had planned to publish the book, retracted, not willing to take the financial risk. The manuscript was published instead by the widow and heirs of Hillebrant Jacobsz. van Wouw in 1631 in a beautiful print with Latin characters.

A second, cheaper edition, this time in gothic characters, appeared with the same widow van Wouw, still in 1631. Van Wouw probably took that step once she had heard that other printers were also preparing a publication of the *Inleidinge*. Van Wouw warned her readers that the versions of the other printers were incorrect. Van Wouw's premonition was justified, as, still in the same year 1631, and without Grotius' authorisation, his *Inleidinge* was also printed by Frans Pels and Cornelis Willemsz. Blaeu-Laken in Amsterdam, by Adriaen Roman in Haarlem and by Pieter Corssen in Rotterdam. In 1636, printer Adriaen Roman took care of his second edition of Grotius' *Inleidinge*. Interestingly, a copy of that 1636 edition – that has been preserved in the university library of Lund – was read and annotated by Hugo Grotius himself in July 1639. That document formed the basis for the 1965 critical edition of the *Inleidinge* by Dovring, Fischer and Meijers, which was used for the present chapter.

19.3 Aim, Style, Structure and Sources

Grotius' *Inleidinge* was clearly meant for teaching purposes, to prepare students for legal practice. The work should fill a gap in legal literature, which had almost exclusively been focused on Roman law. He originally planned to write a logical and well-structured systematic and introductory synthesis of all fields of Hollandic jurisprudence, *i.e.* the law of persons, the law of goods, the law of obligations, procedural law and public law. The circumstances in prison, however, did not simplify that task, and the two latter parts were never completed. In his letter of 9 January 1629, Grotius explained that, for the fourth part on procedural law, the reader could be referred to Paulus Merula's *Synopsis*, first published in 1592. The overview of public law would merit a separate publication and would first of all require that Grotius had access to the archives of the charters, which – given his imprisonment and his later banishment – was not the case (4 BW 1364).

Grotius focused on the law that was applied in the province of Holland. In his view, however, that law was based on natural law, princely ordinances, local statutes, 'old Germanic law', Roman law and – albeit to a lesser extent – canon law. The *Inleidinge* takes into account the legislation of the Burgundians, of Charles V (1500–58) and Philip II (1527–98), and of the States of Holland, as well as different statutes of local towns, from which he tried to derive a common law of the land. In his *Inleidinge*, Grotius did not explicitly refer to other authors or to specific passages from the *Corpus Juris Civilis*. That is why lawyers and legal historians have since tried to find out what sources Grotius had at his disposal.[8] From some of his letters, we are informed of the works he could consult in the prison of Loevestein. That library was rather limited, but contained *inter alia* Filips Wielant's *Practijcke civile* and Domingo de Soto's (1494–1560) tract *De justitia et jure*.[9] Feenstra has also demonstrated that Grotius had been familiar with the teachings of the French jurist, Hugues Doneau (Hugo Donellus, 1527–91), possibly through his uncle, Cornelius (1546–1610) – a colleague of Doneau at Leiden University – or through Doneau's student, Gerardus Tuning (1566–1610).[10] To a large extent, Grotius must have worked from memory or from notes he had made when he was still active in legal practice. Thus, as an 'advocaat-fiscaal' at the Court of Holland from 1599 to 1613, he had had access to the customs of Hollandic towns, which had been sent to the court in the aftermath of Philip II's homologation programme of 1569–70. Grotius also had access to a few books of princely ordinances and regulations *(placcaet-boeken)*.

Grotius did not at all wish to disregard Roman law. The book contains a lot of Roman legal principles, which were dealt with 'to the extent that they were still applicable' (IHR 2.17.9). Grotius described Roman law, and especially Justinianic law, as 'full of wisdom and equity' (IHR 1.2.22). What is even more, our author drew much of his inspiration for the structure of his *Inleidinge* from the *Institutes* of the Roman Emperor Justinian. In his Latin letters, he tellingly referred to the *Inleidinge* as his *Institutiones juris Batavici*. The structure, indeed, often resembles that of Justinian's *Institutes*. At several instances, typical institutes of local law are introduced, as far as possible by linking them to a related Roman legal concept. Thus, for instance, the law of admiralty was linked to that of a partnership (*societas*), and feudal law to the law of emphyteusis.

Notwithstanding all of the above, Grotius' approach was not identical to Justinian's *Institutes*. Grotius more clearly distinguished the law of property from the law of obligations. Moreover, the *Inleidinge* consistently applied dichotomic categorisations: main concepts were subdivided into two sub-concepts, which in their turn were again subdivided into two sub-categories, and so on. The synoptic tables from Grotius' own hand clearly illustrate this technique. For that method, our author was most probably inspired by the works of Pierre de la Ramée (Petrus Ramus, 1515–72). The first scholars to apply that method in a legal or political context were Hieronymus Treutler (1565–1607) and Johannes Althusius (1557–1638). In Holland, the ramist method won influence through the theologian Jacobus Arminius (1559–1609), and his followers, the Arminianists.[11]

19.4 The *Inleidinge*'s Introductory Paragraphs

The *Inleidinge* starts off with a few general definitions and subdivisions of justice (*rechtvaerdigheid*) and right (*recht*) (IHR 1.1). According to Grotius, a distinction must first be made between right 'in the broad sense' (*ruim*) and right 'in the narrow sense' (*eng*). When an act of a rational being corresponds to what is reasonable, it is right in the broad sense. When a reasonable being receives what is due to him according to his personal merits (*waerdigheid*), or according to his subjective real or personal rights (*toebehooren*: 'what is said to be ours'), it is right in the narrow sense. The *Inleidinge* would only deal with right in the narrow sense.

In a second step, Grotius defines the concept of 'law' (*wet*). In his definition, the law stems from reason, is just and aims at the common good. It is enacted by someone or by those with whom the authority over a certain community resides (IHR 1.2.1). Our author describes the threefold effect of laws. First, they create obligations (*verbintenisse*), even in conscience. Second, they enable the imposition of penalties (*straffe*). Third, they lead to the annulment of acts that breach the law. A fundamental distinction is further made between natural ('innate', *aengeboren*) law and positive (*gegeven*) law. The natural law, which is innate in every human being, is the reasonable judgment on what is out of its nature just or unjust. Some just acts are related to what human beings have in common with all creatures, like the urge to procreate and to nourish one's family. Others stem from the relational nature of human beings, who live in a community. This includes the golden rule, as well as virtues such as obedience and gratitude (IHR 1.2.5–6). Positive law is established either by God himself, as revealed in the teachings of Jesus, or by men. Once, through human procreation, the community of men had become too large to be governed by one single polity, a further categorisation was necessary, namely that between the law of (all) peoples (*volcker-wet, jus gentium*) and civil law (*burger-wet, jus civile*). Though not identical, the law of peoples has many similarities with natural law; it is common to all communities and cannot easily be adapted (IHR 1.2.11–12). Civil law, by contrast, is limited to one particular community of citizens, and can be changed by that community. It is either written or non-written. Both kinds of civil law are either regional or local. The judge should not opt for a literal interpretation of the abovementioned regional or local civil laws, but instead for an interpretation in the light of the legislator's intention (IHR 1.2.23).

If a legal question cannot be answered with reference to the abovementioned laws, a judge should decide in accordance with 'reason', as interpreted in his wisdom and modesty. He should, therefore, search for inspiration in Roman law. Even canon law and pontifical law can serve as sources of inspiration, or have received the force of law through their customary use (IHR 1.2.22).

Finally, Grotius introduced the distinction between public law (*wet raeckende lands-stand*) and private law (*wet raeckende byzonder burger-recht*). In the remainder of his introductory textbook, our author only deals with private law. Grotius divides private law into two subcategories, which one could translate as substantive law (*recht tot eenige zaecken*) and procedural law (*middelen om 't zelve rechtelick voor te staen ende te vervolgen*) (IHR 1.2.24–8). Although, originally, a fourth book had been planned, the *Inleidinge* only deals with substantive law, namely with persons, goods and obligations. Real subjective rights (*beheeringe*) are distinguished from personal subjective rights (*inschuld*).

19.5 The Law of Persons

In his first book on the law of persons, Grotius argues that all human beings are equal by birth, except for a child's natural duty of obedience, gratitude and respect towards his or her parents. In what follows, however, he gives a pseudo-historical overview to justify why some people are – nonetheless – ruled over by others (IHR 1.3.8). He states that men are naturally more capable of taking wise decisions than women. Therefore, men ruled over women. In order, however, to avoid confusion over the parenthood of children if several men rule over the same woman, women were prohibited from having intercourse with more than one man. As monogamous relationships turned out to be the most stable ones for the education of children, marriage was developed as a monogamous and indissoluble institute. Marriage formed the basis for a family. In Grotius' reasoning, gradually some weaker people joined the family of a stronger and wiser *pater familias*. Parents often also asked their friends to take care of their children in case they died earlier, i.e. the origin of tutelage. Once ever more families were living together in order to help each other out, it became more difficult for them to deliberate and decide upon all their common affairs together. In some small towns, they opted for a government elected by and answerable to the people (*volcks-regieringe, democratia*). In mercantile towns, the wisest and richest men were left with the authority to rule the town (*bester-regieringe, aristocratia*). Elsewhere, only one monarch was appointed (*Eens-regieringe, monarchia*).

All people in Holland were free, even if some were still bound by a few feudal remnants of the past. Although they were free, minors, mentally ill and married women were not capable of contracting (IHR 1.4). That is why the married status was an essential legal issue. Grotius deals with the institute of marriage, and describes how the 'old Germanic law' (*oude Duitsche wetten*) and canon law had ruled that area of law before the States of Holland enacted regulations in 1580. He describes in detail the different impediments related to agnation and cognation, the requirements of parental consent, as well as the formalities of marrying (IHR 1.5.6–17).

Except in cases of adultery, marriage was only dissolved at the death of one of the partners. The canon law institution of the separation of bed and board is mentioned, too. Husbands were tutors of their wives and had the full and exclusive administration of their wives' patrimony (IHR 1.5.20–3). In principle, married women were not capable of contracting, except for business transactions made by public tradeswomen and for household expenses. If the husband abused his position or risked ruining his wife's patrimony, she could file a claim for separation of goods (*boedel-schei-dinge*). Grotius also mentions the validity of a premarital agreement to avoid that the husband act as tutor, and emphasises the testamentary freedom of all married women (IHR 1.5.24–5). The father also administered the goods of his children until they married or were emancipated. Adoption was not common in Holland (IHR 1.6).

Children who had lost at least one of their parents were called orphans (*wezen*). For orphans younger than 25 years of age, tutors were appointed, either on the basis of a parent's last will or by government. Interestingly, Grotius noted that – based on natural and positive divine law – the surviving parent retained an important say as to the child's education and marriage, even if he or she would not be named tutor. Tutors particularly took care of their pupils' patrimony. Whereas, for the sale of movables, a mere notification of the orphan chamber was required, a sale of immovables and annuities was only allowed after a prior permission by the Court of Holland or the city magistrates. Annually, tutors had to send their accounts to the closest family members of the pupil and to the orphan chamber. Once the pupils reached the age of majority, or once they married or were emancipated by a court's decision, the tutorship came to an end. Orphans who were deaf or not able to speak remained under tutelage even after they reached the age of majority. The same was true for mentally ill or spendthrift orphans (IHR 1.7–11).

In the final part of book 1, Grotius makes some further distinctions between legitimate and illegitimate children depending on the married status of their parents at the time of their conception (IHR 1.12), between autochtonous people and foreigners depending on their place of birth (IHR 1.13), and between nobles and others depending on their family background (IHR 1.14). Given the adoption of the 'purified religion' (*ghesui-verde gods-dienst*), i.e. Calvinism, the distinction between religious (*geestelicken*) and secular people (*wereldlicken*) was no longer relevant as the religious had lost all their privileges (IHR 1.15).

19.6 Property Law

Grotius' second book concerns the law of goods. Before going into the different forms of real rights and the modes of acquisition of goods, our Hollandic author first introduces some important twofold categorisations of goods. Out of their very nature, a distinction has to be made between singular goods and universal ones. Singular goods are either incorporeal (e.g. rights) or corporeal, which – at their turn – are either movable or immovable. Remarkably, Grotius then rejects the opinion according to which some goods belong to God, such as sacred goods or graveyards. According to Grotius, all goods belong either to all people (like the sea[12] and the sky), to a large group of people, to specific persons or to no one at all (IHR 2.1.15–16). Goods that belong to specific persons are either alienable or inalienable. Inalienable are life, body, freedom and honour (IHR 2.1.41–48).

In what follows, Grotius discusses the different forms of real rights and first makes a fundamental distinction between a right of possession (*bezit-recht*) and ownership (*eigendom*). Possession is the actual detention of a good with the intention to keep it for one's own sake. Possession *bonae fidei* requires that the possessor truly believes that he is the owner of the good he possesses. In case of *malae fidei* possession, that conviction is absent (IHR 2.2). Grotius defines ownership as the right by a non-possessor to claim a good as his own. Again, our Hollandic scholar includes a pseudohistorical overview of the origins and development of the legal institute of ownership (IHR 2.3.2).[13] God created all goods for the use of humanity as a whole, without preferring one person over another. Although some creatures, such as the sun, the moon and the stars, are and can be used by all simultaneously, some categories of created goods – such as food and drink – cannot, out of their very nature, be consumed by several people together. Eating or drinking – which are necessary for human nature – can be considered as acts of ownership. Thus, natural law does not exclude ownership. Clothes and houses cannot be shared by all either. Once human beings left the grottos and started to build their own huts and small houses, the ones who had built them became the owners thereof. As the lands and natural fruits were not sufficient to feed everyone without any labour, the lands were divided and agricultural techniques developed in order to increase the amount of fruits. The agriculturers became the owners of the lands and their fruits.

A common ownership was doomed to lead to disputes. Therefore, unattended goods could be occupied by persons who subsequently became the owners thereof. In conclusion, natural law did not create ownership, but did not prohibit it either. Natural causes even gave rise to the development of ownership. Once someone had become an owner, natural law required that his right of ownership was respected by the others. Nevertheless, the civil community always had a higher right than the individual citizen-owners. The civil community could, therefore, regulate private ownership. The law prevailed. Originally, an owner would have been allowed to take possession of his property by force, but that method was changed in favour of a legal procedure. An owner can claim the actual possession of his property, even with a possessor *bonae fidei*, unless that possessor was a privileged moneylender or unless he had bought the goods on an open market (IHR 2.3.3–6).

Grotius then discusses the different ways to acquire ownership of individual goods. First, he considers the possibility of acquisition of goods that are not yet owned by someone else, like wild animals and goods cast up by the sea. He warns, however, that special legislation often attributed those goods to the court of Holland or to beneficiaries of hunting privileges (IHR 2.4). Second, an owner can transfer property to an acquirer. Under natural law, the owner's will to transfer suffices. Civil law, however, introduced the additional requirements of actual delivery (*leevering, traditio*) and of a relevant cause (*oorzaecke*). Only those capable of contracting were allowed to transfer property. Clerics and churches could not validly receive immovable property. Neither could those who had married a young man or daughter without his or her parents' consent and/or explicit approval by a judge (IHR 2.5). Third, in certain circumstances, property could be acquired without the consent of the previous owner. Thus, possessors of good faith acquired ownership of the fruits (IHR 2.6). Acquisitive prescription by a possessor with a valid legal title (*rechtelicke aenkomste*) is another example (IHR 2.7). Fourth, property could be acquired through an act of an acquirer of good faith, e.g. by painting on someone else's paper. Fifth, acquisition was possible through an act of another person, like a testamentary bequest (IHR 2.8.1–6). Sixth, property could be acquired through mixture, confusion or accession of several goods, a situation that was governed by the principle of *accessorium sequitur principale*. Given the importance of dykes and polders for the Republic, Grotius takes some care in describing different situations and local customs in cases of accretion, flooding and island formation (IHR 2.8.7–2.10), three institutions that originated already in ancient Roman law.[14]

In a next step, our author singles out some specific ways to acquire ownership of a universality of goods, insofar as they differ from the abovementioned. One such specific way is marriage. Except for feudal goods or unless minors had married without parental consent, married partners in principle are the co-owners of one single universality of both assets and liabilities. Thus, a wife is bound by the liabilities of her husband, even after the latter's death, although she is generally granted the benefit of cession of goods (IHR 2.11). Before marriage, a prenuptial agreement may deviate from these default rules, as long as this agreement does not entail any leonine clause (IHR 2.12). Another typical situation to acquire ownership of a universality is, as a matter of course, hereditary succession. In Holland, a *decujus* can draw up a last will (*uiterste wille*). If no last will has been made, the *ab intestato* succession benefits mostly close family members, first of all parents and children, in accordance with their natural obligations of alimentation and gratitude. Moreover, some civil laws limit the testamentary freedom to the benefit of those parents and children, precisely with an eye to their natural obligations. Grotius attributes long passages to the law of succession (IHR 2.14–31). They respectively deal with the formalities for a last will, with the necessity to provide for parents, children and siblings, with direct and indirect succession, with the acceptance and refusal of an inheritance, with the content, beneficiaries and formalities of testamentary bequests, with the nullity and annulment of testaments, and with succession *ab intestato*. In those parts, reference is often made to the local law. A lot of attention is, for instance, paid to the double origin of the Hollandic law of intestate succession, namely on the one hand the Frisian neighbours' laws (*aesdomsrecht*) that were in force in the northern part of the county of Holland, and on the other hand the Zeeland laws of the aldermen (*schependomsrecht*) that applied in Southern Holland.[15] In 1580, the States of Holland had tried to harmonise both systems, but several exceptions had been granted to particular areas of the county. Moreover, in their prenuptial agreement or in a last will, married partners could opt for either of those systems of intestate succession.

Interestingly, Grotius distinguishes between full ownership (*volle eigendom*) and limited ownership (*gebreckelicke eigendom*) (2.33.1, cfr. 2.3.9–11). Full ownership implies the right to do everything with the good that is not prohibited by law. A limited owner lacks a part of that right, for instance as he is not allowed to dispose of the good, or to enjoy the fruits thereof. Although strictly speaking the presence of one 'limited owner' of a particular good necessarily implies the presence of another 'limited owner' of that same good, Grotius proposes instead to call the limited ownership of the highest value simply the 'ownership' and the limited ownership of a lower value a 'right' (*gerechtigheid*) to someone else's property (IHR 2.33.1), a distinction that Grotius had borrowed from Doneau.[16] These 'rights' are divided in those that depend on the land itself, such as real servitudes (IHR 2.34–37), and those that do not depend on the land. Within the latter category, a further distinction was made between (i) rights that serve a particular utility on the one hand, either a present utility like '*tocht*' and '*minder als tocht*' or a future utility like expected ownership on the basis of a *fideicommissum* or on the basis of a right of *retractus* (*naasting*) (IHR 2.47), and (ii) rights that serve as a security on the other hand. With *tocht*, which Grotius uses as a translation of *dominium utile*, he refers to the right to enjoy the fruits of someone else's property without reduction of that property (IHR 2.38.5). Usufruct, *emphyteusis* and feudal vassalship are the typical examples thereof. In his *Inleidinge*, Grotius pays special attention to the feudal law and expands on the hereditary succession of feudal goods (IHR 2.41–43). *Minder als tocht* refers to lesser rights, like a right of use (IHR 2.44), a right to tithes (IHR 2.45), a right to a census (IHR 2.46.1–7) and building rights (*huisgebou-recht*, IHR 2.46.8–12). Interestingly, Grotius catalogues a lease (*huir*) as a right of use for a limited time, although he knows that – according to the learned law – a lease merely gives rise to a personal claim (*actio in personam, opspraeck*). Our scholar argues that, in case the lease contract had been written, a lessee keeps his rights even after the lessor has sold the good to a new owner (IHR 2.44.9). At times, Grotius also includes legal historical arguments. Thus, with reference to several legal historical documents, Grotius argues that the right to tithes in Holland is not related to canon law, but rather to old Germanic law. Curiously, it does not entail a right to a tenth part of the fruits, but instead only to an eleventh part. Also, elsewhere in these sections, Grotius focuses on the particularities of Hollandic law. In his discussion of real securities, he makes a fundamental distinction between silent and express securities. Many of the listed silent security rights are related to the Republic's maritime industry (IHR 2.48.10–21). Grotius was the first legal author to consistently categorise those silent securities as a form of limited owner-ship.[17] He also points at the specific Amsterdam custom to put general and specific securities on the same level, whereas elsewhere in Holland and according to Roman law a younger specific security prevails over an older general one (IHR 2.48.40).

19.7 The Law of Obligations

In the final book of his *Inleidinge*, Grotius analyses the law of obligations. He carefully introduces several terms.[18] Not all of them are easily translatable into English. Broadly speaking, *schuld* (obligation) refers to all acts that are befitting to a human being on the basis of some virtues. In that broad interpretation, *schuld* with reference to another person is either a *weldaed-schuld* (obligation on the basis of a benefaction), a *trouw-schuld* (obligation on the basis of fidelity) or a *misdaed-schuld* (obligation because of a delict) (IHR 3.1.3–5). Many of those *schulden* in the broad sense were not enforceable in court. For instance, a mere promise (*belofte, pollicitatio*) did not yet give rise to an enforceable *trouwschuld*. In the remainder of this book, Grotius only deals with *schulden* that did grant a right to someone else. He called such a right an *inschuld* or – from the perspective of the debtor – a *verbintenisse* (obligation, IHR 3.1.7).

Natural law recognised two different sources of *inschuld*. First, a special kind of promise, namely a so-called *toezegging* (*promissio*), could create such an *inschuld*. That is a promise by a promisor with the intention that the promisee accept the promise and be granted a right (IHR 3.1.10). Grotius would further develop his ideas on the binding nature of these *toezeggingen* (*promissiones*) in his *De jure belli ac pacis*.[19] Second, an *inschuld* could also be created through an *onevenheid* (*disequilibrium*, inequality).[20] The disequilibrium could originate when someone was enriched unexpectedly and without reason, when someone was given something or something was done in favour of someone, or – finally – when someone had been harmed through another's delict (IHR 3.1.14–18). Except for the case of the unexpected enrichment, natural law only created a binding obligation (*inschuld*) if the act had been done on the basis of the free will. Very young children, or those who erred or had been deceived, were therefore not liable (IHR 3.1.19).

Civil law had created some new obligations and had limited the enforceability of some of the abovementioned obligations that originated from natural law. In his overview, Grotius especially focuses on civil law and only mentions natural law in passing (IHR 3.1.21–22). His treatment of this issue is divided into three main steps: a discussion of the origins and existence of obligations (*verbintenissen*) in general, followed by an analysis of the parties, the content and the effects of some specific contracts (*afcomste*), and finally by a discussion of the termination of obligations.

In a first step, Grotius deals with the origins and existence of obligations. He explains that, on the one hand, in principle everyone can bind himself, but that, on the other hand, no one can validly bind another, at least in principle. Some exceptions are made, mainly for parents, tutors, shop managers (*winckel-houdende luiden*) and shipowners (*reders*) (IHR 3.1.28–38). Obligations can pertain to one's own goods and goods of others, but not – except upon prior consent by government – goods that are used for religious service or burials. Obligations could not concern the inheritance of a person who is still alive, except in case of prenuptial agreements. Neither can they concern impossible acts. Obligations that are based on an unfair cause are invalid too (IHR 3.1.39–43). Whereas natural law, as aforementioned, does not grant binding force to a mere promise (*belofte*), civil law additionally grants enforceability to mere promises in honour of God or one's land or town (IHR 3.1.48). Nevertheless, like in natural law, also under civil law, obligations mainly emerge either from a special promise (*toezegging*) or from a disequilibrium (*onevenheid*).

Among the *toezeggingen* (henceforth: promises), some are done expressly, others are based on an interpretation of the law. Explicit promises are made either orally or in writing. As to the oral promises, Grotius points at a distinction between Roman law, where mere pacts are not binding, and old Germanic law that – in Grotius' view, who on this issue does not give due credits to canon law – considers as valid all promises based on a reasonable cause (IHR 3.1.51–52).[21] A typical example of a reasonable cause is a donation (IHR 3.2). A reasonable cause can also be the procurement of an act (IHR 3.3.1). Oral promises can be made both by a main debtor (*zaeckweldige*) and by a personal surety (*borge*). In principle, according to the learned law, a third party cannot derive an enforceable right from an agreement between two other contracting parties. Under Hollandic law, however, such a third-party clause is valid and does grant a right to a third party once they have accepted it. That deviation from Roman law is arguably based on equity (IHR 3.3.37–38).[22] Unlike Roman law, oral promises and acceptances do not have to happen at the same moment and at the same place; they can even be done through proctors (IHR 3.3.45). Grotius then discusses the possible content of promises, including the possibility of conditional promises (IHR 3.3.47). Gambling obligations are invalid, unless both parties risk liability, e.g. in case of insurances (IHR 3.3.48). Aleatory contracts based on games are subject to limitations set by local and regional governments (IHR 3.3.49). Grotius qualifies a settlement (*dading, transactio*) as a special kind of promise (IHR 3.4). Promises in writing, which are made by the aldermen, by a notary or by the promisor himself, are in general subject to the same rules that govern oral promises. Written documents are considered as full proof, unless the contrary is demonstrated. A party who contests the truth of a written bond has to do a consignment (*hand-vulling, namptissement*) first. Interestingly, Grotius also accepts the right of a bearer of a bearer bond to claim payment against the debtor, except if the latter can prove that the bearer has received the bond *malae fide* (IHR 3.5).[23]

In a second step, Grotius deals with some specific contracts. Promises that are based on an interpretation of the law (*toezegging door wetduiding*) can be divided into contractual and quasi-contractual obligations. Before going into the special contracts, Grotius gives a pseudohistorical overview of how men in prehistory needed each other's help. Sometimes, they helped each other gratuitously. Sometimes, they stipulated a *quid pro quo*. That gave rise to the barter economy. Once the relationships became more complex, men sought for a common measure, money (IHR 3.6.3). Some promises were gratuitous, others were made for consideration. Promises consisted either of the transfer of full or limited ownership, of the granting of a right of usage, or of the performance of an act (i.e. to do something). A gratuitous promise to transfer full or limited ownership was called a gift (*schencking*) or a testamentary bequest (*making*), one to grant a right of usage a loan for use (*bruickleening*), and one to do something a mandate (*lastaenvaerding*), a deposit (*bewaeraenneeming*) or a pledge (*pandaenvaerding*). A promise for consideration that consisted of the transfer of full ownership was called a loan for consumption (*verbruicklening*), a barter (*reuling*), an exchange (*wisseling*), a purchase (*koop*) or a sale (*verkooping*). A typical example of a promise for consideration to transfer limited ownership was a contract of *emphyteusis* (*erfpacht-gunning*). Lease entails a promise to grant a right of usage in return for a promise to pay a monthly rent. A contract of partnership (including one of marriage) entails promises by both parties to do something. An insurer promises to take over someone's risk, which is also qualified as an obligation to do something. A vassal is bound by an obligation to do something, too, namely to honour his lord and to support him militarily (IHR 3.6.5–8).

As some contracts are used daily, the law has provided for certain standard provisions. If parties do not agree otherwise, those standard provisions apply. That is why they are called promises based on an interpretation of the law (*toezegging door wetduiding*). Two main categories have to be distinguished. First, some of those promises come into being through delivery of a good (*door zaecks-overgeving*), as is the case for deposits, pledges, loans for use and loans for consumption. These are the so-called *contractus re* of the Roman law tradition. Grotius briefly discusses those four contracts, and especially points out the different burdens of liability (IHR 3.7–11). Grotius pays special attention to the permissibility of the taking of interest on a loan for consumption. He argues in favour of such permissibility, as long as the virtue of charity is respected. Interestingly, Grotius *inter alia* refers to the uncontested possibility to conclude three separate agreements with different parties, namely a partnership, a sale of the hope for profit and an insurance. Why, then, our scholar reasons, probably with the discussions on the triple contract (*contractus triplex*) by the Spanish neo-scholastics in mind, not to allow that a similar effect is reached through one single contract (IHR 3.10.10)?[24] Second, other promises based on an interpretation of the law originate through the mere consent of both parties (*door overkominge alleen*). These are the so-called *contractus consensu* of the Roman law tradition. Examples of the latter are mandate, purchase and sale, granting of *emphyteusis*, lease (both of goods and of services), partnership, insurance and granting of a feud. In what follows, Grotius offers a brief discussion of those contracts. Interestingly, he considers the relationship between the drawer and the drawee of a bill of exchange as a mandate too (IHR 3.13). Special attention is paid to the purchase and sale contract, where he also mentions the sale of annuities (IHR 3.14.13–21). As to the sale of immovable property, a right of *retractus* (*naesting*) has to be observed (IHR 3.16). An extensive section deals with leasing contracts in a specific maritime context, between shippers (*bevrachters*) and shipmasters (*schippers*), between shipmasters and ordinary sailors (*schipsgesellen*), and sometimes also between shipmasters and shipowners (*reders*) (IHR 3.20). After a brief discussion of partnerships in general, Grotius deals with three special kinds of partnerships: marriage – for which he mainly refers to his earlier dealings in the first book, admiralty (*amiraelschap*) and co-ship-ownership (*mede-rederschap*). Admiralty is a partnership of several ships for reasons of protection and defence of the merchant navy (IHR 3.22). Co-ship-ownership is, in principle, governed by the regular rules on partnership. Special provisions apply when the shipmaster is one of the co-owners of the ship (IHR 3.23). Whereas Roman law did not know a contract of insurance, Grotius includes the insurance as one of the special contracts (IHR 3.24).

Quasicontractual obligations (*verbintenisse als of daer toe-zegginghe ware*) are also based on an interpretation of the law (*wet-duiding*). These quasicontracts are similar to some of the abovementioned contracts. Thus, the position of an heir with regard to the testamentary bequests made by the testator is similar to that of a donor. The position of a tutor (*voogd*) and acting manager (*onderwinder, negotiorum gestor*) is similar to that of a mandatary. Similar to a partnership is a community of several people, not based on a contract, either with respect to a good (*gemeenschap des zaecs*) or with respect to a result (*gemeenschap des uitkomsts*). Examples of the former are the situation of co-heirs (*mede-erfenis*) or of owners of neighbouring plots without fences and of which the borders are unclear (*t'saem-belending*). Examples of the latter are the community between a shipowner and ordinary seamen, and also the community between all those that are physically present on a ship or have property loaded onto that ship (IHR 3.26–29).

Grotius deals with obligations that arise from a disequilibrium or inequality (*onevenheid*), a concept taken from Thomistic thought. Some are based on unjust enrichment ('the deriving of profit', *baet-trecking*), others on the causation of a disequilibrium (*veroorzaecking van onevenheid*). Grotius was the first to consider unjust enrichment as a source of obligation.[25] He sums up three typical examples of means to claim restitution: the *condictio indebiti*, the *condictio sine causa* and the *condictio ex turpi causa*. He also mentions a fourth, more general, description, which is followed by the illustration of someone whose money has been lent without his knowledge: the borrower has then been unjustly enriched out of that person's patrimony and is liable for restitution (IHR 3.30). Obligations also arise when someone has caused a disequilibrium, either by granting a favour without intention of donation (*ter minne*) or by causing damage (*ter onminne*). The first subcategory resembles the

Roman legal theory on the *actio praescriptis verbis* for the innominate agreements (IHR 3.31.2–11). The second sub-category includes both delictual (*door blijckelicke misdaed*) and quasidelictual liability (*door wetduidinge*). A delict is defined as an act or an omission that is unlawful out of its very nature or out of any legal regulation.[26] A delict gives rise to two separate obligations, one to a penalty and another to restitution. The obligation to a penalty can only be based on civil law, and in Grotius' time, in principle, had to be claimed by the government and could not be forced upon the heirs of the perpetrator. Our author nonetheless describes the old Hollandic procedure to deal with homicide, which involves the family members of the victim and the perpetrator. He also set out the famous *talio*-principle, as well as a procedure of atonement (*zoen*). Moreover, in case of scorn and slander, the injured party can claim a private penalty; a reminiscence of the old *actio iniuriarum* (IHR 3.32.7). Probably with the theories of the Spanish neo-scholastics in mind, Grotius argues that the obligation to restitution is founded on natural law, as adapted by civil law (IHR 3.32.9). Restitution can be claimed by the injured party, and can be enforced vis-à-vis the perpetrator's heirs too. Grotius then discusses the delicts against life, body, freedom, honour and property (IHR 3.33–37). By discussing them in relationship to Aquilian liability, Grotius clearly deviates from the Roman law of Antiquity, possibly again under inspiration from Donellus.[27] Quasidelictual liability does not require any fault. This kind of liability is ascribed to someone by law if a certain result has taken place (IHR 3.38).[28]

In a third and final step (IHR 3.39–52), Grotius analyses the extinction of obligations. Obligations either 'die out' (*'t eenemael sterven*) by dissolution (*rechts-ontbindinge*) or destruction of the good (*des zaecks ondergang*), or 'lose their binding force' (*werden gemaeckt krachteloos*). Dissolution entails both discharge (*quiting*) – payment (*betalinge*) or the like (*betalingsgeliick*), such as consignment (*onderrecht-legginge*), confusion (*vermenging*) and set-off (*verliking*) – and remission (*quiitschelding*). Remission often happens through a human act (*menschen-daed*), without novation, or with novation or delegation (*overzetting*). Assignment (*aenwijzinge*) does not have novatory effect; Grotius digresses briefly on assignment in the context of bills of exchange. Remission can also happen by the force of law, i.e. as a consequence of prescription. This is interesting, as in Roman law prescription was merely a defence that could be invoked in court and did not terminate the obligation (IHR 3.46.2). Obligations lose their binding force, either in general or partly. Such a general loss of force is either due to internal causes, such as fear, fraud and young age, or to external causes, such as *res judicata* or oath. A partial loss of force is caused by a cession of goods (*boedel-affstand*) or by a reparation in case of a prejudice of more than one half (*herstellinge uit verkorting over de helft, laesio enormis*).

19.8 The Fate and Influence of the *Inleidinge* After Grotius' Death

Grotius' *Inleidinge* was an immediate success in the Republic upon its publication in 1631. It soon became a standard introductory work to Hollandic legal practice, and was frequently re-issued. A new impulse was given when Simon van Groenewegen van der Made (1613–52) annotated Grotius' *Inleidinge* and inserted references to some of the sources (ordinances, statutes, etc.). Groenewegen, who would later author a well-known treatise on abrogated Roman laws,[29] also pointed out where Hollandic law differed from Roman law, or where Grotius' positions deviated from the Hollandic jurisprudence actually practiced by the courts.[30] That first annotated edition appeared in Dordrecht in 1644 and took Grotius by surprise. In a letter to his brother, Willem, of 17 December 1644, Hugo complained that it contained a lot of errors (16 BW 7199). In 1652, after Grotius' death, Groenewegen himself prepared a new edition with Aernold Bon in Delft, probably with Willem's support. In the meantime, in the Republic the statists had taken power, who were more favourable to (the memory of) Grotius. For the first time, the States General granted a privilege for the publication of the (annotated) *Inleidinge*. That annotated version went through another eight publications between 1657 and 1767. The 1767 edition additionally contained notes by Willem Schorer (1717–1800), president of the Court of Flanders.[31]

All these prints are proof of the continued importance of the *Inleidinge* for Dutch practising lawyers from across the Republic until the late-eighteenth century. Grotius' work also inspired the Southern Netherlandish practising jurist and canonist Franciscus Zypaeus (1580–1650), who wrote a *Notitia iuris Belgici*, first published in 1635. The attention was, however, not limited to legal practitioners. The *Inleidinge* was also read at the universities. Already before 1636, Petrus Cunaeus (1586–1638), professor of law at the University of Leiden, referred to Grotius' *Inleidinge*.[32] Famous Dutch scholars, professors of law and legal practitioners, such as Arnoldus Vinnius (1588–1657), Antonius II Matthaeus (1601–45), Simon van Leeuwen (1626–82), Ulrik Huber (1636–94) and Johannes Voet (1647–1713) had read the *Inleidinge* too, and referred to it in their writings. It is no exaggeration to state that Grotius' *Inleidinge* is one of the founding works of the 'elegant' Roman-Dutch school, the distinctive type of practice-oriented Roman law scholarship in the seventeenth- and eighteenth-century Dutch Republic that was profoundly influenced by the humanist tradition, too.[33]

The *Inleidinge* was introduced as a textbook on 'contemporary law' (*jus hodiernum*) at universities, possibly for the first time by Bernardus Schotanus (1595–1652) in Leiden in 1648,[34] definitely by Johannes Voet as of 1688. We know of a manuscript commentary to the *Inleidinge* by the Leiden law professor, Gerlach Scheltinga (1708–65), which was taught a few times from 1752 to 1762.[35] Course notes by Professor Dionysius Godefridus van der Keessel (1738–1816) have also been preserved. A summary of van der Keessel's course notes was published in Leiden in 1800.[36] Moreover, in 1776–8, a few learned observations ('*Rechtsgeleerde observatien*') on the *Inleidinge* were printed in The Hague.[37] At the end of the eighteenth century, the *Inleidinge* was also taught in Amsterdam, and even outside of Holland in Utrecht and Groningen.[38]

Contrary to the later Roman-Hollandic works by Vinnius and Voetius – and unlike Grotius' own juridical masterpiece, *De jure belli ac pacis* – the *Inleidinge* was written in the vernacular. Grotius carefully developed a whole range of new Dutch legal terms, and mentioned their Latin translation or more common loan words in the margins. Thus, Grotius had a major impact on the development of the Dutch juridical terminology,[39] but the other side of the coin is that the *Inleidinge* was never made available to a wider European public and could thus only indirectly influence the international academic debates.[40]

In the nineteenth century, the *Inleidinge* lost its importance for legal practice in the Netherlands. Later editions of the Dutch text were prepared by legal historians. Important is the newly annotated version by S.J. Fockema Andreae (Arnhem, 1895). That was different in the former Dutch colonies, where the interest for the Roman-Dutch law remained important.[41] Many of those colonies, like Guyana, Ceylon and South Africa, had been taken over by the British or become independent. The need for English translations grew. A first English translation appeared in London in 1845, prepared by Charles Herbert, a barrister, active in British

Guyana.[42] Another translation by Andries F.S. Maasdorp was published in Cape Town in 1878.[43] The legal historian, R.W. Lee, Rhodes Professor of Roman-Dutch Law at Oxford, prepared a new translation of the *Inleidinge* and the notes by Schorer, which was first published in 1926.[44] The interest for the *Inleidinge* remains even today. Thus, Dominique Gaurier, emeritus professor of law at the University of Nantes, is currently preparing a French translation of the *Inleidinge*.[45]

Further Reading

Ahsmann, M., 'Teaching the ius hodiernum: legal education of advocates in the Northern Netherlands (1575-1800)', *Legal History Review* 65 (1997), 423-57.

Feenstra, R., 'La systématique du droit dans l'oeuvre de Grotius', in: *La sistematica giuridica: Storia, teoria e problemi attuali* (Rome, 1991), 333-43.

Feenstra, R. and R. Zimmermann (eds.), *Das römisch-holländische Recht. Fortschritte des Zivilrechts im 17. und 18. Jahrhundert* (Berlin, 1992).

Fruin, R., 'Geschiedenis der Inleidinge tot de Hollandsche Rechts-geleerdheid gedurende het leven des auteurs', in: S.J. Fockema Andreae (ed.), *Inleidinge tot de Hollandsche Rechts-geleerdheid* (Arnhem, 1895), XV.

Pont, D., 'Die Inleydinge tot de Hollandsche Rechts-Geleerdheyd van Hugo de Groot', *Tydskrif vir hedendaagse Romeins-Hollandse Reg* 9 (1945), 182-203.

Wellschmied, K., 'Zur Inleidinge tot de Hollandsche Rechts-geleerdheid des Hugo Grotius', *Legal History Review* 20 (1952), 389-440.

Notes

1 See, for instance: H. Grotius, *Bewijs van den waren Godsdienst* (Rotterdam, 1622).

2 On the consultation practice in the Low Countries, see: W. Druwé, *Loans and Credit in Consilia and Decisiones in the Low Countries (c. 1500-1680)* (Leiden 2020).

3 P. Busius, *In Pandectas, cum differentiis consuetudinum communium et ... iuris canonici* (Franeker, 1614); P. Gudelinus, *Commentariorum de iure novissimo libri sex* (Antwerp, 1620).

4 E.g. F. Wielant, *Corte instructie in materie criminele*, ed. J. Monballyu (Brussels, 1995); J. de Damhouder, *Practycke ende handbouck in criminele zaeken*, eds. J. Dauwe and J. Monballyu (Roeselare, 1981); P. Merula, *Synopsis Praxeos Civilis, manier van procederen in dese provintiën, Hollandt, Zeelandt ende West-Vrieslandt, belanghende civile saken* (Amsterdam, 1592).

5 H. Grotius, 'Memoriën van mijne Intentiën en van mijne Bejegening', in R. Fruin (ed.), *Verhooren en andere bescheiden betreffende het rechtsgeding van Hugo de Groot* (Werken van het Historisch Genootschap N.S. 14; Utrecht, 1871), 79.

6 'Brief des heeren Hugo de Groot aen zijne kinderen, Kornelis, Pieter, en Diederik de Groot', in: H. Grotius, *Bewys van den waren godsdienst* (4th edn., Amsterdam, 1720).

7 See, for this discussion: R. Feenstra, 'Een tweede handschrift van de Inleidinge van Hugo de Groot en een dito van de Prolegomena juri Hollandico praemittenda', in R. van den Bergh *et al.* (eds.), *Ex iusta causa traditum. Essays in honour of Eric H. Pool* (Pretoria, 2005), 81–91; R. Feenstra and J.E. Scholtens, 'Hugo de Groot's *De aequitate*, tekstuitgave en tekstgeschiedenis, met bijdragen over Nicolaas Blanckaert en over de voorrede tot de Inleidinge', *Legal History Review* 42 (1974), 201–42.

8 See especially: K. Wellschmied, 'Zur Inleidinge tot de Hollandsche Rechtsgeleerdheid des Hugo Grotius', *Legal History Review* 20 (1952), 389–440, at 395–414.

9 Ibid., 410–11.

10 R. Feenstra, 'La systématique du droit dans l'oeuvre de Grotius', in: *La sistematica giuridica: Storia, teoria e problemi attuali* (Rome, 1991), 333–43; Feenstra, 'Hugues Doneau et les juristes néerlandais du XVIIe siècle: L'influence de son système sur l'évolution du droit privé avant le Pandectisme', in B. Schmidlin and A. Dufour (eds.), *Jacques Godefroy (1587-1652) et l'humanisme juridique à Genève* (Basel 1991), 231–43.

11 Wellschmied, 'Zur Inleidinge', 392-95.

12 W. Zwalve, 'The *Introduction to the Jurisprudence of Holland* and the Doctrine of the Free Seas', *Grotiana* 30 (2009), 49–64.

13 See also Bart Wauters' chapter on Grotius' views on property law.

14 See e.g. the *Institutes* of Justinian 2.1.20–4 and D. 41.1.7.

15 R. Feenstra, 'Family, property and succession in the province of Holland during the sixteenth, seventeenth and eighteenth centuries', in L. Bonfield (ed.), *Marriage, Property, and Succession* (Berlin, 1992), 37–52.

16 R. Feenstra, 'La sytématique', 339–40; Feenstra, 'Dominium and ius in re aliena: The Origins of a Civil Law Distinction', in P. Birks (*ed.*), *New Perspectives in the Roman Law of Property. Essays for Barry Nicholas* (Oxford, 1989), 111–22.

17 D. De ruysscher and I. Kotlyar, 'Local traditions v. academic law: collateral rights on movables in Holland (c. 1300-c. 1700)', *Legal History Review* 86 (2018), 365–403, at 392–8.

18 See on the terminology: R. Feenstra, ''Inschuld', 'Schuld' en 'Verbintenisse' bij Hugo de Groot', in F. Stevens and D. van den Auweele (eds.), *Houd voet bij stuk. Xenia iuris historiae G. van Dievoet oblata* (Leuven, 1990), 455–70.

19 See Paolo Astorri's chapter on the law of contracts and treaties.

20 On the importance of equality in contracts, see Astorri's chapter.

21 On this passage and its reception, see: R. Feenstra, 'Pact and contract in the Low Countries from the 16th to the 18th century', in J. Barton (*ed.*), *Towards a General Law of Contract* (Berlin, 1990), 197–213, at 204–13.

22 See: L. Waelkens, 'Ius Quaesitum Tertio, Dutch Influences on Grotius', in: E.J.H. Schrage (*ed.*), *Ius quaesitum tertio* (Berlin, 2008), 175–89; H. Dondorp and J. Hallebeek, 'Grotius' doctrine on 'adquisitio obligationis per alterum' and its roots in the legal past of Europe', in O. Condorelli (ed.), *'Panta rei'. Studi dedicati a Manlio Bellomo* (Rome, 2004), 205–44, at 234–42. For a discussion of Grotius' analysis of promises in favour of a third party in his *De jure belli ac pacis*, see also Astorri's chapter.

23 On bearer clauses in the Low Countries, see: W. Druwé, 'La clause au porteur dans les *consilia et decisiones* aux Pays-Bas méridionaux (XVIe siècle)', in L. Brunori *et al.* (eds.), *Le droit face à l'économie sans travail* (Paris, 2019), vol. 1, 343–60.

24 W. Decock, 'In defense of commercial capitalism: Lessius, partnerships and the contractus trinus', in: B. Van Hofstraeten and W. Decock (eds.), *Companies and Company Law in Late Medieval and Early Modern Europe* (Leuven, 2016), 55–90.

25 R. Feenstra, 'Grotius' doctrine of unjust enrichment as a source of obligation: its origin and its influence in Roman-Dutch law', in E.J.H. Schrage (*ed.*), *Unjust Enrichment: The Comparative Lagel History of the Law of Restitution* (Berlin, 1995), 37–52.

26 See J. Sampson, *The Historical Foundations of Grotius' Analysis of Delict* (Leiden, 2018).

27 Feenstra, 'La systématique', 341.

28 See: R. Feenstra, 'Die Quasi-Delikte bei Hugo Grotius', in M. J. Schermaier *et al.* (eds.), *Iurisprudentia universalis. Festschrift für Theo Mayer-Maly zum 70. Geburtstag* (Cologne, 2002), 175–89.

29 S. van Groenewegen van der Made, *Tractatus de legibus abrogatis et inusitatis in Hollandia vicinisque regionibus* (Leiden, 1649).

30 B.Z. Beinart, 'Simon van Groenewegen van der Made', *Legal History Review* 56 (1988), 333–40.

31 For an overview of these and other bibliographical references: J. ter Meulen and P.J.J. Diermanse, *Bibliographie des écrits imprimés de Hugo Grotius* (The Hague, 1950).

32 M. Ahsmann, 'Teaching the Ius hodiernum: legal education of advocates in the Northern Netherlands (1575-1800)', *Legal History Review* 65 (1997), 423–57, at 431.

33 See, for some general remarks on Roman-Dutch law: R. Zimmermann, 'Römisch-holländisches Recht - ein Überblick', in R. Feenstra and R. Zimmermann (eds.), *Das römisch-holländische Recht. Fortschritte des Zivilrechts im 17. und 18. Jahrhundert* (Berlin, 1992), 9–58.

34 Ibid., 433. The manuscript (preserved in the university library of Leiden, 70 J 28) contains a *cursus praxeos* of 1648. The ascription to Schotanus is controversial:

R. Feenstra, 'De *Inleidinge* van Hugo de Groot in het juridisch onderwijs van de zeventiende en achttiende eeuw. Aanvullingen op een studie over *dictata* van Johannes Voet en Gerlach Scheltinga', *Fundamina* 16/1 (2010), 90-8, at 91-3.

35 P. van Warmelo and C.J. Visser (eds.), *Observationes ad Hugonis Grotii manudictionem ex collegio Iohannis Voet* (Pretoria, 1987); W. de Vos and G.G. Visagie (eds.), *Scheltinga se 'Dictata' oor Hugo de Groot se 'Inleiding tot de Hollandsche rechtsgeleerdheid'* (Johannesburg, 1986); Feenstra, 'De *Inleidinge*', 93; Feenstra, 'Dictata van Johannes Voet en Gerlach Scheltinga op de Inleidinge van Hugo de Groot (naar aanleiding van twee recente uitgaven)', *Legal History Review* 93 (1988), 93-133.

36 D.G. van der Keessel, *Theses selectae juris Hollandici et Zelandici, ad supplendam Hugonis Grotii introductionem ad jurisprudentiam hollandicam, et definiendas celebriores juris Hollandici controversias* (Leiden, 1800).

37 *Honderd rechtsgeleerde observatien, dienende tot opheldering van verscheide duistere, en tot nog toe voor het grootste gedeelte onbewezene passagien uyt de Inleidinge tot de Hollandsche Rechtsgeleerdheid van wylen Mr Hugo de Groot door een genootschap van rechtsgeleerden* (The Hague, 1776-8).

38 Ahsmann, 'Teaching the Ius hodiernum', 441-2.

39 S. Vissering, 'De rechts-taal van H. de Groot's Inleiding tot de Hollandsche rechtsgeleertheid', *Verslagen en mededeelingen der Koninklijke Akademie van Wetenschappen. Afdeling Letterkunde,* 2nd series 12 (1883), 372-441.

40 The first and only Latin translation was written by Joannes van der Linden (*c.* 1830-5), and published as: H.F.W.D. Fischer (*ed.*), *Hugonis Grotii Institutiones juris hollandici* (Leiden, 1962).

41 P. van Warmelo, 'Hugo de Groot se betekenis vir die moderne Suid-Afrikaanse reg', *Tydskrif vir hedendaagse Romeins-Hollandse Reg* 46 (1983), 185-204.

42 C. Herbert (transl.), *The Introduction to Dutch Jurisprudence of Hugo Grotius* (London, 1845).

43 A.F.S. Maasdorp (transl.), *The Introduction to Dutch Jurisprudence* (Cape Town, 1878).

44 R.W. Lee *(transl.), The Jurisprudence of Holland* (Oxford, 1926).

45 https://globalhistoryofinternationallaw.wordpress.com/a-propos/dominique-gaurier/ (last consultation: 2 August 2019).

The Laws of War- and Peace-Making

Randall Lesaffer

20.1 Introduction

Ever since the birth of international law as an established academic discipline at the end of the nineteenth century, Hugo Grotius has been widely acclaimed as the foremost among its historic ancestors. Among the many, at times contradictory, arguments that have been forwarded to sustain Grotius' 'fatherhood' of international law stands out the claim that his major relevant treatise, *De jure belli ac pacis libri tres* of 1625, was – in the words of Hersch Lauterpacht (1897–1960) – 'the first comprehensive and systematic treatise on international law'. However, even a staunch defender of Grotius such as Lauterpacht had to backtrack on this claim in the face of reality. He reluctantly conceded that the treatise did cover many subjects of general, private law that did not belong in a text on international law, while Grotius' treatment of international law remained incomplete.[1] Other modern international lawyers proved more critical, arguing that Grotius had not lived up to the title of the book, as the *jus pacis* remained largely uncovered. With this, they referred to the *summa divisio* of international law, which became the backbone of the structure of many textbooks during the late nineteenth century, between the regime of international law that applied under the state of peace and that which applied under the state of war.[2]

These international lawyers were misled by Grotius' choice of title. With the title, which he took from a speech by Roman orator Marcus Tullius Cicero (106–43 BCE),[3] the Dutch humanist did not suggest that he would cover the whole width and breadth of relations among states. His aim was to write a treatise on the legal regulation of war in its three dimensions: the making of war, the waging of war and the ending of war. 'Peace' in the title referred to the latter subject, the ending of war and the restoration of peace, and not to the body of law that regulated relations among polities in times of peace.[4] With this choice of subject, Grotius placed himself in a tradition that went back to the writings of the late-medieval canonists and civilians. The legal literature of the medieval *jus commune* had dealt with each of these subjects, but separately and in a casuistic manner. Grotius was not the first to bring them together and expound them in a systematic manner. Here he followed in the footsteps of Alberico Gentili (1552–1608), Regius professor of civil law at Oxford, who in 1598 had brought out his major treatise on war, *De jure belli libri tres*. The treatise, which figured among Grotius' sources, was the first to bring together what later became the three parts of the laws of war and to deal with them in logical sequence. With Gentili, the sequential division of the laws of war in *jus ad bellum, jus in bello* and *jus post bellum* – the Latin terminology was coined around the turn of the twentieth century – was reflected in the separation of his work in three books.[5] While Grotius followed the same ordering of the material, he chose not to distribute it in the same manner over the three books of his treatise. Whereas Book 1 dealt with the concept of war and with the question who could wage war and the *jus ad bellum* was covered in Book 2, the *jus in bello* and *jus post bellum* were the subjects of Book 3 (for *jus post bellum* DJBP 3.1–19 and 21, respectively 3.20). Grotius thus adhered to the newly emerging systematisation of private law in persons – who may wage war, things and obligations – about what can one wage war – and actions – how to wage and end war. This new systematisation of private law had been construed by humanist jurists such as Hugues Doneau (1527–91), at one time professor at Leiden, on the basis of the system of *Institutes* of Justinian (r. 527–65).[6]

When Grotius took up the pen to write on the laws of war in 1623, it was not the first time he turned to the subject. In the fall of 1604, the directors of the Amsterdam Chamber of the Dutch East India Company (VOC) commissioned the young lawyer to author a memoir on the taking of the Portuguese carrack, *Santa Catarina*, in the Strait of Singapore the previous year by ships belonging to the company. This ship, with its rich cargo, had been towed to Amsterdam, where the Admiralty Court had assigned it as lawful prize to the VOC in its ruling of 9 September 1604. This did not settle the matter as the case had stirred up public debate about the VOC's role in the fight against the Spanish-Portuguese monarchy. Between 1604 and 1606, Grotius produced a lengthy treatise in which he argued that the ship was a lawful prize in a just war. The first ten out of fifteen chapters did not directly deal with the case, but entailed a systematic and theoretical exposition and reinterpretation of the just war doctrine, the hallmark of the medieval laws of war. Except for its chapter 12, which Grotius brought out as a pamphlet under the title *Mare liberum* in the context of truce negotiations with Spain in 1609, the memoir remained unpublished. It was only discovered in 1864, after which it was given the title *De jure praedae commentarius*. Only then did it become clear to what extent Grotius had borrowed from this earlier work for his *De jure belli ac pacis*.[7]

20.2 The Just War in Medieval Law and Theology

Although they did so on the basis of some text fragments from classical Antiquity – such as from Cicero, the *Digest*, Saint Augustine (354–430) and Saint Isidorus of Seville (560–636) – it was the canonists, theologians and civilians of the twelfth to fourteenth centuries who fleshed out the just war doctrine. The doctrine found its first authoritative articulation in the *Decretum* of the canon lawyer Gratian around 1140.[8] Theologians and civilians adopted the canonist elucidations of the theory during the thirteenth century and gave it their particular twists and interpretations.[9] The Dominican theologian, Saint Thomas Aquinas (*c.* 1225–74) poured it into its most familiar mould by listing three conditions for a war to be just: sovereignty (*auctoritas principis*), just cause (*causa justa*) and righteous intention (*recta intentio*).[10] Thomas' conditions reflected three of the four causes of Aristotle, the *causa efficiens* – who can wage war, the *causa materialis* – about what – and the *causa finalis* – for what purpose. The *causa formalis* – how to wage war – entailed that all hostile action had to be necessary and proportionate to its object and purpose.

Late-medieval doctrine understood the just war as a one-sided action of self-help (*executio juris*) to enforce a right after its violation (*iniuria*) by the enemy. It was an instrument of law enforcement for princes and rulers who recognised no higher secular authority and could thus not resort to the judiciary to enforce their rights. It was not a substitute for a legal trial, a trial by battle. A just war did not settle the title over a disputed right; it sanctioned the violation of a pre-established title. It was not a substitute for a judicial verdict, but for the enforcement of a verdict.

Gratian used Saint Augustine's definition of just war as an action 'to avenge injuries' (*ulcisci iniurias*).[11] With Augustine, he distinguished between three causes of war: to defend one's own against unjustified attack (*ad propulsandam homines*), to retrieve property (*res repetenda*) and to enact punishment.[12] Whereas the former two derived from Roman texts, the latter was introduced into the discourse of war by Saint Augustine. In the view of the Church Father, the punishment of an enemy, who had committed sin and violated the will of God, by inflicting damage beyond what was proportional to the injury was actually an act of love. Later, under the mainstream theology of the late middle ages, expiation of sin during life was considered to lessen divine retribution in the afterlife.[13] Writers from the thirteenth and fourteenth centuries, in particular the civilians, underplayed the importance of punishment and underscored the function of war as an instrument of self-help. Self-defence was not well regarded by Saint Augustine and his canonist and theological followers, as it was a selfish act. It might endanger the soul if one acted out of hatred. The civilians, however, gave it a more central place in their doctrine. For this, they could fall back on the *Digest*. Roman jurists, and their late-medieval interpreters, understood self-defence to fall under the remit of natural law. Following Bartolus of Saxoferrato (1313/1314–57), civilians began applying the natural law of self-defence to polities as well as to individuals.[14]

The canon lawyers who first framed the just war doctrine, and the theologians who followed in their footsteps, were concerned with the question what the waging of war would do to the eternal fate, the chances of salvation for individuals, whether rulers, soldiers or subjects. As Thomas Aquinas stated, the pertinent question was 'whether it [was] always a sin to wage war'.[15] What Thomas labelled as righteous intention had already been a central tenet of the doctrine of Saint Augustine, Gratian and the decretists. Participation in war could only be free from sin if one had the right moral disposition. This implied that one could not fight a war out of hatred or greed, but had to aim for the restoration of peace and justice. Already Augustine had judged that, because such disposition was unlikely in individuals, wars should only be waged by the command of the emperor and one should only engage in war, not for private purpose, but as an agent of the empire. Thomas Aquinas linked the righteous purpose of war on behalf of the polity with the common good (*bonum commune*) of the polity, and by extension to that of the whole Christian community.[16]

The just war doctrine discriminated between a just and unjust belligerent. As the cause of war was the prior violation of a right by one side, it was logically impossible that a war could be just on both sides. Under a consequential application of the doctrine, this implied that only the just belligerent had a right to use force and that all hostilities on the part of the unjust belligerent were *ipso facto* illegal. At the level of conscience, in the internal forum of spiritual relations between God and men with which canonists and theologians were primarily concerned, this meant that all hostile actions were additional sins on the part of the unjust belligerent, with the possible exception of personal self-defence.[17] In the domain of the civilians, that of the war's legal effects in the external forum of relations among men, this meant that only the just belligerents benefited from the rights of war (*jura belli*) such as the right to kill, plunder, conquer and to hold prisoners for ransom or to be released for ransom.[18] In its consequential reading, the just war doctrine dictated, furthermore, that the belligerent could only do as much damage and take as much property as was necessary and proportional to make the enemy account for the consequences of his injurious actions, with maybe a measure of punishment on top. This had the potential of continuously escalating the war as this extended to all costs and damages inflicted during the war by the unjust belligerent. At the end of a just war came a just peace. The object of contention would be attributed to the just belligerent – regardless of the outcome of the war – and he would be compensated for all costs and damages inflicted by the enemy before and during the war.[19]

The discriminatory nature of the just war vexed canonists, theologians and civil lawyers. The canonist and theological literature had to deal with the question of uncertainty about the claims to the justice of war and the underlying rights. Late-medieval authors debated this primarily through the question whether a soldier or subject had to obey his ruler if he ordered him to participate in an unjust war. The mainstream held that, only in case of manifest injustice, one could disobey. In case of doubt, the command by the superior shielded the subject from sin.[20] Before the Reformation, the 'universal' – in the sense of the whole Latin West – acknowledgment of the validity of canon law and the jurisdiction of the ecclesiastical courts, and in particular the papal court, provided – at least in theory – a legal framework and judicial venue to evaluate opposing claims to justice among belligerents, even if – in practice – this rarely led to a clear answer to the question who had justice on his side. The split of the Church in the first half of the sixteenth century and the rejection by over a third of Christian Europe of canon law and the papal court system exacerbated the problem of uncertainty. In the absence of a common law and a common, neutral court to judge, it was impossible for human beings – the belligerents, their subjects and allies as well as third powers – to establish who had right on their side in most cases of war among sovereigns. The Thomist theologian, Francisco de Vitoria (c. 1483–1546), from Salamanca most famously provided a solution by extending the traditional doctrine of manifest injustice to rulers. Whereas he stood by the classical view that a war could not be just on both sides in the eyes of God, he stated that a belligerent who, after diligent scrutiny and advice, mistakenly believed in good faith (*bona fide*) on the basis of provable ignorance that he was waging a just war was nevertheless excused from sin.[21]

For civil lawyers, the discriminatory nature of the just war held highly undesirable consequences. The proposition to apply the *jura belli*, as embodied in the code of chivalry, only to the benefit of the just belligerent was impractical as reciprocity formed the ultimate motivation for warriors to adhere to the code.[22] The civilians found an answer to this problem in the Roman conception of a public war (*bellum publicum*) between independent polities. In opposition to the case of private violence (*guerra*), Roman soldiers in a public war benefited from the *jus postliminii* – the right of captives to regain their status as free citizens and property upon their return.[23] Late-medieval lawyers interpreted this to mean that, in a public war, both sides could benefit from the *jura belli*.[24] The canonist and civilian, Raphael Fulgosius (1367–1427), was most eloquent on this. He argued that, since it was generally impossible for humans to judge over the claims to justice of sovereign belligerents in the absence of a common judge, one had to suspend this judgment and allow both sides to gain title over property in war.[25] Gentili, as the Spanish civilian Balthasar de Ayala (1548–84) had done before,[26] moulded this into an alternative conception of war: legal war (*bellum legale*) as opposed to just war. For war to be 'legal', and trigger the application of the *jura belli* for both sides, it sufficed that all belligerents were sovereign and that the war had been declared. The latter condition referred to the Roman usage to declare war in a formal, ritualistic manner under the *jus fetiale* with which humanists had become familiar through Roman historical sources, chiefly Livy.[27] The demand was also instrumental in a more material manner as a declaration of war commonly spelled out a justification for the resort to war. This was also the practice among European powers from the sixteenth to the eighteenth centuries. During this period, all belligerents generally forwarded justifications of war in the declarations of war and in the more extensive manifestos that they commonly released at the inception of war. These declarations and manifestos deployed the language of just war.[28] The resulting opposing claims of justice by sovereign belligerents made it impossible for fallible human beings – as Gentili would have it with reference to Fulgosius – to judge on the justice of war and necessitated treating both sides as if they were the just side and extending to them the benefits of the *jura belli*. In Gentili's reading, a legal war thus became a substitutive for a civil trial, a trial by battle. In view of the impossibility for any human to rule authoritatively over the opposed claims of the belligerents, it had to be left to the war itself to settle the dispute. The outcome of the war, victory, would attribute title to the disputed rights. As in a civil trial, both sides had the right to enter the fray of war and did so without fault. By consequence, their war actions were covered by the law and were not illegal by themselves. In case victory proved elusive, the negotiated settlement at the end of war, embodied in the peace treaty, would decide who held title.[29]

The late-medieval and sixteenth-century precursors to Grotius bequeathed two different conceptions of war. On the one hand, there was the canonist conception of just war as one-sided law enforcement. On the other hand, there was the civilian conception of legal war as an equal contention to settle a dispute about a right. Whereas the just war was relevant both in the internal and external forum, the Roman doctrine of the legality of war only pertained to its legal effects on the external relations among men and states. It did not regard the spiritual domain of eternal salvation.

20.3 Just War in *De Jure Praedae*

Grotius' brief for writing *De jure praedae* was to defend the capture of the *Santa Catarina* and its rich cargo by the VOC. He harnessed two crucial legal arguments to this cause. First, he tried to reject the Portuguese claim on the monopoly of trade and navigation in the East Indies; second, he tried to persuade his audience that the *Santa Catarina* was a good and lawful prize, as it had been taken under the extant laws of war in a just war. The former argument he made in chapter 12 of the memoir, of which he later published a version separately under the title of *Mare liberum*, and in which he contended that the sea was not open to appropriation and was common property. For the purpose of the latter argument, Grotius reached back to the doctrine of just war, of which he expounded his own version in the first ten chapters of the treatise. Making the case that the capture of the Portuguese carrack by the VOC was a lawful act in a just war was less straightforward than it might seem at first sight. The obvious argument to make was that the VOC fleet had acted as an agent of the Dutch Republic, or the sovereign province of Holland from which it held a commission, in a state-to-state war against the Kingdom of Portugal. Grotius applied this line of reasoning (DJPC 3, ff. 137-8 and 140).[30] However, this did not suffice to make his legal case foolproof. At the time of his writing, the major powers of Europe did not recognise the independence of the province of Holland or the Dutch Republic, although England and France were its allies. While the armed forces of the Spanish monarchy generally applied the laws of war to their Dutch enemies, they still considered the Dutch fight for independence a rebellion rather than a war. This meant that, to the Portuguese, the captors of the *Santa Catarina* were mere pirates, and not men-of-war or privateers acting under the cover of a state. For this reason, Grotius chose to develop, in what amounted to a highly original departure from established doctrine, the subsidiary argument that the Dutch ships had lawfully acted in a just, private war.

For the exposition of his theory of just war in the first ten chapters of *De jure praedae*, the young Grotius drew heavily on the classical just war doctrine, as developed by the canonists, theologians and civilians of the twelfth to fifteenth centuries, and on the works of the neo-scholastic and humanist writers of the sixteenth century. He, however, made some significant intellectual moves, which at one time allowed him to argue the case of private war and offered an innovative systematisation of the just war doctrine.

First, just as Vitoria and other neo-scholastic thinkers of the sixteenth century had done, Grotius placed the just war under the remit of natural law. In line with a medieval tradition that could be traced back to the Roman jurist Ulpian's (c. 170–223) distinction between *jus naturale* and *jus gentium*,[31] Grotius used two different categories of natural law: primary (*primaevum*) and secondary (*secundarium*) natural law. The latter he equated, as some civilians had done before, with the primary law of nations (*jus gentium primarium*).[32] Whereas the first category applied to the whole of creation and all living beings, the second was particular to humankind. Whereas the first category was directed towards self-preservation, the second was premised on man's sociability and rationality

(DJPC 2, ff. 5'a–6').[33] By placing the just war doctrine under natural law and giving it a more secular reading than most neo-scholastic writers, Grotius disentangled the just war from the amalgam of canon law, moral theology, Roman law and the customs and practices of war of which it historically formed part. Natural law offered him a framework of abstract, general principles and precepts that allowed for a novel, logical system-atisation of the just war doctrine. Although his treatise followed the traditional order of the four Aristotelian causes (DJPC chapters 6–9), this was overridden by a different logic, which allowed him to loosen the ties between just war and Christianity.

Grotius' natural law was not fully secular. He insisted on the divine origins of nature (DJPC 2, f. 5'). In Grotius' legal theory, all law derived its authority from the will of the lawmaker, God in the case of natural law. However, once God had finished the act of creation, even he would nor could intervene to alter natural law. Its enduring validity did not depend on divine will, but on its accordance with rationality. This implied that natural law was intelligible to all humankind, whether one was Christian or not. With this, Grotius separated natural law from divine (positive) law, which emerged through God's historic interventions in the world. For Gratian and many medieval scholars after him, natural law had been part and parcel of divine law. With divine law, Grotius particu-larly meant the Law of Moses, or the Decalogue, and the Law of the Gospels. Whereas the first only applied to the Hebrews, and thus was tantamount to municipal law (*jus civile*) of the Jewish people, the latter applied to all Christians. These 'laws', to Grotius, however, rather per-tained to the world of morality (*honestum*) than to that of proper, enforceable law (*justum*) (DJPC 1, f. 4' and 2, f. 14).[34]

Second, the disentanglement of just war and Christian morality provided Grotius with a platform to consider war as a mere instrument for the enforcement of subjective rights by persons or states. Late-medieval doc-trine also saw war as the enforcement of injured rights *(executio juris)*. However, the just cause (*causa justa*), which flowed from the enemy's injurious act, did not suffice to make a war just. For this, the belligerent also needed to be morally disposed (*recta intentio*) towards rendering justice, not only to oneself, but also to the opponent and, in the Thomist reading of the doctrine, towards the good of the commonwealth. Grotius reduced the material justification of war to the enforcement and restor-ation of the just belligerent's own rights.

In Grotius' system, each individual – or state – held a set of natural rights, which derived from a set of natural laws (*leges*). These granted people and states the right to defend themselves and to acquire all that was useful for their self-preservation and life (Laws 1 and 2); they forbade injuring another or taking away their possessions (Laws 3 and 4); and dictated the correction of evil deeds and the rewarding of good deeds (Laws 5 and 6) (DJPC 2). The rights, which individuals derived from these natural laws, Grotius thought of in terms of subjective rights, a conception that he may have taken from Doneau.[35] To Grotius, subjective rights were rights that pertained to the person and to which corresponded an obligation by others to respect them. With these rights also came the right to enforce them against the perpetrator of a violation – they were individual as well as individually enforceable. If necessary, this licensed resort to force, or war.

The sole condition and purpose for war under the perspective of natural law were, thus, the violation of right and its enforcement through seeking its restoration, compensation or punishment. Grotius made clear how this distanced his theory from classical, canonist and theological expositions by pointing out that all this was a matter of corrective justice (*justitia compensatrix*) and not of distributive justice (*justitia proportionalis*) (DJPC 2, f. 8). The kind of justice war was used to attain did not reflect an equal or honest distribution of rights among the members of the natural society, but only the reparation of individual rights to the extent of their violation.[36]

Third, Grotius used his theory of natural just war to justify private resort to war even after states had been created. This he based on the equation of the rights of states under natural law with those of private persons. To argue this, Grotius developed a three-step argumentation. *Primo,* under the state of nature before the creation of states, each person held license to defend, uphold and enforce his rights, by force if necessary. *Secundo,* through the agreement by which they created the state, people transferred their natural rights to the state. This implied that their right of self-enforcement now devolved onto the state, and its judicial institutions. For the relations between the states, the state of nature endured. In the sphere of international relations, the states had fallen heir to exactly the same rights that had previously accrued to individuals. This meant that the right of enforcement through war of the natural person had been transferred to the state. It now befell to the state and its agents to wage war in order to enforce its rights, and those of its citizens (Law 9). However, *tertio,* in exceptional cases where no appeal to the state was possible, the higher laws of self-defence and the right to protect one's property and rights revived and private persons resumed their right to use force (Law 13). Such exceptional circumstances could either occur when the protection of the state was temporarily unavailable – as under the direct necessity of self-defence against an attack – or in places where no state held jurisdiction, such as on the seas. With this, Grotius provided a platform to argue that the VOC ships had been acting in the context of a private war against the Portuguese (DJPC 8, ff. 37–8).

Fourth, whereas his predecessors had largely sufficed with indicating the material cause of war in general terms, Grotius provided his readers with a more systematic exposition of the different material causes for war. For this, he referred to the novel systematisation of Roman law, which humanist jurists such as Doneau had developed on the basis of the *Institutes* of Justinian in order to replace the medieval ordering following the *Digest*. This divided civil law into persons, rights to things (property), rights against other persons (obligations) and actions (remedies). With Grotius, this system returned in the right to self-defence, the right to recover or seek compensation for property and the right to enforce obligations, contractual or otherwise. To this, Grotius added the right to punish the perpetrator of a violation of rights, by doing damage or seeking retribution beyond the extent of the injury (DJPC 7, ff. 29'–30). Whereas both real and personal rights were covered under the notion of *res repetenda* in late-medieval doctrine, Grotius' careful distinction of these two categories was significant as it strengthened the association between the rights to war by states and the subjective rights of individuals. Every right and remedy persons had under Roman private law coincided with a just cause for war for the state. To do this, Grotius poured the system of remedies of Roman private law, through the sieve of its novel systematisation by humanist jurisprudents such as Doneau, into the vessel of his natural law theory.[37] Grotius further strengthened the association of war with judicial trial by his reading of declarations of war between states. Referring to Livy's exposition of the different steps of the fetial procedure to declare war in archaic Rome, Grotius pointed out that it served two functions: to make demands for satisfaction on the enemy and, absent the willingness of the opponent to comply, to declare war. Under the logic of Grotius' just war doctrine, the declaration of war took the place of a judicial verdict in the face of the enemy's refusal to convict himself. In his view, the war was the execution of this verdict (DJPC 8, ff. 45–6). This idea of self-judgment had already found expression with Bartolus.[38]

With this, Grotius made an extensive case for the VOC's right to wage war, whether as an agent of Holland or on its own. As the late-medieval and Renaissance jurists before, he needed to trouble himself with the undesirable consequences of his conception of war as law enforcement. The discrimination between the just and unjust belligerent at the level of the *jura belli*, combined with the uncertainty about the belligerents' claims to justice, made the question whether a prize was lawful almost impossible to settle outside an agreement between the parties themselves. As long as both the Republic and Portugal made a plausible argument for fighting a just war, it was impossible for humans to decide who had right on their side. It meant the attribution of the *Santa Catarina* would never be certain under natural law.

To solve this riddle, Grotius turned to the distinction between rulers and subjects, which canon lawyers had already made when addressing the question of the effects of participation in an unjust war. Late-medieval canonists had lowered the threshold of certainty about the justice of war for subjects, stating that they acted without sin if the cause of their prince was not manifestly unjust and doubts persisted. In his treatise, Grotius defended the thesis that subjects on both sides, regardless of the ultimate justice of their ruler's cause, could obtain rights in war as long as they believed in good faith in the justice of their war. Because they acted under orders and were liable to obey, except in cases of manifest injustice, they participated in the war with right and could thus gain title through their wartime actions. Sovereign command on behalf of the state brought their actions, however, outside the remit of natural law and into that of positive law (DJPC 8, ff. 52'–3' and 10, f. 56–58'). The equal application of the *jura belli* to subjects did not pertain to natural law. For this reason, Grotius introduced a different category of law: that of the secondary law of nations (*jus gentium secundarium*). In the more maturated exposition of the *nova declaratio*, an addition to the manuscript Grotius made in the years after 1606, he defined this as a law, which exclusively applied to states and derived from the consent between states (DJPC 2, f. 12).[39] Logically, as the justification for the equal application of the right to plunder was sovereign command, and as it concerned a rule of the positive law of nations and not of natural law, it only pertained to subjects fighting in a public war, and not to private war.

20.4 The Laws of War- and Peace-Making
in *De Jure Belli ac Pacis*

When Grotius returned to the subject of the laws of war and peace in 1623, his purpose was to promote the cause of peace. For this, he needed to defuse the claims by sceptic thinkers that international relations were ultimately dictated by sheer self-interest and could, thus, not be legally controlled.[40] The major thrust of Grotius' new foray into the subject was to prove that war was legally regulated and restricted (DJBP Prol. 3 and 5).[41] Grotius set out to prove this under four different categories of 'law': natural law, the law of nations, the law of Moses and the law of the Gospel. Only the first two categories, however, he considered in terms of universal enforceable rights and obligations, and thus of proper law. Whereas the law of Moses was particular to the Jews, the law of the Gospel, which did apply to all Christians, only imposed moral obligations. Adherence to the precepts of the Gospel might lead to heavenly rewards, but, inasmuch as they did not coincide with natural law, they could not be enforced and their violation would not meet with punishment (DJBP Prol. 50).[42] Here Grotius distinguished between *facultas*, or enforceable, subjective rights and obligations, and *aptitudo*, or moral disposition. The former was a matter of corrective justice; the latter of distributive justice (DJBP 1.1.4–9).[43]

In the *Prolegomena* to *De jure belli ac pacis*, Grotius expounded his general theory of law. He resorted to a simpler classification of the law of nature and of nations than the one from *De jure praedae*. He collapsed the primary and secondary law of nature into a single category of natural law (*jus naturale*), freeing the term law of nations (*jus gentium*) for exclusive reference to what he had called the secondary law of nations before. Grotius sometimes used the term volitional law of nations (*jus gentium voluntarium*). With this choice of wording, he emphasised that the law of nations was autonomous from natural law and that it was positive, human-made law. The basis of its validity was consent, as expressed in the customs of states (DJPB Prol. 17). Although the instinct of self-preservation was also caught under the now generic term of natural law, Grotius used the term mainly to refer to the law, which was particular to humankind's sociability (*appetitus socialis*) and rationality (DJBP Prol. 6–7 and 1.2.1.1–2). Grotius placed himself here in the Stoic tradition of *oikeiosis* (οἰκείωσις), which he knew best through Cicero.[44]

Grotius devoted the first book of his treatise to the definition of war, the question whether war could ever be lawful and to the question who could wage war. At the inception of the first chapter, he defined war as 'the condition of those contending by force' ('status per vim certantium', DJPB 1.1.2.1). In defining war as a condition or state rather than a set of hostile actions, Grotius purported to catch different categories of war, public and private, perfect and imperfect, under it. In doing so, however, he also suggested that one could think of war as a legal state separated from another, the state of peace, and that different laws applied to these two states. In this manner, Grotius, albeit involuntarily, contributed to the later emergence of the *summa divisio* of international law into the law of peace (*jus pacis*) and the law of war (*jus belli*).[45] In chapter 3 of Book 1, Grotius repeated his theory that – even after the emergence of states – private persons could resort to war in exceptional circumstances (DJPB 1.3.1–2). However, private war played a far smaller role in *De jure belli ac pacis* than in the Dutch writer's earlier memoir; the focus now lay squarely with interstate war.

Book 2 formed the backbone of the treatise. Here Grotius elaborated on his doctrine of just war as an instrument for the enforcement of subjective rights by expounding in fine detail the laws from which these rights emerged. Grotius distinguished five rather than four categories of material causes of war, by splitting obligations into obligations out of contract and out of delict, thus again closely adhering to the humanist system of Roman private law (DJBP Prol. 8). The discussion on the five causes for war and the subjective rights that war sustained induced Grotius to expound large areas of private law doctrine, albeit under the heading of natural law.[46] In case of punitive war, Grotius made an exception to the rule that war was a form of self-help. Under natural law, anyone had a right, albeit not an obligation, to punish those who had committed grave violations of natural law, whether one was a victim of these crimes or not. Whereas this right now accrued to sovereign states, in regions where the jurisdiction of the state did not reach – such as on the seas, it reverted to private persons (DJBP 2.20.7–8, also DJPC 8, ff. 39'–44). This theory has merited Grotius, together with some writers from the sixteenth century, acclamation among international lawyers for being one of the earlier proponents of universal, criminal jurisdiction and of the doctrine of humanitarian intervention.[47]

The most significant difference between Grotius' two treatises came in Book 3, which dealt with the laws regulating warfare itself as well as peace-making. Grotius introduced a second conception of war, next to just war: that of solemn war, formal war or war in due form (*bellum solemne*). This war corresponded to the conception of legal war of Gentili. For a war to be formal, it had to be waged between sovereign powers and it needed a formal declaration (DJBP 3.3.4–5). Like Ayala and Gentili before, Grotius drew on the Roman notion of a public war.[48] The effect of fighting in a formal war was that all belligerents enjoyed an equal right to wage the war and benefited equally from the *jura belli.* With this, Grotius moved beyond what he had conceded in *De jure praedae,* where he had only exempted subjects from the discriminatory application of just war (DJBP 3.4.1.1).

In this manner, Grotius dealt with the undesirable consequences of the discriminatory nature of just war by resorting to the solution, which the civilians of the late middle ages and the Renaissance had crafted from passages from the *Digest* and from what they knew of the *jus fetiale.* This, however, he combined with Vitoria's doctrine of ignorance.[49] The impossibility, in many cases, to discern the justice of war necessitated the equal treatment of sovereign belligerents with regards to the effects of war (DJBP 2.23.13). This equality was, however, restricted to the external forum. Grotius placed the conception of *bellum solemne* within the remit of the volitional law of nations, whereas the just war fell under the law of nature. This implied that, although in a formal war the discriminatory effects of the justice of war were superseded at the level of creating enforceable rights and obligations in the relations among states, the justice or injustice of war retained its relevance in the internal forum of conscience.

To Grotius, this did not mean the pure and utter degradation of the question of justice from the sphere of enforceable, perfect law into that of mere moral obligation, without risk of sanction.[50] First, there was the risk of human sanctioning as, so Grotius admonished, 'justice is approved, and injustice condemned, by the common agreement of men' (DJBP Prol. 20). This implied that perpetrators of natural law who resorted to unjust war risked the disapproval and, possibly, enmity of third powers. Such sanction was a choice, however, not an obligation. With this, Grotius was not far off the mark of reality as the discourse of just war remained a powerful language of persuasion and diplomacy in Europe until the early twentieth century, which states readily deployed to convince their own populations and their allies, as well as neutral powers, of the righteousness of their actions.[51]

Second, there was the risk of divine sanction. Much has been made, in particular by international law scholars, of the secularism of Grotius' natural law because of the 'Etiamsi daremus [. . .] non esse deum' passage, the so-called impious hypothesis, from the *Prolegomena* (DJBP Prol. 11). However, this passage did not purport anything more than the acknow- ledgment that it was not necessary to be a Christian and to accept the truth of the Christian religion to know natural law. Grotius' earlier views on the relation between God as creator and (secondary) natural law from *De jure praedae* had not fundamentally altered, even if they had matured and become part of a more complex and sophisticated theology. In the years before he started writing *De jure belli ac pacis,* Grotius had devoted himself to developing his theological views, which he finally unpacked in *De veritate religionis Christianae* (1627/1629).[52] Essential to Grotius' under- standing of natural law was that, although God had created nature and human nature so that natural law took its original validity from divine will, God did not interfere with natural law throughout history. Moreover, knowledge of Christianity was not innate to human nature. Hence, the rejection of Christian truths was not a punishable offence under natural law. Nature only dictated some very general truths about religion, such as the existence of God, the fact of creation and of God's enduring care for mankind. Natural law thus escaped and transcended the differences between the various Christian confessions and most other religions of the world.[53] However, the confessional neutrality of Grotius' natural law did not separate it completely from Christian moral theology. For Grotius, the violation of natural law constituted sin. By consequence, natural law remained enforceable law, even in the case of a formal war when its practical effects were suspended by the volitional law of nations. Whereas it could not any longer be enforced in the external relations among states, it could very well be enforced by the supreme judge at the Last Judgment (DJBP Prol. 20 and 3.10.3).[54]

A significant consequence of the introduction of the conception of formal war was that it created a space for a situation whereby states were not formally at war – because they had not formally declared war – but wherein hostile actions were taking place. Herewith, Grotius gave another push to the distinction between state of war and state to peace, and to the distinction between perfect and imperfect wars, which in the nineteenth century would become known as measures short of war.[55] Of the different categories of imperfect war that would develop in seventeenth- and eighteenth-century scholarship and practice, such as self-defence, auxil- iary participation in war and reprisal, Grotius' work held most relevance to the latter. Reprisal constituted a violent action by a private individual under license of his own sovereign against the co-nationals of the subject of another sovereign who had injured his rights. Grotius justified the widespread practice of reprisal, which formed a legal underpinning of privateering and thus, ultimately, of the taking of the *Santa Catarina,* by referring to the widely accepted rule that subjects were liable for the debts of their sovereign. Failure of a sovereign to do justice to a foreign subject for the injuries committed by his own subject made all his subjects liable for compensation of the inflicted damage (DJBP 3.2.2–4).[56]

The duality between natural justice and formal law not only applied to the lawfulness of war and of wartime actions, but also returned with regards to peace-making, a subject with which Grotius dealt in chapter 20 of Book 3. Under the perspective of natural law, a peace should do justice to the just belligerent by attributing to him the claim for which he had entered the war and granting compensation for all the costs and damages suffered because of the war. Because, however, it hardly ever occurred – and, in the practice among European sovereigns at the time, actually never occurred – that a belligerent confessed to injustice, the logic of formal war had to be extended to peace. This implied that all wartime actions were considered legal and retained their effect. This altered the nature of war from an instrument of the enforcement of right – just war – to an instrument of dispute settlement – formal war. Grotius translated this in the general application of the principle of *uti possedetis* at the end of war: the belligerents retained their conquests and plunder inasmuch as the peace treaty did not deviate from this principle (DJBP 3.20.11–2). Furthermore, Grotius opined that, because of the inherent uncertainty about the justice of claims for war damages, states needed to waive these. With this, he voiced support for the widespread practice of including an amnesty clause in peace treaties whereby the signatory powers agreed to cede all claims for reparation for costs or damages suffered because of the war (DJBP 3.20.15). To the general application of *uti possidetis* and the general inclusion of amnesty, the peace treaties of the early modern age commonly made an exception by stipulating the restitution of confiscated realty and debts. Grotius' dual logic of just and formal war also provided a theoretical foundation for this. Grotius justified the confiscation of all enemy property at the start of war under the just war doctrine as a measure to secure the later payment of all war damages and costs arising from the war. However, because the peace treaty did not settle who had justice on his side and it waived all claims for reparation, the legal basis for confiscation collapsed. Hence, restitution of the confiscated realty – which in contrast to personal was still retrievable – and debts was indicated (DJBP 3.13.1 and 3).[57]

20.5 Conclusion

In recent decades, students of Grotius' theory of the laws of war and peace have hotly debated its intellectual genealogy. On one side of the debate stand those, such as Haggenmacher, who underline Grotius' indebtedness to the late-medieval, scholastic just war doctrine. On the other side stand those, foremost among them Tuck, who place Grotius in a humanist tradition that premised international relations on the right of self-preservation. More recently, Straumann steered a middle course by forwarding the claim that the key role of human sociability in Grotius' theory of war did not so much derive from late-medieval scholasticism, but from the direct, unmediated exposure to the Stoic tradition that permeated some of his most frequently quoted sources, Cicero and the *Digest*.

Grotius based his two major treatises on the laws of war- and peace-making on an eclectic reading and use of Roman law, canon law, theological and a wide array of other textual sources that ranged from the Old Testament through classical Antiquity and the middle ages to his immediate neo-scholastic and humanist predecessors. This eclecticism was rooted in his humanist epistemology. Although Grotius was critical of the late-medieval lawyers and theologians, this did not stop him from drawing on them. As a humanist, Grotius only attached relative authority to his sources, this in contrast to his late-medieval scholastic predecessors who had granted absolute authority to texts such as the Bible, the writings of Aristotle or the *Digest*. For him, these sources bore witness to human achievements from the past, rather than to an unchangeable, eternal truth. As such, he considered them examples and guidelines, rather than absolute directives. This allowed him to draw on a great variety of textual traditions and sources, and mould them together in a systematic theory guided by the abstract principles and precepts of natural law. In this respect, the emancipation of just war from its entanglement with canon law, moral theology and Roman law also served as a methodological device to pour it into a new mould of logic.[58]

Among the different contributions Grotius made to the further development of the laws of war- and peace-making and to general international law, one stands out for its impact on later writers and on state practice: his dualist theory of just and formal war. To Grotius falls the merit of having brought the two strands of the canonist just war doctrine and the civilian doctrine of legal war together and reordered it into a new system. Grotius' systematisation was there to endure. By the end of the seventeenth century, both the duality of the law of nature and the law of nations, and of two conceptions of war, had become mainstream in international legal scholarship. It would remain so until deep into the nineteenth century.[59] In this, Grotius, like his successors, did nothing but follow the directives of state practice and provide them with a theoretical justification. For the whole early modern age and beyond, state practice indeed adhered to the dual logic of just and formal war. Whereas states did apply the *jus in bello* and *jus post bellum* in wars between them without any regard for claims of justice under the logic of formal war, they did continue to operate the language of just war for the justification of their own resort to war and force, and for their reactions to third states' actions. Although devoid of sanction under the law of nations, as long as natural law remained connected with Christianity and the belief persisted that a violation of natural justice equalled sin and would meet with divine retribution, the language of the justice of war served to reassure the conscience of European rulers, soldiers and subjects. As most defensive alliances presupposed just cause to trigger the *casus foederis*, just war endured as an essential feature, as Grotius well understood, to the workings of European diplomacy.[60]

Further Reading

Aure, A.H., *The Right to Wage War (jus ad bellum). The German Reception of Grotius 50 Years after De Iure Belli ac Pacis* (Berlin, 2015).

Haggenmacher, P., *Grotius et la doctrine de la guerre juste* (Paris, 1983).

Hathaway, O., and S. Shapiro, *The Internationalists and Their Plan to Outlaw War* (New York/London, 2017).

Lauterpacht, H., 'The Grotian tradition in international law', *British Yearbook of International Law* 23 (1946) 1–51.

Lesaffer, R., 'Too much history. From war as sanction to the sanctioning of war', in M. Weller (ed.), *The Oxford Handbook of the Use of Force in International Law* (Oxford, 2015), 35–55.

Lesaffer, R., 'Roman law and the intellectual history of international law', in A. Orford and F. Hoffmann (eds.), *The Oxford Handbook of the Theory of International Law* (Oxford, 2016), 38–58.

Neff, S.C., *War and the Law of Nations. A General History* (Cambridge, 2005).

Onuma, Y. (ed.), *A Normative Approach to War. Peace, War, and Justice in Hugo Grotius* (Oxford, 1993).

Reichberg, G.M., *Thomas Aquinas on War and Peace* (Cambridge, 2017).

Russell, F.H., *The Just War in the Middle Ages* (Cambridge, 1975).

Scattola, M., 'Law, war and method in the *Commentary on the Law of Prize* by Hugo Grotius', *Grotiana* N.S. 26–8 (2005–7) 79–103.

Straumann, B., *Roman Law in the State of Nature. The Classical Foundations of Hugo Grotius' Natural Law* (Cambridge, 2015).

Stumpf, C.A., *The Grotian Theology of International Law. Hugo Grotius and the Moral Foundations of International Relations* (Berlin and New York, 2006).

Tuck, R., *The Rights of War and Peace. Political Thought and the International Order from Grotius to Kant* (Oxford, 1999).

Whitman, J.Q., *The Verdict of Battle. The Law of Victory and the Making of Modern War* (Cambridge, MA and London, 2012).

Notes

1 H. Lauterpacht, 'The Grotian tradition in international law', *British Yearbook of International Law* 23 (1946) 1–51, at 17.

2 E.g. Lassa Oppenheim, *International Law, A Treatise* (London/New York, 1905–6), vol. 1: Peace and vol. 2: War and Neutrality; M.J. Van Ittersum, 'Hugo Grotius: the making of a founding father of international law', in A. Orford and F. Hoffmann (eds.), *The Oxford Handbook of the Theory of International Law* (Oxford, 2016), 82–100.

3 *Pro Balbo* 6.15.

4 P. Haggenmacher, *Grotius et la doctrine de la guerre juste* (Paris, 1983), 8 and 563–4; Haggenmacher, 'La paix dans la pensée de Grotius', in L. Bély (ed.), *L'Europe des traités de Westphalie. Esprit de la diplomatie et diplomatie de l'esprit* (Paris, 2000), 67–79, at 70.

5 A. Gentili, *De jure belli libri tres* (1598, text of 1612, Oxford/London 1933); P. Haggenmacher, 'Grotius and Gentili: a reassessment of Thomas E. Holland's inaugural lecture', in H. Bull, B. Kingsbury and A. Roberts (eds.), *Hugo Grotius and International Relations* (Oxford, 1990), 133–76.

6 Haggenmacher, *Grotius*, 178–9; L. Winkel, 'Problems of legal systematization from *De iure praedae* to *De iure belli ac pacis*. *De iure praedae* chapter II and the *Prolegomena* of *De iure belli ac pacis* compared', *Grotiana* N.S. 26–8 (2005–7) 61–78, at 76.

7 P. Borschberg, 'Grotius, maritime intra-Asia trade and the Portuguese Estado de India: problems, perspectives and insights from *De iure praedae*', *Grotiana* N.S. 26-8 (2005-7) 31-60; M.J. Van Ittersum, *Profit and Principle. Hugo Grotius, Natural Rights Theories and the Rise of Dutch Power in the East Indies (1595-1615)* (Leiden and Boston, 2006), 1-43 and 105-88.

8 Causa 23.

9 F.H. Russell, *The Just War in the Middle Ages* (Cambridge, 1975).

10 ST IIaIIae 40.1; G.M. Reichberg, *Thomas Aquinas on War and Peace* (Cambridge, 2017).

11 Augustine, *Quaestiones in Heptateuchum* 6.10; C. 23 q. 2 c. 2.

12 C. 23 q. 2 c. 1-2; see Cicero, *De Officiis* 1.11.36, but punishment in *De re publica* 2.23.25.

13 Haggenmacher, *Grotius*, 154-9; Russell, *Just War*, 16-27 and 57-68.

14 In particular D. 9.2.45.4; R. Greenwood, 'War and sovereignty in medieval Roman law', *Law and History Review* 32 (2014) 31-63, at 48-50; Russell, *Just War*, 41-5.

15 ST IIaIIae 40.1, translation from R.W. Dyson (ed.), *Aquinas. Political Writings* (Cambridge Texts in the History of Political Thought; Cambridge, 2002), 239.

16 Reichberg, *Aquinas*, 17-41; Russell, *Just War*, 261-2.

17 Greenwood, 'War and sovereignty', 34-5 and 50.

18 P. Haggenmacher, 'On the doctrinal origins of *ius in bello*: from the right of war to the laws of war', in T. Marauhn and H. Steiger (eds.), *Universality and Continuity in International Law* (The Hague, 2011), 325-58.

19 Haggenmacher, *Grotius*, 253-79; e.g. Francisco de Vitoria, *De jure belli*, 60.

20 Russell, *Just war*, 147.

21 Vitoria, *De jure belli*, 32.

22 R. Ambühl, *Prisoners of War in the Hundred Years War* (Cambridge, 2013), 19-45; M.H. Keen, *The Laws of War in the Late Middle Ages* (Aldershot, 1965), 7-22.

23 D. 49.15.24.

24 Bartolus, ad D. 49.15.24.

25 Raphael Fulgosius, ad D. 1.1.5; Greenwood, 'War and sovereignty', 51-2; Haggenmacher, *Grotius*, 279-88.

26 Balthasar de Ayala, *De jure et officiis bellicis et disciplina militari libri III* (text of 1582, Washington, 1912), 1 and 2.7.

27 Livy 1.32.

28 A. Tischer, *Offizielle Kriegsbegründungen in der frühen Neuzeit. Hersscherkommunikation in Europa zwischen Souveränität und korporativem Selbstverständnis* (Berlin, 2012).

29 Gentili, *De jure belli*, 1.2.17-8; R. Lesaffer, 'Alberico Gentili's *ius post bellum* and early modern peace treaties', in B. Kingsbury and B. Straumann (eds.), *The Roman Foundations of the Law of Nations. Alberico Gentili on the Justice of Empire* (Oxford, 2010), 210-40, at 221-6.

30 Van Ittersum, *Profit and Principle*, 45-6.

31 D. 1.1.1.3-4.

32 Like Paulus de Castro (d. 1441), ad D. 1.1.1.3 and 1.1.4.

33 Haggenmacher, *Grotius*, 331–2; M. Scattola, 'Law, war and method in the Commentary on the Law of Prize by Hugo Grotius', *Grotiana* N.S. 26–8 (2005–7) 79–103, at 98–100.

34 Haggenmacher, *Grotius*, 471 and 591–4; Scattola, 'Law, war and method', 97; M. Somos, 'Secularization in *De Iure Praedae*: from Bible criticism to international law', *Grotiana* N.S. 26–8 (2005–7) 147–91; B. Straumann, *Roman Law in the State of Nature. The Classical Foundations of Hugo Grotius' Natural Law* (Cambridge, 2015), 39–41; F. Todescan, '*Sequuntur Dogmatica De Iure Praedae*: law and theology in Grotius's use of sources in *De Iure Praedae*', *Grotiana* N.S. 26–8 (2005–7) 281–309.

35 Haggenmacher, 'Droits subjectifs et système juridique chez Grotius', in L. Foisneau (ed.), *Politique, droit et théologie chez Bodin, Grotius et Hobbes* (Paris, 1997), 73–130, at 112–3.

36 B. Straumann, 'Natural rights and Roman law in Hugo Grotius's *Theses LVI, De iure Praedae* and *Defensio capitis quinti maris liberi*', *Grotiana* N.S. 26–8 (2005–7) 341–65, at 349–9; Straumann, *Roman Law*, 103–29.

37 B. Straumann, 'Ancient Caesarian lawyers in a state of nature. Roman tradition and natural rights in Hugo Grotius's *De iure praedae*', *Political Theory* 34 (2006) 328–50, at 339; Straumann, 'Is modern liberty ancient? Roman remedies and natural rights in Hugo Grotius's early work on natural law', *Law and History Review* 27 (2009) 55–85; Straumann, *Roman Law*, 170–206.

38 Bartolus, *Tractatus represaliarum, in Omnia, quae extant, opera* (Venice, 1590–1602), vol. 10, ff. 119vb; Greenwood, 'War and sovereignty', 48; Haggenmacher, *Grotius*, 223–47.

39 Haggenmacher, *Grotius*, 331–99; Haggenmacher, 'Génèse et signification du concept de "ius gentium" chez Grotius', *Grotiana* N.S. 2 (1981) 44–102.

40 H.J. Nellen, *Hugo Grotius. A Lifelong Struggle for Peace in Church and State, 1583–1645* (Leiden and Boston, 2014), 370–2.

41 Straumann, *Roman Law*, 55–61; for a different interpretation: Richard Tuck, 'Grotius, Carneades and Hobbes', *Grotiana* N.S. 4 (1983) 43–62; Tuck, *The Rights of War and Peace. Political Thought and the International Order from Grotius to Kant* (Oxford, 1999), 94–102.

42 M. de Blois, 'Blessed [are] the peacemakers ... Grotius on the just war and Christian pacifism', *Grotiana* N.S. 32 (2011) 20–39; T. Tanaka, 'Temperamenta *(Moderation)*', in Y. Onuma (ed.), *A Normative Approach to War. Peace, War, and Justice in Hugo Grotius* (Oxford, 1993), 276–307, at 296–304.

43 M. Koskenniemi, 'Imagining the rule of law: rereading the Grotian tradition', *European Journal of International Law* 30 (2019) 17–52; C.A. Stumpf, *The Grotian Theology of International Law. Hugo Grotius and the Moral Foundations of International Relations* (Berlin and New York, 2006), 44–51.

44 Cicero, *De finibus* 3.5.16–9; B. Straumann, '*Oikeiosis* and *appetitus socialis*. Hugo Grotius' Ciceronian argument for natural law and just war', *Grotiana* N.S. 24–6 (2003–4) 41–66; Straumann, *Roman Law*, 88–107.

45 S.C. Neff, *War and the Law of Nations. A General History* (Cambridge, 2005), 102.

46 R. Lesaffer, 'Roman law and the intellectual history of international law', in A. Orford and F. Hoffmann (eds.), *The Oxford Handbook of the Theory of International Law* (Oxford, 2016), 38–58, at 45–57.

47 T. Furukawa, 'Punishment', in Onuma, *Normative Approach,* 221–43, at 231–40; D.J.B. Trimm, 'If a prince use tyrannie towards his people: interventions on behalf of foreign populations in early modern Europe', in B. Simms and D.J.B. Trimm (eds.), *Humanitarian Intervention. A History* (Cambridge, 2011), 29–66, at 39–41; R. Tuck, 'Grotius, Hobbes and Pufendorf on humanitarian intervention', in S. Recchia and J.M. Welsh (eds.), *Just and Unjust Military Intervention. European Thinkers from Vitoria to Mill* (Cambridge, 2013), 96–112.

48 D. 49.15.24.

49 With reference to Vitoria, *De jure belli* 32; A.H. Aure, *The Right to Wage War (jus ad bellum). The German Reception of Grotius 50 Years after De Jure Belli ac Pacis* (Berlin, 2015), 173–5.

50 Aure, *Right to Wage War*, 43.

51 R. Lesaffer, 'Too much history. From war as sanction to the sanctioning of war', in M. Weller (ed.), *The Oxford Handbook of the Use of Force in International Law* (Oxford, 2015), 35–55; Lesaffer, 'Aggression before Versailles', *European Journal of International Law* 29 (2018) 773–808.

52 M.A. Antognazza, 'Introduction', in Hugo Grotius, *The Truth of the Christian Religion, with Jean Le Clerc's Notes and Additions* (Natural Law and Enlightenment Classics; Indianapolis, 2012), ix–xx, at xii–xiii; Nellen, *Grotius*, 422–30.

53 J.P. Heering, *Hugo Grotius as Apologist for the Christian Religion. A Study of his Work* De Veritate Religionis Christianae *(1640)* (Leiden and Boston, 2004), 47–63; S. Mortimer, '*De Veritate*, Christianity and human nature', *Grotiana* N.S. 35 (2014) 75–94; H. Nellen, 'Minimal religion, deism and Socianism: on Grotius's motives for writing *De Veritate,' Grotiana* N.S. 33 (2012) 25–57; Nellen, 'Hugo Grotius on religion as a motive for waging war', in R. von Friedeburg and M. Schmoeckel (eds.), *Recht, Konfession und Verfassung im 17. Jahrhundert. West- und mitteleuropäische Entwicklungen* (Berlin, 2015), 261–8; Stumpf, *Grotian Theology*, 51–8.

54 Aure, *Right to Wage War*, 43–54; N. Kasai, 'The laws of war', in Onuma, *Normative Approach*, 244–75, at 273–5; Tanaka, 'Temperamenta', 298–302.

55 Neff, *War*, 100–2, 119–30 and 215–49.

56 Haggenmacher, *Grotius*, 586–7; R. Lesaffer, 'Grotius on reprisal', *Grotiana* N.S. 41 (2020) 330–48; Neff, *War*, 120–6.

57 R. Lesaffer and E.-J. Broers, 'Private property in the Dutch-Spanish peace treaty of Münster (30 January 1648)', in M. Jucker, M. Kintzinger and R.C. Schwinges (eds.), *Rechtsformen internationaler Politik. Theorie, Norm und Praxis vom 12. bis 18. Jahrhundert* (Zeitschrift für Historische Forschung, Beihefte 45; Berlin,

2011), 165–96, at 188–95; R. Lesaffer, 'Peace treaties and the formation of international law', in A. Peters and B Fassbender (eds.), *The Oxford Handbook of the History of International Law* (Oxford, 2012), 71–94, at 87–9.

58 D.J. Bederman, 'Reception of the classical tradition in international law: Grotius's *De jure belli ac pacis'*, *Grotiana* N.S. 16–17 (1995–6) 3–34.

59 S.C. Neff, *Justice among Nations. A History of International Law* (Cambridge, MA and London, 2014), 170–3 and 182–98.

60 J. Cornette, *Le roi de guerre. Essai sur la souveraineté dans la France du Grand-Siècle* (Paris, 1993), 141–60; N. Reinhardt, *Voices of Conscience. Royal Confessors and Political Counsel in Seventeenth-Century Spain and France* (Oxford, 2016), 106–21.

Stephen C. Neff

21.1 Introduction

To expound the law relating to war was a primary purpose of Hugo Grotius in the writing of his famous treatise, *De jure belli ac pacis* (1625). In Grotius' opinion, a 'very serious error' had taken hold of the popular mind, to the effect that there was no law regulating the manner in which the combatants went about their deadly business (DJBP, Prol. 2). The events of the Thirty Years War, raging in central Europe at the time the book was written, could easily have given rise to such a notion. Be that as it may, one of Grotius' central concerns was to refute this pernicious misconception. Even in time of war, he insisted, the opposing sides remain part of a common moral community, governed by the general law of nature, and also by the body of customary and contractual law known as the law of nations (DJBP 3.19.1; 3.1.18–20).

It would be an exaggeration to see Grotius as an innovator in the laws of war. He is better seen as a systematiser, with clarity and thoroughness, rather than innovation, as his intellectual hallmarks. One of the important sources of his thought was the medieval heritage of just war doctrine, which had reached its mature form by the thirteenth century.[1] That august body of work, however, had comparatively little to say about the *conduct* of war (or *jus in bello* in Latin legal parlance). Its focus had been largely on the lawfulness of *resorting* to war (or *jus ad bellum* to the lawyers). Concerning the conduct of war, its most relevant feature was the principle of *animus*: the idea that war must be waged with the proper mental attitude, meaning a selfless desire to do justice. A just war should be regarded as a regrettably necessary form of self-help, in the vindication of the rule of law. That meant that it must not be waged for greed or glory or the sheer joy of plunder. Beyond that very general principle, though, traditional just war offered little guidance. A second important source of ideas on the conduct of war was the body of law known as the law of arms, which was essentially a code of conduct for medieval knights. Its best-known exposition was Raymond Lull's (1232–1316) *Order of Chivalry*, written in the 1270s.

A number of major works on the laws of war, drawing on these two sources, had long preceded Grotius. The earliest one was *The Treatise on War, Reprisals and Duels* of the Italian scholar, John of Legnano, published in about 1360. This was followed up by two more books that were rather more accessible to average readers: *The Tree of Battles* (c. 1386) by French monk Honoré de Bonet (or Bouvet, c. 1340–c. 1410) and *The Book of Deeds of Arms and of Chivalry* (c. 1410) by Christine de Pisan (1364–1430).[2] More recent commentators, to whom Grotius accorded some grudging praise, included Balthasar de Ayala (1548–84) from the Spanish Netherlands and, most notably, Italian scholar Alberico Gentili (1552–1608).[3] Where Grotius differed from these predecessors was not so much regarding the substantive content of the laws of war, but rather in the extent to which his ideas about war were integrated into a massive and systematic treatment of natural law in general.

The following discussion will first delineate the two bodies of law – the law of nature and the law of nations – that governed the conduct of war, and then proceed to look briefly at some of the more general considerations governing the law of warfare in Grotius' *De jure belli ac pacis* – the principle of equality of status of the belligerents, the concept of belligerents' rights and general considerations of necessity and proportionality or moderation in warfare. There will then be brief discussions of the more specific issues treated by Grotius, including ruses of war and good faith between enemies, the taking of property, prisoners of war, the protection of civilians, assassination and the law of neutrality.

21.2 The Dual Nature of the Law of Armed Conflict

Grotius' view of the law of armed conflict directly reflected his view of international law in general. This view was dualistic, in which international law was regarded as a partnership between two quite distinct bodies of law, having different sources and different substantive rules. First was the law of nature, or natural law, which was a fixed, ineluctable set of rules, valid for all human cultures at all times in history – and, crucially, applicable in war as in peace. It was a reflection of eternal and immutable ideas of right and wrong that were ultimately rooted in the very nature of the moral universe and were neither human inventions nor subject to alteration by humans.

The other body of law was the law of nations – sometimes called the 'volitional' law of nations - which was a human-created body of rules of a basically contractual character. This body of law was utilitarian in nature and subject to alteration at the will of the nations of the world. Because this law of nations was largely contractual in character, its rules were not necessarily binding on the entire human race, as natural law definitely is. Rather, it is binding only on states that could be deemed to be parties to the agreement. Consequently, there were some restraints imposed by the law of nations that applied to conflicts between European or Christian states, but not necessarily when other states were involved. One of these was the substitution of ransom for enslavement as the fate of prisoners of war. Another was the use of poison-tipped javelins in war. Grotius stated this to be prohibited by the law of nations only in conflicts among European powers – plus 'such others as attain to the higher standard of Europe' – but not otherwise (DJBP 3.4.16).

These two bodies of law were seen as complementary rather than competitive – somewhat in the nature of law and equity in Anglo-American legal systems. Broadly speaking, the law of nations was brought into play in situations in which, for various practical reasons, it was difficult or impossible to apply the law of nature in its full rigour. In such instances, the law of nations operated to effect modifications to the law of nature – sometimes to permit what natural law forbade by pointedly withholding punishment for departures from natural law and sometimes acting oppositely, to forbid things that natural law permitted (e.g. DJBP 3.4.15). There was, however, no general or mechanical rule of precedence or hierarchy between the two. The fine eye and the honed mind of the skilled lawyer was needed in the application of these two bodies of law to specific issues – as will be seen below.

The single most prominent case of modification of natural law by the law of nations concerned the overarching question of the rights of contending states during war. This is a matter of such importance as to merit some special attention.

21.3 Equality of Legal Status of Belligerents

The medieval just war doctrine, to which Grotius was strongly committed, arose out of natural law and regarded a just war as an exercise in forcible self-help – i.e., as the enforcement of a legal right by the use of armed force when a less drastic means of enforcement was not available. It was, therefore, by its nature, a clash between good and evil. Moreover, the determination of the just cause was, according to natural law, a strictly objective question. A war could not be just on both sides, just as both sides could not be held to be in the right in ordinary litigation (DJBP 2.23.13).

Because of this right-versus-wrong character of warfare, the rights accorded to the two belligerent parties were, in modern parlance, radically asymmetrical. The just side was allowed to employ whatever degree of force was necessary under the circumstances to bring its foe to brook; while the unjust side had no right to use force at all. Any resort to force by the unjust side merely added to that side's original wrongdoing – with the logical effect that the unjust party became liable to indemnify the just one for the expenses undertaken in the contest itself.

The severe practical problem in applying this doctrine was the difficulty – if not the outright impossibility – of determining, at the time of the struggle, which party was the just side and which was the unjust one. To deal with this conundrum, the law of nations was brought to bear. The law of nations allowed a war to be regarded as just on both sides provided that both sides fought in the good-faith belief that right was on their side. In Grotius' explanation, there would be an absence of blame in such a case, even though, strictly speaking, it remained the case that one side was objectively in the right and the other in the wrong. But, in the absence of blame on either side, the law of nations would treat both sides as equally fighting a just war (DJBP 2.23.13). This crucial change is sometimes stated in terms of a shift in focus from just war to formal war, or what Grotius referred to as a *bellum solemne*. That is, that, so long as a war was formally declared by a lawful sovereign and carried out in accordance with the relevant laws of war, it would be treated as a just war on the part of both contenders by the law of nations (DJBP 1.2.4).

The immediate logical consequence of this change was that both sides became equally entitled, under the law of nations, to exercise what came to be called the rights of war (*jura belli*), or belligerents' rights (to be discussed more fully below) (DJBP 3.4.3). Ever since the time of Grotius, this basic principle has lain at the core of the laws governing the conduct of war: that those laws are fully symmetrical, applying with strict equality to the contending parties, without regard to the underlying justice or injustice of their causes.

This grand, overarching principle of equality between the belligerents may be marked as Grotius' single greatest contribution to the development of the law of armed conflict. Even here, though, he had important predecessors. Most notably, the Spanish Dominican writer, Francisco de Vitoria, writing in the sixteenth century, had allowed that a war could be regarded as just on both sides in cases of 'provable ignorance either of fact or of law' concerning which side was in the right.[4] To Vitoria, however, that was an exceptional and marginal matter. The contribution of Grotius lay in the assertion that the equality of belligerents was *always* a feature of war, as a general principle of the law of nations – though not, admittedly, of the law of nature, where the rule of justice on one side only continued in force.[5]

21.4 The Concept of Belligerents' Rights

The rights of belligerents in wartime were divided by Grotius into two categories. First were the rights belonging to belligerents *per se*, which were exercisable against the enemy armed force and those who provided material assistance to it. These were determined by the law of nations. Second were the rights arising from the principle of necessity, which was part of natural law. The principle of necessity will be discussed below. Here, the focus is on belligerents' rights as such.

The basic idea behind belligerents' rights was succinctly stated by Grotius: that 'it is permitted to harm an enemy' (DJBP 3.4.3). That is to say, that, once a formal state of war is in force, acts may be committed against the opposing side – such as killing, capturing and occupying territory – that would be unlawful if committed in time of peace. Outside of a state of war, intentional killing is murder; capture is kidnapping; and occupation of territory is trespass. Moreover, as noted above, this right to injure the opposing side belongs equally to both sides, without regard to the legal merits of the dispute that gave rise to the war.

An important question – so important as virtually to comprise the whole subject of the law of armed conflict – is whether, in the Grotian scheme, there were any limitations on the exercise of these key belligerents' rights; and, if so, what those limits were. The answer is that there were limitations, with the result that the law of armed conflict – in Grotius' time and still in our own – is Janus-faced. At the very same time, it grants extraordinary legal prerogatives to soldiers and places important restrictions on the exercise of those very rights. The law of armed conflict is, therefore, a subtle interplay of permissiveness and restriction, a continuous, and sometimes confusing, dance between barbarism and humanity.

Speaking broadly, the limitations on the exercise of belligerents' rights, as set out by Grotius, were of two quite distinct types. One type of limitation comprised rules specifically concerning war as such – for example, prohibiting the use of a particular type of weapon or tactic. Rules of this kind came from the law of nations. The other type of limitation comprised rules from the law of nature, applicable in time of both war and peace.

Of these two categories of limitation, the war-specific rules derived from the law of nations were, by a very large margin, the less important. With the sole notable exception of a prohibition against the use of poison as a weapon of war, Grotius did not recognise prohibitions by the law of nations against particular weapons or tactics *per se*. By far the greater constraints on belligerents' freedom of action came from the law of nature – and specifically from the principle of necessity, which is discussed below.

Just a brief observation may be offered by way of comparison between Grotius' views and those of the present day. We no longer make the Grotian distinction between natural law and the law of nations; but the law of armed conflict – or international humanitarian law as it is now commonly labelled – still retains the two-fold character of combining specific provisions about weapons and tactics with general considerations. The chief difference between then and now lies in the balance between the two. Modern international law, in contrast to that of Grotius, contains a very large body of specific prohibitions – though not large enough in the opinion of many. For example, there are explicit prohibitions relating to chemical and biological weapons, anti-personnel mines and the starvation of civilian populations.[6]

For Grotius, the law of nature, rather than the law of nations, was the more fertile source of restrictions on the freedom of action of belligerents. Most important in this regard was the principle of necessity.

21.5 The Principle of Necessity

The role of necessity in law is a subject of vast richness and complexity, so that only the most salient points will be possible in the present discussion. In its most general form, it was pithily stated by Grotius to be 'a right to those things which are necessary for the purpose of securing a right' (DJBP 3.1.2). This was regarded as a general principle of natural law, not limited to warfare *per se*. When applied in the context of warfare, however, it meant that the just party was entitled to use whatever degree of force was necessary under the prevailing circumstances to impose its will onto its enemy – and no more. As noted above, the law of nations made the important modification of granting this right to both sides equally in an armed conflict, rather than to the just side only.

It should be appreciated that this general natural-law principle of necessity – like the law of armed conflict in general – was, simultaneously, both permissive and restrictive in character. It was permissive in that it placed no defined ceiling on the amount of violence that could be employed in warfare, nor any express general restriction as to who the victims of that violence might be. Necessity, in other words, could – and did – justify the infliction of violence against entirely innocent persons, such as civilians. The reason for this drastic conclusion, Grotius explained, is that necessity arises purely from a party's condition of need or distress and therefore does not depend on or require an act of wrongdoing on the part of the party that is affected (DJBP 3.1.2). Consequently, if it is necessary for victory, in a given struggle, to bombard a city with its civilian population penned inside, then so be it. Similarly, if it is necessary, in a given struggle, to mount a scorched-earth campaign against a large agricultural area, then the law placed no barrier in the way. In this respect, the law of armed conflict, as expounded by Grotius, accorded a worryingly large scope for licensed brutality.

There are, however, some very important caveats to be borne in mind. For one thing, there was a duty on the part of a party invoking the principle of necessity to pay compensation to any innocent party whose rights or interests were prejudiced. More important is the other side of the concept of necessity itself – its restrictive aspect. Just as necessity allowed anything that furthered a belligerent's war effort, so – by the very same token – it prohibited any action that did not further that end. The effect, then, is that purely gratuitous damage in warfare is prohibited. This principle continues to play a fundamental role in the modern law of war, though now stated as a prohibition against unnecessary suffering. It is also known, though somewhat confusingly, as the principle of military necessity.[7]

By logical extension, it is easily seen that any act that, by its intrinsic nature, cannot contribute to success in war becomes, in effect, flatly prohibited – not, strictly speaking, on the basis of a specific rule against the act *per se*, but rather on the basis that the act is incapable of meeting the test of necessity (i.e., materially contributing to the war effort). It was on this basis that Grotius favoured exempting sacred sites from attack – on the assumption that they pose no actual military danger (DJBP 3.12.6). Similarly, rape was held by Grotius to be impermissible on the ground that, by its nature, it does not further the belligerent side's war effort (DJBP 3.4.19).

Admittedly, Grotius was not as explicit on this question of gratuitous damage – or unnecessary suffering – as he should have been. For example, in his discussion of the devastation of enemy territory, he only said that it would be 'foolish to injure another without securing any good for oneself' (DJBP 3.12.1). In another place, he denounced 'all engagements, which are of no use for obtaining a right or putting an end to a war, but have as their purpose a mere display of strength'. But, here too, he confined himself to stating that such actions 'are incompatible both with the duty of a Christian and with humanity itself' (DJBP 3.11.19). The logic of the concept of necessity, however, surely dictates a stronger statement: that such actions are outright violations of natural law.

Finally, it should be noted that necessity, in both its permissive and its restrictive guises, was highly context-bound. That is to say, it was never possible to determine *a priori* whether a given tactic, such as the bombardment of a town, was lawful or not. Tactics were, basically, never lawful or unlawful *per se*. Rather, they were lawful or unlawful, as the case may be, depending on the specific circumstances at hand in the particular conflict. If the contemplated action actually contributed to the successful outcome of the particular struggle, then it was lawful. Conversely, if it made no actual contribution to victory, then it was unlawful.

21.6 Proportionality and Moderation

In the modern law of war, proportionality plays an important, though also much contested, part.[8] In Grotius' time, proportionality played an explicit part only in one aspect of armed conflict. This is with regard to one of the three categories of just war that Grotius recognised: punitive war. The other two kinds, it will be recalled, were defensive war and war to obtain something that is owed (DJBP 2.1.2). It was a general principle of natural law, much discussed by Grotius, that any punishment inflicted for wrongdoing should be proportionate to the wrong done (DJBP 2.20.28–37). This principle was applicable – like all of natural law – in time of war and peace alike.

Otherwise, proportionality played no overt role in Grotius' exposition of the law of war. In particular, proportionality did not act as a constraint on the exercise of the principle of necessity. One important reason for this has already been touched upon: the existence of an obligation upon a party acting on the basis of necessity to compensate any non-wrongdoing parties – i.e., non-enemies – who might thereby suffer injury. As a result, those parties, at least in principle, would not be made worse off and therefore could have no just ground for complaint. For this reason, there was not seen to be a need for any kind of balancing of interests between belligerents and innocent parties as there is in modern law.

At the same time, though, proportionality had an important implicit role in Grotius' thought, by virtue of his staunch support for moderation in the waging of war – i.e., for refraining, whenever feasible, from exercising the rights of belligerents to their fullest possible extent. '[L]ove for our neighbour' was one factor mentioned by Grotius as militating against a full exercise of legal rights. This principle of neighbourly love introduces a kind of implicit consideration of proportionality into the calculus of warfare. Belligerents, Grotius cautioned, should carefully consider the material consequences of the actions that they took. The good that was envisaged to flow from a belligerent action should be greater than the evil that was anticipated to accompany it. In cases where the anticipated material good and evil were equal, the governing consideration should be the probability: if the good effects appeared more likely to occur than the evil ones, then the contemplated operation could proceed; otherwise not. More generally, advised Grotius, 'prudent judgement' as well as strict legal right should guide belligerents. And in cases of doubt, 'we should favour that course, as the more safe, which has regard for the interest of another rather than our own' (DJBP 3.1.4).

A good example of this consideration in action is found in the discussion by Grotius of the violent sacking of cities. He noted, with stern disapproval, that '[s]uch actions cannot take place without very serious harm to many innocent persons, and often are of little consequence for the result of the war' (DJBP 3.12.8). In a similar vein, while Grotius conceded that a policy of general devastation of enemy territory 'must be tolerated [when it] compels the enemy to sue for peace in a short time', he also pointed out that, in sorry reality, devastation more commonly occurs 'from motives of hatred rather than from considerations of prudence' (DJBP 3.12.1).

Grotius also touted the practical advantages of moderation. For example, in considering the devastation of enemy territory, Grotius maintained that a policy of forbearance would often be wise from a utilitarian standpoint. For one thing, a campaign of devastation risked making victory in the struggle less likely by instilling in the enemy a sense of despair, which could become 'a great weapon' in his hands. In this same vein, Grotius speculated that a policy of clemency could serve to demonstrate confidence in victory and thereby weaken the morale of the enemy (DJBP 3.12.8).

21.7 Ruses, Perfidy and Faith between Enemies

Questions of deception and honesty in war are somewhat delicate. In general, as noted at the outset, the contending belligerents were regarded by Grotius as forming part of a single moral and legal community – with the consequence that the general natural law duties of good faith continued to be binding. More specifically, the general natural law duty faithfully to observe promises made continued to apply between enemies during war. This was what made truces, cease-fires, safe-conducts and the like possible. Grotius even went so far as to maintain that this obligation to carry out promises applies to non-sovereign enemies such as robbers and brigands (DJBP 3.18.2).

At the same time, Grotius held ruses of war to be lawful. These were basically signs given to an enemy, by way of action rather than words, that the enemy was left to interpret as he would. The classic example, given by Grotius, is a feigned retreat. The opposing side may interpret this, on his own assessment, as a genuine retreat and respond accordingly. But, if the enemy thereby comes to grief, he has only himself to blame for what is, in essence, a misreading of a state of affairs (DJBP 3.1.8). In other words, it was seen as permissible to induce or manoeuvre the opposing side into committing errors on its own initiative, or errors of its own judgment.

A different question was whether false explicit statements could be conveyed to the enemy to gain a military advantage. Grotius himself was not in favour of allowing this. He did, however, concede that writers generally permitted the making of statements that were misleading while being technically true – i.e., statements that are ambiguous and that the enemy might therefore interpret in the wrong manner to his later chagrin. Here, too, the basic principle was that, so long as the error could credibly be said to be the enemy's own, no legal wrong was done (DJBP 3.1.17).

21.8 The Taking of Enemy Property

Perhaps no area of the laws of war illustrates so vividly the key Grotian distinction between the law of nature and the law of nations, or voluntary law, as that concerned with the capture of enemy property. The law of nature imposed, as will be seen, some rather strict constraints on such capture. The law of nations, in contrast, allowed rather greater latitude.

The position under natural law differed somewhat as between state-owned and privately owned property. Regarding state-owned property, an injured party engaging in forcible self-help – i.e., a just belligerent – was permitted to capture and confiscate property belonging to the wrongdoer – but only up to an amount equal to the value of the injury that they suffered. The victim or just belligerent, in other words, was entitled to be made whole, but not to make any 'excess profit' at the expense of the wrongdoer. In the context of armed conflict, however, the principle of necessity could confer slight latitude onto the just party. It might be the case that, in the context of a particular conflict, a greater amount of enemy property would need to be taken in order to attain victory. That excess property, however, could only be sequestered and not confiscated, with a view to returning it to the other side at the conclusion of the hostilities (DJBP 3.13.1).

Regarding privately owned property, the basic rule was that, as a basic natural law principle, private property could not be taken from persons who had not been party to the original wrongdoing. Here, too, however, necessity could act to expand the rights of just belligerents. If, in the particular circumstances of the conflict, the taking of private property was required to bring about victory, then that property could be taken – but subject to an obligation to compensate the owner (DJBP 3.12.1).

All of this was a matter of basic natural law principles, applied in the context of armed conflict. These natural law limitations, however, were regarded as being too exacting to apply in practice in the heat of armed conflict. As a result, nations generally agreed on a simpler set of rules – which gave rather greater rights to belligerents than natural law did (DJBP 3.4.4).

One important change introduced by the law of nations was to abandon the natural law ceiling on the quantity of state-owned property that could be taken. Regarding privately owned property, the change made by the law of nations was more drastic. Private property of enemy nationals, according to this law, was subject to capture and confiscation on the same basis as state-owned property, i.e., without any quantitative limit (DJBP 3.6.2). There was also no requirement of compensation, as there was under natural law. In expounding this rule, Grotius explicitly referred to private citizens as functioning, in this respect, as sureties for their sovereigns (DJBP 3.13.1).

It may be noted that the modern laws of war are kinder to civilians – a development that would have met with the wholehearted approval of Grotius. In land warfare, private property is not any longer subject to capture – though, in maritime warfare, the capture of enemy-owned private property continues to be allowed. The Hague Rules on Land Warfare contain a specific prohibition against pillage.[9] Requisition of private property is allowed in cases of actual need, but only subject to compensation.

21.9 Protection of Civilians

Regarding the protection of civilians from the horrors of war, the distinction between the two concepts of belligerents' rights and necessity becomes very instructively apparent. Speaking from the standpoint of belligerents' rights as such, the position is that all nationals of the enemy state are themselves enemies and, as such, are fair targets for attack. This includes civilians of all descriptions, including the decrepit, the disabled and infants (DJBP 3.4.6 and 9). When belligerents' rights are considered, there is no sign of moderation.

The obvious harshness of this conclusion was, however, considerably mitigated by the application of the principle of necessity in its restrictive mode. Grotius was conscious that, in practice, the killing of innocent non-combatants would make no contribution to military victory and consequently could not be permitted. On this basis, women and children are to be exempt from attack, as are religious figures, farmers, merchants, prisoners of war and, thankfully, persons 'who direct their energies to literary pursuits, which are honourable and useful to the human race' (DJBP 3.11.8–13). The immunity of civilians, however, was subject to the key caveat, rooted in the principle of necessity, that 'reasons that are weighty and will affect the safety of many' can justify attacks on civilians (DJBP 3.11.8). Grotius did not give any examples of cases in which this consideration would come into play.

To one of the most emotive and contentious of issues regarding protection of civilians in modern warfare – the question of collateral damage to civilians arising from bona fide military operations – Grotius had nothing in detail to say, at least explicitly. His general exhortations in favour of moderation, as noted above, were his only contribution to this (now) very prominent issue of the laws of war.

In modern international law, the protection of civilians in armed conflict is treated somewhat differently. For one thing, there is an absolute prohibition against the targeting of civilian populations as such – with no exception granted for cases of necessity. Regarding the important question of collateral damage to civilians from bona fide military operations, an explicit rule of proportionality is the governing consideration: whenever the anticipated damage to civilians, from a planned military operation, is 'excessive in relation to the concrete and direct military advantage anticipated', the contemplated action must not take place.[10]

21.10 Prisoners of War

In no area was Grotius' treatment of the laws of war so much indebted to medieval practice – and, correspondingly, so much at variance with modern practice – as in the area of the treatment of prisoners of war. He endorsed the longstanding position of Roman law that slavery was not part of the law of nature, but only of the law of nations. But, as noted above, it was the law of nations that made provision for the rights of belligerents. Among these was a right to put captive enemies to death. An alternative – held by Grotius to be justified because it was more merciful than killing – was enslavement. Regarding enslaved prisoners, there was no limit, in the law of nations, to the cruelties and indignities that the new owners were allowed to inflict upon their charges. All of the captive soldier's property was also held to belong to their new owner, with all of their descendants becoming slaves (DJBP 3.7.3).

Grotius then proceeded, however, to emphasise that, even though the enslavement of prisoners of war was a feature of the general law of nations, the European countries have, *inter se*, agreed to adopt more merciful practices. The European custom, he explained, was to hold prisoners under guard and to ransom them. This is a reflection of a long-standing practice from the European middle ages, upon which a very elaborate body of law had grown up.[11] The modern law, in which prisoners of war are sequestered in a non-punitive fashion for the duration of the conflict and then released, had no foreshadowing in the writing of Grotius.

21.11 Some Specific Issues: Targeted Killing, Poisoning, Spying

The question of assassinating enemy belligerents away from a battlefield was considered by Grotius. He expressly held it to be lawful. '[I]t is … permissible', he pronounced, 'to kill an enemy in any place whatsoever' (DJBP 3.4.18). The one limit that he placed on the use of assassination as a technique of war was that assassination must not involve a resort to a violation of good faith. This meant that it was not permissible, in Grotius' view, to suborn a subject to murder his own sovereign because the subject owes to his sovereign a duty of good-faith loyalty and obedience. By the same token, it was not permissible to induce a soldier in the enemy's ranks to kill his commander. If, on the other hand, the killers relied, in their deadly mission, entirely on their own boldness and cunning – say, by slipping surreptitiously into an enemy's army camp – then no law was violated (DJBP 3.4.18).

On the question of hiring assassins to kill members of a non-state enemy force, such as pirate or terrorist bands, Grotius allowed greater latitude. Hiring someone to carry out such a killing who was under an obligation not to do such an act was blameworthy under natural law, as in the case of hiring a soldier to kill his commander. In the case of the pirate or terrorist, however, the law of nations altered the position by refraining from imposing any punishment on the hirer of the assassin. This impunity was justified by Grotius on the basis of the general 'hatred' of such scoundrels by people at large (DJBP 3.4.18).

Grotius' view of the use of poison in warfare is particularly instructive, as it provides an excellent illustration of the parting of ways between the laws of nature and of nations. According to natural law, Grotius explained, the use of poison to kill an enemy belligerent was permissible. '[I]t makes no difference', he asserted, 'whether you kill him by the sword or by poison' (DJBP 3.4.15). He conceded that killing by the sword was more noble than killing by poison, in that the victims thereby had a chance to defend themselves – as they were assumed not to have in the case of poison – but there was no natural law obligation to afford an enemy a means of defence.

The law of nations, however, held otherwise and forbade the use of poison as a weapon. This was according to the general agreement of nations – 'if not of all nations, certainly of those of the better sort' (DJBP 3.4.15). It is interesting to note that, in this instance, the law of nations allowed less leeway to belligerents than natural law, whereas in the case of property capture the position was the opposite, with the law of nations granting larger rights to belligerents than natural law. Grotius speculated that this agreement to prohibit the use of poison arose from the self-interest of rulers, who saw themselves at greater personal risk from poison than from conventional weaponry (DJBP 3.4.15).

On the subject of spying, Grotius' views are, for all intents and purposes, the same as our modern law. He was explicit and emphatic that spying – meaning the clandestine gathering of information behind enemy lines – was not forbidden by the law of nations. Any forbearance from resorting to this practice is to be put down to 'loftiness of mind' rather than to any legal prohibition. At the same time, though, Grotius recognised that spies, when caught, were typically treated with great severity. Our modern explanation for this is the existence of a specific rule that spies, if caught in the act, are not entitled to combatant status and, consequently, are liable to be prosecuted as common criminals.[12]

21.12 Neutrality

The subject of neutrality was the only one in which Grotius looked to (relatively) recent state practice for illustrations of his points, as well as to biblical and classical examples. In fact, so new was the topic that even the word 'neutral' was not in general circulation. Grotius instead spoke – more clumsily – of 'those who are of neither side in war'.

Interestingly, Grotius singled out this topic as one in which the law of nations had developed no body of rules – with the result that this part of the law of armed conflict, uniquely, was determined solely by natural law on its own (DJBP 3.1.5). A notable consequence of this was that, in this area, the general principle of equality of rights between the belligerents, without regard to the justice of their causes, did not apply, since that was a principle of the law of nations rather than of natural law. As a result, non-belligerent states, according to Grotius, were not expected to be strictly impartial – as the later, developed law of neutrality would require. Instead, neutral states were under a duty to refrain from doing anything that would interfere with or impede the war effort of a just belligerent – with no parallel duty owed to the unjust side (DJBP 3.17.3).

The law of neutrality has, broadly speaking, two chief areas of concern: the extent to which belligerents may lawfully restrict or reduce the normal peacetime rights of neutral states; and the question of what additional legal obligations the law imposed onto neutral states by virtue of the war. The views of Grotius on each of these will be considered in turn.

First, regarding the prerogatives of belligerents vis-à-vis neutrals. The basic principle of natural law prohibited any targeting of neutrals, on the ground that they were, by definition, innocent of any wrongdoing to the just side in the war and did not qualify as enemies. Neutrals were, therefore, exempt from attack and neutral-owned property was not subject to capture, even if it was located in enemy territory (DJBP 3.6.5). In addition, belligerents were not allowed to conduct military operations in neutral territory (DJBP 3.4.8).

Here too, however, the ever-present principle of necessity operated in the belligerent's favour. In the face of true necessity, a just belligerent could acquire legal rights to dispose of the property of neutral persons, in the interest of successful prosecution of its war effort (DJBP 3.17.1). This was justifiable because, as noted above, the principle of necessity did not require wrongdoing on the part of persons who were adversely affected – i.e., neutrals in the present context. It only required the existence of a genuine state of need or distress on the part of the belligerent – i.e., an actual furthering of the belligerent's war effort. The payment of compensation to the affected party was, however, required.

As for the legal duties of neutrals, Grotius identified one single outstanding one, noted above: that a neutral must not do anything that would prejudice the war effort of the just belligerent. It is only necessary to add here that Grotius considered the situation – that would, in fact, have been very common – in which it was unclear which belligerent was the just one. In such an unhappy event, the neutral should adopt a policy of impartiality (DJBP 3.17.3). But, this should be seen as a matter of prudence rather than of true legal obligation.

The particular question of contraband of war was discussed by Grotius (DJBP 3.1.5). He made a three-fold classification of goods that a neutral might supply to an enemy: goods that are useful solely for war, such as arms and ammunition; goods whose uses are wholly peaceful, such as religious items; and goods that have a dual use, such as money, foodstuffs, ships and naval stores. The first two of these categories were easily dealt with. Trade in non-war-related goods between a neutral and an enemy must be left entirely unmolested. The supplying of war-related materials – i.e., contraband of war – however, had a drastic consequence: that the supposedly neutral supplier thereby took the side of the enemy (DJBP 3.1.5). The implication seems to be – although Grotius did not explicitly state it – that the supplier forfeited its status as a neutral and became an actual enemy in its own right. More specifically, a purportedly neutral party whose contraband goods were captured and confiscated by a belligerent was not entitled to compensation. The reason was that the carriage of the goods was regarded as a wrongful act on the part of the supposed neutral.

The middle category, of dual-use goods – what came later to be labelled as 'conditional contraband' – posed somewhat greater problems. Here, Grotius explained, the presence or absence of necessity on the belligerent's part was the determining factor. If the stopping of the trade would actually further the belligerent's war effort, then the stoppage could be justified. In this case, however, the neutral was entitled to compensation for any damage suffered, if the neutral party had no actual knowledge that his actions were adversely affecting the belligerent's war effort (DJBP 3.1.5). If, however, the neutral did have such knowledge, then he was not entitled to compensation. As an example of this point in practice, Grotius posited a neutral who sought to bring food supplies into a town while it was being besieged. The supplier would know that he was hindering a military operation and so would be committing a wrongful act against the besieging army, thereby forfeiting any right to compensation for his losses.

21.13 Conclusion

The reader of Grotius' great treatise *De jure belli ac pacis* gains little (or even no) impression of the fact that, as it was being written, central

Europe was engulfed in the most terrible war of its history – a collective horror not to be surpassed until the Great War of 1914–18. Grotius was a calm and isolated voice of scholarly reason in this world of turmoil and brutality. His stature in the scholarly world was large, but it would be difficult to detect any discernible impact on the statesmen or military leaders of his period – although the Swedish king, Gustavus Adolphus (1594–1632), was a devotee of Grotius' writings, which he reportedly carried with him on his travels.

Despite a lack of perceptible influence over the daily affairs of his time, our cerebral hero's travails have stood the test of time remarkably well. There is much of the present-day law of armed conflict that Grotius would have no trouble recognising – from the broad structural division into specific rules and general principles, to the welter of specific rules set forth in the ever-thickening web of international conventions. He certainly would applaud the efforts of humanitarian-law activists to wage long-term campaigns to mitigate the horrors of war. Indeed, it was in the years following the founding of the International Committee of the Red Cross in 1863 that Grotius was re-discovered and adopted as a founding father of international law – in contrast to his then better-known roles as a political thinker and natural law philosopher.

It only remains to take note of one important change that has occurred since Grotius wrote: the thesis that, as a matter of principle, the general natural law principle of necessity should be reduced to its smallest possible compass, in favour of as-comprehensive-as-possible a code of specific rules that are not context-bound in their application. The ambition of the modern law of war, in other words, is to be more like a criminal code and less like a philosophical treatise. This change was articulated, though not actually brought about, over a century after Grotius wrote, by Swiss writer Emmerich de Vattel (1714–67), who therefore – more than Grotius – merits the title of the intellectual father of the modern law of war.[13]

Nevertheless, if Grotius' innovations were modest, his range was vast. If his legal labours were carried out largely in solitude, he had all of humanity for a client – not only in his own time, but for centuries to come. He resolutely strode a middle way, between the warmonger and the pacifist; and for that he has earned scant thanks from either. His goal was the relatively unheroic one of bringing incremental change for the better to a brutally imperfect world. For this earnest service, he merits, if not our love, at least our thanks.

Translation of Grotius' Works Used

On the Law of War and Peace. Student Edition, ed. S.C. Neff (Cambridge, 2012)

Further Reading

Ambühl, R., *Prisoners of War in the Hundred Years War; Ransom Culture in the Late Middle Ages* (Cambridge, 2013).

Clapham, A., and P. Gaeta (eds.), *The Oxford Handbook of International Law in Armed Conflict* (Oxford, 2014).

Dinstein, Y., *The Conduct of Hostilities under the International Law of Armed Conflict* (3rd edn., Cambridge, 2016).

Keen, M.H., *The Laws of War in the Late Middle Ages* (London, 1965).

Neff, S.C., 'Vattel and the Laws of War. A Tale of Three Circles', in V. Chetail and P. Haggenmacher (eds.), *Vattel's International Law in a XXIst Century Perspective/Le droit international de Vattel vu du XXIe siècle* (Leiden and Boston 2011), 317–33.

Notes

1 For a thorough treatment of medieval just war doctrine, see F.H. Russell, *The Just War in the Middle Ages* (Cambridge, 1975).

2 See John of Legnano, *Tractatus de bello, de represaliis et de duello* (c. 1360, Classics of International Law; Washington DC, 1917); Honoré Bonet, *The Tree of Battles*, ed. and transl. G.W. Coopland (c. 1386, Liverpool, 1949); Christine de Pisan, *The Book of Deeds of Arms and of Chivalry*, ed. and transl. Sumner Willard and Charity Cannon Willard (c. 1410, University Park, PA., 1999).

3 Balthasar de Ayala, *De jure et officiis bellicis et disciplina militari* (1582, Classics of International Law; Washington, DC, 1912); Alberico Gentili, *De jure belli* (1598, text of 1612, Classics of International Law; Oxford/London, 1933).

4 Francisco de Vitoria, 'On the law of war', in *Political Writings*, eds. A. Pagden and J. Lawrance (1539, Cambridge, 1991), 313.

5 For a more detailed treatment of this point, see Chapter 20 by Randall Lesaffer.

6 There are many fine treatments of the modern law of armed conflict. See, for example, A. Clapham and P. Gaeta (eds.), *The Oxford Handbook of International Law in Armed Conflict* (Oxford, 2014); Y. Dinstein, *The Conduct of Hostilities under the International Law of Armed Conflict* (3rd edn., Cambridge, 2016).

7 For the ban on unnecessary suffering, see Convention Concerning the Laws and Customs of War on Land, 18 October 1907, 205 CTS 277, Art. 23; Protocol I to

the Geneva Conventions, 12 December 1977, 1125 UNTS 3, Art. 35(2); and *Legality of Nuclear Weapons*, International Court of Justice (ICJ) advisory opinion, 1996 ICJ Rep. 226, Para 78. On military necessity, see Dinstein, *The Conduct of Hostilities*, 63–7.

8 E.g., Enzo Cannizzaro, 'Proportionality', in Clapham and Gaeta, *The Oxford Handbook of International Law in Armed Conflict,* 332–52.

9 Convention on the Laws and Customs of War on Land, Art. 28.

10 Protocol I to the Geneva Conventions, Art. 57(2).

11 See generally M.H. Keen, *The Laws of War in the Late Middle Ages* (London, 1965), 156–85; and Remy Ambühl, *Prisoners of War in the Hundred Years War: Ransom Culture in the Late Middle Ages* (Cambridge, 2013).

12 Convention on the Laws and Customs of War on Land, Art. 29; and Protocol I to the Geneva Conventions, Art. 46(1).

13 See S.C. Neff, 'Vattel and the laws of war: A tale of three circles', in V. Chetail and P. Haggenmacher (eds.), *Vattel's International Law in a XXIst Century Perspective/Le droit international de Vattel vu du XXIe siècle* (Leiden and Boston, 2011), 317–33.

William E. Butler[1]

22.1 Introduction

Of all the doctrines of the law of nations that have come down to the present day, few, if any, have been as closely identified with a single individual as the freedom of the seas has with Hugo Grotius. The legal status of the seas and oceans engaged the attention of writers and statesmen long before Grotius appeared on the scene. It is presumed that the limitations of marine technologies required trading, fishing and warships to remain, as a rule, within sight of land in the pre-Roman and Roman eras, with the possible exception of the Mediterranean, Black, Baltic and East Asian regional seas.[2] Fishing was largely a coastal operation, with minor coastal areas making forays into coal, salt, mineral and oyster or related offshore beds. From the standpoint of ocean boundaries and maritime jurisdiction, these eras have been called 'primitive'.[3]

As state formation proceeded in the medieval era, so, too, was extravagant maritime dominion asserted. Venice had, since the Crusades, pretended to vast dominion in the Adriatic Sea, until the seventeenth century Denmark wished to control the Baltic Sea, China asserted special interests in its coastal waters and Portugal and Spain were prepared to divide the oceans in the late fifteenth century to the exclusion of all other powers. Although, in this last-mentioned instance, these claims were intended to lend stability to colonial expansion, for the most part expansive claims to sea space frustrated maritime commerce, interfered with the age of discovery and provoked hostile legal commentary.[4]

22.2 Development of the Principle of the Freedom of the Seas

Grotius entered the scene as a young lawyer engaged by the Dutch East India Company to elaborate a case on behalf of the principle of the freedom of the seas in a brief on the law of prize to justify the capture of a Portuguese galleon, the *Santa Catarina*, by a company vessel in the Straits of Singapore in 1603. The full text of Grotius' work, *De jure praedae commentarius*, remained unknown even in manuscript until discovered in 1864 and published four years later.[5] One chapter (12) was published as a separate work under the title *Mare liberum* in 1609, anonymously.[6] *Mare liberum* was issued during, and prompted by, the negotiations between Spain and the Dutch Republic culminating in the Truce of Antwerp (1609). Spain sought during these negotiations to persuade the Dutch to renounce their right to trade in the West and East Indies. Spain was unsuccessful in this, and the Dutch East India Company is believed to have requested Grotius publish his revised and excerpted essay in order to strengthen the argumentation on behalf of the Dutch position.

In style and substance, *Mare liberum* was intended for an international readership. Tactically, it was considered to be shrewd, as Grotius, a Calvinist of sorts, based his argument on the works of the Spanish School of Salamanca and other Catholic writers, among them Francisco de Vitoria (c. 1483–1546) and Fernando Vázquez de Menchaca (1512–69).[7] A request came on 4 November 1608 from the Zeeland Chamber of the Dutch East India Company to prepare a treatise on the freedom of navigation;[8] as Grotius already had written a brief on the subject, he was able to produce a chapter from the brief, insert a new introduction, omit some pages at the end and pass the manuscript through a friend to his publisher, Louis Elzevier (1540–1617). In fact, publication proceeded more slowly than anticipated and, ultimately, it appeared in April 1609 so as not to interfere with the truce negotiations.[9]

Grotius entered a debate that fostered a substantial literature during the early decades of the seventeenth century, a period replete with conflicting claims to dominion over seas and oceans, not merely by the Spanish and Portuguese, but also by the English and by some of the Mediterranean powers.[10] Shortly after the appearance of Grotius' work, in May 1609, King James I/VI (1566–1625) proclaimed that foreigners would be allowed to fish in the seas of England, Scotland and Ireland only when authorised by the British crown; four years later, he granted to the Muscovy Company an exclusive monopoly over whaling in the Arctic seas around Spitzbergen. With regard to claims of this nature and magnitude, the arguments of *Mare liberum* were apt and quickly pursued by Dutch negotiators in their discussions with the English. A Scottish jurist and professor of civil law at the

University of Aberdeen, William Welwood (*fl.* 1578–1622), published a partial response to Grotius,[11] wherein he challenged Grotius' thesis that the sea could not be the subject of ownership by a single sovereign. Grotius' reply, *Defensis capitis quinti maris liberi*, remained uncompleted, unpublished and undiscovered until 1864. Welwood returned to the issue two years later,[12] but the most celebrated response to *Mare liberum* came around 1617–18 from the pen of John Selden (1584–1654).[13]

Although not published until 1635, Selden's *Mare clausum* defended British claims: the sea, Selden said, under the law of nations is as capable of private dominion as is the land, and the king of Great Britain is lord of all the sea inseparably and perpetually appendant to the British Empire.[14] Others entered the lists on both sides, including Serafim de Freitas (1570–1633), whose *De justo imperio Lusitanorum Asiatico* appeared in 1625, the same year as Grotius' *De jure belli ac pacis*, containing his matured views on the freedom of the seas as part of his longer, more systematic exposition of the law of nations.

The heart of Grotius' position, set out in both *Mare liberum* and again in *De jure belli ac pacis*, came to be the foundation of the modern regime of the high seas: namely, that states may not individually or collectively acquire the high seas areas by occupation because they are *res communis omnium* – a thing belonging to the world community at large – or *res extra commercium* – a thing outside commerce and property that may be appropriated by no one. It took some considerable time for this principle to be accepted in state practice as customary international law: for much of the seventeenth century, claims to closed seas were advanced by Denmark, Spain, the Ottoman Empire, Portugal, Genoa, Tuscany, the papacy and Venice. Russia affirmed the principle of freedom of the sea in 1587 in diplomatic correspondence with England: 'The sea is God's road … '.[15] Queen Elizabeth I (1533–1603) in 1602 affirmed the same principle in reply to a Spanish protest against Sir Francis Drake's (*c.* 1540–96) expedition. But, Stuart policies, as we have seen, reversed the trend. Only after William III of Orange (1650–1702) succeeded to the English throne in 1689 did Britain join the Dutch in championing the freedom of the seas. By the late eighteenth century, most claims to vast sea areas abated or became special jurisdictional claims – although Russia, under Emperor Alexander I (1777–1825), asserted claims to enormous expanses of the Pacific in 1821.[16] Naval power and commercial shipping interests in the nineteenth century ensured European and American support for, indeed insistence upon, the principle of freedom of the seas. In the twentieth and twenty-first centuries, the freedom of the seas has come to be accepted as a 'general', 'basic' or 'fundamental' principle of international law; some are prepared to treat this principle as *jus cogens*.

22.3 The Grotian Concept of Freedom of the Seas

The basis of the principle of freedom of the sea, its spatial parameters and its functional limitations today demonstrate the Grotian tradition in the law of the sea to be obsolete or inappropriate in some respects. There are, however, important elements of continuity. An examination of all aspects is essential if we are to understand the legacy of Grotius and his times.

Grotius' approach to the law of nations reflected the larger literary tradition followed by international legal publicists long before and after him, aptly characterised as an 'underlying structure of thought and argument ... more literary than scientific and more businesslike than concerned'.[17] In *De jure belli ac pacis,* he made evident at the outset his intention to avoid intellectual confusion: 'to make the reasons for my conclusions as evident as possible, to set forth in definite order the matters which needed to be treated; and to distinguish clearly between things which seemed to be the same and were not' (DJBP Prol. 56).[18]

Grotius commenced this work, just as he did *Mare liberum,* by explaining the process through which he found rules of the law of nations; among all the writers on the subject before or since, he remains exemplary for his care in precisely indicating the nature of the authority or source – be it a principle of natural law or philosophy, Roman *jus gentium,* morality, holy scripture or self-evident truth – on which his argument rested. From diverse places and various epochs, he amassed 'testimonies' of authorities whose coincident statements can be attributed to some universal cause or element – which, in Grotius' view, was nothing other than a 'correct conclusion drawn from the principles of nature, or common consent'.

The law of nations, he said, rests on the last-mentioned, 'for whatever cannot be deduced from certain principles by a sure process of reasoning, and yet is clearly observed everywhere, must have its origin in the free will of man' (DJBP Prol. 40). Grotius' method of finding rules of international law, widely followed in doctrinal writings on the subject, requires – and disposes – the reader to perform two mental processes. The first is to make the inductive jump from an accumulation of data of various kinds to a conclusion about the truth or falsity of the proposition being discussed. The second is the leap from a series of 'is' propositions to an 'ought' proposition derived, in the instance of Grotius, from the historical record of state practice, the attitudes of poets, orators, jurists, statesmen, diplomats, princes and other worthies, and sometimes his own personal judgments as to where appropriate basic patterns of relationships lie.[19]

How does this style of presentation relate to the principle of the freedom of the seas? In *Mare Liberum*, Grotius based his argument that, by the law of nations, navigation is free to all persons whatsoever on what he characterised as a:

most specific and unimpeachable axion of the Law of Nations, called a primary rule or first principle, the spirit of which is self-evident and immutable, to wit: every nation is free to travel to every other nation, and to trade with it. (ML 1, 7)[20]

The axiom was laid down by God himself through nature, for, because not every place is supplied with the necessaries of life, some excel in some things and others in something else. By 'divine justice', it was brought about that one people should supply the needs of others. Those who deny this law and remove the opportunities for mutual service do violence to nature herself.

Grotius then turned to the physical properties of water. Navigable in every direction, constantly in motion, encompassing the entire planet, the seas of the world, just as the air, belonged to the *communia*. In his draft reply to Welwood, Grotius elaborated on the reasons why, according to the law of nature and nations, the seas cannot be divided and owned as other property can. Use of the sea by one country for navigation does not make the sea unnavigable for others, whereas, in the case of most moveables, the contrary is true. Moreover, Grotius added, actual occupation of the seas accompanied by a situation of custody or possession of the seas is physically impossible: it is the seas that limit land expanses rather than the contrary. Likewise, parts of the oceans or seas cannot be owned: for they are part of a corporeal whole, and lines demarcating them express merely a desire or intention to occupy rather than the capability to do so. Those who build structures at sea occupy merely the sea-bed, and their right of possession exists only so long as the structure itself. Minor coastal appropriations of seas were conceded for purposes of use, but these could not be appropriated by prescription, for, unlike the civil law, the law of nations gave special protection to the *communia*. Once the use had lapsed, the minor appropriations revert to *communia* again.[21]

The substance and qualities of water being what they are, Grotius continued, no part of the seas, irrespective of how large or small, can be in exclusive ownership.[22] If a line is conceded at three, twelve or one hundred nautical miles, why not beyond? The ruler of a maritime state has the duty to protect the right of all nations to free navigation in adjacent waters, from which it follows that navigation is free, not by command of the ruler, but by command of the law of nations. In denying the right of any state to assert rights of ownership to the sea, however, which Grotius characterised as *dominium*, he recognised the coastal state's right of *imperium*, or sovereignty, defined by Grotius as rights of protection and jurisdiction. The distinction was not drawn as sharply as might have been done in this early work – many writers do not attach the same consequences to the terms in any event – and it is probable that, by maritime jurisdiction, Grotius had in view piracy and the law of prize. If so, those were forms of maritime jurisdiction that any power might exercise at sea, although presumably the coastal state would be most likely to do so. Insofar as the coastal state legislated in furtherance of these jurisdictional rights, it must act so as to protect the basic principles of the law of nations and not to diminish them. To Grotius, that position meant the coastal state had no jurisdiction over non-subjects except insofar as an explicit or tacit agreement with other rulers admitted such jurisdiction. The sea-bed, in Grotius' view, had the same status as the sea waters above and was open to common use provided that such use did not prejudice others.

That, in brief summary, was Grotius' view of the freedom of the seas and the basic underlying reasoning. One does not need to be an international lawyer to realise that the principle no longer has, if indeed it ever did have, the meaning attached to it in Grotius' writings. Natural law in its divine and secular senses, although enjoying a renaissance in the post-Second World War era largely because of advances in human rights, is no longer understood in its seventeenth-century meanings; to the extent that international law as a legal system can be said to derive from or conform to some underlying basic pattern or principle, modern theories of international law, at least in the West, tend to stress rules whose ultimate raison d'être inheres in the international system itself, such as the principle *pacta sunt servanda*. The freedom of the seas may have been axiomatic to

Grotius, but the international system, for all its deference to the principle in the abstract, has never elevated the freedom of the seas to quite that level.

Grotius' method of finding the law by mixing together a vast assemblage of historical events from remotest Antiquity to the seventeenth century, quotations from or references to poets, orators, politicians, statesmen, lawmakers and princes from all historical eras, leavened with his own views as appropriate – a dazzling display of learning and erudition from an acknowledged genius – had been overtaken even by the eighteenth century by a more rigorous level of scientific enquiry and exposition. What persuaded Grotius' contemporaries to make the logical leap from evidence to conclusion was seen by later generations as implausible, unscientific, unresponsive or irrelevant: a principal articulator of modern international legal doctrine, so forward-looking in his ideas, represented the end of an era in scholastic exposition. The ideas lived on through others,[23] even though much in his exposition declined in importance owing to his antiquated method of reasoning and argumentation.

22.4 The Grotian Concept Adapted and Developed

Grotius' arguments rejecting ownership of the seas by reason of the natural properties of water have a compelling logic of their own and considerable physical justification, but the international community has never allowed these to predetermine the exercise of jurisdiction at sea. As maritime powers seized upon the principle of freedom of the seas in the eighteenth century to secure freedom of commerce and links with overseas possessions, or to deploy naval power, coastal states responded by creating coastal zones measured by cannon-range or a specified distance within which certain jurisdictional rights might be exercised. Although the terminology for them varied, it quickly transpired that the areas within these belts of up to three nautical miles or so were regarded as being in the ownership of the coastal state, precisely the kind of claim that Grotius sought to deny in principle.

The international community experienced relatively little difficulty in accommodating such jurisdictional claims by coastal states during the nineteenth and early twentieth centuries, but claims beyond three nautical miles to a territorial sea or to territorial waters provoked sharp protests, as did claims to the ownership of resources, principally fish or other living resources, in waters beyond that limit. It was a measure of Grotius' durable legacy that even the terminological distinction between the 'territorial sea' and 'territorial waters' concealed a conceptual distinction between a 'high seas' and a 'coastal state' approach to jurisdiction at sea.[24] The term 'territorial sea' is believed by many to accentuate limited coastal state jurisdiction over what is otherwise the high seas; the term 'territorial waters' emphasises that the coastal state has either substantial sovereignty or sovereign rights over adjacent waters, which are not part of the high seas. The state practice and treaties of the post-1945 era have seriously eroded the original and uncompromising simplicity of Grotius' view of the high seas. Sovereign rights of coastal states over the continental shelf are recognised; economic zones up to 200 nautical miles have been established by most coastal states, effectively monopolising for the coastal state the greater portion of living and non-living marine resources in and beneath the water column.

22.5 The Grotian Heritage and the 1982 United Nations Convention on the Law of the Sea

The 1982 Convention on the Law of the Sea (1982 LOS Convention) constitutes a continuation of the balancing process between coastal and high seas interests to which Grotius had responded so unequivocally. The measure of how far the international community has departed from Grotius' spatial conception of high seas is expressed in Article 86 of the 1982 LOS Convention: the provisions regarding the high seas apply to all parts of the sea 'that are not included in the exclusive economic zone, in the territorial sea or in the internal waters of a State, or in the archipelagic waters of an archipelagic State'.[25] The high seas is, in effect, the residuum of that which is not claimed in some fashion by coastal states.

Functionally, however, much remains of Grotius' original concept of freedom of the seas.[26] In several key respects, that concept has been clarified and strengthened. Although the high seas are spatially more limited, under the 1982 LOS Convention they are 'open to all States, whether coastal or land-locked' (Article 87). The freedom of the high seas is not an absolute freedom under the convention, but one that is to be exercised under the conditions laid down by the convention and other rules of customary international law and/or contained in treaties.

In Grotius' day, the freedom of the seas meant – for all practical purposes – the freedom of navigation and, more contentiously, the freedom of fishing. It was the freedom of navigation Grotius defended so rigorously in *Mare liberum* and distinguished from a related freedom, the freedom of commerce. The 1982 LOS Convention enumerates six freedoms of the high seas without purporting to be exhaustive: freedom of navigation, freedom of overflight, freedom to lay submarine cables and pipelines, freedom to construct artificial islands and other installations permitted under international law, freedom of fishing and freedom of scientific research. The last four are subject to conditions or circumstances elaborated in other parts of the convention. All freedoms must be exercised with due regard for the interests of other states in their exercise of the freedom of the high seas and also with due regard for the rights under the convention with respect to deep sea-bed activities. The convention imposes another general restriction, namely that the high seas are reserved for peaceful purposes. Of the six enumerated freedoms, four were not practically possible in Grotius' day, and the other two were traditionally conducted mostly close to the coast.

The freedom of navigation encompasses rights and duties of navigation for states, whether coastal or land-locked. International law requires, for example, a genuine link between the flag state and the ship; the issuance of ship's documents certifying the right to fly that state's flag; and the duty to exercise effective jurisdiction and control in administrative, technical and social matters over ships flying its flag, to minimise pollution from sea-going vessels,[27] and to ensure safety at sea. The 'regime of the high seas' is the expression widely used for the conditions and rules governing the exercise of the freedom of the seas and to emphasise that the high seas are not a legal vacuum where states may do as they please, but an expanse open to all to engage in lawful activities with due regard to rules developed to protect the interests of other users and the safe exercise of the activities being carried on. The rules comprising this regime comply with the spirit of the Grotian tradition, irrespective of how far removed they may be from the technology of navigation in the early seventeenth century.

Expanded use of the high seas, in ways and on a scale unimaginable in Grotius' day, necessarily have led to greater regulation of high seas operations, but principally in the spirit of reinforcing the freedom by Grotius rather than diminishing it.[28] Directly linked to the Grotian tradition is the 1982 LOS Convention provision that 'No State may validly purport to subject any part of the high seas to its sovereignty' (Article 89). States, on the other hand, are obliged, as they were in Grotius' day, to assist in suppressing piracy at sea, and in the course of time the list of responsibilities has been enlarged to encompass the suppression of the transport of slaves, illicit traffic of drugs or psychotropic substances, and unauthorised broadcasting from the high seas. The performance of enforcement duties is facilitated by an express, but limited, right of visit on the high seas.

A thorough examination of the 1982 LOS Convention discloses dozens of instances of the Grotian tradition of the freedom of the seas exercising some influence upon the drafters, not least in the provisions relative to the deep sea-bed, the peaceful settlement of disputes and the rights of non-coastal powers in the jurisdictional and resource zones or the territorial seas of coastal states.[29]

22.6 Continuing Vitality of the Grotian Heritage

We are faced with something of a paradox. Among the major developments in the law of the sea over the past century has been the 'significant reduction in the area of the high seas'.[30] But, the sea has been taking its own revenge, for as coastal jurisdictional claims have expanded to take into account what is permissible under the 1982 LOS Convention, the sea level is rising for a complex of reasons, including the melting of the Arctic and Antarctic polar regions. Thus, does the expanse of high seas increase at the expense of land and ice-covered territories.

Merely to compare the origins and spatial reach of Grotius' notion of the freedom of the seas to that of today, instructive as such a comparison is, would understate the continuing vitality of the Grotian heritage in the law of the sea. The principle of freedom of the seas expounded by Grotius has served, and continues to serve, as rhetorical reinforcement for the point of departure when deliberating about matters of maritime jurisdiction. Rather like the presumption of innocence in criminal proceedings, we invoke the freedom of the seas principle constantly to remind ourselves that, whatever developments in the law of the sea are to be contemplated, we should measure their validity and impact with reference to that principle. Grotius left embedded in our legal consciousness a phrase and a standard of community awareness on the international level: anyone doubting the magnificence of that legacy need merely contemplate what might have been if adherents of *Mare clausum* had triumphed in their seventeenth-century conception. On the whole, we have been well-served by a doctrine that has required us to evaluate the propriety and legitimacy of individual claims against the international community interest, rather than the opposite process of carving out an area of community concern from a myriad of conflicting claims to ownership of the seas.

Translations of Grotius' Works Used

H. Grotius, *The Freedom of the Seas, or the Right Which Belongs to the Dutch to take part in the East Indian Trade,* transl. Ralph Van Deman Magoffin (New York, 1916)

    Hugo Grotius, *On the Law of War and Peace*, ed. S.C. Neff (Cambridge, 2012)

Further Reading

Diesselhorst, M., 'Hugo Grotius and the freedom of the seas', *Grotiana* N.S. 3 (1983) 11–26.

Oudendijk, J.K., *The Status and Extent of Adjacent Waters: A Historical Orientation* (London, 1970).

Pinto, M.W.C., 'The new law of the sea and the Grotian heritage', in Asser Instituut (ed.), *International Law and the Grotian Heritage* (The Hague, 1985), 54–93.

Simmonds, K.R., 'Grotius and the law of the sea: a reassessment', in A. Dufour, P. Haggenmacher and J. Toman (eds.), *Grotius et l'ordre juridique international* (Lausanne, 1985), 43–8.

Thornton, H., 'John Selden's response to Hugo Grotius: The argument for closed seas', *International Journal of Maritime History* 18 (2006) 105–27.

Notes

1 This chapter is a reworked, expanded and updated version of W.E. Butler, 'Grotius and the law of the sea', in H. Bull, B. Kingsbury and A. Roberts (eds.), *Hugo Grotius and International Relations* (Oxford, 1990), 209–20, under copyright with the author.

2 See R.P. Anand, 'Freedom of the seas: past, present and future', in H. Caminos (ed.), *Law of the Sea* (Ashgate, 2001), 215. Also see L. Casson, *The Ancient*

Mariners: Seafarers and Sea Fighters of the Mediterranean in Ancient Times (2nd edn.; Princeton, 1991), which will have been in many respects overtaken by more recent archaeological advances. For studies of Venetian, Portuguese, Byzantine, Barbary, Viking, English, African, Meso-American, Caribbean, Mongol Empire, Islamic, Chinese, Indian and Korean maritime activities, see the volumes under the general editorship of C. Buchet, *The Sea in History* (4 vols., Woodbridge, 2017).

3 See D.M. Johnston, *The Theory and History of Ocean Boundary-Making* (Quebec, 1988), 75. For this author's mature views on the origins of the law of nations, see *The Historical Foundations of World Order: The Tower and the Arena* (Leiden and Boston, 2008). More generally, see L. Paine, *The Sea and Civilization: A Maritime History of the World* (New York, 2013).

4 See K.R. Simmonds, 'Grotius and the law of the sea: a reassessment', in A. Dufour, P. Haggenmacher and J. Toman (eds.), *Grotius et l'ordre juridique international* (Lausanne, 1985), 43–8, at 43; Lauren Benton, 'Legalities of the sea in Gentili's *Hispanica Advocatio*', in B. Kingsbury and B. Straumann (eds.), *The Roman Foundations of the Law of Nations: Alberico Gentili and the Justice of Empire* (Oxford, 2010), 269–86, at 275–6.

5 The manuscript remained with the descendants of Hugo Grotius until his personal papers appeared at auction in 1864 and were acquired by Leiden University. The Latin text was published in 1868 and an English translation in 1950. The last is collected with additional materials in Hugo Grotius, *Commentary on the Law of Prize and Booty*, ed. Marine Julia van Ittersum (Indianapolis, 2006).

6 The full title is *Mare liberum sive de iure quod Batavia competit ad Indicana commercia dissertatio* (Leiden, 1609).

7 See H. Nellen, *Hugo Grotius: A Lifelong Struggle for Peace in Church and State, 1583–1645* (Leiden and Boston, 2015), 107.

8 See the Introductory Note by James Brown Scott to H. Grotius, *The Freedom of the Seas or the Right Which Belongs to the Dutch to Take Part in the East Indian Trade*, transl. R. Magoffin (New York, 1916); J.K. Oudendijk, *The Status and Extent of Adjacent Waters: A Historical Orientation* (London, 1970); C.G. Roelofsen, 'Grotius and international law', in L.E. van Holk and C.G. Roelofsen (eds.), *Grotius Reader* (The Hague, 1983), 3–21, at 5–15; M. Ahsmann, 'Grotius as a jurist', in *Hugo Grotius: A Great European* (The Hague, 1983), 38–9.

9 On the printing history, see ibid., 108–9; M.J. van Ittersum, 'Preparing Mare Liberum for the press: Hugo Grotius' rewriting of Chapter 12 of De iure praedae in November-December 1608', *Grotiana*, N.S. 26–8 (2005–7), 246–80.

10 Simmonds, 'Grotius and the law of the sea', 43–5.

11 W. Welwood, *An Abridgement of All Sea Laws: Gathered Forth of All Writings and Monuments Which Are to Be Found among Any People or Nation upon the Coasts of the Great Ocean and Mediterranean Sea, and Specially Ordered and Disposed for the Use and Benefit of All Benevolent Sea-Farers within His*

Majesties Dominions of Great Britainne, Ireland and the Adjacent Isles Thereof (London, 1613).

12 W. Welwood, *De dominio maris: ivribvsqve ad dominivm praecipve spectantibvs assertion brevis et methodica* ([London], 1615). *Mare liberum*, Welwood's response and Grotius' previously unpublished reply to Welwood have been collected in H. Grotius, *The Free Sea*, ed. D. Armitage (Indianapolis, 2004). Armitage works from the first English translation of *Mare liberum* undertaken by Richard Hakluyt (1553–1616) on the basis of the manuscript held by the Inner Temple Library.

13 Although the Grotius-Selden controversy is best known as the 'battle of the books' regarding jurisdiction at sea, a number of individuals from the mid-sixteenth century onward had exercised their minds with the issue. In England these included Edmund Plowden (1518–85), John Dee (1527–1608) and Sir Thomas Craig (1538–1608), but none so prominent in this matter as Welwood, Alberico Gentili (1552–1608), Robert Copland (*fl.* 1508–47), Nicholas Carr (1524–68) and Thomas Rowghton (*fl.* 1530–40). On the continent, there were many others, including Vitoria and Serafim de Freitas.

14 On this history of publication, see G.J. Toomer, *John Selden: A Life in Scholarship* (Oxford, 2009), vol. 1, 388–437.

15 See V.E. Grabar, *The History of International Law in Russia, 1647–1917: A Bio-Bibliographical Study*, transl. W.E. Butler (Oxford, 1990).

16 See W.E. Butler, *The Soviet Union and the Law of the Sea* (Baltimore, 1971), 27–8.

17 P. Allott, 'Language, Method and the Nature of International Law', *British Year Book of International Law* 45 (1971) 79–135.

18 Quotes from Hugo Grotius, *On the Law of War and Peace*, ed. S.C. Neff (Cambridge, 2012). Neff edited and annotated the translation by Francis W. Kelsey and published under the auspices of The Carnegie Endowment by the Oxford University Press in 1925, although, as Neff pointed out, in fact the publishing year is later and presumably the date 1925 was chosen to coincide with the 300th anniversary of the first edition of the work. The English translations of Grotius – Clement Barksdale (1654); William Evats (1682); John Morrice and others (1715 and 1738); A.C. Campbell (1814); and William Whewell (1853) – have been reprinted in facsimile, each with an introduction by W.E. Butler, by Lawbook Exchange Ltd., Clark, NJ.

19 Allott, 'Language', 100–2.

20 An alternative translation is: 'We will lay this certain rule of the law of nations (which they call primary) as the foundation, the reason whereof is clear and immutable: that it is lawful for any nation to go to any other and to trade with it', ML 1, 10 from Grotius, *The Free Sea,* note 11 above.

21 Oudendijk, 'Status and extent', 180–91.

22 Grotius later modified, or retracted, his view in subsequent writings, making an exception for inland seas, bays and straits in DJBP and a territorial sea in that work's version of 1637. See Ahsmann, 'Grotius as a jurist'.

23 Later writers reiterated Grotius' basic reasoning about the nature of the sea and came to the same conclusion; see, for example, the detailed analysis of the positions taken by Grotius and Selden, in J.-M. Gérard de Rayneval, *On the Freedom of the Sea*, ed. W. E. Butler (Clark, NJ, 2013), 1–31.

24 'Territorial sea' historically has tended to connote an expanse of the high seas subject to coastal state jurisdiction for certain purposes. It represented a kind of 'carving out' of an expanse of high seas permitted by international law for the protection of specific coastal interests. 'Territorial waters' tended to convey the opposite presumption: an expanse of coastal waters subject to coastal state sovereignty, the latter, however, being limited by international law to protect certain interests of the international community, for example, innocent passage. In time the juxtaposed presumptions conveyed by the terminology were lost sight of, and many writers used the expressions interchangeably and synonymously without regard to the original implications. Some have found it useful to speak of 'navigational servitudes'. See R.J. Gillis, *Navigational Servitudes: Sources, Applications, Paradigms* (The Hague, 2007), 5.

25 1833 UNTS 3.

26 Doctrinal writings occasioned by the quadricentenary of Grotius' birth exhibited confusion and inconsistency on this point. One writer claimed that two fundamental Grotian principles – that the sea cannot be appropriated and that the freedom of the seas serves the common good – have been 'reaffirmed by the new Convention on the Law of the Sea', citing Articles 78(1) and 89. See B. Kwiatkowska, 'Hugo Grotius and the freedom of the seas', in J.L.M. Elders *et alii* (eds.), *Hugo Grotius: 1583–1983 Maastricht Hugo Grotius Colloquium* (Assen, 1984), 29–30. In fact, as we have learned to our detriment, the sea can be appropriated, despoiled and its resources exhausted. In this sense, the 1982 LOS Convention has been a response to the inadequacy in modern times of the Grotian perception. See B. Vermeulen, review of Elders, in *Grotiana*, N.S. 6 (1985) 94.

27 The human community has belatedly realised that the vast expanses of the seas can nonetheless be irretrievably polluted by the wastes of human civilisation. See, for example, John C. Kunich, *Killing Our Oceans: Dealing with the Mass Extinction of Marine Life* (Westport, 2008).

28 This view is contested with regard to the deep sea-bed and subsoil. 'Appropriation' is physically possible at shallower depths and the Grotian principle of *res communis* continues to be under severe pressure. The promise of technology is responsible for the triumph of 'individual' or 'national' over 'common' use. For views expressed at the time of the LOS Convention, see M. Diesselhorst, 'Hugo Grotius and the freedom of the seas', *Grotiana* N.S. 3 (1983) 11–26. For a vigorous argument that 'ocean nationalism' has triumphed in the 1982 LOS Convention and the international community has squandered an opportunity to pursue a more enlightened policy consistent with Grotian principles, see J.J. Logue, 'The revenge of John Selden: The Draft Convention on the Law of the Sea in the light of Hugo Grotius' Mare liberum', *Grotiana* N.S. 3

(1983) 27–56, and sequel: J.J. Logue, 'A stubborn Dutchman. The attempt to Revive Grotius' common property doctrine in and after the Third United Nations Conference on the Law of the Sea', in Asser Instituut, *International Law and the Grotian Heritage* (The Hague, 1985), 99–108. For an imaginative view of how the oceans and seas may become the principal human environment in the foreseeable future through various forms of occupation, see J. Quick, with P. Friedman, *Seasteading: How Floating Nations Will Restore the Environment, Enrich the Poor, Cure the Sick, and Liberate Humanity from Politicians* (New York, 2017). The argument on behalf of closed seas has been explored by H. Thornton, 'John Selden's response to Hugo Grotius: The argument for closed seas', *International Journal of Maritime History* 18 (2006) 105–27.

29 See M.W.C. Pinto, 'The new law of the sea and the Grotian heritage', in Asser Instituut, *Grotian Heritage*, 54–93. Also see F. Ito, 'The thought of Hugo Grotius on the Mare liberum', *Japanese Annual of International Law* 18 (1974) 1–15; and a subsequent article, ibid. 20 (1976) 1–16.

30 D. Anderson, 'Freedoms of the high seas in the modern law of the sea', in D. Freestone, R. Barnes and D. Ong (eds.), *The Law of the Sea: Progress and Prospects* (Oxford, 2006), 327–46, 328.

23 Property

Bart Wauters

23.1 Introduction

Property was at the heart of Hugo Grotius' theory of war and peace. The primary goal of *De jure belli ac pacis* was to offer a broad theoretical framework with practical guidance on what kinds of infringements on property rights would legitimate war and be permissible during episodes of war. In this sense, *De jure belli ac pacis* built on the approach of *De jure praedae commentarius*, where the Dutch master first developed his theory of ownership for the practical purpose of defending the seizure of the *Santa Catarina* by Jacob Van Heemskerck (1567–1607). When analysing Grotius' property theory, one should not overlook this eminently practical approach.

Both in his early and mature works of political theory, as well as in his more theological and jurisprudential writings such as *De veritate religionis Christianae* and *Inleidinge tot de Hollandsche rechts-geleertheid*, Grotius maintained a remarkable consistency in his account of the foundations of private property. He conceived the emergence of private property as the outcome of an historical evolution. History in itself was not normative, in the sense that history alone was not sufficient to justify the existence of private property regimes, but, for Grotius, it was clear that conceptually the relationship of man and his holdings had evolved over time. The recourse to the evolutionary account allowed Grotius to demonstrate and prove that his premises were not accidental, but were rather the necessary result of practical and rational reasoning, by pointing to certain facts of human nature that reduced the options of how to organise society.[1] The same reasoning lies behind his use of examples from America (e.g. DJBP 2.2.2.1). Historical events were proof of his theorising and made it palpable. However, it would be one-sided to reduce Grotius' historicising approach to a secularised narrative, where it did not matter much whether his sources were biblical, classical or contemporary. Even if this secularised approach has been identified as one of the factors that made Grotius' account so innovative and compelling for the generations of political thinkers after him,[2] we would nevertheless be profoundly mistaken in ignoring the theological dimension of Grotius' thinking on property.[3] When Grotius quoted biblical sources, he did not merely use them as an historical account, but often also as an expression of his deep belief in their normative force. For a full understanding of Grotius' theory of property, it is indispensable to take into account Grotius' theological convictions.

For Grotius, there were roughly two stages in history related to property: a pre-civil state of nature, where things were held in common, and a civil regime of property rights that were held privately. In the first stage, men lived 'at their ease on what the Earth, untilled, did naturally provide them with' (DJBP 2.2.2.1). It was a life of subsistence, with man sleeping in caves, running around naked or in animal skins, and eating what he could gather. In the second stage, man instituted a civil regime of private property. The transition from the first to the second stage was a gradual process. In order to lift his way of life above a level of subsistence, man started to work the land and raise cattle. This, in turn, generated the display of all kinds of human vices such as jealousy, attachment to pleasure and freeriding, which made the common holding of things unsustainable. Therefore, goods, first movables and then land, were divided in virtue of 'a certain compact and agreement, either expressly, as by division; or else tacitly, as by seizure' (DJBP 2.2.2.5). This agreement to the principle of occupation was the last step before people became aware of 'a new sort or right', civil property rights.

Among modern commentators on Grotius' theory of property, there is disagreement about the institutional character of the Grotian conception of property. On the one hand, Marcelo de Araujo and Richard Schlatter argue that Grotius does not conceive of property as a natural right, but rather as a manmade institution based on convention.[4] At the other side of the spectrum, there are authors like Benjamin Straumann, who claims that – for Grotius – private property is a full and complete institution in the state of nature, the existence of which does not require a political community.[5] Likewise, Richard Tuck thinks that the agreement introducing a civil regime of property only recognises a natural right to appropriate, but is not constitutive of a new right.[6] As will be explained more fully below, my own reading of Grotius implies him to say that the normative ground of a civil regime of private property is *consent* to a hypothetical agreement to introduce the regime. While this agreement marks the end of the emergence of man from the state of nature, consent cannot be presumed unless the agreement includes some essential features of the original, primeval use-right.

It is not within the scope of this chapter to enter into a detailed dialogue with the above-mentioned and other authors. However, the discussion is of relevance for a proper understanding of Grotius' conception on justice in the allocation of goods and resources, or, to use an anachronism, 'distributive justice'. If Grotius indeed elaborated private property as a full and complete natural right, existing prior to the state and its legal system, there is nothing that stands in the way of considering him a libertarian or harsh capitalist in the line of Robert Nozick.[7] If, on the other hand, Grotius' property theory is based on convention only, there are no such absolute pre-existing property rights. In that case, the convention regulates the acquisition and transfer of goods, and can include limits as to the extent and scope of property rights. As we will see, there are good reasons to bolster the claim that Grotius was prepared to accept a certain degree of inequality in holdings, although that did not stop him from criticising an unbridled accumulation of wealth. In that respect, it is important to focus on the right of necessity,[8] which entitles persons in extreme need to take someone else's property to save themselves. A proper understanding of this right of necessity allows us to grasp the precise normative basis of the convention introducing the civil regime of private property. Simultaneously, it enables us to reconstruct Grotius' idea of distributive justice by taking into account his interpretation of related values such as liberty, autonomy, equality, sociability and universal fellowship of humankind. Again, for a proper appreciation of these values, an understanding of Grotius' theological views is crucial. In this chapter, I will eventually arrive at an interpretation linking the Grotian conception of these values to his theory of property, but first I have to examine the theory itself. Therefore, in what follows, I will first describe the Grotian conception of *dominium* in the state of nature. Then, I'll proceed with the transition towards the civil regime of private property, where I'll analyse more closely the agreement to the principle of occupation. Finally, I'll have a look at some of the practical outcomes of Grotius' property theory, such as his defence of the principle of freedom of the seas, and his justification of conduct of belligerents in war, more specifically their option to occupy territory of non-belligerents. For the purpose of this chapter, I take Grotius' account to be largely consistent throughout his writings, although where necessary I will point to the evolution in his thinking.

23.2 The State of Nature

How did Grotius conceive the holding of things in common in the state of nature? What rights did men have to the goods they were consuming? First, some terminology. In relation to the state of nature, Grotius used the word 'ownership' (*dominium*) because of a lack of alternative: 'owing to the poverty of human speech, it has become necessary to employ identical terms for concepts which are not identical' (DJPC 12, f. 100ᵛ; ML 5, 21). In the state of nature, some kind of ownership (*dominium quoddam*) did exist, but it was 'ownership in a universal and indefinite sense' (DJPC 12, f. 101; ML 5, 22). 'Common' referred to the fact that the produce of the earth was up for grabs by anyone and that no individual could exclude others from the use of it; common meant undivided. Individuals had no specific rights or claims on particular goods, but each was at liberty to use the common. In this sense, it was 'common' because everyone had this original use-right. To define the exact structure of this original use-right, Grotius referred to technical terms that could be traced back to the Franciscan poverty disputes.[9] In the thirteenth and fourteenth centuries, the friars had entered into a series of controversies with the papacy about the exact nature of their relationship with the goods that had been given to the order by pious donors. Given their vow of absolute poverty, the Franciscans denied having any property rights over these goods and only claimed a *usus facti*, a factual use. This meant that the friars had no civil right to the use of the goods and, by consequence, could not claim or protect it in court.[10] It was this same *usus facti* that Grotius had in mind to define the relationship of the individuals with the common in the state of nature: absence of the power to exclude others, absence of civil protection and only factual detention over the goods while the individual was in a situation of control over them.

Even if *usus facti* as a way to structure the rights of individuals to the common in the state of nature sounds simple enough, there were some complications as to the exclusivity of certain goods, above all, but not only, consumables. The use of consumables such as food and drink inevitably meant *using them up*, thereby denying others from making use of the same thing. Therefore, 'a certain form of private property was inseparable from use'. What made this use a *kind* of private property right was primarily the exclusion of others, 'for the essential characteristic of private property is the fact that it belongs to a given individual in such a way as to be incapable of belonging to any other individual' (DJPC 12, f. 101; ML5, 22). Once an individual was in control over a thing, 'no man could justly take from another what [the latter] had thus first taken to himself' (DJBP 2.2.2.1). To illustrate this, Grotius introduced the example of the seats in the theatre: the seats are open to all citizens, but, once a citizen occupies a seat, he cannot be evicted from it (DJPC 12, f. 101^v; DJBP 2.2.2.1).

What excluded others from the use of the seat in the theatre is the fact that it was taken before they arrived. Why was seizure, the 'joining of body to body' (DJBP 2.8.6), legitimate? Why could people in the state of nature seize and bring under their physical control the earth's resources? Basically, it was because God 'bestowed upon living creatures their very existence' and, therefore, also 'bestowed the things necessary for existence' (DJPC 2, f. 6). Seizure or occupation was the only way to turn the natural resources to use, and therefore it was licit. This power to seize things from the common was held equally by every individual in the state of nature. No individual could stop another from accessing the common, and everyone could use the world's resources as they saw fit.[11]

In *De jure praedae*, where a youthful Grotius presented his system of nine rules and thirteen laws as the basis for a new jurisprudence, the idea of self-preservation as the ground for seizure was made more explicit. The first rule of the Grotian system of jurisprudence is that what God has shown to be his will, is law. One could learn the will of God by empirical observation of nature. As self-love is one of nature's primary principles, it is a clear sign of God's design. All things in nature, not only the human race, 'are tenderly regardful of self, and seek their own happiness and security' (DJPC 2, f. 5^{v}a). Grotius distinguished between 'true and divinely inspired self-love' (*verus et divinus sui amor*), and the vicious 'φιλαυτία', or immoderate and excessive self-love. The just man's highest concern ought to be for himself. However, self-love is not the same as self-interest. Hence, the first two laws of the Grotian system: it is 'permissible to defend one's own life' and 'to acquire for oneself, and to retain, those things which are useful for life' (DJPC 2, f. 6). Self-love, or responsibility over one's own life, thus entails not only the duty of self-preservation, but also the capacity to acquire things that allow one to reach one's purposes in life.

In the state of nature, seizure of the earth's resources is perfectly legitimate. Once an individual seizes or occupies a thing, it enters into the sphere of the *suum*, sometimes even up to the point of a complete identification. That is the case of consumables, for instance, which are 'converted into the very substance of the user' (DJPC 12, f. 101; ML 5, 22). Because the thing enters into the sphere of what is one's own, one can licitly defend it against attempts to snatch it away, and inflict punishment on the intruder, probably even to the point of killing him (DJBP 2.1.11–3, see also 1.2.1.5).[12]

As stated above, Grotius' theory of property cannot fully be grasped without a deep understanding of his theological beliefs. This theological framework is often overlooked by modern scholars. For instance, when Grotius said that God had bestowed the earth upon the human race as a whole, and 'not upon individual men' (DJPC 2, f. 6), he implicitly rejected the theory of Adam's sole *dominium*, which asserts that God had given individual ownership over the whole world to Adam. This theory was still controversial in the seventeenth century, when Robert Filmer (1588–1653) based his notorious political theology of patriarchal kingship on the idea of Adam's sole *dominium*.[13] Its roots lay in the fourteenth-century Franciscan poverty dispute. Pope John XXII (1244–1334) had asserted that God had given individual ownership over the whole world to Adam, in support of his claim against the Franciscans that private ownership existed by divine law, and was thus legitimate, even in the age of innocence. At stake was the soundness of the Franciscan repudiation of private property and its implied criticism of the wealth of the Church. For John XXII, when God transferred *dominium* over temporal goods, Adam could not have had anything in common because he was alone and there was no one to have things in common with. The Franciscan champion, William of Ockham (1285–1347), rejected this argument. If Adam had ownership over the whole earth, he would have had the right to exclude Eve from its use, which was inconceivable. Ockham did agree with John XXII that *dominium* could not have been introduced without a gift from God, but what God had granted was the power to appropriate, the original use-right.[14]

The idea that God had granted to Adam a civil right of *dominium* over the entire world became especially problematic after the Council of Constance (1415) condemned the theses of John Wycliff (1330–84). Wycliff had stated that only those in a state of grace could hold true *dominium*.[15] Even though Wycliff was condemned, theologians still had to come up with an answer to Wycliff's theory as to what extent the Fall of Adam affected man's capacity for true *dominium*. They did so by stressing the idea that God had given the world to man as a natural creature, not as a special gift to the prelapsarian man. Francisco Suárez (1548–1617), for instance, based this conclusion on a profound analysis of Genesis, and more specifically the idea of man having been created in the image of God and being the master of all creatures.[16] That man was created in the image of God touched upon his very nature and essence and did not restrict his capacity for mastery to the state of innocence. Grotius thus referred to standard Thomist doctrine when he said that 'inferior things were given for use by their superiors', and therefore the earth's fruits and resources were at the service of man (DJPC 2, f. 6; IHR 2.3.2). This Thomist tradition was compatible with Grotius' own Arminian convictions.[17]

23.3 Towards a Regime of Civil Property

In Grotius' account, the original use-right transitioned into the modern property regime, following a gradual process 'under the guidance of nature itself' (DJPC 12, f. 101; ML 5, 22). The core of the civil property regime was already included in the original use-right: individuals had a right to both occupy, use and consume goods to the exclusion of others, and defend them. This was primarily the case for consumables such as food and water, but, in a second step, it was logical also to apply the basic concept to goods such as clothing and other movable goods: the use by the first occupier rendered them less fit for subsequent use by others (DJPC 12, f. 101; ML 5, 22). The division of land was the next step, and it was also related to consumption, because arable lands were used for pasture or to obtain food. Grotius employed a biblical account to relate the division of land. First, there was a rough division, between Abel and Cain, and later between 'nations' after the Flood, the Tower of Babel and the parting of Abraham and Lot (Gen. 10.32; 11.8; 13.9). Within each nation, citizens still kept a community of pastures, because, in proportion to the small number of people and cattle, the extent of the land was still large enough. Following the increase in the number of people, and in a subsequent step, a portion of land was assigned to each family. Then everyone rushed to appropriate those water-wells that each could seize, a scarce, but necessary, good in the dry countries that formed the background of Old-Testament history (DJBP 2.2.2.3). The division of land was the last step; once land was divided, people recognised that 'a new sort of right' had been produced (DJBP 2.2.2.5) and that a law should be established to regulate the new regime of private property (DJPC 12, f. 101^v; ML 5, 22). For Grotius, then, the normative basis of the regime of private property was this law, which, as we will see, he based on consent.

It had been necessary to introduce the law regulating private property because of the emergence of material scarcity. There was just not enough land and drinkable water for a growing number of people and cattle. Men could not remain in common 'any longer than whilst [its] fruits are sufficient for the wants of men, and which, after the increase of mankind ... could not long continue' (IHR 2.3.2). It is in this sense that the gradual transition towards a regime of civil property happened under the 'guidance of nature itself'. While nature provides for sufficient resources, there is no need to divide the common; if there is scarcity, the common necessarily needs to be divided. Therefore, goods such as the sun, the moon, the stars and, to a certain extent, the air and the sea – 'things of such a nature as to be sufficient for the purposes of every one' (IHR 2.3.2; DJBP 2.2.3.1) – cannot be divided.

Not only scarcity, but also the corrupt nature of man, prompted the end of common possession. In the state of nature, man was 'ignorant of vice and unacquainted with deceit' (DJBP 2.2.2.1), but man lost his integrity and innocence once he was capable of distinguishing between good and evil. This knowledge opened up a new world of vices, where man would primarily pursue pleasures, wine and 'abominable lusts', leading to jealousy, murder and a 'savage sort of life' (DJBP 2.2.2.2). A regime of private property as an answer to man's sinfulness tapped into a canonistic tradition that went back as far back as the twelfth century,[18] and was moreover consistent with Protestant ideas on the relationship between industriousness and the fallen nature of man.[19] However, while these traditions consider the regime of civil property primarily as a kind of second-best scenario, because man's fallen condition disqualifies him from living in a prelapsarian regime of common *dominium*, Grotius highlighted two positive reasons why a regime of private property is not so bad. First, man, unlike beasts, has the capacity to solve his conflicts by reasoning and argument. Recourse to force should not occur, except 'when [argument] can not be employed' (DJBP 1.2.1.6). Quarrels over goods are thus likely in view of man's greedy nature, but the civil property regime is instrumental in settling such quarrels in a non-violent way. Second, man also has a 'more noble vice': ambition (DJBP 2.2.2.3). It was ambition that made people abandon their caves and pursue a lifestyle above the level of subsistence. As David Hume (1711–76) later remarked, this search for pleasure and 'innocent' luxury need not be entirely negative because it had been the spark of human progress and increasing refinement.[20] Grotius, too, did not seem sorry to have left the 'state of simplicity' with its common possession and its lack of 'knowledge of virtue' (DJBP 2.2.2.2). Moreover, a regime of private property has enabled trade (ML 5, 44) and industry (DJBP 2.2.2.3).

Industriousness and trade require effort and work. Unlike John Locke (1632–1704), who would more explicitly identify labour as the direct foundation of individual property rights, for Grotius labour was only the expression of the ambition to overcome scarcity and subsistence, 'because the earth, not producing by its spontaneous produce sufficient for the wants of mankind, has been rendered more fruitful by skill and labour' (IHR 2.3.2). Due to a 'defect in equity and love, whereby a just equality would not have been observed, either in their labour, or in the consumption of their fruits and revenues' (DJBP 2.2.2.4), things could no longer be held in common. Grotius referred here to the problem of 'free riding'. Under a regime of common possessions, where some people work and others do not, the overall output goes up, increasing the common and thus benefiting those who do not work as well.

Fundamental to the Grotian property theory is the conception of man's autonomy and liberty: 'liberty in regard to actions is equivalent to ownership in regard to property'. God had created man 'free and *sui juris*, so that the actions of each individual and the use of his possessions were made subject not to another's will but to his own'. At the heart of the requirement of self-love lies the power and responsibility to choose one's own purposes and not to be subject to those of others. Natural liberty is, then, 'nothing else than the power of the individual to act in accordance with his own will'. One's possessions are the means by which to reach one's purposes; interference with one's possessions therefore interferes with one's liberty. In this sense, 'every man is the governor and arbiter of affairs relative to his own property' (DJPC 2, f. 10, quoting C. 4.35.21). This focus on man's autonomy links back to the Arminian and Thomist theology of man having been shaped in the image of God and man's capacities for reason, free will and intellect.[21] Freedom over one's actions not only explains man's capacity for *dominium*, but also plays a role in the establishment of a private property regime. Man started to labour because he wanted to overcome his life of subsistence. Some men chose to employ their labour and industry 'for one thing, and others for another' (DJBP

2.2.2.4). The capacity of autonomous choice was thus one of the driving factors behind the transition towards a regime of private property.

23.4 Agreement

The transition from the state of nature, with a regime of common possessions, to a civil regime of private ownership happened step-by-step. Somewhere along this gradual process there were one or more agreements about the allocation of resources; 'pacts' that could be explicit, as in the case of a division such as between Abraham and Lot (Gen. 13.9), or rather tacit. The tacit agreement presupposed that 'each should appropriate to himself, by right of first possession, what could not have been divided' (DJBP 2.2.2.5).

Grotius' idea of an agreement to divide land and other goods is not entirely straightforward. In *De jure praedae* and *Inleidinge*, Grotius avoided the idea of an agreement, and only in *De jure belli ac pacis* does he explicitly use the term *pactum*. This change did not go unnoticed to some of Grotius' early critics, such as John Selden (1584–1654) in his *Mare clausum*: if the division of goods is based on agreement and consent after all, then why can the sea not be an object of such an agreement?[22] A later critic, Immanuel Kant (1724–1804), wondered why future generations should feel bound by agreements to which they were not a party.[23] It is interesting to have a closer look at possible answers to these criticisms, because they allow us better to grasp the Grotian conception of the agreement. In this section, we will have a look at a possible reply to Selden, including an answer to the question why Grotius introduced the idea of an agreement only in his more mature work. In the following section, we will discuss an answer to the criticism of Kant.

Although Selden ascribed to Grotius a strong, almost contractual version of the agreement introducing a regime of private property,[24] and Filmer made fun imagining it as an historical event,[25] it is unlikely that Grotius himself would have agreed with this characterisation. True enough, for Grotius, the agreement comes with clauses and restrictions, such as the right of necessity, which we will discuss below, and the right of free passage over land and rivers by migrants having just cause (DJBP 2.2.13.1). Using clauses and restrictions might create the impression that he envisioned something like a hard contract. Moreover, he did say that the establishment of property 'seems to have extinguished all the right that arose from the state of community', thus suggesting that the agreement was a strong fissure. However, ascribing the idea of a hard agreement to Grotius is probably too simplistic. In the sentence quoted above, the essential word is *seems* ('videatur'). Grotius went on to *deny* that the establishment of private property extinguishes the property regime of the state of nature (DJBP 2.2.6.1).

That Selden's understanding of the Grotian agreement does not match Grotius' own is also supported by the historical account of the development of private property. The development of a private property regime was a very gradual process, and it is not at all evident where in the account a 'hard' agreement should be situated. In each of the steps in the account, we can find some kind of explicit division or tacit acceptance of *faits accomplis*: the organic division into 'nations' after the Flood and the Tower of Babel, the explicit agreement to divide land between Abraham and Lot, the decision to assign land to particular households and, crucially, the recognition – *a posteriori* – that a new sort of right had been developed. These events all are significant in the development of private property, and involved either explicit agreements or, more often, an inarticulate acknowledgement by the community of factual situations. When Grotius spoke of an agreement, *pactum*, he did not refer to an identifiable historical event, but rather to an indeterminate set of hypothetical arrangements, or 'a custom not written' (DJBP 2.2.6.1).

For Grotius, the core of the agreement was the consent to the principle of first occupation. It is not an agreement assigning specific goods to particular persons. To the extent that Grotius did speak about explicit division, it is only another expression of the underlying principle 'that each should appropriate to himself, by right of first possession, what could not have been divided' (DJBP 2.2.2.5). Crucially, the agreement 'was patterned after nature's plan' (DJPC 12, f. 101^v; ML 5, 22). The essential feature in that pattern, as we have seen, is *seizure* as the primary means of acquiring things. Seizure of a thing excluded others from its use, and this exclusivity is what property is all about (DJPC 12, f. 101; ML 5, 22). Seizure is, of course, very close to civil *occupatio*[26]. What the conventional, civil *occupatio* adds to physical control is the possibility to recover goods once one's physical control over them is lost. In the state of nature, others can be excluded from the use of one's goods only while one has physical control, because of one's natural right to defend one's personal integrity or *suum*.

However, once the individual loses physical control over a thing, they also lose the right to use it, for the use-right is 'derived not from a mere internal act of the mind' (DJBP 2.2.2.5). What the agreement to the principle of first occupation then adds is the possibility to recover lost possessions, for which the 'establishment of courts of justice was undertaken' (DJPC 8, f. 39). The possibility to recover goods in spite of loss of physical control over them requires others to subscribe to the idea of continuation of rights by the mere internal act of the mind. By accepting the idea of continuation of rights in the compact, establishing a regime of private property, the parties give the principle of civil *occupatio* its normative basis.

We do not really know why the idea of the agreement is absent in Grotius' earlier writings. The idea of a compact underlying the regime of private ownership is a standard feature in his sources,[27] so his choice not to include it explicitly in *De jure praedae* may have been deliberate. However, it is more likely that, in the earlier work, Grotius just did not need the idea of an agreement to the principle of first occupation. As seizure of the sea is not possible, it cannot be subject of an agreement anyway, so why bother to theorise about it? However, in *De jure belli ac pacis*, Grotius discussed quite extensively a new feature he had not touched upon in *De jure praedae*: the right of necessity. The right of necessity is the right of persons who are in a situation of extreme need to take out of the surplus of others what is necessary to stay alive. This right has a long tradition in canonical and Thomist thinking about poverty, but, as we will see below, Grotius used it in a novel way, primarily to provide guidance to belligerents about rightful conduct in war. As this right of necessity presupposes the agreement on the principle of first occupation, Grotius had to introduce and discuss the agreement to start with, which is why we find it only in *De jure belli ac pacis*.

23.5 Practical Consequences of the Grotian Property Theory

Grotius wanted his theories to have practical effects. That is clearly so for his property theory, which he elaborated in his *Mare liberum* with the obvious practical purpose to uphold the principle of the freedom of the seas. As seizure is a constituent element of property and exclusivity, no single country has a right to exclude navigators from the open ocean because it is impossible to physically keep control over vast tracts of water:

'no one could possibly take possession of it' (DJPC 12, f. 102^V; ML 5, 25). In a similar vein, scarcity has been one of the key drivers in the process of the emergence of a private property regime. However, for those resources of which there is plenty, such as air or water, the use by a single individual does not block other people's use of them. Beyond some well-defined exceptions, such as territorial waters, the process of the emergence of private property on the sea simply cannot be set in motion, as there is no scarcity of the sea and it is impossible to occupy it.

In his later work, Grotius also kept primarily the practical purposes of his property theory in view. The second book of his *De jure belli ac pacis* is entirely devoted to the *jus ad bellum*, and it is not a coincidence that it is in this part of the work that Grotius introduced his property theory. Grotius explained that there are basically three causes for war: defence, punishment and 'recovery of what's our own' (DJBP 2.1.2.2). To define what is one's own, he needed a theory of property. The theory of property is also helpful to explain the behaviour of belligerents at war, the main subject matter of the third book of *De jure belli ac pacis*. It would lead us too far to investigate in close detail all the consequences for the *jus ad bellum* or the *jus in bello*; this section focuses solely on the right of necessity because it is an illuminating feature of the Grotian property theory.

The right of necessity is elaborated in view of a practical purpose. Grotius wanted to show 'how far he that is engaged in a just war may possess himself of any place in a neutral country'. This liberty to take places in neutral countries is, of course, subject to conditions: the belligerent can only invoke it when he is engaged in a just war, when the threat is certain and the injury irreparable were the enemy to take the place first. Moreover, the belligerent can only take what is needed for his security; he can neither take over political power nor tax revenue; and he has to return the place as soon as the danger is over (DJBP 2.2.10). According to Grotius, this right of the belligerent reflects the liberty of a person in extreme need to take from the surplus of others in order to stay alive. In cases of absolute necessity, the 'ancient right of using things, as if they still remained common, must revive, and be in full force' (DJBP 2.2.6.2). The reason is not that there is a charitable duty on the affluent to give some of their surplus to the necessitous. It is rather that, when the agreement to introduce private property was made, it was 'supposed to have been established with this favourable exception, that in such cases one might enter again upon the rights of the primitive community' (DJBP 2.2.6.4). This conclusion is the outcome of an interpretive effort of the hypothetical agreement to the principle of first occupation. Grotius' interpretation of the agreement is based on several arguments. First, there is the intention of those who had made the interpretation. 'For had those that made the first division of common goods been asked their opinion in this matter, they would have answered the same as we now assert' (DJBP 2.2.6.4). It is plain common sense: if the point of dividing the common had been to overcome a life of subsistence and improve the way of life, then no one could be presumed to have agreed to a settlement that would leave him worse off when it matters most. Second, when interpreting the agreement that divided the common one should presuppose that 'they designed to deviate as little as possible from the rules of natural equity' (*aequitas naturalis*) (DJBP 2.2.6.1). This argument refers to the idea that the earth's inferior resources are at the service of superior creatures, and that all had had an equal right to take from the common what was needed to survive.[28] Third, the right of necessity is not something that applies only to private property, but can be more widely used as a private law defence 'in all laws of human institution' (DJBP 2.2.6.2–3).[29] Grotius adduced Roman law examples such as the Rhodian law of jettison (D. 14.2.2.2) to prove the point. Finally, the right of necessity can be linked with the principle of self-preservation: 'In a common calamity, every man looks to himself, and takes care of his own interest' (DJBP 2.2.6.4). The combination of these arguments lead Grotius to conclude that an agreement without a right of necessity is inconceivable.

Grotius presented the right of necessity as a revival of the primitive use-right. However, extreme necessity does not trigger the suspension of the regime of private ownership, nor a return to the state of nature with its regime of common possessions. The right of necessity presupposes the agreement whereupon the private property regime is based; one can look at it as one of the clauses to the agreement. That is also why the very agreement that includes the right of necessity can define its proper limitations. There are three such limitations. First, the necessitous have to make sure that, before taking from others, they have tried everything in their power to avoid the situation of absolute necessity. This includes asking the government for help or trying to convince the affluent to give what is needed (DJBP 2.2.7). Second, the necessitous cannot take from the owner when the latter is himself in a situation of extreme need. This is consistent with the use-right in the state of nature. If both persons are equally in need, one can argue that the ancient use-right has revived for both of them. In that case, 'all things equal the possessor has the advantage' (DJBP 2.2.8), because he has physical control over the thing and *de facto* excludes others. The third limitation is that, once the situation of absolute necessity has passed, the necessitous should reimburse the owner. As Grotius himself anticipated, this statement is open to challenges. Samuel Pufendorf (1632–94), for instance, asked if it was not contradictory to insist on restitution when the necessitous had had a right to the surplus of the legal owner.[30] For the Dutch master, however, there was no contradiction. As we have seen, the right of necessity is an interpretive construction of the agreement underlying the private property regime, which only required subsistence, so there is no problem to construct the right 'so far, and not further, to maintain the laws of natural equity against the rigour of the rights of a proprietor' (DJBP 2.2.9).

The right of necessity, and the way Grotius constructed it, contains the clue of the answer for the Kantian criticism about the binding force of an agreement underlying the civil property regime. When Grotius wrote that 'all men were supposed, and ought to be supposed to have consented' (DJBP 2.2.2.5) to the principle of first occupation, he clearly knew that it was problematic to explain why an explicit division is normative on those who are no party to it, such as future generations or latecomers. His answer is basically that no one has anything to lose by underwriting the principle of first occupation. Everyone receives what he or she would already have in the state of nature: the recognition that seizure of unoccupied goods is rightful. On top of what they already have in the state of nature, the civil property regime adds the possibility to recover goods over which one has lost physical control. This extra feature provides real advantages in terms of economic efficiency and public order, but these positive outcomes are not the only reason why one would subscribe to them because these benefits cannot be expected to be to the equal advantage of all. Even if one did not benefit from these advantageous consequences of the compact, one would still have the right of necessity assuring the same level of subsistence as in the state of nature. No one loses, all stand to gain, there is no reason why we should doubt the consent of all, and thus the validity of the agreement to the principle of occupation.

Even if Grotius was not blind to the self-interested and rational character of man, ultimately he framed the consent to the right of necessity within the theologically conceived requirement of man's self-love and responsibility over one's life. Primarily elaborated to establish the boundaries of belligerent behaviour in war, the right of necessity also had consequences for his ideas on the distribution of wealth. Overcoming a lifestyle at subsistence level has been the point of the introduction of private property, and accumulating more than one needed for current use is therefore legitimate. Accordingly, the ensuing inequality is not unjust. However, this does not mean that Grotius defended an unbridled accumulation of wealth. In *De veritate religionis Christianae*, he said that, if we manage to acquire something more than necessary for mere subsistence, we should 'supply the wants of other men, either by giving or lending to those that ask it'. The reason is that 'the Christian law (...) forbids us setting our affections upon perishing things'. Accumulating and preserving wealth in a way spoils the very pleasures whereto wealth is supposed to lead, because it 'is attended with a certain slavery and uneasiness'. Thus, dependency on the mere accumulation of money is not acceptable from the standpoint of self-love and responsibility over one's life. Not even setting aside money for old age or misfortune is an acceptable excuse for accumulating wealth, because God will provide for us. 'It would be an unworthy thing in us, not to believe so good, so powerful a God, nor to trust him any further than we would do a bad debtor, of whom we never think ourselves secure without a pledge'. For the same reason, love for God, we should not be giving to charity with the calculating purpose of receiving something in return in terms of reputation. The duty to give away from one's surplus even extends to a global level as he reminds his readers of the Pauline epistles where the Christian communities in Macedonia and Achaia sent relief to the poor of Jerusalem (*De veritate* 2.14 – reference to Rom. 15.25–6).

While Grotius thought that the wealthy have a charitable duty to supply the wants of the poor, he explicitly denied that the right of necessity corresponds to such a duty (DJBP 2.2.6.1). A person in extreme need can, therefore, take also from people who have only slightly more than is required to subsist, not only from the wealthy. Conversely, people in need, but not *severe* need, could not raise the right of necessity as a defence when they take from the affluent, even if the affluent do have a moral duty to share.

The right of necessity and the charitable duty of the affluent have in common a concern for the wider community, perhaps typical of

Protestant theology,[31] emphasising mutual assistance between men and identifying it as the main purpose for which political communities are established. Because of the growth in the number of people, 'men were scattered about with vast distances separating them and were being deprived of opportunities for mutual benefaction'. As humankind spread over the world, smaller social units started to emerge 'with the purpose of bringing together under a more convenient arrangement the numerous different products of many persons' labour which are required for the uses of human life' (DJPC 2, f. 10^v). This social unit, large enough 'for self-protection through mutual aid, and for equal acquisition of the necessities of life', then receives its institutional embodiment in the political community. This pooling of resources is necessary for defence against outside menaces. It is also primarily the expression of a principle of 'universal fellowship of mankind and the communion established by nature, that will still cause us to be affected in our turn by ills inflicted upon others' (DJPC 6, f. 27). Universal fellowship is a divine duty, for 'God judged that there would be insufficient provision for the preservation of his works, if he commended to each individual's care only the safety of that particular individual, without also willing that one created being should have regard for the welfare of his fellow beings, in such a way as that all might be linked in mutual harmony as if by an everlasting covenant' (DJPC 2, f. 6^v). Therefore, 'human beings should not hold themselves from anything that is of human import'. However, it is not without some measure of self-love that individuals participate in this universal fellowship. After all, man wants others to treat him the same way when he himself is in distress. There is nothing 'more useful (*utilius*) for man than his fellow man' (DJPC 6, f. 27) and, in that sense, injuries inflicted on others are regarded as injuries to oneself, so while 'striving for the goods of others we are striving for our own good' as well (DJPC 9, f. 54^v). Participating in the universal fellowship of humankind enables each individual freely to fulfil the responsibility over his own life, including the duty to give to those in need. There is no way an individual can opt out. Defining and pursuing one's choices is only possible within the framework of the community. The goal of universal fellowship is the preservation of God's works. This does not entail that each individual must be kept alive whatever the cost, or that the community should act in a paternalistic way towards its most vulnerable participants. Rather, it requires that conditions be set up in such a way that no one, by design, ends up in a situation of dependency, for man is 'free and *sui juris*' (DJPC 2, f. 10). The regime of private property does not contravene the preservation of God's works, provided its design includes some feature to protect people from living a life below subsistence level. The right of necessity is such a provision. When Grotius stated that the right of necessity does not correspond to the charitable duty of the affluent, he was not primarily saying that the rich cannot be legally forced to give to persons in extreme need. He was, rather, emphasising that the survival of the person in extreme need ultimately should not *depend* on the choice of the affluent.

23.6 Conclusion

Grotius was a man of practice. Until his imprisonment, he had been a state official and a practicing lawyer; later in life, he became the diplomatic envoy of the Swedish queen in Paris. As an experienced practitioner, he wanted his theory to yield practical results. In his theory, belligerents could find guidelines about what kind of infringements on property rights justify a just war, and what kind of infringements are allowed during war. The principle of the freedom of the seas and the right of necessity are only two practical outcomes of the theory, but there are many more. The theory is so rich that its application is not limited to early-seventeenth-century warfare. The Grotian theory of the agreement to the principle of first occupation has influenced political thought and social contractarianism from Thomas Hobbes (1588–1679), Samuel Pufendorf and John Locke onwards. Even today, thinking about global justice sometimes takes Grotius' idea of collective *dominium* of the earth as a starting point.[32]

Grotius' theory proved successful not only because it provided real answers, but also because of its methodological and theological sophistication. That Grotius' account allowed for a secularised reading does not mean that the master from Delft forgot about the theological issues at stake. Essential aspects of the property theory, such as man's freedom and autonomy, the universal fellowship of humankind or the equality of the right to take from the common what was needed to survive, are not entirely comprehensible without taking into account this theological context.

Editions and Translations of Grotius' Works Used

Mare liberum sive de iure quod Batavis competit ad Indicana commercia dissertatio (Leiden, 1609)

De Jure Belli ac Pacis Libri Tres, in quibus Jus Naturae & Gentium, item Juris Publici praecipua explicantur (Amsterdam, 1646 (=Washington, 1913))

The Rights of War and Peace, ed. R. Tuck (Indianapolis, 2005)

De veritate religionis Christianae, ed. J. Clericus (Amsterdam, 1709)

The Truth of the Christian Religion, ed. J. Clarke (London, 1829)

Inleiding tot de Hollandsche Rechtsgeleerdheid, ed. S. van Groenewegen van der Made and W. Schorer (Middelburg, 1767)

The Introduction to Dutch Jurisprudence, ed. C. Herbert (London, 1845)

Further Reading

Buckle, S., *Natural Law and the Theory of Property. Grotius to Hume* (Oxford, 1991).

Fitzmaurice, A., *Sovereignty, Property and Empire, 1500–2000* (Cambridge, 2014).

Klimchuk, D., 'Grotius on property and the right of necessity', *Journal for the History of Philosophy* 56 (2018) 239–60.

Nijman, J.E., 'Grotius' *Imago Dei* anthropology: grounding *Ius Naturae et Gentium*', in M. Koskenniemi, M. García-Salmones Rovira and R. Amorosa (eds.), *International Law and Religion. Historical and Contemporary Perspectives* (Oxford, 2017), 87–110.

Salter, J., 'Hugo Grotius: property and consent', *Political Theory* 29 (2001) 537–55.

Straumann, B., *Roman Law in the State of Nature. The Classical Foundations of Hugo Grotius' Natural Law* (Cambridge, 2015).

Tierney, B., *The Idea of Natural Rights. Studies on Natural Rights, Natural Law and Church Law, 1150–1625* (Atlanta, GA, 1997).

Tuck, R., *Natural Rights Theories. Their Origin and Development* (Cambridge, 1979).

Notes

1 S. Buckle, *Natural Law and the Theory of Property. Grotius to Hume* (Oxford, 1991), 4–7.

2 E.g. J. St. Leger, *The 'Etiamsi Daremus' of Hugo Grotius. A Study in the Origins of International Law* (Rome, 1962), 28–36.

3 F. Todescan, *Le radici teologiche del giusnaturalismo laico. Il problema della secolarizzazione nel pensiero giuridico di Ugo Grozio* (Milan, 1983), 103–11.

4 M. de Araujo, 'Hugo Grotius, contractualism, and the concept of private property: an institutionalist interpretation', *History of Philosophy Quarterly* 26 (2009) 353–71; R. Schlatter, *Private Property. The History of an Idea* (London, 1951), 130.

5 B. Straumann, *Roman Law in the State of Nature. The Classical Foundations of Hugo Grotius' Natural Law* (Cambridge, 2015), 176.

6 R. Tuck, *Natural Rights Theories. Their Origin and Development* (Cambridge, 1979), 61, 77 and 79.

7 As Straumann, *Roman Law*, 108, 188, indeed takes him to be. See R. Nozick, *Anarchy, State, and Utopia* (New York, 1974), 150–3.

8 About the term 'right of necessity' (*ius necessitatis*) see B. Wauters, 'Grotius, necessity and the sixteenth-century scholastic tradition', *Grotiana* N.S. 38 (2017) 129–47, at 133.

9 B. Tierney, *The Idea of Natural Rights. Studies on Natural Rights, Natural Law and Church Law, 1150-1625* (Atlanta, GA, 1997), 167.

10 Ibid., 120.

11 D. Klimchuk, 'Grotius on property and the right of necessity', *Journal for the History of Philosophy* 56 (2018) 239–60.

12 A. Mancilla, 'What we own before property: Hugo Grotius and the *suum*', *Grotiana* N.S. 36 (2015) 63–77, at 67.

13 J.P. Sommerville, 'Absolutism and royalism', in J.H. Burns and M. Goldie (eds.), *The Cambridge History of Political Thought, 1450-1700* (Cambridge, 1991), 347–73, at 358.

14 J. Kilcullen, 'The origin of property: Ockham, Grotius, Pufendorf, and some others', in J. Kilcullen and J. Scott (eds.), *A Translation of William of Ockham's Work of Ninety Days* (Lewiston, NY, 2001), vol. 2, 883–931, at 900.

15 I. Wyclif, *De civili dominio liber primus*, ed. R.L. Poole (London, 1885), 1.1.1–2. See also M.J. Wilks, 'Predestination, property, and power: Wyclif's theory of dominion and grace', *Studies in Church History* 2 (1965) 220–36.

16 Gen. 1.26; F. Suárez, *De opere sex dierum*, ed. M. André, *Opera Omnia* (Paris, 1856) 3.16.1–3.

17 J. Nijman, 'Grotius' *Imago Dei* anthropology: Grounding *Ius Naturae et Gentium*', in M. Koskenniemi, M. García-Salmones Rovira and R. Amorosa (eds.), *International Law and Religion. Historical and Contemporary Perspectives* (Oxford, 2017), 87–110.

18 C. Pierson, *Just Property. A History in the Latin West. Volume I: Wealth, Virtue and the Law* (Oxford, 2013), 88–9.

19 A. Fitzmaurice, *Sovereignty, Property and Empire, 1500-2000* (Cambridge, 2014), 95. For a critical appraisal of the Weberian theory on the relationship between Calvinist doctrines and industriousness, see H.J. Berman, *Law and Revolution II: The Impact of the Protestant Reformations on the Western Legal Traditions*, (Cambridge, MA and London, 2003), 24–8.

20 David Hume, *Essays. Moral, Political and Literary*, ed. E.F. Miller (Indianapolis, 1994), 268–80. See also Straumann, *Roman Law*, 185.

21 Nijman, 'Grotius' *Imago Dei* anthropology', 97–101.

22 J. Selden, *Mare clausum, seu de dominio maris libri duo* (London, 1635) 1.4.

23 I. Kant, *The Universal Doctrine of Right*, in *The Metaphysics of Morals*, ed. M. Gregor, *Practical Philosophy* (Cambridge, 1996), 405 (6.251), 411 (6.258); A. Ripstein, *Force and Freedom. Kant's Legal and Political Philosophy* (Cambridge, MA and London, 2009), 155–6.

24 R. Tuck, *Natural Rights Theories. Their Origin and Development* (Cambridge, 1979), 89.

25 Straumann, *Roman Law*, 187.

26 Ibid., 61, 77.

27 Wauters, 'Grotius, necessity', 129–47.

28 Klimchuk, 'Grotius on property', 253–4.

29 D. Recknagel, 'Das Notrecht in der grotianischen Naturrechtstheorie und seine spätscholastischen Quellen', in K. Bunge e.a. (eds.), *The Concept of Law (lex) in the Moral and Political Thought of the 'School of Salamanca'* (Leiden and Boston, 2016), 198–225.

30 S. Pufendorf, *De iure naturae et gentium* (London, 1672), 2.6.6; see also J. Salter, 'Grotius and Pufendorf on the right of necessity', *History of Political Thought* 26 (2005) 284–302, at 285–6.

31 Berman, *Law and Revolution II*, 362–9.

32 M. Risse, *On Global Justice* (Princeton and Oxford, 2012), 89–107.

The Law of Contract and Treaties 24

Paolo Astorri

24.1 Introduction

Hugo Grotius played a fundamental role in the history of contract law. He developed a first draft of the modern general theory of contract law,[1] which influenced Samuel Pufendorf (1632–94), Jean Barbeyrac (1674–1744) and the French scholars, Jean Domat (1625–95) and Robert-Joseph Pothier (1699–1772), who in turn inspired the authors of the French Civil Code.[2] Moreover, the Prussian Civil Code (*Preussisches Allgemeines Landrecht*, ALR) and the Austrian Civil Code (*Allgemeines Bürgerliches Gesetzbuch*, ABGB) followed Grotius' theory,[3] and nineteenth-century English scholars drew from Grotius together with Pufendorf, Domat and Pothier.[4] Grotius derived his thinking from a mixture of traditions on which he invested his original vision. He stood at the crossroads of Roman law and canon law; he was a passionate reader of medieval and early modern Roman-Catholic moral theological works and relied on Aristotelian, Platonic and Stoic philosophy.[5] Most of all, however, he was a humanist scholar,[6] a lawyer and a Protestant theologian.[7]

In this brief essay, we will focus on certain elements of Grotius' teachings on the laws governing contracts and treaties, as expounded in his *De jure belli ac pacis* (1625). Grotius also discusses the same topics in other writings, significantly in his *Inleidinge tot de Hollandsche rechts-geleerdheid* (1631), which here will be only sporadically mentioned. Grotius' analysis of contracts and treaties in *De jure belli ac pacis* is developed on the basis of natural law.[8] It is by referring to natural law that Grotius transforms the *jus commune*. However, the concepts and solutions he uses are often translated from the moral theological universe to his natural law system.[9] The resulting contract doctrine still contains many Christian references, although Grotius' treatise does not intend to instruct men about their salvation, but to promote their peaceful coexistence (DJBP 1.1.1).

The starting point of Grotius' analysis is the doctrine of free will, which, in the scholastic theology, was related to man's salvation. According to

Aristotelian-Thomistic philosophy, man is free to carry out actions that move him away or towards God. Every action is directed towards an end, which is itself a means to man's ultimate end.[10] The immediate end of a contract is determined by the will of the parties, but a contract is also a means to their ultimate end, their union with God. For this reason, compliance with legal rules leads man to gain eternal salvation, while a breach of them leads him to the loss of eternal salvation. This salvific dimension is no longer present in the Grotian treatment of contracts and treaties, which tends to adopt a more secular focus in the maintenance of social order and the protection of the parties' rights.[11]

Grotius dedicates two chapters to contract law in Book 2 of *De jure belli ac pacis*: chapter 11 concerns promises, while chapter 12 addresses issues concerning contracts. Promise and contract are concepts deriving from different traditions. 'Promise' is the standard term used by Roman-Catholic moral theologians and canonists to identify bare agreements, which were enforceable in the court of conscience.[12] The moral rule 'you shall not lie' was the starting point for their reflections. This rule did not distinguish between a sworn promise, a simple promise and a promise with legal requirements.[13] In the eyes of God, the breach of an oath and the breach of a promise are both sins.[14] On the other hand, the Roman jurists used 'contract' as a key term to identify an agreement provided with objective elements necessary to produce legal effects. In Roman law, naked pacts, pacts without the formal requirements for having binding effect, were not actionable.[15] Grotius sought to harmonise these traditions using natural law as a benchmark for his evaluation. Both the treatment of promises and contracts forms the basis for his analysis of treaties, which is mainly addressed in Book 2, chapter 15.

24.2 On Promises

24.2.1 Binding Promises

Grotius has been rightly labelled 'the forerunner of modern consensualism'.[16] In his *Inleidinge*,[17] he defines a promise as a voluntary act, by which the promisor promises something to the promisee, with the intention that the latter accepts and acquires a right against the promisor (IHR 3.1.10). Grotius also declares that this principle is founded on the free power of men over their actions. As men have power over their properties, so they can also transfer their ownership by delivery or consent (IHR 3.1.11). This consensualist approach is restated and reinforced in *De jure belli ac pacis*. In the *Prolegomena*, Grotius affirms that the obligation to fulfil promises derives from natural sociability (DJBP Prol. 8) and is the foundation of the civil laws (DJBP Prol. 16). Then, at the beginning of his chapter dedicated to promises, Grotius strenuously defends the natural obligation to keep promises, while countering the opinion of François Connan (1508–51). Connan, a French erudite jurist, held that a simple agreement is not binding if it does not include a reciprocal exchange ($\sigma\upsilon\nu\acute{\alpha}\lambda\lambda\alpha\gamma\mu\alpha$ – *synallagma*).[18] In other words, a promise that contains an obligation only for one of the parties and not for the other one – who does not promise – would not be binding under natural law. Connan's theory followed the road inaugurated by the Spanish scholastic theologian, Cajetan (Thomas de Vio, 1469–1534), who also assumed that unilateral promises are only morally – and not legally – binding, and referred to Roman law, which required formal elements to establish binding effects for agreements.[19]

Grotius confutes Connan's thesis with a number of arguments. First, he writes, from Connan's opinion it would follow that agreements between kings and people of different nations would have no binding force so long as no part of such agreements had been carried out. Agreements between states would therefore be invalid. Then, Grotius continues, no reason can be found why laws, which are a sort of common agreement between the people of a land, could add to the agreement an obligation for people who do not want that obligation. It is not the civil law that makes agreements binding, but the will of the parties (DJBP 2.11.1). Furthermore, he argues, property rights can be transferred by an act of will, which is sufficiently declared. Natural law does not require the delivery of the thing, but property rights can be transferred with a declared act of will. The delivery of the thing is only a requirement imposed by civil law (DJBP 2.6.1). If men have equal right over their actions and properties, they should be able to transfer their rights as a way to transfer ownership – which is less than the acquisition of the right of property itself – or the right to do something. Finally, Grotius insists on the binding nature of agreements without a reciprocal obligation by quoting examples taken from a number of different sources such as the *Digest*, Cicero, Horatius and Platonic philosophy. In substance, keeping faith is a duty corresponding to nature, human fidelity, moral necessity and justice (DJBP 2.11.1).

Grotius concludes that the fact that the Roman jurists did not consider naked pacts to be enforceable derives from the tradition of Roman law, which introduced the stipulation (*stipulatio*) as a sign of a deliberate intention. As Jørgensen and Deroussin have remarked, he seems not to have correctly interpreted the Roman law teachings on the *stipulatio,* because he considers this only a proof of the intention to be legally bound.[20] For natural law, the deliberate intention can be expressed by other signs besides the stipulation. The deliberate intention is the key element that provides the force of an obligation, and without intent there is no obligation (DJBP 2.11.4). The conclusion of this discussion is that, for Grotius, an accepted promise can produce, not only a moral obligation, but also a legal obligation that is perfectly actionable in the civil courts.

In order to delimit which statements are suitable to transfer property rights, Grotius distinguishes three types of statements.[21] The first type is a statement (*assertio*) that expresses an intention concerning the future. This statement might express an opinion, but does not create a binding agreement. Grotius explains that it requests the truth of the opinion, but not the perseverance of the utterer. In fact, the human mind has the right to change its opinion (DJBP 2.11.2). The second type of statement (*pollicitatio*) is based on the intention to be bound, but it gives no right to the other party. In many cases, Grotius continues, this statement could create a moral obligation, but no right is transferred, as it happens in statements pronounced for gratitude or for mercy (DJBP 2.11.3).

The third type of statement is a perfect promise (*perfecta promissio*). This is a statement by which the utterer adds an external sign to his intention to transfer a property right to another person. The promisor wants to transfer a right and, by his declaration, they assume an obligation. Through this statement, Grotius sustains, we can alienate a thing – i.e. promises to give – or a portion of our personal freedom of action – i.e. promises to perform. The intention triggers the obligation. Indeed, civil law might require certain formalities, but, for natural law, the intention is fundamental for creating the bond (DJBP 2.4.3, 2.6.1). As Decock has suggested, Grotius might have found inspiration in the work of the Leuven theologian, Leonard Lessius (1554–1623), who also defended this solution. Then, an outward sign is necessary, Grotius underscores, because an internal act cannot transfer a right. Human nature requires the act to be declared, because this is the only way it could be recognised by others (DJBP 2.4.3). This issue had also been lavishly discussed by moral theologians.[22]

A perfect promise is not suitable to transfer a right without its acceptance. By requiring acceptance by the promisee, Grotius is adopting the result of a debate that involved the most learned scholastic theologians and canonists. Indeed, he rejects the position of Luis de Molina (1535–1600), who had upheld that a promise is also binding without acceptance (DJBP 2.11.14). To Molina, the fact that Roman law[23] considered the promises to the state valid, without acceptance, was a proof that acceptance is not a requirement of natural law. As Decock has noticed, it is by following Lessius that Grotius reaches the conclusion that Roman law does not say that a promise is binding before acceptance, but only aims to forbid the revocation of the promise at any time.[24] This is specifically an effect stated by civil law, but, for natural law, the promisor can always revoke his promise before the acceptance of the promisee. Since the right of property has not yet been transferred, the promisor can annul his promise. This conclusion was reaffirmed by Pufendorf and became popular among the proponents of the Modern School of Natural Law.[25]

The binding effect of accepted promises is justified by a complex argument. According to Scripture, God is a faithful God and cannot deny Himself.[26] Therefore, Grotius affirms that God would go against His nature if He would not perform what He promised. The binding of promises stems from the immutable nature of justice, which is common to God and all the creatures that have the use of reason (DJBP 2.11.4). According to patristic and scholastic theology, man was created in the *image of God* and retained certain attributes after the introduction of original sin, such as the use of reason, which were in common between God and man.[27] On this basis, Thomas Aquinas (c. 1225–74) conceived of natural law as participation of all rational creatures in God's eternal law.[28] For Grotius, man and God share the same notion of immutable justice, according to which promises must be observed.

24.2.2 The Validity of the Perfect Promise

For the validity of the perfect promise, natural law requires three conditions: the adequate use of reason, the absence of error or fraud and the lawfulness of the subject matter. Concerning the first requirement, Grotius maintains that the promises of madmen, idiots and children are void, while the promises of minors can be valid, if they have the use of reason. The minimal age to determine the use of reason cannot be fixed absolutely, but it must be derived from 'the daily acts of the minors' and from what commonly occurs in a certain region. Agreements made within the jurisdiction of a certain state have to observe the rules with regards age stipulated by the civil law of that state. For agreements made on the sea, on a desert island or by letters (DJBP 2.11.5).

Grotius begins his discourse on error by referring to a number of distinctions, such as whether an error pertains to the substance of a thing or not, whether the deceit has been essential for the conclusion of the contract or not, whether the other party participated in the deceit or not and, finally, whether the agreement was an act of good faith or strict law. These distinctions derive from Roman law. The Roman law of sale distinguished between a mistake related to the substance of the agreement and a mistake related to a quality. If the mistake concerned the substance, the agreement was invalid; if it concerned only an accident, the agreement was valid, but the damaged party had a right to compensation.[29] Furthermore, Roman law distinguished between contracts of good faith (*bonae fidei*) and contracts of strict law (*stricti iuris*). Contracts of strict law were not automatically void in case of deceit, but the offended party could use the remedies of the *exceptio doli* and of the *actio de dolo*. Instead, contracts of good faith were immediately void. This classification was combined with the distinction between a deceit that had been essential for the conclusion of the agreement (*dolus causam dans contractui*) and a deceit that had not been essential (*dolus incidens contractui*).[30]

Grotius argues that the majority of these distinctions are not entirely true or accurate. To prove that they do not comply with natural truth, he puts forward the following reasoning. As a law does not obtain any force if it is based on a presumption of a certain fact, and this fact is not really occurring, so a promise that is based on the presumption of a certain fact, which does not actually occur, does not have binding effect. Indeed, the promisor only consented to the promise under a certain condition that is not met (DJBP 2.11.6). As Gordley has shown, this solution rests on the works of Molina and Lessius, and – in the last instance – on the structure laid down by Aquinas himself. Following Aristotle, Aquinas stated that ignorance has an impact on man's choice when it determines the will, so that a man would not have made such a choice if he were informed of a certain element. Aquinas compared the application of a law with the enforcement of a promise. As a law is not binding under particular circumstances determined by the lawmaker, so a promise is not binding under circumstances under which one would have not agreed to be bound. Grotius adopts the same argument, even though he uses the concept of presumption.[31]

A promise affected by error or fraud is not binding, but there are a couple of caveats. First, if the promisor was careless in investigating the matter or in expressing their thought and, by doing this, they damaged the other, they will be bound to compensate those who suffered for their fault. This bond does not derive from the promise, but from the damage. As Feenstra has noticed, Grotius underscores that this is a fault-based liability, while Lessius did not specify this point.[32] Second, if the promise was not based on the error, the promise will be valid. The error, in other words, must pertain to the substance of the agreement. However, if the promisee caused the error by fraud, they will have to pay for the damages the promisor suffered because of the error (DJBP 2.11.6). As for Lessius, the responsibility of the party only arises if they, and not a third person, caused the damage.[33] Indeed, it is the damage and not the promise that is the source of the obligation.

Grotius deals with the problem of duress (*metus*) by following the lead of the majority of neo-scholastics. He starts again by reporting that several distinctions are usually made in the discussion of duress, such as whether the duress was strong enough to interfere in the decision, whether the duress was just or not, the categories of persons who exercised the duress and, finally, between gratuitous acts and burdensome acts. Then, Grotius states that he accepts the opinion of those – he quotes the Catholic theologian, Sylvester Mazzolini (1456–1523) – according to whom a person is bound to his promise made under duress. In this case, indeed, consent is not based on a presumption of a certain fact, as with regard to the person in error, but it is expressed in an absolute way. Grotius refers here to Aristotle, citing the example of the man who throws his property overboard because he fears shipwreck, but who would wish to save it under the condition there was no danger of shipwreck.[34] Considering the circumstances of the place and time, Grotius comments, this man is willing to risk losing his property (DJBP 2.11.7). For this reason, he concludes that the consent is not vitiated and the promise is binding.

However, Grotius points out, if the person to whom the promise was made provoked an unjust duress, then the promisee is bound to release the promisor, not because of the promise, which was valid, but for the damage they caused (DJBP 2.11.7). As Gordley has evidenced, this is plainly the solution Molina and Lessius found to the problem of oaths extorted by duress. The promisor really consented, even if it was under duress. But the promisee damaged him by making a threat. For this reason, the promisor had the right to choose whether to sustain the agreement or abandon it.[35] The reason of this obligation is the damage, while the promise itself is valid because consent had been expressed.

In addition to the subjective requirement of free will, a promise requires the power of the promisor to be bound and the lawfulness of the subject matter in order to be valid under natural law. Thus, for Grotius, if the promisor does not have the power to be bound at the moment of the promise, the promise will not be valid until they acquire such a power (DJBP 2.11.8). If the thing is not in the possession of the promisor at the time of the promise, but will be in the future, Grotius holds that the validity of the promise will be suspended and the promise ought to be interpreted as conditional to the thing coming within the power of the promisor. But, if the condition implies his power to obtain it, the promisor will be bound to do whatever is morally right to fulfil the promise. Grotius applies here his previous conclusions on the binding force of the perfect promise. He alludes to the case of promises of future marriages, by a man or a woman who is already married, or the promises made by minors. A man is bound by his promise, and therefore natural law obliges him to fulfil the promise, even though the civil law would invalidate these promises (DJBP 2.11.8).

A promise is also invalid if the subject matter is morally wrong by nature, as in the case of a homicide. Grotius does not clarify what he means by saying that a promise is morally wrong by nature. From his definition of natural law, we can infer that it is an act forbidden by God as the author of nature (DJBP 1.1.10). Grotius does not allude to sinful acts, as the moral theologians did. Yet, he is somehow inspired by the theologians, because he adds that, when the morally wrong action is ended, the promise is binding. This thesis circulated in the ambit of neo-scholastics and was defended by Lessius.[36] The effectiveness of the promise would be suspended during the time of the crime, but when the criminal activity is over, the obligation created by the promise would be effective (DJBP 2.11.9). Grotius justifies his conclusion by referring to the prodigal donation and to the biblical example of Tamar in Genesis 38. He insinuates that, once the prodigal donation has been made, there is no more corruption (*vitiositas*), because the things remain with the beneficiary without any vice (DJBP 2.11.9). In the scholastic world, prodigality was a sin and only a few theologians, such as Lessius, defended the contrary opinion. Grotius draws upon Lessius, but avoids the use of the theological concept of 'sin'. As a consequence, the immorality of the action is no longer described with reference to a theological perspective, but to a 'secular' natural law system.

24.2.3 Promises towards a Third Beneficiary

As it appears, Grotius adopts many solutions from the neo-scholastics. However, he gives proof of his original thinking with regards to the so-called contracts for third-party beneficiaries. In Roman law, a principle stated that nobody could demand the execution of a formal promise for the benefit of a third party. A number of exceptions were, however, granted. For example, the agreement to transfer a right to a third beneficiary was allowed only if the promisee had an actionable interest.[37] Another instance of third-party benefit concerned a father who acquired a right through his son or a master through his slave.[38] These exceptions were extended by medieval glossators, but still the principle remained. The canonists, on the other hand, reasoned in a different way. The contract directed towards a third beneficiary produced a natural law obligation.[39] If this obligation was guaranteed by an oath, it could have been actionable in the canon law courts through a remedy called *denunciatio evangelica*. Therefore, by way of an oath, the canonists granted some forms of protection to the third party.[40]

Grotius lays out the fundamental elements towards the modern theory of third-party beneficiary contracts. As Dondorp, Hallebeek, Vogenauer and Waelkens have recently evidenced, he starts from the distinctions elaborated by the neo-scholastics and the tradition of the *jus commune* as enforced in the Dutch courts, but goes beyond this.[41] Grotius distinguishes between the promises made to the promisor, from which the third party will obtain something, and the promises made directly to the third person. In the first case, the promisor promised to the promisee that a right will be conferred to a third beneficiary and the promisee has the right to claim that this right will effectively be given to the third party. This occurs regardless of a particular financial interest of the promisee in the performance for the third party, which the Roman jurists considered as a prerequisite for this type of action. According to natural law, the promisee acquires the right to accept that the right to obtain the performance will be given to a third beneficiary, who can accept or refuse it. To Grotius, this is not against natural law and is congruent with the words of the promise (DJBP 2.11.18). The necessity of the personal interest of the promisee imposed by Roman law is overcome. The rule from natural law establishing a form of respect towards the neighbour, deriving from natural sociability, could possibly have suggested to Grotius that any person can stipulate an agreement for the benefit of a third party.[42]

In the second case, the question turns on whether the promisee has the power to accept the promise. If there is a special mandate to accept, the third person acquires the right. Whoever has received a mandate can accept for the third person. If there is no mandate, the promisor cannot revoke his promise until the promisee has accepted it. The acceptance of the promise, not the beneficiary, is binding for the promisor, but not for the beneficiary, because the promisee does not have a mandate. This is a special bond, Grotius explains, because it is based on good faith. If the promisor revokes his promise, they do not go against the right of anyone, but simply against good faith (DJBP 2.11.18).

24.3 On Contracts

24.3.1 Definition and Classification

To Grotius, a contract is any act destined to the utility of the other party, with the exception of merely beneficial acts (DJBP 2.12.7). Such a definition centres on two elements: the utility or benefit for the other party – Grotius only takes into consideration these types of acts – and the reciprocity of the obligation. The first element seems to characterise contracts as acts directed to the benefit of the other party and not for the sake of personal gain. The second element excludes *merely* beneficial acts, which are *simple* (non-mixed) acts that do not involve a mutual obligation, such as a donation. Apart from the *merely* beneficial acts, many other human acts can be classified as contracts. Simple acts can be merely beneficial, but also entail a reciprocal obligation. Examples of these acts are Roman law contracts of loan for use (*commodatum*), deposit and mandate (DJBP 2.12.2). These contracts are gratuitous, but imply a reciprocal obligation. To Grotius, a merely beneficial act is not a contract, but a beneficial act with a reciprocal obligation is a contract. Furthermore, simple acts can also require an exchange. These acts 'by way of exchange' or 'permutorial' acts (*actus permutatorii*) are intended to benefit the other party because of a benefit received in return. In this category, Grotius includes Roman law nominate and innominate contracts, as well as the agreements the Roman jurists provided with a remedy such as 'I give that you may give, I do that you may do, I do that you may give' (DJBP 2.12.3). In these acts, the parties remain separate, while other reciprocal acts lead to a communion of interests, as in a partnership (DJBP 2.12.4).

Contracts can be *simple* acts, but also *mixed* acts. For Grotius, these acts can be mixed because of the principal act or because of an accessory act. The first category concerns, for instance, a donation mixed with a sale, which occurs when the buyer purchases a thing for a price higher than its worth. This operation could be better understood by looking at the just price theory, formulated in the context of Catholic moral literature and restated by Grotius. According to this theory, a good cannot be sold for more than its market value. But, part of the excessive price could be justified by a sale, and part by a donation; in this way, this agreement would be licit. Grotius, however, also includes in this category a partnership, where one of the parties contributes by giving services and money and another only by giving money (DJBP 2.12.5). Finally, mixed acts by the addition of an accessory act are also to be considered as contracts. The accessory act is added to the original agreement because of gratuity and so transforms the simple act into a mixed act, as for instance by giving a security or a pledge (DJBP 2.12.6).

By nature, contracts must be regulated by equality, which stipulates that the party who has obtained less because of an inequality shall have a right of action (DJBP 2.12.8). Grotius carries on a tradition that harks back to Aristotelian-Thomistic commutative justice cultivated by medieval and early modern scholastics and Protestants, but he goes further by proposing a broader concept of equality. To Grotius, equality concerns several dimensions of the contract: acts preceding the conclusion of a contract, the principal act and the subject matter of the agreement. Moreover, the horizon of Grotius' doctrine of equality is no longer the court of conscience, but his natural law system. Equality is not imposed by the seventh commandment as it is for some Roman-Catholic and Lutheran theologians; it is not even imposed by the Christian tradition, Roman law or other sources used by Catholic moral theologians,[43] but simply by natural law.

24.3.2 Equality Concerning the Acts Preceding the Conclusion of a Contract

First of all, equality involves the duty to inform the other contracting party about known defects to goods. Grotius writes that natural law sets out this obligation because there is a closer union between the contracting parties than among men in general human society. This argument recalls Aristotle's justification of justice in exchange as recycled by some neo-scholastics.[44] Furthermore, as the references to Ambrosius and Lactantius reveal, this duty derives from the regulation of the contract of sale (DJBP 2.12.9). It is, in fact, a generalisation of an obligation formulated for this contract.

The same duty does not hold regarding the circumstances that have no direct connection with the good that is the subject matter of the contract. To Grotius, this information is not demanded by natural justice, but only by the rule of charity (DJBP 2.12.9). He evokes the famous case of the merchant of Rhodes, highly discussed in the scholastic moral theological literature.[45] This case is about a merchant who knows that the price of his goods will decrease, because other merchants will begin selling the same goods. Following the neo-scholastics, Grotius contends that not revealing this information would go against charity, but not against justice.

24.3.3 Equality Concerning the Principal Act

Equality is also required with regards to the main contractual obligations: the parties cannot demand more than what is just. Grotius maintains that this equality rarely concerns beneficial contracts, because if someone accepts a certain recompense for a mandate or a deposit, the contract becomes mixed, partly gratuitous and partly by way of exchange. However, in all contracts requiring an exchange, equality must be respected. If one of the parties promises more than what it is just, it shall not be presumed that this is a donation. Whatever the parties promise or give is to be believed as equal to the performance that is received, and due because of this equality (DJBP 2.12.11). The official rule is, indeed, that the parties shall promise according to equality and only a manifest declaration to the contrary can alter this interpretation. By making this statement, Grotius is probably protecting the parties against a possible violation of the precept of equality.[46] Indeed, the consequence of a breach of equality is a kind of robbery, as he states, quoting John Chrysostom, the writer of

Isidore's life and the Hebrew laws: 'You shall not oppress one another'[47] (DJBP 2.12.11).

24.3.4 Equality Concerning the Subject Matter of a Contract

As a closing point on the treatment of equality in contracts requiring an exchange, Grotius contends that one must return the excess profit if a transaction resulted in unequal gain, even if no more has been pretended than what was due. This applied also in case there was no fault involved (DJBP 2.12.12). In general terms, these teachings appear to be analogous to the doctrine of restitution promoted by both Catholic and Protestant theologians. A similar remedy existed in Roman law, the so-called *laesio enormis*, but in this case the compensation was limited to half of the just price in order to avoid an excessive number of litigations.[48]

Grotius recalls this legislation, but adds that those who are not subject to civil law should follow what is commanded by right reason. The same should be done by those who are subject to civil law, if the subject matter is about 'what is lawful and honourable' and if the law does not give or remove a right (DJBP 2.12.12). Grotius distinguishes between what Roman law establishes and what right reason suggests. He seeks a sort of compromise between restitution operated in the court of conscience and the *laesio enormis* practiced in the civil courts. This compromise is based on an unclarified 'right reason', which is said to induce the parties to offer restitution.

24.3.5 Equality in Beneficial Contracts

Equality in *beneficial* contracts is different from the equality requested in contracts *by way of an exchange*, because it derives from the supporting nature of the agreement and from the fact that the benefactor should not receive any damage from his beneficence. For instance, the mandatary ought to be indemnified from all charges and losses incurred through the execution of the contract of mandate. The recipient of a thing in a loan for use should also make good anything that is lost, because of a contractual obligation, with the exception of the case wherein the thing would equally have perished if it were in the hands of the proprietor. Instead, in a gratuitous deposit, the recipient will not be held responsible for the loss of the thing, because they did not gain any benefits from the contract. Grotius concludes that these rules are all to be found in Roman law, but they derive from natural equity and can also be found among other nations (DJBP 2.12.13).

24.3.6 Price of Goods and Monopolies

The doctrine of equality postulates that the parties must agree on the price of the goods, which has to correspond with a determinate value. Following a tradition that harks back to Aristotle,[49] Grotius affirms that the price of goods should be estimated on the basis of need. Need is, however, not the only criterion, as scarcity and costs should also be considered. Quoting a number of authorities such as Seneca, the jurist Paul and Aristotle, Grotius explains that the price of a thing should correspond to the customary price at a determined place, except when the laws have fixed another price (DJBP 2.12.14). In other words, the *just* price is the market price or the price established by public authority, as it was also held in medieval, neo-scholastic and Protestant traditions.

Among the neo-scholastic theologians, the logical consequence of this theory of price was that private monopolies should be forbidden, because they altered the market price for the benefit of a few people. Conversely, public monopolies could be admitted for a just cause. The neo-scholastics believed that public authority could establish the price, determined by need and scarcity as according to the market.[50] Similarly, Grotius opines that, under natural law, not all monopolies are forbidden; indeed, public authority can admit them for a just cause. Moreover, he claims that only certain types of private monopolies are against natural law, if the price is unjust, while others are only against charity. For instance, when the sellers make an agreement to sell their goods at a price higher than the current price, or by fraud or violence they hinder the supply of goods to be imported, or when they acquire all the goods so that they can sell at a price that is unjust, they are provoking damage and are obliged to repair it. However, if in any other way they hinder the importation of goods, or buy all the goods so that they can sell them at a higher price, but not an unjust one, they are acting against charity, but they do not violate anyone's rights (DJBP 2.12.16). As before when discussing the merchant of Rhodes, Grotius follows the neo-scholastics in distinguishing between justice and charity.[51]

24.4 On Treaties

24.4.1 Definition and Classification

Grotius' teachings on the law of treaties reflect those on agreements in general, but there are some differences. Grotius begins by a systematic analysis of the type of agreements made by nations. Referring to Ulpian, he distinguishes between private and public agreements.[52] Public agreements are those that are made by public authority, either by the sovereign or by a subordinate (DJBP 2.15.1). Public agreements can then be divided into treaties (*foedera*) and *sponsiones* (DJBP 2.15.2). A treaty is made by the sovereign authority or by someone who has the power given by public authority and is binding on the people subjected to that authority. An agreement that is made by people who do not have this power is a *sponsio* (DJBP 2.15.3).

Treaties can be divided into those that only include provisions by natural law and others that add other types of provisions. The first type is generally concluded at the end of a war, but the category also includes treaties for guest friendship and commerce, which are again regulated by natural law (DJBP 2.15.5). The treaties that add something to natural law can be equal or not equal. Grotius restates here the principle of contractual equality expressed before, but with a specific meaning. Indeed, equal treaties are those that have the same conditions for both parties. These are treaties of peace or alliance. Treaties of peace are, for instance, treaties made for returning prisoners or for mutual security. Treaties of alliance impose equal conditions concerning commerce, the sharing of the expenses of war or other matters (DJBP 2.15.6).

Grotius also portrays treaties with unequal terms, but, despite the inequality, he does not condemn them. As Van Hulle suggested, one of the reasons might be that he wanted to defend the treaty practice of the Dutch in the Indies, which included such terms.[53] Treaties with unequal terms are concluded between parties of different rank and are distinguished into two classes: treaties that provide unequal terms for the stronger party and treaties that provide unequal terms for the weaker party. The former category comprises treatises where assistance is promised, but not required in return. The second category concerns treaties where the stronger party makes an imposition on the weaker party. These treaties can diminish the sovereignty of the weaker power. Treaties that diminish sovereign power can provide a clause of conditional surrender, save when this clause transfers the whole of a nation's sovereign power. Unequal treaties without diminution of sovereign power can impose permanent or temporary burdens. Temporary burdens could be the payment of an indemnity, the destruction of fortifications or the giving of hostages or ships. Permanent burdens include the acknowledgement of a duty to render honour to the other sovereign power (DJBP 2.15.7).

24.4.2 Treaties with Infidels

Grotius addresses a number of special questions with regards to treaties. Here we briefly report the issue of the confessional allegiance of the parties.[54] The seventeenth century was a period of confessional tensions. The problem of agreements between Christians and infidels had been long and widely debated.[55] Several Protestant authors argued that only certain types of agreements, such as those concerning boundaries, were permitted, while others even refused the possibility of alliances among Protestants from different confessions.[56] On the opposite side, Grotius holds that, under natural law, agreements with infidels are valid, as this law is common to all men and does not tolerate discrimination based on divine law. The real issue, he writes, is whether these agreements are lawful under divine law. Grotius refers to the debates between theologians and jurists and mentions Oldradus de Ponte (d. 1335) and Tiberio Deciani (1509–82; DJBP 2.15.8).

Grotius examines the question under the Old Testament and the New Testament. He looks at the example of treaties made by Abraham and Isaac with Abimelek, and Jacob with Laban before the establishment of Mosaic law. Then, he argues, Mosaic law did not prohibit agreements with infidels, as the Jews were forbidden to abhor the Egyptians, who were undoubtedly infidels. Treaties for commerce or reciprocal advantage were not banned either, as is demonstrated by the examples of the treaties of David and Solomon with Hiram. Indeed, the law of Moses did not forbid the Jews to do benefits to strangers (DJBP 2.15.9).[57] The law of the Gospel, Grotius continues, does not change what was established by the Old Testament, but encourages Christians to conclude such treaties with infidels. The example of God, who gives sun both to the just and the unjust and sends his rain to the righteous and the wicked, makes clear that every man may benefit from good actions by Christians. Certainly, Grotius points out, good actions should consider in a special way the people of the same religion, but this does not overhaul the precept that one should do good to all men (DJBP 2.15.10).

In conclusion, not only natural law, but also divine law, allows the stipulation of treaties between Christians and infidels. Despite his focus on natural law, Grotius also investigates the moral justification of these agreements according to divine law.[58]

24.5 Conclusion

As previous studies have evidenced, for the construction of his doctrine of contract, Grotius drew extensively on Catholic moral theological works and transferred concepts and solutions borrowed from there into his theory of natural law. The starting point of Grotius' analysis is the doctrine of free will, which, in the scholastic theology, was related to human salvation. For scholastics, compliance or non-compliance with contract obligations and contract law could lead to eternal salvation, or damnation. This connection with human salvation is no longer included in the Grotian vision on contract law.

Although Grotius' theory of contract law derives from moral theology, it is set in the perspective of his 'secular' natural law system. Salvation is not an explicit matter of concern; the focus is on peaceful coexistence among humans. Grotius' natural law system tends, therefore, to eliminate religious elements. The unlawfulness of the promise is not described by referring to 'sins', but to acts morally wrong according to nature. Contractual equality is imposed by natural law and not by Scripture or Christian tradition. While natural law commands that one avoids what is unjust, it does not recommend charity, as evidenced by the cases of the merchant of Rhodes and private monopolies. When choosing between *laesio enormis* from Roman law and the Christian doctrine of restitution, Grotius takes refuge in the concept of *right reason*, which would suggest applying the latter remedy.

On the other hand, the theory Grotius presents is not fully detached from Christian references. For instance, he draws on Scripture to justify the binding force of perfect promises, to sanction the breach of equality and to admit the lawfulness of treaties with infidels. In the final analysis, therefore, Grotius' teachings on the laws governing contracts and treaties are still based on Christian morality, but are not interpreted from the Catholic or the Protestant angle. They assume a neutral position,[59] which might be condensed in the reciprocal respect in human relationships and the protection of individual rights. The morality of contract law is no longer conceived on the basis of man's salvation, but for the sake of conserving men's lives. Contract law is, thus, divorced from soteriology and only retains an immanent dimension.

Further Reading

Augé, G., 'Le contrat et l'évolution du consensualisme chez Grotius', *Archives de Philosophie du Droit* 13 (1968) 99–114.

Decock, W., *Theologians and Contract law: The Moral Transformation of the Ius Commune (ca. 1500-1650)* (Leiden and Boston, 2013).

Deroussin, D., *Histoire du droit des obligations* (Paris, 2012).

Diesselhorst, M., *Die Lehre des Hugo Grotius vom Versprechern* (Köln, 1959).

Dondorp, H., and J. Hallebeek, 'Grotius' doctrine on "adquisitio obligationis per alterum" and its roots in the legal past of Europe', in O. Condorelli (ed.), *Panta rei. Studi dedicati a Manlio Bellomo* (Rome, 2003), vol. 2, 205–44.

Gordley, J., *The Philosophical Origins of Modern Contract Doctrine* (Oxford, 1992).

Jørgensen, S., 'Grotius's doctrine of contract', *Scandinavian Studies in Law* 13 (1969) 109–25, reprinted in *Values and Law: Ideas, Principles and Rules* (København, 1978), 83–101.

Zimmermann, R., *The Law of Obligations: Roman Foundations of the Civilian Tradition* (Oxford, 1996).

Notes

1 M. Diesselhorst, *Die Lehre des Hugo Grotius vom Versprechern* (Köln, 1959); S. Jørgensen, 'Grotius's doctrine of contract', *Scandinavian Studies in Law* 13 (1969) 109–15, reprinted in *Values and Law: Ideas, Principles and Rules,* (København, 1978), 83–101.

2 J. Gordley, *The Philosophical Origins of Modern Contract Doctrine* (Oxford, 1992), 71.

3 A. Diurni and D. Henrich, *Percorsi europei di diritto privato e comparato* (Milan, 2006), 144–6.

4 R. Zimmermann, *The Law of Obligations: Roman Foundations of the Civilian Tradition* (Oxford, 1996), 568–71.

5 G. Augé, 'Le contrat et l'évolution du consensualisme chez Grotius', *Archives de Philosophie du Droit* 13 (1968) 99–114, 113. In general see B. Straumann, *Roman Law in the State of Nature. The Classical Foundations of Hugo Grotius' Natural Law* (Cambridge, 2015).

6 This aspect is pointed out by R. Lesaffer, *European Legal History: A Cultural and Political Perspective* (Cambridge, 2009), 360–1.

7 For the theological roots of Grotius' thought see F. Todescan, *Il problema della secolarizzazione nel pensiero giuridico di Ugo Grozio* (Milan, 1983). See also J. W. Oosterhuis, 'Hugo Grotius', in W. Decock and J.W. Oosterhuis (eds.), *Great Christian Jurists in the Low Countries* (Cambridge, forthcoming).

8 K.P. Nanz, *Die Entstehung des allgemeinen Vertragsbegriffs im 16. bis 18. Jahrhundert* (Munich, 1985), 140.

9 See in general T. Duve, 'Kanonisches Recht und die Ausbildung allgemeiner Vertragslehren in der Spanischen Spätscholastik', in O. Condorelli, F. Roumy and M. Schmoeckel (eds.), *Der Einfluss der Kanonistik auf die europäische Rechtskultur* (Vienna, 2015), vol. 1, 389–408, 389–90.

10 Gordley, *Philosophical Origins*, 21–3.

11 For a general illustration of Grotius' natural law concept see K. Haakonssen, 'Early modern natural law theories', in G. Duke and R.P. George (eds.), *The Cambridge Companion to Natural Law Jurisprudence* (Cambridge, 2017), 76–102, 80–81.

12 M. Schmoeckel, 'Beichtstuhljurisprudenz', in *Handwörterbuch zur deutschen Rechtsgeschichte (HRG)* (Berlin, 2005), vol. 1, 505–8; J. Goering, 'The internal forum and the literature of penance and confession', in W. Hartmann and K. Pennington (eds.), *The History of Medieval Canon Law in the Classical Period, 1140–1234: From Gratian to the decretals of Pope Gregory IX* (Washington, DC, 2008), 379–428.

13 P. Bellini, *L'obbligazione da promessa con oggetto temporale nel sistema canonistico classico: con particolare riferimento ai secoli XII e XIII* (Milan, 1964), 43–7.

14 C.22 q.5 c.12.

15 Zimmermann, *Law of Obligations*, 508.

16 Augé, 'Contrat', 114.

17 On Grotius' contract doctrine in the *Inleidinge* see I. Birocchi, 'La questione dei patti nella dottrina tedesca dell'Usus modernus', in J. Barton (ed.), *Towards a General Law of Contract* (Berlin, 1990), 139–95, 139 note 20 and 153; R. Feenstra, 'Pact and contract in the Low Countries from the 16th to the 18th century', in ibid., 196–213, 197 and 205; U. Petronio, 'Sinallagma e analisi strutturale dei contratti all'origine del sistema contrattuale moderno', in ibid., 215–47, 215 note 20 and 240; R. Zimmermann, 'Roman-Dutch jurisprudence and its contribution to European private law', *Tulane. Law Review* 66 (1991–2), 1685–1721, 1692.

18 Diesselhorst, *Lehre des Hugo Grotius vom Versprechen*, 31–4; Petronio, 'Sinallagma e analisi strutturale', 228–36; I. Birocchi, *Causa e categoria generale*

del contratto. Un problema dogmatico nella cultura privatistica dell'età moderna. I Il cinquecento (Turin, 1997), 95–136.

19 Gordley, *Philosophical Origins*, 73; Birocchi, *Causa e categoria*, 120.

20 Jørgensen, 'Grotius's doctrine of contract', 111; D. Deroussin, *Histoire du droit des obligations* (Paris, 2012), 170.

21 For the reception of this doctrine see: P. Astorri, 'Grotius's contract theory in the works of his German commentators: first explorations', *Grotiana* N.S. 41 (2020), 88–107; S. Koch, 'Grotius's Impact on the Scandinavian theory of contract law', *Grotiana* N.S. 41 (2020), 59–87.

22 W. Decock, *Theologians and Contract Law: The Moral Transformation of the Ius Commune (ca. 1500–1650)* (Leiden and Boston, 2013), 210–11; 182–7; For an in-depth discussion of Lessius see W. Decock, *Le Marché du mérite. Penser le droit et économie avec Léonard Lessius* (Brussels, 2019).

23 D. 50.12.

24 Decock, *Theologians and Contract Law*, 210.

25 F. Wieacker, 'Die vertragliche Obligation bei den Klassikern des Vernunftrechts', in G. Stratenwerth *et alii* (eds.), *Festschrift für Hans Welzel zum 70. Geburtstag am 25. März 1974* (Berlin, 1974), 7–22, 13–16; B. Schmidlin, 'Die beiden Vertragsmodelle des europäischen Zivilrechts: Das naturrechtliche Modell der Versprechensübertragung und das pandektistische Modell der vereingten Willenserklärungen', in R. Zimmermann, R. Knütel and J.P. Meincke (eds.), *Rechtsgeschichte und Privatrechtsdogmatik* (Heidelberg, 1999), 187–206, 192–4.

26 Nehemiah 9.8; Hebrew 6.8; 10.23; 1 Cor. 1.19, 1 Thess. 5.24; 2 Thess. 3.3; 2 Tim. 2.13.

27 J.E. Nijman, 'Grotius' *Imago Dei* anthropology grounding *Ius Naturae et Gentium*', in M. Koskenniemi, M. García-Salmones Rovira and P. Amorosa (eds.), *International Law and Religion. Historical and Contemporary Perspectives* (Oxford, 2017), 87–110, 94.

28 ST I-IIae, q.91 a.2.

29 Zimmermann, *Law of Obligations*, 592–4.

30 Decock, *Theologians and Contract Law*, 274–6.

31 Gordley, *Philosophical Origins*, 85–7.

32 R. Feenstra, 'L'influence de la scolastique espagnole sur Grotius en droit privé: quelques expériences dans des questions de fond et de forme, concernant notamment les doctrines de l'erreur et de l'enrichissement sans cause', in P. Grossi (ed.), *La seconda scolastica nella formazione del diritto privato moderno* (Milan, 1973), 377–400, 386.

33 Jørgensen, 'Grotius's doctrine of contract', 118.

34 Aristotle, *Nicomachean Ethics*, 3.1.

35 Gordley, *Philosophical Origins*, 82–5.

36 Decock, *Theologians and Contract Law*, 483–4 and 494–6.

37 J. Hallebeek, 'Ius Quaesitum Tertio in medieval Roman law', in E.J.H. Schrage (ed.), *Ius quaesitum tertio* (Berlin, 2008), 61–107, 67–8.

38 Hallebeek, 'Ius Quaesitum Tertio', 86.

39 H. Dondorp, 'Ius Quaesitum Tertio in medieval canon Law', in E.J.H. Schrage (ed.), *Ius quaesitum tertio* (Berlin, 2008), 116–41, 122–3; J. Hallebeek, 'Medieval legal scholarship', in J. Hallebeek and H. Dondorp (eds.), *Contracts for a Third-Party Beneficiary* (Leiden and Boston, 2008), 21–46, 22–9.

40 The opinion that by an oath this type of agreement need to be protected was also recognised by the civil lawyers. See Hallebeek, 'Ius Quaesitum Tertio', 102–4.

41 H. Dondorp and J. Hallebeek, 'Grotius' doctrine on "adquisitio obligationis per alterum" and its roots in the legal past of Europe', in O. Condorelli (ed.), *Panta rei. Studi dedicati a Manlio Bellomo* (Rome, 2003), vol. 2, 205–44, 243–4; S. Vogenauer, 'Versprechen der Leistung an einen Dritten' in M. Schmoeckel, J. Rückert and R. Zimmermann (eds.), *Historisch-kritischer Kommentar zum BGB* (Tübingen, 2007), vol. 2–3, 1935–2035, 1963–5; L. Waelkens, 'Ius Quaesitum Tertio, Dutch influences on Grotius', in E.J.H. Schrage (ed.), *Ius quaesitum tertio* (Berlin, 2008), 175–89, 188–9; H. Dondorp, 'The seventh and eighteenth Centuries', in Hallebeek and Dondorp (eds.), *Contracts*, 47–92, 54–8.

42 See the dissertation of Franz Anton Ludovici cited in P. Astorri, 'Le fonti del moderno principio di efficacia del contratto nei confronti dei terzi' in M. Boudot, M. Faure-Abbad and D. Veillon (eds.), *L'effet relatif du contrat* (Poitiers, 2015), 21–34.

43 Decock, *Theologians and Contract Law,* 511–13; P. Astorri, *Lutheran Theology and Contract Law in Early Modern Germany (ca. 1520-1720)* (Paderborn, 2019), 173–85.

44 Decock, *Theologians and Contract Law,* 560.

45 See Cicero, *De officiis* 3.12.50; W. Decock, 'Lessius and the Breakdown of the Scholastic Paradigm', *Journal of the History of Economic Thought* 31 (2009) 57–78, 67–8; Decock, *Theologians and Contract Law,* 601.

46 For a different view, see M. Hogg, *Promises and Contract Law. Comparative Perspectives* (Cambridge, 2011), 129–30. To Hogg, Grotius seems to say here that the parties *can estimate what seems fair to them.*

47 Lev. 25.14 and 17.

48 Zimmermann, *Law of Obligations,* 259–62; J. Gordley, *Foundations of Private Law. Property, Tort, Contract, Unjust Enrichment* (Oxford, 2006), 445 and 453.

49 J. Gordley, 'Equality in exchange', *California Law Review* 69 (1981) 1587–1656; O.F. Hamouda and B.B. Price, 'The justice of the just price', *European Journal of the History of Economic Thought* 4 (1997) 191–216; O. Langholm, *Scholasticism in Economic Thought. Antecedent of Choice and Power* (Cambridge, 1998), 77–89. For more references see A. Del Vigo Gutiérrez, *Economía y ética en el siglo XVI. Estudio comparativo entre los Padres de la Reforma y la Teología española* (Madrid, 2006), 511–719.

50 Gordley, *Philosophical Origins,* 98.

51 This approach is very similar to L. Lessius, *De iustitia et iure* 2.21.21 = L. Lessius, *On Sale, Securities, and Insurance,* transl. W. Decock, N. De Sutter (Grand Rapids, Mich., 2016), 127ff.

52 Ulpian only gave some examples, it is Grotius who formulated the definitions. See B. Vitányi, 'Treaty interpretation in the legal theory of Grotius and its influence on modern doctrine', *Netherlands Yearbook of International Law* 14 (1983) 41–67, 45.

53 I. Van Hulle, 'Grotius, informal empire and the conclusion of unequal treaties', *Grotiana* N.S. 37 (2016) 43–60, 49.

54 For a detailed analysis see O. Condorelli, 'Grotius's doctrine of alliances with infidels and the idea of *Respublica Christiana*' *Grotiana* 41 (2020) 13–39.

55 W. Decock, 'Trust beyond faith: re-thinking contracts with heretics and excommunicates in times of religious war', *Rivista internazionale di diritto comune* 27 (2016) 301–28.

56 R. Tuck, 'Alliances with infidels in the European imperial expansion', in S. Muthu (ed.), *Empire and Modern Political Thought* (Cambridge, 2012), 61–83, 67–74; A. Weststeijn, '"Love alone is not enough": treaties in seventeenth-century Dutch colonial expansion', in S. Belmessous (ed.), *Empire by Treaty. Negotiating European Expansion, 1600–1900* (Oxford, 2015), 19–44, 28.

57 Gen. 21.27; 16.28; 31.44; Deut. 23.7; 2 Sam. 5.11; 1 Kings 5.12; Lev. 19.18; Deut. 22.1.

58 Tuck, 'Alliances with infidels', 75.

59 This feature of Grotius' natural law has been recently highlighted by B. Straumann, 'Is modern liberty ancient? Roman remedies and natural rights in Hugo Grotius's early works on natural law', *Law and History Review* 27 (2009) 55–85.

Dennis Klimchuk[1]

25.1 Introduction

Treatments of Grotius' account of punishment invariably set it in the context of the conceptual architecture of his political philosophy. As with his accounts of property and civil liability, Grotius engages the question of the conceptual foundations and structure of punishment in the service of his account of the just causes of war. On Grotius' understanding, the conduct of private and political actors in the international arena is governed by the very principles to which individuals are subject in their relations to one another. His arguments begin with the latter and move to the former.

Once cast in its place in this conceptual structure, a second context of Grotius' account of punishment calls attention to itself: his motivation, biographical rather than philosophical, for having his investigations yield a particular set of answers. His first treatment of punishment was in a work commissioned by the directors of the Amsterdam Chamber of the Dutch East India Company (VOC), who asked Grotius to provide a brief in defence of the seizure of the Portuguese ship *Santa Catarina* in the straights of Singapore by Jacob van Heemskerk (1567–1607), a Dutch admiral – and, as it happened, Grotius' cousin – acting in service of the United Amsterdam Company, a precursor of the VOC. In *De jure praedae commentarius*, as the lengthy text he produced eventually came to be known, Grotius found the seizure of the *Santa Catarina* to be a justified act of war. Among the different lines of arguments that Grotius develops is that on which it was justified as an exercise of the natural right to punish serious violations of the law of nature.

Certainly, the light cast by these contexts is illuminative of important aspects of the full story of Grotius' account of punishment. It, and indeed his accounts of the domains of private law as well, can be seen as resources deployed in the service of the vindication of Dutch commercial expansion in the Indies, and of violent means taken to that end.[2] But, again, as with his accounts of property and civil liability, Grotius presents his accounts of punishment and crime as complete and defensible on their own, as accounts of the relations among individuals in the state of nature and between a state and its citizens. Though some of his readers will think it mistaken to do so,[3] I will take Grotius at face value here and undertake to treat his accounts of punishment and crime on their own terms. Doing so, we will see, reveals a liberal and egalitarian current in Grotius' treatment of punishment and crime[4] and, I will suggest in conclusion, brings into relief some elements common throughout his account of the principles to which individuals are subject in their relations to one another.

Two prefatory points need to be made. First, Grotius considers punishment in a number of his legal works.[5] I will consider the three principal ones here: *De jure praedae* (1604–6; first published in full[6] in 1868), *Inleidinge tot Hollandsche rechts-geleerdheid* (*Introduction to the Jurisprudence of Holland,* 1621, published 1631) and *De jure belli ac pacis* (1625). My focus will be on his final and most complete statement, in *De jure belli ac pacis*, but I will draw on these earlier works when doing so enriches our understanding of his later view.

Finally, I have so far been talking mostly about punishment and not crime. Punishment was Grotius' focus. But he has interesting things to say about crime as well. One might think that, of the topics of this chapter, it is the more basic: we start with the concept of a wrong, and then consider how it ought to be responded to. But, for reasons that will become clear, Grotius begins with punishment. And so will I, tracing the argument as it unfolds in *De jure belli ac pacis* from punishment to crime to fitting punishment to the crime, and to the criminal.

25.2 Punishment

25.2.1 Torts and Crimes, Compensation and Punishment

The narrative and conceptual starting point of Grotius' treatment of punishment in *De jure belli ac pacis* is a distinction between two respects in which wrongs might be considered: 'either as they may be repaired or [as they may be] punished' (DJBP 20.1.1). There are really two distinctions here. The first is between two sorts of remedies: compensation and punishment. The second is between two sorts of wrongs. Inasmuch as an action is considered 'as it may be repaired', it is a private wrong, a 'tort' in the language of the common law or a 'delict' in the language of the civilian tradition. Inasmuch as an action is considered 'as it may be punished', it is a crime. Not all wrongs can be considered in both respects: some wrongs are torts but not crimes, and some wrongs are crimes but not torts. Grotius is mostly concerned with actions that can be both, as are, for example, theft and assault. I will stick with such cases. In each such case, Grotius argues, 'the Wickedness of the Action is to be distinguished from the Effect it produces. The Punishment answers to the former, and the Reparation of Damage to the latter' (DJBP 20.17.22).

Though he gestures toward them in some passages, Grotius does not clearly draw these foundational distinctions in *De jure praedae*.[7] He does so, in interestingly different but complementary terms, in *Inleidinge tot de Hollandsche rechts-geleerdheid*. Rather than saying wrongs can be considered in two respects, in his *Inleidinge* Grotius claims that a wrong can give rise to two different obligations: to repair the costs arising from it and to suffer punishment for it. There is a significant distinction between the foundations of the two obligations. 'The duty of making amends', Grotius argues, 'arises from the law of nature even without formal demand, much more without judgement' (IHR 3.32.9; see too DJBP 2.17.12). In contrast, 'no one is bound to submit to punishment without previous judgement, unless the law, exceptionally, lays this burden on him' (IHR 3.32.9). There are two reasons why the duty to submit to punishment does not arise directly and merely from the law of nature. The first is that what nature imposes is a 'general obligation' only (IHR 3.32.9); the specific punishment appropriate to a particular crime and criminal must be settled by positive law – supposing we are in civil society: I will consider the circumstances of the state of nature below. The second is that punishment is something to which someone is subjected: there must be someone, or some institution, doing the punishing.[8]

The substantive contrasts Grotius draws here between the obligations to make compensation and to submit to punishment reflects a difference in the formal structures of the relationships between torts and crimes and their respective remedies. One reason one might come to the view that the duty to make compensation arises without the intervention of positive law, but the duty to submit to punishment does not, is that the former, but not the latter, is arguably a matter of what Aristotle called corrective justice. Grotius does not quite say this, but he comes close and this brings us to the next step of his account of punishment.

25.2.2 Distributive v. Corrective, Allocative v. Explicative

In the *Nichomachean Ethics*, Aristotle drew a distinction between two kinds of particular justice, that is, justice operative in the domain of holdings, gains and losses: distributive and corrective justice.[9] Distributive justice is justice in distributions – as one might expect – and corrective justice is justice in transactions. Each is governed by a different kind of formal equality. The equality upheld in distributive justice is geometric. A distribution of some good – material or institutional, such as public offices – is just when it is made in proportion to the merit of the parties. If A is twice as deserving as B on the relevant measure, then distributive justice is done if A receives twice the relevant good as does B. The equality upheld in corrective justice, by contrast, is arithmetic. We can represent a corrective injustice, say a theft, as the taking of some quantity, x, from one party, A, and transferring it to another party, B. Key is that all we need to know about what justice requires is internal to the transaction. A and B are linked as the sufferer and doer of the same wrong, and justice is done when the transfer is undone and x is transferred back from B to A. If, as the theft example invites, one recognises the structure of a claim in tort for compensation in the form of corrective justice, then the idea that the duty to compensate arises without the intervention of positive law makes sense: what justice requires is internal to the form of the disputed transaction itself.

Where punishment fits in this scheme is a question about which Grotius seems to have changed his mind. In *De jure praedae*, he implies that punishment is a matter of corrective justice (DJPC 29). In *De jure belli ac pacis*, he argues that it is neither quite either form of justice, casting the point in the terms he substitutes for Aristotle's, attributive (for distributive) and expletive (for corrective) justice. The principal case in favour of the view that punishment is a matter of attributive justice, Grotius suggests, draws attention to the fact that greater offenders are punished more severely than lesser ones. Thus, the imposition of punishment seems to exhibit the geometric structure constitutive of justice in distributions. However, Grotius argues, the proportionate structure of the relationship between severity of offence and of punishment 'falls out only by Accident, and is not primarily and of itself intended: For that which is simply and in the first Place intended, is the Equality between the Offence and Punishment' (DJBP 2.20.2.2). The principal case in favour of the view that punishment is a matter of expletive justice follows from the observation that it is often said that punishment is due of an offender,[10] which invites an analogy to a debt owed by contract, a paradigmatic instance of a claim in expletive justice. The problem with the analogy, Grotius argues, is that it implies that the criminal has a right to be punished, one akin to the right the creditor has, against the debtor, for repayment.

Grotius seems to take it that the error of this thought speaks for itself, but does it? Not according to some. Herbert Morris, for example,[11] argued that sense *can* be made of the idea that one has a right to be punished: it is a right to be treated as a responsible being, an agent rather than a patient.[12] I don't believe Grotius meant to deny what Morris asserts. A point he makes elsewhere supplies his implicit reasoning here. The problem with the idea that a wrongdoer has a right to be punished is that that implies falsely that they would be wronged were mercy exercised in their case, and, as we will see below, sometimes mercy is deserved. When we say that punishment is due to someone, Grotius says, we mean only that it is right that they be punished: and this undoes the analogy with the creditor and debtor on which the case for the view that punishment is a matter of expletive justice is based.[13]

That said, Grotius argues, the idea that punishment is a matter of expletive justice gets two important things right. The first is that, while the wrongdoer does not have a right to be punished, the person or institution that punishes him must have a right to do so. The second is that there is an illuminating point of analogy with contracts specifically:

> as he who sells a Thing, tho' he mention nothing particularly, is yet presumed to stand obliged to perform the Conditions that naturally belong to such a Sale: So he that commits a Crime, seems voluntarily to submit himself to Punishment, there being no great Crime that is not punishable; so that he who will directly commit it, is by Consequence willing to incur the Punishment; in which Sense some Princes have pronounced Sentence upon a Malefactor thus, *Thou hast brought this Punishment upon thy own Head.* (DJBP 2.20.2.3; see also 2.20.22.1)

'[T]he criminal gives his consent [to punishment] already by his very act', without having also to consent to the institution, argued Gottfried Wilhelm Hegel (1770–1831),[14] and Grotius, I think, is making a similar claim. Drawn together with the view from the *Inleidinge* that natural law imposes only a general obligation to submit to punishment, this second kernel of truth in the expletive justice account yields something like: wrongdoers bring it about that they are vulnerable to being punished.

25.2.3 The Subject of Punishment

A wrongdoer vulnerable to being punished could be justly punished only if someone has a right to punish him. Here we find a second point on which Grotius' view changes between *De jure praedae* and *De jure belli ac pacis*. In *De jure praedae*, he argues that the right to punish derives from a natural right to self-defence (DJPC 8, 136), which we all have (DJPC 2, 23). In *De jure belli ac pacis*, Grotius constructs the right through a series of conceptual stages. The first is a kind of axiom, in which Grotius anchors the justification of punishment: 'Among those things,' he argues, 'which Nature herself tells us to be lawful and just, this is one, That he that doth Evil should suffer Evil' (DJBP 2.20.1.2). A criminal is not wronged by being punished (DJBP 2.20.4.1) and it is permissible that they be punished (DJBP 2.20.3.1). To whom is this permission issued, or, as Grotius casts the question in *De jure belli ac pacis*: who is the subject of the right to punish wrongdoers?

Grotius' main concern in his treatment of this issue in *De jure belli ac pacis* is to establish and then work out the consequences of the indeterminacy of natural law on this question: 'natural Reason informs us, that a Malefactor may be punished but not who ought to punish him' (DJBP 2.20.3.1). In his accounting of this he supposes, but does not defend, the controversial claim that individuals hold the right to punish wrongdoers in the state of nature. He defended that claim explicitly in *De jure praedae*, with two arguments. Each rests on accepting a social contract account of political authority, and then points to a practice that, Grotius argues, could therefore only be explained if the right to punish does not first issue from the authority of the state. The more modest argument – familiar from Locke's version in the *Two Treatises*[15] – points to the fact that the state punishes not only citizens but non-citizens, 'yet it derives no power over the latter from civil law, which is binding upon citizens only because they have given their consent' (DJPC 8, 137). The deeper argument generalises the point to the conditions under which the state can claim to rightfully punish anyone:

[J]ust as every right of the magistrate comes to him from the state, so has the same right come to the state from private individuals; and similarly, the power of the state is the result of collective agreement ... Therefore, since no one is able to transfer a thing that he never possessed,[16] it is evident that the right of chastisement was held by private persons before it was held by the state. (DJPC 8, 137)

Further, as Grotius makes clear in *De jure belli ac pacis*, since 'it is natural for one Man to succour another' (DJBP 2.20.8.2), this right extends to others acting in the crime victim's interests.

Can this argument for the natural right to punish from *De jure praedae* be interpolated into the *De jure belli ac pacis* account of punishment? Grotius does not, in the latter work, explicitly endorse the account of political authority on which what I have called the deeper argument for the natural right to punish in it relies. Indeed, just what the *De jure belli ac pacis* account of political authority consists of is not clear. On this point there is no scholarly consensus.[17] The passage that counts most strongly against integrating the two accounts on this point is this:

[T]he Liberty of consulting the Benefit of human Society, by Punishments, which at first, we have said, was in every particular Person, does now, since Civil Societies, and Courts of Justice, have been instituted, reside in those who are possessed of the supreme Power, and that properly, not as they have an Authority over others, but as they are in Subjection to none. (DJBP 2.20.40.1)

If the argument from *De jure praedae* anticipates Locke, this argument, as Gustaaf van Nifterik points out[18], anticipates Hobbes, who in *Leviathan* argued that:

the subjects did not give the sovereign that right [to punish], but (in laying down theirs) strengthened him to use his own as he should think fit, for the preservation of them all; so that it was not given, but left to him, and to him only.[19]

Either way, there is something disquieting about the conclusion that individuals have a natural right to punish others because, as Immanuel Kant (1724–1804) held, it is difficult to reconcile the right to punish with the equality of the wrongdoer and punisher.[20] Grotius, I want to suggest, felt the force of this worry, and sought to answer it at two steps of the account of punishment in *De jure belli ac pacis*. Here is the first. After finding, as we saw above, that natural reason does not inform us about who ought to punish a wrongdoer, Grotius adds that nonetheless, '[i]t suggests indeed so much, that it is the fittest to be done by a Superior, but yet does not shew that to be absolutely necessary, unless by Superior we mean him who is innocent, and detrude the Guilty below the Rank of Men', as some have argued (DJBP 2.20.3.1). It is not Grotius' view that wrongdoers have lost their humanity,[21] but he seems to endorse the thought that, while punisher and wrongdoer are equal by nature (DJBP 2.20.4.3), there is a sense in which the former's innocence and the latter's guilt place them on unequal footing. Thus he (mis)quotes, with approval, Plutarch saying that nature 'hath designated the good Man to be a Magistrate, and indeed a perpetual one; for, by the Law of Nature itself he who acts justly has a Superiority and Preheminence above others' (DJBP 2.20.9.2).[22]

Grotius draws from this idea a condition imposed upon rightful punishment, the first of two we can think of as aiming to reconcile the natural right to punish with our moral equality: one ought not to be punished by someone who is equally guilty. Let's call this the principle of clean hands. Jean Barbeyrac (1674–1744) argued that Grotius is here referring only to the state of nature. 'Our author', he suggested, 'certainly does not design to extend the Maxim so far as to deprive a Prince, or a Magistrate, of the Right to punish Crimes of which he knows himself guilty.'[23] That is probably right, but perhaps not simply so. Barbeyrac's point rests on the idea that, in political society, the right to punish is invested in the office of the magistrate, and exercised by its holder in that capacity only. I see no reason to think that Grotius would deny this. But, arguably, his account of the source of the magistrate's right to punish serves to qualify it, on both the Locke-anticipating or Hobbes-anticipating versions. If the magistrate bears the right to punish only to the extent that it has been transferred from the subjects, then perhaps it comes with some version of the encumbrance of the principle of clean hands. Maybe a magistrate who, in his capacity as a private person, had committed theft, would not thereby deprive his office of the right to punish thieves. But, it arguably follows that an unjust state might deprive itself of its standing to punish wrongdoers. And, if the Hobbes-anticipating passage in *De jure belli ac pacis* reveals Grotius' later thinking, then the clean hands principle seems to apply in political society even more directly.

25.2.4 The Ends of Punishment

The second condition imposed by our equality on rightful punishment is this: though God may punish persons simply because they have done wrong, 'Because one Man is so linked in Bonds of Consanguinity to another ... he ought never to do him harm, but for the Sake of some

Good' (DJBP 2.20.4.2); only then is punishment lawful (DJBP 2.20.3.4). Grotius identifies three ends for the sake of which punishment for crime may permissibly be undertaken – really, three possible beneficiaries of punishment: the criminal, the victim and everyone.

Both the second and third, for distinct but complementary reasons, are better handled by the state, Grotius argues, but he makes no mention of the question in his discussion of the first. It is tempting to infer that he did not think it fell in the state's purview to punish a wrongdoer for their own sake. His thought seems to be that the wrongdoer is themselves made worse off by their actions. It would not be the only classically liberal current in Grotius' account of punishment were we to find here the thought that it is not the state's business to save persons from themselves. Indeed, in a later passage, concerning fitting punishment to crimes, he says 'we are not treating here of every Sort of Offence, but of those which have Relation to some person besides that of the Offender' (DJBP 2.20.30.1).

'It is lawful', Grotius argues, 'for any one who is judicious and prudent, and not guilty of the same, or of a like Fault, himself, to inflict that Punishment, which is subservient to this End' (DJBP 2.20.7.2), that is, correcting the wrongdoer. This is so, at least, as long as its means are verbal admonition. More serious means of correction are, by convention but not natural law, permitted only to near relations (DJBP 2.20.7.2), and everyone should be sparing of punishing to this end, because 'Charity teaches us not to judge any one rashly to be incorrigible' (2.20.7.4).

The principal benefit of punishment to the victim, and to persons generally, is the same: diminishing the chance of falling victim to the same or another wrong in the future. The means are likewise shared: punishment can either disable the wrongdoer from reoffending – by death, or imprisonment – or deter him and others from offending again (DJBP 2.20.8.1; 2.20.9.1). A second good may accrue to the victim, namely that their dignity is vindicated by the punishment of the criminal who wronged her (DJBP 2.20.8.1). The law of nature has invested in everyone a right to punish to these ends, though it is a right best given up. '[B]ecause we are apt to be partial in our own Cases or of those that belong to us, and to be Hurried on too far by Passion' (DJBP 2.20.8.4), Grotius argues, we rightly passed the right to pursue the victim's cause to the state; we likewise did for the right to punish in the interests of everyone 'since an Examination into the Nature and Circumstances of a Fact, doth other require great Diligence, and the proportioning of Punishment to it, much Prudence and Equity' (DJBP 2.20.9.4), and so it is best to leave it to those we judge the best and most prudent to act on our collective behalf. The right to punish for each of the second and third ends, however, is retained by individuals in the limited sense that it may be rightly exercised where there are no courts that hold jurisdiction, as for example at sea.

25.3 Crime

25.3.1 The Nature of Crime

Grotius spends more space on punishment than on crime, and more on the conceptual foundation of torts than of crimes. To start, we can distil something about the nature of crime from these other discussions. Recall a passage quoted above: in cases of actions that are both crimes and torts, 'the Wickedness of the Action is to be distinguished from the Effect it produces. The Punishment answers to the former, and the Reparation of Damage to the latter' (DJBP 20.17.22). So, we might say, it is the wrongfulness of an action, apart from its harmfulness, in which the crime consists. This is registered in two points of doctrine on which Grotius draws in elucidating the distinction between torts and crimes in the *Inleidinge*. First, one can be punished for wrongful acts even when no one has been injured, and even before the crime has been carried out (IHR 3.32), as in – we would now say – attempts and conspiracy. In contrast, without a loss, there can be no tort. Second, compensation is due from tortfeasors' heirs, but liability to punishment is not inherited (IHR 3.32.10). Criminal responsibility, Grotius says, 'must of Necessity be personal, because it results from out Will, than which nothing can be said to be more strictly ours' (DJBP 2.21.12).

Not all wrongs deserving of moral censure are crimes, including wrongs – imagine some acts of betrayal – whose consequences can be much more devastating than some crimes – consider petty theft. Grotius does not articulate a criterion by which to draw this line, but we can take the lead from the idea in *De jure belli ac pacis* that crimes and torts are two respects of the same set of wrongs, and interpolate here his consideration of the substance of private wrongs. 'The Word *Damnum*, Damage, Grotius speculates, 'probably derived from *demo* to take away ... when a man has less than his Right' (DJBP 2.17.2). A person's rights arise from two sources:

nature, or some human act. Those things that are our own by nature are our lives, bodies, limbs, reputations, honour and actions (DJBP 2.17.2). Among the rights we have that arise from human acts are those that derive from the establishment of property and by stipulation of legislation. An action wrongly depriving another of their due under the entries in this catalogue of rights is a tort, rending one liable for compensation; to the extent that that action is wrongful, apart from being harmful, it is a crime, rending one liable to punishment.

We can draw on one more thing to fill in this picture a bit more. In his later discussion of proportion in punishment, Grotius draws two scales of gravity that imply two axes along which offences can be ordered. One sorts crimes according to the scope of their victims:

that is the most notorious Injustice which disturbs the publick Order, and therefore hurts the most: Next to it is that which touches particular Persons; with Respect, in a first Place, to their Life, in the second, to their Family, the Foundation of which is Marriage; in the last, to particular Goods and Effects whose Possession is desirable. (DJBP 2.20.30.1)

The second sorts each particular crime according to how far along from preparation to execution the criminal managed to get: 'Offences actually consummated hold the first Place, the next those which have proceeded to some Acts but not to the law of all; amongst which that is the most heinous which has proceeded the farthest' (DJBP 2.20.30.1).

25.3.2 The Principles of Criminalisation

Within this scope, Grotius sets our four limits,[24] principles designating categories of actions that cannot, by their nature, be made crimes. First, 'internal Acts of the Mind' cannot be punished by us, even if confessed or otherwise made known. The reason for this is that 'it is not agreeable to human Nature, that any Right or Obligation should rise amongst Men from Acts merely internal' (DJBP 2.20.18), because others' thoughts are knowable to us only through their actions (DJBP 2.4.3). That said, to the extent that one's thoughts manifest themselves in wrongful actions, they are then, as Grotius puts it, 'brought into account', because one's blameworthiness and the appropriate measure of punishment to which one should be subjected will depend, in part, on one's intentions in acting as one did.

Second, 'Those Acts that are unavoidable by human Nature', Grotius argues, 'are not to be punished by human Laws' (DJBP 2.20.19.1). It is impossible for any of us to abstain altogether and at all times from all kinds of sin, and some things perhaps none of us can abstain from – and arguably these might not properly be called sins (DJBP 2.20.19.2). Grotius unfortunately does not give us any examples of this category of action, nor of the third: actions 'which neither directly nor indirectly concern human society nor any Body else' (DJBP 2.20.20.1). Here is another example of a classically liberal current in Grotius' account of crime and punishment. Finally, we cannot make crimes of those wrongs that would not be set right if avoided for the sake of avoiding punishment. Ingratitude, for example, is a vice, but gratitude would not be praiseworthy if one were bound by threat of punishment to show it (DJBP 2.20.20.2.).

25.3.3 Pardoning

Having set out his account of punishment and of the principles of criminalisation, Grotius turns to consider the circumstances under which offences – as he says, though perhaps we might more accurately say 'offenders' – may and ought to be pardoned. The structure and normative content of pardoning is ambiguous, and Grotius is not as careful here as one might wish. Collected under the heading of pardoning are three distinct sorts of considerations, considerations that (a) show the state to be denied standing to punish; that (b) allow the state's standing but defeat or mitigate the offender's responsibility for her actions; and that (c) allow the state's standing and concede the defendant's responsibility, but nonetheless support forgoing or mitigating their punishment. I'll call these 'standing-denying', 'responsibility-defeating' and 'punishment-mitigating' considerations, respectively. Making sense of the first two sorts of considerations contributes to our understanding of Grotius' conception of crime, and so their treatment fits squarely in this section of this chapter; the last anticipates the next section, but I'll consider it here, as it would be tricky to disentangle these threads in his argument.

Grotius begins his treatment of pardoning by posing to himself a challenge for which he credits the Stoics: if punishment is someone's due, why ought he not receive it? His answer recalls a point he made earlier and we saw above: to say that punishment is due to someone is only to say that they would not be wronged by being punished, not that anyone is obligated to punish them, 'and therefore in this Sense Punishment is not always due, but permitted only'. 'And that may be true', Grotius continues, 'as well before the penal Law as afterwards' (DJBP 2.20.21): that is, a criminal may merit pardon both in cases in which a positive law forbidding what they have done has not, or not yet, been passed, and in cases in which they act in violation of the positive law. Grotius treats each in turn.

As to the first: to begin, it would seem to be in plain violation of the rule of law to hold that one can be prosecuted for an offence unnamed in positive law. But Grotius thinks this practice is defensible. Again recalling an idea he defended in his account of punishment, he argues that 'he, who has offended, naturally brings himself into such a Condition, as that he may justly be punished' (DJBP 2.20.22.1). I think we can infer from Grotius' choice of language – 'he, who has offended, *naturally* brings himself into such a Condition, as that he may justly be punished' – that what he has in mind are offences *malum in se*: actions wrong in themselves, knowledge of which everyone can fairly be presumed to have. And, furthermore, punishment in these cases needn't be exacted; 'this depends on the connection of the Ends, for which Punishment was instituted, with the Punishment itself' (DJBP 2.20.22.1). This connection would fail to obtain, Grotius tells us, when an offence is committed so privately that few know of it and more harm than good would come from its public discovery, when the criminal's offence is overbalanced by their ancestors' merit or when the victim grants a pardon. In each case, the state's standing is allowed and the offender's responsibility is conceded. So, here pardoning is a kind of punishment-mitigation.

Grotius adduces these considerations specifically in respect of offences *malum in se* and not expressly prohibited by positive law, and this might be thought to raise a puzzle. He here invokes a principle one might think would apply in all cases, namely that punishment ought to be forgone when its pursuit would be unconnected with the ends whose pursuit makes punishment lawful. Let's call this the 'ends principle'. The answer to the puzzle is that the ends principle *does* apply in cases in which the offender has violated a provision of positive law, but it does so in a particular way. There is, on this point, an important difference between the two categories of cases. Or so I think we can find Grotius to say, though only implicitly. Let's look at this more closely.

One might think the Stoic concern with pardoning would reappear in the category of cases in which the offender has violated a provision of positive law in a form more difficult to answer. The legislator, some argue and Grotius earlier claims, is bound by their own laws: and so how can the state release the offender? Grotius' answer is that the legislator indeed binds themselves, but only in their private capacity. If the legislature can repeal laws, then it follows that it can make provision for their suspension in particular cases. But this cannot be done 'without reasonable Cause', because – and this is the key point distinguishing such cases from offences *malum in se*, but not prohibited by positive law – 'the Authority of the Law, which it is fit should be maintained, is superadded to the other Causes of punishing' (DJBP 2.20.24). This gives us part of an accounting of the difference between the two categories of cases. It explains why there might be more generous pardoning conditions in cases 'before the penal Law is made': there the authority of the legal order is not, in the same way, seemingly impugned by the suspension of punishment in particular cases. But this does not yet show whether and, if so, how, the ends principle applies in cases involving offences committed 'after the penal Law is made'.

Grotius tells us that, in these cases, one can be exempted from the penalty of law for two sorts of causes: intrinsic or extrinsic. The cause is intrinsic when the punishment compared with the law is, if not unjust, too severe. So, here is an operation of the ends principle: 'too severe' could only mean greater than is necessary to realise the ends whose pursuit makes the punishment lawful. This can be consistent with the authority of law if we can treat this as a miscalculation on the legislature's part. So understood, pardoning in this category of cases functions by denying the state's standing to punish: to punish beyond what the pursuit of the ends appropriate to punishment licences is, Grotius' reasoning implies, to act unlawfully, something we cannot suppose we have given the state permission to do.

Extrinsic causes, Grotius says, are those 'from a Man's former Merit, or some other Thing that speaks in his Favour; or even from some Great Hopes of him for the future' (DJBP 2.20.26). At a glance, these seem quite like the conditions he adduced in the case of offences committed 'before the penal Law is made'. But, as he explains, the category turns out to be narrower. The two best illustrations are cases in which an offence was committed through ignorance, even if not altogether blameless, or through 'Infirmity of the Mind', even if it was surmountable with great difficulty. These are conditions that defeat, or diminish, responsibility. And, so, in such cases pardon – full or partial – can be granted without diminishing the authority of law.

Now, one might, as Jeremy Bentham (1748–1832) for one did, undertake to explain such defences in terms of the impossibility to deter offenders.[25] On that explanation, one might subsume them under the ends principle. But Grotius makes no mention of this. We can supply his implicit reasoning here on an analogy with his argument in defence of the prohibition of punishing an innocent person for another's crime. '[T]he true reason' for this principle, Grotius argues:

is not that … all *Punishment is designed for Mens Reformation*, for one may make an Example with the Person of the Criminal, provided it be in the Person of one who nearly touches him … *but because all Obligation to Punishment is grounded upon Guilt.* (DJBP 2.21.12)

Similarly, I suggest we can attribute to Grotius the view that offences committed in ignorance or owing to the offender's infirmity of mind ought to be pardoned because these circumstances defeat or mitigate the wrongdoer's responsibility – and this can be granted without impugning the law's authority.

25.4 Fitting Punishment to the Crime and Criminal

25.4.1 To the Crime

While punishment is to be undertaken with an eye to the good it may bring, that does not, as we have seen, justify its imposition; nor, Grotius explains, is it the measure of its just quantum. 'No Body,' he holds, 'is to be punished above his Desert' (DJBP 2.20.28), and we ought, as a general rule, to err on the side of moderation in punishment (DJBP 2.20. 36.1). But it does not follow from either of these principles that the criminal ought to suffer no more than he caused the victim to suffer: sometimes, Grotius tells us, he ought to suffer more. This is a striking claim, and one could have hoped for more argument in its favour. What Grotius does is list some concurring practices – for example, the Athenian law of theft – and quote some supporting texts. He seems to be moved principally by two thoughts. The first, from Saint Ambrose (c. 340–97), is that imposing a greater cost on a thief than the return of the stolen goods would aid in deterring theft

(DJBP 2.20.32.1). This may seem at odds with my claim that, for Grotius, the ends of punishment, which as we saw above include diminishing future incidents of crime, do not set the quantum of punishment. But we might resolve the apparent tension on his behalf by saying that the wrongdoer has brought upon himself the burden of being made an example of. The second thought, from Philo of Alexandria (c. 25 BCE–c. 50 CE), implies that it is not equitable that the injured and injurious person should suffer the same (DJBP 2.20.32.2).

Three factors ought to be considered, Grotius argues, in determining what he calls 'the Demerit of the Crime' – of the particular crime, that is: (a) the criminal's motive; (b) the reasons that ought to have restrained him; and (c) his disposition to commit the offence. As to (a): hardly anyone, Grotius tells us, sets out to do wrong for its own sake; and those who do are monsters. For the most part, persons are drawn to commit crime by their Affections, and these come in a moral ordering. Least blameworthy is the desire to escape harms, including extreme poverty;[26] at the other end of the spectrum are the desires of wealth, pleasure and honour. As to (b): 'The Cause which in general ought to restrain a Person from offending', Grotius argues, 'is Injustice' (DJBP 2.20.30.1) and the more damage an offence causes and the more important the institution or interest affected – recall the discussion of the ranking of crimes above – the more unjust. Grotius' thought seems to be that the seriousness of a crime is reason for not committing it and so the criminal is blameworthy, not only for doing something serious, but for doing it despite its seriousness. Other aggravating factors include vices displayed in the crime, for example want of affection toward one's parents and ingratitude to one's benefactors (DJBP 2.20.30.3). And, finally, as to (c): various factors, such as age and education, affect persons' ability to manage the affections that lead to crime and to reflect on the reasons to refrain from committing it. Some persons are, for example, quicker to anger (DJBP 2.20.31.1). The general principle is this: 'the more the Judgment is hindered in making its Choice, the more natural the Causes are by which it is hindered, the less is the Offence' (DJBP 2.20.31.2).

25.4.2 To the Criminal

'[T]he Greatness of a Punishment,' Grotius argues, 'is not to be estimated from what it is simply in itself, but with respect to the Person, who suffers it'

(DJBP 2.20.33). His example is of a fine, which might be a great burden for a poor person to pay, but little for a wealthy one. And, so, in this respect punishment should be made to fit the criminal as well as the crime.[27]

There are subtler and perhaps somewhat more inadvertent ways in which, for Grotius, the punishment appropriate in a particular case is indexed to the criminal as well as the crime. I have a couple things in mind. The first is intimated in his quoting with approval, in his discussion of the motives of crime, Demosthenes saying 'If a rich Man be unjust, it is fit that he should be much more severely punished, than a poor Fellow whose Poverty forces him to commit the same Crime' (DJBP 2.20.29.2). We shouldn't read too much into this: the crucial idea in the end is that poverty compels wrong. But, there is a hint, perhaps, of the thought that the identity of the hypothetical criminals – a wealthy and a poor man – itself bears on their blameworthiness. We see a clearer blurring, so to speak, of the act/actor line in Grotius' discussion of aggravating factors in sentencing. Among these, he tells us, are the criminal's past offences: 'The frequency of the Offence is still a stronger Indication of a depraved Mind [than the viciousness of the particular act]; because an evil Habit is worse than a single Act' (DJBP 2.20.30.1). In treating the habit revealed in a criminal's record as a factor in determining the sentencing in a particular occasion, Grotius comes close to saying that we ought to punish the criminal not only for what they have done, but for who they have revealed themselves to be – though only as revealed through their wrongful actions.

25.5 Conclusion

In sum, for Grotius, punishment is the remedial response to the wrongfulness, rather than cost, of a wrongful act. Wrongdoers make themselves vulnerable to punishment; they are not wronged if punished by someone who bears the right to do so. The right to punish is held by individuals by natural law, but can only be rightly exercised by those with clean hands, and in any case, is best left to the state, which can only rightfully punish in pursuit of the future interests of its citizens. So conditioned, the right to punish is made compatible with our moral equality. Here Grotius' egalitarianism comes to the fore. The liberal current in his thinking is expressed in his account of crime. Crimes are wrongs to others: the state does not have standing to save persons from themselves or to promote virtue.

On these terms, there are illuminating substantive and structural parallels with other parts of Grotius' account of the principles governing individuals' interactions with one another. Consider, for example, his account of property. According to Grotius, private property exists as a matter of convention, permitted but not required by natural law, and subject to its principles if instituted. The theory of property does not tell us what goods are appropriate to human life, or which we ought otherwise to pursue, but conditions the terms on which we may permissibly pursue those ends compatible with a life together. The principal condition is respect for the equality we enjoy in the original community of property, where no one's use of the commons is subject to another's will. In Grotius' account, the conventions of private property adopted by a community through its positive law must depart as little as possible from what he calls the 'natural equity' that characterises the original community of property (DJBP 2.20.6.1). While enabling a materially richer life, private property also increases the ways in which we can be made vulnerable to others. The principles of natural law impose limits on the rights of property that protect us against this vulnerability, through, for example, preserving a right of necessity and imposing obligations on finders. It, thus, is a common theme of Grotius' legal theory that our institutions are conditioned by consistency with our moral equality.[28]

But, again, that is not the whole story: recall the bigger picture I sketched in the introduction. In a memorable turn of phrase, Richard Tuck concluded a treatment of Grotius' account of sovereignty by saying that *De jure belli ac pacis* 'is Janus-faced, and its two mouths speak the language of both absolutism and liberty'.[29] Grotius' accounts of punishment and crime are likewise burdened with moral ambiguity.

Translations of Grotius's Worked Used

The Rights of War and Peace ed. R. Tuck (Indianapolis, 2005)

Further Reading

Blom, A., 'Owning punishment: Grotius on right and merit' *Grotiana* N.S., 36 (2005) 3–27.

Geddert, J.S., 'Beyond strict justice: Hugo Grotius on punishment and natural right (s)', *The Review of Politics* 76 (2014) 559–88.

Hinshelwood, B. 'Punishment and sovereignty in *De Indis* and *De iure belli ac pacis*', *Grotiana* N.S., 38(2007) 1–35.

Salter, J., 'Sympathy with the poor: theories of punishment in Hugo Grotius and Adam Smith', *History of Political Thought* 20 (1999) 205–24.

Straumann, B., 'The right to punish as a just cause of war in Hugo Grotius' natural law', *Studies in the History of Ethics* (2006), www.historyofethics.org/022006/022006Straumann.shtml.

Straumann, B., *Roman Law in the State of Nature: The Classical Foundations of Hugo Grotius' Natural Law* (Cambridge, 2015).

Terumi, F., 'Punishment', in O. Yasuaki (ed.), *A Normative Approach to War. Peace, War and Justice in Grotius* (Oxford, 1993), 221–43.

Tuck, R., *Natural Rights Theories: Their Origin and Development* (Cambridge, 1979).

Tuck, R., *The Right of War and Peace. Political Thought and the International Order from Grotius to Kant* (Oxford, 1999).

Van Nifterik, G.P., 'Grotius and the origin of the ruler's right to punish', *Grotiana* N.S. 26–8 (2005–7) 396–415.

Notes

1 Many thanks to Cecilia Li for her excellent research assistance.

2 See the chapter on Grotius in R. Tuck, *The Rights of War and Peace. Political Thought and the International Order from Grotius to Kant* (Oxford, 1999), 78–108, for an accounting of Grotius' theory of property as well as of punishment in these terms.

3 For example, Furukawa Terumi begins his treatment of Grotius' account by arguing that '[i]t is misleading to interpret the chapter [of DJBP] as an independent criminal-law theory'. F. Terumi, 'Punishment', in O. Yasuaki (ed.), *A Normative Approach to War: War, Peace, and Justice in Grotius* (Oxford, 1993), 221–43, at 221.

4 Cf. J.S. Geddert, 'Beyond strict justice: Hugo Grotius on punishment and natural right(s)' *The Review of Politics* 76 (2014) 559–88.

5 For a thorough overview, including of works I do not discuss in this chapter, see G.P. van Nifterik, 'Grotius and the origin of the ruler's right to punish', *Grotiana* N.S. 26–8 (2007–7) 396–415.

6 One chapter of DJPC was published as *Mare liberum* (*The Free Sea*) in 1609.

7 Benjamin Straumann shows that this transition is reflected in the vocabulary Grotius chooses. In DJBP, but not in DJPC, Grotius consistently uses one word to refer to private wrong (*maleficium*) and another to crime (*delictum*). B. Straumann, *Roman Law in the State of Nature: The Classical Foundations of Hugo Grotius' Natural Law* (Cambridge, 2015), 212–13.

8 Grotius does not make this second point explicitly, but I think that's what he has in mind when he says, in the passage from IHR I'm discussing, that the natural law obligation to submit to punishment can be applied in a particular case only with the intervention of some understanding *and* will (IHR 3.32.7).

9 Aristotle, *Nicomachean Ethics*, 5.2–4.

10 'Punishment is due an offender' does not ring as colloquial to our ears, but the thought that, in being punished, offenders 'get their due' does, I think.

11 And earlier, Hegel. See G.W.F. Hegel, *Philosophy of Right*, transl. T.M. Knox (1821; Oxford, 1952), para. 100, 70.

12 H. Morris, 'Persons and punishment', *The Monist* 52 (1968) 475–550.

13 For a careful consideration of the debtor/creditor analogy and its role in Grotius' account of punishment see A. Blom, 'Owning punishment: Grotius on right and merit' *Grotiana* N.S., 36 (2005) 3–27, 12–19. For its roots in earlier work of Grotius' not treated here, see Van Nifterik, 'Grotius and the origin', 402–3.

14 Hegel, *Philosophy of Right,* addition to para. 100, 246.

15 J. Locke, *Two Treatises of Government*, ed. P. Laslett (1690; Cambridge, 1960) 2.2.9. As Tuck notes, Grotius could not have read this in DJPB because it was not yet published: 'This,' then, 'must count as one of the most striking examples of intellectual convergence'; Tuck, *Rights of War and Peace*, 82.

16 As Straumann points out, here Grotius invokes a principle of Roman Law, that no one can transfer greater rights to someone than they possess; Straumann, *Roman Law*, 208.

17 For a helpful survey and compelling entry in the debate see B. Hinshelwood, 'Punishment and sovereignty in *De Indis* and *De iure belli ac pacis*' *Grotiana* N.S. 26–8 (2005–7) 1–35, at 17–33.

18 Van Nifterik, 'Grotius and the Origin', 411.

19 T. Hobbes, *Leviathan* (1649; Indianapolis, 1994), 28.2. Hobbes can't quite be taken to mean what he says here, because, though he argues that individuals in the state of nature have a right to everything 'even to one another's body' (*Leviathan* 14.4), he casts this as a right of self-preservation and never as a right of punishment, which, to further complicate matters, he later defines as an exercise of public authority (28.1).

20 'No war of independent states against each other can be a *punitive war*', Kant argues, '[f]or punishment occurs only in the relation of a superior . . . to those subject to him . . . and states do not stand in that relation to each other.' I. Kant, *The Metaphysics of Morals* (1797) in M. Gregor (ed.), *Practical Philosophy* (Cambridge 1996), Ak. 6:347.

21 As Locke implies: Locke, *Two Treatises*, 2.2.10.

22 The claim that this is a misquotation was Jean Barbeyrac's, made in his notes to a French translation in 1724. Barbeyrac's notes were translated into English and added to the English edition from London, 1738 that is the source for the translation I am using in this chapter, p. 973, n. 3.

23 Ibid., 955, n. 5.

24 Grotius in fact enumerates three, but the last splits into two irreducibly distinct ideas, the third and fourth on my list.

25 J. Bentham, *The Principles of Morals and Legislation* (1789; Oxford, 1970), 13.9–10.

26 On which see J. Salter, 'Sympathy with the poor: theories of punishment in Hugo Grotius and Adam Smith', *History of Political Thought* 20 (1999) 205–224.

27 An idea further developed by Kant: Kant, *Metaphysics of Morals*, Ak. 6:332–34.

28 Or so I argue in 'Grotius on property and the right of necessity', *Journal of the History of Philosophy* 56 (2018), 239–60.

29 R. Tuck, *Natural Rights Theories: Their Origin and Development* (Cambridge, 1979), 79.

Part V

The Reception of Grotius

Grotius and the Enlightenment 26

Marco Barducci[1]

26.1 Introduction

Grotius' intellectual legacy cannot be separated from the Enlightenment. From his natural law theory to his biblical exegesis, Grotius contributed to some of the constituent ideas of this epoch-making period in Western intellectual tradition, such as religious toleration, the contractual origins of civil society and its separation from religious community. These aspects of Grotius' thought, which culminated in the Enlightenment, have been examined individually by existing scholarship and by previous contributions in this book. However, as we start to dig down into the processes of transmission of Grotius' works and ideas across a large span of time and focus on their reception in a range of different – although connected – national and intellectual contexts, we immediately realise that any attempt to chart Grotius' contribution to the Enlightenment is dependent on a series of factors that include the temporal and cultural contexts of Grotius' works, the specific vision of the Enlightenment that we presuppose, and the mechanisms of transmission and reception of his ideas and works across space and time. So, if Grotius was one of the intellectual sources of the Enlightenment, the overall nature and extent of his contribution resists assessment.

Although there is little consensus about the precise start date of the Enlightenment, scholars rarely trace its origins earlier than the mid-seventeenth century. By that time, Grotius was already dead. His chronological lifespan and the persistence in his work of neo-scholastic and neo-Stoic themes and ideas thus falls within the remit of late Dutch humanism.[2] It was only with the appearance of the 'histories of moralities' inaugurated in 1678 by Samuel Pufendorf's (1632–94) *Specimen controversiarum circa jus naturale* that Grotius officially became one of the sources of the Enlightenment. In this text, Pufendorf situated himself within a tradition of thought aiming to separate ethics from theology, whose initiator was Grotius' treatment of natural law in *De jure belli ac pacis*.[3] But, which

Enlightenment? Existing narratives of this intellectual and philosophical movement have tended to trace dividing lines between 'cosmopolitan' and 'national' dimensions, as well as between 'moderate' and 'radical' mainstreams. As in a game of mirrors, these narratives have retrospectively determined the role attributed to Grotius in contributing to the intellectual foundations of this epoch-making period in Western history. According to Michael Zuckert, 'Grotius' theologically neutral natural law' acted as a link between neo-scholasticism and Aristotelianism and John Locke's (1632–1704) natural rights theory, thereby contributing, through the latter's mediation, to the foundations of Anglo-American Enlightenment and to the political philosophy of the American constitution in particular.[4] To Jonathan Israel, instead, during the eighteenth century, Grotius' Bible criticism inspired some of the most subversive criticisms of the era, thus contributing to the background of 'radical Enlightenment'.[5]

As it emerges from this brief outline, Grotius' intellectual legacy to the Enlightenment was multifaceted, not only because his work confronted the main themes of early modern political and religious thought, but also because, as is typical of any history of reception, it was the object of either separate or overlapping processes of transmission and re-adaption in different national and intellectual contexts until at least the mid-eighteenth century. These processes of re-adaptation and interpretation often departed from Grotius' own original intentions in writing his works, and putting his source texts in different contexts imparted different meanings to them accordingly. The 'legend' of Grotius as forefather of modern natural law was developed by German and Huguenot jurists who selected Grotius' *De jure belli ac pacis* out of his much broader output, which included seminal works like *De veritate religionis Christianæ* (1627) and the *Annotationes* to the Old (1644) and New Testament (1641, 1646, 1650). In England, where Grotius was particularly influential for Enlightenment debates on the authenticity of the Bible and the existence of universal moral precepts, his theology and biblical criticism were utilised both by post-Restoration Anglicans against the scepticism of Pierre Bayle (1647–1706) and the relativistic implications of Cartesian and Spinozistic materialism, and by the Deists to criticise organised Christianity and support natural religion.

Moderate and radical receptions, national and cosmopolitan contexts overlapped in the circulation of Grotius' works and ideas across the European continent and its British appendages, thus making it difficult to locate Grotius' legacy within a specific strand of the Enlightenment. This chapter aims to provide a synopsis of the multifaceted nature of Grotius' contribution to the Enlightenment against the backdrop of the tension existing between the notion of 'Enlightenments' in the plural, and of '*the* Enlightenment' as a cosmopolitan movement of ideas, with a special focus on natural law, social contract theory and biblical exegesis. However, the importance of Grotius lays not just in his capacity to attract consensus around his doctrines, or in the Janus-faced reputation of some of his ideas on ethics, politics and religion, but rather in his capacity to pave the way for later discussion about the foundations of ethics and religion, which would imbibe Enlightenment debates on natural law, the origins of society, the authenticity of the Bible and the ability of human reason to interpret its essentially ethical message.

26.2 Natural Law: Moral Philosophy, Sociability and Colonialism

The area where Grotius' contribution to the intellectual roots of the Enlightenment is known to be most significant is 'modern' natural law and natural rights theory. Unlike the tradition of 'classical' natural law stretching from Thomas Aquinas (1225-74) to Francisco Suárez (1548-1617), which presupposed a continuity and interdependence between God-derived natural law and morals, the 'modern' natural law theory, of which Grotius was considered the founder, and which was a vital part of the Enlightenment, in general tended to separate natural law from Christian religion.[6] Modern natural law was not an organic tradition of thought. It accommodated a variety of different perspectives ranging from Pufendorf's voluntarism to Christian Wolff's (1679-1754) rationalism, which underpinned either contractarian or absolutist views of civil society and the state.[7] Besides, the natural law tradition was not unchallenged within the Enlightenment debates on the relationship between morality and theology, as it encountered the opposition of many critics, not only among Lutheran and Catholic orthodox theologians, but also among those, like Gottfried Wilhelm Leibniz (1646-1716), who distinguished Grotius from moral 'voluntarism'.[8] Furthermore, notwithstanding the traditional association of natural law tradition and modern classical liberalism, Grotius' ideas played a role in the justification of colonialism. I will now outline these different – though interconnected – strands of reception of Grotius' natural law theory in the Enlightenment, focusing particularly, although not solely, on its reception in some countries where the natural law tradition significantly influenced the academic, juridical and political debate, such as Germany, Scotland and the Kingdom of Naples.

The connection between the natural law theory of Grotius and its development in the early Enlightenment was originally traced by Pufendorf, and successively consolidated in eighteenth-century Germany by Christian Thomasius (1655–1728), who in 1707 devised the first German translation of *De jure belli ac pacis*. The lineage Grotius-Pufendorf-Thomasius purposely minimised the differences that existed between them, as these particularly concerned the issue of the obligation to the law of nature, in order to break with the previous scholastic and Protestant traditions.[9] Of particular relevance to the transmission of Grotius to the Enlightenment was also the work of Jean Barbeyrac (1674–1744), who distinguished himself as the translator and propagator in French of *De jure belli ac pacis*. The work of Grotius, as mediated by Pufendorf and Barbeyrac in particular, fostered an interest in natural law theories in Scotland and Naples. From the 1690s, natural law theories became an integral part of the moral philosophy curriculum in the Scottish universities of Glasgow, Edinburgh and Aberdeen. Familiarity with the natural law theory of Grotius was enhanced by the practice of studying law in the Netherlands, which became particularly popular between 1680 and 1730. Scottish law students were in the habit of attending a *Collegium Grotianum*, i.e. a class on natural law, while some went to Groningen to study natural law with Barbeyrac.[10] Notwithstanding the tendency to emphasise the role of Pufendorf as a source of natural law in Scotland, also due to Gershom Carmichael's edition of *De officio* (1718), a compendium of Grotius' *De jure belli ac pacis* was published by William Scott (1672–1735) in 1707 for his students in the University of Edinburgh. Adam Smith (1723–90) wrote in his *Theory of Moral Sentiments* (1758) that 'Grotius seems to have been the first who attempted to give the world anything like a system of those principles which ought to run through, and be the foundation of, the laws of all nations'.[11]

According to Knud Haakonssen, Grotius' subjectivisation of 'right' (*jus*) as a moral quality of the person rather than the accordance between action and law, and his theory of rights, sharpened the division between justice and other virtues, thus making an important contribution towards the separation of law and morals.[12] In this respect, David Hume (1711–76) and Smith followed Grotius closely 'when they characterize justice as a mere negative virtue concerned with what not to do, whereas the other virtues are positive guides to action'.[13] Grotius also remained influential on Smith's mature theory of property, which he illustrated in his lectures delivered at Glasgow in 1762. Smith took from Grotius some aspects of his theory, such as the account of property in the first age of society as a community of goods, and the role of agreements in the subsequent development of private ownership.[14] Grotius' view of natural law had 'the enforcement of expediency', so the insistence of some leading exponents of the Scottish Enlightenment on the utilitarian aspects of Grotius' natural rights in relation to property did not constitute a departure from his theory of right but the development of an aspect of it.[15] More generally, the interest in the natural law tradition in Enlightenment Scotland was prompted by a post-revolutionary search for healing and settling and by a reaction to patriarchal and feudal institutions in terms of contract and consent.[16]

A similar situation occurred in Naples from the second half of the seventeenth century, when the doctrines of natural law circulated and were deployed in the antithesis of royal law and customary law. Jurist Francesco D'Andrea (1625–98) argued that the law of the princes, insofar as it was public law, was inspired by the same needs as natural law, namely common interest. Drawing on Grotius, D'Andrea proposed to re-enforce royal legislation according to subjective natural law against the customary law, which had become 'baronial' right.[17] *De jure belli ac pacis* had an early reception in Neapolitan culture, but it was especially through Barbeyrac's translation, as anticipated by the diffusion of the latter's translations of Pufendorf's *De jure naturali et gentium* and *De officio* respectively in 1706 and 1707, that Grotius made his major contribution to the lively Enlightenment culture of Naples. The reputation of Grotius had been promoted in Southern Italy mainly by jurists belonging to the 'ceto civile' (civil class), who wished to undermine the old aristocratic superstructure and promote a renewal of society in which they would play a protagonist role. In the second half of the eighteenth century, Catholic apologists in Naples as well as in other Italian states increasingly used the name of Grotius: on the basis of Barbeyrac's own commentaries and critical remarks,[18] they ended up considering Grotius' natural law theory a development of the neo-scholastic tradition and contrasting it, as in the case of Dominican philosopher Bonifacio Finetti (1705–82), with the essentially atheistic and materialistic doctrines of Thomas Hobbes (1588–1679), Pufendorf and Thomasius.[19]

From a different perspective, but reaching a similar conclusion, on the continent Leibniz backed the opinion of 'the incomparable Grotius' against Pufendorf's 'voluntarist' approach to natural law theory, in that he had 'justly observed ... that there would be a natural obligation even on the hypothesis – which is impossible – that God does not exist'.[20]

The impact of Grotius' natural law theory on the Enlightenment debates on religion and morality was, therefore, not limited solely to those who indicated him as a forerunner of a rational universal ethic separated from religion and alternative to customary right, but involved also those who considered Grotius a *novatore* (innovator) capable of elaborating a Christian undogmatic ethics on which to build a pacified Christian society.

One of the central tenets of the Enlightenment was that governments originated from a social contract to secure people's rights. Grotius is often considered a precursor of social contract theory.[21] This notwithstanding, he actually elaborated a very elementary theory of sociability based on natural law, which was deemed as foundational only with hindsight in the writings of the 'golden age of social contract theory' beginning with Hobbes' *Leviathan* (1651) and ending with Immanuel Kant's (1724–1804) *Metaphysics of Morals* (1797).[22] So, how was it that a rudimentary theory of contract theory, which basically consisted in a remark on *appetitus societatis* in the *Prolegomena* to *De jure belli ac pacis*,[23] became one of the sources of the Enlightenment discourse on the contractual origins of society and constitutionalism?

At a more general level, Grotius provided moral philosophers and jurists in Scotland and in Germany, from the late seventeenth century onwards, with a framework for the solution to the tension existing between individuals bargaining to defend their rights and the possibility of a society erected around the pursuit of the common good. The latter consisted of the combination of a new idea of subjective natural rights with a more traditional, mainly neo-Stoic, natural law theory.[24] Grotius' ideas on sociability were also seen to be relevant to the process of separation of religious and civil governance that he had started in humanism in conjunction with other exponents of the so-called Leiden Circle,[25] and that culminated in the Enlightenment. Grotius believed that self-preservation was a common feature of all living creatures, while a peculiar trait of humanity was 'sociability'. Pufendorf and Barbeyrac instead propagated the idea that, according to Grotius' natural law, society was created for the defence of self-protection. This interpretation was contested by Lutheran and Catholic Aristotelian scholars who detected in Grotius' theory a Christian commitment to piety and love consistent with the Ten Commandments.[26]

As for his natural law theory, then, Grotius' *appetitus societatis* aroused divergent interpretations about the ethical foundations of society at the threshold of the Enlightenment. But, there are two other aspects of Grotius' sociability in particular that informed later discussion on the origins of society and constitutionalism: one is related to what has been defined as the 'Grotian problem', which consisted in an attempt to admit rebellion while banning private warfare in society. The second concerned the complex and sometimes contradictory relationship between social contract and the particular form of civil polity erected by the people. Grotius was a theorist of state sovereignty who affirmed the necessity of surrendering the right of resistance upon entering society in return for peace and stability. But, he also affirmed that sovereignty ultimately resided in the people and justified resistance in extreme circumstances. According to Deborah Baumgold, Grotius' main intellectual project in *De jure belli ac pacis* was to set the principles of a pacified society, and this project was taken up and further developed by Hobbes and Locke. Baumgold argues that, in conflating political resistance with the individual's right of self-defence and with accountable government, Grotius was still moving within a medieval framework, but that he paved the way for further discussion on how to disentangle 'the separate issues of political violence, self-defense, and governmental accountability'.[27] Hobbes and Locke inherited the Grotian problem and worked out two different solutions to it: Hobbes' formulation of the social contract in *The Elements of Law* (1640) and *De cive* (1642) tackled the problem of distinguishing the individual's right of self-defence from political resistance, showing that the former, but not the latter, was compatible with the requirements of a pacified society. Locke's achievement, instead, 'was to strip the idea of a pacified society of its absolutist implications by showing how it could be rendered consistent with the principles of governmental accountability and an ultimate, popular right of rebellion'.[28]

Notwithstanding his preference for a fundamentally absolutist and anti-democratic view of civil and ecclesiastical polities, and his attempt to defuse the destabilising propensities of popular sovereignty by re-casting the connected issue of resistance theory within the casuistry of positive just war, Grotius' work, and particularly *De jure belli ac pacis*, have been regarded by his later readers as containing traces of both 'constitutional-ism' and 'absolutism'.[29] From 1746 to 1776, North American colonists regarded Grotius' social contract theory as one of America's founding political ideas,[30] while the former was seen in Italy as a juridical source of enlightened absolutism until the mid-eighteenth century, being thus eventually replaced by Pufendorf. A 'proto-liberal' version of Grotian natural law theory was developed by French Huguenot authors Pierre Jurieu (1637–1713) and Pierre Bayle. In his *Lettres pastorales* (1689), Jurieu adapted Grotius' natural rights to the political discourse about resistance to Louis XIV (1638–1715), while Bayle used Grotius to combine absolutism and religious tolerance and to justify the latter as a remedy to anarchy and religious war.[31] Due both to the shift of Grotius' interests in state sovereignty in *De jure belli ac pacis* with respect to his earlier historical-constitutional writings in justification of the Dutch republic, and to his claim that the people had eventually the right to choose the form of government that best suited them, his ideas on sociability were utilised to underpin different forms of civil government: a case in point was England during the 'century of revolution', when Grotius was used to justify either monarchy or republic.

What Grotius therefore passed on to later Enlightenment's debates about the contractual origins of society and the related relationship between state sovereignty, the form of civil government, and the rights of subjects/citizens, was a set of open questions concerning 'alienable versus inalien-able rights; ... consent given once and for all versus consent reaffirmed with each generation; ... the sovereignty of the various states versus the sovereignty of the people of the nation'.[32] Jean-Jacques Rousseau (1712–78) affirmed that 'Grotius denies that all human authority is estab-lished for the benefit of the governed, and he cites slavery as an instance. His invariable mode of reasoning is to establish right by fact. One could use a more consistent method, but not one more favourable to tyrants'.[33] Such an assertion was certainly unfair, in that Grotius' aversion to government by the people and his preference for either aristocratic or monarchical forms of government, derived from an emphasis on stability and peace in state and Church that aligned him more closely with the tradition of contractarian absolutism rather than of classical liberalism personified by

Locke.[34] Locke's doctrine of natural law, his analysis of property and his approach to Christian religion based on a combination of reason and revelation, were significantly influenced by Grotius' work. However, one the aspects of Locke's thought on which the influence of Grotius' natural law theory was particularly significant was his justification of colonialism and slavery. This topic deserves a particular attention as it tells us a different story about the contribution of Grotius to the intellectual origins of the Enlightenment, which concerned the relationships between natural law and colonialism.

The relationship between the Enlightenment and colonialism has been the object of contrasting interpretations, with scholars dividing themselves between those who see this intellectual movement as inherently anti-colonialist and those, instead, who point out its endorsement of dividing lines between 'civilisation' and 'barbarism' as *de facto* justifying modern colonialism.[35] According to Barbara Arneil, unlike his predecessors, Grotius' natural law theory, particularly his treatment of property rights, was originally developed in the context of the conflict between England and the United Provinces for the monopoly of commerce and trade in the East Indies.[36] The legacy of the duplicitous nature of Grotius' natural law theory is exemplified by the work of Locke. Locke's engagement with Grotius' natural law theory dated to the early 1660s, when he wrote the *Essays on the Law of Nature,* and it culminated in the development of the 'new republicanism' based on natural law that would come to underpin the political philosophy of the American constitution.[37] In recent years, however, the importance of Locke's natural law theory as a source of Anglo-American liberalism has been questioned in consequence of his direct involvement in the British colonisation and exploitation of North America. Locke's experience in colonial administration and his involvement in the Royal African Company, which was a slave-trading enterprise, had important repercussions for his political writings, particularly in the treatment of slavery, property and conquest in the *Two Treatises of Government.*[38] The influence of Grotius is particularly relevant in Locke's views on punishment and slavery. Locke did not admit 'voluntary slavery' on the basis of the supposition that men are naturally and equally free. However, like Grotius, Locke admitted that 'captives taken in a just war' could be enslaved.[39] While slavery was not permissible in English society, it was justifiable in the territories of Africa and North America, where people lived in 'the state of Nature'. 'These Men having, as I say, forfeited their Lives, and with it their

Liberties, and lost their Estates; and being in the state of slavery, not capable of any property, cannot in that state be considered as any part of Civil Society'.[40] Since neither the North American Indians nor the Africans had waged war against the English settlers, Locke drew from Grotius' analysis of punishment in *Mare liberum* and *De jure belli ac pacis*, as it allowed for restraint of the offender's liberty through enslavement.[41]

Like Grotius, Locke was a colonial thinker, although not one of empire.[42] His example confirms Sankhar Muthu's view that the modern natural law tradition that started from Grotius, although in principle agnostic about imperialism due to the intrinsic egalitarian understanding of human nature implied by natural rights, eventually underpinned the European justification of empire,[43] thus confirming the connection between Enlightenment and colonialism.

26.3 Biblical Exegesis and Natural Religion

Grotius' interest in moral philosophy, which earned him a reputation as the father of modern natural law theory, also found expression in his personal elaboration of Christian ethics. In *De veritate*, he set out the fundamentals of Christian religion to accommodate reason and revelation; in the *Annotationes*, he adopted an historical and philological approach to separate the ethical core of Scripture based on 'the central commandment to love one's neighbour from secondary doctrines unnecessary to salvation'.[44] It has been justly observed that Grotius was 'a representative of a late humanistic tradition that supported a historical approach to the Bible, but was loath to enforce a drastic and irreversible break with orthodoxy'.[45] This notwithstanding, during the eighteenth century, due particularly to his 'widely-suspected and commented on tendency towards Socinianism' and 'to the uses to which he put his Bible criticism' and particularly his refusal 'to concede that the Old Testament prophecies announce and point to the coming of Christ', Grotius was greatly appreciated by some of the most subversive critics of organised Christianity of the era, such as the Deists Anthony Collins (1676–1729) and Hermann Samuel Reimarus (1694–1768). According to this interpretation, Grotius contributed to the 'philosophical' strand of Socinianism. Drawing on the work of Faustus Socinus (1539–1604), Socinianism basically promoted a rational approach to Scripture, on which basis it denied the doctrine of the Trinity and the divinity of Christ. To Jonathan Israel, Socinianism was a stepping stone to radically enlightened thought for the 'obvious relationship' that it had with 'naturalism and materialism, on the one hand, and the origins of modern democracy and equality on the other'.[46] *De veritate* became popular among both Catholics and Protestants on the continent.[47] The radical reception of Grotius, as exemplified by his association with Socinianism, was a significant aspect of his broader and multifarious legacy to the Enlightenment. However, one of the main differences between Grotius and Socinus concerned their concept of punishment. Socinus described the right of punishment as the right of a creditor, thus implying that decisions over punishment were up to the injured party, with no other consideration regarding other interests or rights. To Grotius, instead, the aim of punishment was common good and the preservation of society.[48] Grotius' different perspective on punishment from Socinus had an impact on the late-eighteenth century Dutch Christian Enlightenment of Dionys Van den Wijnpersse (1724–1808), 'who accepted Grotius' conception of the reception through Christ and his being the father of natural law as well'.[49] In Italy, after the second half of the eighteenth century, Catholic apologists like the Neapolitan Damiano Romano (c.1708–87) stressed the difference between the accommodation of reason and revelation elaborated in *De veritate* by a leading exponent of the 'novatori' of Northern Europe, and the atheistic ideas exposed in Pufendorf's *De habitu religionis Christianæ* 'libro pestilentissimo'.[50] In post-Restoration England, both moderate Nonconformists like Richard Baxter (1615–91) and the so-called 'Latitudinarians' – a group of clergymen and scholars within the Anglican Church who emphasised reason in religion and practical morality over theological speculation – preferred Grotius to the mechanistic conception of God and nature of René Descartes (1596–1650), Thomas Hobbes and Baruch Spinoza (1632–77).[51]

The engagement with Grotius' ideas spanned the spectrum of positions within European-wide debates on morality and biblical exegesis in the late-seventeenth and early-eighteenth centuries, thus making it difficult rigidly to explain his legacy in terms of mutually exclusive visions of the Enlightenment. The case of England, where, in the early eighteenth century, the struggle to defend and transmit the Bible and the nature of revealed religion was particularly heated, exemplifies the extent and pervasiveness of Grotius' reputation especially well. Hugh Trevor-Roper argued that Grotius contributed to the English Enlightenment not only via the moderate and irenic Anglican tradition from the Great Tew Circle to post-Restoration Latitudinarianism, but also through the Remonstrant-Arminian and Deist traditions.[52] According to W.J. Bulman, this vision is one-sided, in that it ignores that there was an 'Anglican Enlightenment' promoted by the Anglican establishment, which came to 'accept for good the idea that civil stability is more important that religious uniformity' and which, especially after the Restoration, instead of a backward-looking persecution of heterodoxy, promoted 'a novel scheme for civil stability and moral improvement drawn from the cutting edge of learned culture'.[53]

What was at stake in the early English Enlightenment's debates on ethics, religion and philosophy was not a single doctrine. It was, rather, the authority of Scripture itself to sustain attacks from either Catholics like Richard Simon or Deists like Collins and John Toland (1670–1722). Anglican scholars, such as William Whiston (1667–1752) and Richard Bentley (1662–1742), were therefore asked to 'rescue' the Bible by restoring its original meaning through the use of philology and history.[54] Within this context, Grotius' humanistic Bible hermeneutics played a prominent role, both in undermining and in defending the authority of the Bible and the clergy. Collins and Toland used Grotius' combination of history and philology against priestcraft, while a majority of authors, including Locke and the Latitudinarians, tended to borrow from Grotius' ecclesiological works a combination of theology and non-divine right ecclesiology in an attempt either to promote an accommodation between the English Episcopal Church and Presbyterian Church or to assimilate the latter into the former. Particularly relevant in this respect was the contribution of Grotius to the 'methodological shift' brought about by Anglican scholars with a view to defending the Bible from Spinoza, Simon, Toland and Collins, accused of promoting universal use of reason and understanding of the Bible.[55] Whiston, a theologian and mathematician who succeeded his mentor, Isaac Newton (1643–1727), as Lucasian Professor of Mathematics at Cambridge – from which he was expelled in 1710 after being accused of Arianism, undertook the study of primitive Christianity and a revision of King James I/VI's still canonical version of the New Testament. Whiston criticised Hobbes and Spinoza for their 'infidelity' with regard to prophecies and for subordinating God and men to 'necessity' and 'fatality'.[56] To this end, he regarded Grotius as an authoritative source, both on philology in ascertaining original passages in Greek or Hebrew and on primitive Christianity. Bentley, one of England's finest classical scholars, who distinguished himself by a philological and historicist investigation aimed to restore the Greek New Testament to its purity, engaged in an invective against Jean Le Clerc (1657–1736), who made several mistakes while publishing fragments of Menander (Amsterdam, 1709), in which Le Clerc had drawn improperly on Grotius' own notes on Stobaeus (fifth century) and Greek dramatists.[57] Furthermore, in his critical *Remarks* on Collins' *Discourse on Free Thinking*, Bentley alias 'Phileleutherus' accused Collins of having plagiarised from other authors and collated their ideas, similarly to what Le Clerc did with Grotius. Grotius – who was either depicted by Collins as a 'free thinker' when he told things contrary to common doctrine or ridiculed as an 'unthinker' when he espoused common opinion – was openly admired by Bentley, who took him as one of the sources for his philological method of enquiry of Scripture, although one to be handled with caution due to his ambiguous attitude towards the Trinity.[58]

The ubiquity of Grotius in English Enlightenment debates on the authenticity of Scripture and the related authority of the clergy as the only interpreter of its original meaning, can be explained by tracing a distinction between his ecclesiology and his biblical criticism. In Britain, the experience of revolution, and the potentially disruptive repercussions of religious dissent, reoriented the discussion towards an accommodation of religion and revelation. In this regard, Grotius' combination of Christian theology, natural religion and natural law, which included a belief in miracles while avoiding dealing with the issue of the Trinity, and his non-divine right ecclesiology, which favoured an accommodation between hierarchical forms of Church government while excluding more democratic ones, were influential among those in the Anglican establishment. This was especially the case of the Latitudinarians, who wanted to pacify the Church and develop the possibility of an undogmatic Christian universal ethics in contrast to the materialism and moral relativism associated with the philosophies of Descartes, Spinoza and the Deists.

26.4 Conclusion

Grotius' work contributed significantly to the Enlightenment debates on natural law, ethics and religion. The peak, in terms of publication and circulation of Grotius' main works, was reached in Germany between about 1680 and 1725;[59] in Italy in the 1740s, when the interest in Grotius was replaced on the one side by Charles de Montesquieu

(1689–1755), and, on the other, by Catholic apologists, who attempted to promote a Christian ethics through an alternative lineage connecting Grotius to Leibniz and Wolff.[60] In England, a veritable turning point in the reception of Grotius at the threshold of the Enlightenment was represented by Locke, whose departing from the former in morals, politics and religion marked the gradual replacement of the Dutchman's intellectual authority in England. Finally, eighteenth-century Scottish moral philosophers inherited from Grotius a debate on whether the universality of morality was 'as in the Common Sense philosophy', or was confined to a set of 'minimal, formal aspect of moral reasoning concerning justice without which human society could not exist'.[61]

During a timespan of a century or so after his death, Grotius' legacies to the Enlightenment appear to be as many as the variants of the Enlightenment itself. Some of the strands of reception of his work, such as those relating to natural law theory developed in *De jure belli ac pacis*, became one of the connecting discourses of the Enlightenment from Scotland to Naples, being re-adapted to the peculiarities of national contexts, from continental academic disputes against dominating neo-Aristotelianism, to juridical reactions to 'baronial' privileges and ecclesiastical rejoinders to the rising tide of scepticism and materialism represented by the philosophies of Descartes, Hobbes, Bayle and Spinoza. *De veritate* instead inaugurated a new type of literature attempting to harmonise reason and revelation, which was to be used by Deists, Catholics and Protestants alike.

However, beyond the fragmentation of the 'radical', 'moderate' or even 'Anglican' interpretations of Grotius within the Enlightenment debates on ethics and religion, an underpinning theme in the reception of his work was the correlation of natural law and natural religion that he traced both in *De jure belli ac pacis* and in *De veritate*.[62] Was there a universal ethics, under the form of a set of individual rights, which was at the same time Christian and consistent with human reason? Could this ethics provide a foundation of a pacified society? What was the role of state sovereignty in securing individual rights? Was it possible to reconcile earthly happiness with the duty to worship God? The influence of these questions for the Enlightenment cannot be explained merely in terms of a contribution to the process of 'rationalisation and secularisation', in that this would end up supporting a divisive vision of Grotius being pulled to one side by those from Pufendorf to Toland, who promoted a de-theologised vision of his work, and to the other by those, such as the Catholic apologists or Anglican scholars, who insisted on considering him a continuator either of neo-scholastic ethics or of Erasmus' irenicism. More broadly, then, if we consider how religion was a constituent of the Enlightenment,[63] it appears that Grotius' attempt to accommodate natural religion and natural law provided his readers with arguments in support of a Christian, but undogmatic, ethics that was rational and universal in its content. Grotius' attempt at reconciling natural religion and natural law was developed primarily in the 1610s during the Dutch controversies between Remonstrants and Counter-Remonstrants, in a context in which the new theories of Descartes, Hobbes and Spinoza were increasingly taken seriously. Grotius' combination of ethics, natural religion and historically-based ecclesiology was, therefore, seen as an alternative to the rising tide of materialism, atheism and moral relativism associated with the development of natural philosophy. In conclusion, Grotius was one of the authors who most contributed to the presence of a Christian minimal religion with a focus on ethics within the Enlightenment, and much less one who, at least in principle, wanted to dismantle organised Christianity.

Further Reading

Barducci, M., *Hugo Grotius and the Century of Revolution, 1613–1718* (Oxford, 2017).

Cairns, J.W., 'The first Edinburgh chair in law: Grotius and the Scottish Enlightenment', *Fundamina. A Journal of Legal History* 11 (2005) 11–43.

Champion, J., '"Socinianism truly stated": John Toland, Jean Leclerc and the eighteenth-century reception of Grotius' *De Veritate*', *Grotiana* N.S. 33 (2012) 119–43.

Conti, V. (ed.), *La recezione di Grozio a Napoli nel Settecento, Argomenti Storici* (Florence, 2002), vol. 2.

Grunert, F., 'The reception of Hugo Grotius' *De Jure Belli ac Pacis* in the early German Enlightenment', in T.J. Hochstrasser and P. Schröder (eds.), *Early Modern Natural Law Theories: Contexts and Strategies in the Early Enlightenment* (International Archives of the History of Ideas 186; *Berlin*, 2003), 89–105.

Haakonssen, K., 'Hugo Grotius and the history of political thought', *Political Theory* 13 (1985) 239–65.

Haakonssen, K., *Natural law and Moral Philosophy: From Grotius to the Scottish Enlightenment* (Cambridge, 1996).

Israel, J., 'Grotius and the rise of Christian 'Radical Enlightenment', *Grotiana* N.S. 35 (2014) 19–31.

Jeffery, R., *Hugo Grotius in International Thought* (Basingstoke, 2006).

Negro, P., 'The reputation of Grotius in Italy', *Grotiana* N.S. 20–1 (1999–2000) 49–75.

Nuttall, G., 'Richard Baxter and the Grotian Religion', in D. Baker (ed.), *Reform and Reformation: England and the Continent, c. 1500–c. 1750* (London, 1979).

Trevor-Roper, H., 'Hugo Grotius and England', in Hugh Trevor-Roper (ed.), *From Counter-Reformation to Glorious Revolution* (London, 1992).

Vermeulen, B.P., and G.A. Van Der Wal, 'Grotius, Aquinas and Hobbes. Grotian natural law between lex aeterna and natural rights', *Grotiana* N.S. 16–7 (1995–6) 55–83.

Notes

1 I would like to express my sincere gratitude to the Interdisciplinary Centre for European Enlightenment Studies – IZEA, Martin-Luther-Universität, Halle-Wittenberg (Germany), Durham University (particularly the Institute of Advanced Study and the Department of History) and the European Union, for having supported the research on which the present chapter is based.

2 W. Van Bunge, *The Early Enlightenment in the Dutch Republic, 1650–1750* (Leiden and Boston, 2003), 8–9.

3 T.J. Hochstrasser, *Natural Law Theories in the Early Enlightenment* (Cambridge, 2000), 1.

4 M. Zuckert, *Natural Rights and the New Republicanism* (Princeton, 1998), xix.

5 J. Israel, 'Grotius and the rise of Christian 'Radical Enlightenment', *Grotiana* N.S., 35 (2014) 19–31, at 20.

6 K. Haakonssen, *Natural law and Moral Philosophy: From Grotius to the Scottish Enlightenment* (Cambridge, 1996), 29.

7 Hochstrasser, *Natural law theories*, 21–2.

8 P. Korkman, 'Voluntarism and moral obligation: Barbeyrac's defence of Pufendorf Revisited', in T.J. Hochstrasser and P. Schröder (eds.), *Early Modern Natural Law Theories: Contexts and Strategies in the Early Enlightenment* (International Archives of the History of Ideas 186; Berlin, 2003), 195–225, at 196–9.

9 F. Grunert, 'The reception of Hugo Grotius's *De Jure Belli ac Pacis* in the early German Enlightenment', in Hochstrasser and Schroder (eds.), *Early Modern Natural Law Theories*, 89–105, at 96–7.

10 J.W. Cairns, 'The first Edinburgh chair in law: Grotius and the Scottish Enlightenment', *Fundamina. A Journal of Legal History*, 11 (2005) 11–43, at 35–6.

11 A. Smith, *The Theory of Moral Sentiments*, ed. D. Stewart (London, 1853), 501.

12 K. Haakonssen, 'Hugo Grotius and the history of political thought', *Political Theory*, 13 (1985) 239–65.

13 Ibid., 257; K. Haakonssen, 'Natural Law and the Scottish Enlightenment', *Man and Nature*, 4 (1985) 47–80, at 62.

14 J. Salter, 'Adam Smith and the Grotian theory of property', *British Journal of Politics and International Relations* 12 (2010) 3–21, at 5.

15 L. Brace, *The Idea of Property in Seventeenth-Century England* (Manchester, 1998), 51.

16 J. Moore, 'Natural rights in the Scottish Enlightenment',in M. Goldie and R. Wokler (eds.), *The Cambridge History of Eighteenth-Century Political Thought* (Cambridge, 2006), 291–316, at 292.

17 P. Negro, 'The reputations of Grotius in Italy. Some notes on Naples in the seventeenth and eighteenth centuries', *Grotiana* N.S. 20–21 (1999–2000) 49–75, at 56–7.

18 G.M. Labriola, 'Barbeyrac traduttore di Grozio', in V. Conti (ed.), *La recezione di Grozio a Napoli nel Settecento, Argomenti Storici* (Florence, 2002), vol. 2, 2.

19 M. Bazzoli, 'Grozio nel Settecento Italiano', in Conti, *La recezione*, vol. 2, 47–8 and 57–8.

20 G.W. Leibniz, 'Opinion on the principles of Pufendorf' (1706), in *Leibniz: Political writings*, ed. P. Riley (Cambridge, 1988), 71.

21 See M. Delon (ed.), *Encyclopedia of the Enlightenment* (Routledge, 2013), 127.

22 P. Riley, 'Social contract theory and its critics', in M. Goldie and R. Wokler (eds.), *The Cambridge History of Eighteenth-Century Political Thought* (Cambridge, 2006), 347–75, at 347.

23 H. Blom, 'Sociability and Hugo Grotius', *History of European Ideas* 41 (2015) 589–604.

24 Haakonssen, 'Hugo Grotius and the history of political thought', 241–2.

25 M. Somos, *Secularisation and the Leiden Circle* (Leiden and Boston, 2011).

26 A. Saether, *Natural Law and the Origin of Political Economy. Samuel Pufendorf and the History of Economics* (London, 2017), 41–2.

27 D. Baumgold, 'Pacifying politics: resistance, violence, and accountability in seventeenth-century contract theory', *Political Theory* 21 (1993) 6–27, at 7–8.

28 Ibid., 12.

29 D. Lee, *Popular Sovereignty in Early Modern Constitutional Thought* (Oxford, 2016), 255–72.

30 M. Hulliung, *The Social Contract in America: From the Revolution to the Present Age* (Lawrence, KS, 2007), vii-viii.

31 T. Hochstrasser, 'The Claims of conscience: natural law theory, obligation, and resistance in the Huguenot diaspora', in J.C. Laursen (ed.), *New Essays on the Political Thought of the Huguenots of the 'Refuge'* (Leiden and Boston, 1995), 15–51, at 32–7.

32 Hulliung, *The Social Contract in America*, vii.

33 *Rousseau: 'The Social Contract' and Other Later Political Writings*, ed. V. Gourevitch (Cambridge, 1997), 42.

34 J. Collins, 'Early modern foundations of classic liberalism', in G. Klosko (ed.) *The Oxford Handbook of the History of Political Philosophy* (Oxford, 2011), 258–81, at 260–1.

35 D. Tricoire, 'Introduction', in Tricoire (ed.), *Enlightened Colonialism: Civilization Narratives and Imperial Politics in the Age of Reason* (Berlin, 2017), 1–22, at 4.

36 B. Arneil, *John Locke and America* (Oxford, 1996), 46–54.

37 Cf. Zuckert, *Natural Rights*.

38 J.R. Milton, 'Dating Locke's Second Treatise', *History of Political Thought* 16 (1995) 356–90, at 372–4.

39 J. Locke, *Two Treatises of Government*, ed. P. Laslett (2nd edition, Cambridge, 1970), 341.

40 Ibid., 340.

41 J. Welchman, 'Locke on slavery and inalienable rights', *Canadian Journal of Philosophy* 25 (1995) 67–81, at 78–81.

42 D. Armitage, 'John Locke. Theorist of empire?', in S. Muthu (ed.), *Empire and Modern Political Thought* (Cambridge, 2012), 84–111.

43 S. Muthu, *Enlightenment against Empire* (Princeton, 2009), 268.

44 H.J.M. Nellen, 'Growing Tension between church doctrines and critical exegesis of the Old Testament', in C. Brekelmans and M. Sæbø (eds.) *Hebrew Bible / Old Testament: The History of Its Interpretation: II: From the Renaissance to the Enlightenment,* ed. M. Haran (Göttingen, 2008), 803–10.

45 Ibid., 814.

46 Israel, 'Grotius and the rise of Christian 'Radical Enlightenment', 20–6.

47 G. Lottes, 'The transformation of apologetical literature in the early Enlightenment. The case of Grotius's *De veritate*', *Grotiana* N.S. 35 (2014) 66–75, at 66–7.

48 S. Mortimer, 'Human liberty and human nature in the works of Faustus Socinus and his readers', *Journal of the History of Ideas* 70 (2009) 191–211, at 201.

49 H. Blom, 'Grotius and Socinianism', in M. Mulsow and J. Rohls (ed.), *Socinianism and Arminianism. Antitrinitarians, Calvinists and Cultural Exchange in Seventeenth-Century Europe* (Leiden and Boston, 2005), 121–47, at 145.

50 Cit. in Bazzoli, 'Grozio nel Settecento italiano', 58.

51 Cf. M. Ignatius and J. Griffin (eds.), *Latitudinarianism in the Seventeenth-Century Church of England* (Leiden and Boston, 1992).

52 H. Trevor-Roper, *Religion the Reformation and Social Change* (3rd edition, London, 1977), chapter 4, 'The religious origins of the Enlightenment', 193–236.

53 W.J. Bulman, *Anglican Enlightenment Orientalism, Religion and Politics in England and its Empire, 1648–1715* (Cambridge, 2016), 4–12.

54 J. Sheehan, *The Enlightenment Bible: Translation, Scholarship, Culture* (Princeton, 2007), 25–33.

55 Ibid., 47–8.

56 *The life and writings of Mr. William Whiston. Containing, memoirs of several of his friends also. Written by himself* (1753), 89, 168.

57 J.H. Monk, *The Life of Richard Bentley* (C.J.G. and F. Rivington, 1830), vol. 1, 209–11.

58 K.-L. Haugen, *Richard Bentley* (Cambridge, MA, 2011), 205–6.

59 Grunert, 'Reception', 92.

60 Bazzoli, 'Grozio nel Settecento italiano', 57.

61 Haakonssen, 'Natural law and the Scottish Enlightenment', 72.

62 Cf. J. Lagree, 'Grotius: natural law and natural religion', in R. Crocker (ed.), *Religion, Reason and Nature in Early Modern Europe* (Berlin, 2001), 17–39.

63 J. Sheehan, 'Enlightenment, religion, and the enigma of secularization: a review essay', *The American Historical Review* 108 (4) (October 2003), 1061–80.

27 Grotian Revivals in the Theory and History of International Law

Ignacio de la Rasilla

27.1 Introduction

Hugo Grotius is a paradigmatic figure in the history and theory of international law in a double and mutually reinforcing sense. Historically, Grotius has for long been considered the founding father of international law because his *De jure belli ac pacis*, first published in 1625, has long passed for the first systematic exposition of international law as an autonomous branch of law with a secularised natural law foundation. As a supposed historical symbol of the transition from a *jus gentium* founded on a natural law of revealed origins to one accessible to human reason regardless of belief – that would be valid, according to the famous passage, 'etiamsi daremus' (even if God did not exist) – Grotius has also often been credited with foreshadowing the international legal order crystallised by the Peace of Westphalia of 1648. Westphalia has traditionally been considered the aetiological birthdate of the modern voluntary law of nations between equal and sovereign European nation-states at the time of the disintegration of the medieval *res publica Christiana*.

Theoretically, Grotius' *De jure belli ac pacis* has also been commonly regarded as a springboard for a modern conceptual world view underlying the theories and methodology of international law. This characterisation owes much to the rendition that a prominent international lawyer of the twentieth century offered of the Grotian tradition in international law in the aftermath of the Second World War. Hersch Lauterpacht (1897–1960) identified eleven tenets or features as appertaining to the Grotian tradition. These included the 'subjection of the totality of international relations to the rule of law', the consideration of the law of nature as 'the ever-present source for supplementing the voluntary law of nations' and Grotius' 'rejection of 'reason of State'. Lauterpacht also portrayed Grotius as a forerunner of the 'fundamental rights and freedoms of the individual' and as a champion of the 'idea of peace'.[1] Since then, international lawyers in Anglo-American academia have generally embraced this cosmopolitan portrayal of the Grotian tradition as an emblem of the tradition of idealism and progress in international relations. Accordingly, they have portrayed Grotius as a short-cut for the main tenets of 'liberal internationalism', within which international law works as a constructive force for progress that effectively mediates between state sovereignty and an interdependent international community, with the human being at its core. This liberal internationalist *via media* matches the portrayal that the English School of International Relations later offered of Grotius as the archetypical thinker of the rational tradition of international thought. In Martin Wight's (1913–72) influential tripartite classification, the Grotian tradition stands as a middle-of-the-road position between the extremes of the Machiavellian and Hobbesian traditions of 'realism' in an anarchical international society and the Kantian tradition of 'revolutionism' or 'utopianism', advocating the progress of the world community toward a *civitas maxima* or global federation.[2]

This chapter examines how the title of founder of the law of nations was bestowed upon Grotius and how the liberal internationalist interpretation of the existence of a Grotian tradition in international law came into being. It also reviews the extent to which both historical constructs have been challenged by new historical research and contemporary re-interpretations of Grotius' works and life. The chapter is divided into three parts. The first part covers the reception of Grotius by international lawyers from the time of the discovery of his *De jure praedae commentarius* in 1864 to the establishment of the Grotius Society in England during the First World War. The second part examines the revivals of Grotius among international lawyers in the aftermaths of both world wars and considers a number of Grotius-related historiographical developments during the Cold War period. The third part examines how, in recent decades, on the one hand Grotius has become more mainstreamed and further institutionalised as a global symbol of international law while, on the other hand, his reputation has suffered from him being labelled a hired pen of European colonialism and exploitation. The concluding section reflects on the lasting fame of the 'miracle of Holland' among international lawyers and suggests that the history of international law as a research field should now take a break from Hugo Grotius.

27.2 The Battle of the Founders of International Law

A measure of the popularity that Emerich de Vattel's (1714–67) *Le droit des gens* soon gained as the standard international law text is that Grotius' *De jure belli ac pacis*, which had been reprinted or translated dozens of times since its first edition in Paris in 1625, 'stopped [being] re-edited at about the same time that the work of Vattel appeared' in 1758.[3] However, the lesser practical relevance that statesmen, diplomats and jurists found in Grotius' juridical *magnum opus* did not prevent him from being commonly regarded as 'the founder of the discipline and, in principle, its only founder' during the first part of the nineteenth century.[4] Grotius owed this attribution of paternity of the *jus naturae et gentium* to his three-volume treatise on the rights and duties of nations in times of war and its aftermath. With this book, Grotius professed to seek to restrain and humanise the chronic recurrence and viciousness of fighting during the Thirty Years War (1618–48).

Grotius' unquestioned status as the father of international law, which was buttressed by his central role in all discussions of the law of nations by successive authors and by his constant presence in all early historical accounts of the discipline, began to change with the discovery of the unpublished manuscript of *De jure praedae* in 1864. *De jure praedae* was a brief he had prepared at the behest of the Dutch East India Company (VOC) to support its colonial competition with Portugal for spheres of commercial influence in East Asia in 1604–6. Its publication in Latin in 1868 made it apparent that Grotius' *Mare liberum*, an influential pamphlet on the freedom of navigation, fishing and trade that lay at the origin of what came to be known as the 'battle of the books'[5] over the dominion of the high seas in the seventeenth century, was not an independent essay, as it had been considered since its original release in 1609, but was originally a chapter – chapter twelve – of a larger work. The publication of *De jure praedae*, other than revealing an early source of reference in the writing of *De jure belli ac pacis*, also made evident, as Peter Haggenmacher points out, 'the decisive influence of Spanish scholars, and especially of Vitoria, on the thought of the Dutch jurist-consult'.[6] This was the beginning of what came to be known as the contest of the putative fathers of the law of peoples, which gained academic credentials when Thomas E. Holland (1835–1926) gave a lecture about Alberico Gentili (1552–1608) in Oxford in 1874. In this famous lecture, Holland stressed that Gentili's *De jure belli libri tres* (1598) had been the model for *De jure belli ac pacis* and that, therefore, 'the first step toward making international law what it is was taken, not by Grotius, but by Gentilis'.[7]

Underlying the battle of the founders of international law – which would rage on until the mid-1930s – lay a consensus among late-nineteenth-century historians of international law on the importance of investigating the forerunners of Grotius and the work of Grotius in the light of his predecessors. By the mid-1870s and 1880s, international law was beginning to become professionalised as a discipline taught at universities, and the codification of international law, based on the gathering of international state practice and legal doctrine, was made the founding purpose of the *Institut de droit international* (IDI, 1873) and the Association for the Reform and Codification of the Law of Nations, later renamed the International Law Association (ILA, 1873), whose professional membership spanned across Europe and North America. During the 1880s, 1890s and early twentieth century, an array of academic publications sought to investigate the historical origins of the rising discipline. Among the most influential were those written by Ernest Nys (1851–1920) who, while considering the Spanish neo-scholastics to be the early architects of international law, credited Grotius with being the founder of its science.[8]

Grotius' reputation at the time of the early rise of international law as an academic discipline was furthered by the transnational influence of the peace movement and by the celebration of the first Peace Conference in The Hague in 1899. Gathering representatives of the main powers, the conference put The Hague on a course that would make it the world capital of international adjudication through the twentieth and early twenty-first centuries. This, in turn, did wonders to anchor the reputation of the celebrated son of the nearby city of Delft as the ultimate historical icon of international law. According to Van Ittersum, the drivers behind the international consecration of Grotius' reputation were the outcome of a 'combination of Dutch nationalism', which found in Grotius a national hero it could associate itself with, and American affinity for the Dutch ancestry of a republican form of government.[9] This was at a time when the USA was developing an informal imperial network and aggrandising its overseas territory, with its commercial universalism requiring a new American enthusiasm for international law.[10] The Hague Peace Conference may have contributed to accelerating the release of *De jure belli ac pacis* in 1900 from the Catholic Church's index of forbidden books, where it had remained since 1627 'until corrected' ('donec corrigantur'). It surely was a factor in the American re-print of the translation that A.C. Campbell had prepared back in 1814. The 1901 edition, the first to appear in English since William Whewell's abridged translation in 1853, was preceded by an introduction written by David J. Hill (1850–1932), assistant secretary of state of the USA. In the early years of the twentieth century, the philanthropy of the American industrialist tycoon, Andrew Carnegie (1835–1921), also made possible the construction of the Peace Palace (to house the Permanent Court of Arbitration (PCA) and other future international courts), of which Grotius has been named the 'patron saint'.[11]

The philanthropy of the Carnegie Institution of Washington and, later, the Carnegie Endowment for International Peace was behind the establishment of the collection of *The Classics of International Law* in 1906. This was at the suggestion of James Brown Scott (1866–1943), the driving force behind the creation of the American Society of International Law (ASIL) in 1906. Scott went on to supervise the collection as general editor over the following four decades. He built his request for financial support to the Carnegie Institution on the importance of making the works of the predecessors of Grotius, a proper edition of the masterpiece of Grotius himself [and] the works of the chief successors of Grotius broadly available to an American audience. This tripartite classification, while retaining Grotius' centrality in the history of international law, was based on the idea that the 'general statement' according to which 'Grotius is universally considered as the founder of international law ... is true enough, but likely to mislead'. Instead, according to Scott, Grotius should be seen as a 'middle point in the development of international law' of which he, nonetheless, remained 'its first and its greatest expounder'.[12] From 1911 to 1950, the collection released twenty-two issues published in 40 volumes, including both the Latin and English editions of Grotius' three major works on international law, as fundamental intellectual landmarks in a historical intellectual evolution from Giovanni de Legnano's *De bello, de repraesaliis et de duello* (fourteenth century) to Henry Wheaton's (1785–1848) *Elements of International Law*, originally published in 1836.

Meanwhile, in the Netherlands, during the first two decades of the twentieth century, a number of factors became aligned to make The Hague a pole for the worldwide diffusion of Grotius' reputation: the Second Peace Conference, which for the first time attracted a truly global representation of states to The Hague in 1907; the construction and inauguration of the Peace Palace in 1913; and the scheduling of a Third Peace Conference, which would have taken place in 1915. These events gave impetus to the establishment of the Netherlands Association of International Law (NAIL) in 1910. Not surprisingly, the first international law periodical published in 1913 under the NAIL's auspices was called *Grotius: international jaarboek* (*Grotius: International Yearbook*). In spite of the backlash of the First World War, Dutch scholars continued to sustain the reputation of Grotius by establishing the Society for the publication of Grotius, which was presided over by Cornelis Van Vollenhoven (1874–1933), in 1917. Van Vollenhoven was Chancellor of Leiden University and, in 1918, published *De Drie Treden van het Volken*recht (*The Three Stages in the Evolution of the Law of Nations*). Originally written in Dutch, but rapidly translated into several other languages, Van Vollenhoven's book has been credited with having revitalised the engagement with the work of Grotius in the aftermath of the First World War. On the basis of a selective reading of Grotius, as much as through an instillation of his own moral ideas into Grotius' opus, Van Vollenhoven rendered an idealised portrayal of Grotius as an apostle of peace and the antithesis of Vattel, traditionally considered an early personi-fication of the positivist method. Although Van Vollenhoven's book was subsequently criticised for its ahistorical character,[13] it set the course for a romanticised Grotian tradition of international peace through law. This is a theme that, as we shall later see, was taken up again by Lauterpacht in the aftermath of the Second World War.

Beyond the Netherlands, the setting up of the Grotius Society in London in 1915 would turn out to be particularly relevant for the international dissemination of Grotius' reputation and for the develop-ment of Grotian scholarship. This was conceived as an exclusively British national society and it aimed to substitute, during the war, the ILA, whose cosmopolitan composition included nationals of both enemy and neutral powers. Its proceedings were successively published as *Problems of War* (1915–17) and as *Transactions of the Grotius Society* (1918–59), with regular contributions devoted to Grotius and his works. The founding of the society signalled a symbolic institutional embrace of Grotius by British international law academia that lasted for almost fifty years until the merging of the Grotius Society and the Society of Comparative Legislation into the British Institute of International and Comparative Law in 1959.

27.3 Grotius Reborn from the Ashes of Two World Wars

The inauguration of the Permanent Court of International Justice (PCIJ) at the Peace Palace in 1920 was followed by the start in the same premises of the courses of The Hague Academy of International Law (HAIL) in 1923 with the financial support of the Carnegie Endowment for International Peace. The HAIL was the brainchild of the Dutch international lawyer, Tobias C.M. Asser (1838–1913), who donated his Nobel Prize for Peace to fund the academy. These two institutions further consolidated the position of The Hague as the judicial and, also now, a significant academic pole of the international legal order presided over by the League of Nations during the interwar years. In this context, it was not long before Grotius was again in the spotlight of international law.

The occasion for this new Grotian revival was the 300th anniversary of Grotius' widely celebrated masterpiece in 1925. The academic festivities surrounding the commemoration of this anniversary were accompanied by a great number of works on Grotius and his oeuvre in books and international law journals.[14] The oldest of these in the English language, *The American Journal of International Law* (AJIL), of which James Brown Scott had become the honorary editor-in-chief after almost two decades at its helm, programmed the publication of a series of essays on Grotius in each of its four issues in 1925. Along with essays by some of the Grotian 'usual suspects', like Van Vollenhoven and Scott himself, there were also pieces from other leading scholars. The long-standing dean of Harvard Law School, Roscoe Pound (1870–1964), despite questioning in his essay the seminal character of Grotius' 'great book of the juristic age of reason', nonetheless highlighted its 'pivotal position in the history of jurisprudence'[15] and its deep influence on US law in its formative period. Part one of a two-part essay by Jesse S. Reeves (1872–1942) offered a historical contextualisation of the coming into being of the first edition of Grotius' *magnum opus* in Paris,[16] barely four years after Grotius' romantic escape inside a book chest from Castle Loevestein in the Dutch Republic, where he was serving a life sentence. The second part of the essay retraced the glorious aftermath of the book's original publication, identifying the dozens of Latin editions and translations into other languages of Grotius works[17] up to the publication scheduled in the collection of *The Classics of International Law* of the seventh independent English translation of *De jure belli ac pacis* in 1925, the first one by an American scholar.

Paradoxically enough, however, the tercentenary of Grotius' *De jure belli ac pacis* also marked the beginning of the end of Grotius as the crowned father of international law in erudite circles. In Spain, the tercentenary fostered the establishment of the Association Francisco de Vitoria, and with it a strong collaboration developed between Camilo Barcia Trelles (1888–1977), a Spanish scholar who went to HAIL to teach on the Spanish classics four times in barely twelve years, and Scott. By the early 1930s, Scott, now the President of the American Society for International Law (ASIL), was intensely engaged in an academic campaign to crown Francisco de Vitoria (c. 1483–1546) as the true founding father of the law of nations. This left Grotius, according to Scott, as a 'populariser in the best sense of the word' and, therefore, 'a member of the Vitorian or, as it is more usually termed, the Spanish school'.[18] This renaissance of Francisco de Vitoria and the School of Salamanca, over which Vitoria was the intellectual trailblazer, took place in the larger context of a widespread revival of natural law doctrines among international lawyers in the interwar period. Across Europe, international law scholars were searching beyond the positivist sovereign-will theory for new theoretical foundations as the source of international obligations for the proto-institutionalised society that emerged from the ashes of the First World War around the League of Nations. In trying, as Lauterpacht himself did, to identify 'a factor superior to and independent of the will of states', which they tended to locate in 'the objective fact of the existence of an interdependent community of states',[19] these legal scholars were naturally attracted to the intellectual constructions of late Spanish scholasticism and, in particular, to the works of Vitoria and Francisco Suárez (1548–1617) in the sixteenth and early seventeenth centuries. Despite the crumbling of the system of the League of Nations after the Spanish Civil War, Spanish international law scholars continued to eulogise and extol Vitoria as the founding father of international law during the forty years of General Franco's (1892–1975) national-Catholicist regime in Spain. The Spanish experience with Vitoria stands as a prime example of the role that cultural patriotism has historically played in the nationalist glorification of classical writers on international law, of which the Dutch appropriation of Grotius' legacy stands, nonetheless, second to none.

Once again, the end of another world war proved decisive in giving the international reputation of Grotius a new boost. Although Lauterpacht's famous article in the *British Yearbook of International Law* resorted to *De jure belli ac pacis* on the three hundredth anniversary of Grotius' death (1945) to 'sustain hope by drawing inspiration from works in which principle has asserted itself against makeshifts', Lauterpacht did not do this uncritically. Instead, after devoting many pages to highlighting the 'faults of method and substance' in *De jure belli ac pacis*, Lauterpacht's purpose seemed to have been to distil his own personal reading of the spirit of the book and discard everything else as mere objects of legal antiquarianism. To fulfil this programme, Lauterpacht extracted eleven tenets or features of what he termed the 'Grotian tradition' as representative of how Grotius had endowed 'international law with unprecedented dignity and authority by making it part not only of a general system of jurisprudence but also of a universal moral code'.[20] Several of these features, such as 'the subjection of the totality of international relations to the rule of law', 'the acceptance of the law of nature as an independent source of international law', 'the distinction between just and unjust war' and the 'binding force of promises' (or the principle of *pacta sunt servanda*), were all central tenets in the theoretical progressive orthodoxy of the interwar period.

The other most important characteristics that Lauterpacht identified as belonging to the Grotian tradition should be seen in the context of the dawn of the age of international human rights law, to the foundations of which Lauterpacht was in parallel greatly contributing at the time with his seminal *An International Bill of the Rights of Man*[21] and other works. This context explains Lauterpacht's efforts to ascribe an essential importance to the 'recognition of the essential identity of states and individuals in Grotius' work', the 'true meaning' of which, according to Lauterpacht, is that 'the individual is the ultimate unit of all law, international and municipal, in the double sense that the obligations of international law are ultimately addressed to him and that the development, the well-being, and the dignity of the individual human being are a matter of direct concern to international law'.[22] This, in combination with the affirmation of the 'social nature of man as the basis of the law of nature' and the denial of 'reason of State' as a basic and decisive factor in international relations went some way to portraying, despite obvious difficulties, Grotius as an early advocate of the fundamental rights and freedoms of the individual and as, ultimately, a representative of the traditions of peace and progress through international law.[23]

This revamped Grotian tradition for the new UN era in Anglo-American academia was retaken by the 'English School of International Relations' – a term that is 'usually construed as signifying an approach to the study of international politics more rooted in historical and humanistic learning than in the social sciences'[24] – as an archetypical middle-of-the-road rationalist tradition in the field of international relations. In the work of Martin Wight (1913–72),[25] later re-elaborated by Hedley Bull (1932–85),[26] Grotius is depicted as embodying 'the golden mean, or Aristotelian moderation', as 'a reconciler and synthesizer'[27] bridging the realist/idealist divide, which had defined the so-called 'first great debate' in international relations. In Wight's path-breaking and influential tripartite organisation of the history of international political thought since Machiavelli, the Grotian tradition stands as the *via media* between the extremes of Machiavellian or Hobbesian 'realism', in which there is anarchical competition and struggle among sovereign states seeking to maximise their interests, and the 'Revolutionist' or 'Kantian' tradition, in which a morally united international community progresses to a *civitas maxima,* or global confederation of states.

Beyond the realm of British academia and successive enquiries in the twin-sister disciplines of international law and international relations into the legacy of Grotius for the idea of a modern international society during the Cold War,[28] the decolonisation process across Africa and Asia also fostered new attention on the part of the newly independent states on the putative founder of the law of nations. A pioneer in the engagement by Asian and African scholars with the historical practices of non-Western peoples against the benchmark of Grotius' work was Charles Henry Alexandrowicz (1902–75),[29] a Polish and subsequently British law scholar who took a professorship of international law in Madras in the aftermath of Indian independence and wrote extensively on the law of nations in the East Indies in the sixteenth, seventeenth and eighteenth centuries. As a result of this work, Alexandrowicz has been retrospectively reclaimed as the starting point of a post-colonial revisionist critique of classical writers, including Grotius himself, as the hirelings of colonial and imperial policies.[30] Alexandrowicz founded a Grotian Society in India in 1960, of which he remained chairman while first in Sydney and then in London until the end of his days, ensuring that the society fulfilled its purposes. These were to 'promote the revival of the much-neglected history of the law of nations',[31] by developing a programme of publications in the form of a homonymous book series and a sequence of supplements to the *Indian Yearbook of International Affairs* devoted to the study of historical topics in international law.

Partly under the influence of the decolonisation decades and the creation of newly independent states through the 1950s, 1960s and 1970s, and partly as a result of the dynamics of evolving research in the traditionally overlooked field of the history of international law, these decades also saw historiographical developments that minimised Grotius' importance in the history of international law. Very broadly speaking, these developed in two directions, as can be seen in the historical work of Wolfgang Preiser (1903–97). On the one hand, there were efforts to retrace the emergence of the nation-state before Westphalia in the Western world, either back to the 1300s or to the early sixteenth century. On the other hand, new works extended the history of international law, both temporally and spatially, far beyond the geographical boundaries of the European world, and therefore of Grotius' own immediate milieu in the early European seventeenth century. Also, owing much to German international legal historiography, there was a new shift of focus that attempted to overcome the biases of an 'idealist intellectual' historiography of international law. This, according to Wilhelm Grewe (1911–2000), had become lost in 'an abstract history of the theory' because it did not take enough account of the 'close connection between legal theory and state practice' or of the 'concrete political and sociological background' to the theories of the most noted writers. In this characterisation, the succession of intellectual landmarks ordered around natural and positivist writers in which Grotius had featured so paradigmatically obscured the real division of the history of international law into epochs characterised by the dominance of particular hegemonic powers. In this periodisation, Grotius belonged to the Spanish Age (1494–1648) and his 'legend' as the father of international law became 'once and for all' (again!) one based on those of his predecessors.[32]

27.4 Debunking the Resilient Myth of Grotius

Since the mid-1980s, Grotius has, on the one hand, become more mainstreamed and further institutionalised globally as a symbol of international law. On the other hand, he has also become the object of a post-colonial historiographical revisionist critique for being a hireling of Dutch imperialism. This has further undermined the interwoven historical and theoretical pillars on which Grotius' time-honoured reputation in the history of international law has long stood.

Since the end of the Cold War, the mainstreamed canonisation of Grotius has largely benefited from a number of interrelated factors. First among these has been the intellectual enlistment of Grotius in the tropes of post-Cold War Anglo-American international liberalism where, as we have seen, he stands as a short-hand symbol for a progressive tradition in international legal thought. In this context, the eponymous adjective 'Grotian' has gained a life of its own as a household scholarly term attached to various intellectual constructs. The cases of the 'Grotian tradition', the 'Grotian moment',[33] the 'Grotian quest'[34] and the several existing 'Grotian theories', ranging from the area of humanitarian intervention[35] to the law of the sea, are sufficient illustration. This is a recurrent scholarly practice whereby modern international lawyers claim to draw insights and inspiration from Grotius to describe and meet contemporary realities or to convey a moralised perspective on the role of international law in world affairs. Second, the study of Grotius' works, life and times has also benefited from the elevation of some of the British, or nationalised-British, champions of his memory to the status of twentieth-century semi-modern classics, thanks – up to a point – to the culturally pervasive influence of English as the contemporary *lingua franca* in international legal practice and its scholarship. The institutionalisation of Grotius in the Anglo-American tradition and its dissemination has also been reflected in the establishment of a Grotius Annual Lecture, which has opened the annual meeting of the ASIL since 1999. Along with the Grotius Lecture, which is hosted annually by the British Institute of Comparative and International Law, the holding of the ASIL's lecture further contributes to a Grotian remembrance that often translates into new efforts to extract lessons from Grotius to tackle 'the major challenges for international law and its practitioners in our time'.[36] Last but not least, with the establishment of new international courts and the reactivation of the PCA, The Hague has further accrued its importance as a pole for the spreading of Grotius' fame as a global symbol of international law. This, alongside the rite of passage for any aspiring international lawyer of visiting the HAIL and the Peace Palace Library, which holds one of the greatest collections in the world of the works of Hugo Grotius, has further amplified the figure of Grotius in the global spotlight of international law.

However, the received interpretation of Grotius among international lawyers has also been critically challenged against the background of the 'turn to history' in international law over recent decades. Authoritative accounts, such as that by Peter Haggenmacher in the early 1980s, have contributed to cutting to size the interpretation of Grotius offered by late-nineteenth-century scholarship.[37] This challenge has, first, further questioned whether Grotius really intended to advocate a new secular conception of international law or whether the formula he used was, in fact, a common *ex hypothesi* formula Christian writers of the times used to reinstate God's unquestionable existence. Furthermore, it has been stated that Grotius' treatise was not a system of international law, as it has often been claimed in order to award him the title of the author of the first systematic treatise in the discipline, but instead that it still remains essentially a generalised theory of just war[38] written in the tradition of a classic genre. Last but not least, Grotius' dominant position – if it ever was really such – as the conceptual founding father of international law seems to have finally reverted to the Dominican friar, Francisco de Vitoria, with the 'Grotian tradition' now being considered by the experts to be 'Vitorian' in almost all but name.[39]

An important source of methodological inspiration for the historiographical revisionism that has swept across Grotius' legacy has come from authors like Richard Tuck, Martine Van Ittersum and others who have explored the 'dark side of rights theories' and tried to show that the political theories of classic seventeenth-century authors provided material for imperial and colonial practice and thought in their home countries and abroad. This line of historiographical thought, which applies the methodology of the Cambridge School of Political Thought to the classics of international law, has been welcomed among critical historians of international law who have presented Grotius, along with other 'classic' writers, starting with Vitoria, as historical accomplices of European colonialism and exploitation.[40] According to this account, as a result of this biographical and historical re-contextualisation, Grotius' title of 'father of international law' should be changed to that of 'godfather of Dutch imperialism'.[41] This biographically driven re-contextualisation of Grotius' work has, in turn, affected the pedigree of the 'Grotian tradition' in international law. Closer readings of Grotius' works have tried to separate the myth from the actual work, concluding that Grotius' writings indicate that he was not really a Grotian, at least not as Lauterpacht defined the term,[42] and that the Grotian tradition was less about Grotius than it is about the ideas and goals of his post-Second World War interlocutors.[43] In this revisionist reading, the Grotian tradition has been portrayed as an intellectual variety of the 'invented tradition' in the sense that Eric Hobsbawm[44] used the term: 'a set of practices, normally governed by overtly or tacitly accepted rules and of a ritual or symbolic nature, which seek to inculcate certain values and norms of behaviour by repetition, which automatically implies continuity with the past'.[45] Last but not least, the growing methodological influence of global history with its focus on connections, networks, entanglements and historical encounters in promoting a new brand of comparative international legal history has also fostered new efforts to 'provincialise' Grotius in the light of non-Western sources.[46]

27.5 Grotius in the *Salon des Pas Perdus* of International Legal History

It is a defining characteristic of all classics, and by implication of the classics of international law, that they and their works become objects of different interpretations and reinterpretations in the light of different background historical circumstances, as well as of the rise and fall of diverse ideologies and trends in international legal thought over time. This chronical re-interpretation particularly affects foundational intellectual myths, such as that of Grotius, that the passing of time has turned into didactic archetypes handed on to incoming generations for them to become intellectually socialised within the tradition of the field. This historical pattern leads, in turn, to efforts to reinterpret the classics and, on occasion, to reimagine them altogether. Not surprisingly, for the most part, the attempts at debunking the Grotian myth have been at the hands of the successors of the representatives of an Anglo-American-Dutch tradition who had previously praised and even iconised Grotius, and on occasion even presented their own ideas cloaked under Grotius' mantle.

The latest critical revival of Grotius is a textbook example of the technique of challenging the received interpretations of a classic figure by putting the accent on his work and biography to help to illuminate alternative historical events. In the traditional interpretation, Grotius' fame was interwoven with the myth of the Peace of Westphalia as a prelude of sorts to modern international law. Admirers of Grotius, such as Martin Wight, went down the line of this 'Westphalia equals Grotius' narrative to signal that 'the prestige of Westphalia was buttressed by that of Grotius, whose reputation as father of international law was due to a work prompted by the same general war that Westphalia ended'.[47] However, as we have seen, in contemporary critical scholarship, Grotius' personal and professional biography and works are instead used to illuminate Dutch imperialism and the Western competition for spheres of colonial influence in East Asia in the seventeenth century. The Eurocentrism of the traditional perspective has been superseded by a post-colonial shift of focus in which the history of Western colonialism and imperialism have become the new *mala malaficiorum* of the contemporary history of international political thought and international law.

However, it is questionable whether this new episode in the chronical revisionism of the work and figure of Grotius is tantamount to a death certificate for Grotius' reputation in international law and its history, which Grotius has almost come to symbolise as a field of study. After more than a century of Western intellectual acculturation and institutional branding of his figure from some of the foremost epicentres of international law – The Hague, London and Washington – Grotius' reputation has irremediably spread far beyond the realm of the historiography of international law. The quasi-industrialisation of knowledge production around Grotius has consisted in multiple editions in English and other languages of his main works, the re-founding of a specialised academic journal, *Grotiana,* which is fully devoted to his figure and works, and the regular release of specialised publications exclusively dedicated to his life and writings. Along with his centrality in virtually all treatises of the history of international law, the extremely extensive body of scholarship that his life and works have attracted and its reception in all the main textbooks of international law, this indeed makes it doubtful whether Grotius' time-honoured reputation in the canon of the history of international law has now been substantially altered beyond the confines of a small and highly specialised revisionist circle of Grotius' *connoisseurs* in the West. Moreover, the widespread acceptability of Grotius as a landmark in the global historical consciousness of the discipline and his role as probably the most familiar historical icon for international lawyers worldwide have also negatively affected a myriad other histories of international law. These have been left untold and forgotten in the overgrown shadow of Grotius and other classic writers. Because Grotius also stands as a symbol of the great historiographical blind spot that the reiterative and overlapping attention given to him and other 'classics of international law' has produced in the discipline for almost a century, one should wonder whether the time has not definitively come for the history of international law as a research field to take a break from Hugo Grotius.

In conclusion, the history of the Grotian revivals in the theory and history of international law is a useful reminder that fame in international law has a life of its own, and that, in spite of the cultural hegemonic ambivalence of its archetypes, they still call for a name tag to be attached to them for ease of recognition. This remains the case as long as it may take for the classical orthodoxy to wither away and to become replaced by newer variations of the same inescapable themes and ideals. This is why, notwithstanding the skeletons in Grotius' closet and in spite of the historical and theoretical increasingly questioned foundations on which his reputation in the discipline lies, the reports of the death of Hugo Grotius as a global symbol of international law are greatly exaggerated.

Further Reading

Cavallar, G., 'Vitoria, Grotius, Pufendorf, Wolff and Vattel: accomplices of European colonialism and exploitation or true cosmopolitans?' *Journal of the History of International Law* 10 (2008) 181–209.

De la Rasilla, I., *In the Shadow of Vitoria. A History of International Law in Spain (1770–1953)* (Leiden and Boston, 2017).

Grewe, W.G., *The Epochs of International Law* (Berlin, 2000).

Haggenmacher, P., *Grotius et la doctrine de la guerre juste* (Paris, 1983).

Keene, E., *Beyond the Anarchical Society: Grotius, Colonialism and Order in World Politics* (Cambridge, 2002).

Koskenniemi, M., 'A history of international law histories', in B. Fassbender and A. Peters (eds.) *The Oxford Handbook of the History of International Law* (Oxford, 2012) 943–71.

Lauterpacht, H., 'The Grotian tradition in international law', *British Yearbook of International Law* 23 (1946)1–53.

Lesaffer, R., 'The Grotian tradition revisited: change and continuity in the history of international law', *British Yearbook of International Law* 73 (2002) 103–39.

Nijman, J.E., 'Grotius' *Imago Dei* anthropology: grounding *ius Naturae et Gentium*', in M. Koskenniemi, M. García-Salmones and P. Amorosa (eds.), *International Law and Religion. Historical and Contemporary Perspectives* (Oxford, 2017) 87–110.

Parry, J.T., 'What is the Grotian tradition in international law?' *University of Pennsylvania Journal of International Law* 35 (2014) 299–377.

Skouteris, T., 'The turn to history in international law', *Oxford Bibliographies of International Law* (2017) 1–20.

Van Ittersum, M.J., 'Hugo Grotius: The making of a founding father of the history of international law', in A. Orford and F. Hoffman (eds.), *The Oxford Handbook of the Theory of International Law* (Oxford, 2016) 82–100.

Wight, M., *Four Seminal Thinkers in International Theory. Machiavelli, Grotius, Kant, and Mazzini*, eds. G. Wight and B. Porter (Oxford, 2005).

Vollerthun, U., *The Idea of International Society: Erasmus, Vitoria, Gentili and Grotius*, ed. J. L. Richardson (Cambridge, 2017).

Wilson, E., *The Savage Republic: De Indis of Hugo Grotius, Republicanism, and Dutch Hegemony within the Early Modern World-System (c. 1600–1619)* (Leiden, 2008).

Notes

1 H. Lauterpacht, 'The Grotian tradition in international law', *British Yearbook of International Law* 23 (1946), 1–53, at 21–22, 30, 43 and 48.

2 M. Wight, *Four Seminal Thinkers in International Theory. Machiavelli, Grotius, Kant, and Mazzini*, eds. G. Wight and B. Porter (Oxford, 2005).

3 J.S. Reeves, 'Grotius De jure belli ac pacis. A bibliographical account', *American Journal of International Law* 19 (1925) 251–62.

4 P. Haggenmacher, 'La place de Francisco de Vitoria parmi les fondateurs du droit international', in *Actualité de la pensée juridique de Francisco de Vitoria* (Brussels, 1988), 27–36, at 29.

5 M. Brito Vieira, 'Mare liberum vs. Mare clausum: Grotius, Freitas and Selden's debate on dominion over the sea', *Journal of the History of Ideas* 64 (2003) 361–377.

6 Haggenmacher, 'La place de Francisco de Vitoria', 29.

7 T.E. Holland, 'Alberico Gentili', in Holland, *Studies in International Law* (Oxford, 1898), 1–39.

8 E. Nys, *Les origines de droit international* (Bruxelles, 1893).

9 M.J. Van Ittersum, 'Hugo Grotius: the making of a founding father of the history of international law', in A. Orford and F. Hoffman (eds.), *The Oxford Handbook of the Theory of International Law* (Oxford, 2016), 82–100, at 84.

10 B.J. Coates, *Legalist Empire. International Law and American Foreign Relations in the Early Twentieth Century* (Oxford, 2016).

11 Van Ittersum, 'Hugo Grotius', 99.

12 'The Classics of International Law', *American Journal of International Law*, 3 (1909) 701–7, at 703 and 706.

13 J.K. Oudendijk, 'Van Vollenhoven's "The Three Stages in the Evolution of the Law of Nations". A case of wishful thinking', *Legal History Review* 48 (1980) 3–27.

14 A. Lysen, (ed.) *Hugo Grotius: Essays on His Life and Works Selected for the Occasion of the Tercentenary of His De Jure Belli Ac Pacis, 1625–1925* (Leiden, 1925).

15 R. Pound, 'Grotius in the science of law', *American Journal of International Law* 19 (1925) 685–8, at 688 and 685.

16 J.S. Reeves, 'The First edition of Grotius' De jure belli ac pacis 1625', *American Journal of International Law* 19 (1925) 12–22.

17 J.S. Reeves, 'Grotius De Jure Belli ac Pacis: a Bibliographical Account', *American Journal of International Law* 19 (1925) 251–62.

18 J.B. Scott, *The Spanish Origins of International Law. Francisco de Vitoria and his Law of Nations* (Oxford, 1934).

19 H. Lauterpacht, *The Function of Law in the International Community* (Oxford, 1933), 58.

20 Lauterpacht, 'Grotian tradition', 1–16 and 51.

21 H. Lauterpacht, *An International Bill of the Rights of Man* (Oxford, 1945).

22 Lauterpacht 'Grotian tradition', 27.

23 Lauterpacht, 'Grotian tradition', 24 and 30.

24 S.D. Yost, 'Introduction: Martin Wight and philosophers of war and peace', in Wight, *Four Seminal Thinkers*, xvii–lii, at xvii.

25 Wight, *Four Seminal Thinkers*.

26 H. Bull, *The Anarchical Society: A Study of Order in World Politics* (London, 1977).

27 Wight, *Four Seminal Thinkers*, 34.

28 H. Bull, B. Kingsbury and A. Roberts (eds.) *Hugo Grotius and International Relations* (Oxford, 1992).

29 C.H. Alexandrowitz, 'Grotius and India', in Alexandrowitz, *The Law of Nations in Global History,* eds. D. Armitage and J. Pitts (Oxford, 2017), 113–20.

30 Scott, *Spanish Origins*, preface.

31 C.H. Alexandrowicz, 'The Grotian Society', *American Journal of International Law*, 61 (1967) 1058.

32 W.G. Grewe, *The Epochs of International Law* (Berlin, 2000), 195.

33 M.P. Scharf, *Customary International Law in Times of Fundamental Change: Recognizing Grotian Moments* (Oxford, 2013).

34 R. Falk, 'The Grotian quest', in R. Falk, F. Kratochwil and S.H. Mendlovitz (eds.), *International Law: A Contemporary Perspective* (1985), 36–42.

35 E.G. Criddle, 'Three Grotian theories of humanitarian intervention' *Theoretical Inquiries in Law* 16 (2015) 473–505.

36 K.J. Keith, 'Some thoughts about Grotius, four hundred years later', *Seventeenth Annual Grotius Lecture, ASIL Proceedings* (2015) 3–13.

37 P. Haggenmacher, *Grotius et la doctrine de la guerre juste* (Paris, 1983).

38 P. Haggenmacher, 'Hugo Grotius', in B. Fassbender and A. Peters (eds.), *The Oxford Handbook of the History of International Law* (Oxford, 2012), 1098–101.

39 R. Lesaffer, 'The Grotian tradition revisited: change and continuity in the history of international law' *British Yearbook of International Law*, 73 (2002) 103–39, at 137–8.

40 G. Cavallar, 'Vitoria, Grotius, Pufendorf, Wolff and Vattel: accomplices of European colonialism and exploitation or true cosmopolitans?', *Journal of the History of International Law* 10 (2008) 181–209.

41 Van Ittersum, 'Hugo Grotius',99.

42 J.T. Parry, 'What is the Grotian tradition in international law?', *University of Pennsylvania Journal of International Law* 35 (2014) 299–377, at 363.

43 Ibid., 304.

44 Ibid., 366–9.

45 E. Hobsbawm, 'Introduction: inventing traditions' in E. Hobsbawn and T. Ranger (eds.), *The Invention of Tradition* (Cambridge, 1983), 1–14, at 1.

46 A. Weststeijn, 'Provincializing Grotius: international law and empire in a seventeenth-century Malay mirror', in M. Koskenniemi, W. Recht and M. Jimenez Fonseca (eds.), *International Law and Empire. Historical Explorations* (Oxford, 2016), 21–38.

47 M. Wight, *Systems of States* (Leicester, 1977), 113.

Grotius in International Relations Theory 28

William Bain

28.1 Introduction

The core concerns of international theory – war, peace, security, cooperation, human well-being and so forth – are comprehended in a fundamental problem, namely reconciling freedom with the requirements of order. Hugo Grotius is hailed for articulating an iconic solution to this problem: independent states, though free to pursue self-defined goals, are in their mutual relations subject to rules of law. This is the basis of Grotius' reputation as the father of international law. Of course, enthusiasm for that title has waned as the weight of anachronism has become too much to bear, even for the Miracle of Holland. Nevertheless, a tradition of international thought bearing Grotius' name is still widely recognised as one of the paradigmatic approaches to theorising international society. The Grotian tradition took shape in the twentieth century as a response to the pessimism of political realism, as espoused by E.H. Carr (1892–1982), for example, and aspirational projects that sought to transcend, if not overthrow, the system of independent states. Grotius, so it is said, provides a *via media* that stands between realism and idealism, on the one hand, and natural law and legal positivism on the other.[1] This approach has been criticised for its state-centrism, especially as it presents in European experience, and for its failure to consider the way in which experience beyond Europe informs the theory of international society. The conclusion to be drawn is that the Grotian tradition is the product of a presentist myth. It is, indeed, a retrospective construction, yet forward-looking in orientation, which is meant to confer authority on arguments that are deployed for present purposes.

The presentist character of this project is further complicated by a failure to theorise an account of obligation that reconciles the demands of freedom with the requirements of order. The central claim of the Grotian tradition – the pursuit of advantage is subject to limits imposed by rules of law – depends fundamentally on a coherent theory of obligation.

Recognising the supreme importance of this issue, some proponents of the Grotian tradition look to a secularised natural law for an answer; others, uncomfortable with the lingering odour of religion in natural law, essentially ignore the question, seeing it as being ultimately unanswerable. Both of these approaches contribute to a stunted caricature of the original source of inspiration.[2] This chapter responds to this problem with a view to restoring a coherence that the Grotian tradition otherwise lacks. I begin by setting out the tradition as it is conventionally understood by international lawyers and, later, theorists of International Relations. However, the twentieth-century incarnation of the Grotian tradition rests on an account of obligation – if there is one at all – that is quite different from what Grotius intended. This matters because, in the absence of such an account, the theory of international society collapses into the moral scepticism of political realism. I argue that engaging Grotius' theology unlocks an account of obligation that rescues the Grotian tradition from the coarse world of power and interest. But the resulting pattern of order is quite different from what is normally derived from Grotius' thought. A properly Grotian theory of international society – one that sheds the sinews of myth – is rooted in a coordination of law and rights that reflects God's rational plan and government of the universe. This translates into a theory that affirms the fundamental value of freedom, and above all else the right of self-preservation, while accommodating common standards of moderation and restraint, and positive obligations of mutual assistance.

28.2 Grotius and the Theory of International Society

Grotius' place in international theory is rooted in two narratives, one legal and the other political in provenance. The legal narrative centres on the progressive development of international law, a project that augured the 'rediscovery' of Grotius by nineteenth- and twentieth-century jurists. Lassa Oppenheim (1858–1919) advances this project by portraying Grotius as the far-sighted jurist who anticipated the shape of the modern states system. The collapse of medieval institutions, inaugurated by the Renaissance and consummated by the Reformation, required a law to regulate the relations of a multitude of independent states. Grotius articulated principles that the newly independent states of early modern Europe gradually accepted as binding, making it possible to speak of a community of states or a family of nations. Law subjects the pursuit of particular interests to common standards of justice and safeguards interests that are common to the community of states considered as a whole.[3] Indeed, Grotius' influence is such that Oppenheim says the science of modern international law begins with the system that is laid out in *De jure belli ac pacis*. Natural law plays an important part in this story insofar as it 'supplied the crutches with whose help history has taught mankind to walk out of the institutions of the Middle Ages into those of modern times'.[4] Crucially, Grotius is alleged to have secularised natural law, emancipating it from theology while keeping it separate from the positive law of custom. This achievement, Oppenheim submits, underpins the 'Grotian school' that stands midway between the naturalists, who deny any positive law of nations, and the positivists who either minimise or deny the importance of natural law. International law takes shape in respect of these schools, albeit with the positivists gradually gaining ascendancy through the nineteenth century and into the early part of the twentieth century.[5]

The distance travelled is illustrated by Thomas Erskine Holland (1835–1926), who observed in 1924 that natural law – the scaffolding that Grotius used to support the science of international law – is little more than rhetoric in modern diplomacy.[6] Yet, dispatching natural law to the margins of international jurisprudence entailed a cost. James Leslie Brierly (1881–1955) laments the triumph of the positivist school for fetishising state sovereignty and asserting will, or volition, as the arbiter of right, obligation and interest. For the dogma of sovereignty assumes that state freedom and international order are ultimately incompatible, as sentiments of nationality pre-empt the fragile bonds of international solidarity and common right. Rejecting this view, Brierly says that – in a well-ordered states system – it is necessary to distinguish a defensible formulation of the national interest, which takes proper account of the interests of others, from anti-social nationalism.[7] Hersch Lauterpacht (1897–1960) turns to Grotius in a bid to resolve the problem of unfettered freedom that animates Brierly's concern. Since Grotius refuses to recognise absolute rights of self-preservation and war, there is no point at which law ends and lawlessness begins. Lauterpacht takes this to mean that principles of restraint repose in obligations that govern 'the totality of the relations of states'.[8] That is, rules of law reconcile the demands of freedom with the requirements of order. Interdependence rather than independence is the condition of international life and law is the source of unity that transcends the parochialism of locality. This, Lauterpacht declares, is the central theme of Grotius' writings, and for his followers, the core commitment of the Grotian tradition.[9]

Of course, much of what Lauterpacht claims for Grotius can be found elsewhere. With Oppenheim, he sees Grotius as a pivotal figure in the transition from medieval to modern. The disintegration of the legal and spiritual unity of Latin Christendom highlighted the need for a law to govern the relations of a multitude of independent states. Important, too, is the Thirty Years War (1618–48), ostensibly a religious conflagration that – whatever the cause – provided a blood-stained reminder of the need for restraint and good faith. Yet, evidence of unoriginality aside, Lauterpacht exerts enormous influence on the political narrative that connects Grotius with the theory of international society.[10] Two points are particularly significant in this regard. First, Lauterpacht's position is heavily coloured by the experience of the Second World War. Grotius provided inspiration and authority at a time when international law, having only just survived the ruin of war, was still fragile and uncertain. He supplied ideas and arguments that could be set against the voluntarist orientation of legal positivism and the moral scepticism of political realism.[11] Second, Lauterpacht looked to rescue natural law from the positivist fixation with ascertainable custom and treaty. Grotius' theory of natural law, purportedly secularised and thereby made fit for the modern world, provided the scientific basis of law grounded in custom and agreement. Moreover, it secured the idea of obligation by affirming the sanctity of promises and the principle of good faith, not only between Christians, but also infidels, tyrants and even pirates. Lauterpacht admits that natural law can appear as vague and arbitrary, but, seeing unfettered freedom as a much greater danger, he insists that these defects are 'preferable to the arbitrariness and insolence of naked force'.[12]

The political narrative associates Grotius with a constitutional discourse – the theory of international society – that qualifies state freedom in respect of the common interest of a greater whole. This discourse owes a great deal to Martin Wight's (1913–72) influential lectures on international theory. In these lectures, delivered at the London School of Economics, Grotius is positioned – along with Francisco de Vitoria (c. 1483–1546), John Locke (1632–1704) and several others – as part of a 'rationalist' *via media* that stands between a 'realist' anarchy, modelled on Thomas Hobbes's (1588–1679) state of nature, and a 'revolutionist' *civitas maxima* that is constituted and legitimised by some kind of ideological homogeneity. This broad middle road, as Wight describes the rationalist tradition, accommodates the moral claims of independent states without according them absolute justification. State freedom is subject to common standards that oblige – rather than merely counsel – moderation and restraint.[13] Here again, the question of obligation is fundamental because the idea of a common interest is sapped of vitality when separated from the idea of common obligation. Convinced that the doctrine of progress and theories of common material interest could not answer this question, and anxious to counter a nihilism that discounted the moral significance of political action, Wight seeks to resurrect natural law to explain why rules of law bind.[14] Grotius, so Wight believes, had done enough to de-Christianise natural law, thereby making it serviceable for a world shot through with difference. Precepts of natural law derive from rational human nature independently of God's will – indeed, his existence; and being concerned with what is required to sustain social life, natural law obliges because keeping promises is an indispensable condition of all society. This reading of Grotius leads Wight to conclude that 'natural law is not necessarily *Christian* theory at all'.[15]

Hedley Bull (1932–85), the most prominent interpreter of the Grotian tradition in the field of International Relations, elaborates the *via media* argument that is found in Oppenheim and Wight. He presents Grotius as the representative of one of the classic paradigms of international theory – together with paradigms named after Hobbes and Immanuel Kant (1724–1804) – which explain the character of the states system. So, against Hobbesian reason of state and Kantian universalism, the Grotian position holds that the relations of states are subject to common rules such that they form a society.[16] For Bull, this pattern of relations provides both a descriptive and a normative account of interstate relations. The analytical purchase of this account is reinforced by a progressive historical story, according to which Grotius is seen as responding to the violence and disorder that convulsed seventeenth-century Europe. Bull argues that the central claim of the political narrative – states form a society despite the absence of government – takes shape with the Peace of Westphalia (1648). This claim does not originate with Grotius and not all that is attributed to Westphalia is present in Grotius' thought. Nevertheless, the general course of international history suggests to Bull that 'the theory of Grotius and the practice of the Peace of Westphalia marched together'.[17] Bull rehearses and, in some cases, refines themes that are common to the legal and political narratives, most significantly the progressive development of international law as the alternative Grotius provides to realism. But, on the issue of natural law, Bull clearly echoes Oppenheim. That is, natural law served as the midwife of international society, but, having been eclipsed by the positivist school, it 'had served its purpose of easing the transition from medieval to modern times and could now be discarded'.[18]

Two observations can be made about Grotius' contribution to International Relations theory. The first is that states, though fundamentally free, are bound in their mutual relations by rules that express a common interest. Of course, there are disagreements as to what the common interest demands, whether it entails extensive obligations of mutual assistance or more modest bonds that disclose a presumption in favour of freedom and coexistence. Yet, disagreement notwithstanding, these differences are broadly intelligible in Bull's interpretation of the Grotian tradition, which is still widely accepted as the standard account.[19] The second observation is that the question of obligation, though vital to the theory of international society, remains largely unanswered. Again, Bull's thinking is instructive. Being committed to practice that is grounded in ascertainable custom and consent, he allows no room for natural law or anything that smells of religion when explaining the binding force of law. He acknowledges that attempts to resurrect natural law arise from the belief that will and consent might not be enough to sustain the regulated intercourse that is distinctive of a society of states. In the end, however, he simply asserts the principle of *pacta sunt servanda* since 'there are no rules that are valid independently of human will, that are part of "nature"'.[20] Here, Bull turns away from one of the core issues of the Grotian tradition. Rules of law oblige in respect of instrumental reciprocity, which pushes the matter back on the ground of power and interest. Obligations voluntarily assumed can be renounced in the same way; hence relief from the finality of human institutions is circumscribed by the fact of contingent belief that is immunised from external critique. In other words, the authority of will and consent, that is, the reason why it should be accepted, is left unexplained.

28.3 Grotius beyond Europe

A body of revisionist scholarship challenges the standard account as put forward by Bull and others. Some of this work challenges the evolutionary story about the expansion and consolidation of purportedly Westphalian institutions and practices throughout the world. The most prominent critique is Edward Keene's exploration of the relationship between Grotius' legal theory and the character of international order. Keene argues that the standard account focuses too much attention on the European states system as an arrangement of coexistence that is grounded in the freedom and equality of its members.[21] This focus, supported by a mistaken interpretation of the Grotian tradition, obscures the pattern of order that obtains beyond European experience. Grotius, as read by Keene, furnishes the ideational materials that constituted a distinctive pattern of relations between Europeans and non-European 'others'. Divisible sovereignty and property rights, which individuals and corporations are entitled to defend by waging war, are the central ideas here. The result is an extra-European pattern of order, based on imperial and colonial relations of hierarchy and civilisation, which contrasts with an intra-European order based on mutual respect and toleration. This, Keene submits, casts doubt on the proposition that Grotius' political and legal thought marched together with the practice of the Peace of Westphalia.[22]

This critique is at once appealing and limited in what it claims. Keene provides a timely reminder of the anachronism that too often colours international legal and political thought. Grotius did not set out to theorise an international legal order, much less a society of states, in response to the collapse of Latin Christendom and the wars of religion that convulsed early modern Europe. Heroic stories that laud Grotius as the father of international law have been rightly denounced as a 'delusion' born of a selective and Whiggish reading of *De jure belli ac pacis*. When read in historical context, a rather different picture emerges. Thus, Martine Van Ittersum suggests that, if Grotius is to be anointed as the father of something, the practices of Dutch imperialism are more plausible descendants. Keene, no doubt, agrees. But, his competing intra-European and extra-European orders based, respectively, on tolerance and civilisation, rests on a problematic application of Grotius' theory of divisible sovereignty. Two observations can be made in this regard. First, this dualistic conception of international order cannot be coherently derived from Grotius' thought. Keene admits as much when he says that Grotius thinks in terms of a universal legal and political order. Second, promiscuous appropriations of Grotius' thought have the effect of directing attention away from a positive argument that articulates what a genuinely Grotian theory of international society might look like. It is to clearing the ground for such an argument that I now turn.

Grotius' theory of divisible sovereignty must be interpreted in light of Jean Bodin's (1530–96) contention that sovereignty consists of an absolute and perpetual power, admitting no division in respect of function or between persons. Sovereignty is complete in itself and, therefore, unconditional. The power to legislate belongs to the prince alone, as does the power to repeal or override ordinary law. A sovereign prince in the Bodinian sense is *legibus solutus* – that is, above all human ordinance, including his own – and subject to no restraint, save only for what is prescribed by divine and natural law.[23] Grotius' understanding of sovereignty, or rather supreme power, closely resembles the Bodinian definition. For example, in *De imperio summarum potestatum circa sacra* he declares: 'I understand the "supreme power" to mean a person or body having authority over the people, and subject only to the authority of God Himself' (DI 1.1). Nothing is exempt from this power and nothing equals or excels it; to say that two supreme powers exist in a people is inconsistent with what it means to be 'supreme'. Indeed, the multiplication of supreme powers is a source of confusion because conflicting commands frustrate the effects of authority, namely obligation and constraint. It is necessary, therefore, to establish a hierarchy of authorities that obliges some to yield to others. In this respect, art imitates nature. The state must be one, the site of one supreme power, because it is impossible to obey the commands of different authorities simultaneously. Thus, Grotius asserts: 'For just as man has an undivided will which commands his members and their actions, similarly in this civil body that which commands is undivided' (DI 1.1).

This position clearly resonates with Bodin. However, as Keene sees it, Grotius hedges his position with several exceptions that, in effect, nullify the indivisibility argument; hence, sovereignty might be indivisible in principle, but it can be divided in theory and practice.[24] To support this claim, Keene adduces evidence from *Commentarius in Theses XI*, where Grotius says that, while supreme power cannot rest with several parties simultaneously, the marks of sovereignty can be distributed among different parties. It is possible, therefore, for some marks to reside in the people and others in the senate or prince: '[t]he people or the senate, or [in fact] any other assembly that possesses full sovereignty, may transfer some of its marks (for example, the rights of supreme judgment and pardon) to the prince, to the extent of retaining none for itself' (CTXI 4.24–5). Marks of sovereignty can be defended by war if necessary, since impeding their exercise involves the commission of injustice. For the right of war derives, not from sovereignty, but from one of its marks. Accordingly, when Fernando Alvarez de Toledo, Duke of Alba (1507–82) and Spanish governor-general of the Netherlands, transgressed lawful precedent in matters of taxation, the States of Holland had cause for war by virtue of being in possession of that particular mark of sovereignty. What is more, marks of sovereignty held by others can be acquired by war. The States waged a just war to defend their mark of sovereignty and, in consequence of this war, 'all the marks of sovereignty that once rested with Philip were [subsequently] acquired by the States of [Holland]' (CTXI 11.83–4). For Keene, this pattern structured relations between Europeans and indigenous rulers in the East Indies and, in time, elsewhere. Treaties divided marks of sovereignty that could be acquired through war in support of colonial and imperial expansion.[25]

But Keene claims too much here. Grotius' discussion of divisible sovereignty and his engagement with Bodin is correctly interpreted as a debate about the best constitution and its corresponding shape. Whereas Bodin insists that all sovereign power should reside in one person or office – the implication being that monarchy is best – Grotius defends the mixed constitution of the States of Holland in which sovereign power is distributed among persons or assemblies. As a result, the parts collectively govern the whole. So, where a prince does not hold a part or mark of sovereign power, 'the constitution is not monarchical properly speaking, but rather aristocratic or democratic' (CTIX 4.26). The point is that there is a difference between what sovereignty is and the way in which it is held. Thus, in ascertaining to whom sovereign power belongs, Grotius says it is necessary to 'distinguish between the Thing itself, and the Manner of enjoying it' (DJBP 1.3.11). Elsewhere he writes: 'Sovereignty ... is one Thing, and the Manner of holding it another' (DJBP 1.4.10). For supreme power refers not to the exercise of authority – making law or raising taxes, for example – but to the person or body that exercises authority. Here it is important to bear in mind that Grotius renders Bodin's *marques de la souveraineté* as 'marks of sovereignty', or *actus summae potestatis*, to denote an active power; and this power, though possessed by a person or body that is sovereign, cannot be alienated in a way that destroys the constitution. Hence, supreme power and divisible sovereignty do not clash as such.

Consider administration of the Roman Empire by two emperors, with marks of sovereignty divided geographically between West and East; Grotius says the Empire remains one as full sovereignty or supreme power resides in both emperors together, and 'the constitution therefore, though superficially monarchical, was aristocratic' (CTIX 4.29).[26]

Keene's extra-European order is explained, not by divisible sovereignty, but by the idea of contract. Contractual relations, Grotius explains, constitute a society between people that is closer than that which is common to all mankind. They involve a method of alienating and acquiring property – corporeal or incorporeal – that rests on a distinctive understanding of 'exchange'. Unlike a gratuitous gift, which is given without consideration, a contract is contrived for the sake of mutual advantage: a thing is given in order to gain a thing in return. Contracts facilitate the disposal of property, as when a seller engages to deliver a thing to a buyer for an agreed price; alternatively, they facilitate the use of property for a period of time through letting and hiring (DJBP 2.12.2, 15). Valid contracts depend on equality of knowledge and mutual freedom. Defects in what is exposed for sale should be disclosed and contracting parties should not be unjustly frightened into coming to terms, by extortion for example (DJBP 2.12.9). The necessity of what is agreed is signified by an external act, namely a promise given in speech or writing that indicates consent. This presupposes the use of reason; hence undertakings given by madmen, idiots and infants impose no necessity. Moreover, what is promised must be lawful and in the power of the person who promises. And from such a declaration follows reciprocal rights and obligations that demand performance of what has been promised. Grotius says that, by this method, it is possible alienate a thing or a part of one's liberty without dividing sovereignty: 'To the former belong our Promises to give, to the latter our Promises to do something' (DJBP 2.11.4–5, 10–11).

It is against this backdrop that Grotius' thinking about relations beyond Europe must be interpreted. Being rational creatures, indigenous rulers are at liberty to declare their will and assume contractual rights and obligations (ML 2, 7). Thus, it was in the power of the Sultan of Ternate, for example, to accept the protection of the Dutch East India Company while agreeing to bear the costs. So, too, was the grant of exclusive contracts in favour of the Dutch to deliver cloves at a fixed price.[27] But, sovereignty is not thereby divided in the way that Keene suggests. Contractual relations do not require an equal distribution of benefits. External actions, which result in inequality, are to be treated as equal when underwritten by consent; otherwise agreements will be quickly abandoned as circumstances change, especially among those who have no common judge (DJBP 2.12.26). Here, Grotius' contention that sovereignty is itself undivided, yet sometimes divided by subject matter, is explained in the relation that obtains between creditor and debtor. An exchange of promises generates rights and obligations that limit the freedom of the contracting parties. The right to compel is conferred by a reciprocal obligation that pertains to something specific rather than general, as when a creditor demands performance of what a debtor has promised. Hence, sovereignty is divided by a superiority that pertains to what has been promised, which originates in the will of the person who assumed a debt (DJBP 1.3.17). However, reciprocal rights and obligations instituted by contract do not make the United Provinces and the Sultan of Ternate one, as is the case of the Roman Empire being ruled by two emperors. Full sovereignty does not rest with buyer and seller together; each remains one in a partnership that regulates freedom rather than divides sovereignty. Indeed, contractual relations entail a self-imposed constraint since entering into partnerships is an expression of natural liberty.

The idea of contract explains relations between Europeans and non-Europeans, not divisible sovereignty. Failure to perform what is agreed is to give injury; and, where argument and persuasion fail and methods of justice have been exhausted, war is the remedy of the injustice that attends the violation of rights. War can be justly waged to recover one's own, such as that which is due by 'Contract, by Default, or by Law' (DJBP 2.1.2). This is so, Grotius insists, because 'the Obligation of fulfilling Promises' is an indispensable condition of society (DJBP Prol. 8; 2.11.4). Shifting the burden of explanation from divisible sovereignty to contract is likely to be of slight significance for the person who is interested in outcomes. True, indigenous rulers entered into contracts with different expectations than their Dutch partners and the resort to war to enforce rights conferred by contracts reduced these rulers to a state of subjection.[28] But, none of this leads to a dualistic conception of international order. Keene is right to question the standard account, as put forward by Bull and others, which portrays Grotius and the Peace of Westphalia as marching together. Likewise, the distinction between a European order based on tolerance and an extra-European order based on civilisation provides an apt description of nineteenth-century international relations. However, to derive this distinction from Grotius' thought is as anachronistic as the anachronism that it seeks to correct. Grotius did not think in terms of a dualistic international order and, if such an order existed, he would not have understood it in terms of divisible sovereignty. Recognising the centrality of contract pushes Grotius' contribution to the theory of international society back onto the ground of obligation. Common standards that enjoin moderation and restraint slide into the abyss of unfettered power and interest in the absence of a coherent account of obligation.

28.4 Theorising International Society – Again

The image of Grotius as an apologist for imperialism centres on a discourse of rights and their enforcement by force if necessary, which together converge on self-preservation. Rights call to mind a faculty or power to act, for example, to acquire, use and dispose of property, within what is permitted by law. Richard Tuck, the foremost proponent of the apologist view, argues that Grotius serves up a minimalist morality that aided the cause of aggressive European expansion. The rights to defend one's life and to acquire things that are necessary to sustain life derive from natural law. Thus, natural law also enjoins inoffensiveness – cause no harm – and abstinence – stability of possession. In contrast, positive obligations of mutual assistance are confined to the organised life of civil society. Outside civil society there is no common good to superintend, as men are required 'merely to abstain from injury, and not to give any positive help to their fellows'.[29] Tuck's reading has not gone unchallenged. Critics argue that the laws of nature do not translate into a spare system of formal rights, but rather they condition what can be done to conserve oneself in being. As natural law commands love of oneself and love of one's neighbour, the pursuit of advantage must be set alongside care for one's fellows.[30] Hence, Grotius asserts that God, having supplied all that is required for existence, judged that the rational plan of the universe would be in vain 'if He commended to each individual's care only the safety of that particular individual, without also willing that one created being should have regard for the welfare of his fellow beings, in such a way that all might be linked in mutual harmony as if by an everlasting covenant' (DJPC 1, 6').

To illuminate the origin and character of this harmony, it is necessary to engage that part of Grotius' intellectual estate that proponents of the

Grotian tradition in International Relations Theory have either neglected or renounced altogether: theology. Interpreting Grotius' political and legal thought in light of his theology resolves the conundrum that has long bedevilled theorists of International Relations, namely the need to reconcile the demands of freedom with genuine obligations of moderation and restraint. The result is a conception of human relations in which rights and law are harmonised in respect of God's nature and the reason of creation. Grotius imagines the universe as a hierarchy of mutually dependent causes that defines the place *and* the purpose of all things (*Meletius* 6–7; DI 1.3). Order thus conceived is no manifestation of chance; it is the consequence of God's intelligence and will, just as a house is the consequence of an architect's plan and a builder's labour. For example, Grotius say the motion of the heavenly bodies is not an effect of matter 'but the appointment of a Free Agent' (*De veritate* 2.7; *Meletius* 6–8). Here, however, freedom or will must be understood in conjunction with reason. God, though all-powerful, is also rational. Thus, the order of the universe is a rational construction that is 'the Appointment of the most excellent Understanding' (*De veritate* 1.7). For God's understanding, or rather reason, is the source of all perfection in things as well as the cause of relations between them. Together, they jointly compose a whole, a union of parts, whereby the good of the part is also ordained to the good of the whole. And God's reason, which disposes all things in a pattern of right order, is the law of this union: 'wherefore they are acted upon by some foreign *Reason*; and what they do, must of necessity proceed from the *efficiency* of that *Reason* impressed upon them: Which *Reason* is no other than what we call *God*' (*De veritate* 1.4 and 7; *Meletius* 27–9).

These theological commitments provide the ground of a properly Grotian theory of international society. Law, both natural and customary, defines a domain of freedom in which rights are exercised. Crucially, the harmonisation of law and rights follows from the teleological significance of creation; for God has endowed all things, animate and inanimate, with an end that promotes the good of the whole. That is, the universe, and every particular in it, is caused by God and continues to exist for the sake of God according to his intention, design and government (*De veritate* 1.10–11; *Meletius* 27–9). However, to suggest that law is embedded in a broader theological framework runs up against the deeply entrenched opinion that a secularised theory of natural law – a theory from which God has been evacuated – furnishes the precept that distinguishes social intercourse from the jungle: *pacta sunt servanda*. Much ink has been spilled on Grotius' invocation of the impious hypotheses in *De jure belli ac pacis* (DJBP Prol. 11), where he says the laws of nature would be valid even if God did not exist. Some interpret this passage to mean that these laws have no meaningful connection to God. Precepts of natural law derive directly from man's sociable nature and in consequence of rational reflection on what is required to maintain society. The implication here is that these precepts arise from a natural and secular starting point, which is independent of God's will or any final end or good that is ordained by God.[31] This view fails to grasp that the impious hypothesis is symptomatic of a schism in Western thought that turns on whether God's reason or will grounds norms of right and wrong. It is, indeed, symptomatic, not of a secularising move, but of a debate over which of the following propositions is correct: something is right or wrong, *therefore*, God wills it; or something is right or wrong *because* God's will it.[32]

God is neither excluded from the identification of natural law nor subject to its precepts. The obligation of fulfilling promises is right in itself, being necessary for social life, and, consequently, 'commanded by God, the Author of Nature' (DJBP 1.1.10; *Meletius* 84). It is not the facts of human nature that give rise to this obligation but the reason of those facts. Having endowed man with a rational and sociable nature, God approves of actions that conform to the reason of that nature. For nature is an order of secondary causes through which God governs the universe, which is distinct from divine positive law that is declared by the divine will. In nature it is God's reason that orders and disposes things into an imperishable harmony; and as a rational being man can comprehend this harmony as it structures his relationship with God and the world.[33] Significantly, Grotius' unrelenting emphasis on God's reason casts light on what it means to say that natural law is impervious to change. To say that keeping promises is good or meritorious in itself does not mean that God's will is determined by an extrinsic precept. Grotius' reference to mathematics, 'God himself cannot effect, that twice two should not be four' (DJBP 1.1.9.5), is meant to indicate the limit of divine power, rather than to exclude God from the identification of certain laws. Yet, the limit in question is not imposed from without; the truths of mathematics are independent of God's will but dependent on his nature – that is, they are contained *within* the intellect. Thus, God cannot forbid the obligation to fulfil promises, any more than he will twice two to be five, because to do so is contrary to his nature of absolute and eternal goodness. With this established, Grotius says 'that to perform Promises is a Duty arising from the Nature of immutable Justice, which as it is in GOD, so it is in some Measure common to all such as have the Use of Reason' (DJBP 2.11.4).

The law of nations is equally intelligible within the compass of theology, despite the fact that it is concerned with the advantage of all nations in general, irrespective of professions of faith. The law of nations derives its authority from the common consent of all or most nations; in other words, its cause is usage and custom that reflect the common sense of general opinion. Unlike natural law, the law of nations contains probable rather than certain principles: 'For that which cannot be deduced from certain Principles by just Consequences, and yet appears to be every where observed, must owe its rise to a free and arbitrary Will' (DJBP Prol. 41). But the law of nations is not thereby placed outside God's reason or his providential government. What is true of human wisdom is also true of faith because they share a common rationality.[34] By this, Grotius means that God's word supports, and corrects when necessary, the wisdom of usage and custom, and it guarantees the testimony given by philosophers, poets, orators and, above all else, historians, in different times and different places. Therefore, the imperfect truths of philosophy are tested against the prefect truth of revelation. The doctrines of Plato and Aristotle, and those of the Stoics, are to be accepted only so far as they conform to the light of divine reason. For God insinuated the precepts of custom in the minds of men, or as is recorded in Romans 2.15, 'the nations disclose the work of the law written in their hearts, their conscience bearing witness to them'.[35]

This theologically grounded account of law must be set alongside a theologically grounded account of rights. For example, Grotius' defence of the right of free navigation is rooted in beliefs about the appropriate direction of creation, which God bestowed on man in common. Since the principle of common use is easily disrupted by quarrels, the institution of property is an arrangement of peace and security that is occasioned by the disorder caused by sin.[36] This, in turn, had the effect of barring many men from what is necessary for life; the separation and great distance cut them off from what God provided to satisfy the wants of all. Consequently, travel, trade and communication entail harmless use of the sea and the liberty of negotiation – contract – and trade. By these rights, man attends to his own needs and those of his neighbour, and to that extent they are instruments of friendship that cultivate the unity of mankind. This is no fortuitous accident or simply the fact of the matter. Supplying the wants of others is by appointment of divine justice, for 'God speaketh this in nature' (ML 1, 8). The right of war is similarly coloured by theology. War, as Grotius understands it, is undertaken for the sake of peace, although 'peace is not any agreement whatsoever but a well ordered and disposed concord' (ML 1, 13; DJBP 1.2.1.3). The language of order and concord is telling. War is illicit when employed in the service of bare expediency. The use of war to defend the right of free navigation, for example, is concerned with restoring the condition of right order: God's rational plan of the universe that upholds the good of the particular and the good of the whole.

This coordination of rights and law provides the account of obligation that rescues the theory of international society from the abyss of crude power politics. Proponents of the Grotian tradition have failed to provide such an account because they misunderstand Grotius' theory of natural law or they regard the question of obligation as being ultimately unanswerable. Engaging Grotius' theology unlocks an account of obligation that rectifies this failure. The obligation to fulfil promises is contained within God's rational nature and, therefore, it is an inherent part of the rational order of the universe that is caused by God and actively governed by God. Thence follows a properly Grotian theory of international society that recognises joint ends and common standards for their realisation and defence. This theory accommodates the emphasis that Tuck and others place on self-preservation. The first principle of nature obliges man to conserve himself in being, and to impede access to what is essential to life involves injustice that can be redressed through the use of force. Thus, Grotius asserts: '[i]t is not then against the Nature of Human Society, for every one to provide for, and take Care of himself, so it be not to the Prejudice of another's Right; and therefore the Use of Force, which does not invade the Right of another, is not unjust' (DJBP 1.2.1; 2.2.18). In this assertion, Grotius is less the far-sighted innovator than the traditionalist who conceives self-preservation as a duty to God. It is pleasing to God that man should safeguard his welfare; and, when faced with danger, it is right to prefer one's own welfare before the welfare of others: 'we are commanded in the Gospel to love our Neighbours as ourselves, not before ourselves; nay, when an equal Danger threatens us, we are not forbid to take Care of ourselves before other' (DJBP 1.3.3).

Whatever is claimed for self-preservation must be considered in conjunction with the sociability that is a consequence of man's divinely inspired design. It is not the case that love for others is fleeting in the condition of nature. The duty of friendship is owed to all of humanity because of the universal kinship that is rooted in man's creation in the image of God. Nobody is excluded from this love, even those who profess a different religion. It is not enough, moreover, to merely abstain from harm; those who suffer misery are committed to our care and demand payment of natural debt. In this respect, self-love is tempered by the requirements of human sociability. Therefore, outside the civil condition, 'tho' there were no other Obligations, it is enough that we are allied by common humanity. For every Man ought to interest himself in what regards other Men' (DJBP 1.5.2.2; *Meletius* 69). Here, the individual good and the common good are aligned. The same relation can be imagined as reconciling state freedom with the requirements of international order. Contractual relations between states establish obligations for the sake of mutual advantage, and where consent is absent freedom prevails. But, international order demands more than this; there is a common good to superintend that is superior to a mere aggregate of individual goods. Travel, trade and communication exist ultimately, not for the sake of self-preservation or love of one's fellows, but for the supreme good – enjoyment of God. Thus, persons, natural and legal, are intrinsically related in a necessary pattern of place and purpose in which the good of the parts contribute to the good of the whole. The principle here is that God's reason, the principle of order, dictates that 'every part as a part is arranged for the good of the whole' (DI 4.6, *Meletius* 68).

28.5 The Myth of the Grotian Tradition

The reception of Grotius in the field of International Relations has engendered a mythical tradition that is attributed to a mythical man. He is portrayed as a prophet of peace, who furnished the materials necessary to tame the unfettered freedom of the Leviathans, as well as an apologist for European colonialism and imperialism. In both instances, Grotius' contribution to the theory of international society is teased out with reference to Hobbes. Grotius is either the antidote to the profound insecurity that is found in the Hobbesian state of nature or he is a proto-Hobbesian, complicit in furthering the cause of European expansion.[37] Both of these views, though very different in what they claim, raise searching questions about the obligations that are said to distinguish international society from a world that is loosed from all but the most tenuous bonds of restraint. If, as Lauterpacht suggests, Grotius made the obligation of fulfilling promises the pivot of his teaching, adherents of the Grotian tradition have directed the larger portion of their attention elsewhere.[38] Confounded by a world that was neither Christian nor European, theorists like Bull articulate the Grotian paradigm after discarding this crucial pivot. That promises should be kept is simply assumed, leaving the central claim of the tradition – the pursuit of advantage is subject to limits imposed by law – precariously exposed. By the same token, those who see Grotius as an ethical egoist reduce the common interest of international society as a whole to a slender and surely fragile reed. Where self-interest is the principle of conduct, the idea of obligation is given to formal or negative relations that make little room for positive relations of mutual assistance. Hence, the myth of the Grotian tradition is discerned in an interpretation that is substantially at odds with much of Grotius' thought.

I argue that a genuinely Grotian theory of international society follows from Grotius' theology. The result, however, looks quite different from what is normally associated with the Grotian tradition. International society is neither an arrangement of coexistence based on the equal sovereignty nor a bifurcated arrangement of distinct patterns of order. It is, rather, rooted in the idea that things jointly compose a universal community in which the parts are arranged for their own good *and* for the good of the whole. This arrangement imparts a necessary pattern of right order that is both caused and governed by God's reason. It is, indeed, a hierarchical arrangement that proceeds from God as efficient cause and returns to God as final cause. Of course, interrogating theology is unlikely to appeal to the practically-minded theorist. Better readings of Grotius, so the refrain goes, may be of historical interest, but they make little contact with problems in the real world. What is more, an approach that derives its authority from theology is problematic in a world where Christianity is one of many religions and not, as Grotius believed, the most perfect religion (*De veritate* 2.8, *Meletius* 16–7). And, yet, rejoinders of this kind do not bring our inquiry to a hasty close. There is value in engaging his international thought – to put it anachronistically – even if it provides no guide to action. Reading and re-reading Grotius corrects the mythography of the Grotian tradition. What is gained in doing so is as much about 'us' – what we believe and how we have come to see ourselves in the world – as it is about acquiring a more sophisticated reading of a canonical thinker. Engaging with Grotius is productive, not as a guide to executing policy, but in questioning, shaping and repositioning how we imagine and theorise International Relations.[39]

Translation of Grotius' Works Used

The Rights of War and Peace, ed. R. Tuck (Indianapolis, 2005)
'Defense of chapter V of the *Mare liberum*', in *The Free Sea*, ed. D. Armitage (Indianapolis, 2004)

Further Reading

Bull, H., B. Kingsbury and A. Roberts (eds.), *Hugo Grotius and International Relations* (Oxford, 1990).

Bull, H., *The Anarchical Society: A Study of Order in World Politics* (New York, 1977).

Claire Cutler, A. 'The "Grotian tradition" in international relations', *Review of International Studies* 17 (1991) 41–65.

Donelan, M., 'Grotius and the image of war', *Millennium* 12 (1983) 233–43.

George, W., 'Grotius, theology, and international law: overcoming textbook bias', *Journal of Law and Religion* 14 (2000) 605–31.

Jeffery, R., *Hugo Grotius in International Thought* (Basingstoke, 2006).

Keene, E., *Beyond the Anarchical Society: Grotius, Colonialism and Order in World Politics* (Cambridge, 2002).

Lauterpacht, H., 'The Grotian tradition in international law', *British Yearbook of International Law* 23 (1946) 1–53.

Nijman, J.E., 'Images of Grotius, *or* the international rule of law beyond historiographical oscillation', *Journal of the History of International Law* 17 (2015) 83–137.

Tuck, R., *The Rights of War and Peace: Political Thought and the International Order Grotius to Kant* (Oxford, 1999).

Wight, M., *Four Seminal Thinkers in International Theory. Machiavelli, Grotius, Kant, and Mazzini*, eds. G. Wight and B. Porter (Oxford, 2005).

Notes

1 See R. Jeffery, *Hugo Grotius in International Thought* (Basingstoke, 2006), 103, 118–22.

2 M. Wight, *Four Seminal Thinkers in International Theory. Machiavelli, Grotius, Kant, and Mazzini*, eds. G. Wight and B. Porter (Oxford, 2005), 36–41; H. Bull, 'Natural law and international relations', *British Journal of International Relations* 5 (1979) 171–81, at 180–1; H. Bull, 'The importance of Grotius in the study of international relations', in H. Bull, B. Kingsbury, and A. Roberts (eds.), *Hugo Grotius and International Relations* (Oxford, 1990), 65–93, at 79–80; A. Claire Cutler, 'The "Grotian tradition" in international relations', *Review of International Studies* 17 (1991) 41–65.

3 L. Oppenheim, *International Law* (8th edn., ed. H. Lauterpacht, London, 1957), vol. 1, 84–5.

4 Ibid., vol. 1, 89, 93.

5 Ibid., vol. 1, 93–8.

6 T.E. Holland, *The Elements of Jurisprudence* (13th edn., Oxford, 1924), 40.

7 J.L. Brierly, 'The shortcoming of international law', *British Yearbook of International Law* 5 (1924) 4–16, at 7–8, 15–16; Brierly, 'The basis of obligation in international law', *The Basis of Obligation in International Law and Other Papers*, ed. H. Lauterpacht (Oxford, 1958), 1–67, at 42–5.

8 H. Lauterpacht, 'The Grotian tradition in international law', *British Yearbook of International Law* 23 (1946) 1–53, at 19.

9 Lauterpacht, 'Grotian tradition', 19.

10 See Jeffery, *Hugo Grotius*, ch. 4; Janne Nijman, 'Images of Grotius, or the international rule of law beyond historiographical oscillation', *Journal of the History of International Law* 17 (2015) 83–137, at 90–4.

11 Lauterpacht, 'Grotian tradition', 1, 32–5.

12 Lauterpacht, 'Grotian tradition', 24, 42–3.

13 M. Wight, *International Theory: The Three Traditions*, ed. G. Wight and B. Porter (New York, 1991), 15, 37–40.

14 M. Wight, *Power Politics* (2nd edn., ed. H. Bull and C. Holbraad, Harmondsworth, 1986), 293–8; I. Hall, 'Martin Wight, Western values, and the Whig tradition of international thought', *International History Review* 36 (2014) 961–81, at 971.

15 Wight, *Four Seminal Thinkers*, 36–44.

16 See H. Bull, *The Anarchical Society: A Study of Order in World Politics* (New York, 1977), 24–7.

17 Bull, 'Importance of Grotius', 71–2, 77. A critique of this position is found in E. Keene, 'Images of Grotius', in B. Jahn (ed.), *Classical Theory in International Relations* (Cambridge, 2006), 233–52, at 237–43.

18 Bull, 'Importance of Grotius', 79.

19 See R. Jackson, *The Global Covenant: Human Conduct in a World of States*, (Oxford, 2000); A. Hurrell, *On Global Order: Power, Values and the Constitution of International Society*, (Oxford, 2007).

20 Bull, 'Natural Law', 179.

21 E. Keene, *Beyond the Anarchical Society: Grotius, Colonialism and Order in World Politics* (Cambridge, 2002), 3-4, 145-6.

22 Ibid., ch. 2.

23 J. Bodin, *On Sovereignty*, ed. and transl. Julian Franklin (Cambridge, 1992), 1-14.

24 Keene, *Anarchical Society*, 44.

25 Keene, *Anarchical Society*, 58-9.

26 See also, P. Borschberg, 'Introduction', *'Commentarius in Theses XI': An Early Treatise on Sovereignty': The Just War, and the Legitimacy of the Dutch Revolt*, (Bern, 1994), 53-5.

27 'Treaty between admiral Matelieff and sultan Modafar of Ternate and his council, dated 26 May 1607', in P. Borschberg (ed.), *Journal, Memorials, and Letters of Cornelis Matelieff de Jonge: Security, Diplomacy and Commerce in 17th-century Southeast Asia* (Singapore, 2015), 422-3.

28 See P. Borschberg, *Hugo Grotius, the Portuguese and Free Trade in the East Indies* (Singapore, 2011), 157; M.J. van Ittersum, *Profit and Principle: Hugo Grotius, Natural Rights Theories and the Rise of Dutch Power in the East Indies (1595-1615)*, (Leiden, 2006), 329-30, 387.

29 R. Tuck, *Philosophy and Government, 1572-1651* (Cambridge, 1993), 172-5.

30 See Nijman, 'Images of Grotius', 99-100.

31 For a range of perspectives on the *etiamsi daremus* controversy, see B. Straumann, 'Early modern sovereignty and its limits', *Theoretical Inquiries in Law* 6 (2015) 423-46, at 427-8, 431-3; K. Haakonssen, 'Hugo Grotius and the history of political thought', *Political Theory* 13 (1985) 239-65, at 248-50; L. Besselink, 'The Impious Hypothesis revisited', *Grotiana* N.S. 9 (1988) 3-63; C. Edwards, 'The law of nature in the thought of Hugo Grotius', *Journal of Politics* 32 (1970) 784-807; B.P Vermeulen and G.A. Van Der Wal, 'Grotius, Aquinas and Hobbes: Grotian natural law Between *lex aeterna* and natural rights', *Grotiana* N.S. 16-17 (1995-6) 70-82, at 55-84; F. Oakley, 'Secularism in question: Hugo Grotius's "Impious Hypothesis" again', in W. Bain (ed.), *Medieval Foundations of International Relations* (London, 2017), 54-66.

32 Oakley, 'Secularism in question', 61-2.

33 Besselink, 'Impious Hypothesis', 38-9; G.H.M. Posthumus Meyjes, 'Introduction', in H. Grotius, *Meletius Or Letter on the Points of Agreement Between Christians* (Leiden, 1988), 30-1.

34 Ibid., 28.

35 H. Grotius, 'Defense of Chapter V of the *Mare liberum*', in H. Grotius, *The Free Sea*, ed. D. Armitage (Indianapolis, 2004), 105.

36 Ibid., 83, 116–17.
37 Nijman, 'Images of Grotius', 89.
38 Lauterpacht, 'Grotian tradition', 42.
39 W. Bain and T. Nardin, 'International relations and intellectual history', *International Relations* 31 (2017) 213–26, at 215.

Index

Printed in the USA
CPSIA information can be obtained
at www.ICGtesting.com
LVHW012321211123
764607LV00042B/881